AF769853

CIMA

Strategic Paper P3

MANAGEMENT ACCOUNTING – RISK AND CONTROL STRATEGY

For exams in 2009

Practice & Revision Kit

In this January 2009 new edition

- We discuss the **best strategies** for revising and taking your CIMA exams
- We show you how to be well prepared for the **2009 exams**
- We give you **lots of great guidance** on tackling questions
- We show you how you can **build your own exams**
- We provide you with **three** mock exams including the **November 2008 exam**

BPP's **i-Pass** product also supports this paper.

BPP LEARNING MEDIA

First edition 2005
Fifth edition January 2009

ISBN 9780 7517 6547 2
(previous ISBN 9780 7517 5187 1)

British Library Cataloguing-in-Publication Data
A catalogue record for this book
is available from the British Library

Published by

BPP Learning Media Ltd
BPP House, Aldine Place
London W12 8AA

www.bpp.com/learningmedia

Printed in the United Kigdom

Your learning materials, published by BPP Learning Media Ltd, are printed on paper sourced from sustainable, managed forests.

We are grateful to the Chartered Institute of Management Accountants for permission to reproduce past examination questions. The answers to past examination questions have been prepared by BPP Learning Media Ltd.

Contents

Question index

The headings in this checklist/index indicate the main topics of questions, but questions often cover several different topics.

Planning your question practice

Our guidance from page xxviii shows you how to organise your question practice, either by attempting questions from each syllabus area or by **building your own exams** – tackling questions as a series of practice exams.

Extra guidance

You can find additional guidance on a number of questions in this kit on BPP's website: www.bpp.com/cima/extra-question-guidance

Topic index

Listed below are the key Paper P3 syllabus topics and the numbers of the questions in this Kit covering those topics.

If you need to concentrate your practice and revision on certain topics or if you want to attempt all available questions that refer to a particular subject, you will find this index useful.

Syllabus topic	
Sampling	25(b)
Strategic management accounting	9, 74(d)
Substantive audits	68
System-based audits	5(c), 68
Systems development	59, 62, 64-65, 67, Mock exam 3 Q3
Target costing	8(a)
Trading risk	1(b), 69
Transfer prices	10
Transaction risk	53,57
Treasury function	6(b), 39(a), 77
Value at risk	42(c), 47(d)

Using your BPP Learning Media Practice and Revision Kit

Tackling revision and the exam

You can significantly improve your chances of passing by tackling revision and the exam in the right ways. Our advice is based on recent feedback from CIMA examiners.

- We look at the dos and don'ts of revising for, and taking, CIMA exams
- We focus on Paper P3; we discuss revising the syllabus, what to do (and what not to do) in the exam, how to approach different types of question and ways of obtaining easy marks

Selecting questions

We provide signposts to help you plan your revision.

- A full **question index**
- A **topic index** listing all the questions that cover key topics, so that you can locate the questions that provide practice on these topics, and see the different ways in which they might be examined
- A **BPP question plan** highlighting the most important questions and explaining why you should attempt them
- **Build your own exams**, showing you how you can practise questions in a series of exams

Making the most of question practice

At BPP we realise that you need more than just questions and model answers to get the most from your question practice.

- Our **Top tips** provide essential advice on tackling questions, presenting answers and the key points that answers need to include
- We show you how you can pick up **Easy marks** on questions, as we know that picking up all readily available marks often can make the difference between passing and failing
- We summarise **Examiner's comments** to show you how students who sat the exam coped with the questions
- We refer to the **BPP 2008 Study Text** for detailed coverage of the topics covered in each question

Attempting mock exams

There are three mock exams that provide practice at coping with the pressures of the exam day. We strongly recommend that you attempt them under exam conditions. **Mock exams 1 and 2** reflect the question styles and syllabus coverage of the exam; **Mock exam 3** is the actual November 2008 exam. To help you get the most out of doing these exams, we not only provide help with each answer, but also guidance on how you should have approached the whole exam.

How to revise

☑ Plan your revision

At the start of your revision period, you should draw up a **timetable** to plan how long you will spend on each subject and how you will revise each area. You need to consider the total time you have available and also the time that will be required to revise for other exams you're taking.

☑ Practise Practise Practise

The **more exam-standard questions** you do, the **more likely you are to pass** the exam. Practising full questions will mean that you'll get used to the time pressure of the exam. When the time is up, you should note where you've got to and then try to complete the question, giving yourself practice everything that the question tests.

☑ Revise enough

Make sure that your revision covers the breadth of the syllabus, as in most papers most topics could be examined in a compulsory question. However it is true that some topics are **key** – they often appear in compulsory questions or are a particular interest of the examiner – and you need to spend sufficient time revising these. Make sure you know the **basics** – the fundamental calculations, proformas and report layouts.

☑ Deal with your difficulties

Difficult areas are topics you find dull and pointless, or subjects that you found problematic when you were studying them. You mustn't become negative about these topics; instead you should build up your knowledge by reading the **Passcards** and using the **Quick quiz** questions in the Study Text to test yourself. When practising questions in the Kit, go back to the Text if you're struggling.

☑ Learn from your mistakes

Having completed a question you must try to look at your answer critically. Always read the **Top tips** guidance in the answers; it's there to help you. Look at **Easy marks** to see how you could have quickly gained credit on the questions that you've done. As you go through the Kit, it's worth noting any traps you've fallen into, and key points in the **Top tips** or **Examiner's comments** sections, and referring to these notes in the days before the exam. Aim to learn at least one new point from each question you attempt, a technical point perhaps or a point on style or approach.

☑ Read the examiners' guidance

We refer throughout this Kit to **Examiner's comments**; these are available on CIMA's website. As well as highlighting weaknesses, examiners' reports often provide clues to future questions, as many examiners will quickly test again areas where problems have arisen. CIMA's website also contains articles that are relevant to this paper, which you should read.

☑ Complete all three mock exams

You should attempt the **Mock exams** at the end of the Kit under **strict exam conditions** to gain experience of selecting questions, managing your time and producing answers.

How NOT to revise

☒ Revise selectively

Examiners are well aware that some students try to forecast the contents of exams, and only revise those areas that they think will be examined. Examiners try to prevent this by doing the unexpected, for example setting the same topic in successive sittings or setting topics in compulsory questions that have previously only been examined in optional questions. Remember you have little choice of questions in most CIMA exams.

☒ Spend all the revision period reading

You cannot pass the exam just by learning the contents of Passcards, Course Notes or Study Texts. You have to develop your **application skills** by practising questions.

☒ Audit the answers

This means reading the answers and guidance without having attempted the questions. Auditing the answers gives you **false reassurance** that you would have tackled the questions in the best way and made the points that our answers do. The feedback we give in our answers will mean more to you if you've attempted the questions and thought through the issues.

☒ Practise some types of question, but not others

Although you may find the numerical parts of certain papers challenging, you shouldn't just practise calculations. These papers will also contain written elements, and you therefore need to spend time practising written question parts as well.

☒ Get bogged down

Don't spend a lot of time worrying about all the minute detail of certain topic areas, and leave yourself insufficient time to cover the rest of the syllabus. Remember that a key skill in the exam is the ability to **concentrate on what's important** and this applies to your revision as well.

☒ Overdo studying

Studying for too long without interruption will mean your studying becomes less effective. A five minute break each hour will help. You should also make sure that you are leading a **healthy lifestyle** (proper meals, good sleep and some times when you're not studying).

How to PASS your exams

☑ Prepare for the day

Make sure you set at least one alarm (or get an alarm call), and allow plenty of time to get to the exam hall. You should have your route planned in advance and should listen on the radio for potential travel problems. You should check the night before to see that you have pens, pencils, erasers, watch, calculator with spare batteries, also exam documentation and evidence of identity.

☑ Select the right questions

You should select the optional questions you feel you can answer **best**, basing your selection on the topics covered, the requirements of the question, how easy it will be to apply the requirements and the availability of easy marks.

☑ Plan your three hours

You need to make sure that you will be answering the correct number of questions, and that you spend the right length of time on each question – this will be determined by the number of marks available. Each mark carries with it a **time allocation** of **1.8 minutes**. A 25 mark question therefore should be selected, completed and checked in 45 minutes. With some papers, it's better to do certain types of question first or last.

☑ Read the questions carefully

To score well, you must follow the requirements of the question, understanding what aspects of the subject area are being covered, and the tasks you will have to carry out. Make sure you are aware of what the **question verbs require**; CIMA provides a table of verbs used together with their meaning as part of the question paper (see p xxviii in this Kit). The requirements will also determine what information and examples you should provide. Reading the question scenarios carefully will help you decide what **issues** to discuss, what **techniques** to use, **information** and **examples** to include and how to **organise** your answer.

☑ Plan your answers

Five minutes of planning plus twenty-five minutes of writing is certain to earn you more marks than thirty minutes of writing. Consider when you're planning how your answer should be **structured**, what the **format** should be and **how long** each part should take.

Confirm before you start writing that your plan makes **sense**, covers **all relevant points** and does not include **irrelevant material.**

☑ Show evidence of judgement

Remember that examiners aren't just looking for a display of knowledge; they want to see how well you can **apply** the knowledge you have. Evidence of application and judgement will include writing answers that only contain **relevant** material, using the material in scenarios to **support** what you say, **criticising** the **limitations** and **assumptions** of the techniques you've used and making **reasonable recommendations** that follow from your discussion.

☑ Stay until the end of the exam

Use any spare time to **check and recheck** your script. This includes checking you have filled out the candidate details correctly, you have labelled question parts and workings clearly, you have used headers and underlining effectively and spelling, grammar and arithmetic are correct.

How to FAIL your exams

☒ Don't do enough questions

If you don't attempt sufficient questions on the paper, you are making it harder for yourself to pass the questions that you do attempt. If for example you don't do a 20 mark question, then you will have to score 50 marks out of 80 marks on the rest of the paper, and therefore have to obtain 63% of the marks on the questions you do attempt. Failing to attempt all of the paper is symptomatic of poor time management, poor question selection or failure to revise the whole syllabus.

☒ Include irrelevant material

Markers are given detailed mark guides and will not give credit for irrelevant content. Therefore you should **NOT** braindump into your answer all you know about a broad subject area; the markers will only give credit for what is **relevant**, and you will also be showing that you lack the ability to **judge what's important.** Similarly forcing irrelevant theory into every answer won't gain you marks, nor will providing uncalled for features such as situation analyses, executive summaries and background information.

☒ Fail to use the details in the scenario

General answers or reproductions of old answers that don't refer to what is in the scenario in **this** question won't score enough marks to pass.

☒ Copy out the scenario details

Examiners see **selective** use of the right information as a key skill. If you copy out chunks of the scenario that aren't relevant to the question, or don't use the information to support your own judgements, you won't achieve good marks.

☒ Don't do what the question asks

Failing to provide all the examiner asks for will limit the marks you score. The question part may include two requirements and you should answer **both**, not just the first one. If the requirements specify you should present your work in a certain format (memo, report) there will be marks for doing so, and you will not obtain these marks if you do not use the format specified. You will also decrease your chances by not providing an answer with enough **depth** – producing a single line bullet point list when the examiner asks for a discussion.

☒ Present your work poorly

Markers will only be able to give you credit if they can read your writing. There are also plenty of other things as well that will make it more difficult for markers to reward you. Examples include:

- Not using black or blue ink
- Not showing clearly which question you're attempting
- Scattering question parts from the same question throughout your answer booklet
- Not showing clearly workings or the results of your calculations

Paragraphs that are too long or which lack headers also won't help markers and hence won't help you.

Revising P3

Risk and control

Risk and control are of course central to this paper and hence should be central to your revision.

On risk you need to know:

- The main risks businesses face, not just accounting risks, but also wider strategic, business, operational, financial and IT risks, also reputation risk (often forgotten by students)
- Components of an organisation's risk management strategy
- All the stages of the risk analysis process
- Types of response to risk

Controls – potentially you may have to discuss and evaluate a wide range of controls in any question:

- Control environment (the examiner has highlighted lack of knowledge of what the control environment is as a serious weakness recently)
- Corporate governance
- Strategic controls
- Accounting area controls
- Organisational controls including appropriate structure and communication, controls over outsourcing
- Human resource and behavioural controls including recruitment and training
- Security controls
- Quality controls
- Business continuity controls
- Information systems controls – does the system produce appropriate information? Is it appropriately used (eg budget and actual figures compared), and is action taken if variances are found? Are there appropriate controls over systems development?
- Customer feedback
- The main internal audit techniques
- The main financial risk hedging instruments
- Management supervision and review
- Ethical codes, including CIMA's ethical codes

Regard this as a checklist to give you ideas but don't expect to use them all in the exam.

A number of recent exam questions have grouped controls under the headers financial, non-financial quantitative and non-financial qualitative; you should be able to think of examples of each (see p136 of the Study Text).

Question practice

You should use the Passcards and any brief notes you have to revise these topics, but you mustn't spend all your revision time passively reading. Question practice is vital; doing as many questions as you can in full will help develop your ability to analyse scenarios and produce relevant discussion and recommendations. The question plan on page xxviii tells you what questions cover so that you can choose questions covering a variety of organisations and risk situations.

You should make sure you leave yourself enough time during your revision to practise 50 mark Section A questions as you cannot avoid them, and the scenarios and requirements of Section A questions are more complex than they are in the optional questions.

Passing the P3 exam

Displaying the right qualities

The examiners will expect you to display the following qualities.

Qualities required	
Show risk-based perspective	You must be able to **identify**, **classify** and **evaluate** major risks in a variety of scenarios, your answers must be **clearly related to the scenarios.**
Make reasonable recommendations	The controls and other measures you recommend must be **appropriate** for the organisation and deal with the risks it faces; you will need to discuss their strengths and weaknesses, as there may be costs of adopting them. The recommendations should clearly state what has to be done.
Synthesise knowledge	You may see questions that relate quite strongly to other Strategic level papers or Managerial level exams. The examiners expect you to use knowledge from these papers to answer questions in P3.
Carry out appropriate calculations	You will need to perform calculations that directly indicate risk levels or that give insights into the scenario described in the question.
Show strategic awareness	Remember this is a Strategic level paper, and the organisation's strategies will determine not only the risks it faces, but also how it responds to those risks.

Avoiding weaknesses

The examiners have identified weaknesses that occur in many students' answers at every sitting. You will enhance your chances significantly if you ensure you avoid these mistakes, in particular:

- Failing to provide what the question verbs require (discussion, evaluation, recommendations) or to write about the topics specified in the question requirements
- Making general points rather than relating answers to the scenario; regurgitation of definitions and lists with no application to the question
- Spending too much time discussing accounting controls and not enough time on other sorts of control

Other weaknesses you should avoid include:

- Unrealistic or impractical recommendations
- Vague recommendations (instead of just saying improve risk management procedures, you should discuss precisely **how** you would improve them)
- Repeating the same material in different parts of answers
- Brain dumping all that is known about a topic (no credit is given for this)
- Listing all possible risks or risks not apparent from the scenario rather than concentrating on the significant ones in the scenario
- Failing to answer sufficient questions because of poor time management
- Not answering all parts of optional questions

Using the reading time

Whilst you're reading the paper, remember to keep thinking risks and controls for every scenario that you read.

We recommend that you spend the first part of the reading time choosing the Section B questions you will do, on the basis of:

- Your **knowledge** of the syllabus area tested
- Your **understanding** of the business and the terms used in the question
- The availability of **easy marks** (see below)
- Whether you can **fulfil all the question requirements** (including any calculations)

We suggest that you should note on the paper any ideas that come to you about these questions.

However don't spend the reading time going through and analysing the Section B question requirements in detail; leave that until the three hours writing time. Normally Section B requirements are more step-by-step than Section A requirements and so require less planning and thinking time. Instead you should be looking to spend as much of the reading time as possible looking at the Section A scenario, highlighting and annotating the key points on the question paper.

Choosing which questions to answer first

Spending most of your reading time on the Section A scenario will mean that you can get underway with planning and writing your answer to the Section A question as soon as the three hours start. It will give you more actual writing time during the one and a half hours you should allocate to it and it's writing time that you'll need.

During the second half of the exam, you can put Section A aside and concentrate on the two Section B questions you've chosen.

However our recommendations are not inflexible. If you really think the Section A question looks a lot harder than the Section B questions you've chosen, then do those first, but **DON'T run over time on them.** You must leave yourself an hour and a half to tackle the Section A question. When you come back to it, having had initial thoughts during the reading time, you should be able to generate more ideas and find the question is not as bad as it looks.

Tackling questions

Scenario questions

You'll improve your chances by following a step-by-step approach to Section A scenarios along the following lines.

Step 1 Read the opening paragraph to set the scene

- Size of the organisation
- Factors influencing the decisions (business strategies, financial resources, constraints)
- Changes in circumstances that are about to take place

Step 2 Read the requirements

You need to identify the knowledge areas being tested and what information will therefore be significant. In particular you need to identify which aspects of risk management you will have to cover in your answer.

Step 3 Identify the action verbs

These convey the level of skill you need to exhibit. See the list on page xxix. Make sure you have highlighted **all** the verbs in the question; often question parts have more than one verb, and students take no notice of the second verb.

Step 4 Identify what each part of the question requires

When planning, you will need to make sure that you aren't reproducing the same material in more than one part of the question.

Step 5 Check the mark allocation to each part

This shows you the depth and number of points anticipated and helps allocate time.

Step 6 Read the scenario carefully

Look out in particular for risks and weaknesses, also procedures, systems and controls that are currently in place. Any risks that have been highlighted in the question are likely to be very relevant to your answer. Terms such as exposure, variable, volatility, uncertainty and probability are likely to highlight key risks.

Put points under headings related to requirements (eg by marginal notes). Consider the techniques you'll need to use.

Step 7 Consider the consequences of the points you've identified

Remember that in the answer you will often have to provide recommendations based on the information you've been given. Consider the limitations of any analysis you undertake or other factors that may impact upon your recommendations.

Also think how significant the points you identify are. Not everything you highlight will be vital to answering the question, and you may need to prioritise the points if you are under time pressure.

Step 8 Write a plan

You may be able to do this on the question paper as often there will be at least one blank page in the question booklet. However any plan you make should be reproduced in the answer booklet when writing time begins.

Assess quickly before you start writing that your plan covers **all necessary points** and **excludes irrelevant material**, and that you are happy with the **structure** of the answer and how much **detail** you will include, bearing in mind the **time constraints.** Make sure also that there is **no duplication** between answers to different question parts.

Step 9 Write the answer

Make every effort to present your answer clearly. Paragraphs should have **headers** that relate to the question requirements or key information in the scenario.

Numerical questions

Expect to see some numbers. The most likely place you will see them is in questions on financial risk. The examiners have stated that financial risk hedging will be examined in the majority of papers. Questions will also be set on expected values and calculation of exposure to other sorts of risk. Questions may include interpretation of data. Don't be put off doing a question by the fact that there are numbers in it, as the techniques may not be too complex, and the numbers may not be worth very many marks.

Discussion questions

Remember that **depth of discussion** is also important. Discussions will often consist of paragraphs containing 2-3 sentences. Each paragraph should:

- **Make a point**
- **Explain the point** (you must demonstrate **why** the point is important)
- **Apply the point** (with material or analysis from the scenario, perhaps an example from real-life)

Gaining the easy marks

There are likely to be easier marks available for stating the risks you've spotted in the scenario, also for defining key topics. The examiner has stated that on some papers you may see an essay question that doesn't link into a scenario and this type of question may well be easier than other scenario-linked questions on that paper.

Often the easier marks will be in the first part(s) of the question. If they are in subsequent parts, we would not recommend that you do these parts first, as question requirements and hence answers will generally have a logical flow to them. However you must give yourself enough time on these parts, and not get bogged down in the more difficult question parts.

There will also be some easy marks available for answering using an appropriate format, for example a report.

Formulae to learn

You will be provided with certain formulae and mathematical tables in the exam paper but the following formulae are not provided and you may need to use them in the exam.

Learn them

- The **expected value** of an opportunity is equal to the sum of the probabilities of an outcome occurring multiplied by the return expected if it does occur

  ie $EV = \Sigma px$

  where p is the probability of an outcome occurring and x is the value (profit or cost) of that outcome

- The accounting rate of return (ARR) = $\left(\frac{\text{average annual profit from an investment}}{\text{average investment}}\right) \times 100\%$

- The **future value** of an investment (X) plus accumulated interest after n time periods is

  $V = X(1 + r)^n$

  where r is the compound rate of return per time period, expressed as a proportion

- The **present value** of a future sum of money (V) at the end of n time periods is

  $X = V/(1 + r)^n$

  where r is the compound rate of return per time period, expressed as a proportion

- The **internal rate of return** (IRR) =

  $$A + \left[\frac{P}{P+N} \times (B - A)\right]\%$$

  where A is the (lower) rate of return with a positive NPV
  B is the (higher) rate of return with a negative NPV
  P is the amount of the positive NPV
  N is the absolute amount of the negative NPV

- (1 + money rate) = (1 + real rate) × (1 + inflation rate) where all rates are expressed as proportions

- Return on investment (ROI) (or return on capital employed (ROCE)) = (profit/capital employed) × 100%

- The **standard deviation**

  $$s = \sqrt{\Sigma p(x - \bar{x})^2}$$

  where $\bar{x}$ is the expected value of the Net Present Value

- **Value at risk**

  Value at risk = Daily volatility × Standard normal value associated with one-tail confidence level where volatility is the standard deviation.

- **Interest rate parity**

  $$\text{Forward rate a/b} = \text{Spot a/b} \times \frac{1 + \text{nominal A interest rate}}{1 + \text{nominal B interest rate}}$$

- **Purchasing power parity**

  $$\text{Forward rate a/b} = \text{Spot a/b} \times \frac{1 + \text{A inflation rate}}{1 + \text{B inflation rate}}$$

Exam information

Format of the paper

		Number of marks
Section A:	A compulsory scenario-based question with up to 5 parts	50
Section B:	2 out of 4 questions, 25 marks each	50
		100

Time allowed: 3 hours, plus 20 minutes reading time.

The examiners have stated that credit will be given for focusing on the right principles and making practical evaluations and recommendations in a variety of different business scenarios, including manufacturing, retailing and financial services. A likely weakness of answers is excessive focus on details. Plausible alternative answers could be given to many questions, so model answers should not be regarded as all-inclusive.

November 2008

Section A

1 Business risks; risk management control; risk personnel

Section B

2 Fair value accounting; commodity futures
3 Systems development controls; IT services
4 Board restructuring; impact of CIMA's ethical principles
5 Fraud and theft; internal policies and controls

The November 2008 exam is Mock exam 3 in this Kit.

May 2008

		Question in this Kit
Section A		
1	Risk assessment, response and control; internal audit ethics	78
Section B		
2	Inventory risks, controls and audit	32
3	Categorisation, identification and management of risk; risk management and internal audit	7
4	Cross-rates; arbitrage; trading limits and value at risk	47
5	Treasury function; reporting on risk and control systems	39

Examiner's comments. Performance was satisfactory. Poorer candidates failed to fulfil the requirements, either through a lack of understanding of what they needed to do or a determination to set out memorised facts and information. Students will only be rewarded for providing specific answers to the questions asked. The time pressure many candidates evidently faced was reflected in a failure to answer the questions. Good use of reading time and proper planning can greatly help students.

Students need to be able to use Managerial level knowledge to enhance their answers, for example knowledge from Paper P5.

Questions 4 and 5 were not as popular as Questions 1 to 3. Students must study all of the syllabus. There will always be some questions including numerical elements in this exam and it narrows students' choice if they cannot attempt the numerical questions.

November 2007

Section A		*Question in this Kit*
1	Business risks; risk ownership; risks of change	77
Section B		
2	Expected values; product risks; interest rate swaps	56
3	Accounts payable controls; information systems; fraud	66
4	Business risks; control environment; performance measurement	21
5	Internal audit; audit committee; corporate governance	26

Examiner's comments. Performance was uninspiring, with few students achieving comfortable passes.

A serious weakness in many answers was failure to relate the answers to the question scenarios. The examiner expects students to use the information given in the scenarios, and students who do so can achieve high marks.

Students must use the reading time to read the questions carefully and plan their answers. Good planning should alleviate the time pressure that many students evidently faced.

May 2007

Section A		*Question in this Kit*
1	Risk management strategy, risks and controls; risk response	76
Section B		
2	Control systems review and audit; control by a governing body	20
3	Pension risks; accounting ethics; internal and financial reporting controls	36
4	Internal control systems and the product lifecycle	13
5	Exchange rates; Currency hedging	52

Examiner's comments. Performance and weaknesses were very much the same as in previous exams. Question 3 was avoided by many students, and the calculations in Question 5 were very weak. Students must ensure that they can answer questions on all areas of the syllabus.

November 2006

Section A		*Question in this Kit*
1	Investment appraisal and information systems risk, audit and controls	75
Section B		
2	Systems development; computer systems audit and controls	65
3	Risk profile; risk measurement; treasury function	6
4	Currency and interest rate hedging	43
5	Board review and reporting on internal controls	19

Examiner's comments. Poorer candidates tended to ignore the question requirements, either because they didn't understand what was required or because they wanted to obtain marks 'for repetition of memorised facts and information'. A significant problem was failing to relate the answers to the question scenario. No questions were noticeably unpopular.

Students should remember that there may be more than one way to tackle a question and that marks are always restricted to the total the question offers; students will not gain an advantage by developing one answer at the expense of another that may appear more difficult.

May 2006

Section A		*Question in this Kit*
1	Risk categorisation, assessment, control; impact of strategy on performance measurement; internal audit	74
Section B		
2	Derivatives; value at risk	42
3	Risk management; management review of controls; corporate governance	18
4	Management controls; types of audit; control costs and benefits	27
5	Information systems; management accounting systems	11

Examiner's comments. Performance was generally poorer than expected, although there were some good scripts. Weaker candidates failed to answer question requirements, either because they didn't understand them or because they were trying to pass on the basis of repetition of memorised facts and information. Many students also failed to relate their answers to the scenario: 'When information is given in the scenario, candidates will be expected to use it to illustrate the main issues in their answer.' Reading time should be used to read the questions carefully.

Candidates tended to prefer the more general risk management questions to the specific questions. Few candidates answered Question 2, but their marks were relatively high, as they tended to be the better-prepared candidates. Candidates who avoided Question 2 because they did not feel well-prepared for it had less choice for the other optional questions.

November 2005

Section A		*Question in this Kit*
1	Controls; corporate governance; risk management; exchange risks	73
Section B		
2	Internal audit; IT risks and controls; audit planning; ethical principles	37
3	Risk management cycle; risk appetite; system-based internal auditing	5
4	Interest rate risk; swaps	55
5	Corporate governance	14

Examiner's comments. Well-prepared candidates passed comfortably. Weaker candidates did not relate their answers to the requirements of the question or the scenarios given, instead trying to pass on the basis of repetition of memorised facts and information. Candidates tended to prefer the discursive questions; future students must be sure they can write about issues covering the whole syllabus.

May 2005

Section A		*Question in this Kit*
1	Risk categorisation; controls; internal audit; risk management; risk hurdle rates	71
Section B		
2	Risks; internal control systems and control environment; analytic review	17
3	Advantages and disadvantages of outsourcing ERPS; risks of outsourcing and mitigation through controls and audit; project management of outsourcing	61
4	Problems with internal control systems; external audit and internal audit co-operation; external audit and fraud; fraud response plan	35
5	Currency hedging; returns from export sales	41

Examiner's comments. Poorer candidates tended to ignore the requirements either because they didn't understand what was required or because they wanted to obtain marks 'for repetition of memorised facts and information'. Candidates tended to prefer the numerical questions; (**BPP note**. The opposite comment to what was made in the November 2005 report) future students must be sure they can write about issues covering the whole syllabus.

Pilot paper

	Section A	*Question in this Kit*
1	Importance of risk management; analysis of risks; identification and quantification of risks; components of management control system and control recommendations	72
	Section B	
2	IM, IS and IT strategy; ERPS and EIS; improvements in budgetary allocations for IT and evaluation of ERPS and EIS	60
3	Types of financial risk; quantification of transaction risk; hedging and derivatives	57
4	Expected values of expansion; risks of franchising; managing and minimising the risks of making loans	58
5	Role and responsibilities of board; role and responsibilities of audit committee; disclosure of corporate governance arrangements	16

What the examiner means

The table below has been prepared by CIMA to help you interpret exam questions.

Learning objective	Verbs used	Definition	Examples in the Kit
1 Knowledge What you are expected to know	• List	• Make a list of	74
	• State	• Express, fully or clearly, the details of/facts of	76
	• Define	• Give the exact meaning of	39
2 Comprehension What you are expected to understand	• Describe	• Communicate the key features of	1
	• Distinguish	• Highlight the differences between	
	• Explain	• Make clear or intelligible/state the meaning of	32
	• Identify	• Recognise, establish or select after consideration	66
	• Illustrate	• Use an example to describe or explain something	44
3 Application How you are expected to apply your knowledge	• Apply	• To put to practical use	78
	• Calculate/compute	• To ascertain or reckon mathematically	47
	• Demonstrate	• To prove the certainty or to exhibit by practical means	3
	• Prepare	• To make or get ready for use	68
	• Reconcile	• To make or prove consistent/ compatible	
	• Solve	• Find an answer to	
	• Tabulate	• Arrange in a table	
4 Analysis How you are expected to analyse the detail of what you have learned	• Analyse	• Examine in detail the structure of	37
	• Categorise	• Place into a defined class or division	72
	• Compare and contrast	• Show the similarities and/or differences between	60
	• Construct	• To build up or complete	78
	• Discuss	• To examine in detail by argument	77
	• Interpret	• To translate into intelligible or familiar terms	
	• Produce	• To create or bring into existence	52
5 Evaluation How you are expected to use your learning to evaluate, make decisions or recommendations	• Advise	• To counsel, inform or notify	65
	• Evaluate	• To appraise or assess the value of	20
	• Recommend	• To advise on a course of action	13

Useful websites

The websites below provide additional sources of information of relevance to your studies for *Management Accounting – Decision Management.*

- BPP — www.bpp.com/learningmedia

  For details of other BPP material for your CIMA studies
- CIMA — www.cimaglobal.com

  The official CIMA website
- *Financial Times* — www.ft.com
- *The Economist* — www.economist.com
- *Wall Street Journal* — www.wsj.com

Using your BPP products

This Kit gives you the question practice and guidance you need in the exam. Our other products can also help you pass:

- **Learning to Learn Accountancy** gives further valuable advice on revision
- **Passcards** provide you with clear topic summaries and exam tips
- **Success CDs** help you revise on the move
- **i-Pass CDs** offer tests of knowledge against the clock
- **Learn Online** is an e-learning resource delivered via the Internet, offering comprehensive tutor support and featuring areas such as study, practice, email service, revision and useful resources

You can purchase these products by visiting www.bpp.com/mybpp.

Visit our website www.bpp.com/cima/learnonline to sample aspects of Learn Online free of charge.

Planning your question practice

We have already stressed that question practice should be right at the centre of your revision. Whilst you will spend some time looking at your notes and the Paper P3 Passcards, you should spend the majority of your revision time practising questions.

We recommend two ways in which you can practise questions.

- Use **BPP's question plan** to work systematically through the syllabus and attempt key and other questions on a section-by-section basis
- **Build your own exams** – attempt the questions as a series of practice exams

These ways are suggestions and simply following them is no guarantee of success. You or your college may prefer an alternative but equally valid approach.

BPP's question plan

The plan below requires you to devote a **minimum of 45 hours** to revision of Paper P3. Any time you can spend over and above this should only increase your chances of success.

Step 1 **Review your notes** and the chapter summaries in the Paper P3 **Passcards** for each section of the syllabus.

Step 2 **Answer the key questions** for that section. These questions have boxes round the question number in the table below and you should answer them in full. Even if you are short of time you must attempt these questions if you want to pass the exam. You should complete your answers without referring to our solutions.

Step 3 **Attempt the other questions** in that section. For some questions we have suggested that you prepare **answer plans or do the calculations** rather than full solutions. Planning an answer means that you should spend about 40% of the time allowance for the questions brainstorming the question and drawing up a list of points to be included in the answer.

Step 4 **Attempt Mock exams 1, 2 and 3** under strict exam conditions.

Syllabus section	2009 Pass cards chapters	Questions in this Kit	Comments	Done ☑
Risks and risk management	1-2	1	Write brief notes as an introduction to your revision.	☐
		4	Answer in full. This is further useful practice in recognising risks, and recommending ways in which organisations can deal with them.	☐
		5	Answer in full. This November 2005 question is a good example of a question about an organisation that is not a business. Identification of key risks requires thought.	☐
		6	Answer in full. This November 2006 question provides links with both of the other Strategic level exams and tests your ability to suggest different kinds of relevant controls.	☐
		7	Answer in full. This May 2008 question illustrates the wide variety of risks businesses can face, and how a systematic approach to categorising risks can help control them.	☐
Management accounting control systems	4	9	Jot down some ideas for this question.	☐
		10	Answer in full. This question tests your knowledge of transfer pricing, which is also important in other Strategic level papers, and requires you to discuss the key process of budget setting.	☐
		11	Answer in full. This May 2006 question shows how management accounting and information systems can be tested together.	☐
		13	Answer in full. This question shows how risk management links in practice with product investment and development.	☐
Corporate governance	5	14	Answer in full. This is a straightforward question on corporate governance from the November 2005 paper that provides good revision of the forces driving development and the main recommendations of the reports.	☐
		15	Prepare a plan for this question.	☐
		18	Answer in full. This May 2006 question is rather tough as it requires application of corporate governance principles to a charity.	☐

Syllabus section	2009 Pass cards chapters	Questions in this Kit	Comments	Done ☑
		19	Answer in full. This November 2006 question provides good coverage of the board's role in internal control.	☐
Internal control and accounting systems	6	17	Answer in full. This May 2005 question requires you to define what internal controls are and apply them to an organisation with some control problems.	☐
		20	Answer in full. This May 2007 question requires quite a lot of thought about the role of a governing body and how it can exercise effective control, since it is set in a school, not a company.	☐
		21	Answer in full. This question tests your ability to assess the control environment, which the examiner has recently highlighted as a problem for many students.	☐
Internal audit	7-8	22	Write a plan. This is a good introduction into this section of the syllabus, testing your understanding of the role of internal audit, and also allowing you to discuss outsourcing, which is important in other contexts in this syllabus.	☑
		24	Prepare a plan for this question.	☐
		25	Answer in full. (a) is a thorough examination of your knowledge of audit risk, whilst (b) tests sampling thoroughly.	☑
		26	Answer in full. This recent question is a good illustration of the examiner's interest in testing your knowledge of how different parts of control systems inter-relate.	☐
		29	Answer in full. This question tests your skill at analysing an audit scenario and coming up with a plan in response.	☐
		30	Answer in full. Another good test of your ability to describe relevant audit work. This question gives you a lot of information which you have to sort out in order to come up with an appropriate plan.	☐

Syllabus section	2009 Pass cards chapters	Questions in this Kit	Comments	Done ☑
		27	Answer in full. This is an interesting recent question that covers management control and audit issues that are relevant to a very small organisation.	☐
		31	Jot down the major weaknesses in this system.	☐
		32	Answer in full. This recent question is a good example of the sort of question that might be asked on operational areas, covering risks, controls and internal audit tests.	☐
Fraud and ethics	9	35	Answer in full. This May 2005 question tests your ability to identify signs of fraud, and come up with a plan in response.	☐
		36	Answer in full. This May 2007 question provides a good ethical problem to be solved, as well as requiring you to think carefully about the relevant risks in the situation.	☐
		37	Answer in full. This is a wide-ranging question that covers a number of issues relevant to the internal audit section of the syllabus and also brings in IT considerations.	☐
Financial risk management	10	39	Answer in full. This May 2008 question asks you to show you understand the role of the treasury function in risk management, and what determines how businesses report risk management.	☐
Currency risk I	11	38	Answer in full. Attempt this preparation question to remind you of the most important currency risk calculations.	☐
		50	Carry out the calculations and jot down ideas for the written elements in this question.	☐
		47	Answer in full. This recent question tests your knowledge of various financial risk management concepts, and also involves calculations that require some thought.	☑
		48	Answer in full. This question tests your knowledge of the simpler numerical techniques, and also demonstrates how IAS 39 might be examined.	☐
		52	Answer in full. This May 2007 question provides good coverage of the theories underlying foreign exchange risk, as well as a look at some of the simpler hedging methods.	☐

Syllabus section	2009 Pass cards chapters	Questions in this Kit	Comments	Done ☑
Currency risk II	12	40	Answer in full. This question tests your knowledge of currency options.	☐
		41	Answer in full. This is the question on this area from the May 2005 exam.	☐
		42	Answer in full. This challenging May 2006 question includes a general discussion on derivatives, but also requires specific knowledge of IAS 39 and value at risk.	☐
		43	Answer in full. This November 2006 question is a good example of how more complex techniques are being examined; as well as calculations being tested, the question provides practice in analysing the most appropriate strategy for different types of company.	☐
		44	Answer part (a).	☐
		46	Do the calculations in part (a).	☐
		53	Answer in full. An illustration of how a question can test your abilities to carry out hedging calculations, and discuss wider risk issues.	☐
Interest rate risk	13	57	Answer in full. This pilot paper question is a good wide-ranging question on different types of financial risk.	☐
Swaps	14	45	Answer in full. This question provides a comprehensive test of your understanding of currency swaps.	☐
		54	Answer in full.	☐
		55	Answer in full.	☐
		56	Answer in full. These questions provide handy practice in interest rate swap calculations, and also require consideration of wider financial risk management issues.	☐
International risks	15	58	Answer in full. The pilot paper question covers quite a tricky situation for you to apply your knowledge of risk, and includes calculations.	☐
Information risks requirements, strategy and systems	16-17	60	Prepare a plan for this fairly straightforward pilot paper question.	☐
		61	Answer in full. This May 2005 question provides good coverage of the important topic of outsourcing.	☐

Syllabus section	2009 Pass cards chapters	Questions in this Kit	Comments	Done ☑
Information technology controls	18	62	Prepare a plan for this question.	☐
		59	Answer in full. This question tests your understanding of the importance of a structured approach to systems development.	☐
		64	Answer in full. This question brings in wider systems development issues as well as project management issues.	☐
		66	Answer in full. This recent question illustrates how IT controls may be tested in the context of specific areas of a company's operations.	☐
		65	Answer in full. A good recent question to finish off your revision of this section, as it covers this part of the syllabus quite widely.	☐
Case study questions		73	Answer in full.	☐
		74	Answer in full.	☐
		75	Answer in full.	☐
		76	Answer in full.	☐
		77	Answer in full.	☐
		78	Answer in full. Answer these wide-ranging case study questions to give yourself practice in tackling lengthy questions.	☐

Build your own exams

Having revised your notes and the BPP Passcards, you can attempt the questions in the Kit as a series of practice exams. You can organise the questions in the following ways:

- Either you can attempt complete old papers; recent papers are listed below.

	P3							
	Pilot paper	May 05	Nov 05	May 06	Nov 06	May 07	Nov 07	May 08
Section A								
1	72	71	73	74	75	76	77	78
Section B								
2	60	17	37	42	65	20	56	32
3	57	61	5	18	6	36	66	7
4	58	35	55	27	43	13	21	47
5	16	41	14	11	19	52	26	39

- Or you can make up practice exams, either yourself or using the mock exams that we have listed below.

	Practice exams								
	1	2	3	4	5	6	7	8	9
Section A									
1	75	76	67	68	71	78	73	74	77
Section B									
2	52	43	17	42	11	5	21	58	7
3	19	20	55	18	30	41	27	61	26
4	36	65	32	35	45	33	57	47	56
5	6	13	39	4	37	16	60	14	66

- Whichever practice exams you use, you must attempt **Mock exams 1, 2 and 3** at the end of your revision.

Questions

Extra guidance

Remember you can find additional guidance on a number of questions in this kit on BPP's website:
www.bpp.com/cima/extra-question-guidance

RISKS

Questions 1 to 7 cover risks, the subject of Part A of the BPP Study Text for Paper P3.

1 Preparation question: Risks

When an organisation undertakes a major investment project, it takes on project risk. The risk in a project comes from various sources, and includes:

(i) Project-specific risk
(ii) Competitive risk
(iii) Industry-specific risk
(iv) Market risk

Required

(a) Describe what is meant by each of these types of risk.

The most important risks that many businesses face are as follows:

(i) Trading risk
(ii) Cultural, country and political risks
(iii) Currency risk
(iv) Interest rate risk
(v) Technological risk

Required

(b) Describe what is meant by each of these types of risk.

(c) Explain how following the principles laid down in the codes of corporate governance can assist in managing risks on a day-to-day basis.

Tutor's hints. The main purpose of this question is to remind you how wide-ranging an organisation's risks are, and also how risk links in with corporate governance. It also revises the basics of risk management, emphasising that risk analysis is only a part of the process.

2 ANG — 45 mins

ANG is a road haulage contractor. The company specialises in collection and delivery of large or heavy items such as railway locomotives and sections of bridges from the manufacturer to the customer. The company owns 49 road vehicles of different sizes to enable transportation of the different goods.

ANG's risk management policy is based on taking out insurance. As well as the standard employer and third party liability classes of insurance, ANG also insures against damage to road infrastructure such as bridges and tunnels from its own vehicles or as a result of goods being carried becoming unstable and falling off ANG's lorries.

ANG's terms and conditions of carriage note that radioactive goods will not be transported under any circumstances. Explosives are carried, but only where the owner accepts liability on their own insurance.

Contingency planning is limited; the Board of ANG believes that if any risks do occur, then ANG has sufficient vehicles to continue operations.

The Board of ANG is also considering a new venture for the same day delivery of goods where the distance to travel is more than its existing fleet of road vehicles could travel in one day. This venture involves the purchase of surplus 'Hercules' transport planes from the army. The Board has recently decided to make the purchase of the planes because they are being offered at a substantial discount. Marketing activities will commence next month.

Required

(a) Explain the features that an organisation needs to have to implement risk management effectively. **(6 marks)**

(b) Explain the risk management strategies available to an organisation. **(10 marks)**

(c) Evaluate the risk management strategy of ANG, explaining any amendments that you consider are necessary. **(9 marks)**

(Total = 25 marks)

3 BEB **45 mins**

BEB is a company whose objective is to promote fair trade and fight poverty. It is associated with a charitable organisation, JFR, which holds one ordinary B share in BEB and has significant powers vested in it by virtue of the constitution of BEB. Such rights include a right of controlling vote on all matters of strategy. NED ?

In the financial year to 30 June 20X4, BEB undertook a share restructure and floated on the Stock Exchange. In the restructure, 20,500 ordinary A 50p shares were bought back by the company and exchanged for 10,250 ordinary American $1 shares. A further 40,750 $1 ordinary shares were sold on the Stock Exchange for $15. The new issue was fully subscribed.

BEB's results show an increase on the previous year. Revenue is $14,080,905 (20X3: $11,898,427) and profit before tax is $612,042 (20X3: $354,000). The cash raised by the flotation enabled the company to pay off some long term debts and still show an improvement in its cash in hand figure.

BEB has two main product divisions: foods and gifts. Foods include a wide range of products, including tea and coffee, rice and pasta, cocoa and various chocolate products, and various mueslis and cereal bars. Gifts includes a wide-ranging combination of craft products from around the third world, including items made from wood, fabrics and paper.

The company has three main sources of revenue: mail order catalogue, supermarkets and personal selling. In the past, the income from these three sources has been fairly comparable. In 20X4, the personal selling revenue has seen a large decrease and the income from mail order (which includes sales made through BEB's new website) has increased substantially. Personal selling is carried out by individuals who receive a discount on items purchased from BEB, which they then sell on to family and friends.

BEB sometimes makes advanced payments to suppliers as is common practice amongst fair trade ventures. Due to BEB's expansion policy and the number of new producers it has forged links with in the year, the figure for advanced payments in the balance sheet is much bigger than it has been in previous years, at $756,234 (20X3: $356,199).

Note: No calculations are required to answer this question.

Required

(a) Explain the principal business risks for BEB. **(13 marks)**

(b) Demonstrate how using an enterprise risk management framework can help BEB overcome the risks it faces. **(12 marks)**

(Total = 25 marks)

4 HOOD **45 mins**

HOOD sells a wide range of coats, anoraks, waterproof trousers and similar outdoor clothing from its 56 stores located in one country. The company is profitable, although the gross profit in some stores has declined recently for no apparent reason.

Each store uses EPOS to maintain control of stock and provides the facility to use EFTPOS for payments. However, about 55% of all transactions are still made by cash. Details of sales made and stock below re-order levels are transferred to head office on a daily basis where management reports are also prepared.

Inventory is ordered centrally from Head Office, details of requirements being obtained from the daily management information provided by each store. Orders are sent to suppliers in the post, with inventory arriving at each store approximately 10 days after the re-order level is reached.

Recent newspaper reports indicate one of the chemicals used to waterproof garments releases toxic fumes after prolonged exposure to sunlight. The board of HOOD are investigating the claim, but are currently treating it with some degree of scepticism. The product range has generally sold well, although there has been little innovation in terms of garment design in the last 4 years.

Required

(a) Identify the different risks facing the HOOD Company, placing the risks into suitable categories. **(10 marks)**

(b) Evaluate the potential effect of each risk on the company, recommending how the impact of that risk can be minimised. **(15 marks)**

(Total = 25 marks)

5 Doctors' practice (11/05) 45 mins

A large doctors' practice, with six partners and two practice nurses, has decided to increase its income by providing day surgery facilities. The existing building would be extended to provide room for the surgical unit and storage facilities for equipment and drugs. The aim is to offer patients the opportunity to have minor surgical procedures conducted by a doctor at their local practice, thus avoiding any unfamiliarity and possible delays to treatment that might result from referral to a hospital. Blood and samples taken during the surgery will be sent away to the local hospital for testing but the patient will get the results from their doctor at the practice. It is anticipated that the introduction of the day surgery facility will increase practice income by approximately 20 per cent.

Required

(a) Identify the additional risks that the doctors' practice may expect to face as a consequence of the introduction of the new facility and explain how a model such as CIMA's risk management cycle might be used to understand and control such risks. **(12 marks)**

(b) Explain the meaning of the term 'risk appetite' and discuss who should take responsibility for defining that appetite in the context of the scenario outlined above. **(5 marks)**

(c) Critically discuss the role of systems-based internal auditing in relation to the assessment of risk management procedures in any organisation. **(8 marks)**

(Total = 25 marks)

6 A and B (11/06) 45 mins

The following information relates to two companies based in the United States of America, both of which are listed on the New York stock exchange. Each company had an annual turnover of approximately $800 million in 20X5.

Company A

This company sells into a mix of business-to-business and end-user markets across a total of 15 countries in North America and Europe. Business-to-business sales predominate and 40% of turnover comes from two key European customers.

Manufacturing, assembly and delivery is managed geographically rather than by product type, via three separate subsidiaries with their own CEO based in Canada, France and the UK respectively. Research and all Treasury operations for the arrangement of loan finance and hedging of foreign exchange risk are both fully centralised.

The company has a diverse shareholder base that includes two major pension funds, one of which has a representative entitled to be present as an observer at the board meetings of Company A.

Company B

This company operates in the same product market as Company A, but earns most of its income from end user sales, many of which are initiated by on-line direct orders. 80% of the internet sales originate in the United States of

America. Company's B's largest single customer, a Canadian company, represents 15% of its annual sales revenue, but no other customer exceeds 1% of total sales. Research and sales facilities are based at the US headquarters, but manufacturing and assembly is all undertaken by separate subsidiaries in China, where the company also has a joint venture business that manages all the global distribution. Treasury operations are fully decentralised, but run as cost rather than profit centres.

The company was started ten years ago, and the Board of Directors remains dominated by members of the founding family. The CEO and the Finance Director are husband and wife, and together own 35% of the company's shares.

Required

Using the information contained in the above scenario to develop your arguments, answer each of the following questions:

(a) Discuss how decisions about company structure, market types and location can impact upon the risk profile of a company. **(12 marks)**

(b) Compare and contrast the risks associated with the differing approaches to the Treasury function adopted by the two companies in the above scenario. **(4 marks)**

(c) For either Company A or Company B as described in the scenario, taking into account its current structure and size, recommend one example of each of financial, non-financial quantitative, and non-financial qualitative controls that may be useful tools in monitoring exposure to either strategic or operational risks. You should briefly justify your choices. **(9 marks)**

(Total = 25 marks)

7 LXY (5/08) 45 mins

LXY is a company, which has a five-year contract to operate buses in and out of the city bus station in Danon, France. The station has 60 bus piers and an average of 90 buses per hour leave Danon for local and national destinations.

Services operate between 06.00 and 22.00 daily. All buses are operated solely by the driver, who loads and unloads luggage and checks that all passengers have a valid ticket. LXY only permits travel with a pre-paid ticket.

Local buses provide a suburban service to areas within a 20 kilometre radius of Danon. The national services cover distances of up to 500 kilometres and so drivers are frequently required to stay overnight at certain destinations before covering the return service the following day.

Required

(a) You have recently been appointed Head of Risk and Internal Audit at LXY.

(i) Identify, with a brief justification, three categories which may be used to classify and manage the risks faced by LXY. **(3 marks)**

(ii) For ONE of the categories that you have selected in (i) above, identify three possible risks and recommend appropriate tools for their control. **(9 marks)**

(b) A café owner in Danon has approached LXY with a proposal to provide food and drink facilities on board long-distance bus services.

Identify the additional risks that need to be considered by LXY in the evaluation of the proposal, and how they might be managed. **(4 marks)**

(c) Many companies are too small to justify the existence of separate risk management and internal audit functions.

Briefly explain the distinctive roles performed by each of these functions and recommend ways of maintaining their separate effectiveness within a combined department. **(9 marks)**

(Total = 25 marks)

MANAGEMENT CONTROL SYSTEMS

Questions 8 to 13 cover management control systems, the subject of Part B of the BPP Study Text for Paper P3.

8 Preparation question: Cost containment

Traditional cost control systems focused on cost containment rather than cost reduction. Today, cost management focuses on process improvement and the identification of how processes can be more effectively and efficiently performed to result in cost reductions.

Required

Discuss how each of the following cost management techniques differs from the traditional cost containment approach and how each seeks to achieve cost reduction.

(a) Target costing
(b) Life cycle costing
(c) Activity based management
(d) Kaizen
(e) Lean management accounting.

Tutor's hints. This question is a reminder of P3's place in the management accounting pillar of the CIMA qualification. Management accounting control systems are a significant control. This question reminds you of:

- The limitations of traditional methods (which may be the methods the organisation in the question scenario is using).
- The advantages of the recently developed methods (which are why you might recommend them as improvements in an answer).

9 CEV **45 mins**

CEV is a large agricultural machinery manufacturing company. The company's new managing director is concerned that the information provided by the company's management accounting system is too limited for the problems that the company now faces. You have recently jointed the company as its management accountant and are concerned that the company lacks a strategic management accounting system.

Required

Prepare a brief report to the managing director which explains the following.

(a) Why traditional management accounting systems are now inadequate **(5 marks)**
(b) The aims of strategic management accounting **(6 marks)**
(c) The characteristics of information flow at the strategic level **(6 marks)**
(d) How an effective strategic management accounting system can provide information which meets the needs of CEV's senior management in seeking to realise its corporate objectives **(8 marks)**

(Total = 25 marks)

10 SCL **45 mins**

The SCL Company manufactures consumer electrical goods (fridges, freezers, washing machines and similar products). The company produces all the parts for its products in five separate divisions. Those parts are then transferred to three assembly divisions and the finished goods are finally transferred to the sales division.

Each division is controlled by a manager. Budgets for the division are set annually based on a percentage increased on the previous year; this budget setting process appears to be appropriate because managers always spend between 95% and 102% of their budget each year.

Budgets are normally imposed by senior management. Surprisingly, there is little dissent from lower level managers. However, senior management are aware that divisional managers share data on a regular basis.

Transfer prices between the divisions are also set by senior management again without consultation with the divisional managers. This does result in some problems, normally when manufacturing divisions have to stop production and the assembly divisions purchase supplies from third parties.

Required

(a) Discuss whether the method of setting transfer prices in the SCL Company would be acceptable to divisional managers. **(8 marks)**

(b) Identify any problems that may arise in the budget setting process in the SCL Company, recommending how those problems can be overcome. **(10 marks)**

(c) Advise whether lean management accounting principles can assist in the setting of an appropriate transfer price. **(7 marks)**

(Total = 25 marks)

11 CDE (5/06) 45 mins

CDE is a manufacturer of almost one hundred different automotive components that are sold in both large and small quantities on a just-in-time (JIT) basis to the major vehicle assemblers. Business is highly competitive and price sensitive. The company is listed on the stock exchange but CDE's share performance has not matched that of its main competitors.

CDE's management accounting system uses a manufacturing resource planning (MRPII) system to control production scheduling, inventory movements and stock control, and labour and machine utilisation. The accounting department carries out a detailed annual budgeting exercise, determines standard costs for labour and materials, and allocates production overhead on the basis of machine utilisation. Strict accounting controls over labour and material costs are managed by the detailed recording of operator and machine timesheets and raw material movements, and by calculating and investigating all significant variances.

While the information from the MRPII system is useful to management, there is an absence of integrated data about customer requirements and suppliers. Some information is contained within spreadsheets and databases held by the Sales and Purchasing departments respectively. One result of this lack of integration is that inventories are higher than they should be in a JIT environment.

The managers of CDE (representing functional areas of sales, production, purchasing, finance and administration) believe that, while costs are strictly controlled, the cost of the accounting department is excessive and significant savings need to be made, even at the expense of data accuracy. Managers believe that there may not be optimum use of the production capacity to generate profits and cash flow and improve shareholder value. CDE's management wants to carry out sensitivity and other analyses of strategic alternatives, but this is difficult when the existing management accounting system is focused on control rather than on decision support.

Required

(a) (i) Outline the different types of information system available to manufacturing firms like CDE; and

(ii) Recommend with reasons the information system that would be appropriate to CDE's needs. **(10 marks)**

(b) Given the business environment that CDE faces, and the desire of management to reduce the cost of accounting,

(i) Critically evaluate the relevance of the current management accounting system; and

(ii) Recommend how the system should be improved. **(15 marks)**

(Total = 25 marks)

12 Controls in new company — 45 mins

A large local government authority has decided to seek competitive tenders for all its internal computer requirements. The present managers of the authority's Computer Services Department have decided that they wish to tender for the work, and if successful, form a company to acquire the existing assets and carry out work for the local government authority and other customers.

They think that the work that they currently do for their own local government authority is technically far in advance of that done by neighbouring local government authorities. They consider that additional volume would allow them to reward more highly the good staff who are currently employed at low public sector rates of pay.

A group of local businessmen and potential investors has discussed this proposal with the Director of Computing, who would lead the proposed management buy-out (MBO). They are quite impressed with the technical competence of the staff, and the prospects for gaining additional work.

However, they have a number of reservations, as the staff have no experience outside information technology, and no commercial experience. Their experience of budgeting is also limited. The local government authority does not subdivide its budget for the Computer Services Department. It manages this department as a cost centre, and receives reports of expenditure against budget at quarterly intervals. In order to address the investors' concerns, the managers have employed consultants to advise on the proposals.

Required

Write a report:

(a) Recommending the form and level of detail of budgetary control required in the new company. **(10 marks)**

(b) Advising on the corporate governance, the board's role in risk management and the information the board will require. **(15 marks)**

(Total = 25 marks)

13 Product choice (5/07) — 45 mins

You work in the new product development division of a USA based global consumer electronics company. You are employed as the accountant responsible for costing and project appraisal of all new product proposals. All costs and revenues are based on information provided by the electronic engineers and marketing staff responsible for each individual project. It is assumed that all development is fully completed prior to initial marketing, and so no redesign costs are allowed once a product is launched. The rapid rate of technology change within the industry has led the company to assume a maximum product life of seven years.

The tables below give details of the company-wide incremental cash flows for two new consumer products. All cash flows are assumed to occur at the year end. Regulatory constraints mean that the company cannot invest in both developments. The company-wide hurdle rate for capital investments is 7.5% per year but the Finance Director is considering introducing risk-adjusted rates, which would give a discount rate of 8.5% per year for Product 1 and 10% per year for Product 2. The net present values generated by each of the products, using both the standard hurdle rate and the risk-adjusted hurdle rates, are also given in the tables.

Product 1 would be manufactured and assembled in China and transferred to company-owned retail outlets in the USA. Product 2 would be assembled in the Czech Republic from components shipped in from Taiwan and then sold to third party distributors across Western Europe.

Product 1	Year(s)	*Annual sales revenue $ Million (based on ex factory prices)*	*Design and development costs $ Million*	*Annual manufacturing and distribution costs $ Million*
	1	Nil	200	Nil
	2	Nil	400	Nil
	3	280		120
	4-7	420		180
NPV at 7.5% pa	$244 million			
NPV at 8.5% pa	$217 million			

Product 2	Year(s)	*Annual sales revenue $ Million (based on ex factory prices)*	*Design and development costs $ Million*	*Annual manufacturing and distribution costs $ Million*
	1	Nil	6,400	Nil
	2	1,250	Nil	600
	3	2,000	Nil	750
	4-6	3,500	nil	1,200
NPV at 7.5% pa	$430 million			
NPV at 10% pa	($45 million)			

Required

(a) Recommend three ways of improving your company's internal control systems to ensure better management of risks throughout the product life cycle. **(10 marks)**

(b) Prepare a memo for your Head of Division recommending which product your company should support. You should clearly explain and justify your recommendations in the context of risk management.

(15 marks)

(Total = 25 marks)

INTERNAL CONTROL AND AUDIT

Question 14 to 37 cover internal control and audit, the subject of Part C of the BPP Study Text for Paper P3.

14 Corporate governance (11/05) — 45 mins

Required

(a) Identify the key reasons for the emergence of corporate governance regulations around the world. **(5 marks)**

(b) Explain the core principles that underpin corporate governance regulations. **(10 marks)**

(c) Discuss the role and responsibilities of audit committees as laid down in the Combined Code. **(10 marks)**

(Total = 25 marks)

15 Preparation question: HiT

HiT is an information technology company set up in the Dotcom boom in the late 1990s. Unlike many other companies, it did not expand too quickly at first as the proprietors were cautious and hence did not seek external funding other than venture capital. As a result the company has been well-placed to pick up business that has become available in the IT sector and has done well since the millennium.

The directors have now decided on a policy of expansion both internally and by acquisition. They appreciate that they will need more external funding, and believe the company will soon be in a healthy enough position for them to seek a stock market listing. They understand that this will mean that the company's corporate governance structures need to become more formal. Previously the board has just consisted of the original shareholders plus a representative from the venture capitalists. The directors appreciate that if the company is listed, they will need to recruit some non-executive directors to the board, but are unclear about their role and why most of them need to be independent.

Required

Prepare a memorandum to the board of HiT explaining:

(a) The position, qualities and role of non-executive directors in the corporate governance of a listed company.

(b) The distinction between independent and non-independent non-executive directors.

(c) The main areas for a potential conflict of interest between the external shareholders of a company and its directors, and how non-executive directors can help deal with this problem.

(d) The objections to paying non-executive directors in shares or share options.

Tutor's hints. This question requires more knowledge statement and less application of knowledge than you would normally see in an exam question. It does however cover the key issues connected with non-executive directors. If you're struggling with (c), think about the main board committees that non-executive directors staff. In (d) consider what will lead to larger rewards and how therefore non-executive directors may have a conflict of interest.

16 Good governance (Pilot paper) — 45 mins

You have recently been appointed as head of the internal audit function for a large UK listed company that trades internationally, having worked within its finance function for two years prior to your new appointment.

Your company has also appointed a new chief executive, headhunted from a large US corporation where she had held the post of vice president, finance.

Required

As part of the new chief executive's orientation programme, you have been asked to prepare a detailed report which provides key information on the principles of good corporate governance for UK listed companies.

You should address the following in your report, remembering that her background is in US governance and procedures.

(a) The role and responsibilities of the board of directors. **(5 marks)**

(b) The role and responsibilities of the audit committee. **(10 marks)**

(c) Disclosure of corporate governance arrangements. **(10 marks)**

(Total = 25 marks)

17 BJP (5/05) — 45 mins

BJP is an organisation involved in making business-to-business sales of industrial products. BJP employs a sales team of 40 representatives and assigns each a geographic territory that is quite large. Sales representatives search for new business and follow up sales leads to win new business, and maintain contact with the existing customer base.

The sales representatives spend almost all their time travelling to visit clients. The only time when they are not doing this is on one day each month when they are required to attend their regional offices for a sales meeting. Sales representatives incur expenses. They have a mobile telephone, a fully maintained company car and a corporate credit card which can be used to pay for vehicle expenses, accommodation and meals and the cost of entertaining potential and existing clients.

The performance appraisal system for each sales representative is based on the number and value of new clients and existing clients in their territory. All sales representatives are required to submit a weekly report to their regional managers which gives details of the new and existing clients that they have visited during that week. The regional managers do not get involved in the daily routines of sales representatives if they are generating sufficient sales. Consequently, sales representatives have a large amount of freedom.

The Head Office Finance department, to which regional managers have a reporting relationship, analyses the volume and value of business won by sales representatives and collects details of their expenses which are then reported back monthly to regional managers. At the last meeting of regional managers, the Head Office Finance department highlighted the increase in sales representatives' expenses as a proportion of sales revenue over the last two years and instructed regional managers to improve their control over the work representatives carry out and the expenses they incur.

Required

(a) Advise regional managers as to the risks facing BJP as a result of the lack of apparent control over sales representatives and their expenses and recommend the controls that should be implemented by regional managers to rectify this situation. **(12 marks)**

(b) Explain what an internal control system is, how it relates to the control environment and its likely costs, benefits and limitations. **(8 marks)**

(c) Recommend how analytic review could be used in the internal audit of BJP's sales representatives' expenses. **(5 marks)**

(Total = 25 marks)

18 LMN (5/06) — 45 mins

LMN is a charity that provides low-cost housing for people on low incomes. The government has privatised much of the home building, maintenance and management in this sector. The sector is heavily regulated and receives some government money but there are significant funds borrowed from banks to invest in new housing developments, on the security of future rent receipts. Government agencies subsidise much of the rental cost for low-income residents.

The board and senior management have identified the major risks to LMN as: having insufficient housing stock of a suitable type to meet the needs of local people on low incomes; making poor property investment decisions; having dissatisfied tenants due to inadequate property maintenance; failing to comply with the requirements of the regulator; having a poor credit rating with lenders; poor cost control; incurring bad debts for rental; and having vacant properties that are not earning income. LMN has produced a risk register as part of its risk management process. For each of more than 200 individual risks, the risk register identifies a description of the risk and the (high, medium or low) likelihood of the risk eventuating and the (high, medium or low) consequences for the organisation if the risk does eventuate.

The management of LMN is carried out by professionally qualified housing executives with wide experience in property development, housing management and maintenance, and financial management. The board of LMN is composed of volunteers with wide experience and an interest in social welfare. The board is representative of the community, tenants and the local authority, any of whom may be shareholders (shareholdings are nominal and the company pays no dividends). The local authority has overall responsibility for housing and social welfare in the area. The audit committee of the board of LMN, which has responsibility for risk management as well as internal control, wants to move towards a system of internal controls that are more closely related to risks identified in the risk register.

Required

For an organisation like LMN:

(a) Discuss the purposes and importance of risk management and its relationship with the internal control system. **(8 marks)**

(b) Explain the importance of a management review of controls for the audit committee. **(5 marks)**

(c) Discuss the principles of good corporate governance as they apply to the Board's role

(i) in conducting a review of internal controls; and
(ii) reporting on compliance. **(12 marks)**

Illustrate your answer with examples from the scenario.

(Total = 25 marks)

19 Board review (11/06) 54 mins

Required

Write a report advising the Board of Directors of a stock market listed company on:

- The key responsibilities of Board members in relation to ensuring the effectiveness of internal controls
- The methods used to assess such effectiveness
- The regulations that govern the reporting to the stock market of the results of internal control reviews.

An indicative mark allocation for the three points above are 5, 10 and 5 marks respectively.

(Total = 25 marks)

(includes 5 marks for report format and style)

20 PKG High School (5/07) 45 mins

The PKG High School has 900 pupils, 40 teachers, 10 support staff and a budget of $3 million per annum, 85% of which represents salary and salary-related costs. The local authority for PKG's area is responsible for 34 schools, of which six are high schools. The local authority allocates government funding for education to schools based on the number of pupils. It ensures that the government-approved curriculum is taught in all schools in its area with the aim of achieving government targets. All schools, including PKG, are subject to an independent financial audit as well as a scrutiny of their education provision by the local authority, and reports of both are presented to the school governing body.

The number of pupils determines the approximate number of teachers, based on class sizes of approximately 30 pupils. The salary costs for teachers are determined nationally and pay scales mean that more experienced teachers receive higher salaries. In addition, some teachers receive school-specific responsibility allowances.

PKG is managed on a day-to-day basis by the head teacher. The governance of each school is carried out by a governing body comprising the head teacher, elected representatives of parents of pupils, and members appointed by the local authority. The principles of good corporate governance apply to school governing bodies which are accountable to parents and the local authority for the performance of the school.

The governing body holds the head teacher accountable for day-to-day school management, but on certain matters such as building maintenance the head teacher will seek expert advice from the local authority.

The governing body meets quarterly and has as its main responsibilities budgetary management, appointment of staff, and education standards. The main control mechanisms exercised by the governing body include scrutiny of a year-to-date financial report, a quarterly non-financial performance report, teacher recruitment and approval of all purchases over $1,000. The head teacher has expenditure authority below this level.

The financial report (which is updated monthly) is presented to each meeting of the governing body. It shows the local authority's budget allocation to the school for the year, the expenditure incurred for each month and the year to data, and any unspent balances. Although there is no external financial reporting requirement for the school, the local authority will not allow any school to overspend its budget allocation in any financial year.

PKG's budget allocation is only just sufficient to provide adequate educational facilities. Additional funds are always required for teaching resources, building maintenance, and to upgrade computer equipment. The only flexibility the school has in budget management is to limit responsibility allowances and delay teacher recruitment. This increases pupil-contact time for individual teachers however, and forces teachers to undertake preparation, marking and administration after school hours.

Note: A local authority (or council) carries out service for the local community and levies local taxes (or council tax) to fund most of its operations. Many of the local authority functions are regulated by central government and considerable funding also comes from that source. The range of local authority services include education, community health, refuse collection, and maintenance of footpaths and public parks.

Required

(a) Explain why the review and audit of control systems is important for the governing body of a school such as PKG. **(5 marks)**

(b) Evaluate the effectiveness of the governing body's control over PKG High School and recommend ways in which it might be improved. **(20 marks)**

(Total = 25 marks)

21 EWC (11/07) — 45 mins

EWC is a large company in an unregulated sector of the telecommunications industry. It has ambitious plans for sales growth and increased profitability. In support of these goals, senior management has established a flat management structure. Budget targets place employees under considerable pressure but success in achieving and surpassing sales and profitability targets is rewarded by bonuses and share options. Employees who do not achieve their targets do not remain with the company for long.

Performance targets exist for expanding EWC's customer base, sales value and profitability per customer, and geographic and product-based expansion. EWC zealously pursues cost reduction with continual efforts to drive down suppliers' prices. The company aims to eliminate any wasteful practices in management and administration, EWC considers any expenditure that does not lead directly to sales growth to be wasteful and the company minimises its corporate policies and procedures. As a result, EWC has tended to overlook unscrupulous practices in its employees' dealings with customers, competitors and suppliers in the pursuit of its goals. The company is unlisted and reports its profits to shareholders once per year.

Required

(a) Identify the major types of risk facing EWC that arise from its style of management. Give reasons to support your answer. **(10 marks)**

(b) Explain the significance of the control environment in EWC. **(5 marks)**

(c) From the perspective of a newly appointed non-executive director, evaluate the financial, non-financial quantitative, and qualitative controls in EWC in the context of EWC's goals and the risks facing EWC. **(10 marks)**

(Total = 25 marks)

22 Preparation question: Role of internal audit

(a) Explain the role of internal audit in the context of:

(i) Corporate governance
(ii) Risk management
(iii) Organisational control

Your answer should include one example of how an internal audit department in a manufacturing company might fulfil its role under each of the headings above.

A recent phenomenon in internal audit is the tendency of companies to outsource their internal audit function to the major accounting firms. One of the major reasons for this appears to be a perceived cost benefit.

Required

(b) Discuss the advantages and disadvantages of outsourcing the internal audit function.

Tutor's hints. This question isn't an exam-standard question for this area of the syllabus because it lacks a scenario. Remember in (a) that you are not just thinking about internal audit's role in checking controls over financial reporting. In (b) it may help to think about other areas of a business that could be outsourced, the arguments for doing so and the problems; many will apply to internal audit as well.

23 Independence of internal audit — 45 mins

The directors of GP are considering establishing an internal audit department and have raised a number of questions. One issue most of them are unsure of is how internal audit differs from external audit.

Required

(a) Identify the principal differences between internal and external (registered) auditors, using the following criteria:

(i) Eligibility to act
(ii) Security of tenure
(iii) Primary objective and the limitations on the scope of the auditor's work in order to achieve this objective. **(9 marks)**

One of the directors has quoted an article saying that the internal auditor should have independence in terms of organisational status and personal objectivity that permits the proper performance of his duties.

Required

(b) (i) Explain what is meant by independence in this context, listing and briefly explaining the freedoms and privileges needed for employees of an organisation to be able to act effectively as internal auditors. **(5 marks)**

(ii) Explain the alternative organisational structures which can help to achieve this independence of internal audit, and the ways in which an audit committee can contribute to this. **(6 marks)**

The chairman has raised the issue of how the chief internal auditor should be remunerated. In GP, bonus payments related to annual profits form a significant part of the total remuneration of all senior managers.

Required

(c) Discuss whether it is appropriate for the chief internal auditor to receive a bonus based on the organisation's profit, or whether it could be seen to compromise his independence. **(5 marks)**

(Total = 25 marks)

24 IA effectiveness — 45 mins

As the newly-appointed finance director of a quoted company, you have just been asked by the chairman to advise him on the effectiveness of the existing internal audit department.

The chairman explained that internal audit has been established in the company for many years. The chief internal auditor, who has held this post for many years, has reported direct to the chairman. He has always had a right of access to the Board, and, since the establishment of an Audit Committee, has worked closely with that committee. However, there had been increasing friction in recent years between the chief internal auditor and your predecessor as finance director. Internal audit had been regarded by your predecessor as expensive, slow and ineffective.

Required

Write a report to the chairman explaining how the effectiveness of the internal audit department should be assessed. Your report should deal specifically with the following issues.

(a) What the objectives of internal audit should be. **(6 marks)**

(b) Whether you should carry out the assessment yourself, or, if not, who should do so. **(6 marks)**

(c) How the detailed work of gathering the appropriate information should be conducted. **(4 marks)**

(d) The information required, and any specific financial or non-financial measures required. **(9 marks)**

(Total = 25 marks)

25 CFB — 45 mins

You work in the Internal Audit department of CFB, a company producing a variety of fruit drinks from cheap orange squash to 100% pure fruit juices. It operates from one location on the edge of a major city.

The main accounting and operational systems of CFB are maintained on an online computer with terminals in all of CFB's departments. The software was written in-house two years ago and is currently supported by a team of 5 programmers, who make amendments to the software as necessary.

Most of the company's sales are made on account to wholesalers and distributors of drinks. However, a small retail shop is maintained on the premises where customers can purchase CFB products. Sales are made on a cash basis with total sales representing about 4% of the total income of the company.

The work of internal audit encompasses not only the financial systems of the company, but also monitoring of the quality of drinks produced in conjunction with the quality control department. Internal audit receives reports on raw materials purchased from the buying department, prices paid from the purchasing department, production quantities from the manufacturing department and quality reports from the quality control department. This information is collated and checked to ensure that poor quality inputs do not result in poor quality outputs. A low price followed by high wastage and poor quality reports could indicate poor quality of product.

The Internal Audit department is required to monitor the cleaning of the vats used for mixing drinks. These vats are cleared every three weeks and discharged into the sewer system. Relatively large amounts of fruit juice are sometimes lost as a result of mixing but no environmental damage has ever occurred.

The Finance Director has recently complained about the efficiency of the Internal Audit department. In his view, the department does not make sufficient use of sampling, and he believes that some members of the internal audit department need to be briefed on how sampling should be used.

Required

(a) Analyse how audit risk can be ranked using the severity/frequency (likelihood/consequences) matrix, using examples from CFB to support your analysis. You should also provide recommendations on how CFB should manage risk. **(17 marks)**

(b) Prepare a briefing for other members of the Internal Audit team explaining the sampling process, covering:

(i) The basis to use to select items for testing
(ii) The number of items that should be tested
(iii) The actions to be taken if errors are found in the test **(8 marks)**

(Total = 25 marks)

26 Governance systems (11/07) 45 mins

Required

'Effective internal control, internal audit, audit committee and corporate governance are all inter-related'.

Discuss this statement with reference to:

(a) How internal audit should contribute to the effectiveness of internal control **(7 marks)**
(b) How an audit committee should contribute to the effectiveness of internal audit **(9 marks)**
(c) The role of an audit committee in promoting good corporate governance **(9 marks)**

(Total = 25 marks)

27 HIJ (5/06) 45 mins

HIJ is a new company that provides professional services to small businesses. Apart from the Principal, a qualified accountant who owns 100% of the business, there are four professionally qualified and two support staff. The business model adopted by HIJ is to charge an annually negotiated fixed monthly retainer to its clients in return for advice and assistance in relation to budgeting, costing, cash management, receivables and inventory control, and monthly and annual management reporting. The work involves weekly visits to each client by a member of staff and a monthly review between HIJ's Principal and the chief executive of the client company. In delivering its client services, HIJ makes extensive use of specialist accounting software.

The Principal continually carries out marketing activity to identify and win new clients. This involves advertising, production of brochures and attending conferences, exhibitions, and various business events where potential clients may be located.

The management of HIJ by its Principal is based on strict cost control, maximising the chargeable hours of staff and ensuring that the retainers charged are sufficient to cover the hours worked for each client over the financial year.

Required

(a) Recommend management controls that would be appropriate for the Principal to have in place for HIJ. **(12 marks)**

(b) Discuss the need for various types of audit that are appropriate for HIJ. **(8 marks)**

(c) Discuss the costs and benefits for HIJ that are likely to arise from a system of internal controls. **(5 marks)**

(Total = 25 marks)

28 Subcontracting services **45 mins**

The company of which you are finance director manufactures and sells branded electronic consumer durables.

It has a large market share in its home market, and good sales in some other markets. However, it is small in terms of the world market.

From small beginnings some years ago it grew rapidly until about five years ago, but then suffered badly from competition from much larger multinational companies.

Devaluation, making competitive imports more expensive, has produced a marked increase in domestic sales over the last two years, and technical advances made by the company suggest buoyant sales and profits in future.

Staff are under acute pressure coping with the volume of business and have little time to plan and develop the profitable opportunities created by new products and improvements to existing products. Departmental heads are pressing for more staff and facilities to enable them to achieve objectives.

However, both the chairman and the managing director are concerned about the risks involved in recruiting new staff. They are aware that the future is far from certain. Therefore, they do not wish to recruit staff and then, in a few years time, find it necessary to make them redundant, unless there is no alternative strategy. They remember the cutbacks and redundancies of two to five years ago as very painful.

They have convened a special conference of the board and senior managers to discuss the internal implications of the planned expansion, and have asked you to prepare certain reports for this meeting.

One solution that has been suggested to the problem of staff recruitment is to outsource various functions:

(i) *Legal services:* primarily patents, trademarks and brands

(ii) *Computing:* the main workload is the integrated system which schedules production at the company's own and suppliers' factories, and controls stock and sales

Required

(a) Write a report discussing the case for subcontracting services, rather than providing these services by the use of full-time staff. **(20 marks)**

(b) Explain how an internal audit approach to controls over a service which can be supplied internally would differ from an internal audit approach to the same service if this were outsourced. **(5 marks)**

(Total = 25 marks)

29 New subsidiary **45 mins**

You are employed as a senior internal auditor in a very large retail conglomerate firm. The chief internal auditor has asked you to carry out the initial internal audit of a newly-acquired subsidiary into which your company has diversified.

The newly-acquired subsidiary imports specialised building products, mainly plumbing and drainage equipment, and sells them through 23 regional warehouses, the majority of which are in the United Kingdom. The head office is small – fewer than 50 people are employed. The regional warehouses employ more people – numbers vary between 20 and 80 at each warehouse, and include salesmen, drivers, storemen, and a small number of office and accounting staff.

Regional warehouse managers have considerable autonomy in buying from approved suppliers, and selling, including negotiating special prices with large customers and allowing credit. They are totally responsible for their local staff. The business has grown rapidly and achieved a significant market share by having good inventory available, and allowing generous credit to small and large builder customers. It has been financed by extended credit from suppliers.

The group is not involved in sales to the same markets as the newly-acquired subsidiary, but similar products are bought and sold to retail customers through stores.

The management team of the subsidiary has remained the same after the acquisition, and will be paid very highly as part of the purchase arrangements if forecast profits are achieved for the first two years after acquisition.

Required

(a) Identify the main potential audit problems for this subsidiary. **(9 marks)**

(b) Explain the framework for your proposed initial audit programme. **(16 marks)**

Note. As part of the purchase agreement for the new subsidiary, extensive work was done by an independent firm of auditors on the inventory and account balances at the date of purchase. You are *not* required to duplicate this work.

(Total = 25 marks)

30 JJ — 45 mins

You are the senior audit officer in the newly formed internal audit department of JJ, a generally well run company which operates a chain of 30 juice bars in the capital city and the South East. Details of the contribution to total revenue that these outlets make is as follows:

Kings Cross Station	24%	Thame Station	8%
Marylebone Station	13%	Bicester Shopping Centre	2%
Hammersmith Station	12%	Banbury Station	2%
Ealing Common Station	10%	Other	19%
Gerrards Cross Café	10%		

The outlets sell fruit and vegetable juices and have more recently introduced a range of smoothies onto the menu. Customers may also choose from a limited range of luxury snacks including muffins and bagels. In a number of locations purchases can be consumed on the premises but the majority operate as kiosks based in shopping centres and railway stations.

Station kiosks are in operation from 6am-12 midnight Monday to Saturday and from 9am-6pm on Sunday. Those in shopping centres are open from 9am-6pm Monday to Saturday. Two members of staff work each shift, one of whom is the manager with responsibility for cash and inventory. Management at Head Office are becoming concerned about the high level of staff turnover at the Ealing kiosk which has had four new managers in the last six months.

All transactions must be paid for in cash. Takings are banked after each nine hour shift. All sales and takings are recorded by computerised tills with the information transferred to Head Office on a daily basis where all the accounting records are maintained.

Reconciliations performed at Head Office have highlighted a number of discrepancies relating to the kiosk at Princes Risborough station, a relatively new outlet which has failed to perform. There have been several instances where there has been a shortfall in cash banked as compared to takings recorded by the till. In addition, information from the till shows that even though the kiosk opens at 6 am often the first transaction is not recorded until 8 am or later.

Standard menus and price lists are used throughout the organisation with the exception of the café style bars whose prices are 10% higher to cover the additional premises cost. On the whole the launch of the smoothie range has been successful. Analysis showing a breakdown of revenue of the five major kiosks has shown the following:

	Juice	*Smoothies*	*Other*
Kings Cross	70%	19%	11%
Hammersmith	69%	21%	10%
Ealing	73%	17%	10%
Gerrards Cross	86%	2%	12%
Marylebone	68%	20%	12%

All ordering and purchases are dealt with from Head Office. The manager of each outlet places an order on a daily basis. The order is processed and delivered from regional warehouses the following day. Detailed inventory records are not maintained.

On a weekly basis a physical inventory count is performed and the results returned to Head Office. Each café and kiosk has a separate storeroom with the exception of the Kings Cross Station site where two kiosks operate and share a store. At Head Office stock reconciliations are performed and stock losses calculated. These reconciliations have shown significant losses at the Kings Cross and Ealing sites.

Required

(a) Explain the matters you would consider in planning the internal audit work for JJ. **(13 marks)**

The directors are considering outsourcing the IT requirement, including the accounting function, of JJ.

Required

(b) Explain how this would affect the internal audit approach. **(12 marks)**

(Total = 25 marks)

31 APS **45 mins**

APS has grown in recent years from a small business to a medium sized manufacturing business.

APS employs over 200 hourly paid staff in the factory. In that period the payroll system, as described below, has remained basically unchanged, except that certain routines are now computerised. Controls over the system include daily backup, and also backup after each payroll is produced.

Payroll system

(i) On Monday mornings each employee takes a blank time card from a pile and writes his or her name and number at the top. Each day of the week they record their starting and finishing times. The following Monday each department supervisor collects the cards and forwards them to the wages clerk.

(ii) Personnel and wages records are maintained by the wages clerk on a personal computer. From the time cards he calculates the hours worked by each employee and enters them into a payroll program on the computer. This program, using data from personnel records as to wage rates and deduction, produces the weekly payroll and a payslip for each employee.

(iii) The wages clerk prepares a cheque requisition for the total net pay for the week, which is sent to the company accountant together with a copy of the payroll. The accountant draws up the cheque, made payable to cash, and has it countersigned by a director. The wages clerk takes the cheque to the bank and uses the cash to prepare the wage packets. Wage packets are given to the department supervisors for distribution to the employees in their department as they see fit.

(iv) There is no personnel department. Each department supervisor has the authority to engage new employees and to determine changes in wage rates with the verbal consent of a director.

(v) Gross weekly wages never exceed $500 for any employee, the total hours never exceed 50 hours a week and increases in hourly rates of pay never exceed 10%.

When APS was a small business it was felt that the directors maintained a reasonable level of supervision over all aspects of the business. Now that the business has expanded, the directors felt that a small internal audit function needed to be set up, and you have recently been recruited to join the newly established internal audit function.

During the planning phase of the first internal audit it became apparent that reliance on management supervision may no longer be sufficient in the area of wages and payroll. There are now too many employees for them to be personally known to the directors who, in any event, now rarely find the time to visit the factory. Recognising this, the directors have appointed a factory manager to oversee the day to day running of the factory. The factory manager's job description includes responsibility for hiring factory staff and determining their rates of pay. Since the directors feel that the company is not sufficiently large to require a separate personnel department, appropriate functions are to be assigned to the factory manager.

The internal audit manager asks you to draft a note to form the basis of a report concerning the wages system. She suggests that the note should identify each of the principal weaknesses of the existing system, possible consequences if the weakness is not remedied and recommend changes that should be made including functions to be assigned to the factory manager.

Required

(a) Prepare the note suggested by the audit manager. (You are not required to draft the report) **(18 marks)**

In their last audit the external auditors recommended the introduction of access controls and programmed application controls into the computer system. If such controls are introduced the external auditors might be able to place more audit reliance on computer controls.

Required

(b) Prepare paragraphs for a report to the directors:

(i) Describing access and programmed application controls that could be included in the computer system **(3 marks)**

(ii) Explaining the use of test data in verifying the computer processing of payroll, including a description of the test data you would use. **(4 marks)**

Note: You do not have to answer part (b) in a report format. **(Total = 25 marks)**

32 CSX (5/08) 45 mins

CSX is a distribution company, which buys and sells small electronic components. The company has sales of $200 million per annum on which it achieves a profit of $12 million.

Central Warehouse Department

The company has a large Central Warehouse Department employing 100 staff over 2 shifts. The warehouse contains 30,000 different components, which are of high value and are readily saleable. Technological change is commonplace and components can become obsolete with little warning. Twice a year, the Purchasing Manager authorises the disposal of obsolete inventory. Inventory control is carried out through a computer system that has been used by the company for the last ten years.

Purchasing and receiving

Inventory is ordered using manual purchase orders based on tender prices. Goods received into the Central Warehouse are recorded on a manual Goods Received Note which is the source document for computer data entry. Data entry is done by clerical staff employed within the Central Warehouse.

Customer orders

Orders from customers are entered into the computer by clerical staff in the Sales Department. The computer checks inventory availability and produces a Picking List which is used by Central Warehouse staff to assemble the order. Frequently, there are differences between the computer inventory record and what is physically in the store. The Picking List (showing the actual quantities ready to be delivered) is used by clerical staff to update the computer records in the Central Warehouse. A combined Delivery Note/Invoice is then printed to accompany the goods.

Accounting

At the end of each financial year, a physical check of inventory is carried out which results in a significant write-off. To allow for these losses, the monthly operating statements to the Board of Directors include a 2% contingency, added to each month's cost of sales.

Internal Audit Department

The company's Internal Audit Department has been asked by the Board to look at the problem of inventory losses. Managers in the Central Warehouse believe that inventory losses are the result of inaccurate data entry, the old and unreliable nature of the computer system and the large number of small inventory items which are easily lost, or which warehouse staff throw away if they are obsolete or damaged.

Required

(a) Explain the risks faced by CSX in relation to its inventory control system and recommend specific improvements to the system's internal controls. **(15 marks)**

(b) Recommend (without being specific to the CSX scenario) the tests or techniques, both manual and computerised, that internal auditors can use in assessing the adequacy of inventory controls. **(10 marks)**

(Total = 25 marks)

33 Purchasing and entertainment **45 mins**

(a) Explain how a management control system can help to minimise the risk of fraud in purchasing. **(11 marks)**

Some codes of conduct appear to have a double standard. One such is quoted below.

Customer and supplier relations

The company does not seek to gain any advantage through the improper use of business courtesies or other inducements. Good judgement and moderation must be exercised to avoid misinterpretation and adverse effect on the reputation of the company and its employees. Offering, giving, soliciting or receiving any form of bribe is prohibited.

Business courtesies

Gifts, favours and entertainment may be given in the following circumstances.

(i) If they are consistent with customary business practices.
(ii) If they are not excessive in value and cannot be construed as a bribe or payoff.
(iii) If they are not in contravention of applicable law or ethical standards.
(iv) If they will not embarrass the company or the employee if publicly disclosed.

Gifts, favours, entertainment or other inducements may not be accepted by employees from any person or organisation that does or seeks business with, or is a competitor of, the company, except as common courtesies usually associated with customary business practices. An especially strict standard applies when suppliers are involved. Favours or entertainment, appropriate in our sales programmes may not be appropriate or acceptable from suppliers. It is never acceptable to accept a gift in cash or cash equivalent.

Required

(b) Discuss the acceptability of the above code of conduct. If you consider it appropriate, suggest with reasons any amendments you would wish to see in the code of conduct. **(14 marks)**

(Total = 25 marks)

34 PNY **45 mins**

PNY is a book publisher. Each year, it publishes over 10,000 new book titles that range from popular fiction through to specialist guides on 120 different towns worldwide. Over 50,000 titles are stocked in its warehouse awaiting sale to book wholesalers, and recently individual consumers via its Internet site.

Over the last few years, significant amounts of new technology in the form of on-line trading with suppliers and use of the Internet as a selling medium have been implemented into PNY by outside contractors. However, no independent audit of the Internet trading site has been carried out and the site is left to run more as a marketing tool than selling media. There have been relatively few sales from the site since it started operating. No specific reasons have been put forward for lack of sales. A perpetual inventory system has also been in use for the last two years, providing real time information on inventory balances with the aim of reduction of inventory losses due to theft.

Four staff are employed in the internal audit department. The staff have worked in the company for 10 years. Important family and social commitments have meant they do not want to move location and they have little ambition for promotion. The chief internal auditor reports to the Financial Director, who also sets the remuneration levels of internal audit department staff. Training within internal audit is limited to one day's update on audit procedures each year, the lack of staff mobility being given as a reason not to provide detailed training schemes.

Internal audit testing methods focus on substantive testing of transactions, tracing those transactions through the accounting system as far as possible. Where there is a break in the audit trail, where possible, the transaction is located again after the break and testing continues. Testing of inventory takes place at the year end when a full inventory count is carried out in association with the external auditors.

Risk management policies in PNY are under the control of the Financial Director. The policy is written by the Head of Accounts and then agreed by the board. The Head of Accounts also acts as the whistle-blowing nominee to hear reports of potential whistle-blowing from employees. The company has not established an audit committee.

Required

(a) Explain the contents of a risk management strategy for fraud. **(10 marks)**

(b) Explain the risks inherent in PNY's systems and the internal audit department recommending how those risks should be overcome. **(15 marks)**

(Total = 25 marks)

35 AL (5/05) 45 mins

AL and Co is a London-based building contractor, with an annual turnover of almost £15 million. The company employs 50 people, the majority of whom are skilled tradesmen or apprentices in the areas of plumbing, electrical work, plastering, carpentry, glazing and hard landscaping. AL and Co specialises in renovation work for private clients by offering a fast 'all service' facility that suits busy professional people seeking to renovate either for their own occupation or for investment purposes. As a result of the property boom, turnover has grown by over 30% in the last two years.

Day-to-day management of the business is shared by two executive directors, one of whom manages the financial and legal aspects of the business (Director X), while the other is responsible for operational activities including work scheduling, agreeing quotes with the sales staff, and all procurement (Director Y). The two directors have a mutual respect and trust for one another and therefore do not check or verify each other's work.

As a medium sized company, AL and Co is subject to an annual external audit, but it has no internal audit function and both its internal control and management accounting systems are very basic. Management accounting procedures record the costs of materials associated with all contracts via a job costing system, but other costs are not charged to individual contracts. The system is thus unable to identify whether any specific contract is profitable, and can only compute aggregate profit. One consequence of this system is that the company profitability depends on there being a close match between the actual time taken to complete jobs and the sales team's estimate of the times required: however, the time variances are neither calculated nor monitored.

The systems have never been questioned or refined because, to date, an average gross markup of 25% has always been achieved. This margin has ensured that both directors earn high salaries which have risen year on year, and there has therefore been little incentive to improve controls and manage costs.

Two staff are employed to issue written quotes in response to customer enquires, with prices being calculated on the basis of estimated labour and material costs plus 25%. The quotes are reviewed by Director Y before they are sent to customers. All payments are due on completion of the work.

In drafting the work schedules Director Y has full knowledge of which quotes are accepted by customers. Additionally, given his role of supervising procurement, he regularly gives administrative staff the names of new suppliers for inclusion in the accounting system.

Six months ago, Director Y found himself over-committed financially, and devised a way of diverting company funds from AL and Co for his own personal use. He began adding 10% to the figures quoted for all jobs requiring the use of more than three separate services (plastering, electrical etc), thereby raising the gross markup to 37.5% in such cases. The intention was to fraudulently redirect the additional income for his personal use. This was achieved by the submission to AL and Co, on the completion of the job, of an invoice (for the 10% additional charge) in the name of a fictitious supplier of small tools and consumables. Director Y would code the associated costs as variable overhead in the accounting system. The timing of the invoices could easily be matched to the job completion dates in view of his knowledge of work schedules, and he set up a separate bank account in the fictitious name to receive these payments.

You are an accountant in AL and Co and have been assigned responsibility for liaison with the external auditors. You find that you are unable to resolve their concerns about the escalation in variable overhead expenses over the course of the last year, most of which have been charged to a non-local supplier's account. You are having difficulty clarifying the precise nature of the expenses incurred because telephone calls to the business number always request that a message be left but no calls are ever returned. All other aspects of the audit are satisfactory.

Required

Write a report for the directors of AL and Co that:

(a) Details the inadequacies of the current 'internal control' system within the company and possible changes that could be made to improve the system. **(10 marks)**

(b) Explains why the rise in variable overhead costs is a matter of concern from both an external audit and an internal control perspective, and thus requires immediate agreement on a co-ordinated response to investigate the possibility of fraud. **(5 marks)**

(c) Briefly explains the limits of the responsibility of external auditors to detect fraud. **(5 marks)**

(d) Explains why the company should prepare a fraud response plan, and outlines the issues to be considered in drafting such a plan. **(5 marks)**

(Total = 25 marks)

36 Pensions (5/07) — 45 mins

Under international accounting conventions, the rules on accounting for employee benefits are based upon the principle that the cost of providing such benefits, should be recognised in the period in which the benefit is earned by the employee, rather than when it is paid or payable. The rules laid down in International Accounting Standard 19 (IAS 19) *Employee benefits* apply to a wide range of employee benefits, of which the most common form is pensions.

A significant number of pension plans are classed as defined benefit plans, under which the pension payable by the organisation on the retirement of an employee is linked to his/her salary. The salary used for the calculation of the benefit may be either an average or a final salary, although final salary is still the most common.

Under IAS 19, a company's balance sheet must record the present value of the future benefits payable, net of the value of the pension fund assets. The discount rate used to arrive at a present value for the liabilities is equal to the interest rate payable on AA rated corporate bonds. The valuation are carried out by actuaries, who are required to make a number of assumptions about current economic conditions, life expectancy, the rate of salary increase over time, and the expected rate of return on the pension fund assets.

In the UK, the requirement to put the value of the pension fund's net assets or liabilities on the face of the balance sheet has resulted in a number of companies reporting pension fund deficits in excess of £1 billion and has led to concerns over a 'pensions crisis'.

Required

(a) A company has a pension fund deficit equal to ten per cent of its market capitalisation. Explain and discuss the nature of the risks posed to **both** the company and its current employees by the existence of such a substantial pension fund deficit. **(10 marks)**

The Finance Director of a UK listed company is concerned about the sensitivity of the company's pension fund deficit to changes in life expectancy. If the company's advising actuaries use the most up-to-date life expectancy table, the company's pension deficit will increase by 30%, to approximately 60% of its market capitalisation. The Head of Financial Reporting is therefore considering requesting the actuaries to continue using tables which are now deemed out of date.

Required

(b) (i) Discuss the proposal to request the actuaries to use out-of-date tables. **(8 marks)**

(ii) Identify the internal and external financial reporting controls that could be used to prevent the manipulation of the liability valuation in the manner suggested by the Head of Financial Reporting. **(7 marks)**

(Total = 25 marks)

37 SPQ (11/05) — 45 mins

As a CIMA member, you have recently been appointed as the Head of Internal Audit for SPQ, a multinational listed company that carries out a large volume of internet sales to customers who place their orders using their home or work computers. You report to the Chief Executive, although you work closely with the Finance Director. You have direct access to the Chair of the Audit committee whenever you consider it necessary.

One of your internal audit teams has been conducting a review of IT security for a system which has been in operation for 18 months and which is integral to internet sales. The audit was included in the internal audit plan following a request by the chief accountant. Sample testing by the internal audit team has revealed several transactions over the last three months which have raised concerns about possible hacking or fraudulent access to the customer/order database. Each of these transactions has disappeared from the database after deliveries have been made but without sales being recorded or funds collected from the customer. Each of the identified transactions was for a different customer and there seems to be no relationship between any of the transactions.

You have received a draft report from the internal audit manager responsible for this audit which suggests serious weaknesses in the design of the system. You have discussed this informally with senior managers who have told you that such a report will be politically very unpopular with the chief executive as he was significantly involved in the design and approval of the new system and insisted it be implemented earlier than the IT department considered was advisable. No post-implementation review of the system has taken place.

You have been informally advised by several senior managers to lessen the criticism and work with the IT department to correct any deficiencies within the system and to produce a report to the audit committee that is less critical and merely identifies the need for some improvement. They suggest that these actions would avoid criticism of the chief executive by the Board of SPQ.

Required

(a) Explain the role of internal audit in internal control and risk management. **(5 marks)**

(b) Analyse the potential risks faced by SPQ that have been exposed by the review of IT security and recommend controls that should be implemented to reduce them. **(8 marks)**

(c) Discuss the issues that need to be considered when planning an audit of activities and systems such as the one undertaken at SPQ. **(5 marks)**

(d) Explain the ethical principles you should apply as the head of internal audit for SPQ when reporting the results of this internal review and how any ethical conflicts should be resolved. **(7 marks)**

(Total = 25 marks)

FINANCIAL RISKS AND CONTROLS

Questions 38 to 57 cover financial risks and controls, the subject of Part D of the BPP Study Text for Paper P3.

38 Preparation question: Bruce SA

14 June data

Bruce SA, a French company, makes a sale of $2,350,000 to a US company on 3 months' credit.

Currency Market Rates

Spot Rate $/€	1.2354 – 1.2362
Forward $/€ premium	0.0035 – 0.0028

Money Market Rates p.a.

Euro	2.2%
US	1.2%

Futures Prices (contract size = €125,000)

June	1.2347
September	1.2321

Currency options (contract size = €62,500; premia stated in cents per Euro)

	CALLS		PUTS	
Strike	*June*	*September*	*June*	*September*
12300	2.51	3.59	2.24	3.55
12350	2.27	3.36	2.50	3.82
12400	2.04	3.15	2.77	4.10
12450	1.83	2.75	3.06	4.70

Bruce receives the payment in mid-September when the spot rate is $1.2450/€.

The September futures price in mid-September is 1.2439.

Required

Recommend the most appropriate methods for Bruce SA to use to hedge its foreign exchange risk for the next three months. Your answer should include appropriate calculations to support your recommendation.

Tutor's hints. This question gives you enough data to consider all the main methods of hedging currency risks other than swaps. The key things you have to consider include;

- Which spot and forward rate to use if you are receiving dollars when you want Euros?
- If you're using the money markets, is the first stage to invest or borrow in the home or foreign markets?
- For futures, which contract to choose?
- For options do you choose a June or September, and a put or a call option?
- For options, would you exercise the option you've chosen given what you know about the closing spot rate?

39 Treasury and risk reporting (5/08) — 45 mins

(a) With specific reference to risk management:

(i) Define and discuss the role of the Treasury function within an organisation; and **(6 marks)**

(ii) Discuss the arguments for and against operating a Treasury function as a profit centre. **(6 marks)**

(b) Explain the factors a Board of Directors should consider when deciding what to include in the section entitled 'Risk Exposure and Control Systems', in their company's report. **(13 marks)**

(Total = 25 marks)

40 PS **45 mins**

(a) Explain the five input variables involved in the Black-Scholes pricing model. **(5 marks)**

PS is a medium-sized UK-based company that trades mainly in the UK and the US. In the past, PS has not hedged its currency risks but movements in the exchange rate have recently become more volatile. Assume it is now 30 September. The company expects net cash inflow in US$ (sales receipts less purchases) on 31 December of US$2,350,000.

The current quoted spot rate of exchange is US$1.4180 – 1.4220 to the £1.

The US$ discount on the three-month forward rate of exchange is 0.36 to 0.46 cents.

Option prices (cents per £, payable on purchase of the option, contract size £31,250):

Strike price	*September contracts*	
$	Calls	Puts
1.41	2.28	1.69
1.42	1.77	2.19
1.43	1.36	2.68

Assume there are three months from now to the expiry of the September contracts and that the spot rate in three months' time is $1.4400:£1.

The company plans to hedge the risk using either a fixed forward contract or a European currency option. Ignore transaction costs.

Required

(b) Recommend with reasons, the most appropriate methods for PS to use to hedge its foreign exchange risk for the next three months. Your answer should include appropriate calculations to support your recommendations. **(20 marks)**

(Total = 25 marks)

41 SDT (5/05) **45 mins**

SDT plc is a UK based manufacturer of a wide range of printed circuit boards (PCBs) that are used in a variety of electrical products. SDT exports over 90% of its production to assembly plants owned by large multinational electronics companies all around the world. Two companies (A and B) require SDT to invoice them in a single currency, regardless of the export destination of the PCBs. The chosen currencies are the Japanese Yen (Company A) and the US$ (Company B) respectively. The remaining export sales all go to European customers and are invoiced in Euros.

The variable cost and export price per unit PCB are shown below.

Market	*Unit variable cost (£)*	*Unit export sales price*
Company A	2.75	Yen 632.50
Company B	4.80	US$ 10.2678
Europe	6.25	Euro 12.033

Goods are supplied on 60 day credit terms.

The following receipts for export sales are due in 60 days:

Company A	Yen 9,487,500
Company B	US$ 82,142
Europe	Euro 66,181

The foreign exchange rates to be used by SDT in evaluating its revenue from the export sales are as follows.

	Yen/£	*US$/£*	*Euro/£*
Spot market	198.987 – 200.787	1.7620 – 1.7826	1.4603 – 1.4813
2 months forward	197.667 – 200.032	1.7550 – 1.7775	1.4504 – 1.4784
3 months forward	196.028 – 198.432	1.7440 – 1.7677	1.4410 – 1.4721
1 year forward	188.158 – 190.992	1.6950 – 1.7311	1.4076 – 1.4426

The Managing Director of SDT believes that the foreign exchange markets are efficient and so the likelihood that SDT will make foreign exchange gains is the same as the likelihood that it will make foreign exchange losses. Furthermore, any exchange risk is already diversified across three currencies, each from countries in very different economic regions of the world. The Managing Director has therefore recommended that the Treasury Department should not hedge any foreign exchange risks arising from export sales.

Required

(a) Critically comment on the validity of the views and recommendations expressed by the Managing Director and explain how currency hedging might nevertheless be beneficial to SDT. **(6 marks)**

(b) (i) Calculate the sterling value of the contribution earned from exports to each of the customers (A, B and Europe) assuming that SDT:

(1) Hedges the risk in the forward market; **(3 marks)**

(2) Does not hedge the risk and the relevant spot exchange rates in two months' time are as follows:

Two month spot
Yen/£ 200.18 – 202.63
US$/£ 1.7650 – 1.7750
Euro/£ 1.4600 – 1.4680

(3 marks)

(ii) Calculate the average contribution to sales ratio in each of the above scenarios and advise SDT accordingly on whether to hedge its foreign exchange exposure. **(3 marks)**

(c) Comment on why (based on relative risk analysis) a company might seek to generate higher rates of return from export sales compared to domestic sales. **(6 marks)**

(d) If the payment from Company B is received late, briefly explain what risk SDT is taking in hedging B's payment in the forward market, and how this risk could be avoided. **(4 marks)**

(Total = 25 marks)

42 Derivatives (5/06) 45 mins

Warren Buffett, the stock market investor, views derivatives as a 'time bomb', but many corporate treasurers clearly perceive them as very useful tools for reducing risk.

Required

(a) Explain and discuss the reasons for such divergent viewpoints. **(13 marks)**

The International Accounting Standard on Financial Instrument Recognition and Measurement (IAS 39) includes a fair value option that permits a company to designate certain types of financial instruments as ones to be measured at fair value on initial recognition, with changes in fair value recognised in profit or loss. The designation is irrevocable. Additionally, all financial assets and liabilities held for trading are measured at fair value with the associated changes in value passing through profit and loss.

This method of accounting is defended on the grounds that it ensures that the disclosures better reflect the risks that are being taken, thereby improving the information available to the stock market.

Required

(b) Explain the additional risks arising from these rules that may be faced by companies which choose to exercise the fair value option and/or regularly trade derivatives for profit. **(5 marks)**

An investor owns a portfolio of shares that has varied in value over the last twelve months between £1·5 million and £1·8 million. All stock is highly liquid and can be sold within one day. The daily profit and loss distribution is assumed to be normally distributed with a mean of zero and a standard deviation of £60,000.

Required

(c) (i) Explain the meaning of the term 'value at risk' from the perspective of a fund manager. **(4 marks)**

(ii) Calculate and comment upon the value at risk of the portfolio, assuming a 95% confidence level and a one day holding period. **(3 marks)**

(Total = 25 marks)

43 MNO (11/06) 45 mins

MNO is a UK based company that has delivered goods, invoiced at $1,800,000 US dollars to a customer in Singapore. Payment is due in three months' time, that is, in February 20X7. The finance director of MNO is concerned about the potential exchange risk resulting from the transaction and wishes to hedge the risk in either the futures or the options market.

The current spot rate is $1·695/£. A three month futures contract is quoted at $1·690/£, and the contract size for $/£ futures contracts is £62,500.

A three month put option is available at a price of $1·675.

Required

(a) Assuming that the spot rate and the futures rate turn out to be the same in February 20X7, indicating that there is no basis risk, identify the lowest cost way of hedging the exchange rate risk (using either futures or options) where the exchange rate at the time of payment is:

(i) $1·665/£

(ii) $1·720/£

Note: Your answer should show all the calculations used to reach your answer, including the extent (if any) of the uncovered risk. **(10 marks)**

(b) Briefly discuss the problems of using futures contracts to hedge exchange rate risks. **(6 marks)**

(c) Identify and explain the key reasons why small versus large companies may differ in terms of both the extent of foreign exchange and interest rate hedging that is undertaken, and the tools used by management for such purposes. **(9 marks)**

(Total = 25 marks)

44 GOH 45 mins

Assume you are the financial manager with GOH, a large, multinational company. The company wishes to raise finance to fund an increase in working capital requirements, caused by a decision to implement a more aggressive sales and marketing policy. Its current finance is largely US$ denominated although it has some borrowing in £ sterling. The company treasurer believes there are advantages to borrowing at a floating rate of interest in the Eurobond market and entering into a swap arrangement with JJ, a UK-based company in the same industry but which, because of its smaller size, has a lower credit rating. JJ would prefer to borrow at fixed rates to finance an acquisition.

GOH currently has a credit rating of AAA and is able to raise fixed-rate finance in the Eurobond market at 8.5% and floating rate finance at LIBOR + 0.5%. The smaller company can raise fixed-rate finance at 10.5% and floating rate finance at LIBOR + 1.1%. The swap will be arranged through GOH's bank, which will charge fees of 0.15% of the principal sums. The bank is suggesting the following swap terms to open negotiations:

JJ will pay 9% fixed to GOH
GOH will pay LIBOR + 0.0% to JJ

Required

(a) Explain, in the context of the scenario, the principles and benefits of interest rate swaps and the financial advantages to both GOH and JJ that will result from the swap's interest rate effects. **(12 marks)**

GOH has agreed to sell goods to an importer in the USA at an invoiced price of $150,000. Of this amount, $60,000 will be payable on shipment, $45,000 one month after shipment and $45,000 three months after shipment.

The quoted foreign exchange rates ($ per £) at the date of shipment are as follows.

Spot	1.690 - 1.692
One month	1.687 - 1.690
Three months	1.680 - 1.684

The merchant decides to enter into appropriate forward exchange contracts through his bank to hedge these transactions.

Required

(b) (i) (1) State what are the presumed advantages of doing this.

(2) Calculate the sterling amount that GOH would receive.

(3) Illustrate the wisdom of hedging in this instance, assuming that the spot rates at the dates of receipt of the two instalments of $45,000 were as follows.

First instalment	1.694 - 1.696
Second instalment	1.700 - 1.704

(9 marks)

(ii) (1) Explain how foreign exchange transactions using futures would differ from those assumed in part (b)(i) of this question.

(2) Describe what other types of contract (apart from those in foreign currencies) are available on the market and how they can assist the financial management of commercial undertakings.

(4 marks)

(Total = 25 marks)

*

45 BB

45 mins

BB is a UK-based construction company that operates internationally, mainly in the Middle and Far East. It has recently obtained a contract to build a number of electricity generating stations (EGSs) in an Eastern European country (EE). The EGSs will be paid for by the EE government at a fixed price of 2,000 million EE marks 12 months after the start of the contract. BB will need to spend 750 million EE marks immediately and an additional 750 million EE marks in 6 months' time. The company has not worked in Eastern Europe before and has no other business in this region. no matching possible

The treasurer of BB is discussing the possibility of a fixed-rate currency swap with an EE-based company that trades in the UK. The swap would be taken out immediately for the full expected expenditure of 1,500 million EE marks at a swap rate of 15 EE marks to the £ sterling.

Interest of 20% each year would be payable on the full 1,500 million EE mark swap by BB to the EE-based company. Payment would be in EE marks. The EE-based company will pay interest to BB on the sterling value of the swap at 12%. Payment would be in £ sterling. Assume interest payments are made annually at the end of the year.

There are no formal capital markets in the EE country and therefore no forward rates are available for the EE mark against the £. Forecasts of inflation rates for next year are 3% in the UK and 25% in the EE country.

Assume the value of the EE mark is allowed to float freely by the EE government. The current spot rate is 18 EE marks to the £.

Required

(a) Explain the procedure for a currency swap, and recommend, with appropriate supporting calculations, whether BB should enter into the currency swap with the EE-based company. **(15 marks)**

(b) Discuss the advantages and disadvantages to a company such as BB of using swap arrangements as part of its treasury management strategies, in general and in the circumstances of the proposed contract. **(10 marks)**

(Total = 25 marks)

46 RET **45 mins**

RET Inc is a medium sized US company that trades with companies in several European countries. Trade deals over the next three months are shown below. Assume that it is now 20 April.

	Two months time		*Three months time*	
	Receipts	*Payments*	*Receipts*	*Payments*
France	–	€393,265	€491,011	€60,505
Germany	–	–	€890,217	€1,997,651
Denmark	–	–	Kr 8.6m	–

Foreign exchange rates

	Dkroner/$	*Euro €/$*
Spot	10.68 – 10.71	1.439 – 1.465
Two months forward	10.74 – 10.77	1.433 – 1.459
Three months forward	10.78 – 10.83	1.431 – 1.456

Annual interest rates (valid for 2 months or 3 months)

	Borrowing	*Investing*
	%	%
USA	7.50	5.50
France	5.75	3.50
Germany	5.75	3.50
Denmark	8.00	6.00

Futures market rates:

Three month Euro contracts (125,000 Euro contract size)

Contracts are for buying or selling Euros. Futures prices are in $ per Euro.

June	0.6964
September	0.6983
December	0.7013

Required

(a) Construct, using the forward market, money market and currency futures market as appropriate, a foreign exchange hedging strategy that is expected to maximise the cash flows of RET at the end of the three month period. Assume closing futures price is the same as the spot price at 0.6667 $:€ on the day the contract is closed out. **(17 marks)**

(b) List the advantages and disadvantages of forward contracts and currency futures for hedging against foreign exchange risk. **(8 marks)**

(Total = 25 marks)

work out result using futures of the two and 3 mth position

47 Arbitrage (5/08) — 45 mins

A foreign exchange dealer working in a London-based investment bank wishes to take advantage of arbitrage opportunities in the international money markets.

The following data is available relating to interest rates and exchange rates for Australia and the USA:

	US$/£	AUS$/£
Spot	2.0254	2.3180
6 Month Forward	1.9971	2.3602

The effective six-month Australian dollar interest rate is 3.32% and the equivalent US $ rate is 3.68%. These rates apply to both borrowing and lending.

Assume that in six months' time the actual exchange rate between sterling and Australian dollars is Aus$ 2.32/£.

The dealer is authorised to buy or sell up to US$5 million per transaction. The costs for this type of currency trading are charged in sterling at a rate of £3,000 per transaction.

Note. Each currency conversion counts as one transaction.

Required

(a) Calculate the spot and six-month forward cross rates between the Australian and US dollar. **(4 marks)**

(b) Explain the meaning of the term "arbitrage profit" and explain why such profits may be available in the scenario outlined above. (No illustrative calculations are required). **(6 marks)**

(c) Calculate the profit available to the dealer from exploiting the opportunity shown above, clearly showing all of your calculations. **(10 marks)**

(d) Explain the importance of "trading limits" and "value at risk" as tools for managing the risks within a financial trading operation. **(5 marks)**

(Total = 25 marks)

48 EX — 45 mins

EX is an importer/exporter of textiles and textile machinery. It is based in the UK but trades extensively with countries throughout Europe. It has a small subsidiary based in Switzerland. The company is about to invoice a customer in Switzerland 750,000 Swiss Francs, payable in three months' time. EX's treasurer is considering two methods of hedging the exchange risk. These are:

Method 1

Borrow SFr for three months on the money markets, convert the loan into sterling and repay the loan out of eventual receipts.

Method 2

Enter into a 3-month forward exchange contract with the company's bank to sell SFr 750,000.

The spot rate of exchange is SFr 2.3834 to £1.
The 3-month forward rate of exchange is SFr 2.3688 to £1.
Annual interest rates for 3 months are: Switzerland 3%, UK 6%.

Required

(a) Advise the treasurer on:

(i) Which of the two methods is the most financially advantageous for EX, and

(ii) The factors to consider before deciding whether to hedge the risk using the foreign currency markets

Include relevant calculations in your advice. **(14 marks)**

Assume that EX is trading in and with developing countries rather than Europe and has a subsidiary in a country with no developed capital or currency markets. EX is now about to invoice a customer in that country in the local currency.

Required

(b) Advise EX's treasurer about ways in which the risk can be managed in these circumstances.

Note: No calculations are required for this part of this question. **(6 marks)**

EX's directors have recently attended a course on the introduction of IASs 32 and 39 and are concerned about the impact these standards will have upon the company.

Required

(c) Describe the main impacts the standards will have on EX's accounting systems and risk management strategies. **(5 marks)**

(Total = 25 marks)

49 OJ — 45 mins

OJ is a supplier of leather goods to retailers in the UK and other western European countries. The company is considering entering into a joint venture with a manufacturer in South America. The two companies will each own 50% of the limited liability company JV (SA) and will share profits equally. £450,000 of the initial capital is being provided by OJ, and the equivalent in South American dollars (SA$) is being provided by the foreign partner. The managers of the joint venture expect the following net operating cash flows which are in nominal terms.

	SA$'000	*Forward rates of exchange to the £ Sterling*
Year 1	4,250	10
Year 2	6,500	15
Year 3	8,350	21

For tax reasons JV (SA), the company to be formed specifically for the joint venture, will be registered in South America.

Ignore taxation in your calculations.

Assume you are a financial adviser retained by OJ to advise on the proposed joint venture.

Required

(a) (i) Calculate the NPV of the project under the two assumptions explained below. Use a discount rate of 16% for both assumptions.

Assumption 1
The South American country has exchange controls which prohibit the payment of dividends above 50% of the annual cash flows for the first three years of the project. The accumulated balance can be repatriated at the end of the third year.

Assumption 2
The government of the South American country is considering removing exchange controls and restrictions on repatriation of profits. If this happens all cash flows will be distributed as dividends to the partner companies at the end of each year.

(ii) Recommend whether or not the joint venture should proceed based solely on these calculations. **(7 marks)**

During a meeting to discuss the joint venture, the following questions are raised by the managers of OJ.

(i) 'In reality we will exchange our SA$ cash flows into Sterling at the spot rate prevailing at the end of each year. How reliable are forward rates of exchange as predictors of spot rates?'

(ii) 'If exchange controls exist we will not get much of our cash for three years. Surely we should be using a higher discount rate for Assumption 1?'

(iii) 'Under either assumption we have to accept substantial exchange rate risk. Could we use a currency swap to help us minimise this risk?'

Required

(b) Discuss the three questions raised by the managers of OJ and advise them of any other practical issues which should be considered before they decide to proceed. **(18 marks)**

(Total = 25 marks)

50 ADB 45 mins

ADB is bidding for a contract to supply and install air conditioning equipment to a hotel chain in a Middle Eastern country where there is no interest rate. The variable cost of manufacture and installation was estimated at £640,000 and the contract will take 12 months to complete. The company typically requires a 20% contribution on contracts such as this (ie the contribution to fixed costs is equal to 20% of sales revenue). The contract states that payment will be made in the local currency 15 months after the contract is signed. There are penalty clauses in the contract.

ADB finances its working capital by bank overdraft or short-term loans raised in the UK. The current cost to the company of borrowing this type of finance is 8% per annum.

The company does not always hedge its exchange risks, especially with trades within the European common currency area. Some managers believe there is no merit in hedging currency risk with *any* contract. The spot exchange rate is 5.89 local currency units to £1 sterling. No forward rate is available for the local currency. Annual inflation rates are forecast as 3% in the UK and 5% in the Middle Eastern country. The company treasurer's view is that the local currency will steadily weaken against the pound sterling by 2% per annum.

One of the countries bordering the country with which ADB is dealing has recently imposed restrictions on the monies that can be sent overseas to foreign investors. If ADB is to extend its operations in this region the restrictions may prove problematic.

Required

Assume you are a newly-appointed financial controller of ADB's export division. Write a report to ADB's managing director that includes the following.

(a) A calculation of the estimated price that ADB might tender for this contract assuming you do not anticipate any over-runs. Include brief comments on the assumptions you have made to arrive at this price. **(5 marks)**

(b) An explanation of how the company might protect itself against exchange rate movements using external and/or internal hedging techniques as appropriate. **(4 marks)**

(c) A discussion of the issues that need to be considered before deciding not to hedge currency risk, in the circumstances here and as a general policy. **(9 marks)**

(d) An explanation of how the control of remittances by a government overseas may affect ADB, and the steps ADB can take. **(7 marks)**

(Total = 25 marks)

51 YZ 45 mins

YZ is a specialist food manufacturing company based in the south of England. It trades with companies within the European common currency area. The following receipts and payments are due within the next three months:

	Euros (€)
Due in 1 month:	
Payments to suppliers	600,000
Receipts from customers	400,000
Due in 3 months	
Payments to suppliers	800,000
Receipts from customers	1,200,000

Do again

Exchange rates as at today:	€/£	
Spot	1.6186 – 1.6202	
1 month forward	0.0006 – 0.0002 premium	
3 months forward	0.0013 – 0.0008 premium	
Interest rates (annual)		
(assumed to apply throughout the common currency area)	*Borrowing*	*Lending*
£ sterling	4.25	3.75
€ (Euro)	3.50	3.00

Required

(a) Calculate the *net* Sterling currency receipts or payments that YZ might expect for *both* its one-month and three-month transactions if it:

(i) Hedges the risk using the forward market

(ii) Hedges the risk using the money market

(iii) Does not hedge the risk and the €/£ spot exchange rates in one and three months' time are 1·6192 – 1·6208 and 1·6200 – 1·6220 respectively **(14 marks)**

(b) Discuss the advantages and disadvantages of the three courses of action being considered in (a) and recommend which you consider to be the most appropriate for YZ.

[Note: alternative (iii) is not to hedge. You would not of course know what the actual exchange rates will be when you offer this advice.] **(11 marks)**

Note: A report format is NOT required in answering this question. **(Total = 25 marks)**

52 VQR (5/07) 45 mins

You are the newly-appointed treasurer of VQR Ltd, a medium-sized importing and exporting company, based in Singapore. The company imports goods from Australia and New Zealand and exports these goods to the United States. A subsidiary company, based in Sydney, Australia is partly financed by an Australian dollar denominated floating rate bank loan. VQR uses the forward or money markets to hedge its foreign currency risk. Most customers are allowed, and take, 3 months' credit.

You need to respond to the points raised in the following memo from your Chief Executive Officer:

MEMORANDUM

From: CEO
To: Treasurer
Date: 24 May 20X7

I have been reading the financial section of the local business press and note the following in respect of interest rates and other economic data:

Exchange rates	*Sing $/US$*	*Aust $/US$*	
Spot rate	1.565	1.311	
1 month forward	1.562	1.312	
	Singapore	*USA*	*Australia*
Annual inter-bank offer rate	3.44%	5.38%	6.2%

Annual inflation for Singapore over the next 12 months in Singapore is forecast at 0.5%, compared with forecast rates of 1.3% for Australia and 1.86% for the USA.

(a) As interest rates are higher in the USA than here in Singapore, surely the US$ should be trading forward at a premium to the Sing$, not at a discount?

(b) The newspaper did not quote a 3-month forward rate. We have recently sold goods to a customer in the US to the value of US$ 3 million. What 3 month forward rate of exchange is implied by the information we do have, and therefore what will be the receipt in Singapore dollars in 3 months' time?

(c) Can we save money by buying Aust$ on the spot market as and when we need them to pay for imports, rather than taking out forward contracts, and are there any disadvantages to this strategy?

(d) Would it be in our interests to borrow Sing$ and use the proceeds to pay off our Aust$ loan given that rates of interest in Australia are higher than those in Singapore?

Please respond to these questions by the close of today.

Required

Produce a response to the CEO.

Note. Your response should include a brief explanation of theories and appropriate calculations to support your discussion. 5 marks will be allocated for explanation of appropriate theories. The balance of 20 marks is for application of those theories and relevant calculations. **(25 marks)**

53 IOU ✱ 45 mins

IOU Inc is a large company based in the USA that trades mainly within the USA and with the UK. It has a significant amount of borrowing in £ sterling. Debt interest of £725,000 is due to be paid on 31 October and a further £530,000 on 31 December. IOU Inc's policy is to hedge the risks involved in all foreign currency transactions.

Assume it is now 30 September. The company's bank quotes the following rates of exchange, US$ per £:

Spot	*1 month forward (mid rate)*	*3 months forward (mid rate)*
1.5584 – 1.5590	1.5601	1.5655

Prices for a £/US$ option on a US Stock Exchange (cents per £, payable on purchase of the option, contract size £31,250) are:

Strike price	*Calls*		*Puts*	
(US$/£)	*October*	*December*	*October*	*December*
1.56	2.02	3.00	1.00	2.16
1.57	1.32	n/a	n/a	n/a
1.58	0.84	2.12	2.18	3.14

The Treasurer is considering two methods of hedging the risk, fixed forward or option contracts. Market expectations, based on current published economic forecasts, are that sterling will appreciate against the US$ over the next three months. The Treasurer thinks it might weaken or at least remain stable against the $. He suggests that if options are to be used, one-month options should be bought at a strike price of 1.57 and three-month options at a strike price of 1.58.

You can assume for the purposes of the calculation that the forward rates are accurate predictors of future spot rates. Ignore transaction costs.

Required

(a) Recommend, with reasons, the most appropriate method for IOU Inc to hedge its foreign exchange risk on the two interest payments due in one and three months time. Your answer should include appropriate calculations, using the figures in the question, to support your recommendation and a discussion of the factors to consider when choosing between the two hedging mechanisms. **(15 marks)**

Assume you are a financial manager with the nationally-owned postal and telecommunications company in Zorro, a country in Asia. In organisations such as this, periodic settlements are made between local and foreign operators. Net receipts or payments are in US$.

Required

(b) Explain the main types of foreign exchange risk exposure that are likely to affect the organisation and advise the company on policies it could consider to reduce exposure to these risks. **(10 marks)**

(Total = 25 marks)

54 QW — 45 mins

Assume that you are treasurer of QW, a company with diversified, international interests. The company wishes to borrow £10 million for a period of three years. Your company's credit rating is good and current market data suggests that you could borrow at a fixed rate of interest at 8 per cent per annum or at a floating rate of LIBOR + 0.2 per cent per annum. You believe that interest rates are likely to fall over the next three years, and favour borrowing at a floating rate.

Your company's bankers are currently working on raising a three-year loan for £10 million for another of their customers, ER. This company is smaller and less well known than QW, and its credit rating is not as high. ER could borrow at a fixed rate of 9.5 per cent per annum or a floating rate of LIBOR + 0.5 per cent. ER has indicated to the bank that it would prefer a fixed-rate loan. Your bankers have suggested you engage in a swap which might benefit both companies. The bank's commission would be 0.2 per cent of the amount borrowed in total by both parties. Your counterpart in ER suggests that the commission fees and swap benefits should be shared equally.

Assume that interest is paid at the end of each twelve-month period of the loan's duration and that the principal is repaid on maturity (ie at the end of three years).

You have been in the post for twelve months, having been recruited from a large financial institution. You have a keen interest in using financial derivatives (such as futures and options) to both manage risk and generate revenue. Some board members have expressed concern that your activities may be involving the company in unnecessary risk.

Required

Write a report to the board which:

(a) Explains the meaning and use of financial derivatives, in general terms, and the advantages and disadvantages of their use for companies such as QW. **(8 marks)**

(b) Describes the characteristics and benefits of interest rate swaps compared with other forms of interest-rate-risk management, such as forward rate agreements and interest rate futures **(8 marks)**

(c) Explains the course of action necessary to implement the swap being considered with ER, and calculates and comments on the financial benefits to be gained **(9 marks)**

(Total = 25 marks)

55 LXN (11/05) — 45 mins

LXN is a large book retailer in France and as a result of recent rapid sales growth has decided to expand by opening six new branches in the south of France. The estimated set up cost per branch is €250,000 and LXN wishes to raise the required funding (plus an additional 20 per cent for increased working capital requirements) via borrowing. The Treasurer of LXN is concerned about interest rate risk however, and is unsure about whether to opt for a fixed or floating rate loan. LXN's Board of Directors has indicated that it wishes to maximise the company's use of opportunities to hedge interest rate risk.

LXN currently has €2,000 million of assets and the following long-term debt in its balance sheet.

€15 million [(6% fixed rate) redeemable 20X9]
€18 million [(Sterling LIBOR plus 3%) redeemable 20X7]

All rates are quoted as an annual rate. The current exchange rate is £/€0.684.

Required

(a) Discuss the factors that should be taken into account by the Treasurer of LXN when deciding whether to raise fixed rate or floating rate debt for the expansion project and whether to hedge the resulting interest rate exposure. **(10 marks)**

LXN's Treasurer has negotiated a fixed rate of 6% or a variable rate of Euro LIBOR plus 1.5% for the required borrowing. In addition, a counterparty (MGV) has offered to convert any new fixed rate debt that LXN takes on into synthetic floating rate debt via a swap arrangement in which the two companies will share the quality spread differential equally.

MGV, the counterparty, can borrow at a fixed rate of 7.2% or at a variable rate of Euro LIBOR plus 2.5%.

Euro LIBOR is currently 5%. All rates are quoted as an annual rate.

Required

(b) (i) Briefly discuss the advantages and disadvantages of interest rate swaps as a tool for managing interest rate risk. **(5 marks)**

(ii) Draw a diagram to illustrate how the transactions between LXN and MGV and the two lenders will operate if the swap is agreed. **(4 marks)**

(iii) Calculate the interest rate terms payable by LXN. Evaluate the potential annual saving resulting from borrowing at a fixed rate and engaging in an interest rate swap, as against a straightforward floating rate loan. **(6 marks)**

(Total = 25 marks)

56 X (11/07) — 45 mins

X is a small company based in England. The company had the choice of launching a new product in either England or France but lack of funding meant that it could not do both. The company bases its decisions on Expected Net Present Value (ENPV) and current exchange rates. As a result of this methodology, and the details shown below, it was decided to launch in England (with an ENPV of £28,392) and not France (with an ENPV of £25,560).

England	*Probability*	**France**	*Probability*
Launch costs		**Launch costs**	
£145,000	0.1	£190,000	1.0
£120,000	0.9		
Annual cash flows		**Annual cash flows**	
£65,000	0.4	£90,000	0.5
£42,000	0.4	£70,000	0.2
£24,000	0.2	£30,000	0.3

The annual cash flows are based on contribution margins of 10% for England and 20% for France where it is expected that sales volumes will be lower. It is thought that the product will sell for four years only.

The monetary values are express in the home currency of the company and have been converted (where necessary) at the current exchange rate of €1.47/£1.

The company has discounted the cash flows using a cost of capital of 10% per year.

Required

(a) It has now been forecast that the Euro is likely to strengthen against sterling by 5% in each of the next four years.

Calculate and briefly comment upon the revised Expected Net Present Value if the product is launched in France. **(5 marks)**

(b) Identify the different risks associated with each launch option and discuss how these may be managed by the company. **(8 marks)**

Company X wishes to raise a £500,000 floating rate bank loan to fund the product launch and additional capital investments. Company X is able to obtain fixed rate finance at 8.5% or a variable rate loan at LIBOR + 0.5%. Using its bank as an intermediary, Company X has been offered a swap arrangement with HTM, a smaller company that wishes to borrow at a fixed rate. HTM has been quoted a rate of 10.5% for a fixed rate loan or LIBOR + 1.1% for a floating rate loan. The bank charge for arranging a swap is 0.2% of the principal £500,000, and it is assumed that the net benefits will be shared equally between Company X and HTM.

Required

(c) (i) Briefly discuss the potential benefits and hazards of interest rate swaps as a tool for managing interest rate risk. **(6 marks)**

(ii) Show the transactions involved, the bank charges and the interest terms payable if X and HTM agree to the swap. **(6 marks)**

(Total = 25 marks)

57 Listed services group (Pilot paper) 45 mins

A listed services group with a UK head office and subsidiaries throughout the world reports in Sterling and shows the following liabilities in its notes to the accounts.

Liabilities All figures are in £ million	*Total liabilities*	*Floating rate*	*Fixed rate liabilities*	*Weighted average interest rate*	*Weighted average years for which rate is fixed*
£ Sterling	98	98			
$ US	41	8	33	7.25%	5
Euro	4	4			
Total	143	110	33		

Maturity All figures are in £ million	*Total*	*Maturing within 1 year*	*Within 1-2 years*	*Within 2-5 years*	*Over 5 years*
£ Sterling	98	73	3	18	4
$ US	41				41
Euro	4	1	1	1	1
Total	143	74	4	19	46

Interest rates are currently about 5%.

Required

(a) (i) Evaluate the main sources of financial risk for this group (assuming there are no offsetting assets that might provide a hedge against the liabilities).

(ii) Quantify the transaction risk faced by the group if sterling was to depreciate against the $US and Euro by 10%.

(iii) Evaluate how transaction risk relates to translation risk and economic risk in this example. **(13 marks)**

(b) Discuss the use of exchange traded and Over The Counter (OTC) derivatives for hedging and how they may be used to reduce the exchange rate and interest rate risks the group faces. Illustrate your answer by comparing and contrasting the main features of appropriate derivatives. **(12 marks)**

(Total = 25 marks)

INTERNATIONAL RISKS AND CONTROLS

Question 58 covers international risks and controls, the subject of Part E of the BPP Study Text for Paper P3.

58 ZX (Pilot paper) 45 mins

ZX is a UK-based retailer and manufacturer that also owns a limited number of outlets in the USA, but is anxious to expand internationally via the use of franchising agreements. The enterprise plans to open five franchised shops in each of France, Italy, Germany, Belgium and Holland over the course of the next twelve months. ZX will provide loan finance to assist individuals wishing to purchase a franchise, the average cost of which will be €100,000. Loans will also be available (up to a maximum of 50% of the purchase price) to cover the cost of the franchisee acquiring suitable freehold or leasehold premises. The total sum required for the property loan facility is estimated by the treasurer of ZX to equal €4.8 million. The opportunity cost of capital in the UK is 10% per annum but, in recognition of the lower rates of interest available in the Eurozone, ZX will only charge the franchisees a fixed rate of 7.0% each year on all loans. Repayments will be made in equal Euro-denominated instalments.

ZX charges commission to the franchisees at a rate of 1% of sales revenue, and also earns a net margin of 12% (of retail value) on the products supplied to the outlets from its UK manufacturing plant.

Planned sales from the new European outlets equal €26 million over the next twelve months, but the enterprise recognises that its profits are dependent upon both sales revenue and the extent of loan defaults amongst franchisees (if any). Estimates of the likelihood of a range of scenarios are detailed below.

Probability	*Sales*	*Number of loan defaults*	*Comment*
0.1	10% below plan	2	Economic difficulties reduce sales and cause problems for some franchisees
0.3	20% below plan	4	Severe economic problems lead to low sales and higher loan defaults
0.4	As per plan	0	'Base case'
0.2	As per plan	1	The weak German economy causes problems for one franchisee

Loan default is assumed to mean total write-off and ZX expects 80% of the new franchisees to take full advantage of the loan facilities offered to them.

The current Euro:Sterling exchange rate is €1.3939/£ and the Euro is expected to strengthen against Sterling by 5% over the next twelve months.

In addition to the cash required to fund the foreign loan facility, a further £3.65 million of working capital will be required for the expansion project and the treasury department of ZX requires a minimum annualised return of 15% on all overseas projects.

Required

(a) Use the table of possible scenarios given above to calculate the expected sterling value of the additional profit that ZX will earn if the store openings are completed as planned and the foreign exchange rate forecast is fulfilled. (You should use the average exchange rate over the year for the calculation.)

You should evaluate whether this profit yields the return required for international operations. **(7 marks)**

(b) Discuss the risks that ZX might face in choosing to expand into Europe via the use of franchising. **(8 marks)**

(c) Evaluate methods of managing/minimising the risks involved in granting Euro denominated loans to the franchisees. **(10 marks)**

(Total = 25 marks)

INFORMATION SYSTEMS RISKS AND CONTROLS

Questions 59 to 66 cover information systems risks and controls, the subject of Part F of the BPP Study Text for Paper P3.

59 WRF — 45 mins

WRF Inc trades in a dynamic environment where it is essential that information is presented quickly and clearly to its staff. The information can come from the company's database or from other staff members. Significant processing of the information is also required on each individual's Personal Computer (PC) before effective decisions can be made.

WRF Inc intends to upgrade its computer system to improve speed and clarity of information. Each member of staff will have a PC linked to a Local Area Network (LAN). The network will be used for centralised backup, access to a central database, and storage of data files. The LAN will also be used for communication within the office by e-mail.

The network will incorporate a central file server. The systems analyst is on a fixed term contract which terminates when the system installation is complete.

Users have broadly welcomed the move although they have not been formally told of the system change. However the head of internal audit has queried the ordering process and the lack of authorisation from the board, and has also pointed out that the plans for implementing the system do not provide for sufficient documentation nor testing, nor is there any provision for a post-implementation review.

Required

As assistant to the head of internal audit, explain:

(a) The problems with the current process, showing why the systems development lifecycle would be preferable. **(13 marks)**

(b) The significance of systems and user acceptance testing. **(7 marks)**

(c) The need for a post-implementation review. **(5 marks)**

(Total = 25 marks)

60 MG II (Pilot paper) — 45 mins

The information systems strategy within the MG organisation has been developed over a number of years. However, the basic approach has always remained unchanged. An IT budget is agreed by the board each year. The budget is normally 5% to 10% higher than the previous year's to allow for increases in prices and upgrades to computer systems.

Systems are upgraded in accordance with user requirements. Most users see IT systems as tools for recording day-to-day transactions and providing access to accounting and other information as necessary. There is no Enterprise Resource Planning System (ERPS) or Executive Information System (EIS).

The board tends to rely on reports from junior managers to control the business. While these reports generally provide the information requested by the board, they are focused at a tactical level and do not contribute to strategy formulation or implementation.

Required

(a) Compare and contrast information systems strategy, information technology strategy and information management strategy and explain how these contribute to the business. **(10 marks)**

(b) Advise the board on how an ERPS and EIS could provide benefits over and above those provided by transaction processing systems. **(10 marks)**

(c) Recommend to the board how it should go about improving its budgetary allocations for IT and how it should evaluate the benefits of ERPS and EIS. **(5 marks)**

(Total = 25 marks)

61 AMF (5/05) 45 mins

AMF is a market leading, high technology manufacturing organisation producing components for the computer industry. AMF has adopted a 'lean' approach to all its functions and has already made a decision to implement a new enterprise resource planning system (ERPS) to support the management of its customers, suppliers, inventory, capacity planning, production scheduling, distribution and accounting functions. The Board of AMF is considering the outsourcing of the design, delivery, implementation and operation of the ERPS to a specialist contractor that has an excellent reputation within the computer industry. A team would be set up within AMF to manage the transition.

Required

Write a formal report to the Board of AMF that:

(a) Discusses the advantages and disadvantages of outsourcing the ERPS system as suggested above. **(5 marks)**

(b) Identifies the main risks involving in outsourcing the ERPS and suggests how these risks might be mitigated through internal controls and internal audit. **(10 marks)**

(c) Recommends the processes and controls that AMF should adopt to manage a project for successful transition to a chosen outsource supplier should that be the decision of the Board. **(5 marks)**

(Total = 25 marks)

(Total marks include 5 marks for style, coherence and presentation of the report.)

62 Computer problems 45 mins

On your first morning as financial controller of a large manufacturing division of a group of companies, you meet, for the first time, some of the key staff reporting to you.

The manager of the divisional computer installation (the computer services manager) announces that he wishes to give one month's notice and resign to take up another post.

Discussions with him produce the following information.

(i) Much of the computer's work is on an integrated system of inventory and production control and invoicing.

(ii) This system was bought from a large firm of consultants, which installed the system, five years ago.

(iii) After the consultants had installed the system there was a disagreement over their fees and the system has since been maintained by the operating staff. The computer services manager had done most of the system modification, and had been helped by one of the shift supervisors. The computer services manager considered that the shift supervisor could continue to make any necessary changes.

(iv) The computer services manager had a file of his (handwritten) amendment notes, but did not have an up-to-date set of system operating instructions.

(v) The computer services manager is concerned that there is no back-up system. Until a year ago there had been reciprocal emergency arrangements with a firm in a similar industry, but not a competitor, some twenty miles away. However, it had now closed, and no alternative arrangements had been made.

You are due to meet the key group staff, including the finance director, internal audit manager, and group IT (Information Technology) adviser (who has responsibility for IT policy within the group) tomorrow.

Required

Write a memorandum to your managing director

(a) Explaining the most significant risks that affect the company's computerised operations. **(7 marks)**

(b) Explaining what action you need to take during the next month. **(12 marks)**

(c) Explaining what action the Internal Audit Department should have taken in recent years. **(6 marks)**

(Total = 25 marks)

63 Lottery **45 mins**

The government department responsible for handing out lottery funding to deserving causes has recently overhauled its information systems, because the old systems were unable to cope with the volume of claims that were being processed. Smaller awards are based on information supplied by the bodies applying for grants, supported by independent testimonials. Larger awards are made after visits to the applicants by assessors employed by the department.

The new system is based on a unified database system with real-time processing, run by a central department based in the capital city. In this system all claims are entered on the database when received, and the progress of all claims is tracked. The government is particularly concerned that the assessors' reports and other details about the assessment process are kept secure, since problems with the old system allowed data to be leaked, resulting in much adverse press comment.

Because of the importance of the new system, the Minister responsible for the lottery has ordered that a detailed review be made of the new system by the Government's audit office.

Required

(a) Explain the main risks of the system and recommend the main internal controls that should be in place over the database system and processing facility. **(15 marks)**

(b) Describe the main organisational controls that should be in operation over the central department, including the role that internal audit might play. **(10 marks)**

(Total = 25 marks)

64 KL **45 mins**

KL Group has developed rapidly from a wholesaler supplying specialist stores in one region of the country into a much larger organisation with a significant share of the national market. This has been achieved by:

(a) Acquiring other regional wholesalers
(b) Acquiring local groups of retail shops
(c) Making long-term agreements with stores to act as exclusive suppliers

The group is in the process of consolidating its position, and plans to introduce as quickly as possible an integrated computer system for the whole business, to replace all the current mixture of systems. The main justification for this is to enable central purchasing to use the combined volumes to obtain the best prices and minimise stockholdings. It is envisaged that the integrated system will enable the number of warehouses to be rationalised and reduced.

The finance director has expressed his concern to you, as chief internal auditor, regarding the progress of the project. He fully agrees the need for speed, and the general direction of the project, but does not consider he is adequately informed of the progress made, or of the steps taken to ensure that accounting (and audit) problems will not arise on implementation of the integrated system.

Required

(a) Explain what steps should be taken in the management of a major project, such as the project described above, to ensure that all senior managers are fully aware of the progress made, and any problems arising. **(7 marks)**

(b) Explain briefly the potential accounting and audit problems arising from the implementation of the new integrated system, and recommend the actions required to deal with these problems. **(18 marks)**

Note. You are not required to discuss the design of the new integrated systems.

(Total = 25 marks)

65 STU (11/06) 45 mins

STU is a large distribution business which provides logistical support to large retail chains. A significant problem currently faced by STU is the number of legacy systems[1] in use throughout the organisation. The various legacy systems, each of which tends to be used by a single business function, hold data that is inconsistent with other systems, leading to an inconsistent approach to decision making across the business. The problem is made worse by many managers having developed their own PC-based databases and spreadsheets because of the lack of suitable information produced by the legacy systems.

STU's Board of Directors has recently approved the feasibility study presented by the Finance Director for the in-house development of a new Strategic Enterprise Management (SEM) system. The SEM system will use real-time data entry to collect transaction data from remote sites to maintain a data warehouse storing all business information which can then be accessed by various analytical tools to support strategic decision making. The SEM system will be developed and implemented over a three year period within a budget approved by the Board. Three phases have been identified: design of the new system; development of the software; and delivery of the finished system into business units. The Board considers that designing, developing and delivering the SEM system will be crucial to business growth plans in a competitive environment.

[1]Note: A legacy system is a computer system which continues to be used because the information it provides is critical to a business. However, the high cost of replacing or redesigning the system has led to it being retained by the business. It is typically an older design, is not compatible with more up-to-date software, and because of its age, provides information that is not as complete or reliable as it should be.

Required

(a) Assuming that you are STU's Head of Internal Audit, recommend the actions that should be taken in connection with the design, development and delivery of the SEM system. **(13 marks)**

(b) Advise the audit committee of STU about:

(i) Possible approaches to auditing computer systems; and
(ii) The controls that should exist in an IT environment. **(12 marks)**

(Total = 25 marks)

66 VWS (11/07) 45 mins

VWS is a company manufacturing and selling a wide range of industrial products to a large number of businesses throughout the country. VWS is a significant local employer, with 2,500 people working out of several locations around the region, all linked by a networked computer system.

VWS purchases numerous components from 750 local and regional suppliers, receiving these components into a central warehouse. The company carries about 10,000 different inventory items, placing 25,000 orders with its suppliers each year.

The accounts payable department of VWS has six staff who process all supplier invoices through the company's computer system and make payment to suppliers by cheque or electronic remittance.

Required

(a) Discuss the purpose and value of an internal control system for accounts payable to a company like VWS. **(10 marks)**

(b) Identify the information systems controls that should be in place for accounts payable in a company like VWS. **(10 marks)**

(c) Explain the risks of fraud in a computerised accounts payable system for a company like VWS and how that risk can be mitigated. **(5 marks)**

(Total = 25 marks)

CASE STUDY QUESTIONS

Questions 67 to 78 are 50 marks case study questions.

67 VSYS — 90 mins

VSYS Inc manufactures a range of computer products including silicon chips, hard drives and advanced graphic cards from its single factory located in a medium-sized town in central USA. About 20% of the working population are employed at VSYS, and the company has a reputation for being a good employer with specific focus on maintaining and enhancing benefits for its employees. A local university runs courses specifically for potential employees of VSYS.

Although the company is profitable, the recent management accounts show falling margins with the possibility of a loss being made next year; the first in the 25 year history of the company. The main reasons for the falling profits have been identified as increasing competition from manufacturers in the Far East, and ongoing quality control issues with several key manufacturers. A recent feasibility study shows that moving production to a Far Eastern country would enable VSYS to take advantage of lower labour costs and proximity to suppliers of high quality components. The administration and marketing functions would remain at their current location. While a final decision has yet to be made, the Board is aware of the negative impact this could have on the image of the company and are therefore reluctant to make a firm commitment.

Movement of production systems to the Far East is seen as a particular problem for VSYS. Specific areas of concern include:

(i) Obtaining and maintaining supplies from new suppliers
(ii) Setting up production lines with new workforce and new machinery
(iii) Maintaining sufficient inventory of materials to meet demand when the delivery times are uncertain
(iv) Ensuring the quality of employees' output
(v) Implementing any necessary revisions to the management accounting systems

However, the Board is confident that the move will be successful and looks forward to a positive response from workers and shareholders.

Required

(a) Discuss the arguments for and against outsourcing the manufacturing in VSYS, briefly explaining how the negative aspects could be alleviated. **(15 marks)**

(b) Recommend appropriate control systems and control procedures for VSYS in the possible new production location in the Far East. **(15 marks)**

(c) (i) Explain the main principles of corporate governance for listed companies, with specific reference to establishing and maintaining an internal control system and the role of internal audit. **(10 marks)**

(ii) Explain the problems with the system of management supervision and review that the decision to outsource to the Far East has highlighted, and briefly advise how these problems can be alleviated. **(10 marks)**

(Total = 50 marks)

68 ONH — 90 mins

Introduction

Our National Heritage (ONH) is a non-profit making organisation. The main aim of ONH is to maintain and provide access to buildings and landscape of cultural and national interest within its country of operation. ONH currently owns about 150 historic buildings (ranging from medieval castles through large 19th Century mansions to a few 20th terraced houses), and over 75 areas of land including sections of coastline, woodlands etc. ONH has an excellent reputation in its country; the organisation is seen to be providing a 'national service' by preserving the country's heritage for future generations.

ONH has over one million 'members' who pay an annual fee and are then granted free access to any ONH properties. Non-members may also visit ONH's properties on payment of an entry fee. However, some properties such as coastlines have effectively free access because of the difficulty of collecting entrance fees.

ONH has a small internal audit department.

Income and expenditure

Many properties are given to ONH as bequests in wills; others are purchased. Income is derived from membership and entry fees, as well as trading income from ONH shops. A significant but highly variable income stream is from bequests of money in wills. Income is supplemented by the government refunding the income tax paid by members (called Gift Aid in some countries) allowing ONH to receive membership income 'gross'. Gift Aid income is around 20% of total income. ONH rarely purchases any building or land; most are left to the organisation in wills or presented as gifts by generous benefactors.

Entry fees are not tightly controlled and many ONH workers are volunteers. Entry fees are collected as visitors enter properties owned by ONH. Receipts are provided on request and monies collected are counted by ONH staff at the end of each day. The majority of entry fees are paid in cash.

The internal audit department has reported that control over income received from visitors is weak and recommended that a more appropriate system is implemented.

Much of ONH's expenditure is essentially fixed. ONH must maintain the properties it owns. Expenditure therefore relates to maintenance costs of buildings, salaries of staff to maintain buildings, administration and finance departments. Repair costs can be significant as ONH aims to retain the original structure and appearance of buildings. For example, hand-made silk curtains may be used rather than cheaper cotton curtains where these were originally used in a building.

Information systems are implemented at each property, although the extent varies considerably from electronic cash registers to use of 'off the shelf' packages to provide basic income and expenditure summaries. There is no Wide Area Network or formal budgetary control over expenditure. Managers at each property are allowed to set their own budgets and monitor actual expenditure against budget using their own systems. The central board of ONH approve, and if necessary, amend the budget each year. The total budget for ONH is approved based on the trend of income from the past five years. The budget is generally set at 95% of the average of this income. Comparison of budget to actual expenditure is carried out at the end of each financial year.

Current situation

In the last financial year, ONH made a small 'loss'. The main reason for this was exceptional expenditure on five important buildings which had to be repaired due to storm damage. However, the trend of expenditure is increasing as more buildings and areas of land need maintaining. The government of the country ONH is based in also sets various regulations regarding repairs to historic properties that ONH is legally obliged to follow.

To an extent, ONH is becoming a victim of its own success. For example, 60,000 visitors attempted to visit one building in the last 12 months, although ONH can only cope with 500 per day in that building. Many visitors left disappointed at not being able to see the inside of the building. Furthermore, only 20% of the furniture, paintings and other contents were actually on display due to lack of display space.

A government press release indicates that Gift Aid will be phased out in 2 years time, due to high costs of administration. Most charities and organisations such as ONH have reacted with horror at the news and are considering putting pressure on the government to reverse this decision. Managers are also looking at other income generating options such as 'buy a brick' and 'adopt a house' – which basically mean members are asked to give additional amounts to support buildings within 20 km of their home.

The managers of ONH have also noted that Buildings In Trust (BIT), another organisation that maintains historic buildings (but not land), has started to diversify its activities. As well as generating income from members and admission fees, BIT also maintains restaurants in all its properties, holds evening 'open air' concerts during warmer months and hires out buildings for civic functions such as weddings. These activities have never been considered by ONH as managers have thought customers wanted to see the buildings, rather than being entertained during their visit.

Required

(a)	(i)	Prepare a SWOT analysis for Our National Heritage.	**(8 marks)**
	(ii)	Identify and explain the risks faced by Our National Heritage.	**(12 marks)**
(b)	(i)	Describe the different types of audit test that an internal audit department can perform on sales and cash receipt systems, explaining the appropriateness of each type to ONH.	**(8 marks)**
	(ii)	List and explain the controls and internal audit tests you would expect to see to determine the completeness and accuracy of income from visitors to ONH properties.	**(7 marks)**
(c)	(i)	Discuss the extent to which ONH needs to have an information strategy.	**(9 marks)**
	(ii)	Assume that ONH wants to implement an information strategy. Explain the different approaches that ONH can use to determine this strategy.	**(6 marks)**
			(Total = 50 marks)

69 PowerS — 90 mins

Background

PowerS supplies washing machines, fridges and similar kitchen equipment to customers. The company purchases goods direct from manufacturers and advertises them for sales on its Internet site. PowerS has been trading for five years and has built up a reputation for quick delivery and keen pricing in a market where there are a significant number of competitors.

Internet configuration

Access to the Internet site is provided by a dedicated leased line which PowerS leases from a specialist Internet services company. Internet servers are maintained in-house by PowerS IT staff. Both leased line and server are configured to ensure that the average number of customers are allowed to be online at any time.

PowerS employs 35 IT staff at its main processing site. Staff are responsible for upgrade and maintenance of the Internet hardware and software. Many staff see PowerS as a good place to gain Internet experience; however, they leave after an average service of two years due to relatively poor wages and lack of potential for advancement to more senior positions in the company.

Backup of all data files takes place at the end of each day with data being stored in a separate off-site location 15 kilometres from PowerS's main data processing centre. Programs are amended on a relatively frequent basis in an attempt to provide additional features on the Internet site.

Anti-virus software and firewalls are maintained for the Internet servers by IT staff. Anti-virus software is updated in-house following security recommendations issued by its Internet service company. Internet access passwords for all staff are changed every four months; the only exception is for new staff who are provided with a new password as soon as they join PowerS.

Sales systems

Customers may purchase from the PowerS Internet site by selecting the goods required, placing them into their 'shopping basket' and then proceeding to a secure payments system. Goods are despatched to customers on the next working day following checks on stock availability and the authenticity of the customer credit card. Credit card details are stored on the Internet server without encryption as they are protected by the firewall.

Goods are denominated in Euros with PowerS only accepting payment in Euros. Goods are despatched from PowerS's warehouse to customers using a third party courier. Next day delivery is available for an extra charge to the customer. Customer details are maintained on PowerS's computer systems for up to six months.

Computer upgrade and corporate culture

The Board of PowerS have recognised that their computer systems may need upgrading in the next six months. The board is also considering adding new product lines such as clothes and fashion accessories at this time as they consider if one product range can be sold in the Internet then others can be as well. The Information Systems director recommends purchasing new hardware from a foreign country, partly due to price comparisons with computers available in the local country, but mainly because of the reliability and suitability of the computer for Internet trading.

The corporate structure within PowerS is to devolve power to the individual divisions in the company. Divisional managers are expected to set budgets with the assistance of their sub-ordinates, and the board review / amend the budgets to ensure that overall corporate policy and objectives are followed. The culture within each department therefore follows this sharing philosophy wherever possible. Departmental budgets include financial and non-financial objectives; the board only amend budgets where necessary and provide clear reasons for each amendment.

However, the IT director has decided to set the budget for the new Internet development himself due to perceived lack of knowledge of accounting issues within the IT department. The director is also concerned that the budget needs to focus on financial objectives and that tight budgetary control is required, rather than the more laissez-faire approach normally adopted by PowerS. The IT manager sees Internet production as a relatively informal process – and while there is a definite outcome, the actual design and content may vary as the project progresses depending on what 'looks good' on the Internet site.

Required

(a) (i) Describe the types of audit an Internal Audit department may carry out in an organisation. **(8 marks)**

(ii) Prepare an internal audit report on the Internet systems in PowerS, which describes the risks in the system and briefly recommends methods of overcoming those risks. **(15 marks)**

(b) Describe the risks affecting PowerS from trading on the Internet, recommending how each risk can be mitigated. **(15 marks)**

(c) Discuss the setting of the budget for the update of the Internet site in terms of contingency theory, briefly noting the possible effects as outlined in the theory on the staff in IT department. **(12 marks)**

(Total = 50 marks)

70 LaPoNa — 90 mins

The current date is 30 June.

Company background

LaPoNa is an importer / exporter of specialist cars. Customers in a number of different countries place requests with LaPoNa for cars manufactured in another country; LaPoNa then locates purchases and arranges delivery of the vehicle to the customer. For example, for customers in the USA, LaPoNa may obtain Jaguar cars from England, while for English customers; LaPoNa may obtain Humbee or similar vehicles from the USA. To finance these transactions, LaPoNa has to arrange payments to and from the USA from its UK base.

LaPoNa maintains an accounting staff in the UK; the chief accountant is qualified CIMA accountant with two junior trainees who are progressing through their studies.

End of June transaction details

To simplify its accounting procedures, LaPoNa has four payment/receipt dates per annum.

The following transactions are expected on 30 September:

Sales receipts	\$750,000
Purchases	\$300,000

The current spot rate of exchange is \$1.755 to \$1.759 to the £. A premium for a 3-month forward rate of exchange is 0.75 to 0.71 cents. Annual interest rates in the USA are

Borrowing	USA 4% and UK 6%.
Lending	USA 3% and UK 4.5%

There is currently three months until the expiry of the September contracts. Transaction costs are 0.002% of the US transactions payable on 1 July.

Sales system

Sales are made to private individuals. Vehicles are ordered from either the UK or the USA after the customers' precise requirements have been determined and payment received. Due to the high value of vehicles, credit cards are used infrequently. Cheques, debit cards and bank transfers are the most common form of payment. Invoice value is cost plus 25% to cover administration fees. Cost includes vehicle purchase and shipping to the customer's home country. Sales invoices are raised manually and then entered into the computerised sales day book. Invoices are pre-numbered.

Future developments

Following the increase in sales over the last 12 months in LaPoNa, the board have decided to open three new divisions; one each in Brazil, South Africa and Singapore. The head office will remain in the UK with the USA office maintaining its division status. The board is split regarding the amount of control which should be delegated to the three new divisions in particular. While decentralisation is an option, many board members are concerned that the specific policies and procedures of LaPoNa will not be implemented if this is allowed.

Required

(a) (i) Calculate the net sterling receipts that LaPoNa can expect from its transactions if the company hedges exchange rate risk using two appropriate methods, recommending the most advantageous method for LaPoNa. **(8 marks)**

(ii) Discuss the factors that LaPoNa should consider in hedging foreign exchange risk and explain any alternative actions that LaPoNa could take to minimise this risk. **(8 marks)**

(b) Discuss the benefits of LaPoNa remaining centralised, and the benefits of allowing divisional autonomy to the three new divisions. **(16 marks)**

(c) (i) List and describe the audit tests expected in the sales system to ensure

- Vehicles are not being supplied to a poor credit risk
- Customers are being invoiced for the correct amount
- All sales are recorded in the books of the division (up to and including the nominal ledger)

(9 marks)

(ii) Explain the concepts of teeming and lading, advance fee fraud and ghost employees, noting whether they could apply to LaPoNa. **(9 marks)**

(Total = 50 marks)

71 IDAN (5/05) — 90 mins

Company overview

IDAN is a large banking and financial services group that is listed on both the London Stock Exchange and the New York Stock Exchange. The group has over 20 million customers throughout the world and operates in 35 countries on four continents. The IDAN Group is composed of a mix of retail and commercial businesses that include corporate and investment banking, private banking and commercial banking.

Trends within the Financial Services Sector

The Board of Directors of IDAN is aware that a number of trends within the sector will require the bank to substantially re-design a number of its operating and information systems and review the nature of the interface between the internal audit and risk management functions. Current issues that are having an impact on the financial services sector include:

- A new European Union law requiring banks to provide details of interest paid on personal savings accounts held by non-residents. A withholding tax of 15% is to be imposed on such income and details must be sent by the bank to the tax authorities in the EU country where the recipient resides.

- Forecast rises in interest rates over the next two years.
- The elimination within the UK of the use of personal signatures as the authorisation for credit and debit card transactions and their replacement with personal identification (PIN) numbers.
- The increasing use, by personal customers, of both telephone and internet banking services. Over 40% of bill payments, standing order amendments and balance transfers by such customers were processed in this way during the last 12 months compared with 28% the previous year.
- A growth in the number of cases being sent to the financial ombudsman or the financial industry regulator relating to claims of mis-selling or incorrect advice on the part of financial services companies in the supply of a range of savings and investment products.
- As a result of threats of terrorist activity, money laundering legislation has been introduced or tightened in all of the countries in which IDAN has banking operations.

Analysis by type of business

(i) **Net assets**

	Year ended 31 December 20X4	*31 December 20X3*
	£m	£m
Corporate and investment banking	15,824	12,286
Personal financial services	9,250	6,400
Private banking	2,320	1,755
Commercial banking	11,186	9,364
	38,580	29,805

(ii) **Profit on ordinary activities before tax**

	Year ended 31 December 20X4	*31 December 20X3*
	£m	£m
Corporate and investment banking	3,416	2,949
Personal financial services	2,427	1,684
Private banking	116	85
Commercial banking	3,356	3,558
	9,315	8,276

(iii) Within the commercial banking portfolio, the allowance for credit losses equalled one per cent of the assets compared with two and a half per cent in personal financial services and private banking.

(iv) Profits from private banking are influenced by a range of factors including the state of the world economy and sentiment and performance in the equity markets. The current outlook for the global economy is uncertain and depressed equity markets are expected to recover slowly over the coming year.

Required

(a) Discuss the main categories of risk that are faced by a bank such as IDAN and the advantages of risk categorisation in the design of a risk management system. **(10 marks)**

(b) For every one of the six issues identified in the question, recommend the controls that might be introduced to minimise IDAN's exposure to such risks. **(15 marks)**

(c) Compare and contrast the roles played by internal audit and risk management in organisations. Discuss the likely nature of the interaction between these two activities. **(10 marks)**

The performance of the Managing Directors of the four types of business is evaluated using the profits of their individual businesses. It has been suggested that the strategy of the group, future investment opportunities and the profitability of each business should be evaluated against a risk-adjusted hurdle rate.

Required

(d) Critically discuss this suggestion by making reference to the information provided in the question.

(15 marks)

(Total = 50 marks)

72 Crashcarts (Pilot paper) **90 mins**

Crashcarts IT Consultancy is a £100 million turnover business listed on the Stock Exchange with a reputation for providing world class IT consultancy services to blue chip clients, predominantly in the retail sector. In 20X0, Crashcarts acquired a new subsidiary for £2 million based on a P/E ratio of 8, which it renamed Crashcarts Call Centre. The call centre subsidiary leased all of its hardware, software and telecommunications equipment over a five-year term. The infrastructure provides the capacity to process three million orders and ten million line items per annum. In addition, maintenance contracts were signed for the full five-year period. These contracts include the provision of a daily backup facility in an off-site location.

Crashcarts Call Centre provides two major services for its clients. First, it holds databases, primarily for large retail chains' catalogue sales, connected in real time to clients' inventory control systems. Second, its call centre operation allows its clients' customers to place orders by telephone. The real-time system determines whether there is stock available and, if so, a shipment is requested. The sophisticated technology in use by the call centre also incorporates a secure payment facility for credit and debit card payments, details of which are transferred to the retail stores' own computer system. The call centre charges each retail client a lump sum each year for the IT and communication infrastructure it provides. There is a 12 month contract in place for each client. In addition, Crashcarts earns a fixed sum for every order it processes, plus an additional amount for every line item. If items are not in stock, Crashcarts earns no processing fee.

Crashcarts Call Centre is staffed by call centre operators (there were 70 in 20X1 and 80 in each of 20X2 and 20X3). In addition, a management team, training staff and administrative personnel are employed. Like other call centres, there is a high turnover of call centre operators (over 100% per annum) and this requires an almost continuous process of staff training and detailed supervision and monitoring.

A summary of Crashcarts Call Centre's financial performance for the last three years:

	20X1	*20X2*	*20X3*
	£'000	£'000	£'000
Revenue			
Contract fixed fee	400	385	385
Order processing fees	2,500	3,025	3,450
Line item processing fees	600	480	390
Total revenue	3,500	3,890	4,225
Expenses			
Office rent and expenses	200	205	210
Operator salaries and salary-related costs	1,550	1,920	2,180
Management, administration and training salaries	1,020	1,070	1,120
IT and telecoms lease and maintenance expenses	300	310	330
Other expenses	150	200	220
Total expenses	3,220	3,705	4,060
Operating profit	280	185	165

Non-financial performance information for the same period is as follows.

	20X1	*20X2*	*20X3*
Number of incoming calls received	1,200,000	1,300,000	1,350,000
Number of orders processed	1,000,000	1,100,000	1,150,000
Order strike rate (orders/calls)	83.3%	84.6%	85.2%
Number of line items processed	3,000,000	3,200,000	3,250,000
Average number of line items per order	3.0	2.9	2.8

	20X1	*20X2*	*20X3*
Number of retail clients	8	7	7
Fixed contract income per client	£50,000	£55,000	£55,000
Income per order processed	£2.50	£2.75	£3.00
Income per line order processed	£0.20	£0.15	£0.12
Average number of orders per operator	15,000	15,000	15,000
Number of operators required	66.7	73.3	76.7
Actual number of operators employed	70.0	80.0	80.0

Required

(a) Discuss the increase in importance of risk management to all businesses (with an emphasis on listed ones) over the last few years and the role of management accountants in risk management. **(10 marks)**

(b) Advise the Crashcarts Call Centre on methods for analysing its risks. **(5 marks)**

(c) Apply appropriate methods to identify and quantify the major risks facing Crashcarts at both parent level and subsidiary level. **(20 marks)**

(d) Categorise the components of a management control system and recommend the main controls that would be appropriate for the Crashcarts Call Centre. **(15 marks)**

(Total = 50 marks)

73 VCF (11/05) — 90 mins

VCF is a small listed company that designs and installs high technology computer numerical control capital equipment used by multinational manufacturing companies. VCF is located in one Pacific country, but almost 90% of its sales are exported. VCF has sales offices in Europe, Asia, the Pacific, Africa, and North and South America and employs about 300 staff around the world.

VCF has annual sales of $200 million but the sales value of each piece of equipment sold is about $3 million so that sales volume is relatively low. Sales are always invoiced in the currency of the country where the equipment is being installed. The time between the order being taken and the final installation is usually several months. However a deposit is taken when the order is placed and progress payments are made by the customer before shipment and upon delivery, with the final payment being made after installation of the equipment.

The company has international patents covering its technology and invests heavily in research and development (R&D about 15% of sales) and marketing costs to develop export markets (about 25% of sales). VCF's manufacturing operations are completely outsourced in its home country and the cost of sales is about 20%. The balance of costs is for installation, servicing and administration, amounting to about 15% of sales. Within each of the cost classifications the major expenses (other than direct costs) are salaries for staff, all of whom are paid well above the industry average, rental of premises in each location and travel costs. Area managers are located in each sales office and have responsibility for achieving sales, installing equipment and maintaining high levels of after-sales service and customer satisfaction.

Although the head office is very small, most of the R&D staff are located in the home country along with purchasing and logistics staff responsible for liaising with the outsource suppliers and a small accounting team that is primarily concerned with monthly management accounts and end of year financial statements.

VCF has a majority shareholding held by Jack Viktor, an entrepreneur who admits to taking high risks, both personally and in business. The Board of four is effectively controlled by Viktor who is both Chairman and Chief Executive. The three other directors were appointed by Viktor. They are his wife, who has a marketing role in the business, and two non-executive directors, one an occasional consultant to VCF and the other a long-term family friend. Board meetings are held quarterly and are informal affairs, largely led by Viktor's verbal review of sales activity.

Viktor is a dominating individual who exercises a high degree of personal control often by-passing his area managers. Because the company is controlled by him Viktor is not especially concerned with short-term profits but with the long-term. He emphasises two objectives: sales growth to generate increased market share and cash flow;

and investment in R&D to ensure the long-term survival of VCF by maintaining patent protection and a technological lead over its competitors.

Viktor is in daily contact with all his offices by telephone. He travels extensively around the world and has an excellent knowledge of VCF's competitors and customers. He uses a limited number of non-financial performance measures, primarily concerned with sales, market share, quality and customer satisfaction. Through his personal contact and his twin objectives, Viktor encourages a culture committed to growth, continual innovation, and high levels of customer satisfaction. This is reinforced by high salary levels, but Viktor readily dismisses those staff not committed to this objectives.

The company has experienced rapid growth over the last 10 years and is very profitable although cash flow is often tight. A high margin is achieved because VCF is able to charge its customers premium prices. The equipment sold by VCF enables faster production and better quality than its competitors can offer.

Viktor has little time for traditional accounting. Product costing is not seen as valuable because the cost of sales is relatively low and most costs incurred by VCF, particularly R&D and export marketing costs, are incurred a long time in advance of sales being made. R&D costs are not capitalised in VCF's balance sheet.

Although budgets are used for expense control and monthly management accounts are produced, they have little relevance to Viktor who recognises the fluctuations in profit caused by the timing of sales of low volume but high value capital equipment. Viktor sees little value in comparing monthly profit figures against budgets because sales are erratic. However Viktor depends heavily on a spreadsheet to manage VCF's cash flow by using sensitivity analysis against his sales and cash flow projects. Cash flow is a major business driver and is controlled tightly using the spreadsheet model.

The major risks facing VCF have been identified by Viktor as:

- Competitor infringement of patents, which VCF always meets by instituting legal actions
- Adverse movements in the exchange rate between the home country and VCF's export markets, which VCF treats as an acceptable risk given that historically, gains and losses have balanced each other out.
- The reduction in demand for the equipment due to economic reasons
- A failure of continued R&D investment to maintain technological leadership; and
- A failure to control costs.

Viktor considers that the last three of these risks are addressed by his policy of outsourcing manufacture and continuous personal contact with staff, customers and competitors.

Required

(a) Identify and evaluate the existing controls within VCF (including those applied by Viktor). **(20 marks)**

(b) Write a report to the Board of VCF recommending improvements to the company's corporate governance, risk management strategy, and internal controls. **(20 marks)**

(c) Identify the exchange risks faced by VCF and recommend the methods that could be used to manage those risks. **(10 marks)**

(Total = 50 marks)

74 GHI (5/06) — 90 mins

The GHI Group is a major listed travel company based in the UK, with a market capitalisation of £200 million, that specialises in the provision of budget-priced short and long haul package holidays targeted at the family market. The term 'package holiday' means that all flights, accommodation and overseas transfers are organised and booked by the tour operator on behalf of the customer.

The GHI Group encompasses a number of separate companies that include a charter airline, a chain of retail travel outlets, and several specialist tour operators who provide package holidays. Each subsidiary is expected to be profit generating, and each company's performance is measured by its residual income. The capital charges for each company are risk adjusted, and new investments are required to achieve a base hurdle rate of 10% before adjustment for risk.

The package holiday market is highly competitive, with fewer than five main players all trying to gain market share in an environment in which margins are continually threatened. The key threats include rising fuel prices, last minute discounting and the growth of the 'self managed' holiday, where individuals by-pass the travel retailers and use the Internet to book low cost flights and hotel rooms directly with the service providers. Also, customer requirements regarding product design and quality are continuously changing, thereby increasing the pressure on travel companies to devise appropriate strategies to maintain profitability.

Sales of long haul packages to North America are relatively static, but the number of people travelling to South East Asian destinations has fallen substantially following the tsunami disaster. Africa, New Zealand, Australia and certain parts of the Caribbean are the only long haul growth areas, but such growth is from a small base. Sales within the European region are shifting in favour of Eastern Mediterranean destinations such as Cyprus and Turkey as the traditional resorts of Spain and the Balearic Islands fall out of favour. Short 'city breaks' are also growing rapidly in popularity, reflecting higher spending power particularly amongst the over 50s.

The shift in patterns of demand has created some problems for GHI in a number of Eastern Mediterranean resorts over the last two summer seasons. There are not many hotels that meet the specified quality standards, and consequently there is fierce competition amongst travel operators to reserve rooms in them. In 20X2 GHI took out a three year contract (20X3-20X5 inclusive) for 10,000 beds in four major hotels over the peak holiday season of mid July – end of August. The contract terms required GHI to pay a 20% refundable deposit at the start of each calendar year, in return for the right to cancel unwanted rooms without penalty at just one week's notice. These contract terms were selected in preference to an alternative which required a 5% guarantee payment at the start of the calendar year, but with two weeks notice for all cancellations, and the payment of a flat fee of £20 per week per cancelled room.

On three occasions in 20X3, and six occasions in 20X4, approximately 150 holidaymakers booked through GHI arrived at their hotels only to find that their rooms were already occupied by clients from a rival company. GHI's resort representative had severe problems relocating their customers, and over half of them were forced to move to inland hotels because all of the beach resorts were fully booked. The total compensation paid out by GHI to dissatisfied customers amounted to £135,000 in 20X3 and £288,000 in 20X4, and these payments were categorised as exceptional costs in the published accounts.

The problems encountered by GHI received extensive coverage in the UK media and a popular television travel programme provided assistance to holidaymakers to compile compensation claims. As a result of all of this adverse publicity, GHI decided in early 20X5 to invest £8 million in purchasing two new hotels in the affected resorts. Sales forecasts indicate demand will grow at approximately 15% per year in the relevant resorts over the next five years. It is anticipated that the hotels will supply 70% of the group's accommodation requirements for the 20X6 season.

The package holidays to the GHI owned hotels will be sold as premium all-inclusive deals that include all food, soft drinks and local beers, wines and spirits. Such all-inclusive deals are not currently offered by other hotels in the target resorts.

Required

(a) Identify and briefly discuss two risks that are likely to be faced by the GHI Group under each of the following categories:

- Financial
- Political
- Environmental
- Economic

(16 marks)

(b) Identify and evaluate risk impact upon GHI's financial statements and cash flow management of choosing to purchase its own overseas hotel properties as opposed to block booking rooms from local suppliers under the terms of the 20X3 – 20X5 contract. **(15 marks)**

(c) Identify and comment upon the changes in risks to GHI Group that might arise from the decision to sell premium all-inclusive deals, and suggest methods by which these risks might be monitored and controlled. **(8 marks)**

(d) Explain, using the investment in the new hotels as an example, how strategic decisions can simultaneously affect both performance measurement and capital allocation across a number of different companies within a group such as GHI. **(6 marks)**

(e) List the tasks that the internal audit department of GHI should have performed to ensure that the risks associated with the new hotel purchases are managed effectively. You should assume that its involvement commenced immediately the strategic decision was made to purchase overseas property – in other words, prior to identification of target sites. **(5 marks)**

(Total = 50 marks)

75 BLU (11/06) — 90 mins

BLU is a stock market listed manufacturing company that has historically invested in computer numerical control (CNC) equipment to manufacture a range of electronic components for the telecommunications industry. BLU's strategic objective is to increase shareholder value through an annual increase in sales revenue of 15% and an annual increase in after-tax profits of 17.5%, both of which have been achieved over the past three years. This objective is strongly promoted within BLU and senior management bonuses are linked to the achievement of those targets.

In early 20X1, the following financial justification was presented to the Board of Directors of BLU to support a proposal for capital investment in new CNC manufacturing equipment:

Projected cash flows for new equipment

	20X2	*20X3*	*20X4*	*20X5*	*20X6*
	£'000	£'000	£'000	£'000	£'000
Additional sales income	12,000	13,000	14,000	15,000	16,000
Additional variable costs	3,600	3,900	4,200	4,500	4,800
Additional fixed costs	1,500	1,500	1,500	1,500	1,500
Additional operating profit	6,900	7,600	8,300	9,000	9,700
Less taxation		2,070	2,280	2,490	2,700
Additional operating cash flow	6,900	5,530	6,020	6,510	7,000
Less additional working capital	1,000	300	400	500	600
Additional cash flow	5,900	5,230	5,620	6,010	6,400

Cost of capital	15%
Present value of future cash flows	19,398
Less capital cost of new equipment	17,500
Net present value	1,898

It is company policy to evaluate investments over the first five years only.

In March 20X1, the Board approved the capital investment as it met its minimum criterion of a positive NPV using a cost of capital of 15%. There was one other project that was competing for funds at that time. This was for a new distribution system. However, this project was rejected by the Board because the NPV was lower than that of the CNC equipment.

Later in 20X1, the audit committee asked a firm of consultants to review BLU's capital investment approval process and the information system that informs that process. As part of the first stage of the consultants' review, a draft report has been received by the Board that describes the process but as yet does not make any recommendations. The following are extracts from the consultants' draft report:

- BLU has a Market Research Department that looks at economic, industry and competitive factors affecting the market demand for its products in order to forecast market growth and likely market share during BLU's strategic planning horizon of five years. As part of its assessment, the Market Research Department asks the Sales Department to liaise with its largest customers to determine their likely requirements. The Sales Department forecasts sales based on its own knowledge of its market, including information from existing customers and its plan to win new customers. Having collated the available information, the Market Research Department provides the Production Department with annually updated forecasts of market demand for the next five years.

- The Production Department compares the Market Research Department's forecasts with its production capacity based on past experience of volumes, product mix, and cycle times. The Production Department then determines the 'capacity gap' over the next five years, which it defines as the difference between the capacity required to satisfy forecasts of market demand and its existing practical capacity.
- Based on the capacity gap, the Production Department conducts a search for new CNC manufacturing equipment that will satisfy projected sales. A range of alternative suppliers is considered and prices for the equipment are compared, after which the Production Department identifies the supplier and the equipment deemed most suitable to bridge the capacity gap. The capital costs of new equipment and the capacity of this new equipment are calculated by the Production Department.
- The Finance Department accepts the forecasts of market demand from the Market Research Department and the cost and capacity information from the Production Department. It then uses historical cost information to update standard costs of labour and materials, with advice from the Human Resources and Purchasing Departments respectively about likely increases in the price of labour and materials. The Finance Department makes its own assessments about the additional working capital requirement.
- The Finance Department then completes a discounted cash flow calculation to assess the investment in new capital equipment, which is then presented to the Board of Directors as part of the annual budget cycle. BLU uses a cost of capital of 15% for the assessment of new capital expenditure proposals. This is the benchmark figure used by the Board, which has been in use for several years. Proposals that show a positive net present value are likely to be approved and where there are competing proposals for limited capital funds, the project with the highest NPV is usually selected. The Board's capital investment approval criteria are well known by BLU's managers.

Required

Note: No calculations are required to answer this question.

(a) Analyse the risks facing BLU in relation to its investment appraisal and approval process and the information system feeding that process. **(20 marks)**

(b) Explain how, as an internal auditor, you would plan an audit of BLU's existing capital investment process (and the information system feeding that process), highlighting those elements of the process that you would pay particular attention to under a risk-based approach. **(10 marks)**

(c) Recommend to the Board of BLU the internal controls that should be introduced to improve BLU's capital investment process (including the information system feeding that process) and explain the benefits of your recommended controls. **(20 marks)**

(Total = 50 marks)

76 ACB (5/07) — 90 mins

ACB is a stock exchange listed company that designs and assembles small passenger aircraft which it sells to regional airlines throughout the world. ACB is highly regarded by its airline customers for the quality of its aircraft. ACB is also recognised for meeting contractual commitments through on-time delivery. The company generates profits before interest and taxes of about 5% of sales. However, due to the depressed nature of the airline industry and competition from foreign manufacturers, the company has modest growth targets. About 60 aircraft are delivered each year.

Competitive advantage

The company's competitive advantage is its ability to take a standard aircraft design and customise it to the varying needs of its customers. This includes, for example, changes in engine size, passenger capacity, configuration, and electronic equipment. The cycle time from signed order to delivery is about 18 months.

Pricing and sales terms

ACB sets the price of its completed aircraft in the customer's currency. The fixed price is converted to ACB's home currency using exchange rates applicable at the time contracts are signed. Progress payments are made on order and throughout the production process, but the balance of approximately 60% of the selling price of the aircraft is made on delivery to the airline. Any delivery delays are classed as a breach of ACB's contract for which it incurs significant financial penalties.

Production and supply chain

The manufacture of all the aircraft components have been subcontracted to about 200 suppliers located across several continents. The cost of purchased components constitutes 70% of the final aircraft selling price. Suppliers are selected on the basis of quality, reliability and cost. Contracts with each supplier include prices established in the supplier's currency and incorporate price increases and anticipated efficiency savings over the next two years. This enables accurate forecasting of material costs by ACB. As each component is produced to satisfy the different requirements of each aircraft, any delay in receipt of any component will delay final assembly. A distribution company has the contract to transport all components to ACB's factory and a combination of bar-coding and satellite tracking technology enables the precise location of all components to be tracked from despatch through to receipt by ACB.

There are five major production operations at ACB's factory: four relate to component assembly and one to final assembly. The four component assembly operations are fuselage, wings, engines, and electronics. All four component assemblies are brought together in a large hanger where the final aircraft assembly takes place. ACB operates its factory on a just-in-time (JIT) basis to minimise inventory. Production scheduling for each of the four component assembly operations must be integrated so that the final assembly can take place on schedule.

IT support

ACB uses a sophisticated enterprise resource planning system (ERPS) to manage its supply chain, purchase ordering, production scheduling, accounting and performance management, and customer relationship management. The company also relies on an electric data interchange (EDI) system to track component purchase orders from their despatch by suppliers to receipt at ACB's factory.

Quality control

Aircraft manufacture is highly regulated with stringent quality control and safety requirements. ACB has always maintained the highest standards. The government's Aircraft Inspection Agency makes regular inspections of component and final assembly quality in order to ensure annual re-licensing of ACB as an aircraft manufacturer.

Costing and pricing

The cost of each aircraft is estimated from a bill of materials for components and a labour routing, both of which take into account the customisation of each aircraft. Price negotiations follow the cost estimation process and discounts are given for quantity and the significance of the customer to ACB in terms of past and anticipated sales.

Overhead costs are traced to products through an activity-based costing system, based on cost drivers established for eight significant business processes. Profits are calculated for each aircraft and each order (which may be for several aircraft) and customer profitability analysis is used to support future sales efforts.

Risk management and governance

The company has a risk management group at senior management level that maintains a register of major risks, carries out risk assessments in terms of their likelihood and consequences, identifies appropriate risk responses, and reports to each meeting of the audit committee. IT risks and foreign currency exposures require highly specialised attention and responsibility for these risks is delegated to the IT Department and Treasury Department respectively.

The ERPS and EDI systems are managed by the in-house IT department which has long-serving and highly skilled staff who have developed comprehensive operating procedures and business continuity plans. ACB's Treasury department primarily uses matching techniques to offset foreign exchange exposures in each currency but does use forward contracts where exposures in some currencies are deemed unacceptable.

The Board of Directors emphasises strategy and monitors sales and delivery performance. It aims to ensure that sales are spread evenly over different regions so as not to be disproportionately affected by political or economic changes. The general approach to risk management is to have a portfolio of customers, product and suppliers, so as to minimise sensitivity to any one factor that might jeopardise the company's success. The Board reviews assessments made by the Aircraft Inspection Agency and is actively involved in rectifying any problems identified.

The company's Audit Committee, comprised of independent directors, monitors the risk assessments made by managers, ensures that internal controls are adequate and approves the company's internal audit plan each year. The Audit Committee also monitors all monthly financial performance information while the internal audit function spends a considerable proportion of its resources ensuring that financial performance information produced by the ERPS is accurate for management decision-making and financial reporting purposes.

Required

(a) State the recommended components of any organisation's risk management strategy and evaluate ACB's approach to risk management in terms of those components. **(12 marks)**

(b) Identify the major categories of risk facing ACB and evaluate the controls adopted by ACB in relation to each category. **(28 marks)**

(c) Risk treatment (or risk response) is an important component of risk management strategy. Explain what is meant by risk treatment and its benefits to a Board of Directors. **(10 marks)**

(Total = 50 marks)

77 NOP (11/07) 90 mins

The NOP Group is one of the world's largest clothing retailers and had a turnover in excess of £2,000 million for the year ended 30 September 20X7. The group's clothes are sold in Europe, East Asia, North America, Australia and New Zealand. The clothes are made for NOP by a number of approved contractors in China, Sri Lanka, Thailand and India. The clothes are designed by employees of NOP at the company's headquarters in London, England. The designers base their ideas on what has attracted them when they have attended the previews of the latest styles at the fashion shows presented by the world's leading fashion houses. NOP operates to a four month lead time which runs from the start of the design process through to the first appearance of the new styles in the retail stores.

NOP's clothes are targeted at the mid to high priced sector of the market and are sold under several brand names. NOP tries to match brands to differing customer profiles, and in doing so recognises that its customers' ages are an important factor. Within the 18 – 25 year customer age group, brands are 'uni-sex'.

NOP operates across four geographic business units, with each managed as a profit centre. The group had differing arrangements for its retail outlets across the world, as shown below:

Business Unit	**Outlet arrangement**
Europe (UK, France, Italy)	Group owned shops
USA and Canada	Franchise agreements
Asia, (Japan, Thailand, China, Singapore)	Joint ventures with department stores
Australia and New Zealand	Joint venture with a distributor

The group is a signatory to an ethical code of conduct (see extracts in the additional information below) which has been developed for use within the clothing sector, and it produces a separate social and environmental report which it views as complementary to its annual report. As part of its environmental protection policy. NOP has also declared a commitment not to send waste to landfill sites from 20X8 onwards and will make arrangements for all company waste to be recycled.

The group's treasurer regards NOP as highly exposed to currency risk, and therefore requires that all open positions with an equivalent value in excess of £100,000 are hedged. Responsibility for hedging arrangements lies with the Finance Director of each of NOP's four regional business units. Capital gearing is kept at a low level compared to NOP's competitors, and the market value of debt equalled just 30% of the market value of equity at the balance sheet date of 30 September 20X7. The group directors' remuneration, as detailed in Note 3 below, is linked to medium term financial targets.

The group shares are listed on both the London and the New York stock exchanges. NOP's share price has fallen by 15% over the last six weeks, compared with an average fall of 10% for the general retail sector, and 8% for fashion retailers. A meeting of the board of directors has been called to address the problem.

The group finance director thinks that a share price recovery could be stimulated by a well targeted cost cutting exercise. The production and transportation costs being charged by suppliers are considered too high, as they amount to 75% of the cost of goods sold. Initial estimates suggest there is scope to reduce each of these costs by around 5%. Profit is further eroded by high employee costs, especially in Europe, where they equal 18% of sales, compared to an industry average of 12%. The group finance director believes that increasing the proportion of part-time sales staff could bring employee costs in line with the industry average.

The group marketing director proposes an alternative solution, as he believes that a new advertising campaign would stop the decline in the share price. The campaign would focus on the group's most glamorous product ranges and would use international film stars to promote the clothes. The average gross margin on all clothes sales across the group varies significantly. For some products in the UK and Japan it is 45%, but it is as low as 6% for some products in Thailand and Singapore. The glamour ranges earn an average gross margin of 22% and sales of these ranges account for 15% of group revenue, but it is thought that the advertising campaign could significantly boost global sales of these high mark-up products with no accompanying sales loss elsewhere.

Additional information

1 Extracts from key financial statistics for the preceding two years:

	20X6	*20X7*
	£ million	£ million
Sales*	2,400	3,120
Gross profit (excluding joint ventures)	480	625
Distribution costs	72	50
Profit/loss from joint ventures	(350)	180
Net interest payable	24	22
Dividend yield on year end share price	1.5%	1.5%
UK share price (year end)	465 pence	490 pence
Price index for UK retail shares (Base 100 in 20X0)	680	782

The current (November 20X7) share price is 480 pence.

*Sales are split across the regions as follows: Europe 60%; USA & Canada 20%; Asia 12%; Australia and New Zealand 8%.

2 The Ethical Code of Conduct covers conditions and terms of employment within NOP and in NOP's suppliers, and includes the following requirements:

- Payment of the legal minimum level of wages (or industry average) whichever is higher
- No use of forced labour, and freedom for employees to join a trade union and/or engage in collective bargaining
- Safe and hygienic working conditions
- A commitment not to use child labour, that is, ages below 15
- Working hours kept to normal national levels or local industry standards

3 Remuneration of group executive directors

In addition to a fixed, market based salary, plus pension and health scheme benefits, group directors are entitled to performance related pay. The performance related pay usually represents over 50% of each director's annual remuneration and is based upon the following terms:

- A variable bonus is payable if performance meets or exceeds pre-determined annual targets for NOP's profit before tax. Achieving target performance earns the directors a bonus of 55% of their annual salary, and this rises to a maximum of 150% for performance more than 20% above the target level.
- Half of the variable bonus is granted in cash, and the rest is paid in shares, which must be held for a minimum of three years.

4 Remuneration of business unit directors and other senior managers.

In common with the executive directors, other senior managers in NOP are paid partly on the basis of performance. Senior staff can earn bonuses paid in shares, which carry no minimum holding period requirement. The bonus rates are dependent upon performance relative to earnings per share growth targets set by the board of directors and in recent years have ranged between 50% and 220% of annual salary.

Required

(a) Discuss the extent to which **each** of the following characteristics of NOP creates potential risks for the company's shareholders:

(i) Branding and marketing strategy
(ii) Design and procurement strategy
(iii) Remuneration of senior management and executive directors
(iv) Corporate treasury function
(v) Social and environmental policies

(30 marks)

(b) Prepare a report to be presented at the board meeting that:

(i) Explains why the principle of risk ownership at board of director level is a vital form of control, especially in extremely large companies such as NOP. **(5 marks)**

(ii) Discusses the relative merits of the finance director's and the marketing director's proposals. (Your discussion should be from a risk management perspective, and should therefore focus on the risks created by the share price fall and the impact of each proposal on the group's overall risk profile.)

(15 marks)

(Total = 50 marks)

78 MFT (5/08) — 90 mins

MFT is a publicly listed company, which operates a chain of 74 restaurants throughout the country. The company has built a reputation for quality dining at affordable prices. The business model operated by MFT is to maximise the number of customers within each restaurant's seating capacity and to maximise the amount of money spent by each customer on food and alcohol.

Restaurant management

Each restaurant has a manager. Many of these managers have been with MFT for a long time and are well known to senior management. MFT's Head Office allows managers considerable autonomy in the management of their restaurants. The restaurant manager decides on the menu for his or her restaurant, orders food and alcohol from Head Office and promotes the restaurant locally.

Pricing is the responsibility of each restaurant manager. Price variations depend on location, competition and menu. Each restaurant operates a paper-based, order-taking system. One copy of the order is passed to the kitchen; the other is priced and given to the customer at the end of the meal. About 80% of customers pay their bill by credit card and about 20% pay in cash. The restaurant manager must control costs by balancing staff levels with customer demand. The manager must also minimise food wastage, for example by promoting daily specials.

A market research consultancy carries out annual customer satisfaction and brand recognition surveys for each restaurant.

Central support

MFT's Head Office is responsible for strategic planning, financial management, and legal and governance issues. It also provides marketing support for each restaurant and purchases all food and alcohol through central purchasing arrangements. Sub-contractors are used to deliver fresh food to each restaurant daily. Alcohol is delivered direct by suppliers. Food and alcohol can be signed for by any employee when the deliveries are made to restaurants. Alcohol is stored in a locked storeroom.

fraud?

Financial management

MFT exercises strict financial and reporting controls. Each day, restaurant managers must report the value of sales to Head Office and deposit cash receipts to a central bank account. Each week, restaurant managers must report the number of customers served each day and submit an inventory of unsold food and alcohol to Head Office.

fraud?

The cost of food and alcohol is charged to each restaurant. Staff salaries, based on manual time records, are paid by Head Office into employee bank accounts. Incidental expenses are paid by restaurant managers using a corporate credit card. This permits local payments for advertising, menu printing and so on. The rental and utility costs for each restaurant are paid by Head Office.

A weekly profit statement showing the performance of the restaurant is sent from Head Office to the restaurant manager. Accompanying the report is a comparison against the budget for that restaurant and the average results for all restaurants. Information received by each restaurant manager includes income, gross and operating profits, seating capacity utilisation and spend per customer. MFT defines gross profit as that which is controllable by the restaurant manager, after deducting the cost of food and alcohol, staff salaries and local payments.

The non-controllable expenses of rent and utilities and allocated corporate costs are deducted to arrive at operating profit. The restaurant manager is paid a bonus based on the gross profit earned by his or her restaurant.

Restaurant profitability

The gross profit for MFT as a whole is 35% of sales income, but there is considerable variation between the 74 restaurants. The performance of 5 to 7 restaurants is of concern.

The average sales mix comprises approximately 70% food and 30% alcohol. The gross profit is approximately 30% on food and 50% on alcohol. No restaurant spends more than 1% of sales on local purchases.

Audit and Control

MFT's internal auditor designed the management control and reporting system used by the company. The internal auditor takes a systems approach to auditing and ensures that the weekly management reporting and end-of-year financial reporting is accurate and on time.

MFT has recently received the management letter from its external auditors following the completion of the year-end statutory audit. The auditors have identified a number of risks and have made the following suggestions:

1. There is considerable variation in spend per customer and gross profit margins between individual restaurants. This may be the result of poor restaurant management and/or malpractice. Internal audit should spend more time on checks on individual restaurants that are under-performing compared to the company average. This would allow improvements to be made by utilising best practice from better-performing restaurants.
2. The manual order-taking process has potential for errors in terms of the kitchen fulfilling an order and in pricing. There is also the possibility that the proceeds of bills paid in cash will not be paid into MFT's bank account. MFT should consider a computerised order-taking system in all of its restaurants to eliminate errors, mis-pricing and cash losses.
3. Inventory may be taken by staff for personal use. As most of the value of inventory is alcohol, the suggested computerised order-taking system would also provide a perpetual inventory for alcohol, resulting in more physical control and better management information.
4. Employee time records may not be accurate and employees may be claiming for working longer hours than they have actually worked. MFT should consider an automated time recording system whereby employees enter a code when starting and finishing work.
5. The customer satisfaction and brand awareness survey shows considerable customer dissatisfaction and a negative brand perception in a few areas in which MFT has restaurants. Management should identify the causes and rectify this situation.

6 Restaurant managers may use their corporate credit cards improperly, for example to make personal purchases or to purchase local food and alcohol contrary to corporate guidelines. Credit cards could be replaced with a small petty cash float to eliminate this possibility.

7 There is a risk of short-delivery of food and alcohol by sub-contractors and suppliers when any employee can sign for the delivery, as the quantities and condition may not be checked. This can lead to significant stock losses. All deliveries should be checked as to quality and quantity by the restaurant manager.

Required

(a) (i) Construct a 2×2 likelihood/consequences matrix according to whether they are high, medium and low. **(4 marks)**

(ii) Explain, with examples, an appropriate responses for each of the risk categories. **(4 marks)**

(iii) Apply the matrix to categorise each of the seven risks identified by the MFT's auditors and state your reasons. **(11 marks)**

(b) As the sole internal auditor within MFT, write a report recommending to the Audit Committee which of the external auditor's suggestions should be adopted and which should be rejected. Give reasons to support your recommendations. **(26 marks including 5 marks for report style)**

(c) Explain the ethical issue faced by the internal auditor when responding to the external auditor's report. **(5 marks)**

(Total = 50 marks)

Answers

Extra guidance

Remember you can find additional guidance on a number of questions in this kit on BPP's website: www.bpp.com/cima/extra-question-guidance

1 Preparation question: Risks

Text references. Chapter 1 lists the main risks which are developed in other chapters; Chapters 2 and 5 deal with the risk management and corporate governance issues.

Top tips. This question is simpler than you would expect to see in your exam, but it does provide a good introduction to this section. It emphasises that you need wide-ranging knowledge of the risks an organisation could face to do well in the exam and emphasises that adherence to the corporate governance codes will be a central part of risk management. The verb describe means you need to state what may cause the risk to materialise.

Easy marks. The risks discussed in (b) may come to mind easier than those in (a), as sections of the BPP Study Text are grouped round them. However, don't forget the business and strategic risks in (a) as they are likely to be included somewhere in the paper.

(a) **Project risk**

The project-specific risk for an individual investment project occurs because the **cash flows from the project** might be **higher or lower than expected**, for reasons that are specific to the project. The cash flows might have been **estimated incorrectly**, such as an under-estimate of operating costs or an over-estimate of market demand. (However, if a company invests in a wide range of similar projects, it can be argued that much of this project risk will be diversified away in the normal course of business.) Other risk factors specific to a project could be the location of the project, or the quality of personnel, or the reliability of the equipment to be used.

Competitive risk

This is the possibility of **unexpected effects** on the project cash flows (positive or negative), due to the **actions of competitors**. The actual actions of competitors might differ from the assumptions made by the company when it takes its project investment decision. Companies cannot diversify away competitive risk, but shareholders can, by investing in the shares of the competitor companies.

Industry-specific risk

This is the risk of unexpected changes to a project's cash flows (positive or negative) from **events or changing circumstances in the industry** in which the investment is made. Unexpected changes can arise, for example, due to new technology, or a change in the law, or a rise or fall in the price of a key commodity.

Market risk

This refers to changes that could occur in market conditions, that will affect the cash flows from the project. These could be unexpected changes in **interest rates**, or in the **rate of inflation**, or in the **state of the economy**.

Two-way risks

Each of these risks is a **two-way risk**, in the sense that the actual cash flows could be either better or worse than expected. For example sales demand could be higher than forecast, a competitor might over-price a rival product, a new law might be introduced that has the effect of boosting demand for the output produced by the project, and exchange rates or interest rates might move favourably.

(b) **Trading risks**

Both domestic and international traders will face trading risks, although those faced by the latter will generally be greater due to the increased distances and times involved. The types of trading risk include:

(i) **Physical risk** – the risk of goods being lost or stolen in transit, or the documents accompanying the goods going astray

(ii) **Credit risk** – the possibility of payment default by the customer. This is discussed further below.

(iii) **Trade risk** – the risk of the customer refusing to accept the goods on delivery (due to sub-standard/ inappropriate goods or other reasons), or the cancellation of the order in transit

(iv) **Liquidity risk** – the inability to finance the credit

Cultural, country and political risks

(i) **Cultural risk** – where a business trades with, or invests in, a foreign country **cultural risk** is introduced by the existence of different customs, laws and language. Communication between parties can be hindered, and potential deals put into jeopardy by ignorance of the expected manner in which such transactions should be conducted.

(ii) **Country risk** is the risk associated with undertaking transactions with, or holding assets in, a particular country. Sources of risk might be political, economic or regulatory instability affecting overseas taxation, repatriation of profits, nationalisation, currency instability etc.

(iii) **Political risk** is the risk that political action (exchange controls, tax changes, pricing regulations etc) will affect the position and value of a company.

Currency risk

Currency risk is the **possibility of loss or gain** due to **future changes** in **exchange rates**. When a firm trades with an overseas supplier or customer, and the invoice is in the overseas currency, it will expose itself to exchange rate or currency risk. Movements in the foreign exchange rates will create risk in the settlement of the debt – ie the final amount payable/receivable in the home currency will be uncertain at the time of entering into the transaction.

Investment in a foreign country or borrowing in a foreign currency will also carry this risk.

Interest rate risk

As with foreign exchange rates, future **interest rates cannot be easily predicted**. If a firm has a significant amount of variable (floating)-rate debt, interest rate movements will give rise to uncertainty about the cost of servicing this debt.

Conversely, if a company uses a lot of fixed-rate debt, it will lose out if interest rates begin to fall.

Technological risk

All businesses **depend to some extent on technology**, either in the support of its business activities (eg the computers used by the accounts, stores and treasury departments), or more directly in its production or marketing activities.

As technology evolves and develops, firms can find themselves using out of date equipment and marketing methods, which may leave them at a **competitive disadvantage**. Products in a high-tech industry have very short life-cycles, and a firm must recognise and plan for continual replacement and upgrading of products if it is not to lose market share.

(c) **How the codes of corporate governance can assist in managing the risks**

Corporate governance is concerned with the control and influence exerted over a company's operations and its employees by the decisions of top management, usually the Board of Directors.

The UK's Turnbull Report included recommendations that:

(i) **Role of management**

Management should define the company's risk **appetite**, the level of risks they wish the company to take based on its strategic choices and the returns it requires.

Management should **identify** and **evaluate** the risks to which they will be exposed in the achievement of their corporate objectives. These will include both the traditional areas of risk discussed above, but also those increasingly arising from intangible assets, such as reputation and branding.

(ii) **Embedding risk**

Risk control should be **embedded in the culture and processes of the business**, rather than being the subject of a completely separate management system. Each person in the organisation should be aware of, and manage, the significant risks related to the tasks they perform.

(iii) **Risk analysis**

Risk analysis and assessment should form part of the evaluation of every major capital investment or proposed acquisition.

(iv) **Financial risk analysis**

Financial risk analysis will very much depend upon commercial judgement, but should include assessment of effect on cash flow, profitability, liquidity and gearing.

(v) **Risk profiling**

The **relative likelihood** of the events giving rise to the risks also need to be assessed.

(vi) **Risk management**

Once risks have been prioritised, management needs to decide what to do about them, and how they can be managed and monitored in the future. Strategies for management of a given risk include **acceptance**, **transfer**, **abandonment and control**.

(vii) **Review by directors**

Directors should continually review and monitor risk control issues. It should regularly review **reports on internal control** from line managers and, where appropriate, from internal auditors and other specialists. **Regular discussion** of risk and control issues at board meetings should be encouraged.

2 ANG

Text references. Chapter 2.

Top tips. Overall the question demonstrates how to approach a general question on risk management ((a) and (b)) and then apply the general points to a specific situation in (c).

(a) doesn't ask for a description of a risk management framework but what is required for a framework to operate effectively. To get into this answer, think what a company must do to have risk management in place. This should draw your attention to the need to have a risk management strategy, and staff being aware of that strategy. The point about allocating budgets and having the appropriate tools available then follows on from this. This section is linked to the CIMA idea of world class risk management.

(b) is a fairly standard question on the types of risk management. You need to explain the four main types in your answer. Being able to do this on risk questions will be a big help towards passing them.

(c) is more complicated because it involves the application of the different risk management strategies to a specific company. The requirement word to evaluate means to look for the good and bad elements in the strategy. Don't assume that the company is doing everything wrong; in the real world this would be very unlikely anyway. Areas to focus on the scenario include the appropriateness of existing policies and whether enough is being done to cope with the major risks that the scenario identifies. Also important in this and many other questions is how the organisation will cope with a forthcoming change in business circumstances. You should clearly state the elements of risk management with reasoned comments as to whether they are appropriate. Where you think changes are needed, state these clearly in your answer with justification.

You could pass this question without making any reference in the scenario, but the mark allocation for the general parts of the question is quite generous. In most exam questions, you will need to refer to the organisation's circumstances to pass – and the examiner identifies not doing so as a frequent reason for failure.

Easy marks. (b) is a straightforward discussion on methods of dealing with risk.

(a) **Information management**

The organisation needs a structure to **facilitate and communicate information about risks**. A system such as an Intranet or groupware product would be suitable as it connects all the individuals in an organisation, allowing access to shared databases where information about risks can be stored.

Resources

Sufficient resources are required to support effective risk management. This means that the Board of an organisation must allocate **an appropriate budget for risk management**, and then the budget should be spent on appropriate areas. The appointment of a risk management officer will help to ensure budgeted amounts are spent appropriately.

Risk culture

The culture of the organisation should be developed as far as possible to ensure employees are **aware of risk and to act to avoid risks where possible**. Having a risk avoidance culture will help to ensure that management decisions taken focus on and avoid important risks.

Tools and techniques

Appropriate tools and techniques are available in the organisation to enable the **efficient and consistent management of risks across an organisation**. Tools and techniques available may include obtaining **appropriate insurance** against risks and having a **clear risk management policy in place**.

(b) **Avoidance**

In this situation, the organisation attempts to determine whether the possible **losses avoided from not undertaking a risky activity are greater than the advantages that can be gained from carrying out the activity**. If the losses avoided appear to outweigh the benefits of carrying out the activity, then the activity may not take place. In an extreme situation, entire sections of the business may be closed down if the risk or loss is considered to be too great.

Reduction

Risks are avoided in part but not reduced to zero. For example, the risk of launching a new product can be reduced by obtaining market research on possible demand for the product prior to manufacture and launch.

Risk reduction will also involve **contingency planning** to ensure that if a risk does crystallise, then the damage from that risk is minimised. For example, most companies will have a contingency plan against their computer systems failing. Files will be backed-up regularly, and alternative processing locations will be available if one centre becomes unavailable eg due to fire or flood.

Acceptance

Risk retention is where the **organisation bears the risk itself**. This means that if the unfavourable outcome occurs, then the organisation will suffer the full loss of that event.

Risk retention normally occurs in two situations. Firstly, where some **risk occurs** which the organisation's **risk management policy did not detect**. Secondly, where risk was **classified as insignificant** or **the cost of the risk** was deemed to be **too great compared to the likelihood of that risk occurring**.

Risk retention may also involve **self-insurance**. This means that funds are placed into some fund against risks actually occurring.

Transfer

The last risk management strategy is to **transfer the risk to a third party**. The most commonly used risk transfer policy is take out **insurance** against a risk occurring. However, **risks may also be transferred to other third parties, often without the knowledge of that party**. For example, there may be a minimal risk of errors occurring in some software. The cost of carrying out additional testing may be more than any compensation that may be payable if the error occurs and the customer makes a successful complaint. In this situation, risk has been transferred to the customer without the customer's knowledge.

(c) **Transfer**

The **overall risk management strategy** of ANG appears to be one of **risk transfer**. This is the policy adopted by most businesses and is appropriate given the **likelihood of many risks occurring is low, but if they do occur then significant expenditure would be involved**. For example, if a load did fall off one of ANG's lorries, then the damage caused could be considerable, not only to the load itself, but also to other vehicles, people and even the roads being used. ANG would not be able to operate legally without this insurance, and so it is essential to obtain it.

Insurance

Whether ANG needs to insure against damage to roads, bridges etc. is unclear. The government of the country is normally responsible for maintaining the transport infrastructure. ANG could probably withdraw this insurance and effectively **transfer the risk to the government**. Some cost savings would accrue from this move.

Self-insurance

It appears that ANG effectively **self-insures against loss of vehicles** in respect of being able to provide a replacement vehicle at short notice. This may be acceptable in the case of individual losses. However, it may be inappropriate in situations where, for example, a **significant number of ANG's vehicles are destroyed** in a fire or flood. Where haulage contracts are signed for time critical delivery of goods, then some **reciprocal agreement with another haulage company may be appropriate**.

Avoidance

The decision by ANG to **avoid risk** completely in the **transfer of hazardous materials** seems sensible. There has been some bad publicity about the transfer of radioactive goods by road, and the potential for claims, particularly if an accident occurred in an area of high population density, could be excessive and the damage to ANG's reputation would be considerable. In the case of **explosives**, ANG would need to ensure that the contract for carriage clearer stated that the **owner of the goods was responsible for insurance**. ANG may also want to obtain a copy of the insurance contract to confirm this.

Acceptance

There appears to be some risk in purchasing the transport planes prior to any market appraisal of the new venture. Normally the risk of a new venture would be reduced by carrying out market research prior to significant expenditure being incurred. The Board would normally be advised to check whether there was a demand for this service prior to expenditure being committed.

3 BEB

Text references. Chapter 1 and 2.

Top tips. This question is a typical business risks question. It is important not only to identify but also explain risks and why they are important very clearly in order to score marks. This answer includes company status and aims, products sold, sales methods, and relations with suppliers.

The requirements of (b) are fairly specific. Firstly in order to demonstrate how a framework can help, you need to choose a framework and structure your answer around that framework; throwing in random suggestions in no apparent order would not earned you marks. We've chosen the COSO enterprise risk management framework, but other frameworks, such as CIMA's risk management cycle, would be equally acceptable. However you wouldn't pass (b) if you just went through all stages of the risk management cycle; every stage clearly has to relate to BEB and how it responds to the risks explained in (a) that it faces.

Easy marks. The COSO framework is a very logical progression through all stages of developing an approach to risk and if you can remember the headers, you should be able to develop the discussion sufficiently to gain good marks.

(a) **Business risks**

Stock Exchange listing

The fact that the company has achieved Stock Exchange listing in the year brings a high level of **additional compliance risk** to the company. Failing to comply with corporate governance requirements imposed on listed companies could **compromise the investment potential** of BEB's shares for the market.

As a small company by listed company standards, BEB is likely to encounter particular difficulty meeting some of the requirements, particularly obtaining **suitable non-executive directors**. This problem is exacerbated that the company is an unusual company, with a charitable foundation, and therefore **specific skills** may be required from non-executive directors.

Charitable aims

The fact that **company strategy** is directed and **controlled by the charity** JFR, by virtue of the clause in the company's memorandum, may represent a **financial risk**. This is because it may **restrict the attractiveness of the shares** in the market, as shareholders are going to be **unable to influence** policy with regard to **capital growth and dividends**. However, given the charitable foundation of the company, it is equally possible that its shares will be held and traded by people in sympathy with its aims rather than for any significant hope of gain from the investment.

Products

Another risk, with both compliance and operational elements is the fact that one of BEB's major operations is to **import foodstuffs** from **developing countries**. Risks are breaking **food hygiene regulations** and **deterioration** of food in poor transport and storage conditions.

Change in sales mix

The company has experienced a change in sales mix during the year, although in the past the sales mix has been stable. This may be as a result of the new website being a new source of sales. This is an operational risk as the **systems** of the company **may not be flexible** enough to adjust to changes in the sales mix, which could result in loss to the company and **customer dissatisfaction**. It is also possible that the company could **waste resources** directing marketing and selling effort in the wrong areas.

Personal selling

In the past the company has relied to an extent on **personal selling**, where individuals sold BEB products on behalf of the company. This source of income appears to have fallen in this year. The company should monitor this situation, and try to see whether all sellers, or just a few, are selling less.

There is likely to be a **degree of informality** in the arrangements with personal sellers and without monitoring, the company could find that it experiences big changes in this source of income which it has **very little control** over.

Website

In opening this new avenue of selling, Buy Fair has opened itself up to a significant number of **risks associated with information technology**. These include the **high level of technological intelligence** the company will require to maintain the web facility and any related systems, the risk of **business interruption** due to technological failure, for example, caused by viruses. There is also increased risk of the company being subject to **credit card frauds**, although it will already be exposed to such risks in its mail order division.

Advanced payments to suppliers

It is common practice amongst such fair trade enterprises to make advanced payments to suppliers in order to enable them to produce the goods. However, this practice puts BEB at risk of having made payments to a supplier that **does not produce the goods**, for which the company may have very little come back, given the implied financial situation of the suppliers that it deals with. It also puts the company at risk of **paying in advance for goods which do not come up to quality standards**, with similar effect for the company.

This risk is currently particularly high due to the **number of new suppliers** that the company is dealing with. Although BEB is likely to have carried out significant research before dealing with the suppliers, it will still be learning through the course of its trading relationship with them.

(b) COSO has suggested an eight-stage method for managing risks.

(i) **Internal environment**

This represents the overall style and tone of BEB, and provides the context within which controls are operated. A key aspect is **attitudes to risk**, including risk management philosophy and appetite, integrity and ethical values. Clearly **integrity** is key to BEB's mission, but the company must also bear in mind its attitudes to risk. Although it seems fairly well diversified, BEB should consider whether the change in the relative importance of different sources of sales affects its risk profile.

(ii) **Objective setting**

BEB, and ultimately JER, needs to ensure that there is a **process in place for setting objectives**, and that the chosen objectives support BEB's mission and are consistent with its risk appetite. The objective setting process and how objectives are communicated will need to be reviewed now that the company is listed, with changes in the composition of the board and pattern of shareholdings.

(iii) **Event identification**

BEB needs to **identify internal and external events** that affect the achievement of the company's objectives, **distinguishing between risks** and **opportunities**. Events that have impacted recently have included the reduction in personal selling, so the company needs to identify whether increasing the number of personal sellers by recruitment represents a sufficient opportunity to warrant investment.

(iv) **Risk assessment**

Risk analysis, considering **likelihood and impact**, should form the basis of risk management. For example BEB could look at the experience of other listed companies controlled by charities, to see whether this arrangement has lessened their appeal to 'ordinary' investors, or enhanced their appeal to ethically sensitive investors.

(v) **Risk response**

BEB needs to respond to risks by **avoiding, accepting, controlling or transferring** them, its policies being consistent with its risk appetites. An important area is relationships with suppliers. The board must consider what level of payments BEB is prepared to make in advance and what resources it is prepared to devote to ensuring suppliers fulfil the terms of their contracts.

(vi) **Control activities**

Controls should be designed to ensure that risk management **policies and procedures** are **effectively implemented**. Important procedures will include controls ensuring that BEB meets regulatory requirements affecting food hygiene and controls over the transport and storage of food. Other areas include authorisation of advance payment to suppliers and computer protection controls including measures against viruses.

(vii) **Information and communication**

This means ensuring that BEB's managers and employees have **sufficient, relevant information** to be able to carry out their duties. This includes for example giving personal sellers sufficient information about BEB and other methods of sales so that they can maximise customer awareness.

(viii) **Monitoring**

Monitoring by the board and senior managers is a key part of the whole corporate governance process, encompassing **ongoing review** and regular (annual) or **one-off separate evaluations**. Listing will mean that BEB has to get its arrangements up to the required level, and in many areas increased monitoring may directly benefit the business. For example the directors need to ensure that they are keeping track of the company's changing sales patterns and directing resources accordingly.

4 HOOD

Text references. Chapter 1, with Chapter 16 also being particularly relevant on IT risks.

Top tips. A definition of a key subject relating to the answer can add value; however don't just repeat the requirement. The framework used of Operational, Non-Business (Strategic) and Business (Strategic), is a good way of identifying the most important risks. Other frameworks may be used, although it will be important to ensure that the risks identified are clearly related to the situation outlined in the scenario. Business Strategy knowledge about the influences on demand is helpful here.

In (a) where you're asked to identify the risks, you should focus on what causes them to arise. In (b) evaluate requires assessment of financial consequences.

For (b) if you are faced with a question of the format:

Part (a) Identify risks

Part (b) Evaluate effects of identified risks and recommend what the organisation can do to mitigate them, ensure your answer plan shows consistency in format. Your answer to (b) needs to be a mirror image of your answer to (a).

Don't worry also if you haven't thought of all the possible risks we have. Remember a score of 15 out of 25 is a comfortable pass. It's safer from the viewpoint of passing to cover each risk in reasonable depth, making reference to the scenario rather than just briefly listing all possible risks. A long list of risks without any explanation carries the possibility of obtaining no marks as you haven't shown why what you said is relevant.

Easy marks. Evidence suggests most students find it easier to identify risks than to come up with ways of reducing and controlling them. However to improve your chances of passing, you must be able to come up with ways of tackling risks that are realistic for the company described in the scenario.

Risk can defined as the possibility that events or results will turn out differently from is expected.

(a) The risks facing the HOOD Company are outlined below.

Operational risks

These are risks relating to the business's day-to-day operations.

(i) **Accounting irregularities**

The unexplained fall in gross profit in some stores may be indicative of **fraud** or **other accounting irregularities**. Low gross profit in itself may be caused by **incorrect inventory values** or loss of **sale income**. Incorrect stock levels in turn can be caused by **incorrect inventory counting** or **actual stealing of inventory** by employees. Similarly, **loss of sales income** could result from **accounting errors** or employees **fraudulently removing cash** from the business rather than recording it as a sale.

(ii) **Delays in inventory ordering**

Although inventory information is collected using the EPOS system, **re-ordering of inventory takes** a **significant amount of time**. Transferring data to head office for central purchasing may result in some discounts on purchase. However, the average 10 days before inventory is received at the store could result in **the company running out of inventory**.

(iii) **Event**

HOOD may be vulnerable to losses in a **warehouse fire**.

Non-business (strategic) risks

These are risks that arise for reasons beyond the normal operations of the company or the business environment within which it operates.

(i) **Production**

The possibility of sunlight making some of HOOD Company's products potentially dangerous may give rise to **loss of sales** also inventory recall.

(ii) **Corporate reputation**

Risks in this category relate to the overall **perception of HOOD in the marketplace** as a supplier of (hopefully) good quality clothing. However, this reputation could be damaged by **problems with the manufacturing process** and a consequent high level of returns.

Business (strategic) risks

External risks relate to the **business**; they are essentially **uncontrollable** by the company.

(i) **Macro-economic risk**

The company is dependent on one market sector and vulnerable to competition in that sector.

(ii) **Product demand**

The most important social change is probably a **change in fashion**. HOOD has not changed its product designs for 4 years indicating some lack of investment in this area. Given that fashions tend to change more frequently than every four years, HOOD may experience falling sales as customers seek new designs for their outdoor clothing. HOOD may also be vulnerable to **seasonal variations** in demand.

(b) The potential effects of the risks on HOOD and methods of overcoming those risks are explained below.

Operational risks

(i) **Accounting irregularities**

The potential effect on HOOD is **loss of income** either from stock not being available for sale or cash not being recorded. The overall amount is unlikely to be significant as employees would be concerned about being caught stealing.

The risk can be minimised by introducing additional controls including the necessity of producing a **receipt for each sale** and the **agreement of cash received** to the **till roll** by the shop manager. Loss of stock may be identified by more frequent stock checks in the stores or closed-circuit television.

(ii) **Delays in inventory ordering**

The potential effect on HOOD is **immediate loss of sales** as customers cannot purchase the garments that they require. In the longer term, if stock outs become more frequent, **customers may not visit** the store because they believe stock will not be available.

The risk can be minimised by letting the stores **order goods directly** from the manufacturers, using an extension of the EPOS system. Costs incurred relate to the provision of Internet access for the shops and possible increase in cost of goods supplied. However, this may be acceptable compared to overall loss of reputation.

(iii) **Event**

The main effects of a warehouse fire will be a **loss of inventory** and the incurring of costs to replace it. There will also be a **loss of sales** as the inventory is not there to fulfil customer demand, and perhaps also a loss of subsequent sales as customers continue to shop elsewhere,

Potential losses of sales could be avoided by **holding contingency inventory** elsewhere, and losses from the fire could be reduced by **insurance.**

Non-business (strategic) risks

(i) **Production**

The effect on HOOD is the possibility of having to **reimburse customers** and the loss of income from the product until the problems are resolved.

The risk can be minimised by HOOD taking the claim seriously and **investigating its validity**, rather than ignoring it. For the future, **guarantees** should be obtained from suppliers to confirm that products are safe and **insurance** taken out against possible claims from customers for damage or distress.

(ii) **Corporate reputation**

As well as **immediate losses of contribution from products** that have been returned, HOOD faces the consequence of loss of future sales from customers who believe their products no longer offer quality. Other clothing retailers have found this to be very serious; a **reputation for quality**, once lost, undoubtedly **cannot easily be regained**. The potential effect of a drop in overall corporate reputation will be falling sales for HOOD, resulting eventually in a **going concern problem**.

HOOD can guard against this loss of reputation by **enhanced quality control procedures**, and introducing processes such as **total quality management**.

Business (strategic) risks

(i) **Macro-economic risk**

The potential effect on HOOD largely depends on HOOD's **ability to provide an appropriate selection of clothes**. It is unlikely that demand for coats etc. will fall to zero, so some sales will be expected. However, an **increase in competition** may result in **falling sales,** and without some diversification, this will automatically affect the overall sales of HOOD.

HOOD can minimise the risk in two ways: by **diversifying into other areas**. Given that the company sells outdoor clothes, then commencing sales of other outdoor goods such as camping equipment may be one way of diversifying risk. It can also look to **reduce operational gearing**, fixed cost as a proportion of turnover.

(ii) **Product demand**

Again the **risk of loss of demand and business to competitors** may undermine HOOD's ability to continue in business.

This risk can be minimised by having a **broad strategy** to **maintain** and **develop** the **brand** of HOOD. Not updating the product range would appear to be a mistake in this context as the brand may be devalued as products may not meet changing tastes of customers. The board must therefore allocate appropriate investment funds to updating the products and **introduce new products** to maintain the company's image.

5 Doctors' practice

Text references. Chapter 1 discusses controls and general risk issues. Chapter 7 describes different types of audit.

Top tips. (a) requires imagination, but the way to think is simply to ask what could go wrong. Although this question is about a doctors'surgery, many of the risks are much the same as the risks for any venture undertaken by a business, such as anticipating demand or obtaining finance. A good method of analysis is therefore split the risks up into operational, non-business strategic and business strategic as we have done in our answer. Note that the second part of (a) does **not** ask you to describe CIMA's model in detail, rather to **explain** the uses of it or any other similar model. Elements to emphasise include assessment, coverage, profiling and action. This question reinforces our comments in the front pages that you need to think widely about risks.

In (b) the risks are such that a risk manager needs to be appointed, although the practice is small enough for everyone to be involved in the decision to define risk appetite. Given the significant adverse consequences that could occur for all partners, it is important to involve them all if possible. You also need to bring into your discussion the constraints on decision-making.

The most important point in (c) is that systems auditing may focus on systems, not the risks that drive those systems. A critical discussion requires fair coverage of the benefits and drawbacks. The examiner's comments about students lacking basic knowledge of auditing are worrying and have been repeated in other reports, for example in May 2008. Knowledge of the main types of audit and principal audit tests is important in P3.

Our answers to (b) and (c) are rather shorter than some of the other parts for equivalent marks in this paper. In the exam you may well come across some disparities in the length of answer required to obtain a good mark.

Easy marks. (c) should be easiest, as it's a general part not related to the circumstances described in the question.

Examiner's comments. This question was unpopular and poorly done. In (a) students showed a lack of understanding of what a doctor's practice does, and demonstrated a lack of knowledge of CIMA's risk management cycle or other risk management models. (b) was well done but many answers to (c) were very bad indeed, with students demonstrating a lack of knowledge of systems or other types of auditing.

(a) (i) **Additional risks**

A number of additional risks arise from the introduction of the new facility, including the following.

Operational risks

Surgical equipment failure

The practice may face threats to its income through **failures of its surgical equipment**, meaning that it cannot provide surgical procedures whilst the equipment is unavailable.

Storage facilities failure

Environmental failures in the storage facilities for equipment and drugs may also lead to a **loss of income** if surgical procedures cannot be provided. The practice may also face the **costs of replacing the equipment** and drugs that have been contaminated.

You would also have gained marks if you discussed the following operational risks:

Security

The additional equipment and drugs stored may make the practice more vulnerable to theft.

Transportation risks

The blood and samples taken may be contaminated by storage facilities problems at the surgery, and also by deterioration during transportation. This may result in misdiagnosis of illness and hence the costs of giving patients the wrong treatment.

High demand

High demand at certain times of the year may mean that the practice loses income through being unable to meet the demand, or incurs increased costs through having to pay for extra medical and nursing care.

Hospital delays

The practice may lose income through not being able to provide care because of delays in testing blood and samples at the local hospital.

Staff

Existing staff may not have the collective skills necessary to operate the new unit. If new staff are employed, there may be a risk of staff dissatisfaction and hence retention problems with existing staff if new staff are employed on better terms.

Effect on existing care

The resources required by the new facilities may mean less resources are available for existing work; hence the areas of care currently provided may suffer and income from these be threatened.

Non-business risks

Legal risks

Providing more procedures may increase the risk of problems arising during treatment, and hence losses through the **costs of fighting or settling negligence claims**.

Financial risks

The new **facilities** will have to be **financed**. As the practice buildings will need to be extended, the partners will have to borrow, probably from a bank. The partners, not the practice, will have **ultimate liability** for this debt. The partners may face problems in **meeting any finance costs** that it has to incur, particularly if the return on investment is not as good as forecast. Financing the investment may mean funds are lacking when required for other purposes, such as buying out a retiring partner.

Business risks

Practice development risks

The practice may not achieve the income growth expected if the **standard of treatment is believed to be lower** than would be available in the hospital, or if because of operational difficulties **patients were forced to wait longer** for treatment than they would in a hospital.

Regulatory risks

If shortcomings arise in the treatment provided, the practice's **regulatory body** may **intervene** and prevent the practice providing the surgical procedures it currently wishes to offer.

(ii) **Uses of risk management model**

Iterative model

The most important feature of models such as CIMA's is that it demonstrates how risk management is a **continual process** and experience gained from carrying out all stages can impact upon all other stages of the cycle. Review by the **risk manager** or all of the doctors of the **effectiveness of risk management** needs to be built into the process.

Organisation– wide application

Models are used to assess **organisation-wide risks** and also **specific process or unit risks**. They also are used to assess the **interaction** between risks.

Logical process

Models show that risk management is a logical process, taking the organisation through **initial risk identification,** then **identification of events** that may cause **risks to crystallise, assessment** of **how great losses** might be and in the light of these how best to **respond to risks**. This will help identify who should be responsible for which aspects of the risk management cycle.

Role of monitoring and feedback

Models emphasise the importance of **monitoring risk management procedures** and controls once they are in place. The feedback from this monitoring will **impact upon future risk assessments** and also lead to **continuous improvements in processes**, following the **principles of feedforward control**.

Decision-making

Models emphasise that the results of all stages of the risk management process should impact upon **the organisation's decision-making process** and consequently **affect strategy** and also **the appetite the organisation has for risk.** The decisions taken as a result of this will in turn feed through to the risk assessment and management processes, modifying the views taken on **key risks** and the best ways to **respond to them.**

(b) **Risk appetite**

Risk appetite is the amount of risk that the team of doctors **as a whole** is prepared to **accept in exchange for returns** (the clientele effect). The new arrangements here are expected to **increase income**, and the risk appetite defines what risk levels will be acceptable in exchange for the increased income. Risk appetite also infers that the practice is willing to accept that risk has a downside as well as an upside, and the consequences of both are culturally acceptable.

Risk appetite decisions

In this situation, one of the senior partners in the practice would act as the risk manager and be responsible for analysing risk and recommending what **acceptable risk levels** might be in the **changed circumstances** for each of the major risks. However as the decision results from a major change in what the practice is doing, the recommendations should certainly be approved by a majority of the doctors, and preferably be unanimous. If risks materialise, it could have **significant adverse financial and reputational consequences** for all the partners. The practice may also have to act within **constraints** imposed by government or regulator, which effectively limit the maximum amount of risk the practice can bear.

(c) **Purposes of systems-based auditing**

Systems-based auditing focuses on the **overall functioning of the organisation's systems**. The level of risk of each of the systems that the organisation operates is assessed, the resources required to audit each system are determined and a decision to taken on how often each system should be audited.

Usefulness of systems-based auditing

Systems-based auditing concentrates on:

(i) **Procedures** in place to **achieve an organisation's objectives**
(ii) **Controls** that are in place to **manage the risks** that threaten the achievement of objectives

The systems-based audit will assess whether the **controls and procedures** in place are **appropriate** in the light of the **objectives management has decided** and the **risk management procedures** that managers have adopted. It then tests whether procedures and controls are operating effectively.

Limitations of systems-based audits

A major limitation of systems-based auditing can be a **lack of focus** on the **underlying risk-taking decisions** and **risk management framework.** A risk-based approach would assess whether the risk management processes are sufficient to **assess and manage risk.** A risk-based audit would question the **appropriateness of each system** as a means of managing risk and would question whether the **assessment of each system's risk** on which systems-based audits are based was itself appropriate. Audit of operational systems therefore needs to be combined with an **audit of the risk management system** itself.

6 A and B

Text references. Chapter 1 on risks for (a) and Chapter 4 on control measures for (c), though other chapters are relevant (Chapter 3 contains material on the impact of organisational structure, Chapter 6 on research and development). Chapter 14 of the P9 text covers the issues discussed in (b).

Top tips. This is a good example of a question where material from all three Strategic level papers is relevant, also material from Managerial level papers. Remember that RCS is in the management accounting pillar of the exam structure so you will need to remember what you learnt in P1 and P2, but this questions also illustrates the need to retain financial accounting knowledge from P7 and P8.

(a) may appear to belong on P6 rather than this paper. However before you start bringing in all the P6 theories, you must remember that this is an RCS paper. This should lead you to read the question as saying what do the strategic decisions the boards take on structure, markets and location imply for the risk profile, the nature and level of risks that the two companies bear. It is a good example of what we stressed in the front pages about demonstrating strategic awareness.

(b) is a very standard question on the key decisions about the treasury function. 4 marks is not a very generous mark allocation and it would be easy to run over time on this part. The question requirement **Compare and contrast** means that the best answer structure is a point-by-point comparison under the same headings.

Areas other than those covered in our answer that would have gained you credit include centralisation increasing opportunities for fraud and demotivating local staff, decentralisation meaning greater responsiveness to local needs.

In (c) you were asked to give three controls for Company A or three controls for Company B; we have given three for both companies to cover both possibilities. The question is looking for performance measures that indicate risk levels. What is important is that you don't just state the measure, you also explain what it is and you **justify using the data in the scenario**, why the measure is important.

Note the stress in the question requirements on taking into account current structure and size. Markers will be alert for recommendations that are unrealistic for the company you choose, and will not reward them. You should mark your answers against those criteria, as obviously there are other controls that you could have included that we haven't mentioned.

Other possibilities for A include:

- Financial – transfer pricing, responsibility accounting in subsidiaries
- Non-financial quantitative – sales targets in different market segments
- Non-financial qualitative – repeat business

Other possibilities for B include:

- Financial – profit margin per customer, on-line sales revenue
- Non-financial quantitative – % of sales on-line
- Non-financial qualitative – mystery shopper

Interestingly the question does not tell us what the two companies actually manufacture!

Easy marks. If you remembered what you learnt in P9, (b) should be an easy 4 marks.

Examiner's comments. Most students answered this question reasonably well, although some failed to make the link to strategy. Some students' discussion of pros and cons in (b) was limited.

(a) (i) **Company structure**

The decisions the boards make on company structure will have a particular influence on the following issues.

Effectiveness of risk management

The extent to which decision-making is diversified can determine the ways in which risks are managed. The more autonomy local managers have, the more they are likely to develop **differing risk appetites** and also **differing ways of managing risks**. A also has to ensure that effective control is maintained over the **central functions** of treasury and research and development. In B's case this is complicated by distribution being run as a joint venture. The joint venture partner may have attitudes to risk management and the relationship between risk and return with which B's central management differs, and the partner's attitude may influence the joint venture's activities.

Cooperation between subsidiaries

The board of A's decision to structure its operations geographically rather than by product indicates that it believes that there is a low risk of **production inefficiencies** caused by lack of co-ordination and co-operation between the different subsidiaries. A's board appears to believe that running the company using autonomous subsidiaries for different parts of its operations will not result in dysfunctional behaviour.

Performance measurement systems

The significance of the structure will depend on the performance measurement systems used as means of management control, and whether these are appropriate. **Profit centres, cost or investment centres**, **return on capital employed** and **residual income** all have advantages and disadvantages, but choosing the most appropriate method should reduce organisational risks such as non-congruent behaviour by subsidiaries.

(ii) **Market types**

The type of markets the companies operate in will particularly influence the following risks:

Competition risks

A's greater involvement in the business to business market appears to have had the consequence that it is more dependent than B on demand from one or two **large customers**. This decision may mean that it is **less exposed to the risk of competition** since some potential competitors may not be big enough to service customers of such a size. However the **consequences** of losing either or both of its large customers are likely to be **more damaging to A** than B losing one of its customers other than perhaps the Canadian customer. Similarly the opportunities the two companies have to gain customers from competitors may differ significantly.

Customer risks

The risks of losing customers due to **inadequate service** in the different types of market may differ because of the differing expectations of customers in each market. Evidence suggests that B2B customers have increasingly demanding expectations of what suppliers should offer in terms of use of electronic links and local customer support.

Liquidity risks

Clearly loss of a customer will have a much more **violent effect on A's liquidity** than B. However B may face problems associated with a **higher cost base** necessary to maintain sales, for example the need for advertising spend with uncertain returns to attract more customers.

Information technology controls

B faces costs associated with maintaining an effective on-line presence. These include **security and data integrity risks**. They also include the risks arising from the **need to meet changing expectations of customers**, such as the need to enhance the website to reduce response and transaction times.

(iii) **Locations**

Choice of location may particularly impact on the following risks.

Political risk

Choosing to produce in China indicates that B's board is prepared to tolerate a possibly significant level of **political risk**. Political links between China and the USA are sensitive, and B's links with its subsidiaries may be **forcibly disrupted by the US government** if relations deteriorate. There is also the risk of a change in China to a regime that is **less welcoming to links with western companies**.

Legal risk

Company A may be more likely to suffer **legal compliance costs** in areas such as health and safety to fulfil statutory and regulatory requirements that risks be minimised. The manufacturing and assembly activities of Company B may be subject to a less rigorous regime in China. However the fact that Company A is obliged to adhere to more rigorous regulations may mean that it is **less likely to suffer a major health and safety breakdown** which a strict regime is designed to prevent.

Transportation risk

Both companies appear to be tolerating the risks of transport links being disrupted, as production and sales **take place in different countries**. Company A is possibly more likely to **suffer disruption** at **an earlier stage**, since the major stages of the production process take place in different continents. However B is more likely to **suffer distribution disruption**, since it is distributing from China to the USA whereas much of A's sales are distributed from the UK to elsewhere in Europe.

You would also have scored marks if you had discussed the following risks:

Infrastructure risk

Company B seems to be tolerating the risk that operations may be disrupted by problems with the **Chinese infrastructure**. In Autumn 2006 it was reported that Western companies that were manufacturing in China toys for the Christmas market were facing the risk of being unable to fulfil demand, as problems with the electricity supply had led to electricity rationing and factories only being able to work a certain number of hours per week.

Foreign exchange risks

Both companies make the bulk of their sales in one area, and both will suffer **foreign exchange risks** that are not mitigated by diversification. A will suffer them on sales for which it receives European currencies, B will suffer them on **production costs in China.** Both may be vulnerable to **longer-term economic risks** in the geographical markets in which they sell, and B may also be subject to rising production costs in China as the Chinese economy develops.

Reputation risk

Company B appears to have accepted a risk that its reputation may be damaged because it uses Chinese labour for manufacturing. It may receive **adverse publicity** for using underpaid labour and taking jobs away from the American economy, resulting in consumer boycotts.

(b) **Staff risk**

Company B may be exposed to a greater risk of staff errors; the local divisions may not be able to employ staff with the **expertise necessary** to handle complex treasury issues. As the treasury function is centralised in Company A, resources can be focused on employing treasury specialists and the duplication that decentralising activities will involve should be avoided.

Speculation risk

The recognition of treasury operations as profit making activities implies that treasury activities may be undertaken for the sake of creating profits. **Trading in instruments** such as **derivatives speculatively** implies a **higher risk tolerance** of treasury activities on Company A's part. By contrast in B, treasury is a **service function**; local treasury functions support the activities of local operations and are more likely to use derivatives as a means of **minimising the financial risks** associated with trading.

Organisational risk

Centralisation in A provides a means of exercising **better control through use of standardised procedures** and **pooling and netting; monitoring of operational risks** is likely to be easier if operations are concentrated in one place. Distance may make controls in B weaker. However If the department in Company A's is to be a true profit centre, then **market prices** should be charged for its services to other departments. It may be difficult to decide realistic prices, and this may cause disputes.

Currency risk

Foreign currency risk management is likely to be improved by treasury centralisation. A's central treasury department can **match** foreign currency income earned by one subsidiary with expenditure in the same currency by another subsidiary. In this way, the risk of losses on adverse exchange rate changes can be avoided without the expense of forward exchange contracts or other 'hedging' (risk-reducing) methods. However if wrong decisions are made, the amounts at risk will be greater in A than B.

(c) **Company A**

Financial

A major task of A's treasury department is to manage foreign exchange risk, so therefore A needs to measure what its exposure to financial price risks might be. **Value at risk** calculations indicate the maximum loss that A may incur due to normal market movements in a set period of time with a set probability. The risk of losses greater than the value at risk should under normal market conditions be very small and hence be tolerated by A.

Non-financial quantitative

Monitoring and targeting production lead and waiting times will be key indicators of whether A risks failing to fulfil customer demands. Because of the complications of having manufacturing and assembly on different continents, data is needed on whether **target times for manufacturing and assembly** are being fulfilled, and where any delays are occurring that impact on other stages of the production process.

Non-financial qualitative

A is clearly **dependent on sales from two major customers** and therefore requires controls that will establish as quickly as possible whether these customers are dissatisfied. **Feedback** should therefore be obtained on a regular basis, both by meetings between A's and customers' senior management, and those on both sides who have the main responsibility for maintaining the relationship. These customers should also be able to communicate concerns between meetings, possibly with named managers who are not normally involved in maintaining the relationship. The board should **review** on a regular basis the **feedback** obtained along with **quantitative data** of those customers' demand and how long it has taken to fulfil their requirements.

Company B

Financial

Benchmarking B's cost data against cost data about major competitors will give an indication of how great the threat from competitors is. If competitors have a **high fixed cost structure** then they are likely to respond aggressively to threats to sales volumes; high operational gearing will mean that falls in sales revenues will significantly decrease profits. If competitors appear to have **high unit costs**, there may be a low risk that they can respond effectively to price cuts; this may be a particularly significant issue for B if it has located in China because it wishes to minimise its own unit costs.

Non-financial quantitative

Monitoring and targeting delivery time of completed products is a key measure of risk for B. The transport of goods to different continents may mean that there is a significant risk of delivery delays, and the fact that distribution is handled by a joint venture may mean B is able to exercise less control over it. The directors of B will wish to **measure actual delivery times** against those **budgeted** and also try to **benchmark delivery times against those of competitors**. Possibly cost advantages B gains through manufacturing in China need to be weighed against the risks that competitors will be able to provide a speedier, more reliable delivery service.

Non-financial qualitative

Research and development appears to be a significant area for B; its customer base is more diverse so it is possibly more dependent on new ideas. B's board needs to monitor carefully whether research and development efforts are being wasted, and the possibility that projects are late, over budget or have not delivered the planned benefits. A **post-implementation review** of projects that have been completed is a significant control to assess:

- How **projects performed** against plans
- Whether the R and D department complied with **internal guidelines**

- Whether R and D fulfilled the **strategic objectives** laid down by the board
- Whether **board monitoring** of projects whilst they were going on was regular and rigorous enough

Actions taken as a result of the recommendations of the review should enhance the value given by R and D and also may suggest stronger board monitoring to identify earlier on and terminate R and D activities that will not deliver significant benefits.

7 LXY

Top tips. Two obvious categories in (a) are strategic and operational risks; the answer identifies the COSO ERM model as the source of the third category, compliance. You could also have chosen reporting from the COSO model. Alternatively other classifications of risk include regulatory, health and safety and financial. Given that there are only 3 marks in (a) your justification needs to be short, but you do need at least a sentence on each category.

The best way to plan (a) (ii) would be to choose the category that generates the most risks, bearing in mind that you not only have to discuss the risks, but recommend how they might be controlled. We've chosen operational risks as that seems to us to generate a lot of ideas, but we have listed alternative suggestions for other categories of risk.

(b) offers opportunities to go over time. It's only worth four marks, which means that you would get one mark for the risk and one mark for describing how it could be managed, so just two risks plus good suggestions about how they should be managed should generate maximum marks. It's rather a pity that the examiner did not allocate more marks to this part.

The main point to get across in the first part of (c) is that risk management is primarily responsible for design and implementation, internal audit for confirmation and review. Not auditing one's own work is an ethical, as well as an effectiveness, point. This was also tested in Question 1 of the May exam. The mark scheme gave more credit for discussion of how the two functions should be kept separate, than for the role of each function.

Easy marks. The responsibilities of risk management and internal staff are examined quite frequently, so (c) should have been straightforward, particularly also as no application to the scenario was required.

Examiner's comments. Students generally scored well in (a) and (b), suggesting a wide variety of relevant risks.

In (c) students could describe the roles of the two functions, but struggled to come up with suggestions on how to maintain their separate effectiveness.

(a) (i) The three categories chosen are three categories in the COSO enterprise risk management model.

Strategic – business

Strategic risks are the **risks of volatility in profits** caused by the decisions the directors take about the business activities in which LXY is involved. Taking the wrong strategic decisions, such as deciding to **operate unprofitable routes**, can threaten LXY's existence in the long-term.

Operational

Operational risks are the risks arising from the **day-to-day activities** of LXY. If they are not managed effectively, they can result in significant costs over time, or lost revenue if buses are delayed or cancelled.

Compliance – strategic non-business

Compliance risks are the risks arising from **non-compliance with legislation or other obligations**, such as the contract to provide bus services. LXY should take these risks very seriously, as non-compliance could mean the company being fined heavily or stopped from running buses.

(ii) **Operational risks**

Bus breakdown or accidents

If buses break down or have accidents, LXY faces loss of revenue, customer dissatisfaction and sanctions for breaching its contract. Measures to limit this risk include:

- **A programme of regular inspection and maintenance** so that the engines, tyres are kept in good condition, and **ceasing to operate buses** once they reach a **certain age**
- Having **spare buses and staff available** so that buses that break down can be substituted as quickly as possible. Alternatively **hire contracts** for staff and vehicles may be cheaper and just as effective.

Weather disruption to long-distance routes

Poor weather may cause delays or cancellations, particularly to the national routes that LXY operates, resulting in **lost revenue** from not operating the routes or **customer refunds** on late journeys. Measures to limit this risk include:

- **Monitoring weather and road conditions**, **also vehicle locations** by radio or mobile phone
- **Building slack into bus timetables** to allow for delays at certain times, and having **contingency plans** to operate buses on **alternative routes** if some routes are particularly prone to delay

Poor driver performance

There may be **delays to return journeys on national routes**, and hence customer dissatisfaction, caused by drivers who have stayed away overnight not taking the return journey out on time. Measures to limit this risk include:

- **Making alarm calls** to drivers to ensure that they are awake and **having the driver check in** to central control before he takes the return journey out
- **Surprise inspections** to check buses are departing on time and **disciplinary action** against drivers who consistently take buses out late

Alternative solutions

We summarise below possible risks and controls for other categories of risk:

Risk	Controls
Strategic	
Choosing unprofitable routes	• Detailed management accounting information about profitability • Forecasting of likely future trends in passenger traffic
Competition from other transport providers	• Obtaining intelligence about plans of other providers • Sensitivity analysis of alternative strategies to combat competition
Losing the contract	• Reporting of breaches of contract terms to senior management. • Liaison with key stakeholders (Danon local government, passengers) • Customer complaint scheme and compensation for customers whose journeys are cancelled or delayed
Operational	
Driver fraud by carrying extra passengers/freight/luggage	• References for all new drivers • Spot checks on buses

Risk	Controls
Compliance	
Breaching regulations about the maintenance of buses	• Regular maintenance programme • Service records and testing
Breaching regulations about driver training, licensing or hours	• Training programmes • Checks on police database • Time records, drivers clocking in tacographs
Breaching health and safety regulations – access, facilities, fire protection	• Staff training and manuals • Employment of health and safety specialists • Spot checks of buses by inspectors • Inspection of facilities • Disciplinary action
Breaching environmental regulations on emissions	• Regular vehicle maintenance • Emission monitoring
Failing to fulfil the requirements of the contract	• Monitoring of potential problems, eg bad weather • Spare drivers and buses/hire contracts
Reporting	
Incorrect decisions because of poor quality information	• Detailed breakdown of information from different routes • Information covering qualitative details such as customer satisfaction as well as financial data
Failure to report all income received	• Segregation of ticket issuing from maintenance of records • Reconciliation of passenger numbers with ticket records
Incorrect external reporting of results	• Qualified accounts staff • Internal audit function/audit committee review

(b) **Breaches of food hygiene regulations**

LXY may suffer fines if it is found to have breached hygiene regulations, even if the café owner is **ultimately responsible**.

LXY should ensure that the food and drink the café owner supplies is **regularly checked for quality** by its internal audit function and it has **sufficient storage facilities** for food and drink on buses with overnight stops. Staff responsible for supplying the food and drink during the journey should be given **appropriate training in food hygiene**.

Failure to deliver promised quality

Customers will be **dissatisfied**, and may **demand refunds**, if the food and drink promised by LXY for the journey is not delivered by the café owner.

The **contract** with the café owner should specify strictly what he will provide for each journey. If he fails to reach the standards demanded, LXY should **reduce the amount** he is paid, or make him **liable for any refunds to dissatisfied customers**.

Alternative solutions

You would also have scored marks if you had discussed the following risks and controls.

Damage to vehicles

Spillages of food and drink may cause **damage to buses** and **inconvenience passengers**.

Food and drink should be kept in **secure accommodation** which minimises the risks of leakages. Staff should be trained appropriately in **handling food and drink**. Coaches may need to be modified so that passengers have **enough space** to put their food and drink down safely.

Cafe owner ceasing to trade

If the cafe owner suddenly ceases to trade, LXY will not be able to supply the food and drink it has promised to customers.

LXY may be able to take out insurance against this possibility. The board should also have a **contingency plan** in place, **identifying possible alternative suppliers** so that they can be asked to **substitute quickly** if necessary.

(c) **Risk management**

Objectives

The risk management function has responsibility for **implementing the objectives** of risk management that the board and audit and risk committees have decided.

Role

Risk management will be responsible for **building a risk aware culture** throughout the organisation by **information provision and training.** Risk management will provide **guidelines on overall risk policy** and **coordinate the various functional activities that deal with risks.**

Risk management will also be responsible for **designing and reviewing risk analysis procedures and risk response processes**. They should ensure not only their **recommendations** for improvements, but the recommendations of the board, board committees and internal audit functions are **implemented.**

Internal audit

Objectives

Internal audit will be responsible for **confirming** that appropriate risk management systems are being implemented, and that **risks associated with major business objectives** are being **managed effectively.**

Role

Internal auditors will be looking for evidence that risk management and internal control systems will be **able to take effective steps to counter major risks**. They will also review whether the systems are **working as they are supposed to work**. This includes **reviewing the activities of the risk management function itself.** Internal audit will be responsible for making **recommendations for improvements,** but will not be responsible for implementing these improvements. They should be acting in accordance with **internal auditing standards** as well as the requirements of the organisation.

Maintaining separate effectiveness of both functions

Different staff for risk management and internal audit

Although staff work for a combined department, managers can try to organise the department so that as far as possible **different staff** work on risk management and internal audit activities.

Different training and staff development programmes

Staff could follow **different training programmes** and **train for different qualifications**.

Supervision and management

Different line managers should manage risk management staff and internal audit staff. Risk management staff and managers should report to the **risk committee**, internal audit to the **audit committee**.

Restrictions on what staff can audit

Where staff have both internal audit and risk management responsibilities, they should **not be allowed to review systems in specific functional areas** that they themselves have **designed or implemented.**

8 Preparation question: Cost containment

Text references. Chapter 4.

Top tips. You needed to ensure that you covered each of the techniques (as stressed in the requirements), to mention the relevant traditional cost containment approach for each of the techniques and, it goes without saying, **you had to keep to the point.** By using separate paragraphs and headers, you can demonstrate clearly that you are covering the second part of the requirements, to discuss cost reductions, adequately.

Your discussions need to focus on the limitations of the traditional approach and how the new approaches provide better information for management decision-making and better scrutiny of costs.

Easy marks. This whole question is straightforward as it is not linked to a scenario. However it does highlight what are likely to be the key points if you have to discuss these techniques in the context of a scenario.

(a) **Target costing**

Traditional approach

The traditional approach to product costing, which is dominated by **standard costing**, is first to **develop a product**. An **expected standard cost is then determined** and a **selling price** (probably based on cost) is **set**, with a **resulting profit or loss**.

Target costing approach

This is to **develop a product concept** and then **determine the price** that **customers** would be **willing to pay for it. A desired profit margin** is then **deducted** from the price to **leave a total cost figure**. This is the **target cost**. If the target cost is vastly different from the cost at which the product can be produced, the product may need to be redesigned or may even be scrapped if the target is impossible to achieve.

Management may decide to go ahead and manufacture a product with **a target cost well below the currently attainable cost**. In such circumstances they will set **benchmarks for improvement** towards the target cost, by specified dates. Reducing the number of components, cutting out non-value-added activities and so on are possible cost reduction approaches. Once the product goes into production, the target cost will gradually be reduced, the reductions being incorporated into the budgeting process.

Target costing and cost reduction

To remain competitive, organisations must continually **redesign** their products. Far more so than in the past, when cost reduction during the production process was important, a product's **planning, development and design stages are therefore critical to an organisation's cost reduction process**. Target costing, by focusing on costs incurred at all steps of a product's life (not just the production stage), gives added emphasis to cost reduction at this vital stage.

(b) **Life cycle costing**

Traditional approach

Traditional management accounting practice is, in general, to **report costs at the physical production stage** of the life cycle of a product; cost are **not accumulated over the entire life cycle**. This means a product's **profitability** is not assessed over its entire life but rather on a **periodic basis**. Costs tend to be **accumulated according to function**; research, design, development and customer service costs incurred on all products during a period are totalled and are recorded as a period expense, effectively **hiding them from cost reduction opportunities.**

Life cycle approach

Using life cycle costing, however, such **costs** are **traced to individual products over complete life cycles** (from the product's inception to its decline). This overview of a product's profitability is of utmost importance when assessing cost reduction opportunities.

Life cycle costing and cost reduction

One of the principal ideas of life cycle costing is that the **profit generated by a product** must **cover** not only **production costs**, but the **costs associated with the pre- and post-production stages** (such as costs of research, design and testing, and costs of distribution and customer service). It has been claimed that up to 90% of a product's life cycle costs will be determined 'up front' by decisions made very early within the life cycle (production costs are based on design decisions, for example). The application of life cycle costing will therefore ensure that **cost control and cost reduction** will be **carried out at the early stages**, as well as during the production stage.

(c) **Activity based management**

Traditional approach

Traditional costing systems, notably **absorption costing, assume** that all products **consume resources in proportion to their production volumes**. While this may be true for overheads such as power costs, it does not necessarily hold for all overheads, or an increasing proportion of them, especially those connected with support services. The amount of **overhead allocated** to individual products by absorption costing therefore bears **very little resemblance** to the **amount of overhead actually incurred** by the products and hence gives management **minimal understanding of the behaviour of overhead costs** and, consequently, they have a **lack of ability to control/reduce them.**

ABC/ABM approach

Activity based costing (ABC) attempts to overcome this problem by identifying the activities or transactions **cost drivers**, which underlie an organisation's activities and which cause the incidence of the activity, and hence the cost of the activity (overheads) to increase. Costs can then be attributed to products according to the number of cost drivers they cause/consume using cost driver rates.

Activity based management (ABM) is the term given to those **management processes that use the information provided by an activity-based cost analysis to improve organisational profitability.**

ABM and cost reduction

Because ABM analyses costs on the basis of what causes them, rather than on the basis of type of expense/cost centre, it provides management with vital information on why costs are being incurred. If management can **reduce the incidence of the cost driver, they can reduce the associated cost.**

ABM involves a variety of **cost reduction techniques**.

- Ensuring activities are performed as efficiently as possible
- Controlling, reducing or eliminating the need to perform activities that do not add value for customers
- Minimising cost drivers
- Improving the design of products

In short, it aims to **ensure that customer needs are met while fewer demands are made on organisational resources.**

(d) **Kaizen**

Traditional approach

Costs are **controlled** at **monthly intervals through variance analysis**. The **standard cost**, once set, is only revised for changes of a **permanent or reasonably long-term nature**.

Kaizen

The Kaizen method is applied during the production process when it is difficult to make really big changes. Kaizen focuses on the **key elements of operations, production, purchasing** and **distribution**. Kaizen aims to achieve a **specified cost reduction**, but to do so through continuous improvements rather than one-off changes.

Kaizen and cost reduction

Though managers may seek to establish the targets, **employees** working in the **production process** will ensure that those targets are met. The logic of this approach is that those involved in production will be best able to see how to achieve the necessary economies effectively but with minimum disruption. Often these targets will be achieved in **collaboration with suppliers**.

(e) **Lean management accounting**

Traditional approach

The traditional approach takes insufficient account of the dynamic nature of customer requirements, with customers demanding **continuous improvement**. By concentrating on departments, it is not the best mechanism for determining where value is added within an organisation, or on the other hand value lost through waste. Instead it leads production to produce large batches and hold large quantities of inventory. It can in fact obscure waste within overheads, and the elaborate systems required are themselves a source of waste.

Lean management accounting

Lean management accounting is driven by customer demand, both in terms of the **prices customers are prepared to pay** (target costing considerations) and the processes and value streams that are derived from customer requirements.

Lean management accounting and cost reduction

By focusing on processes, lean management accounting systems can **highlight waste** and hence enable the business to focus on eliminating excessive expenditure and continually improving the service offered.

9 CEV

Text references. Chapter 4.

Top tips. This question is clearly one where you may have to bring in knowledge from lower level papers, particularly Decision Making. The examiner has stressed recently that you will need to use Managerial level knowledge when answering P3 questions. In this paper we are more concerned with management accounting's contribution to top-level decision-making, hence the emphasis on customers, competitive advantage and internal goal congruence, all of which are important at this level. (c) is particularly important, and you will need to consider whether information systems fulfil these criteria in various contexts and provide a means of carrying out the tasks efficiently and effectively.

Easy marks. (d) is a list of the main features of a strategic management accounting system; however, we wouldn't advise doing it until last as the question requirements flow through easily.

To: Managing director
From: Management accountant
Date: 17 July 20X1
Subject: The need for strategic management accounting

(a) **Inadequacy 1 Competitive environment**

Traditional management accounting grew out of **cost accounting** and hence its roots are in **manufacturing**. For much of the twentieth century, manufacturing operated in a business environment in which the **supplier** was of utmost importance, **competition** was largely **local** and the **speed of technical and social development**, although rapid compared with earlier eras, was far **slower** than at present.

Now however, it is the **customer** who is **king** and the **competitive environment** constantly threatens a product's life cycle. To compete effectively organisations must therefore be **flexible** enough to cope with changes in customer requirements. Such a focus on customers and competition requires a more **forward-looking** approach, which must be **substantially outward looking** and focus on **external information**, as opposed to the backward-looking and inward-looking approach of traditional management accounting.

Inadequacy 2 Changes in cost structure

The 'management' that traditional management accounting was primarily intended to serve was production management, hence the **traditional emphasis** on accounting for **labour** costs, **materials** costs and **production overheads. Changes in organisations' cost structures** and in the **nature of costs** have affected the relevance of such an emphasis, however, and have led to the use of possibly **misleading information**, especially with regard to **overhead absorption.**

Inadequacy 3 Lack of information for decision-making

The **internal information** used by management accounting tended to be sourced from accounting systems which were directed towards financial reporting, but the classifications of transactions for reporting purposes **are not necessarily relevant for decision making**.

(b) **Three possible aims of strategic management accounting**

Aim 1 Competitive advantage

Strategic management accounting differs from other management accounting activities in terms of its **external orientation**, towards customers and competitors, suppliers and other stakeholders, and competitive advantage depends on an organisation's **understanding of its competitors** and **customers**.

If CEV is to survive and grow, management **must be aware** of the **activities and possible plans** of its **competitors**. Management also needs to be aware of the **opportunities available** and the threats to the firm's position from social, economic, political and technical developments. The collection and analysis of large quantities of external information is therefore of high importance.

Aim 2 Improved planning and decision making

Strategic management accounting aims to **support the forward-looking and outward-looking processes of planning and decision making** and to provide the values (not costs) upon which they are based.

For example, strategic management accounting aims to provide senior management with information about **external factors and interest groups** which could have an impact on the organisation's future development. Managers are then in a better position to develop strategic plans than when using entirely internal information focused on the business's own activities and capabilities.

Aim 3 Goal congruence

(i) **Link with performance**. It relates business operations to financial performance and therefore helps to ensure that business activities are **focused on shareholders' needs** for profit.

(ii) **Goal congruence**. It helps to ensure **goal congruence**, again by translating business activities into the common language of finance.

(c) **Characteristics of information flows at strategic level**

Long-term outlook

Information flows at a strategic level will be geared towards information expected to **impact on the long-term future** of the business. High quality information is needed to enable sound long-term decisions to be made.

Flexible

In order to maintain control in a constantly changing organisation the information flows and systems at strategic level need to be **flexible** and able to **respond quickly to new demands**.

For example, if a **new competitor** enters the market place, or **environmental legislation** is introduced affecting production processes or a trading opportunity arises in an overseas territory, strategic decisions must formulate the most appropriate response.

Vertical information flows

In a business organisation, information flows both vertically and horizontally. The complex nature of strategic decisions makes information sharing vital. Information flows at the strategic level **facilitate decision making** that will affect the whole organisation and provide the framework for long-term strategic plans. Internal information will flow vertically from **middle management up to senior management and vice versa**.

Horizontal information flows

Information also flows **horizontally between different activities in a business**. For instance, overtime hours provided by the payroll section may be used by the production department, delivery lead times from warehouses may be used by the sales team and future orders from the sales directors will be used to forecast turnover and cash flows by the accounts department. The quality of these information flows will dictate the **efficiency of business operations** and will impact on the type and quality of information received by senior management.

An external component

Strategic-level information flows will include information from **external sources** (such as government, competitors, customers, suppliers and media).

(d) **Need for better information**

The company's senior management need broader and more forward-looking information than can be provided by the internal management accounting system to enable them to realise corporate objectives.

How a strategic management accounting system can help

(i) **Goals**. Help the company's managers to articulate their strategy by **setting realistic broad goals and objectives** for the firm.

(ii) **Decision-making. Provide information for better strategic decision-making** so that these goals can be achieved.

(iii) **Information**. **Provide timely external information** so that decisions and strategies may be amended in the light of external developments.

(iv) **Performance measures**. **Develop internal measures**, many of which will be non financial (such as speed of delivery to customers), which are **aligned to the strategic aims and objectives** of the business.

(v) **Reporting**. **Provide a reporting system** which permits all levels of management to monitor progress.

(vi) **Forecasting**. **Operate a forecasting system** which allows all levels of management to anticipate problems and opportunities.

(vii) **Improve communication. Close the communication gap** between the management accountant and company management by using reports and measures which are relevant to the user.

(viii) **Use of information**. Ensure that CEV **uses standard costs strategically** (and does not just react to past events) by ensuring that attention is focused on elements, such as a planning price variance, that are connected to the external environment.

10 SCL

Text references. Chapter 4.

Top tips. In (a) be careful not to spend a long time explaining transfer prices. The question requires application of knowledge to SCL. You must read the scenario and then identify reasons why the transfer pricing system may or may not be acceptable. Key questions to ask are who is taking the decisions and on what basis and what are the consequences of each decision. The requirement to discuss means that you need fair consideration of advantages and disadvantages. If you didn't pick up on this, you need to look again at the list of question verbs in the front pages.

In (b) as in (a), the scenario provides clues to the problems in the budget setting process, so a careful read is necessary to identify these. In scenarios like this you should look out for rigidities, lack of incentive to improve and problems with centralised or decentralised budget setting. Ensure that the second part of the requirement on showing how the problems could be overcome is also covered in your answer.

In (c) there may not, initially, appear to be any link between these two areas. However, if you think about what lean management accounting is trying to achieve, then you should be able to see why it may impact on the transfer prices accepted. So have a go – you may get marks for trying – but zero marks for ignoring the question.

Easy marks. (c) is the toughest of the three parts, but don't spend all your time on (a) and (b), as you can certainly score 2-3 marks in (c) for a definition of lean management accounting.

(a) **Setting of transfer prices – supplying division**

Transfer prices are set by senior management. While this may help to maximise the company performance, setting prices in this way will lead to various problems. Firstly, the **divisional managers may not accept the prices** and attempt to ignore them or charge the price they think is 'fair'. Secondly, the **price will provide an artificial profit element in the division supplying goods and services**. If this profit element is too small, or even negative, then the supplying division could consider that it is not worth supplying goods at a loss and effectively cease production.

The main method of **overcoming** these problems is to **allow the divisional managers to be part of the decision making process** so that the transfer prices are accepted. The prices themselves should then be based on actual costs plus an acceptable mark-up.

Transfer pricing – receiving division

Having a transfer price imposed on the receiving division may well result in the same motivational issues as the supplying division. However, another issue is the amount being paid for the goods transferred into the division. If the **price being paid for goods or services is too high**, then the receiving division may opt to **purchase those goods and services from a third party**. While this does not minimise costs for the company overall, the action will minimise costs for the purchasing division.

To avoid this problem, transfer prices must be set at a level which provides the supplying division with **some incentive** to supply the goods, but not too high so that the receiving division obtains supplies more cheaply from a third party.

External sourcing – additional problems

External sourcing of supplies due to weaknesses in the transfer pricing system will have other problems. For example, the **quality of the goods may be more difficult to control** along with the timing of receipt of those goods.

The solution to these problems is to ensure that the **transfer prices are set at an appropriate level** so intra company supply is used.

(b) **Spending allocations at year end**

Within the company, the implication is that unless a budget allocation is **spent this year**, the budget will **not be authorised again next year**. This has led to significant expenditure in many divisions towards the year end as budgets are spent to ensure they are approved again for next year.

This process may be difficult to correct, as it may not be clear what expenditure is actually necessary for the division and what expenditure is being incurred to spend the budget. However, **monitoring the month of expenditure** from previous years may provide an indication of the **'overspend' at the year end**. Managers can then be asked to justify end of year expenditure.

Smoothing

If budgets are not actually spent in one year, the division can still **raise accruals in respect of expenditure** that is **committed for this financial year**, but will not take place until the next. However, some of the 'committed' expenditure may not take place, effectively providing **additional budget** in the next accounting period.

Accrued expenditure must be **monitored** to ensure that it does **actually take place**. If expenditure is cancelled then **additional monitoring** will be necessary to check that cancelled expenditure is not absorbed into other budget headings. Checking invoices against accruals will help to determine whether the accrual is genuine and correctly spent.

Motivational issues

Setting a budget that does not appear to be realistic may have **adverse motivational effects on staff**. If the budget is not seen to be realistic, then staff may simply **ignore the budget** and spend what they think is necessary anyway. When variances occur, the budget is blamed for being incorrect rather than any weakness or failure being attributed to staff.

The main way of avoiding this type of problem is to **involve key staff in the budget planning process**. Involving staff will help to ensure that they 'accept' the budget as part of their own objectives.

Illegal acts

Where one division has a budget surplus and another a budget deficit, the **surplus may effectively be 'swapped' to the deficit division** ensuring that overall both divisions have met budget. In the next year, both divisions should have their budgets approved, rather than one division facing a cut due to less than budgeted spending and another facing an investigation due to high expenditure.

The main way of avoiding swapping of surpluses and deficits is to **monitor intra-division charges** at the year end. Where any occur, **satisfactory explanations** must be sought from the division heads.

(c) **Lean management accounting**

Lean management accounting was developed from the value chain principles of Porter. The business is managed through **value streams** rather than traditional departmental structures. The emphasis is on establishing the flow of products through the value stream while **eliminating waste**, the flow **depending on customer demand** rather than the limitations of production processes.

Advantages of lean management accounting

It may be helpful in setting transfer prices for the following reasons.

(i) **Target costing**
Lean accounting uses a **target costing approach**. This means that the **cost of production** within a division is set taking into account the **price that the customer – the receiving division – is prepared to pay**. The producing division must supply goods for this price. Any efficiency gains would then effectively belong to that division. However, the transfer price would be acceptable to the receiving division and would presumably be less than a third party would charge.

(ii) **Adding value**
The system identifies the value being added to a product, rather than simply focusing on the processes involved in making a product. Divisions adding more value to a product could therefore be 'rewarded' with a **higher transfer price**, effectively making more profit for that division. Conversely, divisions undertaking less value added activities would only be allowed a small profit.

(iii) **Response to demand**
The **reason for producing items is in response to demand**; production does not take place simply because productive capacity is available. The receiving division therefore **dictates what goods are required** – it is not forced to take goods simply because they have been produced. This process will allow more budgetary control for the receiving division, even if the transfer price is still set. Money will not be wasted on purchasing goods that are not required.

(vi) **Improvement in quality**

There is an **emphasis on improvement in quality**. This will benefit all divisions if improved quality results in more sales. There may not initially be any amendments to transfer pricing. In fact setting transfer prices too low may hinder improvements in quality if investment in new equipment is not initially profitable in the supplying division.

11 CDE

Text references. Chapter 17 on the information systems, Chapter 4 on the management accounting systems.

Top tips. In (a) outline means you have to go through all the different systems **quickly**, with a short paragraph on each. (a) contains some very definite hints about what systems to choose based on CDE's requirements; the lack of integrated data and the need for strategic analysis should have directed you towards choosing an appropriate system and being able to **justify** your choice. You'd obtain 7 of the marks available for outlining the systems, 3 of the marks for making appropriate recommendations. In other words you can go most of the way to passing this question with a good part (a).

(b) is a reminder that this paper is part of the CIMA management accounting stream; knowledge acquired in P1 and P2 is useful here. However (b) is also in a standard format for this paper, evaluating the current internal controls and suggesting improvements. The question requirement to **critically** evaluate means that you should focus on the weaknesses.

A good way to get your ideas into shape for (b) is firstly to consider what's there, what is used for, and does it fulfil its current objectives. The second aspect is to consider what's missing – what other objectives should be fulfilled (here long-term decision support), what additional methods should be used, and what information gathered.

Again there are some clear hints in the question about what to evaluate and recommend – the point about sacrifice of data accuracy should have been a hint to consider backflush costing, the hints about inventory and optimum use of capacity should have led you into covering lean management accounting. There is some overlap here between P3 and the material in P9 on the changing role of the finance function, and bringing in relevant P9 material will certainly gain you credit.

This question is a good illustration of what we said in the front pages about how important it is in this exam to make reasonable recommendations.

Easy marks. (a) (i) just requires a description of different management systems that doesn't really need to be connected to the scenario; this is a straightforward question for a strategic level paper.

Examiner's comments. Descriptions of systems in (a) were generally good, but many candidates failed to score well because they did not make a recommendation. In (b) many answers failed to discuss the cost of the accounting function. Students also failed to appreciate the significance of the question requirement to make recommendations; when these are required, it suggests that there is a need for change, however many answers were in favour of retaining the existing system.

(a) (i) **Information systems**

Transaction processing systems (TPS)

TPS are used for **routine tasks** in which data items or operations can continue. They incorporate the detail but do not provide the summaries that managers need.

Knowledge work systems (KWS)

KWS **facilitate the creation and integration** of new information into a system. They provide communication facilities and access to external facilities, also analytical and graphic facilities to analyse data.

Decision support systems (DSS)

DSS provide a wide range of **alternative information gathering** and **analytical tools** with an emphasis on **flexibility** and **user-friendliness**. They assist in making decisions on issues that are subject to a high level of uncertainty.

Management information systems (MIS)

MIS **transform data** from underlying transaction processing systems into summarised files that are used as the **basis for management reports**. This summarised information is used to assist managers in planning, directing and controlling activities.

Enterprise resource planning systems (ERPS)

ERPS can be used to plan many aspects of operations and support functions. They operate over the whole organisation and across functions, with all departments that are **involved in operations or production** being integrated into one system. Supply chain management software can provide **links with suppliers or customers**. They use **database management systems** so that data is entered once, then transferred across the system, and can be used for **tailored reports**.

Strategic Enterprise Management Systems (SEMS)

SEMS provide data in formats that assist managers in **setting strategic goals, measuring performance** in the light of those goals and **measuring and managing intellectual capital.** They provide more advanced tools such as **balanced scorecard** and **activity-based management** with which to use data, and enable customer, business unit and competitor analysis.

Executive Support Systems (ESS)

ESS summarise and track **strategically critical information** drawn from internal and external sources. They allow managers to move from summarised to more detailed data and also provide facilities such as the ability to **create simulations.** This information is used to help senior managers make **strategic, unstructured decisions.**

(ii) **Recommendation**

At present CDE is operating an MIS that however does **not provide sufficient integrated information across the group** and does not help management take **strategic decisions.** CDE requires a system that provides **SEMS or ESS** functions. A SEMS will be geared towards **decision support** and enable management to carry out the **necessary analysis**. An ESS will provide the **flexible tools** that help managers make decisions in a changing environment and for that reason should be the preferred choice, subject to these benefits justifying the **costs** of investment.

(b) (i) **Relevance of current system**

Use of traditional accounting methods

CDE's accounting department currently provides data in traditional formats – budgets, variance analysis and standard costing. Whilst this provides useful information for short-term operational **control purposes**, it is less helpful in providing integrated information for **strategic and business development,** areas where the stock market may feel CDE's performance is lacking judging by its share price performance.

MRP II

MRP has been criticised as providing a mirror to what happens in practice, and hence **allowing inefficiencies to be perpetuated** rather than encouraging improvements. It has been criticised for accounting for long lead times, high inventory, large batch sizes and quality problems and hence building these into the planning process rather than pushing for their elimination.

Budgetary targets

The focus on budgets as a means of analysing performance may be misplaced. It may encourage excessive focus on direct costs that are **uncontrollable** in the short-term. Managers may focus on achieving budgetary targets and not on other relevant measures such as **customer service measures**. **Budgetary slack** may also be built into the system; we are not told how standard costs are determined by the accounting department, and it may be on the basis of inflated estimates by operational departments.

Rolling budgets

It also appears that **rolling budgets** may not be used, suggesting that the budgeting system may adopt too slowly to the changing environment.

Standard costing

The issue with standards based on material and labour usage is that they may not be revised often enough. Arguably they should be revised as soon as there is any **change in the basis** upon which they are set, which in a changing environment may be quite frequently, to take account of customers' changing demands. In addition standard costing fails to take into account the **balance** between cost control and other aims; it may for example be considered best to pay higher prices for materials to guarantee speedier delivery and hence enhance CDE's ability to operate **just-in-time.**

Cost allocation

The principal problem with using machine hours as a basis for cost allocation is that it suggests that for all CDE's products, machine hours are the **principal determinant** of costs, which is unlikely to be true. There are other factors that will also be significant and will vary between products, such as space, labour or working capital. Using a misleading basis will distort product cost figures.

Role of accounting department

It is felt that the accounting department is too focused on control and analysing past performance. It does not appear to be providing the information about **product market performance** and **customers** that will assist strategic decision-making.

(ii) **Improving the system**

Implications of just-in-time system

The focus of the just-in-time system that CDE has adopted is on **improvements in productivity and elimination of waste** by obtaining quality components at precisely the time when they are required for use. It follows that the management accounting system needs to focus on key indicators of success or failure in implementing just-in-time. The system of variances used at the moment does not provide all of the necessary information, for example changes in inventory levels.

Lean management accounting

Instead the accounting department needs to take a lean management accounting approach, focusing on performance measurement of **value streams**, activities that **add value** for the **customers**, and which are geared to producing for customers rather than inventory. Product cost is the average cost of the value stream for the quantity produced for the period. Standard costs can still be used to determine **pricing**, but there is less emphasis on them as a means of control.

Backflush costing

The pooling of costs can be done using backflush costing. Backflush costing will significantly reduce the detailed work currently carried out by the accounting department. Use of JIT means that all the costing entries are made at virtually the same moment. Therefore under backflush costing costs will be **calculated and charged when the product is sold**, or when it is **transferred to the finished goods store.** The cost data need not be reported in detail, and inaccuracies in inventory valuation will not be a big issue because inventory is being kept to a minimum.

Activity-based costing

Part of the calculation of costing will be the **allocation of overheads**, and activity-based costing will be a fairer way than the current method. An activity based approach can allocate costs according to value added transactions, for example so-called **change transactions**, activities associated with ensuring customers' requirements are met.

Role of accounting department

Changes in the methods will be reflected in changes in the role of the accounting department. The focus is likely to be more on adding value, including **providing information** that will **aid strategic decision-making,** and **appraising investments** by methods such as **sensitivity** and **what-if analysis**. The accounting department can also provide more useful support by producing a wider range of measures, using the framework of the balanced scorecard. However there are dangers in the accounting department being too focused on helping the operational departments. Excessive identification may lead to a **loss of independence** and **failure to provide any control** in financial management. The best solution may be that the accounting department focuses on the plans and strategies of operational departments, but **rigorously reviews** and **challenges** the assumptions made.

12 Controls in new company

Text references. Chapter 4 on budgets, Chapter 5 on controls over the board.

Top tips. The report in (a) starts by stating the main transactions that the system will have to process. It then discusses the key areas of information required and assignment of responsibility. However your answer to (a) should only briefly mention reporting mechanisms as these are dealt with in more detail in part (b). Unusually the scenario mostly relates to the part with less marks (a). To score well in (a) therefore you need to bring in the scenario information and find examples that would be appropriate for this sort of organisation.

Part (b) covers a very important theme for this part of the syllabus, how the board acts as an overall supervisory control on the rest of the business. This involves taking the decisions that follow from the board's responsibility for strategy (such as non-current asset purchases), and also reviewing the operations of the business using internal and external data.

Extra credit would be given for discussion of the uncertainties involved in gathering information in (a), and the need for the system to develop as the company's activities develop in (b) and you may even be able to pass just by performing well in (b).

Easy marks. If you have a good knowledge of corporate governance there are lots of points that can be made in (b).

Examiner's comments. Many candidates did not exploit the scenario to make obvious points on the requirements. A common error in part (a) was failure to point out the need for the reporting of costs and revenues to be more frequent than quarterly. In (b) some candidates failed to answer one or other part of the question. Although knowledge of corporate governance recommendations helped in answering part (b), it would be inappropriate to apply all the recommendations to a small new company.

REPORT

To: Managers
From: Management Consultant
Subject: Controls in the new computer services company
Date: 15 December 20X4

(a) **Form and level of detail of budgetary control**

A useful starting point is to consider the likely revenues and costs that will have to be considered when designing the budgetary control system.

(i) **Revenues**

Income will be derived from two main sources: **existing** local government **work** and **new work** from neighbouring authorities or commercial customers.

The **local government work** could be **subdivided further**, either according to the nature of the work (one-off data processing tasks, long-term systems development etc) and/or according to the particular local government department (education, housing, etc).

The **other work** may also be subdivided according to its nature and/or type of customer. This will aid **analysis** of **profitability**.

(ii) **Costs**

Operational costs are likely to fall into the broad categories listed below. More detailed sub-categories will be desirable in practice. Most costs will be fixed costs, although there will be sundry equipment, administrative and marketing expenses that are variable.

- Technical staff costs
- Equipment costs (depreciation, maintenance, etc)
- Administrative costs (mainly financial management)
- Marketing costs

(Development costs are considered later in this report, as is capital budgeting.)

Areas of concern

(i) **Income from new work**
Forecasting the **level of income** to be derived from **new work** (the level of existing local government should be easy to predict). Assessment of likely new work will include the likely duration of contracts to be carried out, and how new contracts will be priced and billed.

(ii) **New expenditure**
Allocating and **monitoring expenditure** for the **areas** that are **new** to the company, particularly financial administration, working capital management and marketing. Particularly close attention should be paid to the 'set-up' costs of new systems in these areas.

Recommended system of budgetary control

(i) **Recording system**
A recording system capable of **analysing costs and revenues** in the various ways suggested above. (This may seem self-evident but it has not been the norm in public sector bodies in the past.)

(ii) **Responsibility accounting**
Clear assignment of responsibility for controllable costs and revenues to individual managers, using a cost or profit centre system. Again this may seem self-evident, but detailed apportionment of what have previously been regarded as lump-sum allocations has been a serious problem for public sector and former public sector bodies.

(iii) **Weekly reporting**
Operational reports at least **weekly** in the initial stages to catch bugs in the system and spot areas for improvement. Reports may be less regular once the system is up and running, especially for work

that the company is already used to doing. Some of the information collected can be of a non-financial nature, for example staff and computer time for frequently performed tasks.

(iv) **Monthly reporting**

Monthly reports for **submission** to **senior management**, summarising the operational data. This area is addressed in more detail in the second part of this report.

(b) (i) **Structure and formal controls at Board level**

Personnel

The Board is likely to consist of a Managing Director (the current Director of Computing), a Technical Director, a Finance Director and a Marketing Director. **Non-executive directors** should also be appointed. One should represent the interests of investors and may be appointed by the venture capital company involved; a second could bring in commercial sector experience and a third might have local government knowledge.

Focus of board

The Board's responsibility is the **strategy** of the company and this will include the long-term investment strategy. The Board should focus on **recognising future needs** and ensuring that they can be met at the appropriate time.

The Board's focus on strategy should also mean that certain matters are **reserved for decision by the full Board**. Although the company is not a listed company, they could usefully follow the corporate governance recommendations, and reserve the following decisions for full approval.

- Acquisition and disposal of major assets
- Investments, capital projects, authority levels, treasury policies and risk management policies

(ii) **Risk assessment**

Corporate governance reports such as the UK's Turnbull guidance suggests that board review of risk and internal control has two aspects. As a regular item on the board's agenda, directors should be discussing reports covering:

- What the **risks** are and how they have been **identified**, **evaluated** and **managed**
- The **effectiveness** of the internal control system in the management of risk, in particular how any risks have been dealt with
- Whether **actions** are being taken to **reduce** the risks found
- Whether the results indicate that **internal control** should be **monitored more extensively**

Annual review

The directors should conduct an annual review of internal control that is wider-ranging than the regular review. This should cover:

- The **changes** since the **last assessment** in **risks faced**, and the company's **ability** to **respond to changes in the business environment**
- The **scope** and **quality** of **management monitoring** and of **internal audit work**
- The **extent** and **frequency of reports to the board**
- **Significant controls, failings** and **weaknesses** (including **control environment** issues such as **culture, policies and reward systems** and **clear organisational structures**)
- The **effectiveness** of the **public reporting** process

(iii) **Information**

A key part of the control environment is information. The directors need to be sure that they possess **appropriate information** of **sufficient quality**, including financial and non-financial information and information that is relevant not just to the interest of shareholders but also other stakeholders.

Key items of information are considered further below.

Scrutiny of budget reports

One of the key controls operated at board level will be the **monthly budget report**. Particular attention should be paid to the areas that are new to the proposed company, especially **control of finance** and **cash flow**. Given the Board's lack of commercial experience, an **internal auditor** should be appointed to provide reassurance that unfamiliar areas are being properly managed from day to day.

External monitoring

Presumably in the medium term the company will wish to reduce its reliance on existing local government work. **External monitoring** of **potential markets**, **competitors' activities** and of the **political environment** will therefore be crucial. This can be in the form of SWOT analysis or similar.

Analytical measures

Likewise **measurement** of **current performance** in terms of **market share**, new **business won** and so on will help to guide the overall strategy. In any case, local authorities are likely to set their own performance criteria. Board level checks therefore need to be in place to ensure that the required standards are being maintained.

Future developments

If the company is likely to be taking on new work such as systems development, there should be **formal controls** in this area, since this type of work tends to be long-term. **Separate reports** in addition to the main monthly package may be called for, here.

Appraisal of board

Appraisal of the board's performance as a unit should be carried out once a year. **Separate appraisal** should also be carried out of the **chairman** and **chief executive** with links into the remuneration process.

Signed: Management Accountant

13 Product choice

Text references. Chapters 2 and 4

Top tips. You are not told very much about the system you are meant to be criticising in (a). You therefore have to assume that what you are not told about isn't there and that in this question gives you a lot of potential suggestions for improvements. Possible traps in (a) include spending too much time on the theory (BPP covers the theory in a couple of lines). Your answer needed to explain why controls were needed and to give examples of what should happen; just saying there should be a control wouldn't gain you any credit.

10 marks is quite a generous mark allocation for (a).

You may have written similar answers to (b) when answering the written parts of investment appraisal questions in P9 *Financial Strategy* where interpretation of calculations is very important. For this paper, you have to bring risk considerations into all parts of your discussion.

Our answer spreads out by starting with the financial risk elements, then moving on to consider other business risks. Some of these could have been generated from your P6 knowledge, illustrating what we say in the Study Text and the front pages of the kit about the links between the three Strategic level exams.

Although 3 marks were available specifically for discussion of risk adjusted rates, the majority of the marks were available for other risk factors. Whichever risks you discussed, it's important to use the data selectively to demonstrate why the risks you're discussing are important . Although one mark would have been available for presentation, you could also easily have spent too much time on a lengthy introduction and conclusion.

Easy marks. As starters, the marking scheme for (a) allocated one mark for a definition of the product life cycle, and for (b) one mark was given for the use of a memo format.

Examiners' comments. The examiner emphasised that this question was designed to test ability to apply control principles to a work-based scenario. Therefore students should not just reproduce a rote-learn list of controls. Answers to (a) were generally poor with a lack of focus on the product life cycle. Answers to (b) were better.

(a) **Product lifecycle definition**

The product lifecycle begins with the initial product specification and ends with the withdrawal of the product from the market. Stages include development, introduction, growth, maturity, decline and senility.

Criteria used to judge products

The criteria being used to judge the investments prior to their **introduction** appear to be based on the financial net present value technique. Products also need to be evaluated against clearly-established criteria that take into account **the company's strategy**. The level of **initial costs** also needs careful consideration. For Product 2 $6,400 million is a large amount of development costs so may cause **significant cash-flow problems.** The issue then arises of how important profits over the whole lifecycle are against the need to recoup the costs quickly. Also significant will be how the knowledge gained from the design and development work may influence the **development of other projects**.

Verification of information

The **realism of the net present value analysis** is very dependent on the quality of the information supplied by the engineering staff and marketing staff. The figures they supply need to be verified, by staff not involved in their production or by internal auditors. They will need to review the **justification behind the assumptions** made, whether the figures appear to be based on **expected, best-case or worst-case** forecasts and how much uncertainty lies behind the figures provided. They also must consider whether some **relevant costs** have been omitted from the analysis, for example costs of establishing new supplier relationships.

The verifiers should also take into account how **accurate previous forecasts** made by the departments have been and whether there are **weaknesses in their information gathering or forecasting processes** that have been identified by previous internal audits but not corrected.

Use of other appraisal methods

Using a higher risk-discounted factor as in the scenario takes into account the risks of the specific investment appraisal. However the **discount factor** is only one of a number of figures in the discount analysis. The company needs to carry out additional **investment appraisals,** using **different assumptions** about marketing and engineering figures, also examining the impact on the figures if the **launch of products is postponed.**

It needs to use other methods of risk analysis to analyse the risks involved. **Sensitivity analysis** will indicate by how much figures have to change before the products make a loss. It also ideally needs some idea of the probabilities of different outcomes, as this will help **calculate expected values** and the **chances of making a loss. Worst-case scenario analysis** will indicate maximum risk levels, which may also influence decisions.

You would also have scored marks if you had discussed these issues.

Further analysis

The **decision to commit** to the product over its life cycle is not **irrevocable** as the lifecycle is expected to last some years. **Real options**, including abandonment, may be available during the growth and maturity phase of the lifecycle, and changes in the initial assumptions caused by developments in the fast-moving industry environment may need to be taken into account. The company should therefore have a system in place for **assessing future success** at various stages of the product life cycle. These include when **commitment needs to be made to further costs** beyond the initial costs (for example the Year 2 costs for Product 1) and when **competition** begins to **increase significantly** during the growth stage. The company may also wish to reconsider its policy and maybe **modify the design of the product** to counter competition or to prolong the original expected lifecycle.

Target costing

The quality of the financial analysis may be improved if target or lifecycle costing are used. **Target costing** implies the analysis being **driven by the sales price** that consumers are prepared to pay and the desired profit margin. If costs exceed what is required to achieve the margin, the product will not be manufactured. Assuming the product is manufactured, the company will not be concerned with meeting the initial cost estimates; rather it will be concerned with changing its expectations of what customers are prepared to pay. As customers expect falling prices, so planned costs will have to fall regularly as well. In this example there would be pressure to reduce the manufacturing and distribution costs in later years.

Lifecycle costing

Lifecycle costing would imply going beyond the **development, manufacturing and distribution costs** that are clearly linked in with the product and **tracing elements of all business costs** to the products. Comparison of the total cost figures with expected revenues should give a better understanding of product profitability. Using the complete lifecycle rather than the same base period for each investment will also give a better indication of the investment's long-term importance.

(b) To: Head of Division
From: Accountant
Date: 20 July 20X7
Subject: Choice between Product 1 and Product 2

You have asked me for a comparison of Product 1 and Product 2 and recommendations about which to choose.

(i) **Financial data**

Figures at risk-adjusted discount rate

Assuming use of the risk-adjusted discount factor fairly indicates risk would mean accepting Product 1 with a positive NPV and rejecting Product 2 because it has a negative NPV. The **risk-adjusted hurdle rate** represents a method of taking into account the risks associated with the development of a specific project and quantifying their significance based on how seriously the company views them. However the variety of risks involved (discussed further below), and the difficulty of estimating their importance and ranking arguably means that the risk-adjusted rate fails to give a more reliable guide than using the company-wide hurdle rate would.

Sensitivity analysis

Simple sensitivity analysis reveals that Product 2 is much more vulnerable to making a loss if cost or revenue estimates turn out to be **over-optimistic.** Using the hurdle rate Product 1's NPV is $244 million against initial costs of $600 million, whereas Product 2's NPV is $430 million against initial costs of $6,400 million. Therefore the percentage by which Product 1's initial costs would have to increase before it made a loss is much higher than the % that Product 2's costs would have to increase.

Financial risk of Product 2

Having to meet the higher costs of Product 2 may increase the company's financial risk if loan finance is used and **gearing rises.**

Figures at hurdle rate

If however the hurdle rate of 7.5% is used to appraise investments, then Product 2 shows a **higher net present value**. This indicates that the company may be able to make higher net revenues if it chooses Product 2 so long as it accepts the significant risk of making a loss. Whether the company opts for Product 1 or Product 2 will depend on its **risk appetite**; will it prefer higher returns even though it takes greater risks to achieve them.

Product life cycle

Given the industry is changing rapidly, there is a risk that products may become **obsolete before seven years**. The estimated net present value of Product 1 is more vulnerable to a change in its life cycle, since it has the longer life cycle. Revenues from Product 2 begin to flow earlier than from Product 1, although at a fairly low level.

Use of surplus funds

As noted, Product 1 requires a much smaller early investment than Product 2. To improve the comparisons between the two products, we should consider how the spare funds (the funds that would not be needed for Product 1 but would be for Product 2) would be used. We need therefore to consider the **rate of return** and **risk** of other investments for which the surplus funds could be used.

Postponement of Product 1

As Product 1 is a smaller-scale investment, it may be possible to **postpone** it until some years in the future, and fund it out of the eventual receipts from Product 2.

(ii) **Business risks**

As mentioned, the risk-adjusted discount rate is a means of measuring the levels of strategic and business risks. We need to be sure that sufficient account has been taken of the following risks.

Competitor risk

Certainly we need to consider the **different market profiles** for each product, and the risks that **competitors** will **develop their own products** ahead of us or respond more quickly on one rather than the other, accelerating the product life cycle.

Customer risk

We need to consider not only the likely reactions of customers but the **different profiles of the customer base** for each product.

Supply and manufacturing risk

The **reliability of suppliers and manufacturing arrangements,** and the local infrastructure, needs to be considered carefully. Supply arrangements from China for some companies have been disrupted by problems within China such as electricity rationing. For Product 1 the consequences of problems in China will probably be more severe than problems in Taiwan for Product 2. If manufacturing is taking place in China, disruption there will clearly affect sales, whereas if there are problems with component suppliers in Taiwan, it may be possible to reduce the risk of lost sales by making contingency arrangements to buy components from suppliers in other countries.

Foreign exchange risk

With both products, there may be foreign exchange risks from settling in their suppliers' currencies. However **exchange risk relating to sales** will only apply to Product 2, since Product 1 sales will be in the home market.

(iii) **Compatibility with strategy**

The investment decision must be **compatible with the company's strategy.** For example we need to assess whether the products are a breakthrough into a new market sector, or whether there is **potential to expand** into other geographical markets. Whether the proposed products are **significantly differentiated** from what the competition is offering may be significant. Product 1 is being sold in the company's retail outlets and the strategic impact on these outlets needs to be considered; will it require them to change their focus or will it utilise any spare capacity that they have.

Recommendations

I would recommend we **choose Product 1** because the risk-adjusted discount rate gives a negative answer for Product 2, and Product 2's profits appear to be much more volatile than Product 1. However I recommend that the final decision is not made until after further consideration is given to whether the risk-adjusted discount rate fairly reflects all the risks involved, and alternative scenarios, based on other assumptions about the figures, are examined.

You would also have scored marks in (b) for discussing the risk management process.

Risk management process

Aspects of risk management are also important, particularly risk avoidance and portfolio management.

Risk avoidance

As part of the risk mapping process that we undertake we should have defined what constitute **high likelihood-high consequences risks** that the company should avoid by, for example, not undertaking investment. We need to compare the possible magnitude and the likelihood of making a loss on both products, particularly Product 2, against these criteria to decide whether the risks are too high.

Portfolio management

The company should view investment in both products in the light of its overall portfolio of investments. It should consider how both investments would contribute to ensuring that the company had an optimum mix of **low and high risk investments.** It should also consider the **correlation of both products** with the existing product portfolio – would investing in one ensure that risks were much better spread than investing in the other.

International diversification

The extent of international diversification may be an issue. Product 1 will be sold in the American markets so may be **vulnerable to the American economic cycle**, whereas Product 2 will be sold all over Western Europe and hence diversified over countries with different cycles. Another point is that the risk borne by the retailer will be suffered by our company's outlets for Product 1, but will be shared with third-party retailers for Product 2.

14 Corporate governance

Text references. Chapter 5.

Top tips. The lack of scenario attached to this question is surprising, and unusual for a Strategic level paper. The question is a good reminder of what corporate governance is all about and how it is used as a high level control by some companies.

Brief examples are helpful in (a) and (b), but overall you can't say much on any individual point in (a) since it's only worth five marks in total. Remember we stressed in the front pages that you must note carefully how many marks are available for each part and plan your time accordingly.

Our answer to (b) takes a strict view of the word principles, although you would gain credit for considering corporate governance under the main areas the reports cover. You would also gain credit for bringing in the various perspectives of corporate governance, such as agency, stewardship and stakeholder theory.

(c) deals with the major areas covered in the Combined Code, with most focus on audit committee's liaison with external auditors, which reflects the weight of guidance in the Code. Here the verb discuss means you need to show how the audit committee can be most effective.

Easy marks. Perhaps the role of the audit committee is the area that's best known, but overall this question is one of the most straightforward questions you are likely to see on a Strategic level paper.

Examiner's comments. This question was mostly very well-answered. The only issue was an over-concentration on corporate scandals in (a) in some scripts.

(a) **Reasons for emergence of corporate governance**

Corporate governance was defined in the Cadbury report as 'the system by which companies are directed and controlled'.

Corporate governance has developed because of a number of developments and events over the last twenty years.

Abuses by individuals

In the UK a key influence on the development of the Cadbury framework was the financial scandals of the late 1980s and the abuses exposed. A number of provisions have been designed to counter situations where a **single individual** has dominated a company and has abused his position.

Financial reporting

A key problem in many financial scandals has been **misleading financial accounting practices**. Whilst these have resulted in strengthened international financial regulations, they have also impacted on corporate governance regulations because of the perceived **failure of auditors** to address these problems.

Risks and controls

Again poor controls have been a symptom of poor corporate governance with for example **inadequate management control of individuals** such as Nick Leeson. In addition the development of risk management frameworks such as the COSO guidance has impacted upon regulations.

Internationalisation

More investors, in particular institutional investors, have begun to **invest outside their home countries**. In order to limit the risks of their investments, they seek to promote a common **international governance framework**.

Cultural reasons

Some corporate governance guidance has been driven by **developments in the business environment** in local economies and the **response of the country's culture** to these. South Africa's King report in particular has stressed the influence of corporate governance on qualities that are fundamental to the South African culture. The US has used a strict regulatory approach, embodied in Sarbanes-Oxley to achieve its ends.

(b) **Principles of corporate governance**

The requirements of the corporate governance reports can be grouped under a number of headings relating to the principles with which they attempt to comply.

Ensuring integrity

A basic aim of all governance guidance has been to promote **ethical fair dealing by companies**. An important aspect has been stressing the role of directors in influencing the **culture**, **tone and core values** of the company.

Promotion of strategic objectives

Reports have sought to ensure **adherence to, and satisfaction of, the strategic objectives** of the organisation, thus aiding effective management. CIMA/IFAC guidance has stressed how analysis of how strategic decision-making and activities will **enhance performance**. This should be balanced with the **conformance** requirements of corporate governance reports.

Control of companies

Corporate governance regulations can be seen as creating a framework for the **control of multinational companies** whose interests may not coincide with the national interests. Corporate governance provides a framework for enforcing **compliance with worldwide laws** on this sort of company.

Enhancing risk management

Corporate governance guidelines have promoted **risk management principles, especially financial, legal and reputation risks**. They have required **compliance with accepted good practice** in the jurisdiction in question and **ensuring appropriate systems of control** are in place, in particular systems for monitoring risk, financial control and compliance with the law.

Protection of shareholders

The corporate governance reports aim to **protect shareholders** in the same way that investors are protected who buy any other financial investment product, such as insurance or a pension.

Involvement of shareholders

As well as protecting shareholders, the governance recommendations are designed to **enhance shareholder involvement**, particularly institutional shareholder involvement, in companies. This is achieved by giving them **more details about company activities**, and improving proceedings at annual general meetings by recommending **votes on remuneration policy** and the **report and accounts**.

Protection of stakeholders

Corporate governance reports are also concerned with **fulfilling responsibilities to all stakeholders**. This includes **minimising potential conflicts of interest** between the owners, managers and wider stakeholder community, and **treating each category of stakeholder fairly**.

Establishment of accountability

Governance reports are designed to address the problem of **the over-mighty managing director by emphasising the role of the whole board in major decisions**, and a need for a **clear division of responsibilities** at the head of companies so that one person does not enjoy unfettered power. It also means the **involvement of non-executive directors** through committees in delicate decisions such as recruitment to the board, and **remuneration** of executive directors.

Maintenance of effective scrutiny

Governance provisions have aimed to **ensure the independence** of those with **primary responsibility** for **scrutinising company activities**. This includes prescribing what constitutes, or what might **jeopardise, the independence** of non-executive directors. It also means **enhancing their position** by prescribing that a **certain number of directors be non-executive**.

Provision of accurate and timely information

Governance reports are designed to **complement developments in financial reporting guidance** by emphasising the need for accounts to present a **true and balanced picture of what is happening in the organisation**. They also emphasise the **importance of timely information** as an aid enabling directors to supervise company activities better.

(c) **Audit committee**

The Combined Code requires the audit committee to consist of independent non-executive directors. The role and responsibilities of the audit committee can be grouped under the following headers.

Monitoring financial statements and announcements of financial performance

The audit committee should review all announcements, concentrating in particular on:

- **Significant financial reporting judgements**
- **Key accounting policies**
- **Overall appearance and presentation** of the accounts

To order to carry out this review effectively, the audit committee must include members with **sufficient financial expertise and qualifications.**

Reviewing internal controls and risk management

The committee should **review the system of financial controls** and may also be responsible for **reviewing internal control and risk management systems**. This includes continual monitoring of the **overall adequacy of the internal control systems** and **management's attitude towards control**. The committee should also focus on specific aspects, such as **legal and ethical compliance** and **fraud reduction measures**.

Review of internal audit

As part of their review of the adequacy of internal controls, the audit committee should **assess the need for an internal audit function** in the context of the overall risk management framework. If internal audit is to be used, the committee should **approve the appointment of the head of internal audit**.

If the organisation has internal auditors, the committee should supervise its work including:

- The **standards** it follows
- Its **scope**
- Its **resources**
- **Work plan**
- **Liaison with external audit**
- **Results**

The committee should **monitor management's responsiveness** to internal audit's work. To protect the independence of the internal audit function, the chief internal auditor should be able to **report directly** to the **committee** and should with the external auditors meet the committee at least once a year without the presence of executive management.

Liaison with external audit

The committee's role in connection with external audit has a number of aspects:

(i) **Appointment and removal**

The audit committee should be responsible for recommending the **appointment, reappointment and removal** of external auditors. The audit committee should also approve the **remuneration and terms of engagement** of the external auditor.

(ii) **Audit effectiveness**

The audit committee should be particularly concerned with the **effectiveness** of the **external audit process** and also the **independence and objectivity** of external audit. The committee should especially consider whether it is appropriate to use external audit to **supply non-audit services.**

(iii) **Audit scope**

The committee should **discuss the external audit's scope with the auditors** before it starts. The committee should also aid the external auditors by helping them **obtain the information** they require, act as a **forum for liaison** between the external and internal auditors and audit committee, and be available for consultation with external auditors. The audit committee should **review the results of external audit's work** and **pursue any serious concerns** the external auditors have.

(iv) **Audit review**

At the end of the audit, the audit committee should **assess the effectiveness of external audit** by obtaining feedback and considering whether external audit has shown good understanding of the business, and robust handling of the key audit judgements.

Dealing with staff concerns and investigations

The audit committee should review arrangements by which staff can raise concerns about **improprieties.** The committee should be able to ensure that appropriate **investigations** are made of concerns, whether raised by staff or through other sources.

15 Preparation question: HiT

Text references. Chapter 5.

Top tips. Whilst CIMA has stated that you need awareness of the general principles of corporate governance without getting too involved in the details of individual reports, in practice the major reports are central to corporate governance development. Therefore it is fine to quote from them as we have done. The business background of the company is not very important, but you needed to highlight in the scenario what the directors are uncertain about, and should have included in your answer examples of the consequences of greater formality.

Note how the system of committee (audit, remuneration, nomination) is designed to counter key threats to independence. The most basic control though is recruiting sufficient independent non-executive directors, so look out for threats to non-executive independence if you are given scenarios about the corporate governance situation in a particular organisation.

Easy marks. All parts require some thought: even in (a) you could obtain some credit through quoting the corporate governance reports, but would need to go beyond these to score well.

To: Directors of HiT
From: Consultant
Date: 3 February 20X4
Subject: Non-executive directors (NEDs)

(a) **Position of NEDs**

The board of directors of a listed company has the purpose of leading and controlling the company. The board will normally be made up of **executive directors** who work full time for the company and have specific roles, such as finance director or sales director. The board should also consist of **some NEDs** who will be part-time and have no specific operational role in the company.

The board should include a **balance of executive and NEDs** (and in particular independent NEDs) such that no individual or small group of individuals can dominate the board's decision taking. Some corporate governance guidelines suggest that at least half the board should be NEDs.

Qualities of NEDs

NEDs should be **independent in judgement** (even if they are not independent according to governance guidance) and have **enquiring minds**. They need to be **well-informed** about the **company and the external environment** in which it operates, with a strong command of issues relevant to the business.

Role of NEDs

The main roles of NEDs are **to develop strategy** and **monitor performance**.

(i) **Development of strategy**

In terms of their strategic role they are working with the executive directors in order to **determine the future** of the company.

(ii) **Monitoring**

The monitoring role of NEDs takes on many forms. In general terms they are there to **challenge the decisions** of executive directors where they do not agree and to highlight any bad practice or poor performance.

NEDs should also **satisfy themselves** on the **integrity of financial information** and that **financial controls and systems of risk management** are **robust and defensible**. They therefore need to ensure that **sufficient**, **accurate**, **clear and timely information** is **provided** sufficiently in advance of meetings to enable thorough consideration of the issues facing the board.

(b) **Non-independent NEDs**

A NED is not independent if he or she is on the board **representing** the **interests** of a **major shareholder**, because the views given by the director will be made in the interests of that shareholder. Similarly, it is debatable whether a director is independent when he or she has a **close relationship** with the company or any other executive director. For example, a former chief executive of a company might be given a non-executive role after retirement. He would not be independent.

Independent NEDs

In contrast, an independent NED is a person who has no connection with the company other than as a non-executive director, and who should be able to give an **independent opinion** on the affairs of the company, without influence from any other director or any shareholder.

(c) **Conflicts of interest**

A potential conflict of interest occurs when the executive directors or senior management of a company might be inclined to take decisions that would **not be in the interests** of the **company's shareholders**. Although there are several areas where a conflict of interest could arise, the major problem areas are those of remuneration of the directors and senior managers, financial reporting, and nominations of new board members.

Remuneration

If executive directors are allowed to decide their own remuneration, they could be inclined to pay themselves as much as possible, without having to hold themselves to account or to justify their high pay. Where incentive schemes are in place, there is a risk that incentive schemes devised by the executive directors for themselves will be linked to **achieving performance targets** that are not necessarily in the shareholders' interests. For example, rewarding directors with a bonus for achieving profit growth is of no value to shareholders if the result is **higher business risk** and a **lower share price**.

Remuneration committee

Corporate governance in many countries, such as the UK's Combined Code, calls for a remuneration committee of the board to be established to decide on **directors' pay**, including **incentive schemes**, and for this committee to comprise at least three, or in the case of smaller companies two, members, who should all be **independent non-executive directors**.

The remuneration committee should have **delegated responsibility** for **setting remuneration** for all **executive directors** and the chairman, including pension rights and any compensation payments. The committee should also recommend and monitor the **level and structure** of **remuneration** for **senior management**. The NEDs should, in principle, be able to devise fair remuneration packages that include an incentive element, in which the performance targets bring the objectives of the executive directors more into line with those of the shareholders.

Financial reporting

A second potential area for conflict of interest is financial reporting. The executive directors might be tempted to **'window dress'** the results of the company, in order to present the financial results in a way that reflects better on themselves and their achievements.

Audit committee

There should be an audit committee of the board, consisting of non-executive directors, whose task should be to consider issues relating to financial reporting and financial control systems. This committee **should be responsible for maintaining regular liaison with the external auditors**. The Combined Code says that the audit committee should comprise at least three, or in the case of smaller companies two, members, who should all be **independent NEDs**. The board should satisfy itself that at least one member of the audit committee has recent and relevant financial experience.

Nominations to board

A third potential area for conflict is **nominations of new board members**. A powerful chairman or chief executive could be tempted to **appoint their supporters** or 'yes men' to the board, and so strengthen their position on the board. The Combined Code recommends that there should be a nominations committee of the board, manned by NEDs.

Other areas

Other areas of potential conflict of interest can be identified, such as **succession planning**, and the board's decisions on **making acquisitions** or in preparing defences against a takeover bid. In each of these areas, NEDs should be able to provide a counter-balance to the self-interested views of executive directors.

(d) **Share payments**

In many companies, NEDs receive a fixed cash payment for their services, without any incentives. However, some companies pay their NEDs in shares.

They would argue that the more equity the NEDs hold, the more likely they will be to look at issues from the point of view of the shareholders. There is a risk that a NED holding shares could become more concerned with **short-term movements** in the share price and the opportunity of making a **short-term profit from selling their shares**. However, a suitable precaution against this could be to obtain the agreement of a NED **not to sell his or her shares** until after leaving the board.

Share options

The argument that NEDs should be rewarded with share options is more contentious, but it has been widely practised in the UK and is even more common in the US. The argument against rewarding NEDs with share options is that this form of remuneration could **align the interests of the NEDs more closely with the executive directors**, who also hold share options. NEDs should give independent advice, and it can be argued that it is therefore not appropriate to incentivise them in the same way as the executives.

The Combined Code points out that holding of share options could be relevant to the determination of a non-executive director's independence. It states that remuneration for non-executive directors **should not include share options**. If, exceptionally, options are granted, **shareholder approval** should be **sought in advance** and any shares acquired by exercise of the options should be held until at least one year after the non-executive director leaves the board.

16 Good governance

> **Text references.** Chapter 5.
>
> **Top tips**. You need to know about the UK's Combined Code since it represents best practice in one of the major stock markets in the world.
>
> The answer to (b) is organised round the major headings in the Combined Code, the Code providing a good framework to explain the committee's role. Although the disclosures in (c) are taken from the Combined Code, it's better to think of them as setting out the details necessary to explain the corporate governance arrangements.
>
> **Easy marks**. The whole question, requiring listing of the main corporate governance requirements, appears to be very straightforward for a Strategic level paper.

To: Chief Executive
From: Accountant
Date: 2 August 20X4
Subject: Corporate Governance

The Combined Code was originally published in the UK in 1998 to bring together the recommendations of the Cadbury, Greenbury and Hampel reports. It was updated in 2003. The UK guidance in some ways is less prescriptive than the Sarbanes Oxley guidance in America and elsewhere, being based more on companies disclosing reasons for any non-compliance with the guidelines in the Code.

(a) **Role of board**

All listed companies should be led by an **effective board**. The board should meet regularly and have **certain matters** reserved for its decision such as mergers and major asset acquisitions and disposals.

Responsibilities of board

The board should present a **balanced and understandable assessment** of the **company's position and prospects** in the annual accounts and other reports such as interim reports and reports to regulators.

The board should **review the effectiveness of internal control** annually and report to shareholders that they have done so. The review should cover all controls including financial, operational and compliance controls and risk management.

As part of their responsibility for ensuring that internal controls are effective, the board should appoint an **audit committee.**

(b) **Role and responsibilities of the audit committee**

The audit committee should consist of at least three independent non-executive directors, at least one of whom has relevant and recent accounting experience.

(i) **Review of financial statements and systems**

The committee should review the **interim and annual accounts**. This should involve:

- Judgements made about the **overall appearance** and **presentation** of the accounts,
- **Any changes in accounting policies and practices**
- **Major judgmental areas**
- **Compliance with standards and legal requirements**

As well as reviewing the accounts, the committee's review should cover the financial reporting and budgetary systems. This involves considering **performance indicators** and **information systems** that allow **monitoring** of the **most significant business and financial risks**.

(ii) **Liaison with external auditors**

The audit committee will be responsible for the **appointment or removal of the external auditors** as well as fixing their remuneration. They should consider whether there are **threats to the independence** of external audit, in particular whether the **provision of non-audit services may lead to a conflict of interest.**

The audit committee should **discuss the scope of the external audit** prior to the start of the audit. The committee should also act as a **forum for liaison** between the external auditors, the internal auditors and the finance director and **help the external auditors to obtain the information** they require. If problems arise during the audit, the audit committee should be available for **consultation,** and see that the **concerns raised by the external auditors are resolved.**

(iii) **Review of internal audit**

The audit committee should review on an annual basis the work of internal audit .The review should cover the following aspects.

- **Standards** including objectivity, technical knowledge and professional standards
- **Scope** including how much emphasis is given to different types of review
- **Resources**
- **Reporting arrangements**
- **Work plan**, especially review of controls and coverage of high risk areas
- **Liaison** with external auditors
- **Results**

(iv) **Review of internal control**

The audit committee should **monitor** continually the **adequacy of internal control systems**, focusing particularly on the **control environment**, management's attitude towards controls and overall management controls. They should review reports on the operation of **codes of conduct** and review violations. Each year the committee should be responsible for **reviewing the company's statement on internal controls** prior to its approval by the board.

The committee should also address the risk of **fraud**, ensuring employees are aware of risks, there are mechanisms in place for staff to report fraud, and fraud to be investigated. Audit committees should be given specific authority to investigate matters of concern, and in doing so have access to sufficient resources, appropriate information and outside professional help.

(v) **Review of risk management**

The audit committee can play an important part in the review of risk recommended by the Turnbull report. This includes confirming that there is a **formal policy** in place for **risk management** and that the policy is **backed** and **regularly monitored by the board**. They should also review the arrangements for ensuring that managers and staff are **aware of their responsibilities**. They should also ensure that there are channels for staff to **report improprieties.**

(c) **General disclosures**

The Combined Code requires the following general disclosures:

(i) **Application of principles**

A **narrative statement** of how they **applied the principles** set out in the Combined Code, providing explanations which enable their shareholders to assess how the principles have been applied.

(ii) **Compliance with Combined Code**
A **statement** as to whether or not they **complied** throughout the accounting period with the **provisions** set out in the Combined Code. Listed companies that did not comply throughout the accounting period with all the provisions must specify the provisions with which they did not comply, and give reasons for non-compliance.

Explanation of responsibilities

The directors should **explain** their **responsibility for preparing accounts**. They should **report that the business is a going concern**, with supporting assumptions and qualifications as necessary.

Further statements

(i) **Board**
Information about the board of directors: changes in the composition of the board in the year, the identity of the leading directors and information about the independence of the non-executives, attendance at board meetings, how the board's performance has been evaluated.

(ii) **Committees**
Brief report on the **remuneration, audit and nomination committees** covering terms of reference, composition and frequency of meetings

(iii) **Auditors**
Information about **relations with auditors** including reasons for change and steps taken to ensure auditor objectivity and independence when non-audit services have been provided

(iv) **Control review**
A statement that the directors have reviewed the **effectiveness** of **internal controls**, including risk management, within the framework of the Turnbull guidelines

(v) **Shareholders**
A statement on relations and dialogue with shareholders

(vi) **Going concern**
A statement that the company is a **going concern**

(vii) **OFR**
An operating and financial review.

Please contact me if you have any further queries.

17 BJP

Text references. Chapter 6 covers the main elements of internal control. Chapters 3 and 4 are also helpful on specific controls.

Top tips. (a) is a good example of a question part with more than one verb (advise and recommend). You can't afford not to register the second verb and fail to recommend controls. Our answer to (a) contains more controls than you would have had time to discuss or needed to for full marks. The examiner wanted 3-4 examples of controls. Your answer however should have covered not just control of expenses but control of salesmen's time, as the finance department raised the issue of control over work as well as expenses. Some of the controls we recommend are general, some are standard accounting system controls; some seek to prevent problems by taking away from salesmen the decisions over expenses, and some seek to identify problems (principally the review by regional managers).

In (b) there are a lot of different elements that a definition of control can bring out. Make sure you understand how wide systems are. Benefits include improved performance as well as elimination of loss, costs lost opportunities as well as direct expenditure. Bringing in examples from the scenario could help your answers, although the question requirements don't specify that you should.

In (c) the limited number of marks suggests that your discussion needed to concentrate on reasonableness comparisons; from the scenario there is plenty of evidence available for these. A definition of analytic review may earn 2 marks but no more, so don't spend too much time on this.

Easy marks. The definitions of internal control systems and control environment are pretty much straight quotations from auditing standards – however the marks are only easy if you know the definitions (see examiner's comments). This question is a good illustration of what we said in the front pages about where easy marks are available – and it shows that students don't always have the knowledge to gain them.

Examiner's comments. The examiner stressed that this question required students to think beyond traditional activities. The mark scheme gives scope for different approaches, with 15 marks being identified for (a) (5 marks for each of salesmen's activities, expense claims and general controls) and 10 marks being available for the various elements of question (b).

The main weakness was excessive concentration on expenses and lack of discussion of the freedom granted to sales representatives and how they spent their time. In (b), Some candidates did not know what the control environment was (a comment the examiner has made in other recent reports). Answers to the rest of (b) and (c) were generally good.

(a) **Key risks**

Sales representatives are an important feature of BJP's business. Unless BJP adopts an alternative B2B model, the sales force will have to be maintained. However greater control is needed because of the risks that **excessive costs** are being incurred; salesmen are **spending money inappropriately or inefficiently** and are **not using their time to best effect**.

Claims for expenses not incurred

The risk of this is fairly small, as most of the expenses under scrutiny would be backed by bills or credit card slips, though some **entertaining** might not generate visible records.

Claims for private expenses

The potential for these is much greater. It may be difficult to distinguish how much fuel is purchased for **business use**, how much for **private use**. Salesmen might also claim **entertainment expenses** that are **not linked to specific clients.** As well as incurring expenses that should not be charged to the company, BJP may also be liable to **tax penalties** if the tax authority deems these expenses a benefit-in-kind.

Inappropriate use of time

In pursuit of new customers and hence higher remuneration, salesmen may try to **spend amounts to woo them** that are **higher** than is desirable given the chances of picking up their business or the volume of business they are likely to generate.

Inefficient practices

There is also a **risk of inefficiencies** in salesmen's practices, particularly in the distances they travel; they may be able to concentrate on smaller geographic areas each day.

You would also have scored marks if you had discussed the following risks.

Claims for excessive expenses

Expenses may be incurred for legitimate reasons, but may be **too high**. This is a particular risk for **accommodation** (at hotels which are too expensive) or **entertaining** (too lavishly at expensive restaurants perhaps).

Risk of bribery

The line between legitimate entertainment and bribery is not necessarily clear, and BJP may not easily be **able to identify problems**. However as well as salesmen boosting their income by **illegitimate means**, BJP or its directors may also be liable if corruption is proved.

Controls

Recruitment and training

Proper **references** should be obtained, and salesmen trained in **selling techniques**.

Employment contracts

Salesmen should have **employment contracts** detailing the behaviour expected and how their performance will be measured. There should be **disciplinary procedures** for employees who transgress.

Expense policies

Formal policies should clarify the **distinctions between business and personal expenditure**, and also what else constitutes **acceptable and unacceptable expenditure**. Policies should include recovery of expenditure charged but used for private purposes such as private motoring.

Targets

Employees should be set **budgetary targets** for expenditure and **variances** between **budgeted and actual expenditure** should be **investigated**.

More regular review of expenses

Regional managers could collect the data themselves, and be required to review expenses more regularly than they have been doing, maybe **weekly or fortnightly**. The difficulty may be that regional manager success is primarily judged by **how much** business their salesmen have picked up, so **head office review** will continue to be required and regional managers' performance assessment should be considered (see below).

More detailed review of expenses

However regular they are, manager reviews will only be effective if managers undertake a detailed review of expenses and are prepared to take queries up with the salesmen. Managers should review **records of all expenditure above a certain limit**, and compare salesmen expenses over time and with other salesmen under their authority. Expenses should be **clearly related** to **customers**.

Prior authorisation

Proposed expenditure of certain types, particularly **entertainment**, above a certain limit should require prior authorisation by managers, and would have to be justified by salesmen on the grounds of the business it was expected to generate.

Central control

Certain costs could be limited by taking decisions from salesmen and having them dealt with centrally. **Hotels** for example could be booked by a single employee, who might be able to obtain discounts from hotel chains as well as limiting the hotels salesmen can use.

You would also have scored marks if you had discussed the following controls.

Payment means

The risk of **non-existent expenses** would be **reduced by payment by invoice or credit card settlement** rather than employee reimbursement.

Time spent with customers

Regional managers should review salesmen's call records to see that an **acceptable volume** of calls has been made, and excessive time has not been spent on certain customers. They should monitor how successful the salesman has been in **turning potential customers into actual customers**.

Customer satisfaction

They should also check with customers to confirm their **satisfaction** with the salesman's efforts.

Performance assessment

A key control may be to change the way salesmen and possibly regional management are assessed. Performance measures should be written into salesmen's employment contracts, and should cover:

(i) **Targets for sales calls and business generated**, with assessment being made of whether the salesman has been instrumental in winning the business

(ii) **Comparing the expenses incurred** to generate new and keep existing clients with the **volume of business generated**. Depending on how generous the remuneration is, this should reduce the risk that illegitimate expenses will be charged, and will encourage salesmen not to spend excessive amounts on low volume business.

(b) **Internal control system**

The internal control system includes the **policies and procedures** adopted by the directors and management of an entity to assist in achieving their objective of ensuring the **orderly and efficient conduct of its business**.

The internal control system extends beyond those matters that relate directly to the accounting system and should **evolve over time** in response to changing risks. The internal control system consists of two main elements, the **control environment** and **control procedures**; procedures include operational controls, communication, reporting to management and review.

Control environment

The control environment is the **overall attitude, awareness and actions of directors and management regarding internal controls** and their importance in the entity. The control environment encompasses the **management style**, and **corporate culture and values** shared by all employees. It provides the background against which the various other controls are operated.

Benefits

The benefits of internal control are **avoidance of losses** caused by disruption of operations, assets being stolen or losing their value through neglect, also as here **reducing or eliminating unnecessary expenditure** and **improving the utilisation of resources and employee performance**.

Costs

The main costs of the internal control function are the salary costs of staff employed to operate controls, such as **internal audit or compliance staff**. Other costs include **training** and **IT investment**. The costs are also the **lost revenues** as a result of operational staff operating internal controls such as the managers carrying out expense reviews rather than being employed on profit-making activities. There may also be **intangible costs** such as authorisation procedures **limiting the organisation's flexibility** to respond to new business.

Limitations of internal controls

The main limitations of internal controls are poor design leading to controls being set up which are **inadequate or inappropriate**. Controls that depend on the judgement of those operating them are **vulnerable to human error**. Controls may be overridden as a result of **collusion between employees or bypassed by directors or senior managers**. Even a **well-designed control system** will be designed with **'normal' transactions or 'normal' risks** in mind and may not be able to cope with unusual transactions or unexpected occurrences.

(c) **Analytic review**

Analytic review is a comparison of ratios, trends and patterns **over time** and **between different businesses, eg departments or people**. It can be used by internal audit at the planning stage, as a means of **highlighting key risk areas**. It can also be used as part of detailed audit testing to spot unusual trends, inconsistencies or areas where fraud may have taken place.

Tests at BJP

Auditors should examine the level of salesmen's expenditure and consider whether expenditure levels appear reasonable:

(i) **Over time**, that there are not wide variations in expenditure

(ii) **In comparison with other salesmen** reporting to different regional managers

(iii) **In the light of the salesmen's circumstances**, for example fuel claims fairly reflecting the area the salesman chooses to travel, also the **car make** and **frequency of visits to clients**

18 LMN

Text references. Chapter 2 covers general risk management issues, and Chapter 5 corporate governance.

Top tips. This question is a very good illustration of our comment in the front pages that questions will cover a variety of organisations. The scenario gives lots of detail about risks and how they are controlled, inevitably for a charity where use of funds for proper purposes and value for money are important. In (a) the link between controls and risk management is highlighted in the question details. The discussion in the first part of (a) should be assisted by examples from the scenario, and in the risks-controls you need to include some examples of appropriate controls for LMN. Your answer needs to differentiate clearly, as ours has done by using headers, between purposes and importance so that you can maximise your marks for (a).

It's necessary to read (b) quite carefully to see what the question wants; an assessment of how much a review by the professional managers contributes to the work of the audit committee, and why therefore the review should be carried out. You should start off by defining what the work of the audit committee is, then consider how much managers' review contributes compared with other sources of information.

In (c) again you can't be too theoretical; any discussion of principles has to be related to how they impact on the audit committee and board's reviews. Selected examples from the scenario information are also needed here to boost the discussion. If you can remember that the board needs to carry out a regular and annual review and the main elements you would have scored well in (c) and gone a long way towards passing this question.

Finally note the examiner's comments about the question not being done very well despite being the most popular question in the exam. Some students would have chosen this question because it appeared to be a straightforward corporate question. However the fact that this was a charity does complicate the answer, and the question requirements are quite clear that every part needs to be related to the circumstances of a charity. There are no general parts unrelated to the scenario on which easy marks can be scored. Students should have considered these points when choosing questions in this exam, but it seems that many did not.

Easy marks. No very easy parts, but overall a good example of how to illustrate corporate governance in an organisation with relevant information from a scenario.

Examiner's comments. Although this was the most popular optional question, it wasn't done very well, with students being unable to apply corporate governance principles to an organisation that wasn't a listed company and failing to use the information in the scenario. Many answers to (b) focused on the role of the audit committee when the question was about management evaluation of internal controls.

'Candidates should make full use of the reading time to make sure they understand what is being asked.'

(a) **Purposes of risk management**

Alignment of risk appetite and strategy

LMN's board should consider what **risks** it is prepared to **tolerate** in the light of the organisation's strategy. Risk management comprises the systems and processes for dealing with the risks that the board is prepared to tolerate in order for LMN to fulfil its **strategic objectives**, including its **social goals**.

Develop a consistent framework for dealing with risk

A coherent risk management framework can help LMN **compare risks with obvious financial consequences** (poor cost control, loss of income due to bad debts) with risks whose financial consequences are less obvious (dissatisfied tenants). It also should provide guidelines that can be applied by staff operating across all areas of LMN's activities.

Develop risk response strategies

The risk management process should **identify and evaluate risks** (for example by the high-medium-low method described) and therefore provide the information necessary for management to decide what the best **response to risk** should be – acceptance, control, avoidance or transfer.

Importance of risk management

Improve financial position

The risk management framework can provide a means of judging the **costs of treating the risks** measured against the **benefits**. It can also help LMN's directors judge whether to take advantage of opportunities, for example property investment.

Minimise surprises and losses

By **identifying risks in the risk register**, the risk management process should reduce the occurrence of unexpected shocks. For example identifying **property maintenance** as a risk issue should encourage a programme of regular maintenance designed to deal with the risks associated with the types and ages of property.

Maintain reputation

As LMN is a charity, its reputation as a **good corporate citizen** is very important. Risk management should help it avoid risks to its reputation such as **poor treatment of tenants** or **failing to comply with regulatory requirements**.

Risk management and the internal control system

Internal control is action taken by management to achieve organisational objectives and goals. Internal control thus is bound up with the organisation's strategies, and is therefore also bound up with risk management that is dependent upon the organisation's strategies. Internal control is made up of two elements:

(i) **Control environment**, the framework within which controls operate and within which attitudes towards risk are an important elements. **Communication** between directors and employees is a key element of the control environment.

(ii) **Internal controls**, which should be operated when their **benefits outweigh costs**; controls focused on dealing with the most significant risks will have obvious benefits. Given the risks LMN faces, key controls will include **debtor management**, **maintenance inspections and logs**, **financial appraisal of new investments** and **tenant satisfaction questionnaires**, as well as **accounting**, **compliance** and **cost limitation** controls.

(b) **Audit committee's role in internal control**

Under corporate governance guidelines audit committees are responsible for creating a **climate of discipline and control.** To do this, they have to obtain assurance that internal control is working **effectively** and providing an **adequate response** to the **risks** faced, in particular for LMN, controls over expenditure.

Importance of management review

The management review provides the audit committee with evidence of whether the control systems appear to be **effectively managing the most significant risks**. It also gives the audit committee an indication of the **scope and quality** of management's monitoring of risk and internal control; does it appear to be **adequate** given the risks faced. In the circumstances of LMN, the board of volunteers will wish to gain assurance that the **professional managers** are carrying out their duties effectively and are worth the salaries LMN is paying them. The review should provide **feedback** on weaknesses and should lead to improvements in the control systems.

Other sources of evidence

However management's review of internal control is only one source of evidence that the audit committee should use to gain assurance. LMN's committee should also receive **reports from staff** undertaking important and high-risk activities such as property investment. They should also receive **reports from control functions** such as human resources or internal audit (if any). Feedback from external sources such as **external audit** or **regulatory visits** will also provide information.

(c) (i) **Review of internal controls**

The UK's Turnbull committee emphasises the importance of a regular review and an annual review of internal control as part of an organisation's strategy for **minimising risk**, **ensuring adherence to strategic objectives**, **fulfilling responsibilities to stakeholders** and **establishing accountability at its senior levels.**

Regular review

Regular review is an essential part of the strategy for minimizing risks. The audit committee is likely to have responsibility for this review, and as best practice recommends at least **three audit committee meetings a year**; this is thus how often the review should take place. Its findings should be communicated to the board.

The review should cover the following areas:

(1) **Risk evaluation**
Whether LMN is **identifying** and **evaluating all key risks**, financial and non-financial. This is a very significant task given the variety of risks faced and also the need to devote limited resources to the most important risks.

(2) **Risk responses**
Whether **responses and management** of risks are **appropriate**.

(3) **Effectiveness of internal controls**
The **effectiveness of internal controls in countering the risks**. The board should consider how much controls could be expected to **reduce the incidence of risks**, any evidence that controls have **not been operating effectively** and how **weaknesses are being resolved**. The board would consider evidence such as incidence of bad debts, records of property occupation and complaints from tenants.

Annual review

The annual review of internal control should be more wide-ranging, taking into account the **strategic objectives of the charity** and undertaken by the **whole board** rather than just the audit committee. It should examine controls and risk management systems in all major areas:

(1) **Changes in risks**
The **changes** since the last assessment **in risks faced**, and the charity's ability to **respond to changes in its environment**. For example the board would consider any changes in LMN's credit ratings, also longer-term trends such as changes in the incidence of low income earners.

(2) **Monitoring**
The **scope and quality of management's monitoring of risk and control**, also whether internal audit is required. In particular the review should consider whether the **scope and frequency of the regular review** should be increased.

(3) **Reports**

The **extent and frequency of reports** to the board; should reports on high incidence, high likelihood risks be made more regularly.

(4) **Impact on accounts**

Significant controls, failings and weaknesses that may materially impact on the financial statements, for example problems over its property portfolio management.

(ii) **Disclosures in the annual report**

The report on compliance is a key part of the annual report by which LMN demonstrates its **compliance with regulations** and how it has **fulfilled the differing requirements of its stakeholders**, including tenants, donees, banks and local government.

Responsibility

The board should also **acknowledge its accountability** for LMN's system of control and **reviewing its effectiveness**.

Risk management

The Turnbull report recommends that as a minimum the board should disclose what has been done to **manage risk** and how the board has **reviewed the effectiveness of the risk management process**. The board should explain the limits of the process (it aims at risk management rather than risk elimination) and disclose any **material problems** or **weaknesses** that have been found. It should communicate **risks, objectives, targets** and **measures to counter risks**.

19 Board review

Text references. Chapter 6.

Top tips. The examiners have stated that essay questions without scenarios will occasionally be set. This essay question, like the essay question in November 2005 (Question 14 in the Kit) is on corporate governance, although it is a bit more specific than the 2005 question.

You might have had problems deciding what should go into (a) and what into (b). Our answer to (a) is based on what boards must consider carefully when the system of controls is being established, and a brief note that the board is also responsible for monitoring. Note the examiner's comments highlighting a common problem in this paper, students reading the question requirements too quickly and covering the wrong areas of internal control.

(b) then goes into detail about the two key elements of the monitoring process, the ongoing review by the board and the wider (more strategic) annual review. Because 10 marks are available your advice can go into some detail about what the reviews should cover and how management should use different information sources to carry out an effective review. Remember that corporate governance is essentially a high-level control.

The reference in (c) to reporting to the stock market just means what corporate governance reports need to say about internal controls. Mentioning the Sarbanes-Oxley requirements should gain marks, as these are stricter than most other countries, but have application to companies that trade in America.

Easy marks. If you have good knowledge of the Turnbull recommendations that represent best practice in this area of corporate governance, you should have found most of this question reasonably straightforward. You should certainly have got the full five marks for appropriate report format and style; this question illustrates what we said in the front pages about marks sometimes being specifically available for basic writing skills.

Examiner's comments. Many students failed to answer the question asked, not discussing internal control in detail but instead concentrating on internal audit and audit committees.

REPORT

To: The Board of Directors
From: Accountant
Date: 1 December 20X6
Subject: Board's responsibility for internal control

I am writing to set out what the board should do to fulfil its responsibilities to maintain an appropriate internal control system.

(a) **Key responsibilities of board members**

Sound system of control

Corporate governance guidelines require the board to **maintain a sound system of internal control** to **safeguard shareholders' investments and the company's assets**. A sound system should aid operations by **responding to risks**, should **ensure the quality of reporting**, and help **ensure compliance with laws and regulations**. The board needs to maintain risks within limits desired, so should define the company's **risk appetite** as part of the strategic decision-making process.

Risks

In order to determine what constitutes a sound system, the board should consider the major risks the company faces, concentrating on

- The processes for **identification, evaluation and management of all key risks** affecting the organisation
- The **effectiveness of internal control (see below)**
- **Communication** to employees of risk objectives with targets and indicators
- The **action that needs to be taken if any weaknesses** are found

Effectiveness of internal control

The board should consider the effectiveness of all internal controls, not financial controls but also operational, compliance and risk management controls. Board members need to consider:

- The **nature and extent of the risks** which face the company
- The **threat of such risks becoming** a **reality**
- If that happened, the company's ability to **reduce the incidence and impact** on the business and to adapt to changing risks or operational deficiencies
- The **costs and benefits** related to operating relevant controls

Feedback

The board must not regard establishing a good control system as a one-off exercise. The **risks** that drive the development of the internal control systems will **change** as the company's **strategy** and **business environment changes.** In addition **feedback** on how the controls have been operating is an essential part of a business's control systems; the feedback the board obtains should lead to modifications and improvements.

(b) **Methods used to assess effectiveness of internal control**

Consideration of internal controls should be a regular part of the board's agenda and the board should also conduct a higher level annual review of internal control.

Regular review

The board should regularly consider:

- The effectiveness of **strategies for identifying, evaluating and managing** the major risks
- The **strength of the management and internal control environment and systems**
- The **actions** being taken to **reduce the risks** found

- Whether the results indicate that **internal control** should be **monitored more extensively.**

Annual review

When the board is considering the disclosures about internal controls in the accounts, it should conduct an **annual review** of internal control. This should be wider-ranging than the regular review; in particular it should cover:

- The **changes** since the last **assessment** in **risks** faced, **ability** to **respond to changes** in its business environment and whether the company's **objectives and risk appetite** should be **re-assessed**
- The **scope** and **quality** of management's **monitoring** of risk and internal control, and how well the **information systems** fulfil the board and management's **information needs**
- The **extent and frequency of reports to the board and communication with employees**
- **Significant controls, failings and weaknesses** with **material impacts** upon the accounts
- The **effectiveness of the public reporting processes** in communicating a **balanced and understandable account** of the company's position and prospects

Information for review

To carry out effective reviews, the board needs to use a number of different sources of information. Part of the review of controls should be the quality of the reports the board is receiving.

(i) **Performance measurement and indicators**
Regular reporting of these measures should be built into the control systems. They should include not just **financial data** but also **qualitative measures** such as customer satisfaction.

(ii) **Senior management monitoring**
The board should consider reports on the **monitoring activities** undertaken by senior management below board level, such as control self-assessment and confirmation by employees of compliance with policies and codes of conduct. Management reports should highlight the impact of, and actions taken to remedy, **significant control failings and weaknesses.** Management should also report to the board risk any risk and control matters of particular importance, such as fraud or illegal acts.

(iii) **Audit committee and internal audit**
The board should review regular reports from the audit committee and internal audit. The issues covered should include the committee's review of **control and risk management systems**, and also the **results of internal and external audit**, in particular the **control weaknesses identified.** The audit committee should also **assess the effectiveness of internal audit.**

(iv) **Staff communications**
The board should consider information communicated to them by staff on risk and control weaknesses. There should be channels of communication for staff to use to report **suspected breaches of laws, regulations or other improprieties.**

(v) **Follow-up on problems**
As part of the cycle of continual feedback, the board should **review whether changes have occurred** in response to changes in risk assessment or weaknesses identified in previous reports.

(c) **Reporting on internal control**

The reports the board provides will depend on the stock exchange rules. Two major jurisdictions with differing requirements reflecting a differing approach to corporate governance are the UK and the USA.

UK requirements

The board should disclose, as a minimum, in the accounts the existence of a **process for managing risks**, how the board has **reviewed** the **effectiveness of the process** and that the **process accords** with **UK guidance**. The board should also include:

(i) **Acknowledgement of responsibility**
An **acknowledgement** that they are **responsible for the company's system of internal financial control** and **reviewing its effectiveness.**

(ii) **Aims of system**

An **explanation** that such a system is designed to **manage** rather than eliminate the risk of **failure** to **achieve business objectives**, and can only provide **reasonable,** and not absolute, **assurance** against material misstatement or **loss**.

(iii) **Summary of directors' process**

A **summary** of the process that the directors have used **to review the effectiveness of the system of internal financial control**. There should also be disclosure of the process the board has used to deal with **material internal control aspects of any significant problems** disclosed in the annual accounts.

(iv) **Weaknesses**

Information about those **weaknesses** in internal financial control that have resulted in material losses, contingencies or uncertainties that require disclosure in the financial statements or the auditor's report on the financial statements.

USA requirements

Under the Sarbanes-Oxley requirements, annual reports should contain **internal control reports** that state the responsibility of management for establishing and maintaining an **adequate internal control structure and procedures for financial reporting.** Annual reports should also contain an **assessment of the effectiveness of the internal control structure** and **procedures for financial reporting,** additionally **disclosures of any material weaknesses** in internal control. Auditors should report on this assessment.

If you have any further questions on these issues, please do not hesitate to get in touch.

20 PKG High School

Text references. Chapters 5 and 6.

Top tips. This question is a good test of your understanding of the controls all organisations should have. Remember we stressed in the front pages that you need to know about a large variety of controls.

In (a) the stakeholders are different to those of a company, but they still need the assurance provided by an objective review. Benchmarking is likely to be a particularly important aspect of the audit, given that the governing body is responsible for educational standards.

It is very easy in (b) to stray from the subject and talk too generally about controls – the question asks you to evaluate (often as here concentrate on the weaknesses), and recommend what the governing body should be doing. Our answer is based around the structure of:

- How the governing body is constituted and how it operates
- The data it gets (financial/non-financial, internal-external)
- The decisions it takes and the monitoring it carries out

which is a useful way of analysing how any governing body works.

You may have felt that the question could have given more detail about what the governing body is doing and the information it receives. It is valid to assume that if you're not told anything about key aspects of governance such as a committee system, then they aren't being operated when they should be.

It's also easy in (b) to fail to consider whether financial and other resources are being used to maximum efficiency. Spending limits often mean that expenditure is often made to the limits set down, with little consideration of whether value for money has been obtained.

This question is also a good illustration of the importance of choosing questions carefully. The examiner's comments indicated that the question was popular but not done well, indicating many students made the wrong choice. It seems students had insufficient understanding of the non-corporate sector, and how a governing body would differ from a company board.

Easy marks. Quite difficult to identify on this question.

Examiner's comments. This question was answered poorly. Answers needed to consider a broad range of issues, not just financial ones. However students seemed unable to discuss corporate governance in the context of a school, instead discussing governance procedures that would have been appropriate for a limited company. In (b) students failed to pick up many of the points in the scenario, including the need to control the head teacher and problems with the information received by the governing body.

(a) **Independent and objective assurance**

Having an external review carried out should provide an **unbiased view** of how the school is performing. In particular this provides **reassurance to stakeholders such as parents and the local authority** that the school is providing education of sufficient quality and expenditure is being properly controlled.

Aid to monitoring

Like the board of directors in a listed company, the governors are responsible for establishing and maintaining a sound system of internal control and risk management. The review should provide **feedback** to the head teacher and governing body to enable them to set priorities for systems improvements, based on the areas of **greatest risk.** It should also highlight where the head teacher and governors should **focus their own monitoring activity.**

Expert opinion

The external reviewers can make recommendations based on their **knowledge of best practice in other schools.** This can provide the school with **benchmarks** that it can incorporate into financial and non-financial performance indicators.

(b) (i) **Structure and workings of governing body**

Membership

The governing body includes representatives of the key stakeholder group of parents and the local authority.

However it may be a **more effective monitor** if it includes representation from key internal stakeholders. Certainly it should include staff representatives and perhaps also might include pupil representatives as well.

Committee system

Having the full governing body consider all relevant items at every meeting may not be the most efficient way of operation, and it may mean that some **key risk areas receive insufficient attention.**

Although committees may be difficult to staff, a **committee system** with each committee concentrating on certain key aspects of running the school may be the best way to conduct decision-making, with committees reporting into the main governing body. Certainly it may provide a good mechanism for parent representatives to use their particular expertise.

(1) **Audit committee**

An **audit committee**, including members with financial expertise, could be responsible for detailed scrutiny of expenditure and liasing with auditors. Its remit could also cover **compliance with legislation** and the **operation of internal controls.** This would leave the main governing body to concentrate on the split of expenditure and the overall review of control systems.

(2) **Staff recruitment committee**

Because of the significance of staffing the board should establish a separate recruitment committee. The committee should be involved in specific recruitment decisions, and should also proactively consider **staffing needs.** For example are there **sufficient experienced members** of staff and does the staff body as a whole have an **appropriate range of skills** in key areas such as IT. The committee must consider how **staffing headcount needs** can be **reconciled with planned staff expenditure.**

The committee should also consider the **balance between teachers and other support staff**, whether support staff, with specific skills, need to be recruited or whether their numbers could be reduced and more teachers recruited. It should also be involved in **internal promotion decisions** and consider the effectiveness of the **system of responsibility allowances.**

Induction of governing body members

There appear to be **no induction procedures** for new governing body members that would enhance their knowledge of what the school does and the requirements the governing body has to meet.

Certainly parent governors will need this understanding if they are be **effective governors** (hopefully the local authority will have selected suitably qualified and knowledgeable members).

(ii) **Information received by governing body**

Financial information

It is unclear whether the financial information is sufficiently detailed. The governing body needs to ensure that it receives **sufficient information about expenditure,** particularly because of the wide discretion the Headmaster has and the lack of **segregation of duties.**

Expenditure should be **classified** into **different categories** depending on its materiality and the ways it is controlled. The information should include what **has been spent,** and **expenditure commitments**, also **phasing of expenditure during the year;** not all expenditure will be made in even amounts over the year. The governing body also needs to ensure that the **reliability** of the monthly financial report is reviewed because of its importance for decision-making. As the external auditors may not spend time on this, this review should perhaps be carried out by members of the audit committee.

Financial variances

Although the governors receive information about variances from budgeted expenditure, there is nothing mentioned about how they are, as they should be, informed of action planned if an over-spend appears likely.

They should have input into what should be done.

Non-financial information

There appears to be a lack of non-financial information that the governors need to **ensure educational standards** are being **maintained.** An **annual inspection by the local education authority** would not be frequent enough.

Governors should be supplied with the results of internal methods of assessing the effectiveness of teaching such as **termly exams** and **internal quality reviews** of teaching programmes. Since staffing is both a major element of expenditure and vital in ensuring standards, governors should be receiving details about staff such as **results of appraisals** and **staff development programmes**. Having parent, staff and pupil representatives on the governing body will help measure the **satisfaction levels** of these key stakeholder groups; the governors ought to consider other methods such as regular staff and parent surveys.

External information

No mention is whether the governing body is receiving the external information which it will need for longer-term decision-making.

The governing body should be receiving details of population trends in the area and the impact of changes in schools provisions. It should also be considering specific information about other schools in the area that it can use for **benchmarking purposes** such as pupil numbers, disposition of staff, facilities and exam results.

(iii) **Actions taken by governing body**

Strategic decision-making

The governing body's time horizon appears to be limited to a year, and it does not appear to be considering longer-term issues; there seems to be **no strategic plan.**

Better information should help it **modify** its strategy in response to local issues such as changes in pupil numbers, the opening of new schools, particularly specialist schools or government-promoted schools (such as UK academies) and changes in educational practice (such as increased use of information technology).

Flexibility of decision-making

The governing body needs to consider whether its decision-making is too constricted; the governors may have the flexibility to take decisions that ensure **better use of resources** and **better risk management.**

For example it may consider whether class sizes can be increased in the lower age ranges to allow smaller class sizes and greater preparation time for more advanced teaching. Also it should consider whether to include a **contingency fund** for urgent items of additional expenditure on staff, buildings and IT.

Review of small items of expenditure

The governing body does not appear to take any interest in expenditure under $1,000. There may be scope for the head teacher to abuse this by **spreading significant expenditure** out so that individual items are below $1,000, but the total sum is quite substantial.

The governors should **review all expenditure** below $1,000 even if they don't approve it in advance. There may be scope for raising the limit on certain types of expenditure, so that the governing body does not spend time considering what is essentially non-discretionary expenditure.

Communication

The governing body needs to consider how its **work should be communicated**; there is **no evidence** of how this is happening at present.

Clearly the head teacher will have prime responsibility for communicating and what the governing body publishes should be consistent with what the head teacher is saying. However **communication of what the governing body is doing** and the **issues it is considering** should prove to staff, pupils and current and prospective parents that the school is **well-run.** It should also aid **future recruitment** onto the governing body.

21 EWC

Text references. Chapters 3,4 and 6

Top tips. The scenario is a short one for a 25 mark question. However although it is brief, it is quite concentrated and every sentence contains something of significance for your answer. Because the scenario is short, it's easy to use the same material in different parts of your answer and end up repeating yourself. Hence it's particularly important here to read the requirements and then go through the scenario, allocating all the details to the most relevant question part.

Our answer to (a) starts with the risks connected with staff, then goes on to look at the key risks relating to supplier and customer activity, before focusing on internal and external reporting of this activity and then the external legal risks. Reputation risk is, as often, a good finishing point.

In (b) a brief explanation of the control environment may assist your answer but you can't afford to spend half a page on it. The question part is only worth 5 marks, and 4 of those will be for covering specifically EWC's control environment. Note that the answer points out that EWC, in its own way, does have a strong control environment; however it isn't one that encourages ethical behaviour.

(c) appears to be the most demanding part of the question. The verb evaluate (assess the value of) is a high Level 5 requirement verb, compared with identify and explain in the earlier question parts, which are Level 2 verbs. The examiner requires a realistic assessment of their value and you make the evaluation as a non-executive director interested in higher-level controls and protecting the interests of shareholders and other stakeholders. Key aspects to examine are the impact of controls on strategic decision-making and behaviour.

Easy marks. Hopefully you were able to use the scenario information to generate a number of risks in (a).

Examiner's comments. Answers to (a) were generally stronger than answers to (b) or (c). Many students showed a worrying lack of knowledge of the control environment in (b), and failed to link unethical working practices to the control environment. Although most students identified the controls in (c), far fewer tried to evaluate them. Students who just wrote 'balanced scorecard' without further explanation did not score any marks.

(a) **Staffing risks**

EWC appears to **tolerate high staff turnover**; targets are important, not the people who achieve them. However this may mean that **human resource costs** are **higher** than they need be, with costs involved in recruiting and training new staff.

Staff risks

EWC's tough attitude to its staff is **unlikely to encourage loyalty and trust**. Staff may seek to **enhance their own performance artificially** in order to achieve short-term targets and hence bonuses, by for example focusing on existing profitable customers and not making the same effort to develop new business requiring greater time investment for more risk. Staff may also be more tempted to **join competitors**, and then aim to take the customers with whom they've been dealing away to the competitors.

Supplier risks

EWC's management practices mean that they are unlikely to develop good relationships with their suppliers and hence **may not be able to rely on the supply chain**. The cost pressure EWC is imposing may also lead to a **reduction in service** from their suppliers, and **disputes** that **disrupt** supply.. If EWC changes its suppliers regularly, it will face the **costs of finding new suppliers** and possible problems during the transition if new suppliers have initial difficulties in dealing with EWC's requirements.

Logistics risks

The pressure on costs may increase the risk of **administrative errors** because administration is overworked. This may result in various logistical errors such as not enough inventory being ordered or inventory being sent to the wrong place. These errors may displease customers and result in EWC **losing business.**

Customer risks

The unscrupulous practices towards customers may also **result in lost business**. EWC may have considerable difficulty building up long-term relationships with customers, if they feel that EWC is not treating them fairly, and they can get a better deal from EWC's rivals in a keenly competitive market.

Accounting risks

Failures in the information system may also lead to the accounts **not showing a true and fair view**. If profits and **sales are overstated**, directors and staff may receive **excessive bonuses**.

Legal risks

If staff break the law, then EWC may be at **risk itself from fines and penalties** as well as miscreant staff. This would apply even though EWC is in an unregulated sector, since staff may for example breach **consumer protection legislation** that applies to all businesses.

Reputation risks

If EWC gains a reputation as an unscrupulous operator, then it may find **various business opportunities curtailed**. Potential suppliers and customers may not wish to deal with EWC if they feel the relationship will be unfair. In addition a poor reputation may **jeopardise EWC's chances of obtaining a listing**, which may well be significant to managers and staff holding share options.

(b) **Definition**

The **control environment** is the overall attitudes, awareness and actions of directors and management regarding internal controls, encompassing management style, corporate culture and values. It provides the background for other controls

EWC control environment

Important aspects of EWC's control environment include the following.

Commercial focus

The important values in EWC's control environment are very **commercial**; they include success at all costs, personal wealth and the need to cut costs and find ways of making more profit.

Efficiency of operations

The philosophy that targets are the only controls that matter may mean that the directors believe that they are operating at **maximum efficiency**. However the board may have judged certain necessary expenditure as unimportant such as **quality control**; this may result in poor quality not being identified and hence customer dissatisfaction.

Organisational structure

The **flat structure** should mean that employees have considerable responsibility, which may **improve their motivation**. It should also mean that they can **respond rapidly to customer needs**. However the flat structure may make it easier for individuals to **override controls**. It could mean that they could easily manipulate profits by **entering false sales invoices before the year-end** and **raising credit notes after the year-end**. It also may be a structure that needs **modification as the company expands**. Decisions about **which new product and geographical markets to develop** need to be taken by senior management taking a wider strategic view, not by sales staff.

Ethical values

There is probably a link between the minimisation of corporate policies and the unscrupulous behaviour. The fact that dubious business practices are not forbidden appears to have led staff to believe that **ethical business behaviour** is **much less important than meeting targets**.

(c) **Financial controls**

Quality of information

In order to stay aware of sales, costs and profits, **detailed data** must be being produced and targets be set for each employee. **Value analysis** is also taking place to **identify non-value adding activity**. However the pressure on administration may lead to **poor quality management information** being produced, and lead to managers **taking the wrong business decisions** based on bad information. Although budget targets are tough, they are probably **not considered carefully** and realistic budgets may not be set. There may also be **few or no checks on the quality of the actual information** being compared with budgets.

Sales and profitability targets

Sales and profits targets could complement each other and this would **increase their value**. Setting sales targets means there is an **emphasis on expanding business from existing customers and finding new customers**; profits targets ensure that the **costs of maintaining the customer base are not excessive**. However there is apparently no attempt to address the **undesirable side effects** of these targets. If standards are too demanding, employees may become demotivated and leave. They may also seek to improve their own performance at the expense of other staff, for example **chasing the same customers**.

Non-financial quantitative controls

Expanded geographic and customer base targets

Ambitious targets for expansion appear to be appropriate in a rapidly-developing industry. However targets appear to have been set in every direction without considering whether they can all be achieved together. If cost restrictions mean that not enough time has been spent researching new markets, the targets may turn out to be detrimental because they result in **poor strategic decisions being taken**. EWC may end up **pursuing too many targets** at once or the **wrong targets**, and may as a result lack the resources to service its existing customer base effectively.

Qualitative controls

Lack of balanced scorecard measures

Certain qualitative controls suggested by the balanced scorecard do not appear to be operating, suggesting that qualitative controls will be ineffective, particularly in addressing the risks of losing customers. There seem to be **no attempt to measure business processes** that have the greatest impact on customer satisfaction such as employee performance when dealing with customers. EWC also does not appear to measure what actually matters to customers, for example **customer complaints** and how they are dealt with, or **speed of delivery**. There is also **no mention** of **measuring the quality of supplier's performance**.

Reward mechanisms

The reward mechanisms of bonuses and share options reflect the company's objectives, and **do little to encourage ethical**, **congruent behaviour** as these factors are not taken into account. Arguably they consist of a mix of short-term rewards (bonuses) and longer-term rewards (share options), which make it more likely that successful staff will stay longer. However the **value of share options** is limited at present as EWC is unlisted and there is no ready market for the shares.

Role of non-executive director

Lastly non-executive directors can have an important role in **monitoring strategic development and operations** and **improving the control environment**. The fact that EWC is appointing non-executive directors, when it need not do so as an unlisted company, is a strength. However the corporate governance reports state that non-executive directors need to constitute a **strong and independent body** on the board if they are to be truly effective. A single non-executive director is unlikely to be able to insist on improvements in business ethics. Non-executive directors may **not also be able to obtain assurance about the truth and fairness of the accounts** if the information systems are unreliable.

22 Preparation question: Role of internal audit

Text references. Chapter 7.

Top tips. In (a) try to think of the role of internal audit in your own organisations or other organisations you have worked for. Corporate governance requirements suggest or require listed companies to establish an internal audit function, and an important duty of the internal audit function will be to check compliance with other corporate governance requirements. Remember also risk management covers wider areas than that the standard audit risk model. Internal audit has a key role here in helping management identify, prioritise, assess and deal with risks, and align risk management with competing overall corporate objectives. Remember that internal audit should advise on the processes involved as well as performing the risk management exercise itself.

Outsourcing internal audit is very topical. You might also be asked about outsourcing other functions, for example the information technology function in this paper, or the treasury and financial control functions in the financial strategy paper.

Note the advantages and disadvantages can be considered under much the same headers. Obtaining specialist skills and cost issues will apply to outsourcing other areas; what is specific to internal audit is the need for independence and how the relationship between internal and external audit will work.

Easy marks. (a) is fairly straightforward, so if you couldn't think of much to say you need to go back and revise this area.

(a) **Role of internal audit**

(i) **Corporate governance**

Corporate governance is the **direction of companies**, usually done by the **directors**, in harness with an **audit committee** and other support staff. **Internal auditors** are a significant part of this as they improve accountability and provide a service of check on the functions of the company. Good corporate governance includes a system of **organisational control** and risk management, both of which are discussed more below. Internal audit has a significant role in both areas.

Example

Internal auditors are likely to have a significant role in assessing the major risks the company faces, whether systems and controls are sufficient to address those risks providing greater assurance to stakeholders that the company is managed well.

(ii) **Risk management**

Internal auditors have a role in the **wider risk management** that the directors are charged to undertake as part of good corporate governance. The internal auditors are likely to have a **monitoring role**, to ensure that a risk management policy operates and that employees responsible for **assessing risks** do so on a **timely** basis. Internal audit are also likely to be involved in **providing data** to assess where risks arise and helping to assess risks. They are also likely to be consulted when internal controls are developed to **manage risks**, or as a minimum to assess the controls developed and comment on whether they achieve the risk management objectives.

Example

In a manufacturing company, the areas which risk arises could be assessed in terms of **operational, financial, health and safety**, or other regulatory issues. Internal audit can check the evidence that the company has complied with health and safety requirements.

(iii) **Organisational control**

Traditionally, internal auditors have been involved in organisational control in their activities related to internal controls. They may be involved in the development of these (as discussed above) and also in checking that they **operate effectively** and **achieve company objectives**.

Example

In a manufacturing company, controls should exist over all areas of operation. For example, the company should have controls over the **dispatch of inventory**, in order to ensure that the correct goods are sent to the correct customers who are invoiced for those goods. Such controls would include the use of goods outwards notes and the matching of inventory to invoice and/or order details. The internal auditors, on a routine basis, will conduct tests to ensure that the **controls put into place achieve the objective**. They would observe the system in operation, or select a sample of copy goods outwards notes and ensure that they have been marked by the person despatching to show that goods were checked to invoice and order and that it was signed at the point of delivery.

(b) **Role of internal audit**

As highlighted in (a), the role of internal audit has in recent times been extended.

- Internal controls
- Risk management
- IT strategy and process
- Best Value
- Investigations

This increase in the potential role of the internal auditor has perhaps been behind the trend to outsource the department to the major accountancy firms. The growing popularity of outsourcing suggests that in the main, the disadvantages are outweighed by the advantages. Both are considered in more detail below.

Advantages of outsourcing internal audit

Procuring skill

An advantage of outsourcing is that the company can procure a **high level of skill**, which it might not be able to bring permanently into its business. Outsourced internal auditors are likely to be involved in a number of different businesses, and this **variety** will add to their skills. In house auditors are not in a position to have such variety to call upon, as they are tied to the business which employs them. The firm to which it is outsourced is likely also to use the **best techniques** as that is their business.

Relationship to the company

As outsourced internal auditors are not employed by the company they bring a degree of **independence** to the task which it is impossible for employees of the company to bring. This may enable them to view any issues arising more clearly. It also eliminates the possibility of such issues as internal auditors having difficulty in conducting their task due to **familiarity and personal relationships** with other staff.

As the service has been contracted out, the company has a degree of **legal protection** over the quality of the service. The company is protected against negligent work, for example, to the degree that it can be **compensated** for it, which is not the case if the work is carried out by employees.

Relationship to external audit

The firm providing the service may or may not be the firm that provides external audit services to the company. However, it is likely to be a firm that also specialises in external audit and this may produce **synergies** between the work performed. The auditors will be aware of the work required for the external audit and may ensure that they undertake work that could be used for the external audit. When conducting their **evaluation** of the **quality** of the work of internal audit, the external auditors are likely to be content to rely more on the work of staff of a reputable firm of accountants than might otherwise be the case.

Cost

Purchasing internal audit services means that the company can **focus** on what they want to gain from internal audit and purchase a focused service. It also means that internal audit may be used on a 'part-time' basis, for example, two days a week or four weeks a year, rather than having full time employees. Another consideration with regard to procuring skill is **cost**. It might be prohibitively expensive to buy in the degree of skill required permanently (in the form of an employee), whereas it is cheaper to hire the skill for shorter periods of time.

The fact that the service is being bought from a large organisation dedicated to providing auditing services might also mean that the company will benefit from the **economies of scale** which the service provider creates.

Disadvantages of outsourcing internal audit

Procuring skill

The industry the company is in may require that its internal auditor has **specialised** skills. If the audit is outsourced, and the provider does not have the skills which the company first thought, the cost of changing the service provider could be high, and the company may have lost staff who did possess the relevant skills.

Lack of flexibility

The relationship will be dominated by the contract between the two parties, which will mean that the contract needs to be drafted carefully in the first place and that a **lack of flexibility** may arise in the long term. It may not be possible, for example, under the contract to drop the current programme and conduct a specific investigation if circumstances which required that arose.

Employee morale

Company employees might feel threatened by being asked questions by outsiders, and the internal auditors might find it difficult to carry out their duties effectively or efficiently. Their independence might impose a sometimes **excessive formality**.

Control over internal audit

The audit committee and directors will in practical terms have **less control** over internal audit than they would have done if the department consisted of employees who were required to obey them. In the event of them being unhappy with the service, they might **only have recourse to legal action**, and this could prove costly, and have a detrimental effect on future relations.

Independence of external audit

If the directors of the company wish to use the same audit firm to provide their internal and external audit functions, the audit firm may feel that this would be a threat to their **ethical requirement of independence** as auditors. If the directors then used another firm for either service, this could lead to problems with their external auditors. If the firm determines that no ethical issue arises, it might still appear that the distinction between services is blurred and the **credibility of the audit report** might be affected. In certain jurisdictions, for example America under the Sarbanes-Oxley legislation, a listed company cannot employ the same firm as internal and external auditor.

23 Independence of internal audit

Text references. Chapter 7.

Top tips. Much of (a) relates to the **uncertainties** affecting internal audit. In theory anyone can act as an internal auditor and internal auditors have no statutory security of tenure. Importantly also internal auditors' work may stretch significantly beyond the areas of accounting records and controls in which the external auditors are primarily interested.

(b)-(c) discuss the practical aspects of independence and you should be able to describe the meaning of the term in that context. A good way to approach (b)(i) is to think of the ways in which operational departments can have contact with or influence internal audit. (b)(ii) brings out the important links between internal audit and the audit committee. The threat to independence is fundamental in (c).

Easy marks. Internal-external audit differences are basic knowledge for this area so (a) should have been straightforward.

(a) (i) **Eligibility to act**

External auditors

Under the law in most countries, a person is generally **ineligible** to act as **external** auditor if he is an **officer** or **employee** of the company, a **partner** or **employee** of such a person or a **partnership** in which such a person is a partner. An internal auditor is an employee of the company. External auditors must usually also belong to a **recognised supervisory body**, and this means they must hold an appropriate qualification, follow technical standards and maintain competence.

Internal auditors

By contrast **anyone** can act as an **internal** auditor even if they do not have a formal accounting qualification. It is up to the company's **management** who they appoint.

(ii) **Security of tenure**

External auditors

External auditors are **appointed** to hold office until the conclusion of the **next general meeting**. They can be **dismissed** by an **ordinary resolution of shareholders with special notice** in general meeting, and have the right to make **representations**. External auditors **cannot be dismissed by individual directors** or by a vote of the **board**. The only influence directors can have on the removal of external auditors is through their votes as shareholders. The rules on security of tenure are there because of the need for external auditors to protect the interests of shareholders by reporting on directors' stewardship of the business.

Internal auditors

By contrast, as **internal** auditors are employees of the company, they can be dismissed by the directors or lower level of **management**, subject only to their normal employment rights. The company may have **corporate governance** measures in place to improve the security of internal auditors (discussed further below).

(iii) **Primary objective and limitation on the scope of the audit work**

External auditors

The primary objective of **external** auditors is laid down by statute, to report on whether the company's accounts **show a true and fair view of the state of the company's affairs** at the period-end, and of its **profit or loss** for the period. External auditors are also required to report if certain other criteria have not been met, for example the company **fails to keep proper accounting records** or fails to make **proper disclosure of transactions** with directors. **Statutory rules** mean that management **cannot limit the scope of external auditors' work**. External auditors have the right of access to all a company's books and records, and can demand all the information and explanations they deem necessary.

Internal auditors

Internal auditors' objectives are **whatever** the company's **management decide** they should be. Some of the objectives may be similar to those of external audit, for example to confirm the quality of accounting systems. Other objectives might be in areas which have little or no significance to the external auditor, for example recommending improvements in economy, efficiency and effectiveness. As the objectives of internal audit's work are decided by management, **management** can also decide to **place limitations** on the scope of that work.

(b) (i) **Access and situation**

An internal auditor cannot have the same amount of independence as an external auditor. However, internal audit can be given various **powers and access** to senior managers which allow independent comment about the internal control of the business (or any matter under investigation). In particular, the following points will ensure a satisfactory level of independence within the organisation.

(1) **Role in operations**
Internal auditors should **not act** in any **operational capacity**, particularly at managerial level. They should be concerned *only* with the functioning and management of the internal audit department.

(2) **Control of department**
The internal audit department should **not be controlled** by any **operational managers**. It should be **controlled directly by the board** of directors or **audit committee**.

(3) **Scope of work**
No area of records, personnel or assets should be **closed** to the internal auditor. Any such restrictions would invalidate internal audit's full power of investigation.

(4) **Role of chief internal auditor**
Recruitment, training and other personnel matters within the internal audit department should be **dealt** with only by the **Chief Internal Auditor,** not by outside managers or the board.

(ii) There are two structures in which the internal audit department may operate.

(1) **Reporting to the board**

Even though not a voting board member, the internal auditor will report directly to the **full board**. This is far superior to reporting directly to line management or to the finance director or managing director, as it does not allow an individual manager or director to suppress or neglect an internal audit report.

(2) **Reporting to the audit committee**

The audit committee should consist entirely of independent non-executive directors, and thus internal audit will maintain the independence of his or her report.

This method is advantageous as it brings together people with great expertise in such control matters who have the **time to discuss them** without bias and outside any operating considerations. The committee will also be able to **advise internal audit** on procedures and further action and, because of its seniority, be able to persuade the board to **take action** on any matters raised by internal audit.

A further advantage of an audit committee is that it can act as a **forum for communication** between the various parties involved in financial control.

(c) **Independence**

In external auditing it is considered to be a **compromise of independence** to accept presents, discounts, bonuses or commissions from audit clients. In many ways this will also apply to the chief internal auditor, as an 'officer' of the board.

Reward

Conversely, the chief internal auditor is an employee of the company, which pays a salary to him or her already. As part of the internal control function, helping to **keep down costs and increase profitability**, surely the chief internal auditor should have a reward for adding to the profit of the business.

Conclusion

The problem remains that, if the chief internal auditor receives a bonus based on results, he or she may be tempted to **allow certain actions, practices or transactions** which should be stopped, but which are increasing the profit of the business, and therefore the bonus. The chief internal auditor's remuneration should not therefore be related to the company's profits; instead any bonus should be related to the performance of the internal audit department.

24 IA effectiveness

Text references. Chapter 7.

Top tips. (a) indicates how questions on internal audit will generally concentrate on the strategic and managerial implications of the function, and you must approach the question accordingly.

In (b) you need to state that internal audit's independence must not suffer as a result of the function being audited. One way of ensuring this is the involvement of the audit committee; the corporate governance reports demonstrate that the audit committee and internal audit should be complementary functions.

In (c) a key element of the process is setting objectives.

The hints given in the question about internal audits being expensive, slow and ineffective should have meant your answer to (d) was a discussion of the information needed to assess internal audit's performance on a VFM basis. You need to consider costs and resource usage weighed against benefits, as you would for other aspects of the control system. This is probably the toughest part of the question, but if you scored well in the other parts you would not have needed many marks on it. The headers in (d) are the areas that need to be assessed.

Easy marks. (a) is a fairly basic discussion of what internal audit does.

Examiner's comments. A good answer should have brought in knowledge of the use of VFM audit to assess services in the private sector; the way corporate governance guidance has increased the importance of internal audit; and the guidance given in the question, particularly the emphasis on *effectiveness*.

REPORT

To: Chairman
From: Finance Director
Date: 20 July 20X4
Subject: Effectiveness of the Internal Audit Department (IAD)

(a) **Objectives of internal audit**

Role of internal audit

Internal audit is an **independent appraisal function** established by the management of an organisation for the **review** of the **internal control system** as a service to the organisation. It objectively examines, evaluates and reports on the adequacy of internal control as a contribution to the **proper**, **economic**, **efficient and effective use of resources**. It is an internal control therefore and, like all internal controls, it should be assessed for effectiveness. This appears to be a suitable time for such an investigation.

Review of controls

One aspect of internal audit's work is certainly to **review and report on the adequacy and effectiveness of an organisation's internal controls** The review of controls should cover accounting controls and non-financial controls, controls that ensure compliance with external laws and regulations and internal policies.

Contribution to organisational effectiveness

Internal audit's role should also **contribute** to **overall organisational effectiveness,** by, as the Institute Of Internal Auditors have commented, 'assisting members of the organisation in the effective discharge of their responsibilities...(and furnishing) them with analyses, appraisals, recommendations, counsel and information'. This aspect of internal audit's work will cover recommendations for improvements in the organisation's information systems or its utilisation of resources.

(b) **Who should carry out the assessment?**

Audit committee

The IAD must **maintain** its **independence** from those parts of the organisation which it audits (ie most of the operations of the business). This independence must be maintained when the IAD is itself the subject of the audit for the sake of future IAD audits, and to obtain an objective result in this case. This criteria would exclude me as Finance Director. Other members of the board might be appropriate investigators, but the prime candidate would be a member of the **Audit Committee** (AC) as the IAD acts as almost an executive arm of the committee. A member of the AC with appropriate knowledge and experience would be required.

Another IAD

Alternatives to the AC which we might consider include the **IAD of another company**, which might be approached through contacts of our executive directors. Confidentiality might be an issue here; we would need to make sure that the other company was not a competitor etc.

External audit

Another option would be to use our own **external auditors**. If they were happy with our IAD, then future co-operation between the two sets of auditors might produce a saving in the external audit fee. However, if they were unhappy with the work of our IAD then the external auditors may decide that they need to perform extra audit work in future, and **fees might then rise**.

I do not feel it is appropriate for me to decide who should carry out the investigation of IAD: this is a decision which should be made by the board.

(c) **Detailed work**

Audit objectives

Like any other audit, a management audit involves deciding the **audit objectives** (which managers to audit, what aspects of their work and so on), carrying out an investigation, gathering evidence and reporting the results. The objectives are very important: they must be positive, to encourage co-operation in the IAD staff. The objectives will determine exactly what information is required, but at the least IAD files and reports will be accessed. This will require **explanation and comment** from members of the IAD. Samples will be taken of the IAD's work as it will not be possible to examine all of it.

Collection of information

Information, both written and oral, will also be **collected** from those **outside** the IAD, including the external auditors, the board members of the AC and the operational staff audited by the IAD. In the case of the latter, given the nature of the work, the weight of their evidence will have to be judged according to the level of criticism raised against them by the IAD in the past. In all cases the information collected should be properly recorded, and the documents collected and created should be controlled. This is a sensitive audit, so working papers should remain confidential and kept secure at all times.

(d) **Information required**

Value for money

The audit will seek to determine whether the IAD operates:

(i) **Economically**, producing the appropriate quantity and quality of work at lowest cost
(ii) **Efficiently**, using minimum resources for the quality and quantity of service provided and
(iii) **Effectively**, achieving its set objectives

Comparisons are important for VFM audits. However, it may be difficult to obtain any **industry averages**. Two possible sources are non-executive directors who can gain information on IADs in other companies; and bodies regulating auditing, for example the Institute of Internal Auditors. In addition, **information over time** needs to be collected, again for comparative purposes. Such data should be both quantitative and non-quantitative.

Detailed information

(i) **General set up of the IAD**
This will involve investigating the **structure** of the IAD; what **work** the IAD has been asked to carry out (routine vs specials); **who requests** work to be done; **who receives IA reports**.

(ii) **Resources used by IAD**

The resources used by the IAD should be quantified: **staff**, **equipment** (computers etc), **training**. It should be relatively easy to compare such costs with industry data.

(iii) **Utilisation**

How well is the IAD **utilising** these **resources**? Is training undertaken in slack periods? Are IA staff sitting around the office too much?

(iv) **IA procedures**

The methods and procedures used by IAD to carry out investigations should be examined. Does the IAD use **standardised procedures** and **documentation**? Are **files up to date and well maintained**? Is **staff time recorded accurately and compared to budgets**? Are **audits completed in time and to budget**? Are **review procedures appropriate and effective**?

(v) **Report effectiveness**

The efforts of the IAD must be in vain if the reports **do not reach the appropriate decision-makers**. They in turn must **take action** based on the IAD reports. Assessment is also needed whether, as a result of IAD investigations, **costs** have been **reduced** (including external audit costs).

I hope that this report has provided a good starting point for an assessment of the IAD function and I suggest that you pass it to the Audit Committee with your comments.

Signed: Finance Director

25 CFB

Text references. Chapter 7 covers audit risk, Chapter 2 describes the likelihood-consequences matrix. Chapter 8 covers sampling.

Top tips. (a) focuses on audit risk. You therefore need to remember the definition of audit risk when approaching the answer.

Your answer needs at least to state the likelihood / consequences (frequency/severity) matrix before applying this to CFB. The scenario provides four situations that will no doubt correspond to the four sections of the matrix. For each section of the answer, you should explain audit risk, and then take part of the scenario to show how the internal audit department approaches that risk. You also need to conclude with some comment on how the company should also manage the risk.

Be careful not to be sidetracked into explaining risk from the external audit perspective. Remember, internal audit has a much wider remit than external auditors. Risk analysis is very important in setting priorities and will cover many different areas.

(b) indicates what you are most likely to be asked about sampling; you won't be asked to use one of the sampling methods to select a sample.

Easy marks. You should score well on (b), as this is fairly basic knowledge that does not need to be related to the detail in the scenario.

(a) **Audit risks** can be ranked according to how likely those risks are to occur and the potential consequences of a risk should they occur as shown in the table below.

		Severity (consequences)	
		High	*Low*
Frequency (likelihood)	*High*	Reduce or Avoid	Control systems
	Low	Transfer or reduction	Accept as insignificant

Likelihood High : Consequence High

The risk should be **managed by extensive audit testing**.

Example

This risk is relevant to the **audit of the computer systems** in CFB. There is a **high likelihood of audit risk** occurring because of the **complicated nature of the computer systems** themselves and the fact that amendments are made on an apparently ad hoc basis. The internal auditor could easily reach the wrong opinion in an internal audit report because the systems may not be understood, recorded incorrectly or not sufficiently well tested before implementation that standard audit tests would fail to detect a material error. The **consequence of the incorrect report** could be that **reliance is placed on the computerised systems** when it should not be.

Risk management

The **risk** will need to be **managed** by **eliminating it as far as possible**. Internal audit staff should have sufficient skill and knowledge on auditing computer systems, and appropriate techniques such as computer audit software should be used to audit the computer system. The internal auditor will also need to **recommend that appropriate control systems are put in place to prevent risks materialising**. These systems will range from controls over the input of data into the systems, to appropriate backup facilities should the computer system fail.

Likelihood High : Consequence Low

The risk still needs to be **managed by audit testing**, although there can be a **greater emphasis on the company putting appropriate controls in place**. Audit testing will also be at a lower level than for high consequence situations simply because the effect on the company is reduced if the internal audit report is incorrect.

Example

For example, part of the work of the internal audit department is auditing cash sales. There is a **high likelihood of audit risk** occurring in this area simply because **cash is an asset that can be removed from a company easily**. However, CFB receives only **4% of its total income in cash**, so the **consequence of an error in cash is relatively small**. The company would lose some money, but given that fraud would be limited to a small percentage of the total cash income, then overall loss would be minimal.

Risk management

The internal audit department would carry out **specific tests** such as ensuring that the cash received on any one day in the cash sales office agreed to the till roll and then to the bank statements showing deposit of that cash. **Internal controls** would also be **recommended** to try and ensure that cash was not stolen such as cash being counted by two people to prevent one person removing money, and cash being banked by staff not responsible for sales to introduce appropriate segregation of duties.

Likelihood Low : Consequence High

The risk can be **managed** in various ways including **limited testing** or effectively **transferring that risk**.

The fact that audit risk is low implies that that there is a **low risk** that an internal audit report will **provide an incorrect conclusion on a specific area**. The risk could be managed by **transference** – that is accepting the work of other specialists with internal audit simply monitoring those reports.

However, the fact that the consequence of an **incorrect conclusion is high** (here a fall in consumer confidence) means **some work must still be carried out**. If the audit report is wrong, then significant damage could result to the company as incorrect reliance would be placed on that report.

Example

The audit of the operations of CFB provides a good example of this situation. There is a low likelihood of any of CFB's products being sold where the quality is poor because the quality control department regularly samples products, and the internal audit department monitors overall quality from initial input to final output of drinks. However, because quality control testing is limited, it is still possible for internal audit to identify

potentially poor quality of product from production data but quality control to miss this. It would then be up to internal audit to ask for additional checking.

Risk management

Internal audit work on quality control means that the **quality control process is monitored,** with **reliance being placed on the quality control department**. However, where quality control is limited or the other review indicates a fall in product quality then internal audit must take action.

Likelihood Low : Consequence Low

Appropriate action for internal audit may be simply to **monitor these areas** of the company and provide very **restrictive reporting** on them at all because they are insignificant.

Example

For example, the mixing vats in CFB are **cleaned thoroughly** every three weeks with the discharge being sent into the normal sewer system.

Risk management

Given that the internal audit department has to monitor the effect of CFB's operations on the environment, then this **activity could be checked** to ensure that no harmful chemicals are being released. However, as CFB manufactures fruit drinks, even if a large amount of ingredient was released by accident, it would be **unlikely that any significant environmental damage** would result. The consequence of any over release of product is therefore low – no environment is likely to be affected.

(b) **Purpose of testing**

The purpose of testing is to **test the functioning of the control** on which it has been decided to rely and not the transaction which is the medium of the test. Hence where errors are discovered the monetary value is irrelevant. It is the fact that the error has occurred (and that the control may not be functioning properly) that is important.

(i) **Selection of items**

Items for testing can be **selected** using **random**, **systematic** or **haphazard selection** of the sample. The first two methods are more acceptable as the question of bias in selection is eliminated.

(ii) **Number of items**

The number of items that will be tested will be dependent on the following factors.

(1) **Audit risk** – the sample size will be dependent on the degree of reliance to be placed on a test of control and the assessment of control risk. A high degree of reliance will increase the sample size whilst a low assessment of control risk will reduce it.

(2) **Tolerable error rate** – the higher the rate the lower the sample size.

(3) **Expected error rate** – if errors are expected a larger sample will be needed to ensure the tolerable error rate is not exceeded.

(iii) **Evaluation of errors**

If **errors are found** in testing, they should be **evaluated**. If they all relate to one control, the test may be extended or another control identified upon which reliance can be placed. This would need to be tested in the same way. Alternatively controls may not be relied on if it is felt to be more efficient and effective from an audit point of view to reduce audit risk by extending substantive tests.

26 Governance systems

Text references. Chapters 5-7

Top tips. The lack of a scenario means that you do not have to apply the question to a specific organisation. You are asked to discuss, implying you need to cover the points in reasonable depth.

Control systems theory helps in (a) and you can also generate ideas by remembering internal audit doesn't just check whether controls are operating; it should go deeper and question whether those controls remain appropriate.

These ideas are echoed in (b), with the audit committee not only considering the work internal audit has done (ie how that control has operated) but also whether internal audit as a control is effective. The concepts of independence and authority are key influences on effectiveness.

In (c) the main roles of the audit committee were identified in the Cadbury report. Each paragraph of the answer begins by stating an aspect of good governance as defined in the various reports. We then show how the audit committee contributes to that aspect, stressing that the committee members' position as directors should give them the knowledge and authority to look particularly at strategic and management controls.

Judging by the examiner's comments, a lot of students did not score well on this question. It is likely that they saw it as the easiest question on the paper, and just treated it as a braindump of all they knew about internal audit and the audit committee. The question requirements are specific and you need to pick these up to answer the question well:

- In (a) every paragraph needs to show how internal audit improves internal audit
- In (b) every paragraph should demonstrate how the audit committee enhances internal audit
- In (c) every paragraph should relate to a major aspect of corporate governance and how the audit committee contributes to better governance performance in that area.

Easy marks. If you have revised internal audit and corporate governance well, then all of this question should be fairly straightforward if you fulfil the question requirements.

Examiner's comments. Answers were often far too general, with many students listing the roles of the audit committee without connecting them to corporate governance or internal audit effectiveness. Students must read questions carefully and answer in accordance with the requirements of the question.

(a) **Role of internal audit**

Internal audit has been defined as an **independent appraisal function** established within an organisation to examine and evaluate its activities as a service to the organisation. **Feedback** is a vital element in control systems. The feedback internal audit provides should result in modifications either to the internal control systems or to the behaviour of those operating them.

Review of control design

Internal audit should not merely accept the control systems in place; part of their role will be to **assess the design of control systems** and consider whether they are appropriate. This will be particularly important when **systems are changing**; internal audit's opinion should be sought at every stage of information systems development. Internal audit should also assess whether **information systems**, **organisation structure** and **risk management systems** have **evolved** as necessary in response to changes in business circumstances and particularly risks.

Review of control operation

Internal audit also should be reviewing whether controls are actually operating effectively. One aspect of this is whether controls are operating in the way that they are meant to do. This review is particularly important when staff failure to operate controls could result in **significant loss** to the business; if for example staff are not following **asset security procedures**.

Review of control effectiveness

Internal audit should also consider whether **controls are operating as well as they could be**, for example whether risk management processes have **identified major risks** or **information communication** has been **effective**.

Recommendations for improvements

The improvements internal audit recommend should **be of value and be cost effective**, resulting in **controls being improved** and **operated more effectively**. Internal audit results also provide a **benchmark** against which other data can be judged; the level of bad debts can be compared with internal audit reports on the operation of credit control procedures. Internal audit also provides **information to the board and audit committee**, assisting them in **reviewing regularly the adequacy and effectiveness of internal control systems**.

(b) **Independence of internal audit**

There are obvious threats to the **independence** of many internal auditors which may cast doubts on the **robustness of their work**. Internal auditors may be concerned about reporting on the activities supervised by the finance director who is their ultimate boss.

The audit committee can take various steps to **protect the position of the head of internal audit** and thus the whole department. The head of internal audit should **report to the audit committee**. The audit committee can also review the steps for **guaranteeing the independence of internal auditors**; the committee should ensure that sufficient internal guidance exists to, for example, stop **internal auditors auditing their own work** and ensure **regular rotation of audit staff over operational functions**.

Forum for liaison

Internal auditors' work will be enhanced by strong relations with the external auditors. The audit committee can provide a **forum for liaison** between internal and external audit. Some reports recommend regular meetings between auditors and audit committee without any executive directors being present, as these are a good forum to **raise concerns**.

Direction of internal audit work

The work carried out by internal audit is dependent on the needs of the organisation, and the audit committee needs to ensure that its **work** is **well directed**. The audit committee should **review the workplan for the year** to ensure that there is adequate coverage of key areas such as **safeguarding of assets** and **quality of information systems**.

Review of internal audit work

Internal auditors should **report the results of their work to the audit committee**. As audit committee members are **independent non-executives**, they can take an objective view of the results. As directors also, they are in a position to insist that the **recommendations** of internal auditors are **actioned**; they should **review the responsiveness of executive management to internal audit findings**.

Review of internal audit function

In common with other controls, governance reports recommend that the effectiveness of internal audit will be enhanced by an **annual review** that considers its costs and benefits, and whether it is addressing risks effectively. The audit committee should carry out this review of internal audit. It will be aware of internal audit's activities, and is again in a position to push for changes in its **terms of reference**. It should also consider the **role and effectiveness of the internal audit function** as part of the risk management systems.

(c) **Role of audit committee**

Review of risk management

The Turnbull committee recommends that to manage the business effectively, the board must **review the risks facing the business**. The audit committee is in a good position to help ensure that this review is effective, using its own knowledge of the business to determine whether **risk management is evolving** in line with changes in risks. It should also examine the **overall controls** that ensure everyone is aware of risk, the existence of a **formal policy** and training arrangements for staff.

Monitor internal control

Monitoring of controls is a key component of good control systems. The audit committee has a very significant role in monitoring control systems. As directors, they will be in a good position to judge the **controls exercised by executive management**, **executive management's attitude towards controls** and the **control environment they are promoting**. The audit committee may take a more active look at **control areas of particular concern to stakeholders**, such as controls that ensure compliance with legal requirements and ethics. The committee can also be available to employees who wish to **whistleblow** on questionable practices.

Improve the quality of financial reporting

The corporate governance codes have stressed the importance of accounts as a means of communicating with shareholders, and stated that accounts should show a **balanced and understandable view of a company's position**. The audit committee can help ensure accounts do this by reviewing the contents of the published accounts, focusing on certain key features such as the **overall appearance and presentation of the accounts**, **key accounting policies**, **major areas of judgement** and **compliance with corporate governance codes**. This review will be enhanced if the audit committee includes at least one member with **significant and recent financial experience**.

Review information systems

To gain assurance about the **reliability of the financial accounts**, the audit committee also needs to **review the information systems** that generate those accounts. The review of information systems should also cover their **adequacy as a basis for board decision-making**; do the **performance indicators** show how business risks are being addressed, for example.

Liaison with external audit

Corporate governance reports have highlighted the role of the external auditor in helping to **guarantee to shareholders the quality of financial information**. The audit committee can help **enhance the quality of external audit**. The committee can assist by ensuring that external auditors have all the **information they need**, and the audit committee being available for the external auditors to **raise concerns** that they have. The audit committee should also take a questioning role to the work of external audit, considering whether its **scope is appropriate** and whether there are any **threats to external auditor independence**, particularly the **provision of non-audit services**. The committee should review the work carried out, considering the **judgements** made and **obtaining internal feedback** on the quality of the audit.

27 HIJ

Text references. Chapter 6 gives general guidance on internal controls and Chapter 4 will help with the management accounting aspects. Chapter 7 discusses the approach to different types of audit.

Top tips. Success in this question depends on using your imagination to make the most of the limited data available. (a) asks for management controls; because of the small size of the company the Principal will have to implement most of the controls himself rather than rely on others. There are various ways in which you could group the controls; our broad headings relate to environmental and organisational controls, performance measurement controls and asset protection controls.

To achieve good marks, you need some explanation of each control as you are making recommendations, but it is important also to cover a range of controls. The examiners have stressed the need to cover financial, non-financial but quantitative and qualitative controls. If you define and recommend each control well, you could probably score a couple of marks for each, so would need six controls to score the maximum twelve marks.

(b) requires careful reading. The main point of the question is not a description of various types of audit, but discussion why they are necessary. The areas that will be chosen for audit are those where the risk of loss is high or there may be serious consequences if problems occur. You could have assumed that the organisation was too small for an external audit to be compulsory, in which case you should have suggested that assurance on financial risk management needs to be sought in other ways. There are other different classifications of audit you could have used, such as internal and external, quality and systems. As with (a), you would probably gain two marks for a good discussion of each type of audit so you would need four different types.

Note in (c) that benefits can be classified as positive benefits or means of reducing risks/avoiding losses. For costs your answer needs to mention direct financial costs and opportunity costs.

Easy marks. The discussion of cost-benefits in (c) covers the considerations that you would normally cover on cost-benefit questions.

Examiner's comments. Again many students failed to apply their knowledge to the scenario, with some suggesting an internal audit department (which was unrealistic given the size of the company), others suggested that all expenses over £2 be approved. 'Reading the scenario and planning a sensible answer bearing in mind the organisation in the question would be a huge benefit to candidates.'

In (a) some answers failed to discuss management controls, in (b) some answers just listed the various types of audit rather than using the scenario to discuss the need for audits in terms of the risks identified.

(a) **Exercise of controls**

The small size of the organisation means it is likely that the Principal will operate most of the controls himself, although he will use the support staff to assist him.

Environment and organisational controls

How effective the control environment is and the organisational controls are will be very dependent on the Principal. He will be responsible for **setting standards** (and example) of **client care** and **cost consciousness**, and the **organisational structure** depends on his active involvement, as staff will report into him. If he is busy with marketing activity, it may be appropriate to **delegate certain responsibilities** to another senior member of staff such as guiding newer members of staff.

Budgets and comparison with actual data

Budgets should be prepared annually, and also amended to take account of changes in staff and client based. The following elements will be particularly important:

(i) **Chargeable hours targets** for staff
(ii) **Income and hours targets** for clients
(iii) **Major expenses** including staff salaries, marketing, travel and office upkeep

The Principal should **compare budgeted and actual figures** monthly for hours and income targets, less frequently for less regular expenditure. The Principal should take appropriate action if there are **variances** (counselling staff who are not reaching their chargeable hour targets, using budgeted vs actual data when establishing fees).

Balanced scorecard

Using a balanced scorecard approach should mean using a **variety of indicators** and thinking in terms of **perspectives** across the whole organisation.

(i) **Customer** – measures include **number of new clients won through marketing activity**, whether **any clients have been lost** and **feedback received** at the Principal's meetings with Managing Directors, also the results of **quality reviews** carried out by the Principal.

(ii) **Internal** – measures include **chargeable hours as a percentage of total hours, average charge-out rate** per hour and **comparisons of time spent on each client**, also **deadlines** for producing information are met.

(iii) **Innovation and training** – this can be judged by the **labour turnover rate**, also the **new or improved services** offered to clients.

(iv) **Financial** – apart from total revenues, earnings, cash flow and return on capital employed indicators, other measures include percentage of clients that have not **been profitable**.

Debtor management

Billing must be kept up on a monthly basis, and **credit periods** established as part of the **annual negotiations.** Slow payers should be chased in a series of stages, and these should include **stopping Principal and staff visits** until the debts are paid.

Human resource management

Clearly the employees of HIJ are a key asset and controls are needed over the lifetime of their employment. Recruitment controls should include **references** and also an **interview process** that provides evidence of the **knowledge and communication skills** required. **Training** should include **induction processes** for all new staff and a **personal development programme**. **Remuneration levels** should be influenced by the staff member's success in meeting client profitability and chargeable hours targets. **Employment contracts** should include clauses that prevent staff poaching HIJ's clients if they move elsewhere.

Knowledge management

Human resource management is a key part of knowledge management but there are other issues including **transfer and retention of knowledge.** There should be **specific guidance on the level of detail** that needs to be recorded about each client, and also about the need for **regular updating** of information. Whenever staff are introduced to clients, there should be an **induction process** to ensure they have sufficient knowledge to deal satisfactorily with the clients.

(b) **Need for audit**

Audit work should focus on areas where there is a high risk of loss or serious consequences if risk crystallises, or areas (particularly in dealings with clients) where value could be added.

As the Principal is a qualified accountant, he could carry out internal audit work himself, but given his already extensive role in control, it is difficult to see how additional work by himself will add value, and so the audit should be carried out by external auditors or consultants (the company is too small to warrant an internal audit function).

Financial audit

As cost control is a key priority, audit work needs to cover financial controls. However whether a separate audit is required is doubtful, as assurance can be gained from the work done by the external auditors.

The external auditors will be concerned with the **recoverability of receivables**, and hence will examine the **credit control procedures.** They will also be concerned with the **validity of expenditure,** so will check by reviewing documentation that the expenditure by the Principal and staff is for **business purposes.** Their analytical review should highlight **discrepancies in numerical information**, for example variations in figures between accounting periods, differences between sources of internal data.

Management audit

A management audit is an appraisal of the **effectiveness of managers** and the corporate structure in the achievement of entity and corporate objectives. As there is no effective internal review of the Principal's own role, an **external review by management consultants** will be necessary to highlight any areas of potential weakness. Areas might include:

- **Supervision**. Is the Principal exercising **sufficient supervision** over other staff; are the reviews of their work regular enough and have problems been identified early?
- **Information**. Is the Principal being given sufficient **timely information**?
- **Delegation**. Would management be more **effective** if the Principal **delegated** some of his work to a senior staff member?
- **Decisions**. Do the **judgments** that the Principal has made appear reasonable?

- **Principal's work**. What is the **quality of the Principal's own work** in advising clients in terms of the contents of reports?

Marketing audit

As marketing activity is central to HIJ's expansion, and much of the Principal's time is spent on it, an independent review will provide assurance of its **effectiveness.** A marketing specialist will be able to bring in knowledge of the sector to judge the **activity** at conferences and the **effectiveness of the brochures and advertising** as methods of communication.

Computer security audit

Loss of confidential information could be very serious for HIJ in terms of the **financial compensation** it may have to pay and **loss of reputation**. An independent check on the **robustness of security controls** will be valuable. Other key areas where an IT audit may add value is the **quality of output and adequacy of back-up procedures**.

(c) **Benefits**

Benefits of internal controls will include fulfilment of the objectives established by the Principal including:

- **Cost control**
- All **clients being profitable**
- **Improved chargeable hours of staff**

Other benefits include:

- **Reduced losses through computer or security problems**
- **Bad debts**
- **No loss of clients or key staff**
- Having **motivated staff** working to their full potential
- Producing **reliable financial information**

Costs

There will be costs involved in establishing most of the controls in (a), for example setting up **information sources for the balanced scorecard**. Ongoing costs include **monies paid** to anyone supplying a **control function**, for example a dedicated credit controller or internal auditor, or **fees** paid to an external auditor for services supplied. There may also be costs in **maintaining back-up computer facilities.**

Opportunity costs will include the loss of the **Principal's time**; his **chargeable hours** and hence **fee-earning capacity** will be **reduced** by the time he has to spend on internal controls. There are also the losses involved in diverting other staff to operate controls and away from more profitable activities.

28 Subcontracting services

Text references. Chapter 3 covers organisational issues including a general discussion of outsourcing; outsourcing computer services is covered in detail in Chapter 17. Internal audit is discussed generally in Chapter 7.

Top tips. This question looks at different aspects of the problems of business expansion. (a) examines the issues involved in sub-contracting services, which has become increasingly common in both the private and public sectors. It can be a way of reducing managerial problems in a period of expansion, as well as a possible way of reducing cost in a recession.

The important distinction in (b) is between what should be controlled if the service is provided internally (ie segregation of duties, cash security, etc), and externally (where the key judgement is made at the tendering stage).

Easy marks. You should be able to discuss advantages and disadvantages of outsourcing as these will feature regularly in the P3 exam.

Examiner's comments. Answers to (b) were very weak and they tended to discuss a wide range of irrelevant issues.

(a) REPORT

To: The Board
From: Finance Director
Date: 10 September 20X4
Subject: Sub-contracting services

One possible way of dealing with increased volumes of business without recruiting extra staff is to **contract out** some activities that are presently done in-house.

Advantages and disadvantages

Advantages

(i) **Time**
It would free up time taken by existing staff on these activities. It would also **free up time spent supporting these services** by staff not directly involved, for example supervisory staff, personnel staff. There would also be no need to provide facilities for the service to be performed.

(ii) **Expertise**
It would allow the company to take advantage of **specialist expertise and equipment** rather than investing in these facilities itself and underutilising them. If the contractor is judiciously chosen it is likely that the service will be performed more quickly and to a higher standard than is currently the case.

(iii) **Cost**
It may be **cheaper**, once time savings and opportunity costs are taken into account.

(iv) **Flexibility**
It is particularly appropriate when an organisation is **attempting to expand in a time of uncertainty**. It allows the use of facilities on a short-term (readily cancelled) basis which would only otherwise be available via the relatively long-term investments of a permanent employee and the training he or she requires. In other words it is a way of gaining all the benefits of extra capacity without having to find the full cost.

Disadvantages

(i) **Quality of service**
Without monitoring there is **no guarantee that the service will be performed to the organisation's satisfaction**. There may be penalty clauses built into the contract for poor performance, but financial compensation will not necessarily undo the damage caused. However, if a contract has to be too closely monitored this weakens the argument for contracting out in the first place.

(ii) **Cost**
There is a good chance that **contracting out will be more expensive** than providing the service in-house.

(iii) **Loss of skills**
By performing services itself the organisation retains or develops skills that may be needed in the future and will otherwise be lost.

(iv) **Risks to data**
Contracting out any aspect of information handling carries with it the possibility that **commercially sensitive data will get into the wrong hands.** The contractor will not be able to guarantee absolute security.

(v) **Ethics**

There may be some **ethical reservations**. For example, contract cleaning companies are notorious for exploiting staff, offering inadequate pay and poor conditions. There may even be legal problems: a few years ago the UK Home Office found that it had to dispense with the services of a cleaning company because all of its employees were illegal immigrants!

(vi) **Employee reaction**

There will almost certainly be **opposition from employees** and their representatives if contracting out involves redundancies.

Criteria for selection

There are three main criteria for selection of a service to be contracted out.

(i) **Core activities**

Whether the organisation sees the activity in question as one that is part of its 'core business'. Most organisations do not see the ability to clean offices as one of their main objectives and this is why this service is so commonly contracted out.

(ii) **Cost**

The relative costs (staff, equipment and premises compared with the cost of the service), and **relative benefits** (in-house capabilities compared with external specialisms).

(iii) **Problems**

How serious the **risks or consequences of mistakes** are.

These may be illustrated by the areas in particular that have been suggested for comment.

(i) **Legal services**

Nature of work

Legal services such as handling patents, trademarks and brands are probably **more specialised than a typical organisation's in-house legal experts** (such as accountants, company secretaries, or even the average company solicitor) would have the time or knowledge to handle. In addition these matters often **require the setting up and maintenance of extensive databases and libraries.**

Possible problems

The main problem with contracting out this sort of work is **confidentiality**, a particularly sensitive issue since new products will be the principal subject of the work.

Recommendation

Outsourcing may be the cheapest option. The benefit of having dedicated staff and facilities is likely to be far exceeded by the cost. The likelihood of **mistakes through lack of expertise** is high.

(ii) **Computing services**

Nature of work

Computing services may be contracted nature of work out to advantage where an organisation generates **large volumes of relatively simple processing** which can most effectively be done using **mainframe computers**. Only very large organisations can justify the investment in the computer equipment required. The power of PCs is now enormous, but they **still need staff to operate them** so that there *may* be an overall benefit in contracting out such work.

Possible problems

The **disadvantages** are that the **data** may then **not be available in a form useable** by the organisation's own database, for example for marketing purposes, and once again there may be worries about **confidentiality**.

Recommendation

In the particular case mentioned it is unlikely that **production scheduling** could be done effectively by those not directly in touch with production management. This, surely, is a **core activity of the business**. There may be a much **stronger case for sub-contracting ad hoc computing tasks**, such as systems development and maintenance, or training in the use of new software packages. Mistakes in such tasks can be very costly indeed.

(b) **Internal services**

Segregation of duties

A major concern of internal audit will be **segregation of duties**; internal audit needs to ensure that procedures laid down are reasonable and are being followed. In addition internal audit will be concerned with authorisation controls, which should complement segregation of duties.

Safeguarding of assets

A further concern will be **safeguarding of assets**. This particularly applies for any internal services (for example a staff shop) where significant amounts of cash are handled. Testing of cash receipts and payments is likely to be required.

Outsourced services

Segregation of duties

Internal audit will not generally be concerned with segregation of duties at the external supplier – this will be the responsibility of the external supplier's auditor. As regards authorisation, internal audit should consider procedures when the **supplier is chosen**, and **authorisation of payments** to the supplier.

Supplier choice

With outsourced services, the **choosing of the supplier becomes important**. Hence internal audit will need to check that the **tendering process** has been fair, and that there has been consideration of a range of options. Internal audit will need to consider whether the supplier appears to be a reasonable choice, and that the **terms** are **not unusual**. Once the supplier has been chosen, **authorisation of payments** will need to be checked in the same way that other payments would be checked.

Data controls

Internal audit will have to **consider controls exercised by the external suppliers over data if data processing is outsourced**. The internal auditors would be concerned with **controls over security** as indeed they would be if the service was provided in-house. They would also need to check the controls over the **transfer of data**.

29 New subsidiary

Text references. Chapters 6 and 7.

Top tips. Our answer to (a) focuses on the specific risks and is used as the basis for the initial audit in part (b). You should remember in part (b) that an initial audit should focus on the most serious potential problems. The results can be used as a basis for directing audit work in future years.

Important factors to consider include ensuring effective coverage of all the sites and the actions of managers. They have a lot of responsibility, and significant incentives to distort figures or to attempt to grow too quickly. (The comments about good inventory and generous credit hint at overtrading as well as highlighting specific problems in those areas.)

To score well in (b) you needed not only to discuss controls in specific areas, but also spend time looking at the general control environment, as this potentially is a major problem area here. The answer discusses a number of aspects of the control environment. You should note these carefully, as the examiner has highlighted recently that students do not seem to know what the control environment is, and be able to explain its significance.

Easy marks. The areas discussed in (a)(iii) will be significant on most accounting system audits; likewise, the controls discussed in (b) are normally fundamental.

Examiner's comments. Common faults in (a) were lack of depth and failing to make obvious points. In (b) many answers were too vague and showed a lack of understanding of the aims of the initial audit which should have been to concentrate on systems. Many candidates failed to realise the limits of an initial audit.

Generally many answers were disappointing, some answers displaying little more than rote learning. The question demanded case analysis skills and practical recommendations, as well as knowledge of the objectives of internal audit.

(a) The potential audit problems can be identified by using a **risk-based approach** which concentrates on certain features that the subsidiary has.

(i) **Business risks**

The **features of the market** the subsidiary operates in must be identified since it differs from the retail market in which the rest of the group operates. Although the subsidiary appears to be doing well, the **volatility** of the market should be assessed (would the subsidiary be seriously damaged by a recession in certain sections of the building trade for example?). The subsidiary may be particularly vulnerable because of its reliance on short-term finance.

(ii) **Client management**

An assessment of the **effectiveness of management** will be required. Key issues in this assessment are likely to be:

(1) **The effectiveness of the subsidiary's senior management team**
The fact that management team's remuneration will depend on results may mean there are **pressures to overstate profit**. The lack of detailed controls at head office means the importance of management supervision is enhanced.

(2) **Regional warehouse management**
The most significant issues will be whether monitoring of regional managers appears to mean **potential signs of fraud** can be **identified** quickly, and whether the controls exercised by regional management over their staff are likely to be effective.

(iii) **Accounts areas**

Which **balance sheet areas** are likely to be particularly **prone** to a risk of **material error** should be ascertained by a combination of **analytical review** and use of **knowledge** about the business already possessed. Areas that are likely to be material and important for most or all of the business are as follows.

(1) **Inventory**
Details of **inventory security and recording** procedures will be needed, and also **valuation** since the specialist nature of inventory may mean it is difficult to value.

(2) **Credit control**
The generous terms may mean it is not easy to identify bad debts, and hence **credit limit approval and payment procedures** (including follow-up) of overdue payments should be checked. In particular the consequences of the **largest customers defaulting** should be carefully considered.

(3) **Purchases**
Procedures for choosing suppliers should be confirmed, since although the terms the warehouses are obtaining appear to be good, the prices paid may not be the best available and there is certainly the possibility of collusion between the warehouse managers and suppliers. The warehouses operating abroad may mean there is an element of **exchange risk.**

(iv) **Audit management**

The new subsidiary may pose problems of **audit management** and I would need to identify these. The **independence** of the **regional warehouses** plus the doubts mentioned above about the subsidiary's management may mean it is desirable to **visit a significant proportion** of the warehouses fairly soon after the subsidiary is acquired. However the resources available to internal audit may mean this is difficult to arrange.

(v) **Audit programmes**

Audit programmes will also have to be **re-designed** to reflect the fact that the subsidiary is not selling to retail customers, and also to reflect major differences in the control environment and control procedures between the subsidiary and the rest of the group.

(b) **Aims of initial audit**

These will be to assess:

(i) The strength of the subsidiary's **control environment**
(ii) The **functioning** of **internal controls** and in particular whether assets are properly safeguarded

Both of these will obviously be influenced by the factors identified in (a).

Assessment of control environment

The most important elements of this assessment will be as follows.

(i) **Assessment of head office management**
Assessment would be needed of how head office management **set the tone** of the subsidiary as regards performance standards and commitment to ethical behaviour.

(ii) **Monitoring of warehouses**
Because the subsidiary does not exercise detailed controls at head office level, the procedures for **monitoring the performance** of warehouses would need to be examined. This will involve an assessment of the **management information systems** including how **detailed** the information provided is, how **regularly** it is provided, and what **action is taken if unusual items** are found.

(iii) **Monitoring of warehouse managers**
This will obviously be connected to monitoring of warehouses, but the effectiveness of certain specific controls should be checked because of the considerable autonomy warehouse managers possess. These include **recruitment and training procedures**, how the **performance** of warehouse managers is **assessed** (in particular the use of budgets) and procedures for appraising warehouse managers.

(iv) **Effectiveness of organisational structure**
Although on first glance the organisational structure appears to be uncomplicated (most authority devolved), **certain minimum checks** should be built into the system. These should include clear instructions about the **information** to be **communicated** to head office and which **decisions are reserved for head office management** (for example major asset expenditure). The **communication** of these controls should be checked. Consideration will also be needed of whether **too many responsibilities** are **devolved** upon regional warehouse managers with the result that certain controls which they should be operating fall into abeyance.

Testing of controls

The initial audit should concentrate on the most significant controls which are likely to be as follows.

(i) **Segregation of duties – safeguarding of assets**
This will be a very significant control as regards **safeguarding of assets**, because proper segregation **reduces the risk of collusion**.

(ii) **Segregation of duties – error reduction**

It will also be an important accounting control **reducing the risk of unintentional error** since more staff will be involved in recording the transaction. Segregation of duties is particularly important in the areas of stock, debtors and sales, purchasing, and between all these functions and accounting.

(iii) **Authorisation**

As considerable authority is given to the regional/warehouse managers, the initial audit should check that **transactions are being authorised** and that the managers' overall responsibilities are being exercised effectively.

(iv) **Asset protection**

The most important areas as indicated in (a) will most likely be controls over the **custody of inventory**, the **authorisation of credit terms** and **pursuit of overdue debts**, and **purchasing policies**.

(v) **Accounting systems**

Internal audit will have to record and assess whether the accounting systems **record transactions completely and accurately**.

Strategic audit planning

A final aim of the initial audit will be to use the findings as the basis for **strategic audit planning** of the subsidiary in future years. Regional warehouses may continue to enjoy the degree of autonomy that they do (the subsidiary after all does appear profitable). However this may mean that internal audit itself is an important control, and this will clearly impact on the extent of future audits.

30 JJ

Text references. Chapters 6 and 7.

Top tips. This question deals with internal audit planning matters. This question also looks at the issue of outsourcing finance and other functions, albeit from the internal auditor's perspective.

(a) covers some mainstream asset management issues but also wider human resource and commercial implications which the internal auditors would cover. The scenario quite clearly highlights areas of concern that of course your answer needs to address, and some areas where problems are quite likely (anything involving cash). Commercial issues are important because of the significant consequences if things go wrong, particularly new developments – here a new product.

Similarly, in (b), many of the issues that the internal auditors would be faced with would be similar to those that an external auditor would face. (b) covers overall systems review and operation of the contracts, as well as more detailed review of value for money and information.

Easy marks. There are enough clues in the scenario to enable you to score well in the discussion on cash, inventory and fraud.

(a) **Overall approach**

Both the **compliance based** and **process based approaches** would be **appropriate** here. The business is well run on the whole and there are specific procedures put in place by management, compliance with which could be assessed. In addition however, due to the nature of the business, it is clear that management and control of cash and inventory are key. These could be the focus of a process based approach. In either case, due to the number of sites involved a risk based approach is likely to be the most effective and efficient.

Specific issues to consider

The key decision to be made is to determine **which sites must be visited** and **which areas are of particular concern**.

Financial matters

On the basis of relative significance to the business as a whole the following sites should receive a routine visit: King's Cross, Marylebone, Hammersmith, Ealing, Gerrards Cross and Thame. Together these six sites contribute 77% of the total turnover of the business.

Particular issues to be addressed include:

(i) **Cash management**

Whilst there is no information from Head Office to suggest that there is a problem in this area tests should be performed to ensure that **procedures are being followed consistently and correctly**. Checks should be made to ensure that each kiosk manager is maintaining the **physical security** of the cash by, for example, maintaining the twice daily banking of cash.

(ii) **Inventory losses**

This has been identified as a particular problem at both Kings Cross and Ealing. Work should be performed to try to determine the source of the problems. Possible causes could include:

(1) **Poor inventory control**
Due to the short product life of the inventory consistent overordering is likely to lead to **inventory losses**. This is perhaps heightened at the King's Cross location where two kiosks share the same store. In this situation it is likely that no one individual is taking overall responsibility for the inventory management. Internal auditors should attempt to find out who has responsibility when they visit the site.

(2) **Poor training**
Each product should be made to a standard recipe. Where the recipe is not being followed or where errors are being made this will result in **extra inventory** being **utilised and wasted**. The fact that the Ealing branch has had a high level of staff turnover may suggest that staff have lacked training and that the managers have lacked experience in ordering. Internal auditors should check for a sample of the drinks that the **right recipe** is being followed, and **review the personnel records** of staff employed at Ealing.

(iii) **Fraud**

(1) **All sites**
The possibility of **theft** needs to be considered. The apparent inventory losses mentioned above could in fact be the result of transactions being made without being recorded with the cash received being misappropriated. The **overall performance** of these kiosks should be **reviewed** to determine whether there are any unexpected falls in revenue in comparison to previous periods.

(2) **Princes Risborough**
The Princes Risborough site should receive a **surprise inspection** preferably at the start of the morning shift. Whilst Princes Risborough contributes less than 2% of the total revenue of the business matters identified at Head Office have raised some concerns. The failure of the cash takings to reconcile to the cash bankings could be the result of poor control which should be rectified or potentially due to theft. In addition the timings of the transactions have raised suspicions and it is possible that the kiosk is not in operation for the full period of the shift even though the staff members are paid for the full nine hours.

(iv) **Commercial matters**

The fact that the Gerrards Cross café has failed to sell the newly launched smoothie needs to be **investigated**. At other sites these sales constitute approximately 20% of total revenue and this launch is an important part of the management strategy. Potential reasons could include **poor advertising and promotion** and **inadequate training** on how to make the product. Internal auditors should review **advertising documentation** and **staff training records**.

(v) **Operational**

A number of issues have been identified in relation to **staff recruitment, retention and training**. In particular at the Ealing kiosk an investigation should take place into the reasons behind the recent loss of managerial staff. Internal audit should carry out a **more general review of the human resources function**, looking particularly at the way that candidates are selected and the training process which they are offered.

(b) **Effect on the activities of internal audit**

Review of accounting and internal control systems

Often internal audit is assigned specific responsibility for reviewing the design of the systems, monitoring their operation and recommending improvements. The key difference if the IT function is outsourced is that JJ will **lose control** over these activities thereby **limiting** the **extent of the work** which the internal auditor can perform directly. Instead it will be the internal auditors' responsibility to **manage the relationship** and **monitor the performance of the service provider**.

Terms of contract

Exactly how the internal auditor will do this would depend on the precise nature of the contract between the two parties. The **terms of the contract** would determine for example the extent to which JJ has access to **accounting** records prepared by the service organisation and relevant underlying information. It may be useful, therefore, for the internal auditor to be consulted at this stage.

Design of systems

Once the relationship has been established the internal auditor would only have a **limited impact on the design of the system**. Provided that the end product meets JJ's requirements the way in which these results are achieved and any improvements would be the responsibility of the service organisation. Instead, however it could be the internal auditors role to monitor the **performance of the service organisation** and determine whether the needs of JJ are being met on an ongoing basis.

Control environment

In respect of **controls** the internal auditor would still have **responsibility for checking that the overall control environment is strong**. Where services have been outsourced the control environment will be made up of a combination of those operated by JJ's personnel and those of the service organisation. There are a number of ways in which the internal auditor could monitor the control environment of the service provider including:

- **Information and assurances** regarding the operation of internal controls provided by the service organisation
- **Quality of control**. Assessment of the use of **quality assurance services** (eg the service provider's internal audit function)
- **Actual experience** of adjustments to, or errors in, reports received from the service organisation
- **Reports** from the service providers' external auditors

Examination of financial and operating information

This would normally include **specific enquiry into individual items** including detailed testing of transactions and balances. The result of testing of information provided by the service organisation eg analytical techniques could also be applied to payroll information to establish the validity of processing.

The key issue here is the internal auditors' **access** to the relevant detailed records. In some cases JJ may not maintain detailed records or documentation initiating transactions for example, purchase invoices. If this is the case the information would be sought from the service company.

Review of economy, efficiency and effectiveness of operations

Financial efficiency or cost saving is probably one of the main reasons why JJ is considering the outsourcing of its IT function. The internal auditor would have an **ongoing role** in determining whether the service provider continues to provide **good value for money** by comparing the quality of the service with the negotiated fee.

Special investigations

The internal auditors of JJ would continue to have **full responsibility for non-IT related special investigations**. Any IT related projects are likely to be the remit of the service organisation as access to their expertise will be one of the main advantages of outsourcing in the first place. The internal auditors may, however, have a role in establishing what those projects should be as they have an in-depth knowledge of the detailed operations and needs of the business.

Compliance with regulations

Under company law JJ has certain **obligations to maintain proper accounting records**. If JJ were to use a service organisation the internal audit department might be involved in ensuring that the contractual arrangements are such that company law is complied with. This would include ensuring that the company has **legal ownership of the records and has access to them**.

31 APS

Text references. Chapters 3, 6 and 18 all contain relevant discussion of risks and controls.

Top tips. You should be able to see a number of weaknesses in the payroll system. Try and prioritise your answers, as we have, as that part of the question is worth 18 marks and you might run out of time trying to cover them all. Covering six properly should gain you 18 marks (one each for a weakness, consequence and recommendation). SOAPSPAM may help you think up the necessary controls.

Key elements relate to organisational weaknesses, management failing to exercise supervision and threats to the security of assets and data.

(b) is a good illustration of how computerised controls and computer-assisted audit techniques can be covered in questions.

The reference to access controls follows on from the threats to systems identified in (a).

Easy marks. It's generally easier to identify weaknesses than to discuss what they mean and how they should be countered. However you will get little or no credit if you just list weaknesses, however long that list is. Presenting what you say in the format we have used demonstrates to the examiner that you are thinking through how the weaknesses should be addressed.

(a) **Weaknesses in the payroll system**

Control over time recorded

Weakness

There is apparently **no form of control over what employees record** as their hours. The department supervisors do not appear to authorise the time cards and there is no independent check on whether the hours recorded are the hours worked.

Consequence

The company could be **paying the employee for work which he or she had not done**.

Recommendation

In the first place, the department supervisors should be asked to **authorise the time cards** to ensure that time recorded is reasonable.

However, the supervisor will not always be physically present at the times when employees clock in and out. Therefore in the long term we recommend that the company make use of a **mechanical or computerised clock**, so that employees are required to punch or sign in and out. This will provide an independent check of what hours have been worked.

Segregation of duties

Weakness

There is currently **no segregation of duties** in the wages system. Although the director approves the cheque for the wages, the wages clerk is allowed to create the payroll, which is not authorised until after the cheque has been written, and then put together the wage packets from the cash drawn from the bank.

Consequence

The directors have little control over:

- Whether the **payroll is an accurate reflection** of the clockcards
- Whether the **payslips reflect** what is on the payroll

The wages clerk could **misappropriate cash** from the wages cheque by allocating more cash on the payroll than on the payslips.

Recommendation

In the first instance, some **segregation of duties** should be introduced into the system. Someone other than the person who enters the payroll should make up the wage packets (subject to the point below).

In the longer term, the directors should consider **investing in an integrated payroll system** rather than using a PC. This could automatically record time from the clock machine and create the payroll and the payslips simultaneously.

Cash pay out

Weakness

The wages are **paid in cash** which the wages clerk collects from the bank on wages day.

Consequence

In addition to the possibility of staff misappropriation discussed above, the transfer of a substantial amount of cash between the bank and the premises each week is dangerous and leaves the company highly **susceptible to theft**.

Recommendation

It is common practice for businesses to use **direct bank transfers** to pay wages. We recommend that APS introduces the use of automated banking procedures.

Amendments to wages

Weakness

Wage changes are arranged **informally and orally** with the directors, apparently on an ad hoc basis.

Consequence

This could lead to confusion, particularly given that there are so many staff, and staff **could be paid something other than what has been authorised**. There appears to be **no system for updating the details on the PC** which contains the **payroll details**. It may also lead to some staff receiving wage rises regularly and others being forgotten, which would adversely affect staff morale.

Recommendation

Staff wages should be **reviewed on a systematic basis** (perhaps six monthly) and changes in wages should be authorised in writing. The wages clerk should not process any amendment which is not authorised in writing.

Recruitment

Weakness

Recruitment appears to be undertaken in a **casual, ad hoc manner**.

Consequence

The company could **fall short of the vital resource of staff**, or could employ people of a lower skills than required.

Recommendation

The company should set a **recruitment policy**, involve at least two people in each recruitment and consider employing a **personnel manager**, see below.

Personnel and policies

Weakness

The company employs 200 people. It has **no written policies towards employees** and no personnel department. Personnel duties are being left to the factory manager.

Consequence

Employment law can be complex, particularly in areas like the EC, and the company could find that it falls **short of regulatory requirements**. It may also be at risk from disgruntled employees taking **legal action** in the event of no company policy to deal with problems arising.

Recommendation

The company should consider forming some **formal policies** towards employees and producing an employee handbook. Given the number of staff it now employs, it should consider employing a personnel manager, possibly on a part time basis, who could also assist with recruitment.

(b) (i) **Access controls**

The most common access control to a computer system is the use of **passwords**. This would be the most appropriate strategy for APS, for whom use of controls such as retinal scans might be a little excessive.

Another important consideration for access is the **physical location of the computer terminals**. They should be contained within lockable rooms. Security will be improved if they are **away from windows**, or they are **not kept on the ground floor**.

Application controls

The application controls which would be used in a payroll system are controls such as:

(1) **Data entry checks** (for example, values are within a certain range)
(2) **Total checks** (for example, hash totals, such as the number of employees on the payroll)

(ii) **Test data**

Test data is used to ensure that **data is processed correctly by the system**. There are two types that could be used in the payroll system.

Valid data

Valid data could be entered, to ensure that the results are as predicted and expected. This would involve taking the details of an employee or **creating a new employee** and entering details such as pay rates and hours worked which could be valid, and processing them into the system. The required payroll information could be worked out in advance, and agreed to what the system produced.

Invalid data

Invalid data could be entered, to ensure that the system **rejected it and refused to process it** as valid data. This could be varied in several ways.

Examples of invalid data

For example, the test could involve taking a **genuine employee** and changing one detail which was then invalid. Another error could be added to the same test.

32 CSX

Text references. Chapters 6 – 8.

Top tips. Our answer to (a) links risks with controls designed to counter them, which is the neatest way to tackle this question. The amount of detail given about data entry and the fairly casual attitude to inventory write-offs indicates that these are significant problems. CIMA's model answer also suggested that you would have received credit for discussing various general and application controls over computer activities.

(b) needs to be read quite carefully; the examiner wants a general answer about use of different audit tests in inventory work. You therefore need to think beyond CSX and consider work done at the inventory count. The question requirements include a very strong hint about discussing computer-assisted audit techniques, so you need to spend time describing how they are used to test inventory.

Easy marks. Provided you understood what the examiner wanted, and had a good knowledge of the basics of auditing, (b) should have been quite reasonable.

Examiners' comments. Students scored very well on (a), but disappointedly poorly on (b).

In (b) many answers just discussed internal controls, rather than internal audit tests and techniques, which was what the question required. A number of answers to (b) duplicated the answers to (a) and merely added that the auditors should check whether the control was operating. Students would have gained credit for general suggestions and detailed work on inventory. Future students would be well-advised to study internal audit well.

(a) **Risks and improvements**

Incorrect quantities received

There is no indication that the quantities received are matched with the quantities ordered. Suppliers may **over or under deliver amounts.** If too much inventory is delivered, then **inventory may be held for excessive time and the risk of obsolescence** may **increase.** If inventory is under-ordered, there may be **insufficient quantities in inventory to fulfil customer demand**.

Records of goods received should be **matched with purchase orders and supplier invoices.** The purchasing function should resolve matters with suppliers if incorrect quantities are delivered or deliveries that **do not match orders** could be **refused and returned**.

Incorrect amounts paid

The **actual price paid to suppliers** may be **greater than the tender price** on which the purchase order is based. This could also mean that **inventory is incorrectly valued** if it is valued at tender price.

The purchasing function should **compare the values of purchases invoiced by suppliers** with the **tender prices** to ensure that they are identical.

Misposting of inventory

Clerical staff could post **incorrect quantities of inventory received**. If amounts are over-posted, there is a risk that inventory actually available may be **insufficient to meet customer demand**. If amounts are under-posted, unnecessary extra orders may be made, resulting in **increased purchase and holding costs**, and **greater risk of obsolescence**. If data on picking lists have to be posted manually by warehouse staff, there is also a risk that **quantities delivered to customers** may be entered **wrongly**.

Purchase ordering should be **computerised** and **quantities entered on delivery matched** with **specific purchase orders.** The computer should identify any differences between **amounts ordered** and **deliveries**

entered. The GRNs and picking lists should **automatically update warehouse records** without the need for further data entry by warehouse staff.

Loss of inventory

The company is suffering **increased costs** through inventory **being lost. More orders** may have to be made, and CSX may be **unable to satisfy customer demand** because there is insufficient inventory available. Also staff may be stealing inventory said to be lost, since components are **high value**, **small**, **portable** and **easily saleable**.

Inventory counts should be carried out **monthly due to technological changes** that rapidly render parts obsolete; if costs are an issue, different types of inventory should be counted each month, with all inventory perhaps being counted over a **three month cycle**. Excessive losses should be investigated. Steps taken to **prevent losses** should include **surveillance** by security staff, ensuring that there is **no access to inventory** by unauthorised staff and **searching staff** who are allowed access to inventory.

Collusion between staff

Collusion to hide loss or theft of inventory between staff handling goods and staff entering data may be easy to arrange as they work together in the warehouse.

There should be stricter **segregation of duties,** with staff entering data being based away from the warehouse and reporting to different managers.

Disposal of obsolete inventory

There appears to be no control over staff throwing away inventory that is obsolete or damaged. **Good inventory** could be **incorrectly classified** as obsolete, and again staff could use throwing away inventory as a cover for stealing good items.

Managers **should authorise the disposal of inventory**; staff should **not throw obsolete items away** on their own initiative. **All write-offs** should be **recorded**.

Loss of data

The age of the computer system may make **computer crashes and loss of data** more likely. There is no evidence of controls to counter these threats.

Data should be **backed up daily** and back up copies kept off site. CSX should also have **contingency arrangements** in place for processing data if the computer system breaks down. Other **appropriate general** and **application controls** should be in place to limit risks to data.

Accounting

There are various risks of **incorrect external reporting of accounting data** including **incorrect valuation of inventory** and use of a **potentially inaccurate general provision** of 2%. This provision may be contrary to the **requirements of IAS 37** and in the context of a **profit margin of $12 million** may be **material**. The lack of care taken over it may indicate a **poor control environment in relation to accounting**.

Inventory should be valued at **actual price paid to suppliers or net realisable value** if this is lower due to obsolescence. The provision against inventory should be **limited to specific losses**; this should also emphasise to management the extent of the problem of inventory loss and encourage them to take steps to reduce it.

(b) **Walk through tests**

Auditors should confirm that the systems and documentation for **recording inventory** are operating as it should be. They should **trace** a limited number of items **through inventory records** to see whether their understanding of the system and controls is correct.

Tests of controls

Auditors should carry out **compliance tests** on controls in areas where risks are significant and the organisation needs controls to reduce these risks. Auditors should examine evidence such as **manual signatures or computer cross-references** to see that **comparisons are being made** between different inventory records, for example purchase orders and delivery notes. Auditors should also assess whether **inventory is being kept in secure accommodation**, and **observe security measures** such as **searches of staff** that are in place.

Substantive tests – attendance at inventory counts

Auditors should **observe inventory counts**, seeing whether count procedures are being followed by staff. They should carry out **test counts.** Auditors should also check that **differences between records** and **actual amounts** in inventory are **investigated** and **adequate explanations obtained,** both at the counts they attend and other counts held during the year. They should also check that **cut-off** is **correct,** that inventory movements are recorded in the right period.

Analytic review

Auditors should **review inventory levels at the count** and **records of inventory levels** during the year. They should obtain evidence that inventory is only ordered when amounts held are below **minimum levels. Analytic review** of different inventory figures can also highlight problems with certain types of inventory. Auditors can compare the **holding periods** and **write-offs** of specific types of inventory, inventory held in different locations or inventory ordered from certain suppliers. They can thus highlight areas of concern, poor control of inventory held in certain places for example.

Computer assisted audit techniques

As many inventory systems are computerised, auditors will need to use computer-assisted audit techniques to audit inventory effectively. Examples include:

(i) **Test data**
Test data can be used to test controls over inventory data entry, such as reasonableness checks ensuring that entry of **excessive inventory quantities** is **queried**, or only items with permitted inventory line or supplier codes can be processed.

(ii) **Audit software**
Audit software can be used to **make comparisons**, for example inventory levels at different locations, or **carry out analytic review calculations**, for example ranking inventory lines by % write-offs. Audit software can also be used to **compare versions of programs** that are used at different locations where inventory is held.

(iii) **Integrated test facility**
An integrated test facility involves the creation of a **fictitious entity.** Transactions are put through using existing programs and actual results are compared with predicted results, for example whether inventory has been **costed correctly**.

(iv) **Systems control and review file**
This posts **transactions with certain characteristics**, for example orders above a certain amount or unusual orders from specific suppliers to a file for **later auditor review**.

33 Purchasing and entertainment

Text references. Chapter 6 covers purchases, Chapter 9 discusses the relationship between codes of conduct and ethical issues.

Top tips. The key point in part (a) was a recognition of the risk of collusion between purchasing staff and suppliers. The answer should have discussed controls which minimised this risk, particularly authorisation and monitoring, and also commented on organisation-wide issues such as internal audit or contract management.

In part (b), the verb discuss suggests that there are both good and bad aspects of the code that you need to highlight. Our answer thus looks at the ways in which the code can be seen as acceptable and the ways in which it can be seen as unacceptable, and then we suggest ways in which it could be improved.

Easy marks. There are plenty of controls that could be suggested in (a).

Examiner's comments. Many candidates spent too much time on part (a) and little if any time on part (b), which was worth more marks. The examiner noted that part (b) was significantly harder than part (a). Common errors included repeating the code in the question without adding any substantial commentary and commenting that it was a contentious subject, without either agreeing with the existing approach or proposing an alternative.

(a) The following features of the system should help minimise the risk of fraud.

(i) **Risk assessment**

Examples of purchase fraud include **rigged tendering**, **goods being supplied** for **private purposes** and **fraudulent transactions with connected companies**. Another possible danger is **collusion** between the person authorising purchases and suppliers. Once purchases have been authorised, there may be nothing further that can be done to prevent fraud. The important controls therefore are normally those which are aimed at identifying unusual suppliers or circumstances.

(ii) **Monitoring of suppliers**

The risk of collusion between suppliers and employees can be minimised in a number of ways.

(1) **Approval of suppliers**
The person using the goods should only be able to **choose suppliers from an approved list**.

(2) **Segregation of duties**
The use of new suppliers should be **authorised by someone other than the person using the goods**. The person authorising new suppliers should be particularly wary of **abnormal terms**, suppliers providing goods which they would **not normally supply** and suppliers which **appear too small** to cope with the proposed volume of purchases.

(3) **Management review**
In addition there should be **regular monitoring** by management of arrangements with suppliers. Warning signs should be investigated, such as suppliers handled directly by senior staff, or suppliers handled outside the normal control systems.

(iii) **Controls in the payment cycle**

(1) **Segregation of duties**

Segregation of duties can reduce certain risks. **Segregating the cheque-signing role from the payment authorisation role** can reduce the risk that payments are made out to certain types of bogus supplier, for example those with abbreviated names. Part of the process of reviewing suppliers can be carried out at the payment stage, by checking that **individual or total payments do not appear excessive**.

(2) **Documentation**

Requirements for **full documentation** should be linked to segregation of duties. Full documentation would include **purchase requisitions**, **purchase orders and purchase invoices**. These can help prevent purchases for private use.

Documentation of returns is also important; **credit notes** should always be obtained from suppliers when goods are returned in order to prevent stock losses through bogus returns.

(iv) **Contract management**

Ways of preventing contract fraud include the following.

- An **open competitive tendering** process.
- **Interim payments** being made on **certification from independent valuers**.
- **Changes to terms being authorised independently** of the person who deals with the contractors on a day to day basis.

(v) **Organisation and staff controls**

(1) **Personnel**
References should be obtained for all new staff, and details retained of previous employers so that possible collusion can be checked.

(2) **Ethics**
A **business code of ethics** can remind staff of what constitutes unreasonable inducements.

(vi) **Internal audit**

Internal audit can play a role in a number of the above checks, particularly the following.

- **Detailed checks** of documentation.
- **Scrutiny of suppliers** and payments for suspicious circumstances.

(b) As with many codes of conduct adopted in practice, there are both acceptable and unacceptable aspects to the code in question.

Aspects of the code which are acceptable

(i) **Business custom**
The organisation has adopted a code of conduct which attempts to **conform with customary business practices**. It wishes to behave in a manner consistent with that of others in the market.

(ii) **Risk appetite**
The code appears to imply that employees can take **slight risks** and go beyond behaviour that might be construed as strictly correct in order to secure sales. It would be logical and reasonable to do this in order to gain a sales advantage.

(iii) **Control over conduct**
The conduct of the members of the staff working in the **purchasing function** is **controllable** by the organisation and so the organisation can determine the code of conduct which should apply. The code of conduct covering the **selling operation has to meet the expectations of the market** and **customers**, however. The organisation has **no control over its potential customers**, who can decide whether or not they should accept any gifts, favours or entertainment offered.

(iv) **Who benefits**
Any **gifts, favours and entertainment provided by a supplier benefits an employee** whereas those **provided for customers benefit the customer** rather than the employee (unless the entertainment is lavish). There are therefore stricter controls over purchasing staff than sales staff.

Aspects of the code which are unacceptable

(i) **Lack of detail**

The code **fails to provide sufficient guidance**. For example, it does not specify the nature of customary business practices, common courtesies and so on. Employees have no idea about whether they can offer a potential customer a glass of wine, a bottle of wine or a case of wine.

(ii) **Penalties**

The code gives **no information** about the **repercussions** for employees for contravening the code. There is therefore no indication of the seriousness with which the organisation views breaches of the code.

(iii) **Lack of clarity**

The penultimate sentence about 'favours or entertainment, appropriate in our sales programmes' implies a **double standard** and may encourage sales personnel to adopt a position which could damage the good name of the organisation.

(iv) **Permitting unethical behaviour**

The unclear nature of the code relating to sales means that, because **behaviour is not actually illegal**, it may be **adopted** because it increases the organisation's short-term profits.

(v) **Profit focus**

If **performance measures** are based on **short-term profit**, **employees** may feel **pressurised** into adopting unethical or even illegal behaviour.

Suggested amendments to the code of conduct

Given the above comments there are various amendments which could be made to the code of conduct to increase its acceptability.

(i) **Increased clarity**

Ambiguous terms should be **clarified**.

(ii) **Disciplinary measures**

Penalties for contravening the code could be **included**.

(iii) **Simplification**

It could be drastically **simplified** and the entire **section on business courtesies deleted** since the information provided in the remaining section provides an adequate and concise code of conduct.

(iv) **Provisions affecting sales staff**

The **code relating to the conduct of employees** working in the sales function could be **rewritten** with the intention of making it as **strict and clear** as that covering the purchasing function employees (no entertainment, no gifts and so on). There are commercial problems associated with such an approach, however; the market and customers may expect a more liberal attitude.

Such changes would produce an **unambiguous, clear and concise code of conduct** which will **protect the integrity of the organisation** and allow **employees to be confident** that their efforts for the organisation will remain within acceptable limits.

34 PNY

Text references. Mainly Chapter 9, though Chapter 7 contains useful material on internal audit.

Top tips. In answering (a), you need to identify the three key elements of an anti-fraud strategy that we have identified. Note that most of the factors discussed in connection with prevention of fraud (culture, risk awareness, reporting) are part of the control environment.

You will need to provide 2 or 3 good points on each part of the strategy to obtain a good pass.

For (b) it is critical to review the information being provided in the scenario to identify risks in internal audit and the processes in the company. The scenario does provide plenty of clues (corporate governance shortcomings, independence of internal audit, problems with their work), so identify these and then be sure to link each risk with recommendations for changes within the internal audit department.

Easy marks. The fraud discussion in (a) is fairly general, and the elements should hopefully be familiar.

(a) A **risk management strategy** for fraud will contain three elements:

- Fraud prevention
- Identifying fraud, and
- Responding to fraud

Fraud prevention

The fact that a risk management strategy for fraud is in place within an organisation will itself act as a **deterrent against fraud**. Fraud is less likely to be attempted if the potential perpetrators of that fraud know they are more likely to be caught.

Key methods of preventing fraud

(i) **Having an anti-fraud culture in the organisation**
This means that all staff are encouraged to **treat each other and customers and suppliers with respect** and that reasons for decisions are **transparent**. The policy will be enforced partly by **contracts of employment** that will indicate actions that employees must take, eg ensuring security of client data, and partly by the **overall culture**, such as directors providing an example to staff in their dealings with customers.

(ii) **Risk awareness**
There should be **awareness amongst staff that fraud could be taking place**, which will be reinforced by **appropriate training programmes** within the entity. Where fraud has been identified, appropriate publicity could be given to this, again to maintain awareness of the issue.

(iii) **Whistle blowing**
This relates to **disclosing information on possible frauds** by people not involved in that fraud and where the fraud does not appear to have been identified and acted on by normal channels such as internal audit. **Maintaining an anti-fraud culture** may help whistle-blowers come forward with information, although fear of reprisals by management including inappropriate dismissal may limit the number of disclosures.

(iv) **Internal control systems**
Appropriate internal control systems will also help to prevent and detect fraud. The **use of controls** such as **segregation of duties and authorisation** controls ensure that fraud can only take place by collusion between staff. This will help to minimise the incidence of fraud.

Identifying fraud

As noted above, good internal control systems will assist in preventing and detecting fraud. Fraud identification normally results from the **work of internal audit** and internal investigation, rather than the **work of external auditors**. External auditors in their engagement letter recommend that their work cannot be relied upon to detect fraud.

Specific tasks of internal audit which will help to detect fraud include:

(i) **Checks**
Performing regular checks to ensure that **assets are accounted for** – eg inventory counts and cash counts.

(ii) **Analytical review**
Monitoring key ratios and other accounting indicators and transactions for unusual or unexplained movements eg receivable days increasing, payments made to an overseas subsidiary without justification.

(iii) **Information gathering**
Receiving information from whistle-blowers. The audit committee or the chief internal auditor is normally nominated as the person to receive whistle blowing reports from employees.

Responding to fraud

Where fraud is suspected, then an **appropriate investigation** should be carried out into those suspicions. Actions to be taken will depend on the outcome of the investigation, but could include internal disciplinary and/or legal proceedings.

(b) **Inherent risks and internal audit**

Independence of audit reports

There is **no audit committee** in PNY – **so all internal audit reports are directed to the financial accountant**. This procedure raises **two specific risks** regarding the contents of internal audit reports:

(i) **Finance Director's responsibility for internal audit**
Firstly, as the Finance Director is directly responsible for employing the internal auditors, the internal auditors may feel **uncomfortable about writing reports** that are **critical of the financial accountant**. There is the possibility, real or not, that an adverse report could adversely affect promotion or remuneration prospects of the internal auditors.

(ii) **Lack of action**
Secondly, there is **no guarantee** that the Finance Director will **take action** on the reports. Again, the Finance Director may have a **vested interest** not to make amendments to the control systems and could block or amend any report prior to it being presented to the board.

Resolving independence of audit reports

These problems could be avoided by **establishing an audit committee** or, if this is not feasible within PNY, **by sending internal audit reports to another board director**, possibly the Chairman to maintain a division between the person employing internal auditors and the person reviewing their reports.

Ability and independence of staff in internal audit

The internal audit department employs four staff. As noted in the scenario same staff have been working in the department for the last 10 years. This implies two risks with the work of the internal audit department:

(i) **Lack of continuing professional education**
Staff may **not have kept up-date** with the latest technology and therefore be unable to perform audits sufficiently well to test the newer systems in PNY. This comment is borne out by the lack of training within internal audit.

(ii) **Lack of independence**
The internal audit staff may **no longer be sufficiently independent** of PNY or its staff to be able to produce a completely objective report. Internal audit may be too familiar with some systems to notice mistakes, and certainly too friendly with staff in PNY to want to criticise them.

Resolving ability and independence issues

These problems could be avoided by **introducing new staff** into the internal audit department and possibly by providing internal audit staff with **secondments** into other areas of the company (eg the management accounting department) to ensure that they have an appropriate break from internal audit.

Weaknesses in audit testing

The process of testing in the internal audit department focuses on **substantive testing of transactions**. While this does provide **appropriate evidence** that transactions are being recorded correctly, there are other concerns. The accounting systems in PNY have been **upgraded** in recent years. This indicates a risk that internal audit staff may **not have the skills or abilities** to **audit the new online systems in PNY**. The fact that audit trails are lost and may not be located again tends to confirm this view.

Dealing with testing weaknesses

Audit testing in the department needs to be upgraded to include **computer assisted audit techniques** to ensure that the new computer systems are audited appropriately. This may mean **employing new staff** in internal audit, **training existing staff** and certainly **purchasing new computers and audit software** to be able to carry out internal audits effectively.

Physical inspection of assets

Even with a perpetual inventory system, audit testing of inventory appears to be **limited to the end of the year**. There is a risk that **inventory is misappropriated** during the year and this would not be identified until the year end.

Enhancing physical inspection

The perpetual inventory system does allow **physical inventory to be checked** to the book inventory on a regular basis throughout the year. Internal audit procedures should be amended to take account of this change.

Whistleblowing

The Head of Accounts sets the **risk management policy** in the company and also hears reports from potential whistle blowers. However, given that whistleblowing is not discussed with an audit committee, an independent body in a company, the Head of Accounts may appear to have a vested interest in **not taking action on reports**, especially if this adversely affects PNY.

The **chief internal auditor**, being **independent of the executive board**, may be a more appropriate person to hear reports.

Lack of control testing

There is **limited, or even no control testing being carried out**. This is a **weakness with audit testing** because the control systems within PNY, that are specifically designed to ensure that transactions are **appropriate, authorised and help prevent fraud**, are not being tested. Control weaknesses could be occurring without the internal auditors knowing about them.

Changing focus of testing

To ensure that the **internal control systems in PNY** are working correctly, the internal auditor must **focus audit testing on control tests**. This will provide appropriate audit evidence that controls are working as well as being more time efficient.

35 AL

Text references. Chapter 9 is the most useful.

Top tips. The scenario to this question poses a number of problems. It appears from the last paragraph the external auditors and the report's author are not certain that fraud has taken place though they have suspicions. The information in the penultimate paragraph that there has been a fraud is not apparently known to the report's author, so you can't bring it into the report directly, though you can suggest that an increase in expenses may have been due to the kind of fraudulent behaviour that has in fact taken place.

You also have to assume that the two executive directors are the only two directors, as non-executive directors aren't mentioned. The report is being made to these two directors yet the fact that one of these directors has been acting fraudulently does not appear to impact upon what the accountant is asked to do.

That said, the scenario offers plenty of weaknesses for you to identify in (a). Although you're told that the control systems are weak, you should go into most detail about the areas covered in the scenario. As we stressed at the start of the kit, it's important to analyse the scenario carefully to make sure you've picked everything up. This means focusing more on management information weaknesses than general financial controls. (Remember this exam is part of the management accounting pillar.) A brief mention of internal audit as a possibility would be OK, though it wouldn't be a big department in this business. It's good technique to explain briefly why the weakness is a problem and link the controls in directly. The 10 marks could have been obtained by a brief description of **five** weaknesses and then five **improvements linked in with those weaknesses**.

In (b) external auditors have to take action based on the strangely large increase in expenses and the lack of audit evidence and internal control weaknesses need to be rectified, therefore co-operation is best. The key to (c) is remembering where the focus of external audit's work lies. (d) required a response plan in response to this **specific fraud**, although this might not have been entirely clear from the question. It should include who to investigate, why (the aims), how the investigation should be carried out and what should be done as a result.

Overall, if you focus on the requirements, there is plenty to discuss, but if you see an optional question where the scenario or requirements appear questionable, and these problems are too distracting, it's probably best to avoid it.

Easy marks. (c) if you knew what differences there are in most countries between internal and external audit scope.

Examiner's comments. The examiner emphasised that the situation of a small business was deliberately chosen to emphasise the need for fraud control across all types of business.

This was the least popular question and most answers were too brief. Although in (a) weaknesses were identified, realistic controls were often not discussed, and far too much emphasis was placed on the role of internal audit. The perspectives demanded in (b) (external audit/internal control) were often not addressed. Most answers to (d) showed a minimal knowledge of what a fraud response plan is.

REPORT

To: Directors
From: Accountant
Subject: AL's internal control systems

Introduction

This report is based on concerns raised by the external auditors as a result of their most recent audit. These have to be addressed by yourselves as directors of AL, as it is your responsibility to establish systems that **minimise the risk of fraud or error**, and also ensure the **business** is **operating efficiently**.

(a) The main weaknesses in the system, together with remedies for improving those weaknesses, are set out below.

Checking directors' work

No checks are carried out on the work of executive directors, so that any problems or mistakes made will not be identified.

A system of checking should be introduced, including the **directors carrying out checks** on each other's work, and perhaps internal audit or other financial staff also carrying out some verification.

Lack of internal audit

There is no internal audit department. Internal audit work can **pick up weaknesses in internal control systems and information provided**, and also can **identify significant business and financial risks** and **monitor the organisation's overall risk management policy.**

AL should establish a **small internal audit department**, headed by a qualified accountant.

Cost charging

Because not all costs are charged to contracts, it is impossible to see whether individual contracts are profitable. This means for example that AL may be offering renovation services that may be **unprofitable**, and also that it is **difficult to monitor costs.**

Contracts should therefore be **charged with all direct costs**, not just material costs, and a **relevant share of overheads apportioned**, perhaps on the basis of labour hours, the likely **main driver.**

Pricing decisions

Pricing decisions depend on **predictions of labour times**, but there is no indication of how accurate labour times are.

A system of **labour reporting variances** should be **introduced**, and reasons for variances between planned and actual time investigated. Pricing of contracts should be amended if actual time differs significantly from what has been expected.

Budgets and management accounting

More generally there is no evidence that **budgets are being prepared**, or if they are, that **budgeted and actual performance are being compared. Full management accounts** are also not being prepared regularly.

A **complete review of the management information system** needs to be undertaken, and budgets and management accounts showing a level of detail that is appropriate for maintaining control of the business should be prepared. Exception reports showing **variances and unusual items** should be **prepared and investigated.** Reports need to **include information on the performance of sales staff** (are the quotes realistic) and **staff responsible for work on site**.

You would also have scored marks if you had discussed any of the following risks and controls:

Asset usage

Although jobs have been charged with tools used and consumables, there does not appear to be a system in place for checking **issue and usage of tools**.

Records should be kept of **all assets issued and used** in connection with specific jobs.

Suppliers

There is **no evidence** of checks being carried out on the **reliability of suppliers**. Suppliers who **over-charge** or who provide **no service** may be selected.

Selection of suppliers should be **fully documented**, and evidence obtained of their reliability. As this is an area of concern and as Director Y is responsible for procurement, Director X should approve the selection of suppliers and also certainly large or unusual invoices.

Internal control systems

Other aspects of internal control, including efficient usage of assets such as materials, may also be **lacking.**

Internal audit, possibly with external audit assistance, should carry out an investigation of **all aspects of the control system and recommend improvements.** Any recommendations made for improvements in controls by external auditors should be actioned as appropriate.

(b) **Rise in variable costs**

Most costs have risen in line with increased sales, thus allowing AL to maintain a consistent profit margin. However variable overheads have shown a disproportionate rise, and this is worrying for the following reasons.

(i) **Single supplier**
The rise seems primarily **due to use of a particular supplier**, and there is a **lack of audit trail** of what that supplier has provided, suggesting that payments may have been made for non-existent goods. Not only may AL **have made material expenditure without receiving goods**, but the **accounting records** may be **incorrect** if they record expenditure for legitimate business reasons that in fact was not for the business's benefit.

(ii) **Possibility of overcharging**
Even if the payments are for legitimate reasons, AL may well have been **overcharged**, possibly indicating **deficiencies in supplier procurement**.

Need for external audit work

The external auditors may wish to pursue their investigations further to obtain evidence of why these expenses have risen so much, and ultimately may have to consider how they should report any **suspicions of fraud** they have. I recommend that we cooperate with the external auditors by providing evidence they require in relation to the procurement procedures undertaken, and our dealings with that particular supplier.

(c) **Fraud and financial statements**

External auditors **do not have a general responsibility to detect and prevent fraud**; the requirements they face are more limited. External audit's focus will be on those frauds that lead to **material** (significant) **misstatements** in accounts.

Chances of detection

The external auditors should consider the susceptibility of the entity to these frauds at the planning stage, and should **design procedures to reduce to an acceptably low level the risk** that **material misstatements** will **not be detected**. However external auditors will only ever have a reasonable chance of detecting fraud, particularly as wrongdoers normally seek to hide it.

(d) **Fraud response plan**

A **fraud response plan** is a strategy for **investigating and dealing with the consequences** of fraud. The plan should be implemented if it is believed fraud may have occurred. It is required because the need for **legal action** should fraud be proven, also the threat to the company's **reputation** if management or employees are convicted. Issues include:

(i) **Immediate action**
Actions that have to be taken as soon as the fraud comes to light include **ensuring the security of the records** that will be used to investigate what has happened, and also the **securing of assets** that may be vulnerable to theft.

(ii) **Investigation procedures**
A **senior internal member of staff** who has not dealt with the supplier concerned and who has sufficient expertise might lead the investigation, or better possibly the external auditors. The methods used should aim to **obtain evidence without alerting the suspect**.

(iii) **The aims of the investigation**
These include establishing the **extent of the loss**, **how the fraud occurred**, **who else** may have been **implicated** in the fraud and whether the **fraud was not detected** because **existing controls were not operating properly**, or whether existing controls would have been unlikely to prevent or identify the fraud.

(iv) **Action to be taken if fraud appears to have happened**
This includes **dealing with suspects**, and considering **notification of the police**.

Conclusion

The board should review the evidence presented so far, and should meet with the external auditors to consider further action. Whatever the outcome of the investigation, the board must consider a fundamental overhaul of AL's control systems.

36 Pensions

Text references. Chapter 1, 6, 7 and 9.

Top tips. The key question in (a) is the financial consequences of the actions that need to be taken to combat the risks. Note that employees may suffer even if they are not making any contributions to the scheme themselves. (a) is also a good illustration of reputation risk, where risk levels depend upon the impact stakeholder actions can have on the company.

(b) (i) follows the method suggested in Chapter 9 of the text; identifying the key facts, discussing the ethical issues, looking at possible actions and making justified recommendations. It's easy in ethics questions to fall into the weakness we highlighted in the Passing the P3 exam section of making vague and impractical recommendations. One problem is that it is not clear who the discussion should be aimed at – another member of the Financial Reporting team perhaps?

In (b) (ii) we are talking about how the system deals with a high level accounting issue, and is therefore a good test of top-level internal controls. Most governance reports specifically include consideration of significant accounting treatments within the audit committee's remit. The mention of external controls should indicate the need to discuss what external audit can do. Although knowledge of auditing standards on using the work of an expert would have helped you a bit, application of your general understanding about what external auditors are trying to achieve should hopefully have meant that you came up with the points we made.

The examiner noted that this question was unpopular. It seems many students were put off it by mention of IAS 19 and the fear that they needed detailed knowledge of the standard to pass the question. In fact the question is about risks, ethics and controls, not the fine print of IAS 19.

Easy marks. (b) (ii) is based round the key figures in a large company's system of financial reporting.

Examiner's comments. Despite being the least popular question on the paper, this question was very well-answered.

(a) **Risks to employer**

(i) **Financial risks**

The employer will have to take action to **remedy a long-term deficit**. The nature of the risk will depend on the action taken. A **lump sum payment** will provide a quick fix, but may mean that the employer has **insufficient resources** to take advantage of major profitable investment opportunities. **Gradual repayment** may be easier on cash flow, but represents a **continuing drain** and means that the employer has to live with the other consequences of a deficit. Ultimately if the employer cannot meet the deficit, it could lead to the **employer's insolvency**.

(ii) **Stock market risk**

The company's **market value** may fall as a result of investors perceiving the company to be of **higher risk** because of the deficit. This fall may occur even if the underlying causes of the deficit are not long-term. For example if the pension fund is invested to a significant extent in equities, the effect of a few weeks of falling share prices may give an exaggeratedly pessimistic picture of the scheme funding at the year-end.

(iii) **Financial provider risk**

The reaction of other finance providers is likely to be similar to stock market investors. They may well perceive the employer to be of higher risk because of the liabilities on the balance sheet, and hence be **less willing to provide funds** if they feel that the funds will be diverted to clearing the deficit. Alternatively funds provided may be on less favourable terms, causing **finance costs** to **rise.**

(iv) **Employee risks**

Threats to benefits or the possibility of increased contributions may cause **staff to leave** and make **recruiting new staff more difficult.** Staff who remain may be more unhappy and less co-operative because of the retrenchment necessary to resolve the deficit. Leavers and staff who remain may decide to **transfer their entitlements** out of the pension fund to **another pension arrangement**, putting further pressure on it.

(v) **Information risks**

The employer may take some significant decisions on the basis of actuarial forecasts that include significant uncertainties. In particular if **investment values** are in **flux,** or the **average age and past service of employees alter** as a result of **significant transfers out of the scheme,** the assumptions on which forecasts are made and decisions based may become misleading quite rapidly.

Employee risks

(i) **Increased contributions**

The employees too may face adverse financial consequences from a deficit **having to be remedied**. They may face **increased contributions themselves** to remedy the deficit.

(ii) **Salary costs**

Even if they don't have to contribute, their **salaries** may be **capped**, not only to reduce operating costs, but also to limit the benefits that the scheme will ultimately have to pay. They may face an increased threat of redundancy.

(iii) **Employment risks**

Other employment risks may be more indirect. If the employer is concentrating on resolving the deficit, then there may be **less development opportunities** because of the cutting back of expansion plans or reduction in training.

(iv) **Transfer risks**

If staff member leave the pension scheme, and transfer to another pension arrangement, then there is a risk that the new arrangements will **provide less favourable benefits** than the old scheme at a higher risk. In particular, **transferring to a defined contribution scheme**, where the employee's contributions go into an individual 'pot' of investments out of which benefits are paid, means that the employee **bears the whole risk** of the investments fluctuating in value.

(v) **Non-payment of pensions**

Ultimately if the scheme problems lead to the employer's bankruptcy, there is a risk that the staff will not receive the pensions they expect.

(b) (i) **Action proposed**

The action proposed is problematic in two respects.

(1) The actuary is being asked to prepare a valuation that is clearly not reasonable, since it is **based on out-of-date information**.

(2) The valuation will be used in the accounts in a way that means that the accounts **do not show a true and fair view**.

Although the Finance Director might argue that the high valuation of the deficit is unfair, using the wrong information is clearly unacceptable, as it cannot be seen as reliable. If the accounts contain a lower valuation than appropriate, this will persuade investors that the company's value is higher than it is, also perhaps that it is a lower risk investment. Both of these will **unfairly inflate the share price.**

Ethical principles

A number of ethical issues are at stake in this question. The Head of Financial Reporting is proposing action that will mean that he, and the Finance Director if he agrees, are not acting with **integrity** – acting in a **straightforward and honest manner**. This clearly constitutes **unprofessional behaviour by all parties.** In addition the fact that the Head of Financial Reporting believes that he will be able to influence the actuary may indicate the actuary lacks **objectivity,** something the Head of Financial Reporting is exploiting.

Lastly there is the issue of **confidentiality** that faces other members of the Financial Reporting team that know what has happened. If out-of-date information is used and misleading accounts are prepared, how should they weigh up their duty of confidentiality to their employer against the desirability of reporting unethical, and probably fraudulent, behaviour.

Actions taken

The actuary should obviously decline the request; his **professional ethical code** and **employer's code of conduct** will require him to decline. If he feels that undue pressure is being put upon him he should consider resigning.

Staff members who know about the fraud should consider the internal reporting options available. If the Finance Director has agreed to the arrangement, then the matter cannot be reported to him. The **head of the audit committee** should however have the independence and knowledge to challenge the treatment used. If satisfactory action is not taken internally, the **public interest issue** of the market being misled would appear to override confidentiality, and indicate reporting to the local equivalent of the UK's Financial Reporting Review Panel.

Recommendations

The threat to the actuary's integrity and professional position is such that resignation may be the most sensible course.

For Financial Reporting staff members, they should first consider reporting the situation to the **audit committee**, as an independent audit committee should be able to take action. Not only will this be making use of procedures within the organisation, if done in time publication of the **misleading information** may be **prevented** and the **damage limited**. However **whistleblowing to external regulators** is likely to be necessary if the accounts are published using the wrong information. Either way, staff should consider **resigning** because of possible future problems of working for senior management who lack integrity.

(ii) **Internal financial reporting**

Recruitment of expert

There should be internal procedures in place governing the **recruitment of the expert**, the **qualifications** required, who makes the decision to recruit and retain the expert and to whom the expert reports.

Internal audit

The effectiveness of any internal audit work on the actuary's valuation will depend partly on internal auditors' level of expertise, also whether they themselves can employ external expert help. There are some things that internal audit should be able to assess well, including the **professional competence of the expert** and the **scope of the expert's work**. They may be able to carry out some work on the **data and assumptions** that the expert has used; this may be sufficient to identify the problem over the wrong table being used if internal auditors themselves are able to obtain sufficient information.

Internal audit committee

Corporate governance reports require the audit committee to review the **published accounts**. This should involve assessment of the **key accounting policies** and **major areas of judgement**. Hopefully some committee members should be able to review the actuary's work effectively. In addition, the audit committee should act as a **forum for staff**, internal audit or actuary to raise concerns about being pressurised by senior management.

Financial statement controls

There should be a review of the **financial statements** for **compliance with accounting standards, disclosure requirements** and **consistency with internal information**, undertaken by staff who have not been responsible for its preparation. This review may highlight problems with the underlying evidence that require further investigation.

External financial reporting controls

External audit evidence

The work of the external auditor is a **fall-back** if internal controls have not worked satisfactorily. External auditors will be obliged by auditing standards to obtain sufficient evidence about all material items in the accounts. Clearly the valuation will be very material. External auditors should consider carefully not only the **work** the expert has done, but also the expert's **objectivity**.

External audit valuation

External auditors may need to call upon **expert assistance of their own** if they believe that the actuary's work does not represent sufficient audit evidence, because of doubts about the assumptions used or objectivity.

External reporting

Ultimately external auditors can qualify their audit report if they have not obtained satisfactory evidence. This may act as a **deterrent** preventing manipulation.

37 SPQ

Text references. Chapter 1 lists the main risks, Chapter 7 covers internal audit's role, Chapter 18 is helpful on the controls and Chapter 9 on ethical issues.

Top tips. Note that (a) stresses the work internal audit does in reviewing the overall control and risk management framework as well as the detailed testing. Consideration of the factors in the COSO framework and CIMA's risk management cycle may help you generate ideas.

(b) is a good illustration of what we said in the front pages about understanding what the question verb requires. The analyse (examine in detail) requirement in (b) means that you have to go beyond the problems with the systems and ask what else the systems development demonstrates about SPQ; make sure your answer clearly identifies the control action.

In (c) we cover the issues, particularly the risks, affecting the running of the specific audit, but also consider the issues affecting this audit's place in the overall plan for internal audit.

In (d) you just about have time to use the principles in considering different solutions to the ethical problem, although don't go overboard on these. You should have made a recommendation about resolving the conflicts at the end of your answer.

Easy marks. (a) is a good start to the question. Similar part questions have been asked on other occasions, so a explanation of internal audit's role may well be worth a few marks in your paper as well.

Examiner's comments. There were many good answers. Poorer answers were too general and failed to relate to the case, particularly in (d). In (a) some candidates failed to relate internal audit to internal control and risk management. Answers to (c) were generally good, although there was a lack of focus on planning and many answers regurgitated textbook learning. A large number of answers to (d) consisted of short bullet points and thus lacked appropriate depth.

(a) **Internal audit's role**

Internal audit's evaluation of an organisation's systems and processes is part of the process by which an organisation gains assurance that its **business risks are being effectively managed** and that **internal controls are operating** as planned.

Risk management process

Part of internal audit's remit is to review the **risk management strategies established by management**, the **risk culture** of the organisation and the **reliability of risk assessments** being made. Internal auditors may be able to place reliance on the risk assessments made when planning their own work; however if they are not satisfied, they will have to make their own judgements and report on the inadequacies of the current system to the board and audit committee.

Internal control

Internal audit will also be concerned with how the **systems established by management** to respond to, and manage, risks are working and their work on internal control systems is part of this.

Internal audit will be concerned initially with the **design of internal controls** and the **adequacy of the framework** for reducing risks to acceptable levels. Internal audit will also be concerned with the **operation of controls**, using a combination of **risk assessment and detailed testing**. Not only will internal audit provide a check on operation, it may improve the chances of some controls operating effectively; staff may be more likely to operate controls well if they know that their work might be audited.

Recommendations

The recommendations internal audit make will feed back into the **design and operation** of **risk management and internal control systems**. The recommendations will have regard for the organisation's **strategic objectives** (including the requirement that costs of control are reasonable given benefits) and also the organisation's **risk appetite**.

(b) **Risks**

Data protection risks

SPQ is possibly vulnerable to the **loss of sensitive data** about customers to competitors or other third parties. It may also have **breached data protection legislation**.

Information systems risks

SPQ may also be vulnerable to interference in the data it holds by the introduction of **viruses**. This would severally impact on its ability to trade on-line.

Accounting information risks

If the problems are widespread there is a risk that management decision-making will be **influenced by incorrect data**. There is also a **compliance risk**, that the loss of data will mean SPQ **fails to fulfil legal requirements to maintain proper accounting records**.

Systems development risks

The failure to test systems properly may mean that systems are not fulfilling their objectives and that consequently **resources are being wasted**, either through the systems not providing the **support required** or as here because **resources are having to be used to investigate problems** within the system.

You would also have scored marks if you had discussed any of the following risks.

Revenue and counterparty risks

An obvious risk is the risk of **loss of revenue** through failure of customers (or possibly third parties) to pay for goods that have been delivered. There is also a risk of **customers' dissatisfaction** and **loss of sales** if they have ordered goods, but their orders have been intercepted by **third parties**.

Reputation risks

SPQ will be vulnerable to a **fall in its sales**, if its computer problems are made public and as a result **customers lose confidence** in the security of the system. These developments may ultimately **depress the company's share price**.

Controls

Security controls

The whole security system requires urgent review including whether **staff's rights of access to the system** need to change, and whether any current system of **passwords needs to change**. Possibly the passwords currently required are too easily guessed and more **complex passwords or more frequent changes** should be introduced. Other measures include **firewalls**, preventing public access to certain parts of the system.

Accounting information controls

It should **not be possible to delete transactions completely** without a **record being made in the system**, possibly a **dump file**, the contents of which are regularly reviewed and investigated. Also **order and delivery records** should be **matched** to sales and receipts details, and **unmatched orders and delivery notes investigated**.

System testing

The systems development procedures either need to be improved or implemented better, and in particular should **require the approval of the information technology department** and **other users.** The use of a structured methodology would ensure that the system is designed with both business and users' needs in mind. Clearly also a **system of post-audit reviews** should be introduced. If fundamental failure of the systems occur (as perhaps here), there should be a requirement that the system undergo a **complete re-testing.**

Decision-making and review

The governance procedures requiring change may include the requirement for the whole board to approve decisions such as the **introduction of the new systems**, and **improved access** particularly for internal audit but also for other staff to the audit committee. The UK's Combined Code requires a **regular review** of all internal control systems, including IT systems, by the board.

(c) **Strategic issues**

The overall audit plan will be influenced by the **organisation's objectives, structure and information flows** and the **risk management system** in place. These will determine which **areas of the organisation** and **which risks** it is most important for internal audit work to cover.

Areas to be covered and extent of coverage

The audit **objectives**, the **order of work**, the **areas** to be covered and **how much and what work** is done will depend on:

(i) The organisation's **own risk assessment** and **risk assessments undertaken** by **internal audit**

(ii) The **extent of internal controls** within the area

(iii) Any **specific requests for coverage**, for example by the chief accountant (as here) or the audit committee

(iv) The **work carried out by external audit**

(v) The results of **preliminary work** on the audit area including review of previous results and changes in the business environment

(vi) **Any control breaches identified**

Operational planning

The operational plan will need to cover in detail the **scope and timetabling** of the audit, and also the **staffing and resources** required (including the need for staff with experience or specialist knowledge). If members of the internal audit team have been involved in the design of the system, they should **not** be involved in its audit.

(d) **Ethical principles**

Integrity

The Head of Internal Audit (HIA) is being asked to tone down the criticisms and **therefore produce a report** that is **potentially misleading** to the audit committee. It may affect the decisions and recommendations the committee makes about the company's risk management procedures and framework if committee members do not have a correct understanding of the **level of risks**.

Objectivity

The HIA is coming under pressure from others to **modify internal audit's recommendations** because of **political pressures** within the company. **Ethical objectivity** requires a consideration of the impact on affected third parties who are unable to influence the decision.

Competence

If internal audit does produce a toned-down report and major problems continue, the **competence of the HIA and the rest of the internal audit department** may be called into question when the problems are discovered, possibly by external audit.

Resolving difficulties

Reporting weaknesses to the chief executive

This course of action would be proper in the sense that the chief executive is the HIA's **immediate superior**. If the chief executive is convinced about the seriousness of the problems, it may be easier to get them corrected. However the chief executive's **previous attitude** suggests that he may forbid the HIA to issue the audit committee with the report in its current form. The chief executive's **previous involvement** also means that the HIA could justifiably bypass him.

Reporting weaknesses to the audit committee

This would resolve the issues of **not supplying the audit committee with information** and aspersions being cast on **internal audit's competence**, and also mean that the HIA had taken a robust attitude to the pressures placed on himself. However if there is a **conflict between the audit committee and the chief executive**, it might jeopardise the chances of the necessary improvements being made. **Discussion with audit committee chair** might be a better response than submitting the report directly. As head of the audit committee, the chair has responsibility for **ensuring the findings of internal audit are properly actioned**, and practically he may be able to advise how best to present the recommendations.

Discussion with finance director

Alternatively the HIA could first discuss the matter with the finance director, as he should be aware of the concerns the chief accountant has. The difficulty might be that the finance director may feel **loyalty to the chief executive** and report the conversation to him.

Recommendation

As a first stage, the best solution would be to **discuss the matter with the audit committee chair** for his advice on the best way to proceed. Although this is not a formal report, notes should be taken of this discussion. Subsequent action can be agreed at this meeting.

38 Preparation question: Bruce SA

Text references. Chapters 11 and 12.

Top tips. With the forward contract the question indicates you should subtract the amount (the premium). The rate is use is the unfavourable rate for Bruce SA. As it's based **in Europe** and has **received $**, it wants to **buy €** with **the $** it's received. Hence the rate to use is the **higher** rate that means it has to spend more $ (1.2362 – 0.0028 = 1.2334) to obtain each € that it wants. We subtract the 0.0028 as the forward rate is quoted at a premium.

For the money market calculation

- You have to **borrow** in the **foreign currency** to match the foreign currency **receipt.** You will pay off the borrowing with the receipt.
- The amount you borrow is less than you will receive (hence the division) because you will obtain interest by **investing** the amount borrowed in your home market.

As you'll be **receiving $**, you need to **buy € futures** now, and sell them at the later date when you want to buy € with the $ you receive.

For the futures calculation the date of the contract needs to be **after** the date the transaction is due to be settled. (Here the contract is settled mid-September; the September futures date is at the **end** of September.) The tick size is 0.01% of the contract size, hence we multiply the contract size by 0.0001. The futures gain has to be translated at the **closing spot rate** as the gain is in $ which is the foreign currency in this transaction.

The key decisions in the options calculation are to choose the right date – again it needs to be **after** the date the transaction is due to be settled. (The September option, expiring 30 September, is after the mid-September settlement date.) You need to choose the right type of option – here it's a **call** option enabling you to **buy** the **home currency €** that you want using the **foreign currency $** receipt. The option ensures that you can buy at a reasonable price in the worst possible exchange rate scenario. In some calculations, you may have the information available to be able to calculate which option price to choose, but more often, as you do here, you can choose one as an example (if you're told the closing spot rate, then the example option price you choose will be one where you will exercise the option).

Because you're using a traded option, there will be a difference between what receiving from the customer and the amount covered by the option contract, so you have to calculate the **difference** at the **closing spot rate,** having translated the amount of home currency in the option contracts at the **option strike price.** Remember also that the option premium is translated at the **opening** spot rate.

Easy marks. The forward rate calculation should hopefully be straightforward, and you will get easy marks for making the right decisions about which futures and options to choose, and calculating how many contracts.

Hedging using the forward contract

The company should take out a **three month forward contract** to sell $2,350,000 at $1.2362 – $0.0028 = $1.2334

This rate is agreed today for exchange in 3 months, converting to $2,350,000/1.2334 = **€1,905,302**

Top tip. Remember as the exchange rates are quoted as $X:€1, we have to **divide $** amounts by the exchange rate to obtain amounts in €.

Money market hedging

	Now		*+ 3 months*
$	2 So borrow now $2,342,971	3/12 × 1.2% = 0.3% per 3 months (borrowing rate) × 1/1.003 ←	1 Will receive $2,350,000
↓	To be able to invest $ borrowed, must sell them now @ 1.2362		
€	3 So invest now €1,895,301	On which interest is received at 3/12 × 2.2% = 0.55% per 3 months (lending rate) × 1.0055 →	4 Due to Bruce €1,905,725 (effective receipt from hedge)

Futures market

Set up

(i) We shall be buying September contracts as they mature after payment date

(ii) Buy € futures

(iii) Number of contracts

$$\frac{2,350,000/1.2321}{125,000} = 15.3, \text{ say 15 contracts.}$$

(iv) Tick size 125,000 × 0.0001 = $12.50.

Closing prices

Closing futures price is 1.2439 $/€, closing spot rate is 1.2450 $/€

Outcome

(i) **On futures market**

Opening futures price Buy	1.2321
Closing futures price Sell	1.2439
Movement in ticks	118 ticks gain
Gain on futures market	118 × 12.50 × 15 = $ 22,125 gain

(ii) **Net outcome**

	€
Spot market receipt (2,350,000/1.2450)	1,887,550
Gain on futures market (22,125/1.2450)	17,771
	1,905,321

Option set up

(i) Contract date

September

(ii) Type of option

Buy call option as buying €

(iii) Strike price

Say 1.2350

(iv) Number of contracts

$$\frac{2,350,000 \div 1.2350}{62,500} = 30.4\text{, say } 30$$

(v) Premium

$$\text{Premium} = \frac{30 \times 62,500 \times 0.0336}{1.2354}$$

$$= €50,996$$

Closing spot rate

1.2450 $/€

Outcome

(i) **Options market outcome**

Spot rate	1.2450
Exercise price	1.2350
Exercise	Yes

(ii) **Net outcome**

Outcome of options position 62,500 × 30 = €1,875,000

Balance on spot market

	$
Exercise option 62,500 × 30 × 1.2350	2,315,625
Value of transaction	2,350,000
Balance ($ receipt not covered by option contract)	34,375
Translated at spot rate (34,375/1.2450)	€27,610

	€
Options market	1,875,000
Balance on spot market	27,610
Option premium	(50,996)
Net receipt	1,851,614

39 Treasury and risk reporting

Text references. Chapters 2,5 and 10.

Top tips. The main (possibly the only) danger in (a) is to be sidetracked from the terms of the question; remember you are looking at the treasury function's role with **specific reference to risk management**. Linking risk appetite with the activities of the treasury function is an important consideration here. The arguments against the treasury function acting as a profit centre are derived from the agency problem, which is also an issue in corporate governance. How do the directors (the principals) control the treasury function (the agent)? What are the costs?

To answer (b) well you probably needed to have read risk and control disclosures in one or more sets of listed company accounts. Our answer weighs up the factors that may lead to increased disclosures (regulatory, investor or reputation demands) against factors that may incline the directors to disclose less.

The examiner's comments for (b) are a good illustration of why you need to read questions carefully. It seems that many students focused on the second half of the requirement and wrote all they could think of about Risk Exposure and Control Systems. However the key words were **explain the factors** that determine disclosure. This illustrates the need above all else to focus on the question verb (explain) and the object of the verb (the factors).

Easy marks. You should certainly have had the knowledge from your RCS and FS studies to be able to score heavily in (a).

Examiner's comments. (a) was generally answered well; answers demonstrated thorough revision of this area.

Answers to (b) were generally very poor. Students failed to answer the question, which was the **factors influencing** the content of the report, not the content of the report.

(a) (i) **Definition of role**

The treasury function exists to **manage the risks** that relate to the finance the organisation requires, the organisation's cash flows and funds, and the currency dealings that it undertakes. It is also responsible for **managing the relationship between the organisation and its financial stakeholders** and **assessing the financial viability** of the investments it undertakes.

Discussion of role

Relationships with banks

The treasury function is responsible for **contacting and dealing with banks**, and **diversifying funds** over a number of institutions or markets to minimise the risk of being too reliant on one.

Liquidity management

The treasury function is responsible for ensuring that the organisation has **sufficient liquid funds** available for emergencies and **future cash requirements** are **budgeted**. It should also ensure that **cash surpluses** are **invested** in accordance with corporate objectives and the organisation's **risk appetite.**

Funding management

The treasury function will be responsible for determining the sources of funding the **organisation requires.** It will take into account the risks of:

- The **debt-equity mix** and the combination of different types of debt
- **Committing to making interest payments**
- **Changes in interest rates.**

Bearing these **risks** and the **costs** of different sources in mind, it will select the **sources of funds** and the **capital instruments** that are most appropriate for the organisation, and **organise the raising of finance**.

Currency risk management

The treasury function **supervises currency risk management**. It should ensure efficient use is made of **internal matching of cash flows from different subsidiaries**. It will also be responsible for choosing appropriate **external hedging methods** depending on the **size and length of exposure**, and whether the organisation wishes to make the most of possible **opportunities** presented by favourable exchange rate movements by purchasing options.

(ii) **Arguments for operating the treasury function as a profit centre**

Making the most of opportunities

Running the treasury function as a **profit centre**, and evaluating its performance in terms of how funds are used to generate profits, means that the organisation can take advantage of **lucrative opportunities** that the financial markets offer. The profit motive incentivises the function to take risks which is unlikely if it operates as a cost centre.

Quality of staff

The profits made may enable the company to recruit **knowledgeable and experienced staff** at high salaries. Hopefully this should mean that mistakes are not made through staff not understanding the complexities of the transactions that the organisation is undertaking.

Efficiency of risk management

Having risk management centralised with a profit incentive, should mean that the treasury function manages risks efficiently, ensuring a **balanced relationship** between risk and return. **Unnecessary hedging** should not occur, and the **costs of risk management** should be **reduced** as a centralised department can undertake fewer and larger transactions.

Arguments against operating the treasury function as a profit centre

Inconsistent risk appetite

In order to make profits, treasury officials have the incentive to **speculate large sums of money** on transactions carrying a **significant probability of loss.** These risks may be greater than the board of directors believes is desirable; however the complexities of treasury operations may mean that it is difficult for the board to identify that its wishes are not being followed.

Costs of monitoring

Monitoring treasury activities effectively will be **expensive.** Senior management will need to **spend significant time** reviewing treasury activities. Internal audit involvement may also be necessary; however the **salaries of internal auditors** who understand treasury activities may also need to be **high.**

Costs to subsidiaries

Running the treasury function as a profit centre will mean that subsidiaries can be charged a **realistic rate** for their use of its services. This should enable a fairer assessment of the profitability of both the subsidiaries and the treasury function. However the costs may **discourage the subsidiaries from using the services of the treasury function**, so that they **retain risks** which have not yet crystallised rather than pay for them to be managed. As a result **losses** may be **built up** in **subsidiaries** at a later stage.

(b) **Legal and regulatory requirements**

The board will firstly need to ensure that the company complies with the requirements of legislation, Stock Exchange rules or corporate governance codes. For example, the UK Turnbull report requires the board to:

- Acknowledge its responsibility for ensuring the effectiveness of control systems
- State the existence of a risk management process
- Explain what the board has done to review its effectiveness

It may also mean disclosing the full implications of problems, for example the requirement in the Sarbanes-Oxley legislation for boards to disclose **material weaknesses in internal controls over financial reporting.**

Other accounts disclosures

The risk and control report should **link in with other disclosures** in the accounts about business developments. UK 2008 regulations require disclosure in the directors' report of likely future developments in the business of the company, including presumably changes in risk exposure.

Interests of users

The directors must also take account of the views of shareholders, who will be interested in learning about the risks that could have most impact on the **value of their investment,** and how these risks are being controlled. These would include **principal strategic and financial risks**, and also **operational risks** that could have severe financial consequences; for example a provider of education courses would be severely affected by loss of access to teaching sites. The views of other principal **stakeholders** will also be important.

Risks materialising or changing over the year

Any risks that have crystallised over the year and caused **material losses** will interest users of the accounts, who will also want to see what **improvements in control** have been made or proposed as a consequence. Disclosure of risks that have **significantly changed** will also be important, and how control systems have developed to meet these changes.

Reputation risks

Risks that could cause a significant fall in the organisation's reputation may well be risks about which the board wishes to reassure stakeholders. This will be particularly important if the board wishes to stress the company's **corporate social responsibility or environmental protection** credentials. Disclosures will also focus on threats to reputation that may have a large impact on the business, particularly **product safety.**

Limitations on risk disclosures

The board may be less willing to disclose some risks on the grounds of **commercial confidentiality.** Directors may also fear that **disclosures about certain risks** will be **misinterpreted** by readers of the accounts. However they may also be motivated to include matters included in the reports of competitors or those identified as **best practice** to evidence how they are managing the risks that are common in this industry.

Accountabilities

Although the board has ultimate responsibility for risk management, disclosures ought to cover other accountabilities for risk management. This includes the roles of the **board committees**, and the **role of specialist functions** such as treasury. Disclosure should also show how the board is **identifying and prioritising the most important risks**.

Strong control systems

Evidence suggests that some companies include **detailed disclosures about control systems** and reveal rather less about risks. They appear to be trying to give the impression that they have robust control systems that can cope with all the significant risks that the company faces.

40 PS

Text references. Chapter 12.

Top tips. Forget the complicated Black-Scholes formula – you will not be asked to use it! But appreciation of the five input variables is important when evaluating a number of choices that arise in investment decisions. List them and give brief explanations.

In (b) the forward contract calculation is easy provided you can work out the rate.

For the option, remember that if you are exchanging dollars for £, this means you need to **buy** £ with dollars, so you need a £ **call** option.

The option price to choose can be debated. $1.41 offers the best choice of option on the information given because you are spending as few dollars as possible (effective rate is lowest) when buying £. However an examiner has argued that the spot rate equates to the forward rate of $1.4266 on the terms given in the question. If the exercise price of a currency option is worse than the forward rate, and exchange rates move in the **predicted direction**, ($ falling against £), it doesn't make sense to acquire an option at a price below $1.4266. You will only choose an option price of $1.41 if you expect to exercise it, but you buy an option in the expectation that it will not be exercised.

Remember also that the option premium is a sunk cost that has to be paid **whether or not** the option is exercised; it needs to be included in the calculation to be able to compare the outcome of using options with the outcomes of using other methods. For strict comparability with the forward market, we have taken out a forward contract on the amount unhedged by options. It would have been acceptable to have just taken this amount to the spot market, and that's what you'd probably do in other questions when time is tighter.

Easy marks. You should always be able to obtain marks for discussion in a derivatives question, even if a lot of the marks are available for the calculation. Following the proforma in an options question should ensure you remember all elements of the calculation even if you don't get all the figures right.

In other questions on derivatives, you'll find that the discussion element accounts for rather more of the marks than it does here.

(a) The **Black-Scholes pricing model** was developed to value traded call options on quoted shares and can be adapted to value any options. The input variables are:

(1) **The market price of the underlying share**
If the **share price rises**, the value of the **call option** will **increase**.

(2) **The exercise price (or strike price)**
A **call option** gives the holder the **right to buy** the share at a fixed price, known as the **exercise price**. The **higher the price of the underlying share** compared with the exercise price (above), the **more valuable** is the **option**.

(3) **The time to expiry**
The longer an option has to run before it expires, the more chance there is that the **value of the underlying share will increase**. Time to expiry therefore **adds value** to an option.

(4) **The volatility of the underlying share (standard deviation of share price variations)**
Options provide **unlimited opportunities for gains** but **losses** are **limited to the purchase price**. This asymmetrical probability distribution of gains/losses means that volatility of the underlying share **adds value** to the option.

(5) **The interest rate**
This is the **risk free rate of interest**, which gives the **time value of money** and is relevant because the option is valued today but is exercisable on a future date.

The difference between 1 and 2 is known as the '**intrinsic value**' of the option, but it has a minimum value of zero. The combination of 3, 4 and 5 gives its '**time value**'. The total value of the option is the sum of intrinsic and time values.

(b) The company expects to receive $2,350,000. At today's spot rate this would be converted to £ at $1.4220, giving $2,350,000/1.4220 = £1,652,602. This can be regarded as the company's target receipt.

Hedging using the forward contract

The company should take out a **three month forward contract** to sell $2,350,000 at $1.4220 + $0.0046 = $1.4266. This rate is agreed today for exchange in 3 months, converting to $2,350,000/1.4266 = **£1,647,273**.

This amount is guaranteed, provided the dollars are received as expected.

Option set-up

(i) **Contract date**

3 months time

(ii) **Option type**

Call option; buy £ with $

(iii) **Strike price**

Choose $1.43 because option is not expected to be exercised

(iv) **Number of contracts**

$\frac{2{,}350{,}000 \div 1.43}{31{,}250} \approx 53$ contracts

(v) **Premium**

Premium = 53 × 31,250 × $0.0136
= $22,525 @ 1.4180
= £15,885

Outcome

Option will be exercised if dollar weakens to more than $1.43 in £.

(i) Exercise 53 contracts @ $1.43

Outcome of options position

31,250 × 53 = £1,656,250

Balance on spot market

	$
Exercise option (31,250 × 53 × 1.43)	2,368,438
Value of transaction	2,350,000
Balance overhedged	(18,438)
Translated at spot rate (26,250/1.4400)	£(12,804)

(ii)

	£
Option outcome	1,656,250
Balance received	(12,804)
Option premium (sunk cost)	(15,885)
Net receipt	1,627,561

Conclusion

The **forward contract** provides **better cover** than the option if the dollar weakens (£1,647,273 compared with £1,627,561).

Other influences on policy

(i) **Risk appetite**
The forward rate offers a certain solution that isn't **dependent on movements in exchange** rates.

(ii) **Budgeting**
How important for budgeting and other purposes it is to know the exact amount.

(iii) **Gain**
The fact that the option allows the company to make a **currency gain** which is not possible under the forward contract.

(iv) **Lapse of contract**
A forward contract **cannot be avoided** if the contract is lost and could create a currency loss, compared with translating at spot, whereas a currency option can be allowed to lapse if it is not advantageous.

(v) **Feasibility of dates**
The forward contract has to be settled on a **fixed date**, whereas an option need not be. However the company can take out an **option forward contract** which allows settlement over a range of dates.

41 SDT

Text references. Chapter 11 on the financial risks, Chapter 15 on other relevant risks.

Top tips. Note the requirements in (a) require **critical** commentary, which should have indicated to you the need to explain why the director's views were wrong. The main elements in the answer are market efficiency and (insufficient) diversification, both concepts from Financial Strategy, but remember that you may need to use FS knowledge in this paper as well. Don't forget the second part of the question, to discuss potential benefits.

The main problem in (b) appears to have been identifying which figure you had to calculate, indicating you needed to read the question carefully. The **greater** of the two relevant exchange rates is used in every calculation, as in each case SDT is **receiving the foreign currency**, and is having to pay the **higher amount** to obtain each £ that it wants.

(c) is a straightforward look at the higher risks that mean a higher return is required. (d) can bring in debtor management as well as option forward contracts.

Easy marks. Evidently the calculations, as this was the most popular Section B question and many who answered it scored full marks in (b); those that didn't calculated figures the question didn't require rather than made mistakes in calculating the figures the question did require. (c) is a fairly general risk discussion so shouldn't have presented too many problems,

Examiner's comments. This was by some distance the most popular optional question. The question required candidates to comment critically and interpret currency data. About a third of the marks were available for computation.

The main weakness in (a) were failure to discuss the managing directors' views, as required by the question. Many candidates scored full marks in (b), although some failed to score because they did not follow the requirements of the question, and calculated sales value or contribution per unit rather than total contribution.

(a) The main problems with the Managing Director's views are:

(i) **Conditions for efficiency**
The conditions for efficiency are **market liquidity**, **full information** and **freely floating currencies**. In practice liquidity and information available varies between currencies. Many currencies are at most subject to managed floating, floating within limits decided by governments. However conditions for efficiency will apply more to the major currencies in the scenario, and gains and losses from each individual currency may be equally likely.

(ii) **Limited range of currencies**
Although the managing director is correct in saying that the risk is diversified, it is not diversified across all currencies. It is possible that the £ may move in an **adverse direction** against each of the three currencies, if for example the UK's inflation rate was higher than other major nations. In fact the currencies quoted are known as the Triad because the countries are similar markets, so in practice there might be **positive correlation between the three** and hence diversification over them will increase the risk of losses.

(iii) **Hedging sales only**
Foreign exchange risk is enhanced because it is only in one direction, for **sales**. As purchases are all in £, there is **no matching of sales and purchases** in the same currency which will limit foreign exchange risk.

Currency hedging may be beneficial for the following reasons, although it will incur costs:

(i) **Risk limitation**
Hedging risk can mean that the **amounts SDT** receives can be **fixed**, and SDT is not subject to **adverse fluctuations**. In an efficient market, prices respond to new information, so shocks may have unexpected effects on exchange rates.

(ii) **Size of possible losses**

Because SDT exports over 90% of its production, **potential losses** from adverse events could be **very large**.

(iii) **Improved forecasting**

Fixing the amounts to be received will also help **internal forecasting and budgeting procedures**.

Conclusion

Bearing these considerations in mind, SDT needs to consider hedging risk

(b) (i) (1) **A**

Contribution = Revenue – Costs

$$= \frac{\text{Export sales}}{\text{Exchange rate}} - \left(\text{Unit variable costs} \times \frac{\text{Export sales}}{\text{Unit export sales price}}\right)$$

= (9,487,500/200.032) – (2.75 × 9,487,500/632.50)

= 47,430 – 41,250
= £6,180

B

Contribution = (82,142/1.7775) – (4.80 × 82,142/10.2678)

= 46,212 – 38,400
= £7,812

Euro

Contribution = (66,181/1.4784) – (6.25 × 66,181/12.033)

= 44,765 – 34,375
= £10,390

(2) **A**

Contribution = (9,487,500/202.63) – 41,250

= 46,822 – 41,250
= £5,572

B

Contribution = (82,142/1.7750) – 38,400

= 46,277 – 38,400
= £7,877

Euro

Contribution = (66,181/1.4680) – 34,375

= 45,082 – 34,375
= £10,707

(ii) **Hedging**

$$\text{Contribution to sales ratio} = \frac{6{,}180 + 7{,}812 + 10{,}390}{47{,}430 + 46{,}212 + 44{,}765} = 17.62\%$$

Not hedging

$$\text{Contribution/sales ratio} = \frac{5{,}572 + 7{,}877 + 10{,}707}{46{,}822 + 46{,}277 + 45{,}082} = 17.48\%$$

Hedging leads to a higher contribution per sale than not hedging and accordingly SDT should hedge its foreign exchange exposure.

(c) **Reasons for generating higher rates of return**

Businesses will try to generate higher contributions from export sales as they appear to be riskier than domestic sales.

Foreign exchange risk

Foreign exchange risk will mean that the **receipts are uncertain**, unless the exports are **invoiced in the domestic currency**.

Physical risk

Because of the greater distances, there may be an increased risk of the **goods being lost, damaged or stolen in transit**, or the documents accompanying the goods going astray.

Credit risk

There may be a higher risk in allowing customers credit because **researching their suitability is more difficult** than domestic customers. Payments may be **slower from overseas customers**, and it may be difficult and costly to monitor and pursue customers who fail to pay promptly or at all.

Trade risk

Because of the large distances travelled, there may be a risk that the customers **do not accept the goods** when delivered, or that the order is **cancelled in transit**.

Political risk

Overseas governments may impose a **variety of rules and restrictions**, including **higher quality standards** than are imposed in the company's own domestic market.

Risk mitigation

The effects of all these risks can be mitigated by **hedging techniques** for foreign exchange currency, **insuring against the risks** or reducing the risk of problems by, for example, using **credit reference agencies** to report on customers. However all of these will have **costs**, and increased sales revenues will cover those costs.

(d) **Risk**

The risk is that SDT will be forced to **buy currency at a poorer spot rate**, in order to be able to sell it to the bank at the forward rate. If the customer subsequently fulfils the contract, SDT may not be able to recoup the loss it has made. Alternatively SDT may take out **another forward contract** up until the time that the customer is expected to pay, but this may be on poorer terms than the original contract. **Transaction costs** will also be incurred.

Risk reduction procedures

(i) **Insurance**
The risk can be avoided by taking out **insurance** against the possibility of the customers failing to fulfil their obligations, although a premium will be payable.

(ii) **Discount**
SDT could **reduce the risk of the customers paying late** by offering a **discount for payment on time**; the cost then would be the amount of the discount. Alternatively SDT could specify **penalties** for late payment; this would reduce the cost for SDT if payment was late.

(iii) **Hedging**
SDT could take out an **option forward contract** that would give it some leeway as to the date the contract will be fulfilled. However there would be **increased transaction costs**, and SDT would have to accept the worst exchange rate over the period the option could be exercised.

42 Derivatives

Text references. Chapter 11 covers hedging, Chapter 13 IAS 39 and Chapter 10 value at risk.

Top tips. Note that the answer to (a) doesn't just consider risk from the company's viewpoint but also the investors' viewpoint. The requirement to discuss means that you have to look at both sides of the debate; the basic viewpoints are that Warren Buffett appears to be thinking more of derivatives as means of speculation, whereas corporate treasurers think in terms of derivatives as a method of hedging to **reduce** risks. The 13 marks available mean that you have the chance to discuss in detail the reasoning behind the two viewpoints and reach a conclusion. Hedging may reduce risk, but what problems might involvement in the foreign exchange markets cause? Speculation can lead to excessive losses, but is it possible to reduce risks to a level that's acceptable compared with the returns that may be obtained?

The mention of IAS 39 later in the question should have alerted you to the need to discuss the impact on accounts, but you don't need to go into excessive technical detail; the main points were the problems with measuring fair values and the different treatment of hedging instruments. Bringing in Financial Strategy knowledge of the work of treasury departments is also helpful.

(b) requires a explanation of the impact of fair value accounting on various risks, not just trading risks, again emphasising what we said in the introduction to the kit that you need to think widely about risks. The highlighting of the accounting implications should have led you to cover accounts risks. The question does actually provide the main details of IAS 39 that you need to answer (b).

(c) requires application of the value at risk definition in the context of what a fund manager does. The figure used for standard deviations is the 'one-tail' figure 1.65 standard deviations, corresponding to 0.4500 in the table. We are only interested in one half of the normal curve as we are only worried about a loss. You would have missed marks on (ii) if you failed to comment (explain the implications of) the calculation. This discussion in fact was worth more marks than the calculation.

Easy marks. Some easy marks at the start of the question for explaining the purposes of hedging, but your answer to (a) and (b) needs to go some way beyond that in order to pass. Had this come up in your exam, you also shouldn't have attempted the question if you weren't sure what value at risk was.

Examiner's comments. Some candidates limited their mark-scoring opportunities in (a) by failing to discuss speculation. Answers to (b) were poor with candidates failing to use the details in the question, not understanding the different uses of the derivatives and clearly not knowing the accounting requirements. The straightforward calculation in (c) was done badly and students need to revise this area.

(a) **Definition of derivative**

A **derivative** is a financial instrument **settled at a future date**, the value of which changes in response to changes in an **underlying variable**, and which has a **relatively small initial investment** compared with other contracts that respond in similar ways to changes in market forces. Examples of derivatives include foreign exchange, interest rate and commodity derivatives.

Different reasons for using derivatives

The reasons why different views on the use of derivatives exist is that derivatives are used for different purposes. Some organisations use them as a means of **reducing risk** and to **hedge other transactions** they are undertaking. Other organisations use them for **speculative purposes**. Successful speculation can lead to increased return; however with **increased return** comes **increased risk**. However both hedgers and speculators are necessary for markets in futures to function; the involvement of speculators **increases the liquidity of markets** and bridges the gap between hedgers who are selling and hedgers who are buying.

Hedging

Organisations that use futures to hedge are concerned about **future commitments** they are making to deal in the future in foreign exchange, commodities or financial instruments. Because the deal is taking place some time in advance, the eventual receipt or payment may be uncertain. If for example the deal is in a foreign currency, the amount to be received or paid in the home currency will depend on how the **exchange rate** has **moved** in the meantime.

The company will therefore invest in futures so that losses through adverse movements in exchange rates will be matched by gains on the currency future contracts, brought about by changes in price due to the same exchange rate movements. This should **reduce profit and cash flow risks**. **Options** can be used to reduce these risks as well and also allow organisations to **benefit from favourable movements in rates**.

Hedging risks

The risks from hedging derive from the futures investment **not being an exact match** with the original transaction. **Basis risk,** the risk that the futures price movement and the movement of the price of the original transaction will not correspond, may also be significant. If an instrument is held for hedging purposes, its fair value gain or loss is recognised in the income statement, but so also is the gain or loss on the underlying hedged item. This **limits the effect of uncertainties in measurement** on the accounts.

Speculation

Some organisations **buy or sell futures purely to make profits**. They are **not interested in the commodity or instrument** that **underlies the futures transaction**, but instead attempt to make profits from their ability to predict movements in prices of the futures.

Speculation risks

Because the futures market is **highly leveraged**, the speculator can for a small deposit invest in derivatives, whose movements in price are **proportionally much greater** than those of the underlying commodity. As a result the **profit or loss per pound invested is much greater** than speculating on the underlying commodity. Hence Warren Buffett and others view them as a potential time bomb.

Reduction of speculation risks

Speculation risk can be reduced by employing **treasury specialists** to carry out dealings. However treasury specialists who are employed by an organisation running its treasury department as a **profit centre** may be tempted to **speculate excessively** to improve profits and hence their own reward. In addition even cautious well-informed treasury specialists can be caught by unexpected market changes.

Control of treasury specialists

To reduce this risk the organisation's senior management need to **establish the organisation's risk appetite** in terms of the maximum losses it can sustain and ensure that this is reflected in **effective controls** over the amounts that treasury specialists can risk. However the effectiveness of these controls may be undermined by the difficulties in measuring profits or losses from derivative trading and hence the risks its treasury specialists are taking.

Investors' risks

IAS 39 requires derivatives held for speculation or trading purposes to be carried in accounts at their **fair value**. The risk to investors partly derives from the uncertainties involved in determining fair value. To do so, **significant assumptions** may have to be made, and **judgements** exercised as to what techniques should be used. This means that investors may see a value in the accounts that could have been significantly different under different assumptions, and that accounts **do not disclose fully the risks involved**. This makes judging the balance sheet date position and forecasting the future extremely difficult, and of course the position may have altered significantly since the balance sheet date.

Conclusion

Thus both viewpoints are potentially true. Derivatives can be a means of risk reduction, but they can also have very serious consequences if not used carefully, or used for speculation, and can also lead to problems for investors trying to assess accounts.

(b) **Accounts risks**

The main risk is **loss of reputation or financial penalties** through being found to have produced accounts that give misleading indications of fair value.

Income risks

Income may become **increasingly volatile** depending on the market data and models being used. This volatility is due to a focus on assets and liabilities rather than accounting for income. This may have an **adverse impact on the ability of companies to pay dividends** and on **companies' share price and cost of capital,** as accounts users find it difficult to determine what is causing the volatility.

Systems risks

Adoption of fair value may require investment in new systems, and there may be an **increased risk of systems problems** as systems have to cope with linking of assets with derivatives, accommodating changes in hedge allocations and measuring hedge effectiveness.

(c) (i) **Value at risk**

The **value at risk** model is a statistical method of assessing risk in financial markets. From the viewpoint of the fund manager, value at risk measures the **maximum loss possible due to normal market movements over a given period of time and a given level of probability**, assuming a normal distribution.

In this context the period of time chosen would be one day, reflecting the short length of time financial assets are held before being liquidated. The level of probability chosen will depend on the fund managers' **attitude to risk**; the higher the confidence level, the more **risk averse** the fund manager will be.

Usefulness of value at risk

The value at risk provides an idea of what the potential loss is that is **easily understandable,** and value at risk limits can be used to **control the activities of traders**. A low limit will minimise the risks traders can take. Value at risk does reflect normal market conditions and is less useful in fund markets that could be subject to **sudden shocks**. More sophisticated scenario analysis may also be required.

(ii) If x = 5% and standard deviation = £60,000

Then Confidence level = 1.65 deviations from the mean

VAR = 0 – (1.65 × £60,000)

VAR = £99,000

The 1.65 is the standard normal value associated with the one-tail 5% probability level. There is a 5% chance that the loss of value each day on the shares will be greater than £99,000. In other words the loss would be expected to be greater than £99,000 one day in every twenty. This appears quite small given the size of the portfolio, but the investor may regard it as excessive. Changing the portfolio may **reduce the standard deviation** and hence the **value at risk** to an **acceptable level.**

43 MNO

Text references. Chapters 12 and 13.

Top tips. In (a) for futures, as contracts are in £, you have to **divide the receipt** by the **opening futures price** in order to calculate how many contracts.

The question doesn't say anything about the contract size of the option so the simplest assumption is to assume that it's an over-the-counter (OTC) option. (Further confirmation that it's meant to be an OTC option is that it's a put option, implying a right to sell US $. There are no US$/£ exchange traded option contracts).

The question also does not tell you any direct information about the premium. You don't actually need the premium information to carry out the calculation, although you should certainly mention that there would be a premium as we have done in our answer. Our alternative solution gives the premium calculation suggested by CIMA, although this method has been questioned.

A good way to approach (c) is to consider key elements of the risk management process; company objectives, the risks that need to be managed, and the availability and effectiveness of risk hedging instruments. (c) gives you the chance to demonstrate your strategic awareness, which we stressed as a key skill in the front pages.

Our answer to (c) brings together in each paragraph the different elements of the requirements – that you have to explain how much hedging is undertaken and what instruments are used to hedge. It seems that some students did not go into enough detail about the different methods used.

Easy marks. (b) represents basic knowledge, so should have been very straightforward if you revised this area well.

Examiner's comments. Few candidates used all the correct rates and attempted to calculate the premium. For (c) students were also uncertain about the most appropriate methods of hedging for small and large companies.

(a) **Futures market**

- Buy £ futures
- Number of contracts

  $\frac{1{,}800{,}000/1.690}{62{,}500}$ = 17.04, say 17 contracts.

  This leaves (1,800,000/1.690) – (62,500 × 17) = £2,589 not covered by contracts.
- Tick size 62,500 × 0.0001 = $6.25

On futures market

Opening futures price	1.6900	1.6900
Closing futures price	1.6650	1.7200
Movement in ticks	250 ticks loss	300 ticks profit
Loss on futures market	250 × 6.25 × 17 = $26,563 loss	300 × 6.25 ×17 = $31,875 profit

Net outcome

	$	$
Spot market receipt	1,800,000	1,800,000
Loss/profit on futures market	(26,563)	31,875
	1,773,437	1,831,875
Translated at closing spot rate	1.665	1.720
	£1,065,127	£1,065,044

Option

We assume that MNO is able to purchase an over-the-counter option that means that the exact amount is covered.

Spot rate moves to 1.665 $/£

The option will not be exercised, and MNO will receive $1,800,000/1.665 = £1,081,081

Spot rate moves to 1.720 $/£

The option will be exercised, and MNO will receive $1,800,000/1.675 = £1,074,627.

In practice in either case with the option, MNO will not receive so much because it will have to pay a **premium** for the option. The premium size may well mean that futures are the best method of hedging.

Alternative solution

Premium calculation

Cost = 1.690 – 1.675 = $0.015 per £

Premium = (0.015 × 1,800,000)/1.675 = £16,119

If this figure is used, then the futures market offers the best method of hedging

(b) **Tailoring of contracts**

The contracts cannot be **tailored to the user's exact requirements**. Futures are dealt with on currency exchanges using **standard contract sizes** and the amount to be hedged may not be an amount that can be hedged using a whole number of contracts. In addition futures are only available for **standard delivery dates** that may not correspond to when the company is receiving or paying currency. This means that the company will have to eliminate its commitments under the futures contracts by **closing out**; undertaking a second futures transaction that reverses the effect of the first one.

Hedge inefficiencies

Having to deal in a whole number of contracts means that there may be an amount that is not hedged by futures, or the futures hedge a larger amount than required. The company can leave the **difference unhedged** and exposed to currency risk, or use a **forward contract** to hedge the difference at a different rate. Hedge inefficiencies are also caused by **basis risk**; the risk that the futures contract price will move by a different amount from the price of the underlying currency. Volatile trading conditions on the futures markets mean that the **potential loss** can be **high**.

Market volatility and liquidity

Futures require a **margin payment corresponding to daily price changes in the futures market.** If the market is volatile the **margin payments** may be for significant amounts.

(c) **Objectives and risk appetites**

The strategic objectives and hence the risk appetites of small and large companies are likely to differ significantly. **Small companies** are likely to **concentrate on fewer products and markets**. The key aim is most likely to be using hedging instruments as a means of **minimising exchange transaction risks**. However the risks involved in using some hedging instruments may be considered excessive, for example futures or swaps with significant **counterparty risks**. Small companies may also wish to avoid the **accounting and tax complications** of more complex hedging instruments.

Larger companies by contrast are more likely to achieve their objects by **diversification**, and are likely to tolerate varying levels of risk and return from different activities. This may mean that they are more concerned with being able to take advantage of **possible profits** from derivative usage, for example by using an option so if rates move in a favourable direction the option is not exercised. Ultimately large companies may choose to speculate in **derivatives**, deal in derivatives as a profit-making activity without any link to other underlying transactions.

Incurring exchange risks

Small companies may **incur currency risk** on a limited number of significant transactions in a few currencies. Directors may therefore feel it is worthwhile to **hedge all significant transactions**. To minimise risk, **forward contracts** may well be used as these **guarantee** the exchange rate at which the company will receive or pay monies.

For larger companies, hedging all significant transactions may be **unnecessarily expensive**. Directors will take account of the **currency portfolio** of their transactions. Currency losses through significant payments in a particular currency may be **offset** by significant receipts in the same currency. If the company is undertaking transactions in several major currencies, there is a greater chance that exchange losses on transactions in one currency will be balanced by exchange gains on transactions in another currency.

Incurring interest rate risks

Small companies will be most concerned with the interest rate sensitivities of the debt they need to take out, and their gearing structure is unlikely to be complex. Again they are most likely to be concerned with guaranteeing a borrowing rate on particular sums that they have to borrow and use **forward rate agreements** for that purpose. However they may also want to **use interest rate swaps as** a means of **obtaining finance on better terms**.

Larger companies will be concerned with their overall portfolio, with the **interest rate sensitivities** and **term structure** of their debt and also their investments. This may mean they will use a variety of instruments to hedge different types of finance.

Risk management methods

Smaller companies may not be able to use all the risk management methods available to larger companies. They may not be able to **match receipts and payments** in the same currency for example, or **match investments and borrowings**. The commitment required may be excessive; over-the-counter contracts are often of a **minimum size** that may be too large. The **costs** of certain techniques, for example option premiums, may be considered **too high**.

Large companies may be able to employ **specialist treasury personnel** who have a greater level of expertise in using derivatives than would be found in a smaller general finance function. They are also more likely to have directors or senior managers with sufficient expertise to be able to **monitor** treasury activity effectively. They are therefore more likely to use derivatives such as **futures**, **options** and **swaps**.

44 GOH

Text references. Chapter 11 covers forward exchange contracts, Chapter 14 deals with interest rate swaps.

Top tips. In (a) you need to attempt a calculation, although the terms of the swap are flexible; the gains are unlikely to be split 50:50 because of the inequality in size of the two parties. In other questions you will have to suggest the terms of the swap yourself, but here it is simplest to follow the bank's suggestion that the question has provided.

The question is not completely clear on whether both parties (together) are being charged 0.15%, or each party is being charged 0.15%. We have stated our assumption that each party is being charged 0.15%, but you could have made the other assumption.

You would not need to have drawn a diagram illustrating the swap in this question; we have included the diagram to show clearly the direction of the payments.

Key points in the discussion were the disparity of access to borrowing between the two companies, the principle that the companies should borrow in the market in which they had comparative advantage and using the figures in the question to support the answer.

Other questions on swaps in this kit just ask for advantages in general. Here you are asked for the benefits **in the context of the scenario;** therefore you must bring scenario details in to obtain all the (straightforward) marks.

(b) stresses the key points of certainty and the discussion of futures and other contracts, though brief, covers the major points.

Easy marks. All the discussion parts are straightforward and you could just about pass the question by scoring very high marks on those.

Examiner's comments. Attempts at (a) were in general good; candidates generally coped well with the numerical aspects of swaps, and made valid comments about how gains might be divided.

(a) **Principles of interest rate swaps**

Interest rate swaps are transactions that exploit different interest rates in different markets for borrowing, to **reduce interest costs** for either fixed or floating rate loans. GOH and JJ **swap interest rate commitments** with each other. In a sense, each simulates the other's borrowings, although each party to the swap retains its obligations to the original lenders. This means that the parties must accept **counterparty risk** (the risk of picking up the other's obligations if the other defaults.

Benefits of interest rate swaps

(i) **Transaction of cost**

Transaction costs of 0.15% **are low** compared with other methods, such as options.

(ii) **Flexibility**

Swaps are **flexible**, since GOH and JJ can arrange them in any size, and they can be reversed if necessary.

(iii) **Increased opportunities**

Companies **with different credit ratings** such as GOH and JJ can **borrow in the market** that offers each the best deal and then swap this benefit to reduce the mutual borrowing costs. This is an example of the principle of **comparative advantage**. Here JJ has a comparative advantage in floating rate finance as it can borrow at only 0.6% more than GOH in the floating rate market, compared with 2% in the fixed rate market. GOH therefore has a comparative advantage in the fixed rate market.

(iv) **Capital restructuring**

Swaps allow **capital restructuring** by changing the nature of interest commitments. The implication appears to be that JJ will find it difficult to raise finance at **favourable fixed rates**.

The effects of the swap can be illustrated as follows using the bank's suggestion.

	GOH	*JJ*	*Total*
Wants	Floating	Fixed	
Pays without swap	LIBOR + 0.5%	10.5%	LIBOR + 11
Pays with swap	8.5%	LIBOR + 1.1%	LIBOR + 9.6
Bank fee (assume both are charged 0.15%)	0.15%	0.15%	0.3%
Potential gain			1.1%
Swap			
Pays to bank if swap agreed	(8.5%)	(LIBOR + 1.1%)	
Details of swap			
Floating swap	(LIBOR)	LIBOR	
Fixed swap	9%	(9%)	
Bank fee	(0.15%)	(0.15%)	
Net outcome	(LIBOR – 0.35%)	(10.25%)	
Pays to bank without swap	(LIBOR + 0.5%)	(10.5%)	
Net gain	0.85%	0.25%	1.1%

As the larger company with the better credit rating, GOH received the bulk of the gain.

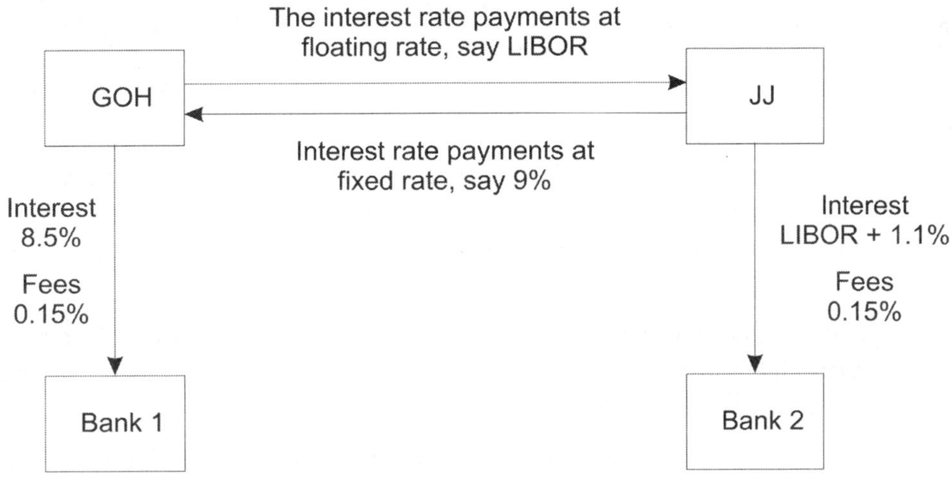

(b) (i) (1) **Advantages of forward exchange contracts for the exporter**

- He can **guarantee** his **profit margin** on a sale by fixing in advance his sterling income.
- He **knows** precisely what his **cash flow** will be **in the future**. This could be important for budgeting.

(2) Assuming the merchant entered into forward contracts to sell dollars to his bank at 1.690 in one month and 1.684 in three months he would receive the following amounts in sterling.

	£
\$60,000 at 1.692	35,461
\$45,000 at 1.690	26,627
\$45,000 at 1.684	26,722
	88,810

(3) Without hedging, the merchant would have received the following amounts in sterling.

	£
\$60,000 at 1.692	35,461
\$45,000 at 1.696	26,533
\$45,000 at 1.704	26,408
	88,402

Clearly the decision to hedge has proved to be beneficial.

(ii) (1) **Transactions in futures**

Transactions in financial futures available on future exchanges are very similar to forward exchange contracts, the main difference being that **futures contracts** are **not individually tailored**. Instead, dealings are in standard contracts for specific future dates. There are also some **administrative differences** between the two forms of contract. On the futures market, participants must lodge a **deposit** to cover possible losses. The open competition leads to **low transaction costs**.

(2) **Other contracts**

Other contracts available include **interest forward rate agreements**. They are advantageous for financial managers because transaction costs are low, competition ensures that the best price is obtained and contracts can be concluded very quickly. Businesses can fix their **interest payments** and therefore **know** what their **cash flow** will be in the future.

45 BB

Text references. Chapter 12.

Top tips. In (a) compare the cash flows of the investment with and without the swap. Note that the risk reduction effect of the swap is just as important as the fact that the expected profitability is higher. Remember also in A that as the exchange rate is quoted at EEX:£1, you need to **divide** the EE amounts by the exchange rate to arrive at the amounts in £.

Your answer to (b) needs to bring out that the main purpose of a swap is to alter risk and/or repayment characteristics of a loan. If this results in gains in expected value then so much the better. You should also be able to comment on disadvantages including counterparty risk.

The marking guide to (a) broke the calculation down in detail. Two marks were available for the net sterling receipts with the swap and one mark available for each of the other points. For the calculation if the swap wasn't used, two marks were available for the end of year receipts, and one mark each for immediate exchange, the position in six months time and the total. Note also that in addition to the marks available for the calculation, two marks were available for an explanation of what was happening and one mark for a recommendation. The marking scheme for (b) allowed a couple of marks for each valid point.

Easy marks. The discussion part of (a) and then most of the discussion in (b). In fact you can gain about half the marks on this question without doing any calculations.

Examiner's comments. In (a) some candidates failed to calculate the expected exchange rate, and failed to recognise the opportunity cost of the swap. Others incorrectly assumed a DCF approach was required.

(a) **Definition**

A currency swap is the exchange between two parties of streams of cash flows denominated in different currencies. In this example the swap takes place as follows:

(i) A **principal amount is exchanged at an agreed exchange rate**: 1,500 million EE marks for £100 million pounds.

(ii) **Interest is paid by the party which received the currency** in the swap: BB plc pays 20% pa on the EE marks and the EE based company pays 12% on the pounds.

(iii) The **principal amounts are swapped back** on agreed terms: in this case it is a straight repayment of the original amount received.

Initial workings

Cash flows occur at three points in time: now, in 6 months and in one year. The spot rate today is EE 18 = £1. Using **purchasing power parity**, which assumes freely floating currencies and bases currency predictions on relative inflation rates,

$$\text{Forward rate currency a/b} = \text{Spot a/b} \times \frac{1+\text{A inflation rate}}{1+\text{B inflation rate}}$$

where EE is A, the UK is B.

$$\text{Forward rate} = 18 \times \frac{1+0.25}{1+0.03}$$

$$= 21.84$$

Assuming a uniform depreciation of the currency, the exchange rate after 6 months would be approximately (21.84 + 18)/2 = 19.92. (Alternatively $18 \times (1.25/1.03)^{1/2} = 19.83$).

In the computations, account will be taken of the interest and opportunity cost of funds by compounding cash flows forward to the end of year 1.

Investment project without the swap

Time		EEm	*Exchange rate*	£m
0	Outlay 1	(750)	18	(41.67)
6 months	Outlay 2	(750)	19.92	(37.65)
1	Project sales receipt from EE govt.	2000	21.84	91.58
	Surplus from project at end of year 1:			12.26

However, this is highly risky as the full amount of project receipts depends on the exchange rate in one year.

Investment project financed by currency swap

Time		EEm	*Exchange* rate	£m.
0	Receive/pay: swap	1,500	15	(100.00)
0	Outlay	(750)		
6 months	Outlay	(750)		
1	Interest paid /received on swap: EE 20%, £ 12%	(300)		12.00
1	Project sales receipt from EE govt.	2,000		
1	Repay swap	(1,500)		100.00
	Net surplus in EE, converted to £	200	21.84	9.16
	Surplus from project:			21.16

The use of the swap **increases the expected value** of the investment. In addition, there is far less currency risk, because only the profit element of 200 EE marks is subject to the exchange rate in one year. The **opportunity costs** will however need to be **evaluated,** and the **credit status** of the EE company reviewed, as the interest burden it is taking on is significant.

(b) **Nature of swap**

A swap is an **exchange** of a stream of **future cash obligations** with another party. For example interest on loans can be swapped in the same currency or different currencies. A swap is particularly useful if **high transactions costs prevent** the **early redemption** of a loan in order to take out one with different characteristics.

Advantages of swaps

Repayment characteristics

If markets are efficient, the main use of a swap is to **alter the risk and/or repayment characteristics** of cash flows to a **more desirable pattern**. For example, floating rate interest may be exchanged for fixed in order to **improve predictability**. In this example, the **currency swap** is used effectively as a **money market hedge**, so that currency fluctuations in foreign earnings are offset by interest costs in the same currency. Swap products have been developed to meet **specific requirements**, for example '**swaptions'** which give the holder the option to swap payment patterns.

Market imperfections

Sometimes **gains** can also be made from **market imperfections**. In the example, the interest charged on the EE loan to BB is not high enough to compensate for the expected depreciation of the EE mark relative to the pound. This is a market imperfection which results in a gain in the net present value of the project.

Comparative advantage

Swaps offer the ability to **take advantage of a relatively better credit rating** in the company's own country than in a foreign country. If two organisations borrow in their home currencies and swap, they may achieve lower interest rates than if they attempt to borrow directly in foreign currencies. Similarly, **comparative advantage of fixed or floating rate borrowing** can also be exploited. For example if a company can obtain

relatively cheaper rates if it borrows at floating rate, but it requires a fixed rate loan, it may achieve a lower fixed interest rate by borrowing at floating rate and swapping into fixed rate.

Disadvantages of swaps

Risk of default by the other party to the swap (counter-party risk)

In the example, if the EE company became **unable** to meet its **swap payment obligations**, this could mean that BB plc risked having to make them itself.

Arrangement fees

Swaps have arrangement fees payable to third parties. Although these may appear to be cheap, this is because the intermediary accepts **no liability** for the swap.

46 RET

Text references. Chapters 11 and 12.

Top tips. In (a) the first stage is to net off the receipts and payments.

It is then very important to note from the question details that:

- This is a US company
- Both exchange rates are quoted at Other currency X: $1

These details will be different in different questions, and you must be sure that they are fixed in your mind as you tackle the question, as they will determine **which exchange rate you use**, and whether you **multiply or divide** by that exchange rate.

In this situation you use the **lower** rates for the forward market hedges as the US company is seeking Euros, and will get **fewer** Euros for each dollar it pays. For the receipts, you use the higher rate, as the company is trying to **sell kroners** to obtain dollars, and will need to provide more kroners to obtain each dollar.

With the money market hedge, you invest in the foreign currency to obtain money to fulfil a payment requirement, but you have to borrow in your own currency. You invest a lower amount now in that foreign currency to obtain the interest and add capital and interest together at the end to obtain the payment you require. However you have to pay back the borrowing plus the interest charged in your own currency.

If you are going to obtain a receipt in a foreign currency, you borrow the lower amount, and the receipt will cover what you borrowed plus the interest. The amount you borrow is converted into your own currency for investment and that amount plus the interest is your ultimate benefit.

We have followed our normal proforma for the futures market calculation for two months to demonstrate how you get the bulk of the marks for that part. Note that the closing spot and futures price being the same simplifies the position.

The advantages and disadvantages in (b) are very important. You need to consider:

- Certainty of receipt
- Timing
- Costs
- Availability
- Complexity
- Any risks

The verb **list** is from the lowest level of CIMA verbs, and indicates quantity, not quality of points is important. You would therefore cover each point in a sentence, no more. Other questions will require you to **explain** which would require a couple of sentences on each point, maybe with a quick example to illustrate. If you'd been asked to **discuss** the methods, you would have to indicate the significance of each point, how much impact each advantage or disadvantage would have on the decision whether to use different methods.

Easy marks. Although you may think that the calculations represent some of the toughest marks on this paper, the discussion marks on derivatives questions are often very easy to obtain as here. It may be worth doing (b) first and ensuring you have enough time to gain virtually all the marks on the discussion, before tackling the calculation.

Examiner's comments. Many candidates wasted time by doing superfluous calculations.

Answers to (a) showed many weaknesses including use of the wrong rates, the wrong number of contracts, the incorrect decision of whether to buy or sell futures, and the wrong month of contract maturity; answers to the futures part of the question were the least convincing.

(a)

Two months payment:	€393,265
Three months receipt:	Kr8.6m
Three months payment:	491,011 + 890,217 – 60,505 – 1,997,651 = €676,928

Forward market hedge

Two months payment

$$\frac{€393{,}265}{1.433} = \$274{,}435$$

Three months payment

$$\text{Payment } \frac{€676{,}928}{1.431} = \$473{,}045$$

Three months receipt

$$\frac{\text{Kr}8{,}600{,}000}{10.83} = \$794{,}090$$

Money market hedge

Two months payment

	Now		+ 2 months
€	2 So invest now €390,984	2/12 × 3.5% = 0.583% per 2 months (lending rate) × 1/1.00583 ←	1 Need to pay €393,265
↓	To be able to invest € must buy them now @1.439		
$	3 So need to borrow now $271,706	On which interest is charged at 2/12 × 7.5% = 1.25% per 2 months (borrowing rate) × 1.0125 →	4 Due to Bank in 2 months $275,102 (effective cost of hedge)

Three months payment

	Now		+ 3 months
€	2 So invest now €671,056	3/12 × 3.5% = 0.875% per 3 months (lending rate) × 1/1.00875 ←	1 Need to pay €676,928
	↓ To be able to invest € must buy them now @ 1.439		
$	3 So need to borrow now $466,335	On which interest is charged at 3/12 × 7.5% = 1.875% per 3 months (borrowing rate) × 1.01875 →	4 Due to Bank in 3 months $475,079 (effective cost of hedge)

Three months receipt

	Now		+ 3 months
Kr	2 So borrow now Kr 8,431,373	3/12 × 8% = 2% per 3 months (borrowing rate) × 1/1.02 ←	1 Will receive Kr 8,600,000
	↓ To be able to invest Kr borrowed, must sell them now @ 10.71		
$	3 So invest now $787,243	On which interest is received at 3/12 × 5.5% = 1.375% per 3 months (lending rate) × 1.01375 →	4 Due to RET $798,068 (effective receipt from hedge)

Futures market

Two months payment

- We shall be buying June contracts as they mature just after payment date
- Buy € futures
- Number of contracts

  $\frac{393,265}{125,000}$ = 3.15, 3 contracts.
- Tick size 125,000 × 0.0001 = $12.50.
- Closing spot rate and closing futures are 1.500 €/$, 0.6667 $/€.

- **On futures market**

Opening futures price	0.6964
Closing futures price	0.6667 (1/1.50)
Movement in ticks	297 ticks loss
Loss on futures market	297 × 12.50 × 3 = $11,138 loss

- **Net outcome**

	$
Spot market payment (€393,265 × 0.6667)	(262,177)
Loss on futures market	(11,138)
	273,315

Three months payment

- Number of contracts

$$\frac{676{,}928}{125{,}000} \approx 5.42\text{, say 5 contracts}$$

- Closing spot rate and closing futures are 1.500 €/$, 0.6667 $/€.
- **On futures market**

Opening futures price	0.6983
Closing futures price	0.6667 (1/1.50)
Movement in ticks	316 ticks loss
Loss on futures market	316 × 12.50 × 5 = $19,750 loss

- **Net outcome**

	$
Spot market payment (€676,928 × 0.6667)	(451,285)
Loss on futures market	(19,750)
	471,035

Conclusion

For the three month Kr receipt, the money market will maximise cash flow. For the two Euro payments, the futures market should maximise cash flow assuming basis risk is negligible. If basis risk does have a significant impact, the forward market may be the best choice.

(b) **Advantages of forward contracts**

- The contract can be **tailored to the user's exact requirements** with quantity to be delivered, date and price all flexible.
- The trader will **know in advance** how much money will be received or paid.
- **Payment is not required** until the contract is settled.

Disadvantages of forward contracts

- The user may **not be able to negotiate good terms**; the price may depend upon the **size** of the **deal** and how the user is rated.
- Users have to **bear the spread** of the contract between the buying and selling price.
- Deals can only be **reversed** by **going back to the original party** and offsetting the original trade.
- The **creditworthiness** of the other party may be a problem.

Advantages of currency futures

- There is a **single specified price** determined by the market, and not the negotiating strength of the customer.
- **Transactions costs** are generally **lower** than for forward contracts.
- The exact date of **receipt or payment** of the currency **does not have to be known**, because the futures contract does not have to be closed out until the actual cash receipt or payment is made.

- **Reversal** can easily take place in the market.
- Because of the process of **marking to market**, there is **no default risk**.

Disadvantages of currency futures

- The **fixing of quantity and delivery dates** that is necessary for the future to be traded means that the customer's risk may not be fully covered.
- Futures contracts may **not be available in the currencies** that the customer requires.
- The procedure for converting between two currencies, neither of which is the US dollar, can be **complex.**
- **Volatile trading conditions** on the futures markets mean that the potential loss can be high.

47 Arbitrage

Text reference. Chapters 10 and 11

Top tips. (a) is simply a question of deciding what to multiply or divide.

The essential point in (b) is that arbitrage relates to exploiting an unexpected difference. The second part of (b) relates to the scenario and hence exchange and interest rates, so you ideally need to use another example in the first half of (b). You may have found it easier to explain how arbitrage works once you had attempted to determine the gain in (c).

Before you get into the calculations for (c), you have to calculate the arbitrage opportunity, using interest rate parity. The opportunity exists because the forward rate suggests that you need more Aus $ to buy each US $ (1.1818) than would be forecast by interest rate parity (1.1405). Curiously interest rate parity not only suggests that the US$ is overvalued; it suggests that the US$ should weaken rather than strengthen forward.

(c) is like a money market hedge, but with complications:

- The US $5,000,000 is the amount you start with now. If we were undertaking a money market hedge, the key amount would be the receipt or payment at the end of the period.
- To take advantage of the arbitrage opportunity, you need to take out a forward contract to convert the US$ deposit into Aus$ after 6 months. This means that you have to start by **borrowing Aus $ now** and **converting Aus $ into US$ now** to be able to convert them back into Aus $ after 6 months.
- The need to convert the surplus after the loan has been repaid into a third currency, £, as the business is based in London, so will account in sterling. Here the question supplying the actual Aus $/£ exchange rate at the end of 6 months is a clue that you have to do this.
- It would also be possible to take out a forward contract **now** for the surplus you expect to receive at the forward rate of Aus $: £ 2.3602. The question details make it clear that you would receive a lower amount of £ if you did this (you'd have to pay Aus $2.3602 for each £ rather than Aus $2.32). However that is with the benefit of hindsight; you wouldn't know what the Aus $: £ spot rate in six months' time would be when you undertook the original transaction.
- The transaction costs for the three foreign exchange transactions

(c) is also made more complicated by the fact that the two principal currencies are both $ so you have to make sure you differentiate clearly between Aus $ and US $.

You could also attempt the question by assuming profits are taken today rather than after 6 months.

The main points to bring out in (d) are what each figure represents, and how fairly they measure risk.

Easy marks. (d) probably if you concentrate on the usefulness to the organisation. Certainly not (c)!

Examiner's comments. In (b) many students confused arbitrage and speculation. Arbitrage involves taking advantage of a short-term opportunity with little speculation being involved.

In (c) only a small number of students produced correct answers. 'It was clear that candidates had not learned this part of the syllabus and did this question out of desperation.'

In (d) most students explained trading limits but not value at risk, probably demonstrating a lack of knowledge of value at risk.

(a) Aus \$: US \$ = AUS \$: £ × £: US\$

For current spot rates

$$\text{Aus \$: US \$} = 2.3180 \times \frac{1}{2.0254}$$

$$= 1.1445$$

For six month forward rates

$$\text{Aus \$: US \$} = 2.3602 \times \frac{1}{1.9971}$$

$$= 1.1818$$

(b) **Arbitrage profit**

Arbitrage means **exploiting short-term differences**, maybe between **two markets**, selling in one market and buying in the other. Alternatively it can mean exploiting price differences between **two products**, where the similarities between those products (for example two bonds having a similar maturity and risk) suggests that they should be traded at the same price. Arbitrage differences are **short-term**; as other traders see the opportunities and exploit them, the laws of supply and demand suggest that prices will converge, and the opportunities for exploiting the differences will disappear as equilibrium is reached.

Relevance to scenario

The opportunity for arbitrage profit in this scenario arises because the **difference between the spot and forward exchange rates** does not mirror **differences in interest rates**. Investors can:

- Borrow in one currency
- Deposit what they have borrowed as an investment in the other currency for (say) six months
- Liquidate their investment and convert the proceeds at the forward rate
- Repay the amount borrowed and retain the surplus

(c) **Ascertain arbitrage opportunity**

Using interest rate parity

$$\text{Forward rate Aus \$: US \$ should} = 1.1445 \times \frac{1+0.0332}{1+0.0368}$$

$$= 1.1405$$

This compares with the rate calculated in (a) of 1.1818 suggesting the US \$ is **overvalued forward**.

Therefore we should buy US \$ at spot and sell them forward.

This locks in with the rate we shall receive in 6 months' time as forward contracts are binding agreements. To obtain US \$5,000,000 now (the maximum permitted for this trader) we need to borrow sufficient Australian \$ at the spot rate calculated in (a).

	Now	Interest rate	+ 6 months
US $	4 Take out forward contract to sell, @ 1.1818, US $5,000,000 (1 + 0.0368) = US $5,184,000 This locks in arbitrage opportunity. 3 Invest US $5,000,000	3.68%	5 Liquidate investment + interest received US $5,184,000
↑	2 Buy US$ @ 1.1445 with Aus $5,722,500 to receive US$5,000,000		6 Sell US $5,184,000 @ 1.1818 to receive = Aus$6,126,451 ↓
Aus $	1 Borrow Aus $ 5,722,500	3.32%	7 Repay Aus$ loan & pay interest Aus $5,722,500(1 + 0.0332) = Aus$5,912,487 Aus$ Surplus = 6,126,451 – 5,912,487 = Aus$213,964
£			8 Sell Aus$213,964 @2.3200 = £92,226 9 Pay costs of investment (3 × £3,000) = £9,000 Surplus = £83,226

Alternative solution

1 **Borrow** Aus $ (5,000,000 × 1.1445) = Aus $5,722,500

2 **Convert to US $** at spot to give US $5,000,000

3 **Invest** US $5,000,000 for 6 months

4 **Take out a forward contract** at 1.1818 to sell the US $ amount expected at the end of 6 months, US $5,000,000 × (1+ 0.0368) = US $ 5,184,000.

5 After 6 months **liquidate investment**

6 **Convert US $ that have been on deposit plus interest to Aus $,** to give Aus $5,184,000 × 1.1818 = Aus $6,126,451

7 **Repay Aus $ loan and pay interest**. Surplus = 6,126,451 – (5,722,500 × 1.0332) = Aus $213,964

8 **Convert to £,** to give £213,964/2.3200 = £92,226

9 Profit needs to be adjusted by the transaction costs of the three foreign currency transactions (Steps 2, 6 and 8)

Profit = 92,226 – (3,000 × 3) = £83,226

Top tips

- As the Aus$:US$ spot rate is quoted at Aus$1.1445:US$1, you **divide** the Aus$ figure by the exchange rate
- As the Aus$:US$ six month forward rate is quoted at Aus$1.1818:US$1, you **multiply** the US$ figure by the exchange rate
- As the Aus$:£ spot rate in six months is quoted at Aus$2.3200:£1, you **divide** the Aus$ figure by the exchange rate

(d) **Nominal value**

A trading limit, $5,000,000 in the question, limits the size of each transaction undertaken to a monetary amount. Capping all traders in this way, maybe with different limits for each trader, will **limit nominal exposure** from operations.

Nominal value only covers the initial payment transactions, and the total payments may be larger, for example there may be additional **margin** payments on futures transactions. The nominal value also may **not fairly represent the risk** of an individual transaction. For example if another trader working at the organisation is undertaking a transaction in the same market in the opposite direction, the two transactions will be **hedged** and the risks **reduced**, though each will have been limited as if the two transactions were independent.

Value at risk

Value at risk works by determining the potential loss, generally over a whole portfolio, based on the principles that the volatility of market transactions is a **normal distribution**. The value at risk is determined by the **% confidence level** that the organisation wishes to have that the loss will not exceed the value at risk, and the **timeframe** over which the loss may be made – the longer the timeframe the bigger the value at risk. Thus a trader could say that with 95% confidence that the daily loss on the portfolio would not exceed $100,000.

However, particularly with large portfolios, the use of value at risk as a control could be undermined by traders **undertaking individual transactions** for which the chances of losses much greater than $100,000 are much higher, these transactions may be affected by abnormal events and so will not follow the assumed normal distribution. These transactions may not affect the value at risk calculations significantly if the portfolio is large enough.

48 EX

Text references. Chapter 11 covers hedging exchange risks, Chapter 13 examines IAS 39.

Top tips. This question is predominantly about the overall strategic approach that the company should take towards foreign currency risk (should it eliminate risk or just partly reduce it?) and the principles of matching assets and liabilities in the same currency. The answer to (a)(ii) starts off by asking whether hedging is necessary at all – would matching be better. It then explains the implications of various strategies and concludes by suggesting a sensible compromise.

In (b) you need to explain three or four different ways. The most important point perhaps is the results of borrowing in a hard currency are not necessarily predictable.

(c) illustrates the probability that questions on IAS 39 won't be about the technical details of the standard, but about the effect on systems, information requirements, financial stakeholder relations and risk management; unusually in fact for a part question most of the major areas of the syllabus are mentioned.

Easy marks. Some marks are available in (a) (ii) for a simple discussion of the more straightforward methods; however the discussion is complicated by the need to consider the company's appetite for risk. Note that you would pass the question on the discussion parts without even attempting the calculations.

(a) To: The Treasurer
From: Assistant
Date: 12 November 20X7
Subject: Hedging exchange risks

(i) **Comparison of two methods of hedging exchange risk**

Method 1

	Now		+ 3 months
S Fr	2 So borrow now SFr 744,417	3/12 × 3% = 0.75% per 3 months (borrowing rate) × 1/1.0075 ←	1 Will receive S Fr 750,000
↓	To be able to invest S Fr borrowed, must sell them now @ S Fr 2.3834		
£	3 So invest now £312,334	On which interest is received at 3/12 × 6% = 1.5% per 3 months (lending rate) × 1.015 →	4 Due to EX £317,019 (effective receipt from hedge)

Method 2

The exchange rate is agreed in advance. Cash received in three months is converted to produce SFr750,000/2.3688 = £316,616.

Top tips. Remember that as the Swiss Francs exchange rate is quoted at SFr 2.3688: £1, you need to **divide** SFr amounts by the exchange rate to calculate the amount in £

Conclusion

On the basis of the above calculations, Method 1 gives a slightly better receipt. Banker's commission has been omitted from the figures.

(ii) **Factors to consider before deciding whether to hedge foreign exchange risk using the foreign currency markets**

Offsetting receipts and payments

Before using any technique to hedge foreign currency transactions, **receipts and payments** in the same currency at the same date should be **offset**. This technique is known as **matching**. For example, if the company is expecting to receive SFr 750,000 on 31 March and to pay SFr 600,000 on the same day, only the net amount of SFr 150,000 needs to be considered.

Matching

Matching can be **extended** to receipts and payments which do not take place on exactly the same day by **simply hedging the period and amount of the difference** between the receipt and payment. A company like ours which has many receipts and payments in European currencies should consider matching assets with liabilities in the same currency.

Defensive strategy

The company should have a clear strategy concerning how much foreign exchange risk it is prepared to bear. A highly risk-averse or **'defensive' strategy** of hedging all transactions is **expensive** in terms of commission costs but recognises that **floating exchange rates** are very **unpredictable** and can cause losses high enough to bankrupt the company.

Predictive strategy

An alternative **'predictive' strategy** recognises that if all transactions are hedged, then the **chance** of **currency gains** is **lost**. The company could therefore **attempt to forecast foreign exchange movements** and only **hedge those transactions where currency losses are predicted**. The fact is that some currencies are relatively predictable (for example, if inflation is high, the currency will devalue and there is little to be gained by hedging payments in that currency). If predictions are made sensibly, the strategy should lead to a **higher expected value** than that of hedging everything and will incur **lower commission costs** as well. The risk remains, though, that a single large uncovered transaction could cause severe problems if the currency moves in the opposite direction to that predicted.

Cash limits

A sensible strategy for our company could be to set a **cash size** for a foreign currency exposure above which all amounts must be hedged, but below this limit a predictive approach is taken or even, possibly, all amounts are left unhedged.

(b) **Matching with a subsidiary**

If the foreign subsidiary is selling predominantly in its own country, the principle of **matching assets and liabilities** says that the subsidiary should be financed as far as possible in the currency of that country. Ideally the **subsidiary** will be **highly geared** with loans and overdrafts in the developing country's currency.

Hard currency

If it is impossible to borrow in the local currency, EX should attempt to find a **hard currency** which is highly **positively correlated** with the local currency. For example, some countries have a policy of pegging their currency to the US dollar. The receipt can then be hedged by selling the US dollar forward.

Risks of devaluation

This technique is, however, open to the risk that the **local currency suddenly devalues against the dollar**, as happened in 1997 with a number of Asian currencies. The likelihood of this happening is high if there is high inflation in the country and it has low reserves.

Other options

If EX is fairly certain that the local currency is going to devalue and that it cannot borrow in that currency other options are:

(i) **Increase the sales price** by the amount of the expected devaluation and bear the risk

(ii) **Invoice in a hard currency**, for example US dollars, which can then be sold forward

(iii) **Arrange a 'counter-trade' agreement** (ie barter) in which the sale of EX's textiles is paid for by the purchase of local raw materials or other products

(c) **Accounting systems**

In order to deal effectively with the accounting issues, the accounting system should be able to produce **journal updates** and **accounting entries** for IAS 39 significant events such as hedge termination.

Accounting statements

EX's directors will also need to consider carefully how IAS 39 requirements impact upon the **statements** they have to produce for various regulatory bodies.

Business processes and systems

EX's directors will need to make sure that its systems are **robust enough** to be able to **process a trade or hedge** from trading through risk management to accounting entry generation. The **market data** and **models** used must be consistent; inaccuracies may result in unnecessary income volatility. The systems must also be able to **link assets and liabilities** with **derivatives, accommodate changes in hedge allocations** and **measure hedge effectiveness**. Because of the requirements to measure instruments at fair value, **sources of fair value information** will need to be identified.

Communication with shareholders

EX's directors will also have to consider its **communication strategies.** Users will be examining a range of disclosures on fair value, hedging and gains and losses, and they need to receive a clear view of what is happening.

Risk management strategies

As well as needing to understand the new rules, the directors must also consider whether **risk management strategies** will need to be **modified**. **Monitoring procedures** will have to be **strengthened**. Risk officers may have to employ different management techniques, **limiting the hedging strategies used or specifying different effectiveness assessment methods for different structures**.

49 OJ

Text references. Chapters 11 and 12.

Top tips. (a) is a computation illustrating how exchange controls can delay the repatriation of cash from foreign investments. The biggest problem you may have found was setting out the layout clearly. It is useful to plan in advance layouts that might be difficult to fit on a page, for instance layouts with lots of columns as in (a).

(b) requires knowledge of the relationship between forward rates and spot rates and the workings of currency swaps, as well as posing an interesting discussion on whether exchange control risk should affect the discount rate used in investment appraisal.

All three statements in (b) merit at least 6 marks to do justice to the discussion, bringing out the qualifications and problems with the views raised, so you could have been hard-pressed to finish this question in time.

In (b) (i) the distinction that your answer needs to bring out is the difference between an **unbiased** and an **accurate** prediction.

In (b) (ii) the key point is that adjusting the discount rate is an alternative to adjusting cash flows for the effects of exchange controls.

(b) (iii) demonstrates how a swap would work, but to get good marks on this part, it is more important to discuss the problems of swaps and whether other methods (forward contracts) might do the job better.

Easy marks. Difficult to identify as neither the calculations nor discussions are straightforward. Quite a tough question.

(a) (i) **OJ Limited: Joint venture NPV**

Assumption 1: exchange controls in operation

Year	*Project cash*	*OJ's 50% share*	*Cash repatriated*	*Exchange rate*		*Discount factor*	*PV*
	SA$'000	SA$'000	SA$'000	SA$/£	£'000	16%	£'000
0					(450.00)	1.000	(450.0)
1	4,250	2,125	1,062.5	10	106.25	0.862	91.6
2	6,500	3,250	1,625.0	15	108.33	0.743	80.5
3	8,350	4,175	6,862.5	21	326.79	0.641	209.5
		9,550	9,550.0				(68.4)

Assumption 2: removal of exchange controls

Year	*Project cash* SA$ '000	*OJ's 50% share* SA$ '000	*Cash repatriated* SA$ '000	*Exchange rate* SA$/£	£'000	*Discount factor* 16%	*PV* £'000
0					(450.00)	1.000	(450.0)
1	4,250	2,125	2,125	10	212.50	0.862	183.2
2	6,500	3,250	3,250	15	216.67	0.743	161.0
3	8,350	4,175	4,175	21	198.81	0.641	127.4
							21.6

(ii) Based solely on these calculations, the joint venture should only proceed if restrictions on repatriation of profits are lifted.

(b) (i) **Reliability of forward rates as predictors of spot rates in the future**

Forward rate

A forward rate is a rate agreed today at which currency will be exchanged on an agreed future date. Forward rates offered by banks are calculated from **today's spot exchange rate** and **the fixed interest rate in each currency** for the period in question. Because these rates are known with certainty, the forward rate can be fixed with accuracy: any variation from the computed rate would allow speculators to engage in risk-free arbitrage between the money markets and currency markets.

Spot rate

In a **floating exchange rate system**, however, the **spot rate** in the future is **dependent** on many **economic factors** affecting supply and demand for the currency, not just current factors but new events that arise between now and the future date. Factors include balance of payments, capital investment cash flows, interest rates, inflation rates and actions by speculators. The future spot rate is therefore subject to significant uncertainty.

Forward rate as predictor

If consistent patterns emerge, forward rates will be adjusted to take account. The forward exchange rate will be as likely to be above the eventual spot rate as below it. This is, however, completely different from saying that the forward rate is a reliable or accurate predictor of the spot rate. It clearly is **not a reliable predictor** because of the uncertainty in events which might arise between now and the future date. This is particularly likely to be true in a volatile currency such as the South American one in this question.

(ii) **Should a higher discount rate be used when there are exchange controls?**

The discount rate of 16% is assumed to allow for the time value of money and the normal business risk of the investment but not for the risk of **exchange controls** being **retained**. Since the company is not a public limited company and shareholders are probably undiversified, they are assumed to be concerned with total risk, not just systematic risk. Exchange controls are therefore a relevant risk which must be accounted for.

Allowing for the uncertainty of exchange controls

(1) **Risk-adjusted discount rate**
The cash flows are **evaluated assuming there are no exchange controls** (Assumption 2) and the **discount rate is increased** to allow for the uncertainty in the timing of the cash flows because of exchange controls.

(2) **Two scenarios**
Two scenarios are postulated, **one with exchange controls** and one **without**, as in the question. Both are discounted at 16% to allow for business risk, but the discount rate does not need to be increased to allow for exchange control risk, which is already being allowed for by the delayed cash flows in Assumption 1. This method, used in the question, is valid and more detailed than the alternative method.

What is *not* valid is to postulate the scenario with **delayed cash flows** and in addition to **increase its discount rate**. This would be double-counting the exchange control risk.

(iii) **Can a currency swap help to minimise the exchange rate risk?**

In a currency swap two parties lend each other agreed amounts of different currencies for a given time, the loans being repaid at the end of this period. This has the effect of **fixing the exchange rate in advance** for the repayment date and therefore reduces currency risk.

Terms of swap

Of course there are no 'free gifts' in foreign exchange and the **interest paid** on OJ's loan in SA$ will probably be **significantly higher** than the interest it receives on its sterling loan. In addition, the **swap exchange rate** may well be **higher than 10**. These factors are subject to negotiation between the parties.

Risks of swap

OJ must also consider the **risk** that its **swap partner defaults** on repayment or that **exchange controls prevent the receipt of interest** on its sterling loan. There will also be commission to pay to the intermediary which arranged the swap.

Forward contract

Given that there is a **forward market** for the SA$ then currency risk can be hedged sufficiently without using a swap. As this is OJ's first venture into South America, forward contracts may be easier to manage.

50 ADB

Text references. Chapter 11 deals with foreign exchange risks, Chapter 15 discusses various political risks.

Top tips. This question deals with a number of important parts of the syllabus: purchasing power parity, the use of a currency option in hedging a tender bid, and arguments for and against hedging in general.

No specific knowledge of the region is necessary. Marks would be lost for discussion of forward contracts because the question specifically states they are not available.

In (a) remember that PPP means that the currency of the country with the **higher** rate of inflation **weakens**.

The discussion in (c) needs to demonstrate that hedging is not a straightforward process. Hedging techniques do not eliminate currency risk and there may be significant costs involved. Hence some companies quite legitimately do not use hedging techniques whereas other companies use them wholesale. In (d) you might also have mentioned the possibility that exchange controls may be symptomatic of wider political risks.

Easy marks. Most of the question is fairly straightforward explanation or discussion that doesn't need to be tied into a scenario.

To: Managing Director
From: Financial Controller
Date: 12 May 20X0
Subject: Bid for air conditioning contract in Middle East

Introduction

This report recommends a tender price for the bid and discusses techniques for hedging against currency risk.

(a) **Price**

Variable costs are estimated at £640,000. For a contribution of 20% of sales, the selling price should be £640,000 × 100/80 = £800,000. This assumes that the **cost estimate** already **allows for inflation** over the next 15 months.

Translation

This sterling price needs to be **translated into the local currency** at the predicted exchange rate in 15 months' time. Assuming that the pound and the local currency are allowed to float freely **purchasing power parity (PPP)** can be applied to estimate the exchange rate in 15 months.

PPP

The inflation in the Middle Eastern country is 5% per annum compared with 3% in the UK. From PPP, this implies that the **foreign currency** will **weaken** by approximately 2% per year, as confirmed by the Treasurer. In 15 months, the overall weakening will be approximately 2% × 15/12 = 2.5%, giving an exchange rate of 5.89 × 1.025 = 6.04 to the pound.

The tender price should therefore be 800,000 × 6.04 = 4,832,000 units of local currency.

(b) **Need for hedging**

Note that the computation of exchange rate above is only an estimate. Many factors might arise to cause the foreign currency to strengthen or weaken to a rate very different from today's. We are particularly concerned that if the foreign currency weakens, the **sterling value** of our sales receipts **will fall** and we may make **significant losses**.

Means of hedging

Although no forward market exists for the currency, it may be possible to hedge by **borrowing** approximately 4.8 million units in the foreign currency, and **converting to sterling** to pay off some of our existing sterling overdraft. On receipt of the contract fee in 15 months, we could repay the foreign loan. Alternatively, if it is impossible to borrow, we may be able to arrange a **currency swap** with a foreign company wishing to sell to the UK or another UK party who wishes to buy from the foreign country.

(c) **Problems with hedging**

The problem with the hedges described above is that if we carry them out today and do not win the tender, we will expose ourselves to **currency risk**. If we wish to hedge today, we would be better to enquire whether an **option** to sell the currency for a fixed price is available from the Bank. This could be for the period until the bid results are announced, or for the full 15 months. If we lose the contract, the option can always be abandoned if necessary.

Costs of hedging

Currency risk is just one of a number of business risks that need to be properly managed, and hedging methods exist to reduce or eliminate it. Like all risk management techniques (for example insurance) **hedging has a cost**. The company must decide whether this cost is justified by the **reduction in risk.**

Wholesale hedging

Some organisations will hedge all currency transactions (except those that are too small) on the grounds that currency risk is not related to the core objectives of the business and should be eliminated. This strategy is, however, **relatively expensive** and such organisations will **lose the opportunity of currency gains** which could offset losses.

Minimising hedging

Other organisations believe they can predict future currency movements and will only hedge those transactions where they believe the currency will move adversely. This type of strategy is probably sensible where **economic factors** such as **large inflation differentials** make the direction of currency movements relatively easy to predict, but evidence shows in other cases that it is easy to make the **wrong prediction** and to **incur significant losses**. It must also be remembered that, for a non-financial company, the embarrassment from making a significant currency loss is usually greater than the advantage of making an equivalent currency gain.

Ease of hedging

Regardless of the overall strategy there are several **easy hedging techniques** (eg matching receipts and payments) that are costless and that should normally be implemented when appropriate. These issues need to be fully discussed before deciding not to hedge.

(d) **Purpose of controlling remittances**

Control of remittances by a government is a form of **exchange control** which stops the currency being fully convertible. Such measures imposed by government as a form of protection in order to rectify, or avoid, a balance of payments deficit and to prevent a depreciation in the nation's currency. Exchange controls are discouraged by the OECD but are still imposed by many developing countries.

Problems for investors

The foreign investor will suffer from the problem that it will be difficult to **'repatriate' dividends** from the investment. Faced with this difficulty, the investor may respond in different ways. If the investor is less concerned about the flow of dividends, he may not see the controls as a major impediment, but ultimately the value of the investment must depend upon the ability to receive distributions of profits.

Avoiding investment

One response of the foreign investor is to **avoid investments** in countries in which **controls over remittances** exist. This could hamper investment in the local economy but on the other hand it may allow local entrepreneurs to operate more easily.

Avoiding exchange controls

Another possible response of the foreign investor is to find ways of avoiding the exchange controls, for example by seeking returns through **royalties** or by setting **transfer prices** for part-processed goods at non-market levels. The government exerting the controls will have to close such 'loopholes' through further control and regulation if it wants the controls to have an effect.

51 YZ

Text references. Chapters 11 and 12.

Top tips. You can avoid wasting time in (a) by netting off receipts and payments in the same currency, and only hedging the net amount. **€** is the **term currency** as it is quoted as €X:£1 and we therefore have to **divide** € amounts by the exchange rate to calculate amounts in £.

Remember that:

- The **bank sells** (and the **company buys**) the **term currency** (€) **low**
- The **bank buys** (and the **company sells**) the **term currency high**

Remember also to **deduct** premiums and **add** discounts from and to the term currency.

When calculating the part year interest rates for the money market hedge, it would be technically better to use the twelfth and fourth roots for 1 and 3 month rates, but the examiner has indicated dividing the annual rates by 12 and 4 is acceptable here.

Don't forget to give a recommendation at the end of your answer to (b). The discussion is primarily about:

- The feasibility of the method
- The certainty of the results
- The ability to benefit from favourable exchange rates (only possible on the spot market here)

Easy marks. As in Question 2, the discussion parts are fairly straightforward and you may want to tackle them first. However, the numerical element is more important in this question, so you will have to attempt the calculations to pass.

Examiner's comments. Many candidates obtained full marks in (a); errors included incorrect treatment of premiums, failing to calculate the interest rates in the money market hedge correctly, and using the wrong spot rate. In (b) some candidates failed to distinguish between forward and money markets, and wasted time by repeating much of their answer under different headings.

(a) The company will be concerned with hedging net amounts:

In one month's time 600,000 – 400,000 = €200,000 payment

In three months' time 1,200,000 – 800,000 = €400,000 receipt

(i) **Forward currency market**

One month

Payment = 200,000/(1.6186 – 0.0006)
= £123,609

Three months

Receipt = 400,000/(1.6202 – 0.0008)
= £247,005

(ii) **Money market**

One month

	Now		+ 1 month
€	2 So invest now €199,501	1/12 x 3% = 0.25% per month (lending rate) × 1/1.0025	1 Need to pay €200,000
	To be able to invest € must buy them now @ $1.6186		
£	3 So need to borrow now £123,255	On which interest is charged at 1/12 × 4.25% = 0.3542% (borrowing rate) × 1.003542	4 Due to Bank in 6 months £123,692 (effective cost of hedge)

Three months

	Now		+ 3 months
€	2 So borrow now €396,530	3/12 × 3.5% = 0.875% per 3 months (borrowing rate) × 1/1.00875	1 Will receive €400,000
	To be able to invest € borrowed, must sell them now @ 1.6202		
£	3 So invest now £244,741	On which interest is received at 3/12 × 3.75% = 0.9375% per 3 months (lending rate) × 1.009375	4 Due to YZ £247,036 (effective receipt from hedge)

(iii) **Not hedge**

One month

Payment = 200,000/1.6192
= £123,518

Three months

Receipt = 400,000/1.6220
= £246,609

(b) (i) **Advantages of using forward market**

If YZ uses the forward market, then the payment is **fixed** and there is no risk of the company suffering losses from adverse movements in the exchange rate. **Cash flow planning** is therefore improved. Evidence suggests that the forward market is an **unbiased predictor** of the spot rate, and anyone using the forward market many times will not lose out compared with not hedging the transactions, and taking a chance on the spot market. Forward contracts can also be **tailor-made** to fit YZ's exact requirements.

Disadvantages of using forward market

A forward exchange contract is binding, and cannot be **terminated** nor its terms **altered** by YZ. For one-off receipts or payments, YZ may lose out on **spot market rates** in one or three months' time not being the same as forward rates. If YZ's customers do not pay on time, YZ will nevertheless have to **honour its own commitment** to the bank. An **option forward exchange contract** (settlement possible on a range of dates) may be available to help overcome this problem.

(ii) **Advantages of using money market**

Market forces will mean that the premium or discount on a forward contract **reflects the interest differential** between the two. Hence the results of a money market hedge will not be very different from the results of using a forward contract, and a money market hedge is thus **low risk**.

Disadvantages of using money market

YZ is committed to a course of action that it cannot change if **exchange rate movements** mean that it would be better to use the spot market. In addition the operation of money market hedges is **more complicated** than the operation of forward exchange contracts, and possibly further expertise will be required.

(iii) **Advantages of using spot market**

Not hedging and using the spot market means that YZ can **benefit from unexpectedly favourable exchange rate movements**. As things happened here, YZ would have been better off not hedging the one month payment, but that is said with hindsight.

Disadvantages of using spot market

The spot market carries the **risk of losses** if exchange rates move adversely. Not hedging means that YZ is **uncertain** about what its future cash flow will be.

Recommendation

Hedging would be a prudent course, given the uncertainty about interest rates. There is not much difference in monetary terms between hedging on the forward and money markets, and the decision may depend on the **incidental costs** of both markets.

52 VQR

Text references. Chapter 11.

Top tips. This question involves discussion of various issues raised by the chief executive officer, who lacks full understanding of how foreign exchange markets work.

The information you are given indicates that you will need to discuss interest rate parity and/or purchasing power parity. Since these concepts are relevant throughout the answer, our answer explains them in detail in the introduction, and refers to them more briefly later on. The marking guide allocated 5 marks for these explanations. The level of detail you are given should have indicated that calculations should be used to support the points you made as relevant.

When dealing with continuously compounded interest rates for part of a year, it is more correct to use x to the power y calculations, but you would also have gained credit if you had adjusted the interest rates by dividing.

You need to assume that there is no concern about the bid/offer spread on the forward exchange rates.

NB This question was nearly identical to a question set in the *Financial Strategy* exam in May 2002. CIMA received some criticism because of the close similarities between the two questions.

Easy marks. Explanations of purchasing power and interest rate parity should be fairly straightforward, also why it is risky not to hedge at all; this will often be a possibility that you have to discuss.

The examiner's comments however indicated that many students were unable to define the terms adequately; remember that in the front pages we said that definitions often provide easy marks, but it seems that many students did not obtain these marks here.

Examiner's comments. Answers were well organised, but calculations were poorly done, indicating inadequate revision of these areas. Written explanations were also often poor.

MEMORANDUM

From: Treasurer
To: Chief Executive Officer
Date: 24 May 20X7
Subject: Financial data

I am writing in response to the questions you raised about the financial data relating to South-East Asia published in the business press. There are two important theories linking exchange rates, interest rates and inflation that need to considered when determining strategies in this area.

Interest rate parity

Interest rate parity is based on the hypothesis that the difference between interest rates in the two countries should offset the difference between the spot rates and the forward foreign exchange rates over the same period. The formula is:

$$\text{Forward rate currency a/b} = \text{Spot a/b} \times \frac{1+\text{nominal A interest rate}}{1+\text{nominal B interest rate}}$$

Purchasing power parity

Purchasing power parity predicts that the exchange value of foreign currency depends on the relative purchasing power of each currency in its own country, and that spot exchange rates will vary over time according to relative price changes. The formula is:

$$\text{Forward rate currency a/b} = \text{Spot a/b} \times \frac{1+\text{A inflation rate}}{1+\text{B inflation rate}}$$

(a) **US $ trading forward**

The forward rate between the Singapore and US dollars is nearly as predicted by interest rate parity.

One month forward rate $= 1.565 \times \frac{1+0.0344/12}{1+0.0538/12}$

$= 1.562$

> **Top tips.** Because the exchange rates are quoted as Sing $ to US $, that means Singapore is Country A in the interest rate parity calculation, the US is Country B.

The reason why the US dollar is quoted forward at a discount or cheaper is that the market has acted to offset the desire that investors in Singapore $ would have to switch to US$, a currency associated with higher interest rates. The Singapore $ has become more expensive in the forward markets to compensate for the lower interest rates in Singapore, a process known as **arbitrage**.

(b) **Forward exchange rates**

Again interest rate parity can be used to estimate the forward rate.

Three month forward rate $= 1.565 \times \frac{1+0.0344/4}{1+0.0538/4}$

$= 1.558$

We can therefore expect US$ 3,000,000 × 1.558 = Sing $ 4,674,000. This compares with a receipt of US$ 3,000,000 × 1.565 = Sing $4,695,000 on the spot market.

> **Top tips.** As the currencies are quoted at Sing$ X: US$ 1, you have to **multiply** amounts quoted in US$ to calculate what they are in Sing$.

To guarantee that we receive the minimum of $ 4,674,000 we should take out a forward contract for the expected receipt at a rate of $1.558, the contract to be performed in three months time.

> **Alternative solution**
>
> The requirements for (a) specify that you need to use interest rates to calculate the forward rate, but the requirements to (b) do not. It would therefore have been acceptable to use inflation rates in the calculation.
>
> Three month forward rate $= 1.565 \times \frac{1+0.005}{1+0.0186}$
>
> $= 1.544$
>
> US$ 3,000,000 × 1.544 = Sing $ 4,632,000.

(c) **Buying Aust$ on spot market**

We need to calculate the Aus $: Sing $ crossrates.

Aus $: Sing $ = US $: Sing $ × Aus $: US $

For current spot rates

Aus $: Sing $ $= \frac{1}{1.565} \times 1.311$

$= 0.838$

For one month forward rates

$$\text{Aus \$: Sing \$} = \frac{1}{1.562} \times 1.312$$

$$= 0.840$$

This indicates that the Australian $ is expected to depreciate against the Singapore dollar so it may be possible to save money by waiting until Australian dollars are needed and buying them on the spot market some time in the future.

Disadvantages of using the spot market

Risk of adverse movements

Purchasing power parity indicates that the forward rates should in real terms be the same as the spot rates. In practice spot rates will differ from forward rates and VQR could make **gains from favourable spot rate movements**. However VQR may equally make **substantial losses** if rates move **adversely**, and because there is no specialist foreign currency manager, the risks of losses will be too great. By contrast VQR's use of forward contracts allows it to **limit its exposure to losses** by fixing in advance the rates it will use when it comes to pay for imports.

Transaction costs

Transaction costs may also be **higher** if VQR uses the spot market.

(d) **Borrowing Sing $ to pay off Aus $**

It is true that we would be paying lower interest rates on a loan in Sing $ than a loan in Aus $. However the difference in the forward rates compensates for this, so it would be **more expensive to buy Aus$ now** (each one would cost Sing $ 1.193) than it would be to set a forward rate to buy them in say a month's time (when each Aus $ would only cost Sing $ 1.190)

In addition if VQR hedges on the money market by buying Aus $ and placing them on deposit, it would be **matching** the amount deposited with the Aus$ loan. Although it would suffer higher interest rates than on a Sing $ loan, it would also benefit from higher interest rates on the deposit. Matching is a further way in which VQR can limit its exposure to losses from exchange rate and interest rate movements.

If you have any further queries, please do not hesitate to get in touch.

Treasurer

53 IOU

Text references. Chapters 11 and 12.

Top tips. The higher price $1.5590 is used as the company has to pay more dollars for the £ it needs to settle the payment. A call option is required as this is a US company seeking to obtain £ with $.With the December payment, there is an over-hedge, thus the company will be obtaining a receipt on the forward market.

Choosing the right option price to use may have given you difficulty. The logic for choosing option prices that are less favourable to the company than forward rates is that the company expects the £ to weaken against the dollar, and hence the options will not need to be exercised. At any rate less than the forward rates, the company will be better off using the spot market. Option prices above 1.5601 and 1.5655 allow the company to choose the spot market (and not exercise the option) for any rate below the forward rate.

The discussion in (b) may appear straightforward, but you could have limited the marks you scored by:

- Failing to bring in any details about the company; although the scenario is short there is information you can use (the company's location, the fact that settlements are in $)
- Failing to advise the company, in other words not picking up the second part of the question requirement

Easy marks. A few discussion points, although you need to think about which methods to discuss; your answer to (b) shouldn't cover options or forward contracts as these are covered in (a).

(a) **Spot market position**

The company expects to pay £1,255,000. At today's spot rate this would be converted to \$ at \$1.5590, giving 1,255,000 × 1.5590 = \$1,956,545.

Top tips. Remember that we have to **multiply** the **£ amount by the exchange rate** as the **£ is the foreign currency**, and the exchange rate is quoted as \$X:£1.

Forward contracts

Forward contracts remove the **risk from future short term currency fluctuations** by fixing an exchange rate in advance. If forward contracts are used, the following dollar costs will be incurred:

One month: £725,000 × 1.5601 = \$1,131,073
Three months: £530,000 × 1.5655 = \$829,715
Total payment: 1,131,073 + 829,715 = \$1,960,788

A forward contract will mean that the interest payment is of a **predictable amount** and the **possibility of exchange losses is eliminated**. However IOU will **not be able to participate in exchange gains** if the pound weakens.

Options

Options can be used to put a **'ceiling'** (or 'cap') on the amount payable while allowing the user to take advantage of **favourable exchange rate movements**.

Option set-up October payment

(i) **Contract date**

October

(ii) **Option type**

Call option; buy £ with \$

(iii) **Strike price**

Choose \$1.57 as recommended by the Treasurer

(iv) **Number of contracts**

$\frac{725{,}000}{31{,}250}$ = 23.2 contracts. Say 23 contracts hedging 31,250 × 23 = £718,750.

(v) **Premium**

Premium = 23 × 31,250 × \$0.0132
= \$9,488

Top tips. Remember that this is a US company, and as the premium is quoted in \$, it does not need to be translated at the opening spot rate.

Outcome

Option will be exercised if dollar weakens to more than \$1.57 in £.

Exercise 23 contracts @ \$1.57

Outcome of options position = 31,250 × 23 × 1.57 = \$1,128,438

Balance on spot market

	£
Exercise option 31,250 × 23	718,750
Value of transaction	725,000
Balance unhedged	6,250
Translated at spot/forward rate 6,250 × 1.5601	$9,751

	$
Option outcome	1,128,438
Option premium	9,488
Unhedged amount at spot forward rate	9,751
	1,147,677

Option set-up December payment

(i) **Contract date**

December contract

(ii) **Option type**

Call option

(iii) **Strike price**

Choose $1.58

(iv) **Number of contracts**

$\frac{530{,}000}{31{,}250}$ = 16.96 contracts, say 17 contracts hedging £31,250 × 17 = £531,250, with difference taken to forward market (531,250 – 530,000 = £1,250)

(v) **Premium**

Premium = 17 × 31,250 × $0.0212
= $11,263

Outcome

Option will be exercised if dollar weakens to more than $1.58 in £.

Outcome of options position = 31,250 × 17 × 1.58 = $839,375

Balance on spot market

	£
Exercise option 31,250 × 17	531,250
Value of transaction	530,000
Balance	(1,250)
Translated at spot/forward rate 1,250 × 1.5655	$(1,957)

	$
Option outcome	839,375
Overhedged amount	(1,957)
Option premium	11,263
Net payment	848,681

Breakeven rate

The disadvantage of options is that they can be **expensive** to buy because of the premium. The breakeven rate, the rate below which options will give a more favourable outcome than a forward contract, can be calculated as follows, ignoring the issue of whole contracts.

(Breakeven rate × Amount hedged) + Premium = Forward contract payment

For October Breakeven rate $= \dfrac{1,131,073 - 9,488}{725,000}$

$= \$1.5470$

For December Breakeven rate $= \dfrac{829,715 - 11,263}{530,000}$

$= \$1.5442$

Recommendation

Options should only be used if it is thought to be a good chance that the **pound** will **weaken** (but protection is still required against its strengthening). If, as the market believes, the pound is likely to strengthen, forward contracts will offer better value.

(b) **Exchange risks in Zorro**

Transactions exposure

This is the risk that the exchange rate **moves unfavourably between the date of agreement** of a contract price and the **date of cash settlement.**

Economic exposure

This is the risk of an **adverse change in the present value** of the organisation's future cash flows as a result of longer term exchange rate movements.

Netting off

The Zorro postal and telecommunications company will receive **domestic income** in its local currency but will make **settlements** (net receipts or payments) with foreign operators in US dollars. It may appear that most of the **currency risk** is **hedged** because **dollar payments** are **balanced against dollar receipts** before settlement. However, although this is a good way of reducing currency transaction costs, it does not remove currency risk.

Residual risk

Although the foreign transactions are denominated in dollars, the exchange risk involves **all the currencies of the countries with which the company deals.** For example, if money is owed to Germany and the euro has strengthened against the dollar, then the dollar cost of the transaction has increased. Also, although all of these transactions are short term, their combined effect is to expose the company to **continuous exchange risk** on many currencies. The company needs to manage this form of **economic exposure**.

Management of currency risk

One way to manage risk is to attempt to **match assets and liabilities** in each currency.

(i) The company needs to examine each country with which it deals and, having selected those with which it has a material volume of transactions, **determine in each case** whether there is a **net receipt or net payment** with that country and the average amount of this net receipt/payment.

(ii) If for a given country there is normally a net receipt, currency risk can be hedged by **borrowing an amount** in that currency equal to the **expected net receipt** for the period for which hedging is required, and **converting this amount** to the home currency.

(iii) For countries where there is **normally a net payment**, a **deposit account** in this currency should be maintained.

This strategy will go some way towards hedging currency risk in the various countries involved, but will involve **increased currency transaction costs** and possibly **increased interest costs**. It is therefore probably only feasible for major currencies (eg dollar, euro, yen) and for currencies of Asian countries with which there are major transaction volumes.

54 QW

Text references. Chapters 13 and 14.

Top tips. This question requires careful reading to ascertain that only just over half the marks are available for interest rate swaps; you also need to explain the use of derivative products generally, and to contrast the merits of the different techniques available for hedging interest rate risk. (a) gives you the chance to explain the purposes of derivatives in detail, showing the possible costs and the effects on risks. Your answer to (b) should concentrate on the main points of comparison (costs, flexibility, what each instrument achieves).

The best way to approach the calculations in (c) is to tabulate the swap under the two alternative arrangements, and then compare your results. You calculate the figure you adjust by taking the fixed/floating rate (whichever is chosen) which the company pays without the swap, and subtracting half the difference between the total the two companies pay with the swap and without the swap. We have included a diagram to help demonstrate what is happening (you weren't required to draw one here).

Don't forget that the question asks for a report format; you would get at least 1 mark for heading the report correctly and using appropriate language throughout.

Easy marks. The swap calculation is fairly straightforward, but if you're not sure of that, the description of the different instruments is not very complicated.

The question is a good illustration of the sort of question we mentioned in the kit front pages, where the techniques are not too complex and most of the marks are for discussion.

To: Board of Directors, QW
From: Treasurer
Date: 30 November 20X1
Subject: The use of financial derivatives and interest rate swaps

1 **Introduction**

1.1 The purpose of this report is to **explain** the **nature and function** of **financial derivatives**, and the benefits that they could offer to QW. The later sections of the report deal in more detail with methods of hedging interest rate risk, and the potential benefits of negotiating an interest rate swap with ER.

2 **Financial derivatives**

2.1 Financial derivatives are **traded products** that have developed from the securities and currency markets. Examples of derivative products include futures and options in currencies and interest rates.

2.2 There are two main purposes for which these products might be used:

1 **Hedging against known risks**

This can best be explained by means of an example. The company might have a **commitment** to **make a payment** in a foreign currency on a **specific date in three months' time**. It knows the amount, but it cannot know what the exchange rate will be at that time. It therefore faces the risk that if the home currency depreciates against the foreign currency, the size of the payment in sterling will be greater than if the payment were made now. This risk could be **hedged** by **using a derivative**. Such a transaction would have a **commission cost associated** with it, but it would **limit the risk** faced by the company.

2 **Speculation**

Derivatives can also be used to **gamble on expectations of movements** in interest and exchange rates. For example, the investor might believe that sterling would weaken against the dollar, and therefore buy dollars futures. These dollars would then be sold on the spot market once the expected movement in rates had taken place. The transactions are made purely with the **motive of making a profit**, and are not linked to any underlying business transactions. They are therefore very risky.

Since QW has diversified, international interests, derivative products offer **significant benefits** in the management of financial risks. The board needs to **determine the level of risk** that it is prepared to accept in these areas so that an integrated set of guidelines can be established.

3 Hedging interest rate risk

The main techniques available to hedge this type of risk are as follows.

3.1 Forward rate agreements

A forward rate agreement (FRA) is an OTC contract to lend or borrow a given sum of money in the future at an interest rate that is agreed today. These contracts can be used to **'fix' interest rates or exchange rates** on future transactions, thus **removing the risk of rate movements** in the intervening period.

3.2 Interest rate futures

These operate in a similar way to forward rate agreements. However, they are not negotiated directly with a bank but are **traded on the futures market**. Consequently, the terms, the amounts and the periods are **standardised**. For this reason, forward rate agreements are normally more appropriate than interest rate futures to non-financial companies such as QW.

3.3 Interest rate options

An interest rate option provides the **right to borrow or to lend a specified amount at a guaranteed rate of interest**. On the date of expiry of the option, or before, the buyer must decide whether or not to **exercise the right**. Thus in a borrowing situation, the option will only be exercised if market interest rates have risen above the option rate. Tailor made contracts can be purchased from major banks, while standardised contracts are traded in a similar way to interest rate futures. The cost of taking out an option is generally higher than for a forward rate agreement.

3.4 Interest rate swaps

These are transactions that exploit different interest rates in different markets for borrowing, to **reduce interest costs** for either fixed or floating rate loans. An interest rate swap is an arrangement whereby two companies, or a company and a bank, **swap interest rate commitments** with each other. In a sense, each simulates the other's borrowings, although each party to the swap retains its obligations to the original lenders. This means that the parties must accept **counterparty risk**.

3.4.1 Benefits of swaps

The main benefits of a swap as compared with other hedging instruments are as follows.

- **Transaction** costs **are low**, being limited to legal fees.
- They are **flexible**, since they can be arranged in any size, and they can be reversed if necessary.
- Companies **with different credit ratings can borrow at the best cost in the market** that is most accessible to them and then swap this benefit with another company to reduce the mutual borrowing costs.
- Swaps allow **capital restructuring** by changing the nature of interest commitments without the need to redeem debt or to issue new debt, thus reducing transaction costs.

4 Implications of an interest rate swap with ER

The proposed swap would involve one company borrowing at a floating rate, and the other at a fixed rate. Each company would enter into an individual loan arrangement with the bank, and the interest rate liabilities would then be swapped. The two options are:

	QW	ER	
Wants	Floating	Fixed	
Pays with Swap	8%	LIBOR + 0.5%	LIBOR + 8.5%
Pays without Swap	LIBOR + 0.2%	9.5%	LIBOR + 9.7%
Bank fee	– 0.2%	– 0.2%	– 0.4%
Potential gain			0.8%

We are told that the commission and gains should be split equally.

	QW	ER
Pays to bank if swap agreed	(8%)	(LIBOR + 0.5%)
Details of Swap		
Floating (W)	(LIBOR – 0.4%)	LIBOR – 0.4%
Fixed	8%	(8%)
Bank fee	(0.2%)	(0.2%)
Net outcome	(LIBOR – 0.2%)	(9.1%)

For QW the net outcome is:

Swap given to ER	LIBOR – 0.4 %
Bank charge	0.2 %
Net outcome	LIBOR – 0.2 %

For ER the net outcome is:

Difference between swap payment (LIBOR + 0.5)% and swap received from QW (LIBOR – 0.4)%	0.9%
Swap given to QW	8%
Bank charge	0.2%
Net outcome	9.1%

Working

$$\text{LIBOR} + 0.2\% - \frac{9.7 - 8.5}{2} = \text{LIBOR} - 0.4\%$$

The starting point for this calculation is what QW pays without the swap.

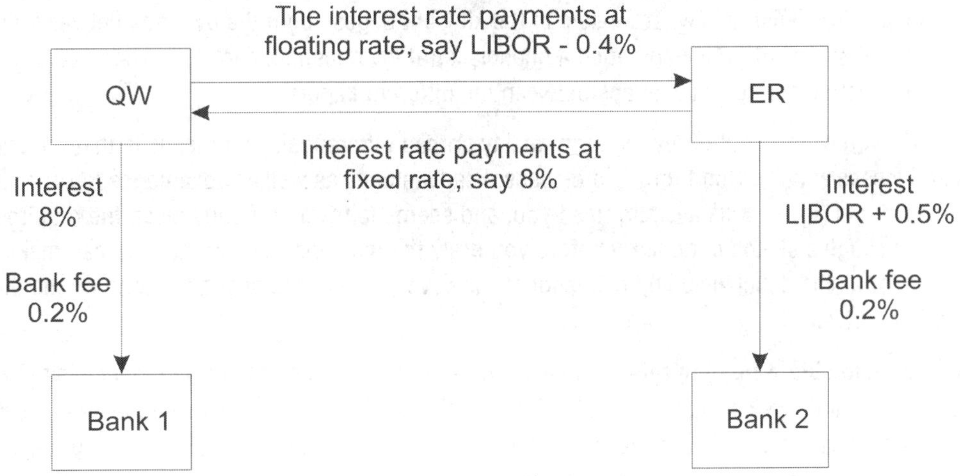

Alternative solution

Details of Swap	*QW*	*ER*
Floating (W)	(LIBOR + 0.5%)	LIBOR + 0.5%
Fixed	8.9%	(8.9%)
Bank fee	(0.2%)	(0.2%)
Net outcome	(LIBOR – 0.2%)	(9.1%)

For ER the net outcome is:

Swap given to QW	8.9%
Bank charge	0.2 %
Net outcome	9.1%

For QW the net outcome is:

Difference between swap payment 8% and swap received from ER 8.9%	– 0.9%
Swap given to ER	LIBOR + 0.5%
Bank charge	0.2%
Net outcome	LIBOR – 0.2%

Working

$$9.5\% - \frac{9.7 - 8.5}{2} = 8.9\%$$

The starting point for this calculation is what ER pays without the swap.

It can be seen that, regardless of the LIBOR rate, the two companies will **save £120,000** (£10 million × 1.2%) per year between them as a result of exploiting QW's ability to borrow at a lower fixed rate than ER plc. Of this, the bank would take a commission of 0.2% of the amount borrowed by both parties, £40,000 (£20 million × 0.2%).

It has been proposed by ER that the costs and gains should be **split equally**, leaving each company with a net benefit of £40,000 per year ((£10 million × 0.4%). However, ER is effectively benefiting from the better credit rating of QW, and therefore QW should be able to negotiate a higher percentage of the benefits.

55 LXN

Text references. Chapters 13 and 14.

Top tips. This question illustrates what we said in the kit front pages about the overlaps between different strategic level exams. The first part of (a) is very much a financial strategy question, and it's perhaps surprising to see it here, but it demonstrates potential overlaps between the different papers.

Hopefully in (b) you weren't put off by the term quality spread differential; all it means is that the two parties share the gains and losses equally. Don't forget to discuss disadvantages as well as advantages in (b)(i). The requirement to draw a diagram in (b) (ii) will have surprised you, and seems fairly superfluous given the requirements in (iii). It's essential to rough a sketch out quickly before you draw the main diagram so that you can make sure you leave enough space for all the detail including two lenders. However, it's easy to spend too long on the diagram so don't got beyond 8 minutes.

In (iii) LXN wants to **obtain floating rate finance** by the synthetic means of the swap, hence initially has to pay **fixed rate**. You should have calculated the total difference as you're asked to evaluate the annual savings. Other methods you could use to calculate the terms of swap are adjusting the fixed rate payment, or saying that the floating rate swap takes place at LIBOR (hence here the fixed rate swap must take place at 4.6%).

You should note that the written parts of this question were worth 15 marks; that's enough to pass it without tackling any of the numbers.

Easy marks. (b) (i) is a straightforward list for five marks.

Examiner's comments. Answers tended to be very good or very bad. Some answers to (a) lacked depth and focus. Poorer answers to (b) showed a lack of understanding of interest rate swaps, whilst some calculations were very badly attempted. 'There are very few numerical topics in the syllabus but it is important that candidates are well-prepared for these.'

(a) **Factors influencing choice of fixed and floating debt**

Cost of debt

The respective **current costs** of fixed and floating rate debt, plus any **arrangement or set-up fees**, will influence the decision.

Interest rate expectations

Expectations will be a significant influence, particularly if LXN borrows locally in Euros. Taking out fixed rate debt will eliminate the risk of changes in interest rates causing changes in finance costs. Higher interest rate costs will **not only increase LXN's cost of finance** if the directors choose floating rate debt, but may **decrease demand**, further decreasing profits. On the other hand, expectations of lower interest rates will mean that **floating rate debt** may be a **better option**.

Mix of debt

One way in which LXN can **limit its exposure to interest rate movements** is by having a **mix of fixed and floating rate debt**. If the funding is raised by fixed rate debt, then because the current floating rate debt is redeemable first, after 20X7 LXN could have just fixed rate debt. It would hence be vulnerable to relatively expensive borrowing if rates do decrease, and **termination costs** if it terminates some or all of its loans.

Factors influencing decision to hedge

Attitudes to risk

LXN seems to be very **risk-averse**, and this may increase the likelihood that it chooses to hedge.

Cost of hedging

Purchasing interest rate derivatives will have a **cost**, and LXN will have to decide whether the cost is worth incurring in the light of the **potential magnitude and likelihood** of **losses**. The proposed expenditure and hence loan funding required is €250,000 × 6 × 1.2 = €1.8 million which does not seem very large in the context of €2,000 million assets. If hedging reduces the possibility of financial losses, the company may feel able to **incur more debt**, and the **cost of borrowing** may **fall** because of the decreased risk. If interest rates are expected to remain stable, the **losses from not hedging** are likely to be **small**, not justifying the cost of hedging.

You would also have gained marks if you had discussed the following points.

Tax

If hedging is likely to **reduce variability of earnings**, this may have tax advantages if the company faces a higher rate of tax for higher earnings levels.

External hedging

The directors may be unwilling to undertake external hedging by purchasing derivatives because of the **monitoring** that will be required and the **need to disclose hedging costs** in the accounts in line with IAS 39.

Benefiting from favourable movements

If an interest rate option is purchased, LXN will be **able to gain from favourable movements in interest rates**, and also be **protected from adverse movements**.

(b) (i) **Advantages of interest rate swaps**

(1) **Flexibility and costs**

Swaps are **flexible**, since they can be arranged in any size, and they can be **reversed** if necessary. **Transaction costs are low**, being limited to legal fees, and are potentially much lower than the costs of terminating one loan and taking out another.

(2) **Credit ratings**

Companies **with different credit ratings** can **borrow in the market** that offers each the best deal and then swap this benefit to reduce the mutual borrowing costs. This is an example of the principle of **comparative advantage**.

(3) **Capital structure**

Swaps allow **capital restructuring** by changing the nature of interest commitments without renegotiating with lenders.

You would also have gained marks if you had discussed the following points.

(1) **Risk management**

Swaps can be used to **manage interest rate risk** by swapping floating for fixed rate debt if rates are expected to rise.

(2) **Convenience**

Swaps are relatively **easy to arrange**.

Disadvantages of interest rate swaps

(1) **Additional risk**

The swap is subject to **counterparty risk;** the risk that the other party will default leaving the first company to bear its obligations.

(2) **Movements in interest rates**

If a company takes on a floating rate commitment, it may be vulnerable to **adverse movements in interest rates.**

(ii)

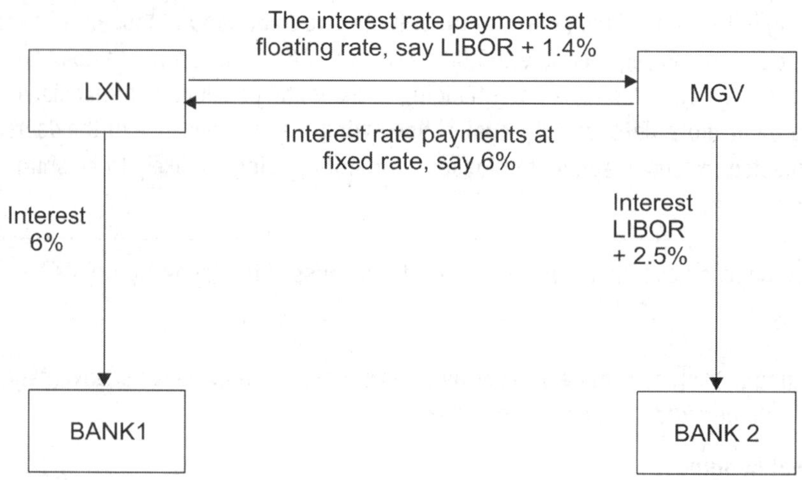

(iii)

	LXN	*MGV*	
Wants	Floating	Fixed	
Could pay with swap	6%	LIBOR + 2.5%	LIBOR + 8.5%
Would pay without swap	LIBOR + 1.5%	7.2%	LIBOR + 8.7%
Benefit	0.1%	0.1%	0.2%

We are told that gains should be split equally.

	LXN	MGV
Pays to bank if swap agreed	(6%)	(LIBOR + 2.5%)
Details of Swap		
Floating (W)	(LIBOR + 1.4%)	LIBOR + 1.4%
Fixed	6%	(6%)
Net outcome	(LIBOR + 1.4%)	(7.1%)

Working

$$\text{LIBOR} + 1.5\% - \frac{8.7-8.5}{2} = \text{LIBOR} + 1.4\%$$

The starting point for this calculation is what LXN pays without the swap.

Without the swap

LXN will pay (5 + 1.5)% × (€250,000 × 6 × 1.2) = €117,000

With the swap

LXN will pay (5 + 1.4)% × (€250,000 × 6 × 1.2) = €115,200

Saving = €1,800

The gain must be considered in the light of the **counterparty risk**, of LXN having to cover payments that MGV has to make. LXN can obviously take steps to assess or limit its exposure, obtaining a credit rating on MGV or seeking an indemnity from MGV's bank.

56 X

Text references. Chapters 10, 14 and 15.

Top tips. In (a) the question details are not completely clear whether all of the costs of production are in £ or €; we have assumed €. The € **strengthening** against the £ means for UK companies that revenues and costs denominated in € will **rise**; therefore you have to multiply the sterling contribution by 1.05 each year. There are various valid ways to do the calculation; another one would be to calculate the expected value of the receipts first, and then use this amount in the NPV calculation.

(b) is asking specifically for risks that differ between launching in France and England. For each risk, you would probably get 1 mark for identifying it, 1 mark for discussing how to manage it but it is not that easy to generate ideas from the limited details given.

In (c) X wants floating rate interest so has to pay fixed rate interest and then swap. Since you are given the amount of the loan, you need to calculate the total benefit.

We have changed the question details in (c), as in the original question both companies wanted fixed interest and the swap wouldn't work. If you come across this situation in the exam, and spot it instantly you may decide to do another question instead. However here as the calculation is only for six marks, it would not be too risky to state that you had identified a problem, and what assumptions you'd made to overcome it. The diagram isn't required by this question, but we have included it to illustrate how the swap works.

Easy marks. The benefits and drawbacks of interest rate swaps have been examined before and should be six of the easiest marks in this exam.

Examiner's comments. In (a) some students confused weakening and strengthening; most students also failed to gain marks because they did not discuss the results. The main weakness in (b) was a failure to discuss the problems of a new product launch in a new country. In (c) candidates showed good knowledge of swaps, although few calculated the bank charges. Candidates who noted that a fixed to fixed swap (see problem discussed above) was not possible were given reasonable marks. However most candidates who did carry out the swap calculations, assuming one company should accept a floating rate, produced correct answers.

(a) Expected annual cash flow = (90,000 × 0.5) + (70,000 × 0.2) + (30,000 × 0.3)
= £68,000

Year (n)	*0*	*1*	*2*	*3*	*4*
	£	£	£	£	£
Original expected annual cash flow	(190,000)	68,000	68,000	68,000	68,000
Original annual cash flow × (1.05)n	(190,000)	71,400	74,970	78,719	82,654
Disc factor 10%	1.000	0.909	0.826	0.751	0.683
Present value	(190,000)	64,903	61,925	59,118	56,453

Expected net present value = £52,399

The appreciation of the € has meant it will now be preferable to launch the product in France.

(b) **Risks associated with product launch in England**

Launch costs

The **actual net present value** will prove significantly **lower** than the expected net present value if launch costs turn out to be the less likely possibility, £145,000.

X should identify the factors that could cause launch costs to be £145,000 and take steps to **avoid these factors materialising**, for example **tight cost control**.

Risks associated with product launch in France

Exchange risks

As illustrated above, a strengthening of the € means that the product launch in France would be worthwhile. However if expectations are wrong and the **€ weakens against the £,** then the wrong decision would have been taken.

X can reduce this risk by **obtaining finance in France in euros** to fund the launch of the product. This would **match costs of finance against cash flows from the product**, and thus provide a **hedge against currency movements**.

Finance risk

Sales volume elasticity

X may find that the **availability of substitutes in France** may mean that the demand for product is more elastic than it anticipated. As a result revenues for new products are more price-sensitive and the higher margins that it is trying to obtain **result in lower annual cash flows than predicted**.

X should **reduce this risk** by being prepared to **vary the price of the product**, perhaps with a lower contribution margin in the first couple of years to get the product established. Possibly it may be able to raise margins in Years 3 and 4 once the product has become established and the demand is perhaps less elastic.

Market risks

As X is based in England, it may find it more difficult than anticipated to break into the French market if it lacks experience of it. It may not have contacts and also lack an appreciation of **different taste and cultural conditions**. X may also find it **more difficult to withdraw** from the French market once it has made the commitment to enter the market, since it may jeopardise its future chances of success abroad.

X should **reduce this risk** by **undertaking market research** and **employing French staff as agents**, to advise on the French market and to provide means of establishing sales and distribution networks.

(c) (i) **Benefits of interest rate swaps**

Flexibility and cost

Swaps are **flexible**, since they can be arranged in any size, and they can be reversed if necessary. **Transactions costs are low**.

Credit ratings

Companies **with different credit ratings** such as X and HTM can borrow in the market that offers each the best deal and then swap this benefit to reduce the mutual borrowing costs. This is an example of the principle of **comparative advantage**.

Capital restructuring

Swaps allow **capital restructuring** by changing the nature of interest commitments. The implication appears to be that HTM will find it difficult to raise finance at favourable fixed rates.

Hazards of interest rate swaps

Risk of default

The swap is subject to **counterparty risk**; the risk that the other party will default leaving the first company to bear its obligations, unless the contract has been guaranteed through an intermediary.

Interest rate risk

If a company takes on a floating rate commitment, it may be vulnerable to **adverse movements in interest rates**.

(ii)

	X	*HTM*	*Total*
Wants	Floating	Fixed	
Pays without swap	LIBOR + 0.5%	10.5%	LIBOR + 11%
Pays with swap	8.5%	LIBOR + 1.1%	LIBOR + 9.6%
Bank fee (assume both are charged 0.1%)	0.1%	0.1%	0.2%
Potential gain	0.6%	0.6%	1.2%
Swap			
Pays to bank if swap agreed	(8.5%)	(LIBOR + 1.1%)	
Details of swap			
Floating	(LIBOR + 1.1%)	LIBOR + 1.1%	
Fixed (W)	9.8%	(9.8%)	
Bank fee	(0.1%)	(0.1%)	
Net outcome	(LIBOR – 0.1%)	(9.9%)	

Working

$$10.5\% - \frac{11 - 9.6}{2} = 9.8\%$$

X and HTM should each make a gain of £500,000 × 0.6% = £3,000

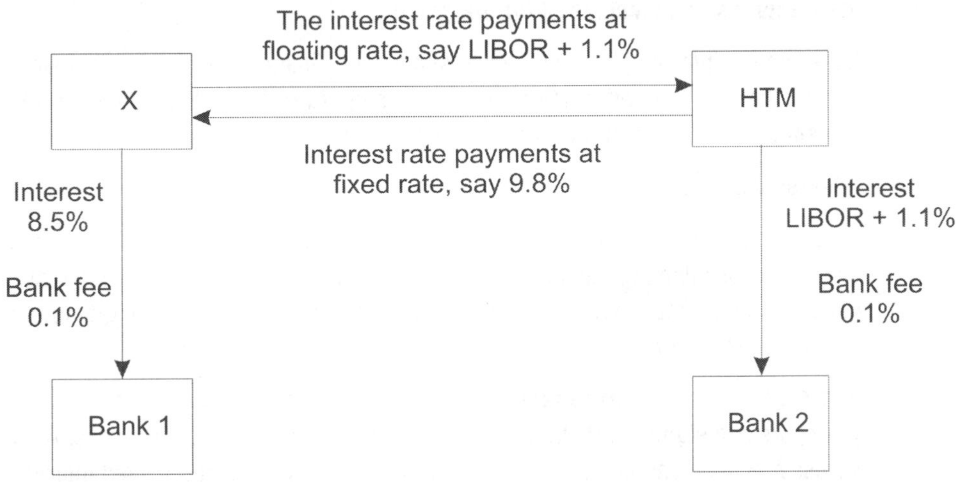

Alternative solution

Swap	*X*	*HTM*
Pays to bank if swap agreed	(8.5%)	(LIBOR + 1.1%)
Details of swap		
Floating (W)	(LIBOR – 0.2%)	LIBOR – 0.2%
Fixed	8.5%	(8.5%)
Bank fee	(0.1%)	(0.1%)
Net outcome	(LIBOR – 0.1%)	(9.9%)

Working

$$\text{LIBOR} + 0.5\% - \frac{11 - 9.6}{2} = \text{LIBOR} - 0.2\%$$

57 Listed services group

Text references. Chapters 11 to 14.

Top tips. If your answer contains most of the points that ours does, you should score well on any questions involving discussion of currency or interest rate risk. Bear in mind however that questions may contain more complex numbers than this one does.

(a) is a general question about financial risks so note in (a) (i) the other sources of financial risk as well as interest rate risk and currency risk. The question illustrates that exchange risk is not just about the risk on individual transactions, but also economic risk (longer-term trends) and translation risk (figures shown in the accounts), although this is arguably cosmetic. Whilst (hopefully) you picked up the requirement in (a) (ii) that you had to carry out a calculation, the requirement in both (a) (i) and (iii) to evaluate may have caused you more difficulties. Evaluate implies giving an idea of the magnitude, if possible using the numbers in the scenario to support what you're saying, even if you can't carry out complicated calculations with them. Thus (a) (i) brings in from the scenario the extent of floating rate, foreign currency and short-term borrowings.

Key pegs to hang your discussion on in (b) are:

- Purpose (swaps need to be distinguished from other instruments)
- Cost
- Matching of exact requirements
- Whether the organisation can benefit from favourable changes in exchange rates.

Easy marks. (b) as you don't need to carry out any calculations. Any questions on derivatives in this paper will include a discussion element on which you should aim to score well.

(a) (i) **Main sources of financial risk for the group**

Based on the information given, which shows only financial liabilities, the main sources of financial risk for the group are **interest rate risk**, **exchange rate risk**, the risk that **short term loans may not be renewed** and the **general financial risk** associated with borrowing (gearing).

Interest rate risk

Most of the group's borrowings are at a **floating rate of interest** (£110 million out of £143 million, or 77%). Because floating rate loans gives the lender the right to increase interest rates in line with general interest rate movements, the company suffers substantial risk that interest rates may increase in the future.

At present the group's **fixed rate loans** (all of which are long term with maturity in more than 5 years) are at a **significantly higher interest rate** than current floating rates. Although part of this excess may be regarded as a premium for the certainty of paying a fixed interest rate, it may also indicate that floating rate interest rates are **likely to rise** in the **medium term** future.

Exchange rate risk

The group reports its results and pays dividends to shareholders in pounds sterling. However, £45 million (31%) of its **borrowings are in foreign currencies** (US dollars and Euros) and there is the risk that the pound will weaken in relation to these currencies, resulting in a higher sterling cost of interest payments and loan repayments.

The group will suffer **similar exchange rate risks** on **its trading transactions** and on its foreign denominated assets.

Risk that short term loans are not renewed

£74m of the group's borrowings (52%) are **due for repayment** within the next year. If the company suffers financial difficulties there may be **difficulty in refinancing its operations**. Further information would be required to evaluate this risk.

Gearing

All companies that borrow suffer from the financial risk that **interest** must be **paid regardless of whether profits are made**. The effect of borrowing is to make the group's profit and cash flow stream more volatile than that of ungeared companies.

(ii) **Exchange rate transaction risk**

The group's transactions over the next 12 months relating to its foreign currency liabilities are predicted to be:

			Loan	*Rate*	*Interest/repayment*
Liabilities			*£m*		*£m*
US $ loans:	Interest	Fixed	33	7.25%	2.3925
		Floating	8	5%	0.4000
Euro loans:	Interest	Floating	4	5%	0.2000
	Repayment				1.0000
Total payments					3.9925

If the pound were to depreciate 10% against the US dollar and the Euro, to 90% of its current value, the cost of the payments in pounds would rise to £3.9925/0.9 = £4.4361 million. Additional payments suffered over the next year would therefore be (£4.4361 – £3.9925) million = **£443,600**, which would be charged directly against group profits as an exchange loss. This is referred to as transaction risk.

(iii) **How transaction risk relates to translation risk and economic risk in this example**

Applied to this example, **translation risk** is the risk that the **balance sheet values of foreign currency liabilities increase** as a result of a decline in the value of the pound. The current sterling value of foreign denominated liabilities is currently £45 million. If the pound depreciated by 10%, these liabilities would be valued at £45/0.9 = £50 million. The increase in the balance sheet value of the liabilities would be **£5 million**, which is the translation risk.

Whereas the translation risk depends entirely on what the exchange rates are at the end of the next financial period (one year), there is also the possibility that the **value of a foreign currency liability increases still further** because of longer term movements in exchange rates. This is an example of **economic risk** that, as applied to this example, can be defined as the risk that the **expected present value of foreign currency liabilities increases** as a result of a long term forecast exchange rates.

(b) **Use of derivatives for hedging**

A derivative is a security whose **value is derived** from the **price of another asset**, known as the underlying asset. In the context of the current example, the underlying assets are bonds (loan stocks) or currencies and the main types of derivative are forward rate agreements, futures, options and swaps. These can all be used to 'hedge risk', that is reduce the risk associated with using loans and/or foreign currencies.

The derivatives can be **purchased** or **sold** '**over the counter'** (OTC), that is by negotiation with a financial institution (a bank), or on **formally regulated exchange markets** which bring together buyers and sellers of standard derivative contracts (futures and options exchanges).

Exchange traded derivatives

The **advantages of exchange traded derivatives** are that they can be **available in smaller contract sizes** and to **organisations with lower credit ratings; transaction costs are low**, and positions can be **closed** at any time by entering into reverse transactions (by selling a futures contract that has previously been purchased). However, because the contract sizes, currencies, time periods and due dates are **standardised** and **limited**, it is usually only possible to obtain approximate hedges.

OTC derivatives

By contrast OTC derivatives can be **tailored by negotiation** to the user's exact hedging requirements. However, positions cannot be so **easily reversed out** if situations change, **regulation is lower**, **transaction costs** can be **higher** and the **starting size for contracts may be too high** for smaller organisations.

Characteristics of the main types of derivative relevant to the example are given below.

Forward rate agreements

A **forward rate agreement** (FRA) is an OTC contract to lend or borrow a given sum of money in the future at an interest rate that is agreed today. For currencies, the equivalent is the **forward contract:** an agreement to buy or sell a given amount of currency in the future at an exchange rate that is agreed today.

These contracts can be used to '**fix' interest rates or exchange rates** on future transactions, thus **removing the risk of rate movements** in the intervening period. In the example, the company needs to repay a euro loan (of approximately £1 million) next year. The risk of the pound weakening against the euro in the period before the loan is repaid can be hedged by entering into a forward contract to buy £1 million worth of euros at an exchange rate agreed today. The money does not need to be paid until next year, but the exchange rate is fixed today.

Note that removing risk is not always beneficial. If the pound were to strengthen against the euro, the company would have lost the opportunity of making an exchange gain if it fixed its exchange rate using a forward contract.

Futures contracts

Futures contracts are **exchange traded versions** of forward rate agreements and are used in a similar way to hedge risk. The markets are mainly for interest rates rather than currencies.

Options

Options can be obtained for **interest rates and currencies**, for both OTC and exchange traded contracts. In contrast to forward or futures contracts, an option need only be **exercised** (used) if it is **advantageous to the user**. For example, the company has a floating rate sterling loan on which it is currently paying 5% interest. It could purchase an option to pay fixed interest of 7% on this loan. The option would only be exercised if the floating rate rose above 7%. In all other situations the option would be allowed to lapse. The option therefore offers a guaranteed maximum to the interest paid, while allowing an unlimited reduction in the interest rate. It is known as a **cap.** Because of this flexibility, options are expensive derivatives to purchase.

Swap

A **swap** involves two parties **agreeing to swap payment obligations** on their loans. For example, if the company wished to **reduce interest rate risk**, it may consider swapping its floating rate sterling payments with a party that that was making fixed rate sterling payments on the same principal value of the loan. To **reduce exchange rate risk**, it may agree to swap its interest and repayment on a US dollar loan with a party that has a sterling loan and prefers an obligation in US dollars. This is called a **currency swap.**

58 ZX

Text references. Mainly Chapter 15, though Chapter 11 deals with currency risk and Chapter 13 covers interest rate risk.

Top tips. Expected values will be a key risk quantification technique in this paper, so make sure you can follow all stages of our answer to (a). (b) brings in control and organisation of the franchisees as well as general issues relating to trading abroad. The verb discuss means that you have to debate whether the risks are significant, bringing in uncertainties and factors that may increase or decrease the risks identified. (c) emphasises that currency and interest rate risks are important topics in this paper. The requirement to evaluate means that you have to show how effective the methods you discuss are likely to be.

Easy marks. (b) is a fairly general discussion on risk. (c) also covers mainstream risks, but with a difference in emphasis to most questions on exchange and interest rate risk which requires thought.

(a) **Expected sterling value of additional profit**

Total **number of franchises offered** = 5 × 5 = 25. Total value = 25 × €100,000 = €2.5m

Value of loans made for franchise costs = 80% ×€2.5 million = €2 million

Value of loans made for property = €4.8 million

Note: It is assumed that this property loan figure does not need to be multiplied by 80%, as it is the treasurer's estimate.

Total value of loans made = €2 million + €4.8 million = €6.8 million

Average loan per franchisee = €6.8 million/25 = €272,000

Annual interest cost of the loans to ZX = 10% × €6.8 million = €680,000

Annual interest charged to franchisees = 7% × €6.8 million = €476,000

Therefore, **net annual interest cost to ZX** is (680 – 476) = €204,000

ZX's income from sales made by franchisees is 1% commission + 12% margin on goods sold = 13% × sales value.

Total planned income is 13% × planned sales = 13% × €26 million = €3, 380,000

Scen -ario	*Sales propor -tion*	*No. of loan defaults*	*Sales* €	*ZX income: 13% × sales,* €	*Net interest cost* €	*Cost of loan write-offs** €	*Net profit**,* €	*Prob*	*Expected value* €
1	90%	2	23,400,000	3,042,000	(204,000)	(544,000)	2,294,000	0.1	229,400
2	80%	4	20,800,000	2,704,000	(204,000)	(1,088,000)	1,412,000	0.3	423,600
3	100%	0	26,000,000	3,380,000	(204,000)	0	3,176,000	0.4	1,270,400
4	100%	1	26,000,000	3,380,000	(204,000)	(272,000)	2,904,000	0.2	580,800
								1.0	2,504,200

* Defaults × average loan per franchisee

** Net profit to ZX is ZX income – net interest cost – cost of loan write-offs.

Note: This figure does not include the receipt of €2.5 million for franchise purchases paid by the franchisees. This receipt should be credited to ZX's income statements over the period of the franchise. However, the question does not say for how many years the franchise is valid.

The expected additional profit for ZX is €2.504 million.

The exchange rate at the start of the year is €1.3939:£1. The Euro is expected to strengthen by 5% over the next year to 1.3939 × 0.95 = €1.3242: £1.

The average exchange rate for the year is approximately (1.3939 + 1.3242)/2 = €1.3591.

The **expected profit** in £ is therefore 2,504,200/1.3591 = **£1.8425 million**.

The **capital invested** by ZX is loans €6.8 million + working capital £3.65 million.
Using the opening exchange rate of €1.3939, this is £4.878 million + £3.65 million = £8.528 million.

The rate of return earned is 1.8425 / 8.528 = **21.6%**, which is comfortably above the minimum required return for international operations of 15%.

Note: If some portion of the €2.5 million receipt from franchisees were included in profit, the rate of return would be correspondingly higher.

(b) **Risks from expanding into Europe using franchising**

Franchising in foreign countries is a form of **foreign direct investment (FDI)** and is subject to the risks associated with this.

Political risk

Because UK is also a member of the European Union (a stable political and economic union), the **political risk** associated with any of the five countries considered is **very small**. The highest risk is probably that increases in corporate or property taxation are introduced in some regions.

Cultural risk

Cultural risk is higher. It is possible that consumers in some locations are **prejudiced** against UK products where there are local alternatives. However, because of this, franchising using national owner-managers may represent a less risky form of investment than the alternative of setting up wholly owned subsidiaries. On the other hand, franchising may prove to be an **unpopular form of business model** in some regions, which is another aspect of cultural risk. In addition it is possible that ZX will **not be able** to attract **sufficient franchisees** as it is not a well-known enough concern. Most franchises are linked to globally known brands.

Currency risk

Any form of investment in Europe will be subject to **currency risk**: the risk that the euro declines in value against the pound, resulting in a **reduced present value of the income stream**. Again, franchising suffers lower risk than investment in wholly owned subsidiaries, although ZX's decision to make **euro loans** to franchisees leaves it exposed (see (c)).

Credit risk

In addition to the normal risks of customers defaulting on debts, ZX bears the risk that its **franchisees will fail** and default on the repayment of the loans it has advanced to them.

Control risk

Franchises are **more difficult to control** than wholly owned investments; in particular they may be unwilling to accept the ZX way of doing things as regards the image projected, store design and product stocking.

Export sales risk

Franchise sales **displace export sales** made by the UK operation or, more indirectly, **divert resources** from the UK.

Lack of goal congruence risk

If franchises are not located carefully, they may end up **competing** with each other.

(c) **Management of risks associated with the euro loans**

ZX intends to advance fixed interest euro-denominated loans to its franchisees. This will result in three types of financial risk: credit risk, currency risk and, possibly, interest rate risk.

Credit risk

This is the risk that some of the franchisees **default** on the **loans**. In the calculations in (a), this has been accepted as a risk.

Reduction of credit risk

It could be reduced by:

(i) **Carrying out standard credit control checks** on franchisees.

(ii) **Requiring guarantees** by the directors of the franchisee companies to bank loans.

(iii) **Taking security for the loans** (in the form of charges over the property used for operating the franchise).

However, in taking action to reduce credit risk, ZX must be prepared to negotiate a **reduced margin** from franchisees, or else run the risk of a lower than expected number of franchise takers.

Currency risk

Currency transaction risk is the risk that the **sterling value of loan interest and repayments** is **eroded** if the euro declines in value against the pound. Although this is not predicted to happen in the calculations, there is a substantial risk that it will. Currency risk also applies to the commission remitted by franchisees.

Reduction of currency risk by euro borrowing

The best way to **reduce currency risk** on the **loans to franchisees** is to **finance these loans out of euro (rather than sterling) borrowings**. In that way, if the euro declines, both receipts and payments are reduced. The disadvantage of borrowing in euros is that ZX may **not be able to obtain such a relatively favourable interest rate** as in pounds.

Other methods of reducing currency risk

Alternative ways of hedging currency risk include:

(i) **Forward currency contracts**
These **fix the exchange rates for future receipts and/or payments**. They can be tailored to suit the company's circumstances, but bind the company into a fixed price.

(ii) **Futures**
These also **fix the price of a transaction** in the future, but as they are only for standardised amounts, there is likely to be some transaction exposure that isn't hedged.

(iii) **Options**
In return for a substantial purchase price, options allow the company to **avoid exchange losses** while **taking advantage of exchange gains**.

(iv) **Matching franchise receipts with payments to short-term payables**
That is **EU based suppliers**. This would however reduce the output required from the UK based factory.

Interest rate risk

ZX will suffer from **interest rate risk** if it **grants fixed interest loans** to franchisees while **paying floating rate interest** on the borrowings it makes to finance them. If interest rates rise, ZX would make a loss on this financing arrangement.

Reduction of interest rate risk

This could be avoided by negotiating with its bankers to exchange some of its floating rate borrowings for fixed rate borrowings (probably at a higher rate of interest). Alternatively it could **reconsider its plans** to offer fixed rate finance, and instead **offer franchisees floating rate loans**.

59 WRF

Text references. Chapter 18.

Top tips. Note when you analyse the scenario for (a), the analysis not only involves picking up the highlighted weaknesses in the scenario (failure to consult users, lack of testing process), but also key business details (the dynamic business environment) and what you're not told (any information about cost!). Even if you hadn't been asked specifically about the systems development lifecycle, you should have recommended it as a key control improvement.

Note in (b) that the process needs to go beyond being a technical review of the system and satisfy the user and business requirements. User involvement in the testing process is thus essential.

Post-implementation reviews should be an integral part of the company's control and audit procedures for the reasons given in (c), and their results should be reviewed as part of the directors' review of the effectiveness of the internal control system.

Easy marks. This is generally a fairly straightforward question. You should be able particularly to list the stages of the systems development lifecycle and discuss post-audits, a favourite topic for part questions.

(a) **Problems with existing approach**

A purchase recommendation has been made for a system using hardware and software that may **already be outdated** in terms of the fast-moving world of IT.

(i) **User requirements**
A **systems investigation** is needed so that account is taken of the **specific requirements of users**. At present, users only know of a proposed change through the grapevine: they do not appear to have been formally consulted. This is particularly regrettable since they seem to be enthusiastic about change and would no doubt have a good deal to contribute to the specification of an ideal system for their needs.

(ii) **Information on problems**
More **systems analysis** is required to determine what are the problems with the existing system. The upgrade is intended to improve the **speed and clarity of information**, but we have no details of how the design of the proposed new system will do this.

(iii) **Future needs**
Account must be taken of the **future needs** of the business. We trade in a dynamic environment and our information needs may well be significantly different in future years. Will the proposed system be able to cope with change and growth?

(iv) **System costs and specification**
There is no indication of system costs, and a detailed specification. We need a **detailed breakdown** of the **initial cost** and also of **ongoing costs** over the life of the proposed system, together with a specification detailing what it is we would receive (eg file server and PC specifications).

(v) **Conversion of information**
Information in the company's **existing database** is likely to have to be **converted** in some way to make it compatible with the new system. What will this entail? Will data have to be entirely restructured and if so how. Will all the data have to be re-input, or is there software available to ease the task.

(vi) **Implementation of system**
Arrangements need to be made for the **implementation** of the system. Even in the short term the analyst's contract ends at the installation stage: does this mean that we will be **without his support** during the early days of the system going live, when it would be unusual for there to be no **teething problems**?

Systems development lifecycle

The **systems development lifecycle** is a disciplined approach intended to reduce the possibility of a result that does not meet the needs of the organisation

(i) **Feasibility study** – review of existing system and identification of alternative solution

(ii) **Systems investigation** – obtaining details of current requirements, problems and alternatives

(iii) **Systems analysis** – identification of better alternatives to current methods

(iv) **Systems design** – determination of inputs, processing and storage facilities required to produce outputs, also design and controls; production of a detailed systems specification

(v) **Systems implementation** – software acquisition, testing, conversion, installation and starting to run the new system

(vi) **Review and maintenance** – ensure the system meets objectives and lessons are learnt for future developments

(b) **Risks of inadequate testing**

If systems testing is inadequate, there is the risk ultimately that the **software will fail to work at all**. There is also the risk that data will be posted incorrectly with consequent **disruption to the company's accounting systems and relations with customers**. There is also the risk that although the system within its limits works accurately, it **fails to meet the specifications required**. If these features are not met, then the software will **fail to meet user expectations** and at worst it may be unusable.

Systems testing

Systems testing will seek assurance that the software **works correctly** in the following areas.

(i) **To ensure that the specification for the system has been met**
This is a key test.

(ii) **To check that the user interface is understandable and usable**
Software must be easy to use; additional checks will be made to ensure that screen formats are consistent and the same keys are pressed to carry out common functions such as closing dialog boxes.

(iii) **To ensure that data is processed correctly**
Checks need to be made to ensure that data is transferred between individual programs (eg the sales program updates the inventory balances in the inventory system). Similarly, processing within one program should operate correctly (eg the correct sales ledger account is updated when an invoice is raised). **Test data** will be prepared and run within the program to meet these objectives. Further work will be necessary to ensure that appropriate error messages are generated.

User acceptance testing

User acceptance testing will take place after systems testing, seeking the following assurance.

(i) **The software meets the systems specification agreed by the users**
This specification will normally be contained in flowcharts or entity-relationship models. Users will therefore want to **check the design of the software**, and in particular will check the individual screens to ensure that they are usable, and whether users need **additional functionality** building into the system that was not in the initial specification.

(ii) **The workflow of each department is accurately reflected in the software**
Although the specification should **reflect work flows**, it is only when the system itself is available that a full check is possible.

(iii) **Appropriate documentation is being generated to provide training and reference material**
Although this material is unlikely to be complete, users may be able to **test the accuracy of draft**

material and provide valuable input into the important points that need to be included in both sets of material.

(c) **Risks of failing to review development**

A **lack of review** may mean that remaining problems with the system which need to be remedied are not identified and **remedial action not taken**. These include not just failure to fulfil user requirements but also **failure to achieve the business benefits**. A lack of review may mean **problems with the development process** itself are **not addressed**, which will have **implications** for the success of future developments.

Post-implementation review

A post-implementation review takes place a few months after system implementation is complete. The review is to receive **feedback** from users on how well the system is working and to check that the **objectives** of the project have been met. The review normally takes the form of a meeting between the project sponsor, systems analyst, developers and users.

Review of procedures and systems

The review will investigate both the **procedures used throughout the project** and the **systems that have been produced**. The purpose of doing this is to identify what features of the project went well, and what went wrong or badly, so that future projects will avoid these problems.

Review of results

In reviewing the objectives of the project, the review will also check whether or not the **business benefits** expected from the project have been **achieved**. Where benefits have not been achieved, or other objectives of the project have not been met, the review may also recommend **remedial action** to ensure that the required benefits are obtained, and that the **systems development process is amended** for future projects.

60 MG II

Text references. Mainly Chapter 16, with Chapter 4 covering budgeting.

Top tips. (a) demonstrates the significance of the different components of information strategy. Note that information systems strategy is primarily to do with **effectiveness** whereas information technology strategy focuses more on **efficiency**.

To give the required advice in (b) you have to have an awareness of what managers' needs are – summarised information, relevant for long-term decision-making, and showing appropriate performance measures.

Note in (c) that you have to use knowledge about budgeting systems that you will be assumed have brought forward from management level papers. The examiner has emphasised in recent examiners' reports that it's important to use this knowledge. The answer links the two requirements: the recommendations about the systems are generated by business use analysis, based on the concepts of zero based budgeting.

Easy marks. You will be fortunate if you get a part like (a) in the exam as all it does is require you to state definitions.

(a) (i) **Information systems strategy**

Information systems strategy refers to the **long-term plan** concerned with **exploiting information systems** either to **support business strategies** or **create new strategic options**. It needs to ensure that information is made available for implementing strategy in all areas of an organisation's activities.

Information strategy is focused ultimately on the **business's long-term objectives**, with information systems being used as a means to achieve those objectives.

(ii) **Information technology strategy**

Information technology strategy involves deciding how **information needs** will be met by balancing **supply and demand of funds and facilities**, and the development of programmes to supply IT.

Information technology strategy ultimately focuses on **investing in the best possible technology including hardware, software and operating systems**. It takes into account risk attitude and technical standards, but also ensuring that the technology supplied is in line with the organisation's **needs, style and structure**.

(iii) **Information management strategy**

Information management strategy refers to the basic approach that an organisation has for managing its information systems, computerised or manual. It includes planning developments, the organisational environment and control. It should ensure that the **right information is provided to users and that irrelevant information is not being produced**.

Information management is primarily concerned with the links between the information technology function and the rest of the organisation. It is also influenced by wider issues such as the **structure** of **the organisation** and **the businesses** that it is in, dealing with **who** should be **responsible** for managing information, **where** the information function should be **located** and **how** information should be stored.

(b) **Transaction processing systems**

Transactions processing systems are designed for the routine processing tasks that the company needs to carry out in order to continue operations. They cover receipts, payments and inventory movements, and are designed to **fulfil the requirements to prepare financial accounts** and to report profits made by the main component parts of the organisation.

Drawbacks of transaction processing systems

The main disadvantage of these systems is that their **output is not summarised** in ways that might help managers make decisions. They can provide excessive detail in certain ways, but fail to provide strategically useful information such as sales or profits by product or by customer.

Need for strategic information systems

Transaction processing systems are basically knowledge systems, designed to integrate knowledge and help in operational tasks. The company however also needs strategic systems, designed to **help senior management with long-term planning** and ensuring that the **business develops successfully** in the light of changes in the external environment, in particular developments affecting suppliers, customers and competitors.

The company therefore needs to consider its information systems strategy carefully and ensure that it invests in management support systems that **enhance strategic decision-making**.

Enterprise resource planning systems

Enterprise resource planning systems are used to **identify and plan the enterprise-wide resources** needed to record, produce, distribute and account for customer orders. They collect accounting, operational, customer and supplier data and **produce reports and update performance measures.**

Advantages of enterprise resource planning systems

The systems can **produce reports that are tailored to managers' needs**, and are sophisticated enough to be able to cope with a range of different performance measures, for example the **balanced scorecard** or **activity-based measures.** Because they provide information about the wider business and competitive environment, they can be used to **develop strategy**, and also in **customer and supplier management**.

Executive information systems

Executive information or executive support systems **pool data** from internal and external systems and make information available to managers in an easy-to-use form.

Advantages of executive information systems

The advantages that should be built into the systems are that they can **identify, track and summarise strategically critical information** from competitors and external information as well as internal sources. They then provide key figures and trends in whatever detail and format are required, and packages can also use these figures in data analysis and models. Executive information systems should also be **flexible** to users' needs and have a **quick response time**. They should provide information in response to **one-off enquiries.**

(c) **Drawbacks of present system**

The present **incremental** budgeting system is unsatisfactory not just in terms of the information technology function but the organisation as a whole. It takes **no account of changes in business strategy** and the expenditure that may be required as a result, and can also **perpetuate inefficiency**.

Alternative methods

(i) **Zero-based budgeting**
This involves **justifying every item of expenditure**, either starting from scratch or looking at all items of current expenditure to see if they are worthwhile. Zero-based budgeting can mean that purposeless expenditure and the budgeting system responds better to changes in the business environment, although it can over-emphasise short-term benefits.

(ii) **Activity-based budgeting**
This means **focusing on the activities that underlie costs** and allocating resources according to the importance of the activities.

Implications for IT investment

Use of either zero-based or activity-based budgeting will imply that a **business case** has to be made for information technology investment. The case should specify **organisation information requirements** in the light of an organisation's plans and objectives, in particular the **critical success factors** of the organisation. These requirements should be linked in with developments in the information technology environment to produce the recommendations for the best systems.

61 AMF

Text references. Chapter 17.

Top tips. Planning (a) and (b) is important to ensure that you don't repeat yourself; some of the disadvantages of outsourcing are the risks of 'letting go' sensitive information. In (a) you would only have had time to consider a limited number of advantages and disadvantages given that the question asked you to discuss. (ie comment on their likely significance).

Note that some of the advantages and disadvantages discussed do not just relate to the ERPS, but apply to whatever is being outsourced. However the strategic significance of the ERPS also requires discussion.

In (b) again you would only have had time to mention a limited number of points as risks, internal controls and internal audit tasks, although the use of the verb identify suggests your comments on each risk should be limited. (Remember that per the table of question verbs in the front pages 'identify' is a lower level verb). The ultimate risks are loss of reputation and financial consequences, and you need to think what could bring them about. The link between risks and controls is not 1:1, as some controls should cover all the risks, above all the service agreement.

Your comments on internal audit need to bring out the auditors' review of the control environment and the detailed control testing that the auditors should carry out. Internal auditors' work will be inadequate unless they are granted access to the supplier's systems.

The recommended transition process in (c) should mostly be the same as for all major systems development, although the initial implementation needs to be considered carefully.

Note the examiner's comments, indicating common weaknesses in student answers, not just for this question. The discussion in (a) and (b) needed to relate to the supplier **described in the scenario**. Clearly some answers failed to mention the supplier at all. Students also failed to read (c) properly and did not pick up the key point in the requirement that the **supplier had been already chosen;** the question was therefore not about choosing the supplier.

Easy marks. Whatever the contents of your report, you should have made sure you obtained the five marks available for a formal report by including an introduction, conclusion, main heading and structure with subheadings. There should also be a logical flow to the report. The marking scheme specified that the five marks were available for 'structure, style, coherence and presentation.'

Examiner's comments. Many candidates did not obtain the marks for the report format. Discussions about outsourcing were often too general. In (c) a lot of candidates wrote about choosing a supplier rather than the transition to an already chosen supplier.

REPORT

To: Board
From: Management Accountant
Date: 17 October 20X5
Subject: Outsourcing the ERPS system.

Introduction

This report covers:

- The advantages and disadvantages of outsourcing the ERPS system
- Risks of outsourcing and mitigation of risks
- Managing the transition to an outsource supplier

The aims of the ERP system will be to **support the management** of **all business functions** by capturing and then making it available for planning and the production of reports. Outsourcing its development and operations enables us to concentrate on **value-added activities**.

(a) **Advantages of outsourcing**

(i) **Consistency with current strategy**
Outsourcing will be consistent with the company's overall strategy of limiting internal staffing and resourcing outside wherever possible. It will mean that we do **not to have expend resources recruiting and employing specialist staff**.

(ii) **Expertise**
The specialist contractor is likely to have undertaken the **whole range of development activities** for other companies, and thus will have **greater expertise and experience** in developing the system, benefiting from **economies of scale**. This should mean that the system is developed **efficiently**, with less chance of error.

(iii) **Costs**
An outsourcing arrangement will mean **costs are easier to predict**, and **budgets easier to control**.

Disadvantages of outsourcing

(i) **Tailoring the system**
The system the consultant develops may **not be geared** enough to our needs, either because the

consultant recommends an already-developed system that is not appropriate for us, or the consultant has **insufficient knowledge** of our requirements. This may be a crucial factor because of the **strategic importance** of the system, and hence the need for extensive knowledge of our requirements.

(ii) **Flexibility**

We may find ourselves tied into a long-term service agreement to use a system that our changing requirements soon **renders inappropriate** for our needs. Although the supplier has a good reputation, there is a risk of **loss of flexibility and inability to respond to changing circumstances**.

You would also have scored marks if you had discussed the following disadvantages.

(i) **Loss of staff**

Contacts with the consultant over the new system may lead to some of our key staff being **lured away** to work for the consultant.

(ii) **Failure of supplier**

If the supplier goes **bankrupt**, AMF's **operations** could be **very seriously disrupted** because of uncertainty over the continued operation of the system.

(iii) **Reputation**

Our company has the reputation of being at the **forefront of IT development**. This reputation may be jeopardised if the industry learns that we have decided not to develop a key internal IT system ourselves.

(iv) **Costs and resource usage**

The arrangement will **not necessarily be cheaper** and, depending on the agreement with the supplier, costs may increase over time. As well as the supplier's charges, we also need to consider **other transaction costs** such as monitoring and insurance, and the internal time resource involved in monitoring the arrangement.

(b) **Risks**

Confidentiality

The specialist contractor will be handling the key information about AMF, and there are thus potentially very serious consequences if this information is **leaked to a competitor**.

Business delays

Failure to update information promptly could result in **delays in operations**, for example billing debtors, or decisions being made based on out-of-date information. Ultimately the disruption to production may mean that **customer requirements are not fulfilled**. This will lead to **financial losses and loss of reputation**.

Dependence

AMF may find itself **locked into the arrangement with the contractor**, and be unable to move to another supplier or to move the system in-house if it's later felt to be desirable.

Controls

Service level agreement

A **tightly drafted service agreement** is the most important control. The agreement should specify **minimum levels of service to be provided**, with **legal guarantees and penalties** for failure to meet those levels of service. Specifications should include **response time** to requests for assistance/information, system uptime percentage and deadlines for performing relevant tasks. The service agreement should also cover **security procedures**, and **make clear the ownership** of the system.

Liaison procedures

A director or senior manager with contract management skills should be responsible for **ongoing liaison arrangements** with the contractor. Staff with **appropriate knowledge** should **liaise on technical aspects** of the system. One possibility would be to **locate a member of staff permanently at the supplier's premises**, to act as liaison between the client and the contractor.

Feedback from operational staff

There should be mechanisms for **feedback from operational staff** so that problems can be quickly rectified. We need to decide whether staff should deal directly with the contractor or use an internal intermediary. An **internal intermediary** has the **advantage** of providing a **single focus for the relationship, better control of costs**, and **better monitoring of usage of service**.

You would also have gained marks if you had discussed the following controls.

Monitoring supplier

Press and other information sources about the contractor should be monitored for evidence of any business difficulties or financial problems.

Information technology function

The specialist function retained in-house is potentially a control, as there will be **greater expertise** to liaise with the supplier.

Computer controls

A range of computer controls should be applied to the outsourced systems.

(i) **Application controls** should be operated over the **input, output and processing** of transaction data by the contractor.

(ii) **General controls** should be in place over the **recruitment of staff handling sensitive information**, and access controls such as **passwords**. AMF should also **review business continuity controls** operated by the contractor, to ensure that the risk of disruption to AMF's operations is minimised.

Data security controls

Network controls should be operated to **secure data** transferred between AMF and the contractor and prevent hacking.

Internal audit

Control framework

Internal auditors should **consider the adequacy of the control framework**. They should confirm that the **service agreement** is **satisfactory** before it is **signed**, and assess the **adequacy of liaison arrangements**. Internal audit will also review the adequacy of computer controls, and test controls in areas where adverse consequences could be significant, for example **confidentiality breaches**.

Ongoing relationships

Internal audit should inspect records of correspondence between AMF and the service provider, and **confirm** that **concerns raised by AMF** have been addressed **adequately and promptly**.

Information

Internal audit should review the **financial and non-financial information** that the contractor produces to ensure that it is **accurate**, **complete and fulfils AMF's requirements**. Internal audit will also be concerned with whether the information is **sufficient** to provide a suitable **audit trail**.

Confidentiality

Internal audit should visit the contractor's premises and inspect the arrangements the contractor has for ensuring **security**, including **provisions in staff contracts**. It should have access to the client's systems and staff and carry out tests on the security procedures employed by the contractor.

(c) **Steering committee**

This should be **headed** by the **director/manager responsible** for the relationship with the supplier, as well as members of the project planning team, IT support staff, representatives of operational departments and senior staff from the contractor. The steering committee should assess whether the proposed system appears to fulfil required criteria, including **level of support** and **security arrangements**, and also consider the **time** and **resources** required for the changeovers, preparing a **budget** for the process.

Project planning team

A **project planning team** should be **responsible** for the transition. Their key tasks will include:

- **Specification** of the **requirements** of AMF that will be embedded in the service agreement of the **internal resources** required to support the project
- **Contacting stakeholders** such as **suppliers and customers** who may be affected
- **Detailed analysis of risk**, and specification of a **risk response plan**

Implementation plan

The implementation plan should specify the changeover method. Since the new system will be a fundamental part of AMF's operations, I recommend:

(i) **Parallel running** be adopted wherever possible, with the complete new and old systems being run in parallel, **processing current data** and **enabling cross checking** to be made. Parallel running should continue until the steering committee is satisfied that the new system is working satisfactorily.

(ii) For those **parts of the new system** which have **no parallels** with the old system, there should be enhanced checks before the system is operated and monitoring by internal specialist staff and internal audit during the first weeks of operation.

Post-audit

Internal audit should carry out a post-audit on the transition process to **identify learning points** to be applied if other activities are outsourced in the future.

Conclusion

It is fundamental that any agreement between AMF and the supplier is satisfactory to ourselves in terms of the **level of service provided** and the **management of risk**. If the supplier cannot provide the guarantees we require, we should tender elsewhere. Adequate internal controls and internal audit involvement will be necessary, and we should seek information about all the likely costs and resource usage before a decision is reached.

62 Computer problems

Text references. Chapters 16 to 18 all contain relevant material.

Top tips. This is a good meaty practical problem, one which occurs all too frequently in real life. You would do well to use common sense and any relevant practical experience when forming your answer. If you get a question like this in the exam, you should assume that all the paragraphs in the scenario will contain something of relevance to your answer.

Note that the answer sets out the key risks in (a) and then in (b) the controls demonstrate how they should be addressed. Note that solution of the personnel problems forms a significant part of the answer to (b), but it is important to include back-up facilities and the wider issue of systems development strategy.

A number of systems development controls are mentioned in (c), but our answer also considers the failure of other general controls, and *why* internal audit has failed to report on the lack of controls.

Easy marks. There are enough hints in the scenario to enable you to identify risks fairly easily. In particular the key involvement of certain staff, the lack of supervision, the information documentation and of course the failure to back up require comment.

Examiner's comments. Common errors included wasting time repeating the question, failing to distinguish between actions and discussions, and failure to distinguish between short-term and long-term actions. In (c) some candidates failed to address the scenario set and some thought that IA could act to correct problems, rather than just reporting them.

CONFIDENTIAL MEMORANDUM

To: Managing Director
From: Financial Controller
Date: 10 September 20X4
Subject: Computer system and departure of the computer services manager (CSM)

Introduction

This report covers

- The key risks we face in relation to our information technology system
- The actions that we need to take
- The role of internal audit

(a) **Key risks**

(i) **Dependence on key staff**

The company has become **very dependent upon** the **CSM's expertise**. He has been mainly responsible for the amendments to the system with some help. The amendments made may well have been beneficial and produced a system more tailored to the company's needs. However the amendments have also made it more difficult for anyone to take over the system. This problem has been enhanced by the **poor documentation of the operating systems and the amendments**.

As well as the problems faced by the IT department, the CSM's departure may have **highlighted wider personnel issues**, including a **lack of succession planning for key staff, and inadequate notice periods**.

(ii) **Vulnerability to disasters**

The CSM was rightly concerned about the **lack of back-up facilities**. The division's computer operations are extremely vulnerable to major disruption due to fire, flood or hardware breakdown.

(iii) **Systems development**

The CSM's departure has highlighted a number of problems with systems development.

(1) Changes made appear to have been **inadequately documented** making them difficult to follow.

(2) There does not appear to have been any consultation with the other operating departments, with the risk that the **changes made may not have been for their benefit**.

(3) There seems to be no overall long-term plan for systems development in line with the company's **overall strategic needs**. The solutions adopted since the break with the consultants have essentially been temporary, **make do and mend alterations**.

(b) **Urgent action**

The CSM's departure, although unfortunate, gives us an opportunity to undertake a **wide-ranging review of the computer system**, covering its operation, control and security. There are some long-term plans which should be made, but of more immediate concern is how the situation should be dealt with before the CSM leaves, ie within the next month. I would therefore like to propose the following.

(i) **Dependence on key staff**

(1) **Replacement CSM**

It is obviously vital that a suitable candidate should be found. To this end a **job specification** should be prepared for the position. As this is, potentially at least, a strategic role within the group, I feel a wide range of views should be heard on this matter. A committee formed for the purpose (me, Chief IA, FD, MD?) could report in, say, one month.

(2) **Temporary CSM**

In view of (i), we should consider appointing a temporary CSM, either externally (from a computer consultancy) or internally (possibly the shift supervisor who was helping the CSM. A temporary CSM would aid the transition and it would also free the current CSM to perform various tasks before he leaves, which I consider to be vital (see below). Also, the **current CSM can be relieved of day-to-day contact** with the system, to avoid any new problems being created and as a general security measure.

(3) **Current CSM's duties**

Before he leaves, the CSM must put his handwritten system amendment notes into a **logical order** and have them typed up. We need a **permanent copy** of amendments made to the system. In addition, any problems or errors which arise under the new (temporary) CSM can be cleared up by the old CSM during his final month.

(4) **Staff planning**

The human resources function should undertake a comprehensive review of staffing, **identifying key members of staff**. The board should consider whether **excessive reliance** is being placed on certain members of staff and if anything can be done to alleviate this. In any event there should be **proper succession planning** so that internal candidates are available as replacements should senior staff leave. In addition **terms and conditions** of senior and key staff's employment should be **reviewed** with a view to increasing their notice period to more than one month.

(ii) **Back-up facilities**

Alternative back-up facilities must be found immediately. A search should commence for some **comparable facilities** to our own. We need to negotiate for use of such facilities, although we may be required to offer reciprocal arrangements.

(iii) **Systems development**

The system we have is now five years old and there have been problems with it since installation. In view of this, and the departure of the CSM, an **information systems development strategy** needs to be **formulated** at divisional board level. This can be commenced at the next board meeting. In fact, the new CSM may be appointed at board level, in order to be involved directly with the control of systems development.

(c) **Internal audit (IA) involvement**

It is disappointing to note that the IA department has not been able or willing to help the computer services department to avoid the crisis situation in which it now finds itself. Obviously I was not present at the time, but it seems that there were some obvious areas to which both the internal and external auditors could have made a direct contribution in terms of **reporting difficulties and problems** encountered and thus aiding their prevention.

(i) **Systems amendments**

These amendments should require **formal authorisation and proper documentation**, but in fact they have been carried out on an *ad hoc*, informal basis for five years. This is a serious breakdown in control over the computer system and its development. The IA department should have reported on this.

(ii) **Operating manual**
The **lack of an operating manual** which is up to date and complete is also a serious breakdown in control. It also implies that, as the internal auditors have not reported on it, they are in fact **ignoring** the **computer system** by auditing 'round' rather than 'through' it.

(iii) **Segregation of duties/personnel**
The operators of the system should **not be able to implement changes** to the system, as has been the case with the shift supervisor helping the CSM. As well as being a grave breach of a key control, this is also a symptom of a **breakdown in personnel policy**.

(iv) **Back-up system**
Given that a back-up system was thought necessary in the past, the IA department should have commented when the division lost such facilities. The **lack of a disaster recovery plan** should have been commented on by both the internal and external auditors.

Summary and conclusions

The situation in the CSD is critical and should be of paramount importance to the board. Any disruption or breakdown in the computer service would disrupt the division's entire operations, affecting as it does sales, production and inventory, and I would therefore appreciate a rapid response to my proposals.

Signed: Financial Controller

63 Lottery

Text references. Chapter 18 on day-to-day controls, Chapters 17 and 18 on the organisational issues.

Top tips. Most of the general framework outlined in (b) can be widely applied. In (a) you needed to discuss a range of controls, but you should have emphasised the importance of specific controls over the database and access controls, since security is mentioned specifically in the scenario. Other controls would not operate very well in the system described or would be undermined by lack of segregation of duties.

Easy marks. As indicated, the framework in (b) will often be useful, so if you struggled on this part, make sure you are happy with the key points discussed.

(a) **Risks of system**

Incorrect data

An important risk is that data will be **wrongly entered and processed**. The **lack of segregation of duties** that is a feature of this system increases the risks of this happening as the involvement of additional staff in processing would increase the chances of errors and misdemeanours being identified. Input and processing of data could result in **incorrect decisions being made about who should receive grants**.

Leaking of data

There is also the **risk of political difficulties** if sensitive information is leaked.

Loss of data

Having a single central system also increases the potential for data to be lost if a disaster occurs, whether through **natural causes or sabotage**. As a government centre, the operations may be particularly threatened by deliberate action.

Key controls

Physical/access controls

There should be physical controls over the computers, with access obtained only by an **entry code**, and the premises being kept shut outside operating hours.

Passwords

A system of passwords should be in operation. This should be hierarchical with one level of password being required for **access to certain information**, another for the user to **be able to process certain information**. Passwords should be **changed regularly** and no-one should use a password that could **easily be guessed**. Terminals should **automatically log off** if no entry is made within a certain time or a wrong password is entered say three times in succession, and all **attempted violations** should be **logged**.

Input controls

Various **accuracy controls** are likely to be required. Examples include:

- **Check digit verification** (a check on the validity of the coding of input)
- Checks that input is within the **permitted range**
- Existence checks that recipients of grants have **valid accounts** within the system
- Checks that **all the necessary information is present**.

Processing controls

Operating instructions should be clearly laid down, and updated whenever significant changes occur such as changes in the data dictionary. Controls should ensure that **all input data is processed** and the **processing of each transaction is accurate**.

Output controls

Output controls may include an **audit trail,** the ability to trace output back to originating documentation. This may be difficult if only summary control totals are produced at the end of daily processing. Hence other controls will be significant. **Exception reports**, highlighting rejected transactions should be printed out on a regular basis and reviewed by management. Management should also **review reports** of **changes to specified files,** particularly standing data files Internal audit can use computer assisted audit techniques to review output, in particular **SCARF**, which automatically writes transactions of certain types or certain amounts to a separate file for later review by the auditors.

Backup and emergency procedures

The department should have backup and emergency procedures in place to ensure data processed is not lost through computer malfunction, and that processing can continue if a disaster occurs. Procedures include daily backup of processing and **storage** of what has been processed in a **remote location. Virus protection controls** should be embedded within the system. There should be **protection of equipment against fire** and other hazards, and arrangements to use **back-up facilities** if processing on the main site has to be suspended.

Controls over programs

These controls are particularly important because errors in programs may impact upon the processing of all transactions. **Password protection** is particularly important; no-one except computer support staff should be able to access live programs. An important review control would be periodic **comparison of live production programs to control copies** and supporting documentation. **Back-up copies** of programs should be stored away from the main site.

Controls over database

The database system will also need controls to **maintain the integrity of the database**. Again restriction of access is vital; **access to the data dictionary** should again be **restricted to computer support staff**, because the dictionary contains what is integral to the running of the system.

(b) **Organisational risks**

The department may be vulnerable to bad publicity if it is poorly organised, since grant applicants may not receive an **acceptable level of service** and the department may be accused of not giving value for money and **wasting the cash generated** by the lottery. There may also be problems of **accountability**, with decisions being taken contrary to the wishes of ministers and civil servants who are held accountable for them.

Important general controls

Organisational structure

Clear systems of **authorisation of transactions and delegation of responsibilities** should be important elements in any organisational structure. A further element is **segregation of duties**. mistakes by allowing cross-checking of work done by a different person. Since there are a significant number of functions involved in data processing, it may be difficult to segregate all the duties. In any event, however, those responsible for maintaining and developing the system should not be responsible for the actual data processing.

Management review

Managers should be responsible for **setting** of **budgets and operational targets**, and reviewing performance against standards set. Management should oversee the overall development of the system. In particular they should be concerned with whether the information produced has resulted in **improved service** for grant recipients and **better information** for management.

Supervision

As well as senior management exercising supervision, certain staff should be exercising full–time supervision over the system, particularly if there is a lack of segregation of duties. Key tasks of the system supervisor include ensuring **authorisation procedures are appropriate** and properly carried out, checking that the **necessary information is available** should problems occur, and **investigating problems.**

Operating manual

Guidance from management covering the system should include the following elements:

- **Targets,** such as length of turnaround period for all documentation
- **Organisational structure**
- **Job descriptions** containing responsibilities and duties of management and staff
- **Controls**, in particular **documentation standards**, security and integrity controls, and back-up procedures
- **Commitment to information security** and details of legal data protection requirements

Staffing controls

Recruitment and training will be key controls. References should be requested for new recruits; this is particularly important because some of the information processed may be quite sensitive. Staff should receive sufficient training in both the technical knowledge required to carry out their work and also internal procedures.

Development controls

The system should be able to develop as the **needs of users change**. Development should however take place in accordance with defined guidelines covering **design standards**, requirements for **adequate documentation, testing procedures and training**. Each stage of development should be **approved by both** the management of the processing function and representatives of users of the information. Internal audit should also be involved in checking development standards have been met.

Internal audit

Internal audit should also be responsible for carrying out regular review. It should consider whether current **controls** are **operating effectively** and are **adequate** in the light of any changes in processing. Internal audit should also carry out **substantive testing** on a selection of **payments** of grants.

64 KL

Text references. Chapter 18.

Top tips. You need to draw on your Performance Evaluation knowledge in (a); this question part is a reminder that RCS is within the CIMA qualification's management accounting pillar.

You should note in (b) the emphasis on *user* needs both as regards the operation of the system and training in it. The answer to (b) also matches the principal accounting and audit problems with their solutions, rather than going into detail about the whole of the systems development process. This demonstrates that the recommendations that (b) requires are relevant for the problems identified.

Easy marks. You can gain credit for using a systematic approach to (b), and linking in problems with corresponding risk reduction measures.

Examiner's comments. A common failing on even good scripts was to write more on part (a) than part (b), which had more than twice as many marks. Other weaknesses in part (a) were writing generally about systems, and proposing that the project start all over again. In (b) many answers failed to discuss how the problems related to the introduction of the new system and standardisation, and the solution of the problems. A number of answers failed to focus on the requirements of the question but were general essays on internal control guidance and computer auditing.

The examiner stated that although the project mentioned in the scenario was the development of a computer system, the question raised a number of points that were applicable generally to project management scenarios.

(a) **Planning the project**

If progress and problems are to be communicated effectively, projects must be properly planned. The choice of the new computer system should have been based on a **feasibility study** with alternative solutions assessed. This study should have highlighted **possible problems** with the implementation of the new system, for example the need to have it fully operational before the next year-end.

Once the system had been decided on, the following should have been approved by management:

- **Overall project targets** for costs, timescale or resource usage should have been **established**.
- **Project division**. The **project** should have been **divided** into **activities**, time and cost budgets set and resources allocated for each activity.
- A **framework** should have been set for **monitoring** the project.

The monitoring process

In order for management to monitor the project effectively, the following must be established.

Measurement mechanisms

Time taken can be measured by reference to network analysis or Gantt charts. **Resources** used can be measured by available resources and percentage utilisation. **Costs** can be measured by reference to budgets.

Lines of reporting

It is necessary to establish to **whom progress** should be **reported** and to **whom problems** should be **reported**. As well as reporting to senior management **user departments** should be contacted if **time and budget constraints** mean that **features** they have **requested cannot be implemented**.

Reporting to management

Reporting to management of progress and expenditure should take place every so often as a matter of course and also at the **completion of every major stage** of the project. Additionally **time or budget overruns** or **excess resource usage** should be **reported as soon as they appear likely** to occur.

(b) The new system may pose the following audit and accounting problems. These are discussed below, together with the actions enabling the risks to be reduced.

Capacity of new system

Assurance is required that the new system will be able to **cope with the volume of processing**.

The **operation** of the whole of the new system should be **tested** prior to implementation using the kind of data volumes from different users that it will have to cope with when operational. In addition the **new system** should be **run in parallel** with the old systems initially, to minimise disruption should the new system be unable to cope with the volume of data.

Local requirements

The new system is replacing a number of systems, and it is possible that **local needs will be ignored**. This may mean the **information available** under the new system is **less** than before, and it may mean the **system cannot cope** with all the **necessary accounting requirements**, for example valuation of stock.

All **users** should be **consulted** about their needs prior to the system being designed. They should also be involved in testing the system to ensure it meets their requirements.

Master files

New master files which contain the appropriate information must be set up but this may be difficult given the **variety of local requirements**.

Design of an appropriate system of master files and coding system should be a **priority** in the development process. Consultation with users is particularly important here.

Transfer of data

There is a risk of **data being lost or corrupted** when being transferred.

Data files from the old system should be **copied** before conversion in the case of failure or corruption. **Master file data** should be **input in stages**, with the data input being copied at each stage. Once the data has been input, it should be printed out and compared with an independent source.

Staff problems

Lack of training of staff and **lack of documentation** of the new system may increase the risk of errors when the system does become operational.

These can be overcome by **proper documentation** and **training**. Documentation of the system should include:

(i) **Listings** of program instructions, flowcharts, file layouts, input and output documentation, and the **procedures which each program module covers**;

(ii) **Details of procedures to be followed if a systems crash** occurs;

(iii) **An operating manual**, containing instructions on setting up and operating the system, and details of error messages and what action to take if they occur.

Training sessions should also help staff. These should include **posting** of **test data**. Attendance records should be kept so that management can ensure that all potential users of the system are trained.

Disaster recovery

Because the group will now be dependent on a single system, the consequences of a **system breakdown** could be **catastrophic**.

There should be **formal plans** for disaster recovery. These should include ongoing controls such as **backup of systems and storage of files** in a remote location. There should also be arrangements for **alternative facilities** to be provided should a catastrophe occur. The plan should cover different types and levels of disruption and should be properly tested.

65 STU

Text references. Chapter 18.

Top tips. This question covers a situation that many organisations face; a poor information strategy even more poorly implemented, plus the controls that can be deployed to remedy this situation. In (a) you have to take on the role of the Head of internal audit, and so your answer needs to consider the audit implications of the systems development. However the question does not appear to restrict the answer to the audit implications, and therefore you should also include the other control actions that should be taken at each stage.

(b) demonstrates what we said in the front pages guidance about the need to plan carefully; (b) (i) should focus on the audit implications, and the discussion of other controls should be included in (b) (ii).

In (b) (ii) you could also have discussed organisation controls, since the changes should mean that the board should re-consider how IT support is organised. Changes may include an enhanced central function providing help and setting standards; performance indicators measuring how well the system and the IT function are performing will also be necessary. Discussion of human resource controls over the operators of the system would also have gained marks.

Easy marks. Potentially lots to talk about for the six or so marks available for (b) (ii). However be careful. Your answer needs to have enough breadth, to include examples of controls on specific applications and over the system in general. You also don't have much chance to go into detail about individual controls because of the limited number of marks available; it's very easy to over-run on time on this part.

Examiner's comments. Generally most students scored well on this question. Problems that arose in (b) included students failing to relate their answers to an IT environment, only discussing general approaches to audit and failing to give sufficient detail about reasons for controls.

(a) (i) **Design**

Systems design involves the conversion of data into a workable format. It needs to cover:

(1) What the **sources of data** used will be

(2) The **format of input**; the same formats will need to be used across the organisation which has not been the case in the past

(3) The **data warehouse structure**, what structure will be most easy for the users to access

(4) The **format of reports** produced, will these provide the level of detail required for strategic decision-making

Guidance on data security and authorisation levels also ought to be developed at the design stage.

Audit work at design stage

Auditors need to review the evidence that the systems design is **acceptable** to all involved in development, including **users**. They also should review the **adequacy of the systems documentation** and whether the **costs** and **benefits** have been estimated accurately.

(ii) **Development**

The system needs to be **thoroughly tested by systems development** and **IT staff.** They should assess the **logic of the systems** and **test the programs using test data**. Given that the system may be processing large volumes of data, the **flexibility of the system to cope with peak-time demand and changes to processing routines** should be **investigated.**

Users also need to be involved in the **testing** to assess whether they are able to use the **analytical tools** provided by the system.

Audit work at development stage

Internal auditors will need to be involved in **testing the system** and **review the testing** carried out by other staff. They also need to **review changes to specifications** and **operating instructions** that have resulted from the development process. They will need to ensure that the **new system provides an adequate trail** for managers, themselves and the external auditors.

(iii) **Delivery**

The **transition** from the current situation will require careful planning. Information on the current systems will have to be transferred, and decisions will be needed on **what information** will be required and **what format** it should be in, as it may not currently be held in a form that can easily used by the new system. In addition all divisions of the company need to start using the SEM at the same time, otherwise the data it uses will not be complete; however this means that the changeover will require a very large IT resource and training commitment.

Audit work at delivery stage

Internal auditors will review whether the **implementation plan is realistic**, particularly given the number of **sites** involved, and that **implementation has been authorised by senior management**. They should again consider the **adequacy** of **documentation** and also the **arrangements** made for maintaining the system once it is operational. The auditors should also be involved in a **post-completion audit,** considering:

- Whether the system has **delivered the expected benefits**
- Whether the **costs have been excessive**
- Any **problems** during the initial operation of the system

(b) To: Audit committee
From: Accountant
Date: 4 December 20X6
Subject: Auditing computer systems and IT controls

(i) **Possible approaches to auditing the system**

Importance of accurate data

STU is heavily dependent on the data processed being **accurate and consistent** across the organisation. This means that the internal auditors need to review **the data** itself and also how the data is **processed** by the system.

Reviewing the data

Audit interrogation software allows auditors to extract data from the system for further work. The data extracted can be printed in a form that can be compared with the **data in management reports** produced by the SEM. Audit interrogation software can also perform procedures such as **calculations on large volumes of data,** and thus provide **statistical analysis** of the data within the system. This may **help to indicate the reliability of the data** from the various sites.

Internal audit may use other forms of software to **highlight certain items of data**. **Resident software** can be used to select automatically certain data for later investigation. **Integrated monitoring software** can highlight certain items (for example certain types of transaction processed at a specific site) if they fall outside limits suggested by the auditors.

Reviewing the system

Test data can be used to check the accuracy of data being produced by the system, by comparing the actual results produced by the system with the expected results. However use of test data may prove problematic in STU's real-time system, as the test data used will have to be reversed.

Embedded audit facilities are audit modules built into the accounting system that allow a continuous review of the data recorded and the manner in which it is treated by the system. An **integrated test facility** creates a **fictitious entity** within the company application; transactions are posted to it alongside regular transactions, and actual results of the fictitious entity compared with what the system should have produced.

(ii) **Testing controls**

In addition internal audit will have to gain assurance on the operation of the key controls that are covered below.

Controls over the IT environment

Application controls

Application controls are controls over each **specific application**, and can be grouped into the following categories.

(1) **Input controls**
Input controls should ensure the **accuracy, completeness and validity of input. Data validation controls** include **check digits, control totals** and checks that the **input is within a reasonable numerical range**.

(2) **Processing controls**
Strong controls over **systems development** should help ensure the **completeness** and **accuracy of processing**. The tests carried out by embedded audit facilities should also provide assurance.

(3) **Output controls**
Controls ensuring the **completeness and accuracy of output** include a list of **transactions processed, and investigation and follow-up of error and exception reports**.

General controls

General controls relate to the **environment** within which the IT systems **operate.**

(1) **Access controls**
Access to the system should be **password protected**; the passwords required should be personal for each user and allow access only to relevant parts of the system. To counter the threat of hacking, passwords should be complex (minimum number of characters, include letters and numbers) and changed regularly.

(2) **Disaster prevention controls**
The key central computer facilities should be located in an environment that minimises physical threats by precautions such as **smoke detectors and fire alarms.** Threats from viruses can be reduced by using the **latest anti-virus software, running virus checks** on files received from outside the organisation and **prohibiting the use of unauthorised software**.

(3) **Contingency controls**
Daily backups should be taken of the information posted to the system. STU also needs to have **alternative arrangements available** should the system break down. However any alternatives need to be centrally controlled; a return to decentralised systems will wipe out the advantages of the SEM system.

66 VWS

Text references. Chapters 6,9 and 18.

Top tips. The scenario does not give very much information about the company and the accounts payable system appears to be a very standard one. You need to try to make the best use of the information to give examples in (a), although there is not that much data you can use. The verb discuss means you have to take the broad purposes and values (mostly derived from the Turnbull guidance) and show that they apply to the accounts payable system.

The scenario provides more material for answering (b). The answer follows a logical sequence, looking firstly at security controls before processing can take place, then controls over processing and lastly controls to minimise threats to the operation of the whole system.

In (c) fraud in a computerised system can come about through false information being input by legitimate means (by staff with the necessary authorisation for example) or altering the programs to generate false payments.

Easy marks. Hopefully you will have revised IT controls well enough to be able to come up with plenty of ideas in (b).

Examiner's comments. Many candidates failed to discuss accounts payable and showed a lack of knowledge of accounts payable systems. Answers were often far too general, with many students just braindumping all they knew about general controls.

(a) **Purposes of internal control system**

The Turnbull report suggests that the main purposes of an internal control system in any area are to **facilitate effective and efficient operations** and **enable the organisation to respond to risks.**

Accounts payable control systems

Safeguarding assets

A key risk for purchases is that payments will be made for **unauthorised or unwarranted purchases**. The control system needs to ensure that payments are:

- **Not made for goods that have not been received**
- Made for orders that have been **properly authorised**
- **Only made to authorised suppliers.**

Another aspect of asset protection is ensuring that supplies are obtained at competitive prices. Given the number of suppliers VWS uses, it should be possible to obtain good terms by threatening to use other suppliers.

Identifying and managing liabilities

Another key risk is that **liabilities** will **not be properly recognised**, leading to disputes with suppliers. Alternatively suppliers may benefit through mistakes, with **cash** being **paid twice** or **being paid to the wrong supplier**.

The system should ensure that **goods and services received are accurately recorded** and that **documentation exists to support all invoices and payments**; accounts payable staff at VWS also need to make sure that invoices and payments are included in the **right suppliers' accounts**. Another part of managing liabilities is to **review regularly suppliers' accounts** to make sure that **available credit** is being **taken**, and **discounts for early payment** are being **accepted**. Staff should also investigate disputed amounts with suppliers to **ensure** that **all credits** to which the business is due **are claimed and received.**

Ensure quality of financial reporting

The accounts payable system is part of the overall accounting system, and it is important for this reason as well that **appropriate liabilities are recognised** and that **payments are recorded.**

Value of internal control system

Reputation and liquidity

Problems with not paying bills mean that suppliers may **decline or tighten credit**, making **trade more difficult** and **impacting on reputation**. Poor cash management can ultimately lead to **liquidity problems**.

Reasonable assurance

Control systems over accounts payable provide reasonable assurance, that the **purposes of the control systems** have been **fulfilled**. They can be undermined by human error, for example entering details into the wrong supplier account. They can also be undermined by **collusion**, for example between accounts payables staff and fake suppliers; **management override of procedures** is also a possible limitation. The control systems may not be able to cope with non-routine transactions, **special one-off orders from suppliers** for example.

Benefits vs costs

The control systems are also only valuable if their **benefits outweigh their costs**. Elaborate authorisation procedures may result in a **lack of flexibility** in dealing with suppliers, and being able to obtain better terms. **Comparison of benefits versus costs** may be **difficult**. Costs of controls, for example salaries, may be apparent, but the benefits, for example in terms of problems prevented, may be difficult to assess since those problems have not materialised.

(b) **Supplier authorisation controls**

Payables staff should only be able to process invoices and payments for suppliers who have been authorised and who have been given a **payables ledger reference**.

Passwords

The system of passwords used should **differentiate** between the requirements of different types of users. Staff other than payables staff should be able to access some of the information on a **read only basis**. However the system should allow only the accounts payable staff to **change details** on the ledger or to **generate payments**. If access is **attempted unsuccessfully**, the system should **log the attempt** and management review this log.

Matching with order

Invoices should only be entered if they can be matched with specific orders that are already on the system. The system should **match the invoice with the order details** that should already be on the system.

Reasonableness controls

The system should **automatically query and report on all unusual transactions**. For example it should **query any invoice number** that has **already been posted**. It should highlight any payment that results in a **debit balance**; this may indicate that the **payment** has been **made twice**. There may be further **reasonableness checks**, for example **range checks** detecting invoices or orders that are very large for that supplier.

Control totals

Totals should be used to **reconcile different data**, for example the **total of cheques and electronic payments** should **agree with the total of cash paid entries** on the payables ledger control account.

Reports generated

A system of **exception reporting** is vital, highlighting payables or specific invoices that have not been paid for a long time, payables accounts over certain limits or orders that have not been delivered.

Encryption

Because payment data is transmitted electronically, it needs to be **encrypted** into a secret code. This should **prevent hackers gaining access to the data transmitted**.

Virus protection

The systems should be protected from disruption by **anti-virus software** and **on-access virus scanning** that prevents infection by disallowing access to infected items. There should also be policies in place to minimise the risks of viruses being introduced, for example a **ban on unauthorised software**.

Backups

Details on the system should be regularly **backed up** during the day, and backup copies kept away from the main site, along with operating system software. This should enable information to be reconstructed if the system does break down.

Contingency plans

There should be contingency plans, for example backup computer facilities, to enable processing to continue if there is a **major systems breakdown**. Because of the large volume of transactions being processed, it is vital that processing continue with a minimum of delay.

(c) **False suppliers**

Payables staff may be able to enter the **details of non-existent suppliers** onto the system, and then enter false invoice details and make payments to that supplier.

Management should consider **greater segregation of duties**, with staff who enter and update supplier details not being able to process payments on those accounts, and also different staff updating invoice details and generating payments. There should also be reports for **management or internal audit** checking, for example reports showing new supplier accounts that have been opened each period. Controls **matching invoices with orders and goods received** are also important.

Payments for goods not received

Payments may be made to legitimate suppliers for **goods that have not been received**.

Requiring links to be made between **invoices and other data** (orders, goods received) should limit this risk.

Program problems

The writer of the payables ledger computer programs could also commit fraud, by for example **generating electronic payments to himself** rather than suppliers, or **rounding up amounts in control accounts** and paying these through the expenses system.

This risk can be mitigated by **independent testing** of **all programs** and **program changes**.

External hacking

Outsiders could **gain access** to the payables system and arrange for payments to be made to themselves. This particularly applies if outsiders have some access to the computer systems through the Internet.

A **firewall** can **restrict access** to only software and files that are available for public use. The firewall only allows access through a single gateway, and restricts access to the rest of the system by establishing user names and passwords.

67 VSYS

Text references. Chapter 2, 4 and 5.

Top tips. There are many arguments for and against outsourcing; however, (a) is quite specific in requiring some comment on the situation in the VSYS company. You must therefore look in the scenario for reasons for outsourcing which specifically affect VSYS, and ensure those reasons are clearly mentioned in the answer. Fortunately the second half of the second paragraph highlights a number of points very clearly.

(b) may appear to be a very open question. However the question requirements state that the discussion should be confined to the new location in the Far East. Very helpfully the scenario provides you with a list of possible problems. You can therefore easily demonstrate that your answer links to the scenario by using the problems identified as the main headers in your answer to (b). You can then go on to discuss the issues related to new systems, suppliers and labour force grouped round these headers.

(c) (i) is mainly theory based, although you will need to read carefully the requirement to ensure that the correct sections of corporate governance are discussed in the answer. Mention can be made of the Turnbull report or similar country specific guidance, although this is not essential to obtain a pass.

Having defined what an internal control system should do in (i), you may have a better idea of the points that can be made in (c) (ii) of the answer. For example, recognising that the board should be making decisions to overcome operational risks in the company may help identify the problem of not taking an appropriate decision concerning movement of production to the Far East.

Easy marks. The discussion on corporate governance in (c)(i) doesn't need to be tied into VSYS's circumstances; you should score most of the marks available for this part.

(a) **Positive aspects of outsourcing**

Cost

Costs are likely to be **lower for a number of reasons** including **cheaper labour** and **less lost production and wasted materials** due to decreased quality problems. Continuing pressure on margins may force the board to accept outsourcing for this reason alone.

Highly educated workforce

Many Far Eastern countries have a **highly skilled workforce** which VSYS could use. It is unlikely that existing employees will want to **relocate**, although transferring some key staff would be an option, ensuring that skills are retained in the company.

Resources scaled up or down according to demand

Given that VSYS would be a **relatively new employer** in the region, there is the possibility of **increasing or decreasing the level of employees** to meet demand without significant interference from the local community. Revising the labour force downwards in its present location would still have the same negative impact on the company's image as relocation, making the option less attractive.

Proximity to local suppliers

VSYS is currently experiencing **quality control problems** with some of its suppliers. While the location of those suppliers is not known, they may well be different from those in the Far East. Relocation to a different country therefore provides the opportunity to **change suppliers**, removing the quality control issues by taking advantage of high quality suppliers in other countries.

Negative aspects of outsourcing

Employee redundancy – morale

Moving production to another country would have a **significant negative impact** on the morale, both of production staff prior to relocation of the facility, and for the administration and marketing staff left in the company. Remaining staff would tend to **fear for their own jobs**, while staff being made redundant would normally have **lower productivity**, and could provide **additional quality control problems**. Some form of incentive in the form of **enhanced working conditions** or reassurance for remaining staff would help alleviate the negative impact of the move.

Bad publicity – nationwide when many jobs being outsourced

Given that VSYS has a reputation for being a good employer and appears to produce high quality products, moving production with the associated loss of jobs could result in **adverse publicity** for the company.

Possible actions against the company could include **boycott** of the company's products by consumers and possible **picketing** of the company to disrupt supplies. There may be little VSYS can do to retain confidence, although some form of publicity marketing exercise focusing on the number of jobs remaining in the USA could be carried out.

Effect on community

The community around VSYS is heavily dependent on the company for employment. Decreasing the number of employees will not only cause bad publicity for the company locally, but also **decrease the amount of disposable income** in the town. Knock-on effects could include **closure of suppliers and retail businesses** used by the local population. Again, there would appear to be little VSYS can to reduce this negative impact.

Inability to return to the USA

Given the significance of the move, VSYS may find it very difficult to return to the USA. **Skills** would be **lost** in their local town (the university course is almost certain to close as demand for workers falls) and employees would relocate to find other jobs. The company therefore needs to be very sure that the production capability in the Far East country can serve its requirements, and is available for the foreseeable future. If this is not the case, the production should not be moved.

(b) **Control systems for the new production location**

Obtaining and maintaining supplies

Inputs will be sourced from effectively unknown suppliers, even though they may have a good reputation. Control systems will be needed to cover the following areas:

(i) **Review of delivery time**
Delivery time from placement of order to arrival of materials at the factory needs to be tracked. This can be tracked simply by maintaining a register of these times.

(ii) **Initial quality testing on inputs to ensure that they meet the company's standards**
This will help to detect errors in quality before the materials are incorporated into VSYS products.

Setting up new production lines

Production systems must be **monitored** to ensure that the computer components being manufactured are **available at the correct time** and are manufactured to the **appropriate quality**. Specific quality control checks include:

(i) **Quality control testing of outputs**
This will ensure that company standards are maintained. If quality errors are found, then **reasons for the errors** will have to be **determined** and **remedial action taken** to ensure that those errors do not continue.

(ii) **Review of individual machine downtime and production quality**
This will help determine the need for maintenance and overhaul of machines.

Maintaining sufficient inventory

Quality control procedures will be required to ensure that inventory is available to meet production requirements. Appropriate quality control procedures will include:

(i) **Determining and maintaining appropriate re-order levels and quantities**
These levels can be determined from previous experience in the USA and will be refined when the delivery time and reliability of local suppliers has been determined.

(ii) **Ability of suppliers to provide stock as requested**
Additional systems may be implemented including Electronic Data Interchange to facilitate communication with suppliers and decrease delays in the transfer of information.

Ensuring quality of output

The workforce in the Far East country will be new, at least to VSYS, even though they may have the necessary skills. **Careful monitoring** will be required to ensure that appropriate production and quality targets are met. Specific quality control procedures required will include:

(i) **Monitoring of time spent on each shift**
This should ensure that workers actually work contracted hours and so VSYS is only paying for work actually done.

(ii) **Monitoring the number of production errors made per shift**
This should ensure that employees are producing components to the appropriate quality.

(iii) **Checking the quality of items produced each shift**
This should detect poor manufacturing quality that could be attributed to employee negligence.

Management accounting systems

Management accounting systems will also be required to set budgets and monitor the costs of the new factory. Specific quality control procedures will include:

(i) **Setting budgets for the manufacture of each product** which can be amalgamated to provide total expected costs for the factory.

(ii) **Recording and monitoring of costs** incurred so actual costs are known.

(iii) **Production of variance analysis** to monitor the accuracy of budgets / whether variances relate to purchase of materials or production inefficiencies.

(iv) **Identification of loss making items** so that either the price can be increased or the product range amended.

(v) **Setting realistic prices** for each computer component taking into account the costs of production.

(vi) **Recording and monitoring prices** to help determine amendments to productive capacity.

(c) (i) **Aim of corporate governance**

Corporate governance **refers to the way in which companies are governed** with the overall aim of implementing practices and procedures to ensure that a company is run in accordance with its objectives.

Agency

The overriding principle of governance relates to the **split between ownership and control** of a company. The shareholders own a company as they purchase shares and as a result of this risk of investment, share in the rewards of ownership, that is dividends received. However, the directors are in charge of and run the company on a day-to-day basis. As the directors are effectively **agents** of the shareholders, they must ensure that the company is run for the shareholders' benefit; corporate governance provides a control and reporting function to show that the shareholders' interests are being met.

Stakeholder interests

There may be other **stakeholder interests** that the board of directors must also take account of in running the company such as employees.

Internal control system

Part of their **overall duty of running the company** will also result in the directors **setting up an internal control system** to help ensure that transactions are recorded and the assets of the company are protected. The main elements of an internal control system were summarised in the UK by the Turnbull report, with other countries having similar guidance.

Aims of internal control system

The internal control system should:

(1) **Facilitate the effective and efficient operation of a company**
This should enable it to **respond to specific risks** that may hinder it from achieving the company's objectives. The risks faced may be operational, financial or compliance, for example, with the objectives relating to minimising loss of assets or ensuring that liabilities are understood and managed.

(2) **Ensure the quality of internal (management) and external reporting**
As well as fulfilling legal requirements relating to financial accounts, management must be able to **rely on the internal information** they use for their decision-making.

(3) **Ensure compliance**
The company must comply **with laws and regulations** and also with the company's internal policies regarding the overall conduct of the business.

However, while a sound system of internal control does not provide complete assurance that situations above will not occur, it does help to ensure that the likelihood of their occurrence is minimised.

Internal audit

One of the key features of an internal control system is the establishment and maintenance of an internal audit department. Internal audit is normally defined as 'an **independent appraisal activity** established within an organisation as a service to it. The internal audit department therefore assists other members of the organisation in discharging their responsibilities, from the board in reviewing the internal control system to more junior managers in monitoring systems. Internal audit will therefore **review the internal control system** over the management and financial accounting systems to identify potential and actual weaknesses. Reports will be made to management on these weaknesses with recommendations for amendment to systems.

(ii) **Potential problems with the system in management in VSYS**

Lack of appropriate action

It appears that the board of VSYS have noted the problem of retaining productive capacity in the USA and at least one possible action of moving that capacity to a Far East country. However, it is not clear whether the board appreciates the seriousness of the situation or whether any other options, such as cutting the cost base in the USA, have been evaluated. What is clear is that some action is needed to ensure that the company remains in existence. Failing to take action may result in the board **failing in their fiduciary duty** to the shareholders causing loss of their investment and future earning stream.

Possible lack of appropriate management experience

The lack of board action leads to another possible internal control weakness; possible lack of appropriate managerial talent and control at board level. The internal control system should **ensure the overall quality of management**. Lack of decision on relocating to the Far East could be caused simply by **lack of managerial ability** or **will** to take that difficult decision. Internal audit may need to report in confidence to the audit committee on this matter and recommend that directors with appropriate decision-making ability are appointed.

Information systems

Setting up a new factory in the Far East will also mean **establishing new management and financial accounting information systems** in that country. Risks inherent in establishing those systems may be minimised by **exporting the systems currently** being **used in the USA**. However, it is unlikely that no modifications will be necessary, as systems will need to be modified to meet the specific situation in the new location. Internal audit will need to review the systems in detail to ensure modifications are **appropriate** and have been **implemented**.

Communication risks – Far East to USA

Establishing a **new production location** will mean that **regular management and other reports** will be **sent between two geographically diverse locations**. This new communication system will run risks such as **communications being lost or intercepted** en route. The board will need to ensure that **appropriate encryption systems** are introduced across the communication system to minimise these risks. Renting time on a virtual private network will help to decrease communication risk where a dedicated link is too expensive to maintain.

Board control

Geographical distance from the USA to the Far East may **limit the board's ability to maintain appropriate control of the new production location**. The risk is that the new factory may manufacture the computer components correctly, but meeting its own constraints regarding mix of components produced or timescales for production. To maintain adequate control, a **director** may have to be appointed to be in **residence** at the new factory to ensure both locations are attempting to meet the objectives of VSYS.

68 ONH

Text references. Chapters 1 and 15 are the most useful chapters on risks, Chapter 6 is the most helpful on audit work. Chapter 16 covers establishment of an IT strategy.

Top tips. You may have been surprised to see a SWOT analysis included in (a). SWOT is included because the examination notes state clearly that the syllabus may not be fully indicative of what might be examined. This is a warning to candidates to expect the unexpected, including elements that may seem more at home in other papers. In addition one of the aims of this paper is to prepare you for the TOPCIMA exam, where a SWOT analysis will be a fundamental part of your preparation for the exam.

(a) (ii) is a more 'standard' risk identification exercise with ideas being placed throughout the case.

You need to look out for factors affecting the key sources of income, significant changes that are likely to occur over the next few years and hints about poor controls and vulnerable areas (anything where cash collection is involved!)

(b) looks at the process of internal audit in the sales system – where controls are poor. You should hopefully have been able to include some basic controls in this section, particularly ticketing, recording and reconciliation. You should get 1 mark for each.

(c) discusses the need for an information strategy in a charity. Again there are pointers in the case that can be used to give reasons for having an information strategy. You should be looking out for data about the use made of information (including how much the board receives), general systems issues such as the degree of centralisation and wider environmental issues such as major competitors. In (b) the main way to score marks is identify controls and audit tests briefly, whereas in (c) (i) you must say more as you're required to discuss.

Easy marks. Probably (a) (ii) and (c), but even these have to be tied into the scenario to score enough marks to pass each part. The best way to pass this question is to allocate your time strictly and make sure you give some points for each part. The points you make first are likely to be your best.

(a) (i) **SWOT analysis for ONH**

Strengths	Weaknesses
• Good image • Large membership base • Provides 'national service' • Very popular – attracts significant number of visitors	• High fixed expenditure • Some income streams uncontrollable (bequests) • Cannot meet customer demand • 'Narrow minded' thinking by managers (lack income generation)
Opportunities	**Threats**
• Many more items available for display (only 20% of furniture etc. on display) • Expand services (restaurant, concerts) • Merge / takeover BIT for economies of scale • Other income generating possibilities (adopt a home)	• Gift aid income to fall – 20% of income base lost. • Victim of own success – too many visitors – go elsewhere? • Competitor providing other services (BIT) • Possible loss of image if BIT continue to expand services?

(ii) **Sources of risk**

Legal risk

ONH must **repair and maintain buildings** in accordance with the **building regulations** issued by the government. At present it appears that ONH is managing to comply with those regulations. However, there is a risk that **new regulations** will become **too onerous** and that ONH may not be able to comply, mainly due to the expense of compliance (older buildings are normally more expensive to maintain). There is a possibly that ONH would have to **deny access to some properties**, limiting its income.

Political risk

A major source of income for ONH is 'gift aid', where the government allows ONH to reclaim income tax paid by 'members'. The government has indicated that **gift aid** is to be **withdrawn** in two years. If this happens then ONH will **lose a significant proportion of its income**. ONH needs to lobby the government now to try and avoid this happening.

Property risks

ONH is at risk from **damage or destruction to property**, as happened in the storms detailed within the scenario. Properties owned by ONH may be more at risk than modern properties due to the older building techniques required to maintain the properties in their current state. Property risk is normally transferred by taking out **insurance**. Again, this option may be limited by ONH depending on whether insurers are willing to take premiums for properties in a high risk bracket.

Income risk

Linked to property risk is the **risk of loss of income**. If ONH cannot provide appropriate properties for people to visit, then **one-off visitor fees** will **fall**. Member fees may be adversely affected if either the range of properties provided is limited, or other organisations provide better 'value for money' as Buildings in Trust appears to be doing.

Reputation risk

ONH is seen to be providing a 'national service'; part of its income is likely to be derived from the fact that members believe in preserving the heritage of the country and therefore support ONH. If ONH does not provide this 'service' then **membership is likely to fall**. While there is no indication of this happening at present, ONH does need to be aware of this fact and try to ensure that it maintains a good reputation. One example of an adverse impact on reputation was when the National Trust in England allowed the Ministry of Defence to build a nuclear shelter within the grounds of one of its properties. Members considered this to be an inappropriate act.

Fraud risk

There is a **lack of control over the collection of entry fees** to ONH properties. Entry fees are normally paid in cash, with receipts only being provided on request. This implies that there is no overall control of cash receipts; ONH staff could easily misappropriate cash and report income below that actually received at the end of the day. This appears to be an area where appropriate control systems need to be implemented (see part (b) below).

(b) (i) Types of audit test that can be used by an internal audit department include:

Compliance tests

Compliance tests are tests of controls. They are used to obtain evidence regarding the effectiveness of:

- **Design of the accounting and internal control systems,** whether they are suitably designed to prevent or detect material misstatements
- **Operation of internal controls** throughout an accounting period

Substantive tests

Substantive tests are tests to obtain audit evidence to **detect material misstatements** in the accounts. There are two main types of test:

- **Analytical procedures** – obtaining explanations for changes in account balances over time.
- **Detailed testing of transactions** and balances by obtaining documents tracing transactions through an accounting system.

Testing in ONH

Problems with compliance testing

It is likely that substantive testing will be more appropriate than compliance testing. The main reason is that the **internal control system** is relatively **informal** which limits the effectiveness of compliance tests. ONH has many volunteers rather than salaried employees. Volunteers may not have the **training or skills** to implement detailed internal controls. Systems in ONH also appear to **lack basic internal controls** (receipts only being provided on request for example), making compliance testing ineffective.

Use of substantive testing

However, substantive testing may be used. For example:

(1) **Analytical procedures** can be used to monitor the amount of entrance fees banked on a daily, weekly or monthly basis. The amounts banked should follow some trends, providing a rough check on the completeness of banking.

(2) **Detailed testing of purchase invoices** can be undertaken with invoices being checked to ensure they relate to specific properties owned by ONH and that the invoice totals have been calculated correctly.

(ii) **Internal controls**

(1) **Provide** all visitors to a property with a **pre-numbered ticket**; this includes both members and non-members. **Maintain ticket sequences** – one for members and one for non-members.

(2) **Record all non-member entrance fees** on an electronic cash register – with ticket sales being allocated to either cash or credit card.

(3) At the end of each day, an employee of ONH not involved in issuing tickets **counts the money in the register** and agrees this to the total maintained by the register. Any discrepancies are investigated. The same employee also **agrees credit card sales** to the **listing of credit card authorisations** obtained by the register. Any discrepancy is investigated.

(4) **Enter cash received** on to the bank paying in slip and bank as soon as possible.

Internal audit tests

(1) **Obtain total number of visitors** each day by comparing the difference between the first and last tickets issued, or by **dividing the total value of ticket sales** by the **ticket value**.

(2) **Compare number of visitors** to the **tickets issued** to ensure all visitors have been charged.

(3) **Note discrepancies** between ticket income and number of visitors. Where discrepancy indicates visitors not charged, monitor against volunteers receiving income to determine patterns over time.

(4) **Agree total on register for cash receipts** to the **bank paying-in slip** and **bank statement**.

(c) (i) ONH is likely to need an **information strategy** for the following reasons.

Cost

IS generally **involves high costs** in terms of **capital expenditure** (purchase of new computers) and **ongoing expenditure** in terms of consumables, support and other running costs.

Within ONH, although there is no central IT systems, expenditure is likely to be relatively high as each property **maintains its own systems**, resulting in **duplication of support costs**. Additional costs will also be incurred, amalgamating data from each property as it is unlikely to be in any standard format. Should ONH decide to **implement a WAN or implement common systems**, this will be expensive; a budget as part of the overall IS strategy will be required.

Critical to success

IT can be critical to the success of many organisations. Within ONH at present, IT appears to be more of a **support activity** with very little information being transferred within the organisation. ONH could still function without IT, as people could still visit ONH's properties even if no IT was available.

Information and competitive advantage

Many organisations recognise the need to use information for competitive advantage. The current situation within ONH appears to be that **information is not used to market the company**. However, ONH does have a 'competitor' Buildings in Trust (BiT). ONH may need to consider using IT more aggressively either to **publicise its activities or inform members of facilities available** at its properties. For example, members who were unable to visit a property because its capacity was exceeded could be allowed to **book online** to ensure that their journey was not wasted next time.

Management information

Very little management information appears to be available to the Board of ONH. For example, although budgets are set, the **budgeting process is not particularly precise** while budget monitoring takes place on an annual basis. ONH needs to have an information strategy to ensure that the Board is provided with **frequent financial information** so that it can make effective decisions. For example, when **urgent repair work** is **needed on a property**, as has happened with recent storm damage, the Board would be aware of the current budgetary position and be able to **allocate surplus funds quickly and efficiently**.

IS and stakeholders

ONH is seen to be providing a 'national service' implying that there are parties outside the organisation who are **interested in its activities** and the services being provided. The implication is that ONH should be **providing information** to these people. However, the lack of internal systems and information for the board implies that **external information provision will also be limited**. ONH therefore needs an IS to ensure that appropriate information is made available to third parties.

(ii) According to Earl, there are three different methods of determining an Information Strategy.

Business Led (top down approach)

In this approach, an organisation:

- **Defines its business objectives**
- **Determines how IS/IT can support** those objectives
- **Involves senior management** and project teams to determine the necessary IS/IT systems

This approach will assist ONH, as the organisation needs to meet the objective of **providing a national service** as well as providing the Board with the information it needs to make effective decisions. Determining the internal and external information requirements will show the **information systems needed**. For example, if the Board requires monthly management accounts, then IS/IT systems must be available to collect the information and send it to the Board.

Infrastructure led (bottom up approach)

In this approach, an organisation:

- **Determines what information systems are currently available**
- **Defines what information is needed at an operational level**
- **Prepares a gap analysis** showing the difference between information required and that actually available.

This approach will also assist ONH. The organisation needs systems to **record the number of visitors, issue tickets, monitor budgets** etc. Current provision is mixed, with many different systems being used. There is a gap between what is required operationally and what ONH currently has. Defining operational requirements will enable ONH to implement common systems across all properties to collect transactional data.

Mixed (inside out)

In this approach, an organisation:

- **Identifies opportunities** for using IS/IT
- **Encourages creative thinking**
- **Uses an innovate approach** to IT

This approach appears to have less value to ONH. Current IS tends to be support systems only with little or no innovative use. It appears that ONH needs to upgrade its systems first before seeking competitive advantage in this approach.

69 PowerS

Text references. Chapter 7 is useful on the role of internal audit. Chapter 18 covers the computer issues. The business risks are covered in Chapters 11 and 15, and Chapter 3 covers the broader systems issues.

Top tips. (a) (i) is a standard theory question, allowing you to explain the usefulness of different types of internal audit. (ii) focuses on the learning outcome indicating that an audit of the information systems in an organisation may be the subject of an examination question. The scenario includes various risks with the control system that you need to identify.

Key elements to highlight in the scenario are what the systems can do, including their capacity, access and data maintenance, back-up procedures and how controls are developed over time. Note that although Power S's systems are undoubtedly strong, even these lead on to consideration of potential problems.

(b) moves the case on to the risks of trading on the Internet. Points for the answer can be obtained from the scenario or from knowledge of Internet trading. You need to identify in the scenario general information about trading (what is trading, where it's traded, who's competing) and think about any special features affecting Internet trading. Data protection is particularly important here; threats to reputation may be more significant than legal consequences.

(c) is potentially the most difficult section; you have to use contingency theory to say why you need to update the Internet site. However, the 12 marks available for (c) means you cannot afford to miss it out totally. The headers to (c) indicate information you're looking to glean from the scenario.

Easy marks. As (a) (i) is a general part that you don't need to relate too closely to the question, it's probably the easiest part though (a) (ii) and (b) are not bad.

(a) (i) **Carry out internal audit work**

The **actual extent and amount of work** internal audit carry out will depend on the internal auditors' **assessment of internal controls** in PowerS. However, the areas where internal auditors will carry out work will include:

Review of the accounting system and internal controls

The internal auditors will:

- **Review the design** of internal control systems
- **Monitor the effectiveness** of those controls by detailed testing
- **Recommend cost effective improvements**

Internal audit reports may also be made **available** to the external auditors to assist in external evaluation of systems and potentially decrease the amount of work carried out by the external auditors.

Review of operating systems and information

In this area, the internal auditors may:

- **Review the systems** used to produce such information
- **Enquire into any potential irregularities or errors** in the information produced prior to management using the information.

Other reviews include:

- **Economy, effectiveness and efficiency** of operations
- **Safeguarding of assets**
- **Compliance with specific laws or regulations**
- **Implementation of corporate objectives**

Risk management

The internal auditors can assist with PowerS's risk management process by assessing control systems within the organisation and then advising how risks can be **managed and controlled**. In general terms, the internal auditors' work will be influenced by PowerS's appetite for risks. However, the work will involve:

- **Reviewing the adequacy of risk management and response processes** for identifying, assessing and managing risk and reporting on risk
- The **risk management and control culture** within PowerS
- The **design and operation of internal controls** within PowerS to limit risks
- The **operation and effectiveness** of the risk management process.

The actual amount of work carried out will depend on the internal auditors' **assessment of the controls** in place within PowerS and the potential risks identified. Where the overall risk management framework is inadequate, then the internal auditors will have to depend on their own risk assessment while recommending that an appropriate risk framework is established.

(ii) **Internal audit report**

To:	Board
From:	Chief Internal Auditor
Date:	5 October 20X6
Subject:	Review of Internet Provision

Introduction

As part of the ongoing review of company systems, the internal audit department performed a review of the Internet provision of PowerS during the month of September 20X6.

Key findings are given below. The main finding of the review is that the Internet site requires urgent upgrade. There is a strong recommendation that the board of PowerS allocates a budget and project team to carry out this upgrade as soon as possible.

Key findings

Bandwidth and server capacity

The bandwidth available for the Internet site should be **sufficient to allow access** to the site from the maximum number of customers. **Current bandwidth** is focused on **providing access** to the site for the **average number of customers. Server capacity** relates to the **number of requests that can be processed**. Again, this is focused on meeting average demands. While this ensures access is available for considerable periods of time, there are two risks affecting the company:

(1) **Access**
Firstly, during busy periods, **customers** will be **denied access** to the site. Given PowerS's products are available from many other suppliers, it is likely that customers will simply switch to the Internet site of a competitor and order from them. PowerS will therefore lose sales.

(2) **Crashing**
Secondly, if the **Internet servers** become **overloaded** there is the possibility that they will 'crash' **denying access to all customers**. Again, this will lose sales for PowerS.

We strongly recommend that the **bandwidth and server capacity** are **upgraded** as soon as possible.

Backup

All data files are **backed up daily on a regular basis** and stored off-site. This is appropriate as it ensures that data can be restored as at the end of the previous day if the main computer at PowerS is damaged.

However, there are specific risks with backup:

(1) **Backup of program files**
Firstly, the **program files are not backed up**, meaning if the main computer at PowerS is damaged it will be **difficult to reconstruct the actual programs used**. This is particularly relevant to PowerS where amendments are made to programs on a relatively frequent basis.

(2) **Backup of data files**
Secondly, there is also **no backup of data files during the day**; again if the **main computer files are damaged or destroyed** during the day prior to the evening backup then all **data** processed up to that point will be **lost**.

We recommend that:

(1) **System backup**
A **full system backup** (data and program files) is **carried out each day and stored offsite**, as occurs for data only at present.

(2) **Ongoing backup**
Backup is maintained during the day, using technology such as mirrored servers. This ensures that if one server is unavailable, then processing continues on the second server as all transactions are processed and stored on both servers simultaneously.

Firewalls and anti-virus software

PowerS correctly maintains firewalls and anti-virus software. However, it appears that there are two risks with the system:

(1) **Software updating**
Firstly, **anti-virus software is maintained in-house** and only updated following recommendations from the Internet service company. Taking this approach may leave PowerS vulnerable to attack from viruses due to the time delays in updating and testing the anti-virus software and the relatively swiftness with which new viruses can be distributed around the Internet.

(2) **Password updating**
Secondly, **passwords** are **only updated every four months**. However, on average, two programmers leave each month. As their passwords will still be operational it is possible that they could **access PowerS's software externally** to the company and amend software or data files, or place viruses into the system.

We recommend that:

(1) **Software updating**
Anti-virus software is **updated on a timely basis**. This may involve purchasing a third party product, with frequent updates available over the Internet.

(2) **Password updating**
Passwords are **changed on a more regular basis**. In particular when IT staff leave their user ids and passwords are immediately deleted from the system.

Customer details/fraud

PowerS correctly uses **encryption of credit card details** as these are transferred over the Internet to pay for purchases. The details are then **stored in the Internet server** in unencrypted format in case they are to be used in repeat purchases. Storing details in this way gives rise to the risk of those **details** being **stolen by a third party** and then used by that third party to obtain goods or services fraudulently.

We recommend that **credit card details** are **not stored on PowerS's servers** which means they cannot be stolen. Alternatively, the credit card details should be stored in **encrypted format**, so if they are stolen, they cannot be used.

Sales system

The Internet sales system allows customers to select purchases from the range of goods offered by PowerS. However, goods are only allocated to the customer overnight implying that the **Internet site** does **not show the real-time inventory levels**. This leads to two risks:

- **Customers pay for goods** that **cannot then be delivered**. This may generate **customer dissatisfaction** as the customer will expect to receive the goods as the order was accepted.
- PowerS will need to ensure that **customers' credit cards** are **not charged** in situations where goods are not despatched. If this happens it will again lead to dissatisfaction.

We recommend that the Internet site is **updated to provide real-time inventory levels** with orders only being accepted where goods are available.

(b) **Currency risks**

Because PowerS has an Internet site, trading can take place in any country. In theory, this could mean that PowerS would receive funds in any currency and therefore be subject to **risks of adverse exchange rate movements**. As PowerS only shows prices in Euros, movements in the value of other currencies against the Euro would mean that PowerS could receive more or less Euros than the stated price for goods sold.

However, this risk is effectively controlled by **PowerS always requesting funds in Euros** – its home currency. The risk can be further mitigated by **PowerS placing conditions of trading** on the Internet site to effectively only trade in Euros.

Competitor risk

The Internet is a competitive market place as prices can be compared between different companies. There is a risk that PowerS will **lose sales to competitors** if it does not maintain reasonable prices.

This risk can be mitigated by **monitoring the prices stated on competitors' websites and adjusting prices on the PowerS website** as appropriate. PowerS may also consider **other forms of price competition** such as free delivery or cheap maintenance contracts to try and obtain some competitive advantage.

Physical risk

This is the **risk that goods will be lost or stolen in transit**; that is transit between PowerS's warehouse and the customer.

As a third party carries out deliveries for PowerS there is little the company can do to mitigate this risk.

Trade risk

There is a trade risk that the customer will **cancel the order** prior to the goods being delivered or **refuse delivery of the goods**. This will involve PowerS in **extra costs of paying the courier** firm for non-delivery as well as refunding the customer.

Again, there may be little that PowerS can do to mitigate this risk as most countries have some form of Sale of Goods Act allowing the customer to return goods. PowerS may be able to insist that the customer **pays the delivery charge** where the return is at the request of the customer rather than the product being faulty.

Liquidity risk

This is the inability of PowerS to **finance credit**.

This risk is effectively minimised as far as possible by customers **paying using credit cards** because the credit card company will normally ensure that the customer's card is valid. However, this does not necessarily ensure that PowerS is protected against fraudulent transactions, and card companies may still charge PowerS for fraudulent use.

Legal risks

As PowerS is obtaining and storing personal data (that is data that can be identified with a living individual) the company is subject to the provisions of relevant Data Protection legislation. There is a risk that **personal data will be accessed by third parties**, with the result that PowerS would be in breach of Data Protection legislation.

PowerS needs to **maintain appropriate firewall software** to prevent unauthorised access to its customer data. There are weaknesses in this area regarding **lack of encryption of details and update of password controls**. These need to be addressed to ensure that PowerS does not breach Data Protection legislation.

Business risks

PowerS is considering expanding its Internet site to include the sale of clothes and fashion accessories. They assume that because one product can be sold on the Internet then others can be also. However, this assumption fails to take into account the **nature of the product being sold**. Potential customers tend to want to touch or try clothes on prior to purchase.

To mitigate this risk, the directors of PowerS need to consider the **option of expanding the website**. Checking the success of diversification by other Internet based companies would be advisable, particularly those involving sale of clothes. A **business plan** will also need to be drawn up to try to confirm the viability of the diversification decision.

Reputation risk

The directors of PowerS must also be aware of reputation risk; that is the risk of **loss of reputation** caused by the adverse consequences of another risk. For example, if customer details are 'stolen' from the company's servers, then potential losses include **payments to credit card companies** for loss of customer details and then the **adverse publicity** resulting from the loss. The latter reputation risk may be more damaging to PowerS as customers will refuse to trade with the company.

There may be little Power S can do to mitigate reputation risk, although **employment of public relations resource** and a **rapid response contingency** plan may help.

(c) **Structure**

The overall structure of PowerS is to **delegate power** to the **individual divisions** of the company. The centre simply reviews reports from each division on a monthly or bi-monthly basis.

In terms of contingency theory, this will mean that members of the IT department will expect to be **involved in the budget setting process**. In fact if they are not involved then there will be some element of **demotivation** and managers/staff may not accept the budget. If this is the case, they will tend to work at their own pace, ignoring any budgetary constraints, which in turn will lead to cost overruns.

Environment

The environment normally relates to the **external competition**, **number of products** produced etc. In the case of the IT department, the external environment is the company itself and then the technology driving the Internet site.

While the company is not changing significantly, the **hardware and software requirements** for the Internet, as well as **customer expectations** for Internet sites tend to **change** at an ever increasing pace. The effect of this on budgeting for the new Internet site is that the **budget** itself may become **out-of-date** very quickly, and that **more frequent reporting** will be required to monitor progress of actual expenditure against budget. This may work to the benefit of IT staff, as newer technology/software may be incorporated into the Internet site, although more frequent reporting may be **de-motivating** as this will take time away from improving the Internet site.

Culture

Culture refers to an **organisation's value systems** and the expectations that staff obtain as a result of those value systems.

In relation to the Internet budget, staff within the IT department would expect to be involved in setting the budget as the corporate culture in PowerS is based on **sharing and involvement**. However, the IT director has decided to set the budget for the new Internet site. This decision goes against the normal corporate culture and the director can expect some **resistance** from staff and potential lack of ownership or following of that budget.

Role of centre

The role of centre refers to the way that **head office attempts to control the wider group**.

Within PowerS, the role of centre normally relates to the **strategic control**; financial targets are set, but there are also significant non-financial targets. The focus on financial targets only for the Internet site along with tight budgetary controls is more indicative of a **financial control style**. Staff within the IT department may not be clear on exactly how to work under this type of control and it is likely to **increase the stress levels** within the department, leading possibly to the loss of key staff during the project.

Technology

The production of the Internet is a relatively informal process that normally indicates that the **budgetary systems** should also be **informal**. The **imposition of strict budgetary controls** may therefore be **resented** by staff.

Similarly, as the production process is less predictable and the content and design of the site may change during production, **budgetary slack** would normally be included in the budget. The decision of the IT director to set a **tight budget** may therefore be correct as this will avoid any slack, providing what is hopefully a realistic budget.

70 LaPoNa

Text references. Chapter 11 deals with hedging currency risk, Chapter 3 centralisation vs decentralisation. Chapter 11 gives examples of controls and Chapter 9 discusses fraud in detail.

Top tips. (a) (i) Is a basic hedging question. It is slightly more difficult because you need to identify other hedging options that are not being used and then comment on those. Note that these include simpler methods than buying derivatives; these may well be appropriate for the company's trading circumstances. As the question requires discussion, the answer indicates how important they are.

The key decision in (b) in relation to the control system is whether to allow centralised or decentralised control. The factors for and against can be obtained from theory but you will need to use the scenario to provide specific comment on the situation in LaPoNa, particularly the issues of geographical diversity and the need to respond to changing sales patterns.

In (c) (i), the plan for an audit relates to a sales system. You are presented with the aims of the audit, but must prepare appropriate tests for each risk. As you're asked to describe the tests, you must say what they're designed to achieve. (ii) focuses on problems in sales and wages systems – only one problem is likely to be relevant to LaPoNa but you must still explain the logic behind this decision.

Easy marks. Really depend on how comfortable you feel with different areas of the syllabus. The numbers in (a) (i) aren't too complicated; discussion in (a) (ii) is a bit wider than in other hedging questions. (b) is a fairly standard discussion on centralisation v decentralisation. Provided you link in the main points of the debate to the company's circumstances, you should score well on this part.

(a) (i) Hedging of net receipts of $450,000 ($750,000 – $300,000) as transactions occur on the same date.

Forward exchange contract

Three month forward contract to sell US$. Rate = $1.759 – $0.0071 = $1.7519/£.

Receipt calculation:

	£
Sterling proceeds in three months' time: \$450,000 / 1.7519	256,864
Transaction costs: \$450,000 × 0.002% / 1.759	512
Net receipt	256,352

Money market hedge

	Now		+ 3 months
\$	2 So borrow now \$445,545	3/12 × 4% = 1% per 3 months (borrowing rate) × 1/1.01 ←	1 Will receive \$450,000
↓	To be able to invest \$ borrowed, must sell them now @ \$1.759		
£	3 So invest now £253,294	On which interest is received at 3/12 × 4.5% = 1.125% per 3 months (lending rate) × 1.01125 →	4 Due to LaPoNa £256,144 - £512 (transaction cost) = £255,632 (effective receipt from hedge)

Receipts are higher using a forward exchange contract – hence this is the preferred method.

(ii) **Factors to consider in hedging risk**

(1) **The ability of staff within LaPoNa to manage the different techniques**
Given that LaPoNa has a **qualified management accountant** then there should be appropriate ability in the company to manage these transactions.

(2) **The attitude of the company to risk**
It is not clear what LaPoNa's **risk appetite** actually is; however, given that the contracts are for relatively short periods of time, and exchange rates US\$ to GBP can be determined relatively well in advance there appears to be little risk with these transactions.

(3) **The size of the transactions compared to the company's total operations**
The larger each transaction then the greater the overall risk. As LaPoNa has four payment receipt dates per annum, each transaction would appear to represent **roughly one quarter of the total receipts and payments for the year**, implying that the risk attached to each set of transactions is relatively high.

(4) **The perceived level of risk attached to the currencies**
Both the US\$ and the GBP are **established currencies** involving minimal risk limiting overall transaction risk for LaPoNa.

(5) **The relative cost of the different options**
Costs are the same, making this factor irrelevant to the calculation.

Alternative methods of minimising the risk

(1) **Opening two bank accounts**
This is a distinct possibility as LaPoNa has regular transactions in both the USA and the UK. Denominating and collecting receipts in the **local currency** at the time of sale would enable LaPoNa to decide when to remit funds between the USA and the UK rather than being dependent on rate movements over three months.

(2) **Denominate all prices in either US$ or GBP**
While this would remove currency risk, the option will only be viable where customers in one country will **accept prices denominated** in a different currency.

(3) **Use of other techniques such as multilateral netting or swaps and option contracts**
LaPoNa would have to **investigate the relative costs and benefits of these options** and ensure **appropriate knowledge** was available in-house to perform these transactions.

(b) **Centralisation/decentralisation**

Centralisation/decentralisation refers to the **amount of authority** which is **delegated** in an organisation and therefore to the level at which decisions are taken within the management hierarchy. In LaPoNa the Board are considering changing the company structure from centralised to decentralised in conjunction with establishing three regional offices as part of an expansion plan. Comments below are made in this context.

Advantages of LaPoNa remaining centralised

Decision making

In a centralised organisation, **all major decisions** are **made in one place**. This tends to make the organisation **easier to co-ordinate and control**.

In LaPoNa, maintaining central decision making may be advisable given that the organisation is expanding. Maintaining central control may be advantageous as head office staff can **set up the new divisions based on their experience** rather than new staff having to learn how to run a division to LaPoNa's requirements on their own.

Quality of decision making

Senior managers in the organisation can take a **wider view of problems** and the consequences of those issues. In theory, the quality of decisions will be higher due to the **skill and knowledge** of managers in the central location.

In LaPoNa, this means that managers can **monitor the business closely** and make decisions based on that knowledge. For example, they can monitor exchange rate movements on an international basis and make appropriate decisions on prices in each region based on that global knowledge.

Allocation of resources

Senior managers can attempt to **maintain a proper balance** between different departments and functions and allocate resources as necessary to each function.

With the new divisions, it may be **useful to set initial budgets** for each division **centrally** for marketing, administration, finance etc. as LaPoNa will have learnt from the initial two centres roughly how much money is needed. If additional resources are then necessary in any location, these can be allocated where these can be justified.

Cost

Maintaining centralised decision making may be **cheaper**, particularly because roles and functions will not be duplicated across the organisation.

This will certainly be the case in LaPoNa given that there may **not be a need** for **separate marketing or finance functions** in the new divisions until it is shown whether that division is financially viable.

Advantages of LaPoNa becoming divisionalised

Avoids overburdening top managers

Establishing a divisionalised structure means that senior managers have **less decision making**, limiting their workload and hopefully **decreasing the stress** of their jobs.

In LaPoNa, there is **no indication that staffing will be increased** at head office; hence incorporating a divisionalised structure will mean top managers will not have to be so concerned about the day-to-day running of the individual divisions.

Improves motivation

Divisionalisation normally **improves motivation** of more junior managers who are therefore given more responsibility.

This will certainly be the case with LaPoNa. As the divisions are new, LaPoNa has the opportunity to **employ staff locally** who appreciate the challenge of establishing a new division. Staff are more likely to be **motivated** knowing that the division will be 'their work' rather than follow guidance from a central location.

Awareness of local problems

Local decision makers are more likely to have awareness of local problems.

Within LaPoNa, top managers may **not be aware of marketing arrangements, local laws on import and export of vehicles etc**. whereas a local manager should be aware of these issues. Using a divisionalised structure will therefore **enable the divisions** to be **established quicker** than using central control.

Speed of decision making

Decision making is quicker as there is **no need to refer decisions upwards** to the head office. However, information technology allows input from head office where required.

This may be particularly important in LaPoNa where new divisions may need **timely decision making** in order to establish the division. For example, decisions may be needed in determining prices with car manufacturers for a customer. However, there is still the issue of **each division being new** and staff within the division therefore **taking time to understand and implement** LaPoNa systems. Provision of good information systems to head office allows queries to be addressed quickly with head office while still allowing local control and decision making.

(c) (i) **Controls**

Vehicles are not being supplied to a poor credit risk

- **Payment by credit card**: ensure that **confirmation has been obtained** from the **credit card company** that the amount of the purchase is within the customer's credit limit and that credit is available.
- **Payment by cheque**: **agree payment details in the cash book to the bank paying in book and bank statements. Check the bank statements** about one week after banking to **ensure that the cheque has not been returned to the bank as uncleared**. Where the customer's order is urgent, **request special clearance of the cheque** with the bank.

Customers are being invoiced for the correct amount

- To **confirm that the price is correct, agree details on the invoice to the customer's order** and then the confirmed price from the vehicle manufacturer. **Ensure that any unique vehicle identity numbers agree** to confirm that the correct vehicle appears on the invoice.
- To **confirm the shipping charge, agree shipping charge on invoice to the shipping invoice** from the transport company. Price will then be the price from the manufacturer, add the shipping charge plus 25%.
- **Cast** the **sales invoice**.

All sales are recorded in the books of the division

- **Review the sales day book to ensure completeness of numbering of sales invoices.** Any omissions should be investigated.
- **Agree details from a number of sales invoices into the sales day book.** Items to be agreed include the customer name, invoice amount (vehicle cost, transport cost, any sales tax and total cost) as well as the vehicle details.
- **Agree details to the individual account in the sales ledger**, confirming that the customer name and invoice details agree.
- **Total sales invoice amounts** for one month to ensure calculations are correct and **agree total amounts to the general ledger** for that month, to ensure records are correct.

(ii) **Teeming and lading**

This occurs when an employee (normally the cashier) has the chance to **misappropriate payments from customers**. Cash received is 'borrowed' by the cashier rather than being kept as petty cash or banked. Cash received the next day is then banked in place of the previous day's cash. Overall, the cash and debtor balances appear to be correct; there is simply a **time delay** of a few days between cash receipts and entry of those receipts into the company's books.

Teeming and lading is unlikely to occur in LaPoNa because **payments are received by credit card or cheque/banker's draft**. There is no cash to misappropriate.

Advance fee fraud

In this situation, a fraudster takes a **fee or deposit up-front** promising to deliver the goods ordered some time in the future. In some situations, taking a part-payment is a legitimate business exercise. However, in the fraud situation, the **goods ordered are never delivered** with the fraudster keeping the money. In many situations, the fraudster sets-up a 'fake' company to obtain the funds, which is then closed down after a few months, making tracing of the money difficult.

In LaPoNa, **no initial deposit** is taken and the **company has been established for a number of years**. Should a customer not receive his vehicle then hopefully there are sufficient staff to alert the directors with the situation. If many vehicles are not delivered then LaPoNa's reputation will decrease significant, again warning the directors of the irregularity.

Ghost employees

In this situation, there are **imaginary or 'ghost' employees** on the payroll. Wages are paid to these employees (perhaps to their bank account) – however, the bank account is also under control of the fraudsters so when funds are received, they are distributed amongst the fraudsters.

There is a risk of ghost employees in LaPoNa, especially with the setting up of the new divisions. It is possible that local managers could **set up some ghost employees** – as long as total staff were in line with divisional budgets then head office may not notice the discrepancy. Controls that the board of LaPoNa could implement include **ensuring appropriate employment documentation is obtained** from each employee (eg P45 in the UK), that **references are filed** and internal audit confirms the **physical existence of employees**.

71 IDAN

Text references. Chapter 1 broadly on risks, with Chapter 15 giving the greater detail that may be helpful. Chapter 7 deals with the role of internal audit.

Top tips. In (a) we have grouped risks round the main categories identified in the text, business strategic, non-business strategic and operational risks. Don't worry too much if your classification of risks differed from ours. An alternative suggested by CIMA is credit, market, operational, reputation, compliance and business risk. Key threats to reputation here would be customers receiving a poor service through operational failures, concerns over systems security and legal penalties being imposed as a result of poor financial services advice.

It's important to link your discussion into the scenario; it's evident for example that IDAN faces a number of legal/compliance risks. Note that the discussion of the advantages of categorisation focuses on key elements of the risk management cycle.

(b) is an interesting mix of a number of controls; you need to give specific examples and also give some consideration to the risks of introducing new systems in response to changes. Note that IT controls are a significant element. You don't need a detailed knowledge of the money laundering regulations to answer that part; a systematic approach to risk management (establishing policies, staffing, training and management review) will get you the majority of marks. You can also use your own experience of dealing with banks when discussing opening an account with a new bank or using pin numbers. The marking guide allowed 3 marks for each risk discussed, with a maximum of 15.

At first glance (c) may seem a rather odd requirement as surely internal audit is part of risk management, not separate from it. What the question was in fact asking was a comparison of the risk management **function** (ie the work of the staff with designated responsibility for risk management) with the internal audit **function**. The scenario details do mention both functions. The main focus of the risk management function will be on **establishing and undertaking** the chosen approach to risk whereas internal audit will be responsible for **reviewing** what has been done. **Compare and contrast** means that the comparison should be done under the same headers. As you're asked to discuss, you need to explain the significance of the links.

In (d) the requirement for you to make reference to the data meant that you were expected to calculate the return on assets, although this is not completely clear in the question. 4 marks were available in total for the calculations. The focus of the discussion could then have been on whether establishment and use of a risk-adjusted discount rate was appropriate, including what other methods could be used to judge between divisions.

Easy marks. Categorisation of risks in (a) should have provided a gentle start to the question as most of the 'normal' major risks apply. In (b), provided you make clear by using headers which risk you're discussing, you don't have to discuss the risks in the order given in the question, and can start with those you find easiest first.

Examiner's comments. The most serious weakness was use of textbook material with lack of thought on how relevant it was and how it should be applied to the scenario.

Answers to (a) were generally good, with risks suitably categorised.

(b) was also answered strongly, with relevant controls and good links to the scenario. However some of the controls suggested were unrealistic.

Some answers to (c) showed good understanding of the internal audit and risk management; however 'far too many answers were based on the regurgitation of definitions and lists from study texts'. They also failed to discuss the links between the two functions.

Answers to (d) showed a lack of understanding of risk-adjusted hurdle rates. Good answers discussed why risks might differ between the units. Few answers calculated the return on net assets.

(a) **Main categories of risk**

Business strategic risks

Competition risks

Business risk is the potential volatility of profits caused by the **nature and type** of **operations** in which the company is involved. The consequences of making the **wrong strategic decisions** may be very significant, since IDAN is faced with choosing in which areas of business to carry out further investment. IDAN also faces business risk through **failing to respond** as quickly as its competitors do to the **current changes in the business environment**. Deregulation means the group faces competition in some areas from outside the banking sector, such as entities other than banks offering more flexible or informal loan arrangements.

Credit risks

Credit risk is the risk of losses through the **bank's customers failing to meet their payment obligations**. This is a major source of risk for a bank, since much business will be loans on which interest and capital repayments have to be made. The risk of losses will depend on whether loans are secured on assets, or have no security backing.

Non-business strategic risks

Financial market risks

Financial market risk is the risk of losses through adverse movements in financial markets. This includes **changes in the foreign currency markets** (exchange risk), **changes in interest rates as expected here** (interest rate risk) and other changes in securities or derivatives markets.

Legal risks

Legal risks are the risk of losses resulting from IDAN **incurring legal penalties**, or having its **operations disrupted by legal action**. IDAN faces several risks in this area, including legal penalties for failure to supply details to the tax authorities or to implement money laundering requirements, and claims against the group for incorrect financial services advice. Because IDAN operates in a number of different countries, the risk of breaches somewhere may be increased.

Operational risks

Systems risks

Systems risks may be significant for IDAN, since it is faced with having to **re-design its operational and information systems**. Problems with the design or implementation of new systems may lead to failure to provide a **proper service to customers** or **failure to supply managers** with the information they need to **supervise the business effectively**. Another significant risk is a **breakdown in the computer systems** resulting in customers being unable to use their credit or debit cards.

Fraud risks

IDAN may be vulnerable to **losses through fraud**, for example use by **unauthorised persons of PIN numbers**, or **fraudulent transactions over the telephone**.

Advantages of categorisation of risks

Event identification

Sorting risks into different categories enables the business to **identify situations or events** that will cause loss, and also **links** between them.

Risk response

Categorising risks should ensure they are dealt with in the most appropriate manner, for example developing systems to eliminate the risk of non-compliance with regulations or transfer of risk by insurance. Even when the same broad method is used for different risks, there may be variations, for example using **different insurers to cover operational and credit risks**.

Responsibility

Grouping risks enables the business to assess who will be responsible for dealing with them. Risks in **specialist areas** of the business may require **internal or external risk management input**, whereas **'mainstream' operational risks** can be dealt with by **operational managers**.

Monitoring

Categorisation of risks makes its easier for the directors to **fulfil their responsibilities** to ensure that the risks are managed to an acceptable level. Not only will it make risk monitoring easier, but the initial process of risk categorisation will require directors to respond to the results by ensuring appropriate systems are developed. Directors will also be able to fulfil their legal obligations to report on risk.

(b) **EU law**

To counter the risks of non-compliance, information systems will have to be amended to:

(i) **Identify accounts held by non-residents**; and also **separately identify accounts held in each European country**

(ii) **Automatically generate a 15% deduction of withholding tax when interest is paid** on these accounts

(iii) **Show details** grouped by each EU country of the **amount of the interest paid and the tax due**

The listing of accounts held by non-residents should be checked independently of the processing function.

(i) **Confirm that interest is shown as paid** on the due dates.

(ii) **Reconcile the list with the previous list sent to the tax authorities**. Any changes should be confirmed to listings of accounts transferred or closed, and any other changes investigated.

Forecast rises in interest rates

Interest rate risk is fundamental to the group's operations, as it may arise through trading activities or traditional banking work. The board therefore needs to consider the **desirable appetite** for this risk. The directors should also regularly **review future prospects for interest rates, IDAN's lending patterns** and **the credit ratings of its borrowers**. Excessive concentration on long-term fixed interest lending will leave IDAN vulnerable to **not benefiting from interest rate increases**.

IDAN's treasury department should be looking to **hedge any of IDAN's own borrowing** that may become more expensive by using appropriate instruments such as interest rate caps.

Elimination of personal signatures

Transition to new arrangements will require controls to ensure that all customers are notified of their PIN numbers. IDAN must also implement appropriate security measures to combat the **risk of fraud**:

(i) **Numbers**
The identification numbers supplied by IDAN to its customers should be reasonably **easy for the customer to remember**, but should **avoid combinations** that **can easily be guessed**. Customers should be instructed to **destroy IDAN's notification** of their pin number.

(ii) **Lost cards**
IDAN should make clear to customers what they should do if their cards are lost or stolen. If customers **report cards** to be **missing**, those cards should be **instantly cancelled**.

(iii) **Pin numbers mislaid**
If customers contact IDAN **claiming to have forgotten their pin numbers**, IDAN staff should ask for **evidence of identification** such as personal details before supplying their pin numbers.

In addition, IDAN will need to ensure that its own cards function properly by **pre-testing** the new arrangements. Once operational, there should be **back-up facilities in place**.

Increasing use of telephone and Internet banking services

Developments in new types of business carry the risk that the company's systems will not be able to cope with **increased demand**. Management therefore **need to monitor call waiting times against targets**, and **Internet response times**. Internal audit may need to carry out **detailed testing of transactions** to ensure that they have been processed accurately. **Extra training** may be required to combat problems.

Verification of identity controls will also be required to counter the risk of security breaches. This can be achieved by requiring a PIN number to be entered or quoted over the phone, along with an item of personal data such as **date of birth**. There should also be controls over the **security of the telephone system** and **encryption and firewall controls** to protect data transmitted by computer.

Misselling claims

Human resource controls are an important element of avoiding the **legal risk** of successful claims:

(i) **Recruitment**
Recruitment processes should ensure the employment of **properly-qualified staff** and **obtaining references** on their experience.

(ii) **Training**
Staff should be trained in **legal requirements**, **appropriate selling techniques and ethical**

behaviour. If staff are found to have fallen below standard, they should incur **remedial training or dismissal** as appropriate.

(iii) **Remuneration**
Staff remuneration schemes should be carefully reviewed to ensure that they do not encourage inappropriate selling.

IDAN should also have controls in place to ensure **staff behaviour is monitored**, for example requiring recording of all phone calls, and written records of all meetings which the customer confirms.

It should also implement a formal **complaints procedure**, which deals with **customer complaints speedily and actions findings**.

Money laundering

The key elements of a money laundering policy are:

(i) **Compliance officer**
Appointing a director or senior manager as **money laundering compliance officer**.

(ii) **Policies**
Establishing written policies and procedures which cover the money laundering regulations, detail the records to be kept and periods of retention and specify when the authorities should be notified

(iii) **Identification procedures**
Verifying identities of new customers can be done for personal customers by a passport or identity card. Similar details should be obtained for companies.

(iv) **Training**
Training all staff so that they are aware of the **signs of money laundering** and know that they are **legally required to report their suspicions**

(v) **Strange transactions**
Tracking large or unusual transactions, especially those taking place over more than one country

(vi) **Policy review**
Regular review of policies to ensure that they are effective and comply with any changes in regulations

(c) **Roles of risk management and internal audit**

Aims and scope

Risk management function

The risk management function's aims will be to assist the directors in fulfilling their obligations to **respond appropriately to significant risks**, **safeguard assets**, **ensure compliance with laws and regulations** and **guarantee the quality of financial reporting**. The risk management function will **oversee risk management systems** over all aspects of the organisation's activities. However the risk management function will **not be solely responsible** for risk management; risk management will be a key part of operational managers' responsibilities, and staff will also have responsibility for limiting some of the risks in their areas of work.

Internal audit

Internal audit's aims will be whatever senior management managers prescribe. It may be **limited to reporting on the operation of the accounting control systems of the business**, although increasingly it will cover non-financial aspects. Its work may not just cover risk issues, but it may also try to **add value** to the organisation by for example suggesting improvements in the economy, efficiency and effectiveness of operations.

Responsibilities

Risk management function

The **risk management function** will be responsible for advising the board on the decisions it takes as to how much **risk** the company is prepared to **bear**. The risk management function will analyse the risks faced on an ongoing basis; this will include consideration of whether **risk limitation targets** have been met. The function will also be responsible for **establishing risk management policy, co-ordinating responses to risks** including **designing risk management processes and systems**, and **promotion of risk-conscious behaviour** within the organisation.

Internal audit

Internal audit is the **responsibility of a dedicated team** with specified roles and agreed work programmes that cover certain areas of the business's operations.

Links between risk management and internal audit

Internal audit links in with a number of areas of risk management:

(i) **Risk analysis impact on audit**
The **risk analysis** undertaken by staff with responsibility for risk management will help determine the areas on which internal audit concentrates and the extent of their work. Internal audit will undertake their own risk analysis as part of audit planning. The results of their work will influence the future work they carry out and impact upon the organisation's overall continuing risk analysis

(ii) **Risk response**
Internal audit is part of the **risk response process**; the risk of fraud by staff may be reduced for example if they know that their work will be subject to stringent internal audit work.

(iii) **Role of internal audit**
Similarly internal audit **testing control procedures** to see if they are working satisfactorily is itself a control procedure.

(iv) **Assessment of risk by internal audit**
Internal audit may have **responsibility** for wider risk assessment tasks including **assessing** the **adequacy and operation of the risk management processes**. Weaknesses identified by internal audit may result in risk management having to strengthen control systems, since they have not proved robust enough to eliminate risks.

(v) **Role in management monitoring**
The **results of internal audit and the risk management function's work** will be used as part of the **overall monitoring** of the organisation by senior managers, and also by external auditors.

(d) **Limitations of using absolute profitability**

Comparing the performance of managers by looking at the profits they make is likely be flawed, since it takes no account of the risks involved in the different types of business. Each business will have a very different **risk profile** and the profits that will be regarded as a satisfactory return for those risks will also differ. Profit levels may also reflect original size rather than better performance.

Return on net assets

If the risk-adjusted hurdle rate is to be used, it has to be compared with a measure of return on capital. Here the return on net assets is used to measure the return on capital.

	20X4	*20X3*
Corporate and investment banking	21.59%	24.00%
Personal financial services	26.24%	26.31%
Private banking	5.00%	4.84%
Commercial banking	30.00%	38.00%

Private banking generates a much lower return than the other sectors and appears to be more vulnerable to external economic factors. However its net assets are only a small part of IDAN's total asset base (6% in 20X4). Thus the most significant judgements in terms of performance and where investment should be are between the other three sectors.

Choosing an appropriate rate

If a risk-adjusted hurdle rate is to be used, the directors will need to determine what the appropriate rate is. Choice of a **common rate over all sectors** would be **inappropriate** given the differing risk profiles of different areas of the business.

Need to measure risks

Therefore required returns will be influenced by risk levels; the higher the risk level the higher required return. IDAN thus has to decide how **risk** should be **measured** and **how exactly differences in risk levels** will affect **required return**. **Credit losses** are one proxy for risk; if they are used then resources are likely to be diverted to commercial banking since the risk of credit losses there is lower and the rate of return is higher. However other business risks should also be taken into account.

Need to link risk and return

IDAN also needs to feed through risk into required return. If equity market performance is judged as a key risk measure, then the **capital asset pricing model** provides a link between risk and return. Other, more subjective, methods of assessing risk may be more difficult to link with returns.

Problems with risk-adjusted rate

The **risk-adjusted rate** is a relative measure that does not take into account the size of profits made by each division. Other measures that do take these into account include:

(i) **Absolute profits**, as before

(ii) **Residual income** or economic value added, which deduct an imputed charge for the capital consumed from operating profits

Other considerations

As well as being determined by risk-return links, investment may also be determined by:

(i) **Minimum investment** required in a particular sector, linked to the finance available; information technology requirements mean that most capital expenditure is likely to be required in the **private banking** and **personal financial services** divisions.

(ii) **Strategic opportunities** each sector offers; private banking, although offering a lower return, may bring customers in who will use other, more profitable, services

The return on net assets figure fails to take account of the **quality** of the asset base, whether the assets are capable of generating long-term profits.

Performance measurement

As well as being used to assess potential investment, the risk-adjusted return is being used to judge management performance. However other measures will need to be considered as well, including **performance against budget**, and **improvement in returns over time**. A **balanced scorecard** may be appropriate as a means of assessing a range of factors.

72 Crashcarts

Text references. Most of the chapters dealing with different types of risk are helpful, but particularly Chapter 2's coverage of the methodology for dealing with risk. Chapter 5 covers corporate governance.

Top tips. The Turnbull and COSO guidance on risk are important in this paper and you should get credit for quoting **relevant** parts. The emphasis that these reports place on accurate and relevant information has obvious implications for the management accountant, both in terms of ensuring the information is correct, and devising new measures.

The calculations in (c) though long-winded are not technically difficult once you realise that shortages of inventory drive the risk. The assumption that enquiries only fail to become orders because of shortages of inventory seems a slightly strange one and certainly worth a comment in the discussion. Otherwise the approach to questions like (c) is to work methodically through the information and assume most of it will be relevant to a discussion of risks; in some cases the risks will be obvious, in others you will need to think and make connections between different pieces of information (such as the client bases of parents and subsidiaries).

It is possible to go into a lot of technical detail about control systems in (d), but remember that this is also a practical paper, and thus suggesting appropriate controls will gain you considerable credit. The best way to emphasise that the controls you recommend are relevant is to group them under the key risk headings identified in (c).

Easy marks. (b) should offer quick, straightforward marks: the temptation is to spend too long on each stage as the part is only worth 5 marks.

(a) **Corporate governance guidance**

Importance of risk management

In America the COSO committee has emphasised the importance of **enterprise risk management**, in particular the links between the organisation's **strategy** and its ability to bear risks, **enhancement** of **risk responses** and **considering opportunities** as well as risks.

The UK's **Turnbull committee** suggested that **review of internal controls** should be an integral part of the company's operations.

Risk perspective

The Turnbull committee emphasised the importance of a risk-based perspective, in particular avoiding **unnecessary financial risks**, risks that **accounting information** may be **unreliable** and threats to the **safeguarding of assets**. Boards need also to be able to make sure that controls are not so restrictive that there is a **risk of missed opportunities**.

Board assessment

In particular the board should consider:

(i) The **identification, evaluation and management of all key risks** affecting the organisation

(ii) The **effectiveness of internal control**; again that does not just mean financial controls but also operational, compliance and risk management controls

(iii) The **action taken** if any **weaknesses** are found

Effectiveness of internal controls

The Turnbull report recommends that when assessing the **effectiveness of internal control**, boards should consider the following:

(i) The **nature and extent of the risks** which face the company and which it regards as **acceptable** for the company to bear within its particular business

(ii) The **threat of such risks becoming a reality**

(iii) The **company's ability to reduce the incidence and impact** of risk on the business

(iv) The **costs and benefits** related to operating relevant controls

Role of management accountants

Providing information

Turnbull recommends that in order to carry out their work effectively, boards need to receive and review reports on internal control. Reports by management accountants could form part of this review, particularly reports on the **operation of the budgeting systems**, **feedback** on the results of comparison between actual and budgeted figures, and details of the **action taken** if significant variances have been identified. Management accountants must also be concerned with the **accuracy of information**.

Risk quantification

Management accountants can also play a key role in **risk quantification**, presenting the results of complex risk quantification techniques in a form that will enable the board to decide on the threats the organisation faces.

Designing systems

Recommendations by management accountants can help ensure that risk avoidance and reduction is built into management accounting control systems. This includes specifying the key information that systems will handle; in an uncertain environment more use will be made of **external, non-financial and projected information**. COSO emphasises the importance of refining large volumes of data into **actionable information**, and changing information systems as required, to support new objectives.

(b) A formal methodology to analyse risk is made up of five stages.

(i) **Risk identification**

The company needs first to identify what potential risks there might be. This can be achieved by:

- **Physical inspection** of, for example, computerised equipment
- **Review of documentation**, for example **correspondence with clients**
- **Brainstorming** with representatives of various departments.

An important part of risk identification is **identifying events** that could cause problems.

(ii) **Risk assessment**

Risk assessment involves ascertaining all the **possible consequences** of the identified risks actually occurring. Sources of information that might need to be reviewed include organisation and production charts, information about major customers and accounting information.

(iii) **Risk profiling**

Risk profiling involves using the results of the risk identification and assessment to group risks according to their **likelihood and consequences**.

(iv) **Risk quantification**

A variety of techniques such as **sensitivity analysis**, **scenarios** and **expected values** can be used to calculate the impact of risks. The company should aim to quantify:

- Average or expected results or losses
- Frequency of losses
- Chances of losses
- Largest predictable losses

(v) **Risk consolidation**

Senior management at the parent must ascertain whether there are any risks that are **common** to both the parent and subsidiary, such as problems with accounting information, and try to ascertain the impact of these risks.

(c) **Risk identification – subsidiary**

Client risk

The major risk the subsidiary faces is the **loss of clients**. The subsidiary has a number of large retail clients, so the loss of even a couple may have a serious impact on profits. The subsidiary may be particularly vulnerable to being **undercut** on price, with cost centres abroad having lower labour costs and hence being able to offer better terms.

Running out of inventory

As indicated below, the subsidiary faces the risk of **major loss of income** through its clients having insufficient inventory

Information technology risks

The subsidiary may be vulnerable to a **major breakdown in technology**. The **maintenance contract** and the **off-site back-up** should help mitigate this risk, although this may make the subsidiary vulnerable to problems with its suppliers. As the subsidiary holds a lot of sensitive data, the consequences of a successful attempt at **hacking** could be serious. In a few years time the technology will need replacing.

Human resource risk

The subsidiary may be vulnerable to loss of orders due to **mistakes or slowness of processing** by inadequately trained or poorly motivated **staff**. The holding of credit and debit card information may make the subsidiary vulnerable to **fraud** by staff members.

Risk identification – parent

Investment risk

The parent faces the risk of **loss of income** if the subsidiary loses clients, and ultimately **impairment, in the value of its investment** in its accounts. However the parent will not be liable for the subsidiary's debts should the subsidiary run into financial difficulties.

Reputation risk

The parent may suffer a loss of reputation if the subsidiary is unable to **provide an adequate service**. This may be quite serious for the parent as there appears to be overlap between the parent and subsidiary's clients and both are providing information technology services. The parent may be more vulnerable as the services it provides seem to be more in the nature of one-off consultancy projects rather than long-term continuing operations.

Control risk

The parent may also face the risk that **controls over the subsidiary fail to work**, resulting in the need for expenditure of time and resources to correct difficulties.

Risk quantification

The company can use a number of **different sensitivity calculations** to assess the impact of for example price changes and loss of customers. Here we shall look at the impact of running out of inventory and of spare operator capacity.

Running out of inventory

	20X1	*20X2*	*20X3*
Number of incoming calls received	1,200,000	1,300,000	1,350,000
Number of orders processed	1,000,000	1,100,000	1,150,000
Out of stock-orders	200,000	200,000	200,000
Average number of line items per order	3.0	2.9	2.8
Out of stock-line items	600,000	580,000	560,000
	£	£	£
Income per order processed	2.50	2.75	3.00
Income per line item processed	0.20	0.15	0.12
Lost income per order	500,000	550,000	600,000
Lost income per line item	120,000	87,000	67,200
Total lost income from running out of inventory	620,000	637,000	667,200

This calculation assumes that the sole reason for the difference between incoming calls and orders is lack of inventory, and ignores the possibility of staff problems.

Spare capacity

	20X1	*20X2*	*20X3*
Number of operators	70	80	80
Capacity (operators x orders per operator)	1,050,000	1,200,000	1,200,000
Actual number of orders	1,000,000	1,100,000	1,150,000

	20X1	20X2	20X3
Spare capacity (orders)	50,000	100,000	50,000
	£	£	£
Cost per order (operator costs/ order capacity)	1.48	1.60	1.82
Cost of spare capacity	73,810	160,000	90,833
Actual number of orders	1,000,000	1,100,000	1,150,000
Number of clients	8	7	7
Orders per client	125,000	157,143	164,286
Actual number of line items	3,000,000	3,200,000	3,250,000
Line items per client	375,000	457,143	464,286
	£	£	£
Income per order processed	2.50	2.75	3.00
Order income per client (A)	312,500	432,143	492,858
Income per line item	0.20	0.15	0.12
Line item income per client (B)	75,000	68,571	55,714
Fixed contract income per client (C)	50,000	55,000	55,000
Value of each client (A + B + C)	437,500	555,714	603,572

Given that net profits fall from £280,000 in 20X1 to only £165,000 in 20X3, the loss of even one client will tip Crashcarts into loss, making client satisfaction a significant part of the company's strategy.

(d) **Elements of management control systems**

In common with other control systems, management accounting control systems have **inputs**, **processes** and **outputs**.

Feedback

The outputs are used by managers to assure themselves that specific tasks are being carried out **efficiently and effectively** (operational control) and assuring themselves that resources have been obtained and used **efficiently and effectively in the accomplishment of the organisation's objectives**. This implies comparison of outputs with predictions/targets, so that there is a **predictive element** built into control systems. It also implies determining the cause of deviation from predictions/targets and taking **corrective action** if necessary.

Feedforward control

As well as taking action based on **feedback** arising from what has happened, management accounting systems also allow **feedforward control**, the forecasting of differences between actual and planned outcomes, and the implementation of action beforehand to avoid differences.

Responsibility centres

As indicated above, there is a risk that controls over the subsidiary will fail to work and that the parent will suffer a **loss of resources**. Responsibility centres are a key component of management accounting systems, but the parent's directors need to decide how much **responsibility** the subsidiary will be allowed, and how much power will be **centralised**.

Key controls

The main controls that Crashcarts should implement are largely based round the key risks identified in (c). A few general measures for reducing risk are also relevant.

General risk reduction measures

(i) There should be procedures in place for identifying and assessing risks (see (b)) and recording risks in a **risk register**.

(ii) It may be economic to appoint a **risk manager** to monitor risk, and deal with serious risks.

(iii) The board and audit committee should maintain awareness of risks, and carry out a formal **review of the company's risk management processes** at least once a year.

(iv) **Internal audit** should concentrate on the key risk areas.

Subsidiaries

Client risk

(i) The subsidiary should have formal arrangements for dealing with each client, including **someone managing the relationship** and periodically **receiving feedback** on service levels.

(ii) Senior managers should receive reports from each client service manager and be alert for any **common problems in relationships**.

(iii) **Formal tendering procedures** should be in place if contracts are periodically re-advertised. These should involve senior management and operational staff. After every tender, **debriefing procedures** should be in place to ensure lessons are learnt.

(iv) There should also be procedures in place for **monitoring trends** in the market, both in terms of identifying which **clients might be vulnerable** and any **opportunities to win new business**.

Running out of inventory

It may seem that clients running out of inventory is something that the subsidiary has no control over. However the subsidiary should keep full records of when **orders** are **lost** through lack of inventory and **inform the clients**; the subsidiary should not assume that the client will automatically act to deal with the problems.

Information technology risks

(i) **Supplier performance** should be **monitored** by having staff appointed to liaise with the supplier.

(ii) In particular the **security** of the system needs to be kept under review and controls against outside hacking tested regularly.

(iii) **Records** should be kept of all problems that arise, how they were dealt with and what the consequences were.

(iv) Full controls should be maintained at the call centre including **passwords** and **other access controls**, **data confirmation**, **backup**, **virus protection**.

(v) **Insurance** against disasters should be taken out.

You would also have scored marks if you had discussed any of the following controls in relation to the risks faced by the subsidiary.

Human resource risks

(i) A **formal induction programme** and **immediate and appropriate training** should ensure that staff reach full competence as quickly as possible.

(ii) **Morale** can be **improved** by obtaining and acting upon feedback from staff (including exit interviews), appraisals and appropriate reward schemes.

(iii) Potential causes of stress should be monitored including **working conditions** and **health and safety considerations**, and **stress counselling be made available if required**.

Parent

Investment risk

The value of the investment is primarily dependent on **maintaining and expanding the client base**. However the value of the investment should be monitored by obtaining **performance information** on a regular basis.

Control risk

(i) The financial performance of the subsidiary should be compared with targets, **variances highlighted** and action taken to correct problems. The senior managers of the parent should receive information that problems have been corrected.

(ii) Similar procedures should apply to **non-financial performance measures**, in particular the calls received, orders and line items processed.

(iii) **Key decisions**, for example major expenditure by the subsidiary, should be **authorised** by the **parent's board**.

You would also have scored marks if you had discussed any of the following controls in relation to the risks faced by the parent.

Reputation risk

(i) **Reputation risk** will of course be **much reduced** if the **risk measures** taken by the subsidiary are **successful**.

(ii) However the parent should also have **contingency plans** for **damage limitation** should problems arise with the subsidiary. This includes acting through news management to maintain its reputation, and also policies to preserve its own relations with specific clients who have had problems with the subsidiary.

73 VCF

Text references. Chapters 3 and 4 should have helped you cover the organisational and management accounting issues, Chapter 5 the corporate governance problems. Chapters 11 and 12 deal with exchange risks.

Top tips. Part of the purpose of this paper is to prepare you for the TOPCIMA exam, and the situation of a single, dynamic, entrepreneur running a company is one that you may well encounter in TOPCIMA.

In (a) it is difficult to get away from the fact that the company is overwhelmingly dependent on Viktor but you have to try to make maximum use of the information in the scenario. Note that as well as identifying risks you need to evaluate them, so you need to say how strong or effective they are. Don't however suggest improvements as you will be doing that in (b). Your assessment has to be clearly grounded in the details in the scenario, so following the process of scenario analysis that we describe in the front pages is very important. You'll need around ten controls to score maximum marks.

There are various ways you can group the controls in (a). Listing them as they appear in the scenario has the benefit of simplicity; listing the most important controls first demonstrates prioritisation skills. Alternatively you can group the controls under the headings of financial, non-financial qualitative and non-financial quantitative as has been required in other questions. We have started off by looking at the governance and board, then the information systems, then other main aspects (human resources, research and development, asset (patent) protection).

In (b) remember that this report is addressed to the board, in particular of course Viktor. Therefore you need to explain your recommendations in terms that make it likely that the board will accept them. However the company is listed, and therefore needs to introduce more formal systems and not be so dominated by a single individual. There are some fairly obvious indications of poor corporate governance. The risk part can (as often) be tackled by following through the main aspects of the risk management cycle. The discussion on controls does link with (a) although there is not a one-to-one matching. This is because as well as suggesting improvements to existing controls, you also need to recommend new controls.

In (c), you can discuss translation risk as many of VCF's transactions are large and may cause distortions in the year-end accounts. Don't forget the other exchange risks though. The size of the transactions also makes it worth using derivatives as well as simpler methods.

Easy marks. (c) is a fairly straightforward discussion of exchange risks.

Examiner's comments. The key difference between strong and weak answers was how well the corporate governance frameworks discussed were linked in with the scenario. In (a) many students identified controls but did not evaluate them, and some unnecessarily went into detail about controls that were not mentioned in the case. (b) was generally well done, with most candidates making the detailed recommendations required, although a few just described PEST and failed to relate it to the question. In (c) many candidates limited their marks by only discussing hedging instruments, or excessive focus on translation risks.

(a) **Introduction**

The main features of the controls are much dependence on one person, and limitations in management accounting and human resource systems.

Dependence on Viktor

The main control and also the main weakness of the system is its **dependence on Viktor's knowledge and experience**. The biggest danger the company faces is that something happens to Viktor, perhaps as a result of the personal risks he takes, and the other directors and the company are left to cope without him. The board appears to play little if any role in **actively supervising** the **company's activities**. Viktor's reports appear to be unquestioned, and the rest of the board appears to have little involvement in decision-taking.

Budgets and management accounts

Although budgets and management accounting are supposedly used for expense control, it appears that not much notice is taken of them. Viktor does not seem very interested and the company is committed to **sales growth and research and development** rather than profit targets. However although profit figures may have the limitations Viktor identifies, excessive expenditure also may be a factor in the shortages of cash that VCF has experienced.

Sensitivity analysis

The analysis undertaken by Viktor to manage cash flow does **not appear to be linked** in with the **budget and management accounts** being produced. In addition VCF seems very dependent on this **analysis being reasonable**, particularly as costs are tight.

Cost analysis

The system for analysing costs appears to be based on the ideas that costs are driven by sales (costs expressed as % of sales). Many of the costs such as staff costs have **other drivers**, and are also incurred a long time in advance of sales being made, so that the link with sales may be fairly tenuous.

Balanced scorecard

Viktor is making some attempt to use a balanced scorecard to assess performance. A model scorecard focuses on four perspectives:

(i) **Customer satisfaction** is being addressed, but it is difficult to see how it is being measured

(ii) **Internal processes**; as suppliers are responsible for delivery of outsource service, VCF's processes need to be concerned with **how relations with suppliers are managed**. This issue does not appear to be considered very much, and may leave VCF vulnerable to problems with suppliers

(iii) **Innovation and learning**; VCF invests heavily in research and development but how the performance of research and development is assessed is unclear, apart from the vague measure of **maintaining technological leadership**

(iv) **Financial**. Financial measures are a **major element in performance assessment**, but the weakness is that shareholders and the stock market may be more concerned with profit measures than Viktor is

Pricing

The pricing system seems based on **customers' willingness to accept high prices**. If there is a risk of economic recession, customers may not be prepared to pay these prices and VCF will be forced to adopt **more sophisticated pricing methods**.

Assessment of managers

Manager assessment appears to depend on Viktor's personal involvement; there seems to be no formal system of **appraising managers**. This is more of a problem as the achievement of many of the responsibilities of management cannot be measured in monetary terms; other than Viktor's knowledge of competitors, it is difficult to see how standards of **after-sales service and customer satisfaction** are being measured. In addition **cost control** does not appear to be a major element in the assessment of managers' performance.

Human resources

Identifying and dismissing staff who are 'not committed to the company's objectives' may be problematic unless carried out formally, and could result in **unfair dismissal claims and dissatisfaction** amongst staff who remain. VCF appears to rely on the assumption that staff will be happy as they are being paid well, which may not be correct.

Research and development controls

The fact that research and development is not linked into any product but is expensed suggests the link with specific product development lacks clarity and the benefits of R&D activity are uncertain. There seem to be risks that **activity is wasted on projects that provide no benefits**, that **projects fail to deliver the planned benefits** and **costs are not adequately controlled**.

Patent protection

The main control is the institution of legal proceedings but this may be a more effective control for limiting losses than **avoiding the risks of competitors using VCF's technology** in the first place. There do not appear to be any restrictions placed on **staff moving to competitors** and taking knowledge with them that competitors can use; the chances of this happening may be enhanced by Viktor's dismissal of unhappy staff.

(b) **Report**

To: Board, VCF
From: Consultant
Date: 15 September 20X8
Subject: Improvements in governance, risk management and internal controls

Introduction

This report offers recommendations for a number of ways in which systems can be improved, to enhance the efficiency of operations, manage risks more effectively and fulfil investor and stock market operations.

(i) **Corporate governance**

VCF fails to fulfil several aspects of corporate governance best practice. These should not just be seen as box-ticking requirements, but as contributing to the **well-running** of the company and its appeal to shareholders.

Board

The board does not appear to be meeting often enough to be exercising effective supervision over the company. In order to operate well, the board should **meet regularly (more than once a quarter)** and that the board's constitution should specify that certain **major business decisions** such as significant investments must be **formally taken by the whole board**.

Lack of division of responsibilities

Currently the board's operation is completely dependent on Viktor, and serious problems may occur if he is **unable to fulfil his responsibilities**. Viktor acting as **chairman and chief executive** does not fulfil the requirements that there is a clear division of responsibilities at the head of the company. Different directors should act as chairman and chief executive.

Non-executive directors

Although two out of four directors are non-executives, the connections both have with the company means that they are not independent. Governance guidelines state that a majority of non-executive directors should be **independent**, and be able to contribute an **objective view** of the company. In addition there is no indication that either of the non-executive directors has **significant financial expertise**; at least one non-executive director ought to have **an accounting qualification** to be able to analyse the accounting information with appropriate knowledge.

Committees

VCF should operate the committee structure recommended by corporate governance guidance:

(1) **Nomination committee**
A nomination committee, would be made up of **non-executive directors** whose role is to oversee the process for board appointments. The committee needs to consider carefully the **best structure of the board** including the balance between executives and non-executives, the range of skills possessed by the board, the need for continuity and the appropriate size of the board.

(2) **Audit committee**
An audit committee would be made up of **independent non-executive directors**. This committee would be responsible for certain control tasks including **reviewing financial information** and VCF's system of **risk management**, and liasing with, and reviewing, the work of **external audit**.

(3) **Remuneration committee**
A remuneration committee again consists of **independent non-executive directors**. Though salaries paid to directors could well be justified, the **increased transparency** that use of a remuneration committee can mean should deflect possible shareholder criticism of high salary levels.

Views of shareholders

The board ought to **consult regularly** with major shareholders; damaging conflict may arise if shareholders are particularly concerned with short-term profitability.

(ii) **Risk management strategy**

Overall VCF does not appear to have a clear risk management framework. Identifying risks is one of the many responsibilities of Viktor, but risk identification and mitigation will be enhanced if VCF **formalises its risk management procedures**.

Risk appetite

It seems that the directors are prepared to tolerate a high level of risk being taken. However they should consider whether the **returns** the company is achieving **justify the level of risks** being taken. In addition the board should also consider whether the **benefits** of countering certain risks **outweigh the costs** – are the costs and resources required to pursue legal action for infringement of patents worth the benefits?

Risk identification

A key aspect of risk identification is **Viktor's analysis** of likely threats to cash flow. As this is so important, this analysis ought to be **checked by someone else** who reviews the figures, and considers the reasonableness of the assumptions made and whether there are any other possible scenarios that have not been analysed.

Risk acceptance

The decisions made on whether to accept exchange risk have been determined by historical balancing out of gains and losses. VCF should also be considering the **likely future movements of exchange rates**.

Failure to reduce certain risks

VCF does not appear to have mitigated the impact of certain risks. Although the company has tight cash flow quite often, there does not appear to be any identified source of **contingency funds**. There also appear to be **no contingency arrangements** if supplier problems arise.

(iii) **Internal controls**

Overall the control system needs to **depend less on Viktor's involvement** and have more formal procedures in place.

Role of board

Expanded board membership should enable the whole board to exercise more effective supervision over the company. This includes carrying out a formal process of **risk identification**, and **monitoring and considering the effectiveness of internal control**, including a formal annual review of internal control.

Internal audit

A small internal audit department could be established. Not only would it fulfil the requirements of corporate governance guidelines, but it could be used to review the **value for money** of a number of aspects of operations, including supplier procurement, marketing and research and development, thus potentially saving the business considerable costs.

Accounting system controls

The budgeting and management accounts system needs to be reviewed to assess whether all the information produced is necessary. **Comparisons** need to be made of **actual costs with budgeted costs and variances investigated.** A more **formal system of responsibility accounting** needs to be introduced with costs allocated to cost centres and ultimately to individuals for control purposes.

Costing system

The accounting system will also be **more effective** if it is more clearly **linked with cost drivers**, the factors influencing costs. More attempts need to be made to link costs into products or groups of products, for example **allocating marketing costs** across the **products promoted** and assessing how far **research and development costs** can be linked into products. This will provide a better idea of product profitability and enable more informed pricing decisions to be taken. Viktor's knowledge of competitors and other available industry information may enable **benchmarking** against competitor best practice.

You would also have scored marks if you had discussed the following controls.

Scorecard

The system Viktor uses needs to be modified with more consideration being given to **supplier performance** and **cost measures**.

Area managers

The **responsibilities** of area managers need to be **clarified**; there appears to be confusion resulting in the managers being bypassed. The **system for appraising managers** needs to be formalised, and the scope of assessment widened, covering control over costs as well as the aspects currently appraised.

Staff controls

All staff ought also to be **formally appraised** and feedback obtained to ascertain whether staff are happy, since departure of dissatisfied staff to competitors may jeopardise VCF's competitive position. VCF should ensure that staff contracts are drafted as tightly as possible as regards use elsewhere of knowledge of VCF's operations, and joining competitors, although local employment law may limit how effective these restrictions can be.

Summary

Overall the company would benefit from more **formalised governance procedures**, a **wider base of directors** and developments in **accounting**, **human resources** and particularly **risk management systems**.

(c) **Exchange risks**

Transaction risks

VCF may suffer from risks on individual sales transactions. Over the period of time that sales are settled VCF's **currency may strengthen** against the currency in which settlement is being made, which will mean that VCF receives less of its own currency in exchange for the foreign receipts than it anticipated doing when the sales terms were agreed. However, **progress payments and deposits** will mitigate this risk.

Economic risks

VCF will also face **economic exposure** as a result of the effect of longer-term exchange rate movements on its competitiveness. If VCF's local currency strengthens against most of the major currencies in the world, the price increases required to maintain its local currency revenues may make it **less competitive**; 90% of its sales are exports. VCF will be more vulnerable as there will not be an equal and opposite effect on costs, since costs of production are incurred in its local currency.

Translation and accounting risks

VCF may be vulnerable to translation risks adversely affecting the appearance of its balance sheet, as it deals in **large transactions in many currencies** that have to be consolidated into the domestic currency. If VCF does use derivatives (see below), it should consider also how the requirements of **IAS 39** will impact on its balance sheet.

Managing risks

Invoice in own currency

One way of VCF avoiding exchange risks would be to **invoice customers in VCF's local currency**. This would effectively transfer the exchange risk to customers, and thus might threaten VCF's sales if the customers were unwilling to accept the risk.

Changing pattern of receipts

If VCF expected adverse exchange rate changes during the course of particular contracts, it could reduce their impact by **insisting on receiving more income at an earlier stage of the contract**. However again this may be unpopular with customers and threaten sales.

Matching receipts and payments

VCF can reduce the level of foreign exchange risk by **using suppliers** in countries where it makes the **bulk of its sales**. However although exchange risks may cancel out, VCF may incur **increased purchasing and transportation costs**, and also suffer **increased risks** arising from **problems during transportation**.

Forward exchange contracts

VCF could enter **forward exchange contracts** against specific receipts, and be able to exchange the currency it planned to receive at a pre-determined rate. VCF would however face the risk of having to **honour the contracts** even if the customer defaulted.

Money market hedging

VCF could hedge against specific receipts by **borrowing in the same currency** as the receipt, converting the borrowing to its own local currency, placing that amount on deposit, and settling the loan with the sale proceeds. Again there may be problems if the customer defaults.

Derivatives

As VCF is dealing in large transactions, it may be worth incurring the costs of using **futures or options** to hedge individual transactions, provided VCF's currency is exchange-traded. Options would also allow **VCF** to make **gains** if currency movements turned out to be favourable.

Restructuring

VCF may be able to **reduce economic risk** by restructuring where it does business, **expanding in some economies** whilst **contracting in others**, although it may be difficult to get reliable information on which to base strategic decisions. VCF might also **outsource its production facilities abroad** as well as locally.

74 GHI

Text references. Chapters 1, 3 and 15 are all helpful on the different risks the organisation faces; Chapter 6 can be used as sources of hints on controls. Chapter 4 is useful for the issues in (d).

Top tips. Very definitely a question that demonstrates what we said in the front pages about how widely you need to look when considering the risks a company faces. The requirement to discuss the risks briefly means you have to mention their impact as well as identifying what they are. In (a) remember that financial risks include any risks associated with business finance, not just foreign exchange. You could have said something about risks associated with sources of finance used for the investment, although we are not told what they were. Political risk includes risks that might alternatively be classified as legal risks; your answer could have included unstable political conditions or holidaymakers not being welcome in certain countries.

CIMA's feedback on this question defines environmental risk as relating to wider issues such as social concerns and position of competitors, and not just 'green' issues. However 'green' risks (such as the risks of environmental taxes on aircraft fuel or water usage controls) are certainly one of the risks you could have mentioned in this wide-ranging category; other possibilities would be changes in income patterns leading to a shift in demand away from the resorts in which GHI currently operates, or the risk that the demand will be affected by economic recession.

CIMA defines economic exposure as risks that a company's future cash flows will vary with changes in exchange rates. Given the question requirements, this is best thought in terms of longer-term risks, with risks on specific transactions being covered as a financial risk.

Risks that aren't discussed in (a) are the risks of having to pay compensation to customers and the risks relating to the investment value, as they need to be discussed in (b) as key points of comparison. This demonstrates the need for careful planning particularly of answers to Section A questions in this paper, to ensure that you don't repeat material. (b) requires an evaluation, but this is somewhat difficult given the limited financial data. Our answer represents probably the most that can be attempted with the available information. The requirement to evaluate means that the answer to (b) has to focus on the financial statements impact; although the data given might have tempted you to attempt an NPV calculation, this was not what was required.

The answer to (c) takes the investment as decided (ie the hotels are there) and focuses on the impacts on revenues and costs of offering all-inclusive deals. For each risk we've identified the problem and explained how the risk should be monitored and controlled; you should obtain 2-3 marks for each risk discussed for doing this.

(d) may have seemed the most unexpected part of this question, but it demonstrates that P3 is part of CIMA's management accounting stream. If you struggled with it, it may be worth revisiting Text or Passcard chapter 4 on management accounting control systems. The key problem is how to ensure that the new business generated by the hotels results in profit maximisation for the group as a whole **and** fair measurement of the performance of all the subsidiaries. Without transfer pricing adjustments, use of residual income means that the division that operates the hotels effectively bears the whole 'cost' of the investment.

5 marks is not a generous allocation for (e); you would only have time to make a limited number of points and not develop them very much, but you need to make clear what internal audit has to do. The scope of the question is not entirely clear, but CIMA's guidance suggests the answer should have covered the set-up of operations as well as hotel purchase procedures. (It seems that the hotels are being purchased already built rather than constructed from scratch.) It's also debatable whether internal audit's role should be restricted to checking compliance with risk management or whether it should also consider if the existing policies are adequate for dealing with risks. Given the significance of the diversification into hotels, it certainly would seem appropriate for internal audit to consider the adequacy of property purchase procedures, since the procedures in existence may not have been tested before.

Easy marks. Difficult to identify, but (a) has to be reckoned easier than (b) as (a) does not require evaluation of risks. You should hopefully have been able to come up with a number of suggestions for (e).

Examiner's comments. 'The question requires application of knowledge rather than regurgitation of facts as is typical of all Section A questions to date.' The most significant failing was not answering the question, particularly (c) and (e) where many answers were a general discussion of risk. In (a) a number of answers did not classify risks correctly. In (b) many candidates carried out calculations that were not required, whilst failing to discuss the impact on the financial statements. Many answers failed to discuss the performance measurement aspects of (d), although discussion of capital rationing was better. In (e) most students failed to appreciate that the majority of risks would occur before the hotels were opened; some discussed controls rather than internal audit verification of risk management.

(a) **Financial risks**

Cash flow risks

GHI has to **pay hotel providers** and **aircraft operators in advance** on the basis of bookings by customers, but the income to meet these payments may be lower than expected because of cancellations by customers. To some extent this risk has been mitigated by the payment of **refundable deposits** on the four hotels (although requiring a high advance payment), and the severity of the risk will also depend on what GHI can recover from customers who cancel their bookings at the last minute.

Exchange risks

Adverse exchange rate movements may make it more expensive for GHI to **settle with foreign suppliers** in their own currency. This risk will be **matched** to some extent by **income in foreign currency** that GHI receives from customers (for example for excursions during their holiday) but the matching is unlikely to be exact.

Political risks

Disruption due to terrorism threat

The disruption in the UK in August 2006 demonstrates that this risk is potentially very serious and unpredictable. It could affect GHI in two ways; firstly the **consequences of having to pay compensation** to travellers whose flights and therefore holidays have to be cancelled. Even if GHI is insured for this risk, its **insurance premiums** are likely to **rise.** Secondly the disruption and restrictions caused by the threat of terrorism may make customers **less willing to undertake long-haul flights** and result in a **long-term loss of income.**

Unfavourable conditions in country where hotels are being built

GHI may be a victim of **discrimination by local or national government,** for example being subject to onerous local regulations or subsidies being given to local businesses. This is most likely if the country concerned is not a member of the EU. GHI may also suffer **penalties** through ignorance of, and hence non-compliance with, local regulations.

Environmental risks

Change in individual preferences

There is a risk that GHI's role as **intermediary** may become **redundant** as customers use the Internet to book flights and accommodation directly.

Competitor action

GHI's all inclusive deals may not achieve the expected sales increases if competitors offer packages that are more in line with customer requirements. Competitors may for example offer **more flexible packages**, just including flights and accommodation, with customers arranging their own drinks and food. However if GHI's all inclusive deals do prove popular, competitors may themselves offer these deals on more favourable terms.

Economic risks

Long-term devaluation of home currency

GHI must consider the potential impact of its **home currency weakening** against the currencies of all the countries with which it does business. The economic impact will depend on the currency in which GHI **settles its liabilities to suppliers**; it will also depend on whether GHI or its suppliers respond to currency movements by **increasing their prices**.

Long-term devaluation of overseas currencies

GHI will also be vulnerable to a **weakening of the currencies of countries in which it currently does not operate**. The weakening may mean **holidays** in these countries become **cheaper**, and demand therefore shifts towards them and away from the countries in which GHI operates.

(b) (i) **Increased risks resulting from investment in hotels**

Income statement

Revenues

The **increased prices** that GHI charges for the all-inclusive service may be **outweighed** by the **decreased demand** because of the greater expense so that **total income falls**.

Fixed costs

As GHI will be incurring hotel running costs that are not dependent on demand, a **greater proportion of its costs will be fixed** and its **operating gearing will rise**. There is therefore a risk of **much lower profits** if demand is not as predicted.

Compensation risk

GHI will be **fully liable for any shortcomings in its own hotels** and will not be able to obtain the compensation that would have been available from the owners of the hotels that it has previously used. This may result in **increased costs**.

Transaction risk

Dealing with an **increased number of foreign suppliers** directly will result in an **increased number of transactions** and hence possibly an increase in the **impact on the accounts of adverse exchange rate movements**.

Balance sheet

Translation risk

A **fall in the value of the currency** of the country in which the hotels are located will cause a **fall in the balance sheet value** for the hotels, when the investment is translated into GHI's home currency. Although this will only affect cash flow if the hotels were sold, the lower value of the investment may have an adverse impact on GHI's share price if the stock market perceives the fall as a loss in real value.

Property value risk

The properties' value may fall for other reasons as well, for example **excessive wear and tear** or a **collapse in local property prices** resulting possibly from a fall in tourism or unstable local conditions.

Cash flows

Increased working capital requirements

The decision to offer all-inclusive deals will mean that **increased working capital** is needed to fund the business, and **cash flow payments are more frequent**. This means that GHI may face liquidity problems sooner, and the problems are more serious, if demand fails to meet forecast levels.

Reduced funds

The volatility in earnings may result in reduced funds being available directly for further investment, and may also **discourage other potential suppliers of finance** from providing funds.

(ii) **Decreased risks resulting from investment in hotels**

Income statement

Compensation risk

GHI will **not face the risk of paying compensation** on the rooms booked in its hotels due to the rooms having also been booked by its competitors.

Relocation expenses risk

GHI will **not be at risk of incurring transport and other arrangement costs** necessary to move its customers from double-booked hotels into other hotels.

Cancellation costs risk

GHI will **not be liable to the owners of the hotels** it uses for compensation if its customers cancel at the last minute.

Balance sheet

Nil. No investment means that the balance sheet impact is zero.

Cash flow

Timing

There will be **no need to pay deposits** to suppliers in January when seasonal cash flow is weak and GHI possibly is more liable to cash flow problems.

(iii) **Financial evaluation**

Magnitude and timing of cash flows

Other than the compensation payments, it is difficult to evaluate in monetary terms the impact of investing vs not investing. However there are clearly a number of issues that could result in significant differences in the figures in the accounts and cash flow forecasts. GHI will not only have to consider the **magnitude** of these differences, but also whether the timing of cash flows will result in **increased or decreased risk of cash flow difficulties**. Timing differences are likely to be significant given the seasonal nature of the travel business.

Supply of funds

The impact on suppliers of funds will also be considered; will the greater commitments of the investment mean that **funds will be more difficult to obtain** and the **cost of capital therefore rise**.

The consequences of any change in the capital structure necessary to fund the investment will also be considered; given increased volatility of earnings financial risk may significantly increase if debt finance is used to fund the investment.

(c) **Revenues**

Justifying increases

A key threat to revenues is that customers will not think that the extra amount charged for the all-inclusive deals represents good value and will go elsewhere. The risk can be **monitored** by **continuous review** of the number of holidays booked and total revenue, and also **measures of customer satisfaction** through focus groups, questionnaires and external sources such as trade reports.

The risk can be **limited by marketing activity** that targets likely (new) customers and sets out the extra services and the quality offered in the all-inclusive package, so that customers are well-informed of what GHI is offering. GHI should investigate through **market research** offering (and marketing) extra benefits in the package over time to maintain and increase its **differentiation** from competitors.

Maximising revenues

Given the nature of the market, it is unlikely that GHI will be able to obtain full revenues on all the inclusive holidays it sells. However unsold holidays increase the risk that fixed costs won't be covered. GHI can **monitor the threat** of cut price holidays by maintaining awareness of the **deals being offered by competitors** and also **take-up of its own packages.**

GHI can **limit the risk** by introducing **flexibility** into the deals it offers that is dependent on time of booking. Last minute deals will be worthwhile for GHI if the income makes a positive contribution, but GHI needs to ensure that it is not offering generous discounts too early when it could still be selling full-price holidays.

Costs

Consumption by customers

The all-inclusive deals offered may mean a risk of significant costs arising from customers eating and drinking excessive amounts; ultimately the income received may not cover the costs of supplying them. Clearly **expenditure and consumption of each category of food and drink consumable** needs to be **budgeted**, **actual figures compared and variances highlighted**.

GHI can **limit the risk** by **control over the portion sizes** that are given to customers, or **providing buffets** which customers are only allowed to visit once each meal. Controlling drinking may be more difficult, and perhaps can be best achieved by **limiting bar opening hours**.

You would also have scored marks if you had discussed any of the following risks.

Procurement policies

GHI faces the risks that costs are higher than necessary because it is **not obtaining supplies on the best terms available**. It should **compare budgeted costs of its supplies against actual costs** and also against what costs could be if other suppliers were used.

GHI can **limit procurement risk by only dealing with certain approved suppliers.** These should be chosen by a **tendering process**, and GHI should seek **significant discounts** in return for long-term commitment to suppliers. **Delivery requirements** must also be established in writing.

Theft by staff

GHI also faces the risk of losses through theft by staff of inventory. This risk is difficult to monitor as the all-inclusive nature of the package means that **consumption is not directly matched with cash receipts**. Again **monitoring consumption** of **each category** of food and drink might highlight problems.

GHI can **limit the risk by limiting access to inventory** to certain individuals, and **obtaining references** for staff who are in positions of trust. **Recording customer orders and matching these with consumption** would be a substitute for not being able to match with cash receipts. Limited internal audit work, particularly surprise visits to count inventory and reconcile with records, should help reduce the risk.

(d) **Impact on performance measurement of subsidiary that owns hotels**

Residual income is profit minus a charge for capital employed in the period (cost of capital × capital employed).

Clearly the **operating income** from the hotels will impact on the residual income of the subsidiary that operates them; the investment will also affect the subsidiary's pre-tax income due to the **depreciation charge and possible translation loss. Residual income** will also be affected by the **amount invested**; the **larger investment** will mean a **larger deduction from profits** and hence a **smaller residual income figure.** Residual income may be affected by an **increase in the risk-adjusted cost of capital** because of the increased risks of the hotel development. Again this will result in a **larger deduction from profits** and **smaller residual income.**

Impact on performance measurement of other subsidiaries

The other companies in the group may receive **benefits of extra income** without having their own residual income affected by the cost of the investment and the extra risks. The airline subsidiary may benefit from more people flying, the retail outlets possibly through more people booking holidays. A system of **transfer pricing** will be required to correct the situation where the costs and risks are just impacting upon the hotel-owning subsidiary.

Capital allocation

Capital allocation may be affected by **changes in residual income** but strategic necessity may be a more significant factor, with the hotel investment being undertaken because it will provide **most strategic benefit** to the group. GHI's managers will need to decide whether the investment in the hotels should result in **changes in capital allocation**. They should consider what will happen if further investment is needed in the hotels, and whether more capital should be allocated to the subsidiaries whose business is linked most closely with the hotel subsidiary.

If capital has to be **rationed**, the group's board will need to show clearly how the **capital allocation will benefit the group** as a whole.

(e) **Risk and control**

Internal audit will seek assurance that business risks are being **managed effectively,** and the controls designed to counter those risks are **operating properly.**

Property purchases

(i) **Confirm that internal procedures for choosing sites and negotiating purchase terms** have been **followed**.

(ii) **Consider whether evaluation of possible sites** has been **sufficient** in terms of number of sources of evidence used and information obtained about each site.

(iii) **Confirm that appropriate legal advice has been sought** in connection with the property purchase and associated matters such as planning permission and that advice given has been **followed**.

(iv) **Consider** whether **investigation of possible sources of finance** has been **sufficient** and **reasons for choosing selected sources** have been **adequately documented**.

Organisation and operation of hotels

(i) **Confirm organisation and staff reporting structure** has been **established** by reviewing organisation charts.

(ii) **Confirm** that evidence exists of GHI's **compliance with health and safety and employment regulations.**

(iii) **Confirm** the **existence of controls over asset security** and **evaluate their adequacy**, by observation or attempting to bypass them.

Review of hotels

(i) **Confirm that all necessary accounting responsibilities have been clearly allocated**.

(ii) **Evaluate adequacy of data that will be provided** about the performance of hotels.

(iii) **Plan timetable and programme** of internal audit work.

75 BLU

Text references. Chapters 4 and 16 on information, Chapter 7 on audit planning.

Top tips. This question is more narrowly focused than previous case studies, and the emphasis on the quality of information differentiates it from most questions on information technology systems where there is more focus on protecting the technology and the information.

The key to doing well in (a) is to try to get as much mileage out of the scenario as possible, adopting a questioning, what's wrong with this, approach. You also need to remember what you've learnt about investment appraisal in P2, particularly the assumptions underlying NPV calculations and also how calculations should be modified when capital is rationed.

The perspective to adopt in (b) is to ask what evidence would lead the auditors to consider, when planning the audit, that an area was of high risk.

Your answer in (c) should link to the problems you've identified in (a); remember to justify the controls. Some of the problems in (a) indicate wider difficulties, such as problems with the whole budgeting and forecasting system and it's fine to discuss controls over these.

Easy marks. If you progress methodically through the elements of the NPV calculation and then think what other considerations should affect investment decisions, that part of (a) shouldn't have been too bad. Overall however this is a tough question.

Examiner's comments. Students must use the reading time to see what's being asked. General answers unrelated to the scenario won't score well.

Problems in (b) included a number of students misreading the question and going into great detail about examining invoices and checking casts. Others produced general answers relating to audit planning, or answers that related to external audit. Students needed to discuss the approach to the audit, including the scope of the audit, and relate their answer to the scenario.

In (c) students often identified controls but failed to gain any of the 10 marks available for describing their benefits. Some students repeated their answer to (a) in (c).

(a) **Investment appraisal risks**

The fundamental risk relating to investment appraisal is that incorrect decisions are made, that

- Investments are made when they should not have been, or are not made when they **should have been**
- When choosing between two investments, the **wrong investment is chosen**

A number of factors affect the decision to invest.

Choice of cost of capital

The historic cost of capital has been used, and this cost **may no longer reflect the risks** BLU now faces nor the **attitude to risk** of its finance suppliers. Choice of an **excessively large cost of capital** may affect the investment decision, as it can lead to a bias towards investments with high short-term returns, against investments with returns further in the future.

Inappropriate appraisal techniques

The Board used total NPV as the criteria when capital is rationed. This fails to take into account the **different level of investment** involved in the two projects, **different funding levels** required, and also the **different lives**; would the manufacturing equipment require replacement sooner than the distribution equipment. Other appraisal techniques such as payback or accounting rate of return should have been used to give a different perspective.

Inappropriate time horizon

Five years may be a fairly arbitrary, **short-term time horizon** to consider investments. The choice between the two investments might have come up with a different outcome if the time horizon had been longer.

Consideration of alternative scenarios

The Board's decision appears to have taken on the basis of a very simple financial justification without any consideration of the **assumptions and data** supporting the forecast. Only one projection appears to have been considered for the CNC investment and presumably one projection for the distribution system investment as well. This implies only **one set of assumptions** has been used when appraising each investment, whereas there may be other, perhaps more likely, assumptions that could have been used.

Consideration of strategic issues and risk

In addition the Board has also taken the decision largely on financial grounds and has ignored other strategic criteria that may be relevant, particularly as the Board is not choosing between two identical choices but between **manufacturing equipment** and a **distribution system**. Risk has only been considered in the context of the long-used cost of capital. The Board does not appear to consider whether each major investment decision is **consistent with the risk appetite** that the directors believe BLU should have and that is **consistent with the overall strategy** they wish to pursue.

Board approval procedures

Certain decisions that the Departments have taken that are **integral to the investment appraisal** should have been considered by the Board. The production system has been chosen on the basis of the Sales Department's plans for **expansion of the customer base**; is the Board happy that these plans are consistent with BLU's overall strategic objectives. The benefits and costs will also be very dependent upon the supplier chosen; the decision about which supplier to choose should have been made by the Board rather than the Production Department.

Information systems risk

The main risk is that the information system produces **inappropriate or misleading data** for the board to use in the investment appraisal process. The data supplied largely appears to follow simple numerical patterns (sales income up by £1 million, variable costs by £300,000, working capital by £100,000) each year, indicating that not enough thought may have been given to estimating the required figures.

The following factors are relevant to this risk.

Use of historic data

Some of the estimates supplied have been based on the assumptions that **historic patterns will continue** or will change in simple ways. The Production Department's capacity forecast is based on past experience. The Finance Department uses historic cost information to update standard costs with limited adjustments for increases in prices. However use of historic data takes no account of **changes in production processes**, **use of different suppliers** or **efficiency** that may result from use of the new equipment.

Consistency of data

There are a number of ways in which inconsistencies could occur, or have occurred, in the data.

(i) **Sales and marketing data**
The Market Research Department appears to **accept the Sales Department's estimates** without considering whether they are **consistent** with its own knowledge.

(ii) **Sales and production data**
The figures supplied by the Sales Department take account of its plans to win new customers, and presumably if the company does win new customers, the **product mix may well change**. However the Sales Department's data has been compared with data complied by the Production Department on the basis that the past product mix will continue.

(iii) **Different assumptions**
More generally, some estimates could be based on a **best-case scenario**, others on a **realistic** scenario. If for example the Sales Department took an optimistic view of how successful they were likely to be in winning new customers, these figures would be compared in the NPV calculation with the estimates of labour and materials cost that have been complied on the basis of the increases that will probably occur. This will make the NPV calculation give an overly favourable picture of what cash flows are likely to be.

Objectivity of data

Managers are well aware of the criteria the Board uses to appraise investments. As they appear to have some leeway in terms of the assumptions on which their forecasts are based, they may be tempted to bias their forecasts by using **generous assumptions** for projects that they believe will yield high short-term returns and hence high bonuses, and stricter assumptions for investments of a longer-term nature that will have less short-term impact on cash flows.

Role of Finance Department

There are a number of checks that should be occurring within the information systems, but do not appear to be.

(i) The Finance Department appears to accept and use the information supplied by the other departments without checking it for **reasonableness**.

(ii) The Finance Department's role as a monitor could be called into question by its involvement in the investment appraisal process, as Finance staff are making significant judgements on the level of working capital required. It may be questionable whether the Finance Department is acting as an **advocate** of new investment or as a **validator** of the cases made by other departments.

(b) **Risk-based approach**

The internal auditors should focus on the key risks of the capital investment process and the information systems that support it. The auditors will be concerned with **areas and decisions** that are **particularly prone to error**, **distortions** or **uncertainty** and areas and decisions where the **consequences of an error could be serious**, for example here deciding to invest in a project the costs of which significantly outweigh its benefits. They will also be concerned with the information systems as reliable information is fundamental to BLU's operations.

Which investments to audit

Capital investments of this sort are likely to be few in number and very significant in their impact on operations. Internal audit should therefore aim for **100% coverage** of those undertaken, verifying the key elements of the calculations (cost of capital) and seeing whether other appraisal techniques or sensitivity analysis give different perspectives on the appraisal.

Assessment of information provided

Assessment of the quality of information provided will be a key part of the audit. The internal audit should focus on the elements of the information supplied that are most likely to be prone to error or distortion. The auditors can assess what these are by considering the following.

(i) **Past performance**
Internal auditors should be aware of how accurate **previous forecasts and budgets** made by the various departments have been, and focus on departments whose forecasts have been **unreliable** in the past.

(ii) **Results of post-completion audits**

Post-completion audits should have taken place after previous major investments. Internal auditors should review the results of those, and in particular whether **any improvements** were made to any parts of the information systems or information supply processes. They should ascertain whether these improvements have been implemented, and if they have not been, what has been the effect on the information supplied.

(iii) **Subjective and uncertain areas**

Internal auditors will be more concerned with **uncertain areas** such as market demand that involve estimates and interpretation. Internal audit will need to see that **appropriate methodologies** have been followed in making assessments of factors such as future demand – are they are in line with established practice. The auditors will also need to **compare investments** that have been **accepted** with **investments** that have been **rejected at the same time**, and see if the information on both was compiled using **consistent data and assumptions**.

Supplier choice

Supplier choice is a particularly high-risk area because the criteria used to choose suppliers appears to be very subjective. The audit will therefore need to consider the reasonableness of the criteria used, and whether the criteria were applied **fairly to the supplier chosen**, and **consistently to all the suppliers that were rejected**.

As the success of the investment is very dependent upon the **reliability of the system** chosen, internal audit work needs to consider the **adequacy of the guarantees given by the supplier**, and ascertain the **adequacy of the system's maintenance arrangements**.

Independence

There is a possibility that staff involved in internal work might also be involved in **Finance Department assessment** of possible investments. It is therefore important to ensure when planning the internal audit that no-one audits their own work; it would be better if the staff responsible for the internal audit of capital investment were not involved in assessing capital investments at all.

(c) **Investment appraisal**

Choice of cost of capital

The Board should reconsider the cost of capital used every time a major investment is undertaken. This should change in the light of the **changes in business risk** that a major investment will cause, also the **changes in financial risk** if BLU's financing mix changes as a result of undertaking the investment.

Appraisal techniques

Single or multi-period capital rationing techniques should have been applied to investments when capital is rationed. These take into account the **efficiency of the investments**, that is the level of returns generated by each pound of scarce capital.

Time horizons

Investment appraisals should be extended over **more than five years**, and the board should assess carefully the implications of a longer horizon appraisal showing a significantly different result to a five-year horizon appraisal.

Consideration of alternative scenarios

When appraising investments, the Board needs to consider various scenarios built on different **possible assumptions**. From this the directors should be able to ascertain the **range of possible outcomes** and the **likelihood** of both projects showing a **negative NPV**.

Consideration of strategic issues and risks

More sophisticated scenario analysis would enable the Board to **reconcile the investment decision** with the **level of risk** that it is prepared to **tolerate**, objectives for growth in sales and profits and other strategic considerations. For example the Board might have been prepared to invest in the manufacturing equipment on the basis that it yielded good prospects of a higher return, even if the risk of a negative NPV was greater than for the distribution system.

Board approval procedures

The Board needs to move away from a simplistic attitude to investment appraisal and to adopt a more **questioning attitude** towards the information it receives. If investments are meant to achieve increases in sales and profits the Board needs to consider **how** the desired increases will be achieved. If for example BLU needs to attract a significant number of new customers in order to achieve its strategic objectives, the Board should certainly have considered whether the new manufacturing equipment or new distribution system was more likely to meet the requirements of the potential customers. The Board also needs to have **input into all the key decisions** involved in the investment, for example deciding between suppliers.

Information systems

Use of historic data and budgeting

The reliance on historic data calls into question BLU's whole system of budgeting and forecasting. BLU's system of budgeting and forecasting should be a **zero-based system**. This means that expenditure should be justified in its entirety each time a budget or forecast is produced rather than historic patterns assumed to continue with maybe minor adjustments. A zero-based system will force managers to take into account efficiencies that are expected to be produced by a major new investment, and take appropriate action.

Consistency of data

Each department that uses data supplied by another department should assess whether it is **consistent with its own knowledge** of the business and industry environment, and the data it prepares itself is prepared on a **consistent basis** with the data that it has been given. The Finance Department should review the forecasts supplied by other departments and check whether they have been produced using common assumptions.

Objectivity of data

Linking with the changes to the overall forecasting and budgeting processes, departments should supply greater detail of the **assumptions and bases** used and the justification for using them, and also be required to supply forecasts using alternative assumptions (for example best-case, worse-case).

Role of Finance Department

The Finance Department should be more **sceptical of the data** that is supplied to it by other departments. It should review the assumptions made in each forecast, and question assumptions that appear to be unrealistic or have been prepared without sufficient care, for example adding a simple mark-up onto historical costs or assuming that fixed costs will be unchanged for a number of years. These steps should improve the realism of the forecasts supplied by the information systems.

Internal audit

Internal audit work, including post-completion audits on all major investments, is important in ensuring that **improvements in systems are identified and implemented**.

76 ACB

Text references. Chapters 1, 2, 4, 11, 15, 17 and 18.

Top tips. The techniques for analysing scenarios covered in the front pages are very helpful for answering this question. Seeing first of all what the requirements say will mean that you ask yourself as you read the scenario to which question part each piece of information relates; this will help you make best use of that information.

The best way to answer questions like (a) systematically is to use one of the risk management models. We've used CIMA's, but equally validly you could have used the COSO model. However even if you didn't use a risk management model you would still have scored high marks if you mentioned the elements stressed by the examiner, namely risk appetite, assessment, treatment, responsibility, reporting and monitoring. One trap in (a) is that you spend most of the time stating what the stages should be and insufficient time on evaluating what ACB was doing; about two thirds of the marks would be available for the evaluation.

By integrating the two question requirements, our answer is time-efficient and also clearly ties in the risk management cycle to what ACB is actually doing.

It is doubtful in (a) whether you can conclude that ACB has a good approach. The company's risk appetite hasn't been clearly defined, and the board's approach to risk does not appear to understood within the company. The delegation of responsibilities means that the specialists are effectively monitoring themselves, thus clearly lacking objectivity. The failure to review risks actively as opposed to maintaining the risk register is also a clear weakness, highlighted in the examiner's report.

In (b) we've structured our answer to start with the strategic risks, then going through the various stages of the supply, delivery, production and sale processes before finishing off with the information risks that relate to the decisions that are made and the monitoring that takes place. Discussion of the probability of the risks materialising and the seriousness of the impacts will help you score well on a discussion of risks like this.

Your answer needs to demonstrate why the controls are important. You may have found it difficult to evaluate controls of which there is little or no detail; generally you have to assume that if you're not told about a control you think should be there, then it's not being operated, which is therefore a potential weakness.

You should certainly get 2 marks for each well-explained, relevant risk category you discuss, and a further 2 marks for suggesting appropriate controls to counter those risks.

Marks in (c) were split evenly between the explanation of risk treatment and discussion of its benefits. This meant that you would have gained credit for giving the detail of the four main methods. Note the discussion on benefits is mainly about control and governance, with links to strategy also being very significant.

Easy marks. The examiner's comments, together with experience of other exams, suggest that most students are able to identify lots of risks in a scenario like this.

Examiner's comments. Surprisingly (a) was poorly answered, with many candidates missing out the review and monitoring stages, and confining their answers to identification and assessment. Most candidates answered (b) well, although some answers lacked structure and consisted of a list of all possible risks. Answers that were closely related to the scenario scored well. Many answers to (c) were good; however others lacked detail, consisting of a list of short bullet points that failed to earn marks.

(a) **CIMA's risk management cycle**

CIMA's risk management cycle, which demonstrates that risk management should be seen as a continuous loop, will be used to analyse the steps ACB is taking.

Establish risk management group and set goals

ACB's establishment of a risk management group of senior staff is an important part of managing risks, since the group can focus on building on ACB's overall risk management framework and prescribe **methods of risk management.** However aspects of the framework lack clarity. In particular the board does not appear to have defined the company's **risk appetite**; this will determine for example what strategies are appropriate, with some risks being accepted without risk limitation measures being taken, since they are well within the company's appetite.

Identify risk areas

The risk management group's methods for **identifying risks** are not defined. The key risks identified should clearly **link into ACB's strategy and its risk appetite.** The group should also be monitoring changes in the business environment that will influence risk levels, for example new competitor activity or information technology developments.

Understand and assess the scale of risks

The risk management group appears to be doing this, using the **standard likelihood-consequences method** of assessing risk.

Develop risk response strategy

Again the **risk management group** has responsibility for doing this, although its role is limited, partly by the general policy imposed by the board of diversification, partly because deciding on action to manage the **IT and treasury risks** is **delegated.** The risk management group should at least be **reviewing the decisions taken by the specialist departments** but this does not appear to be happening.

Implement strategy and allocate responsibilities

Operational managers will have responsibility for implementing risk responses, and the existence of a risk management group should not be seen as limiting the role of operational managers in this respect.

Implement and monitor controls

Clearly directors and managers have introduced controls to counter key risks in different areas. These include controls aimed at addressing various threats to the IT system, and Treasury department consideration of the need for different methods of hedging depending on risk levels. There are also controls over distribution, another key area for the business. However controls appear to be lacking in other significantly risky areas, in particular **day-to-day management of the contracts with suppliers**. Also internal audit and the audit committee seem to focus heavily on **controls over financial information**; IT and treasury appear to be left to manage their control systems without these effectively monitored.

Review and refine process and do it again

The last stage, the **double loop feedback** stage, should ensure that risk management continuously improves. However there is no indication that **changes are made to the risk management process** as a result of **weaknesses** that have been identified and that highlight problems with the process.

(b) **Economic and political risks**

Risks

ACB appears to be vulnerable to a long-term loss of sales. This is partly due to **industry stagnation** but there may also be a **significant threat from competitors.** The cycle time of 18 months may mean that ACB loses customers to competitors who can promise a shorter lead-time. ACB may also be affected by political disruption, either to sales or purchases. Changes in government may lead to tighter controls on aircraft sales because of global warming concerns. **Political turmoil** may disrupt supply or distribution arrangements.

Controls

ACB appears to be aiming to **continuously improve performance**, which should lessen the threat from competitors. However it does not appear to be carrying out active competitor monitoring. There is also no sign that the board is regularly considering **how to respond to the changing environment**, and whether to change strategy by diversifying what it manufactures.

Supply risks

Risks

ACB is incurring very significant **financial and reputation risks** relating to supply. The **complexity of its supply arrangements** means that disruption to one of its many suppliers could lead to construction being delayed on the whole aircraft. This risk is increased by using **just-in-time methods** that mean spare inventory will not be held for emergencies. The consequences of disruption could be very serious if they lead to delays in manufacture, as ACB will suffer **financial penalties** and also a **loss of reputation** for prompt delivery, deterring future customers.

Controls

ACB appears to have stringent arrangements in place for selecting suppliers, with **selection procedures** covering all key areas. **Supply contracts** are designed to encourage **continuous improvements in efficiency** by suppliers. However there is no evidence of **ongoing monitoring of supplier performance**, nor of **penalties** being imposed if suppliers fail to deliver. There also do not appear to be any **contingency arrangements** for obtaining supplies from other sources if suppliers don't deliver.

Distribution risks

Risks

The distances involved may mean that ACB is vulnerable to **disruption of the transport arrangements from its suppliers to its factory** due, for instance, to adverse weather or political problems. The consequences are the same as for supply problems, with **assembly being delayed** and the **finished product not being available** on time.

Controls

ACB appears to have stronger controls over delivery of components than supply, with the **satellite tracking technology** being used. Using one distribution company rather than many suppliers should make managing the relationship simpler, although again there is no evidence of how the company's **performance is measured** and what actions are taken if it fails to perform satisfactorily. In particular ACB does not seem to have obtained **guarantees** that distribution will be effectively monitored if the satellite technology breaks down. Again the just-in-time arrangements mean that there is **no contingency inventory** if problems occur.

Quality risks

Risks

Loss of quality is a risk with potentially the severest possible consequences. A **lack of quality** could cause a collapse in ACB's **reputation and sales** and worst of all lead to it being **closed down** by its government.

Controls

The **regular inspections** by the Agency should help to ensure quality, although ACB would not want these inspections to identify any problems since they might jeopardise its licence. We are not told anything about ACB's **internal procedures**. Clearly however it must have internal procedures in place as a condition of its licence, and presumably also these have been effective in the past since we are told ACB has always **maintained the highest standards.**

Facilities risks

Risks

Damage to any area of the factory may cause **disruption to production**, but perhaps ACB is most vulnerable if its aircraft hanger is put out of action. ACB may have **great difficulties** in **finding an alternative location** to assemble the aircraft.

Controls

We are not told anything about these. ACB needs to have procedures in place to counter natural threats such as **fire and flood, also disruption to power supplies**, should they arise. The factory should be protected by **24 hour security**. ACB also needs to have **contingency plans** if an area of the factory is put out of action, however difficult it may be to find somewhere else.

Bad debt risks

Risks

The payment arrangements may leave ACB vulnerable to **undertaking extensive production** for which **customers never pay**. Payment for the final 60% is not due until the end of the contract, and the length of the contract may mean that customers who appeared financially sound when the contract was signed are in trouble by the time the final payment is due. This risk is increased by the depression affecting the airline industry. ACB will have difficulty limiting losses from **customer bankruptcies** by selling completed aircraft to other airlines, since its key competitive advantage is the customisation that it offers.

Controls

The policy of **diversification** should reduce the size of loss to some extent, since it should mean that ACB is not dependent on sales to one, or a few, airlines and hence particularly vulnerable to one of its key customers collapsing. However there seems to be **no monitoring of customers' ability to pay** before contracts are signed. There also seems to be **no variation in contract terms** depending on the **credit rating** of the customer, with a higher % of sales price being paid as progress payments for customers judged to be higher credit risks.

Currency risks

Risks

ACB is subject to exchange risks because it **sets its prices in its customers' own currencies** and it **agrees contracts with suppliers in their own currencies**. For each customer and supplier there may be adverse exchange rate movements during the production process, which result in ACB receiving less or paying more in its own currency.

Controls

ACB does not appear to consider possibly the most effective way of limiting exchange risks, which is to **invoice customers in its own currency** and negotiate to pay suppliers also in its own currency. There appear to be controls in place for **identifying unacceptable risks** when **forward contracts** are used. The use of **matching** to deal with smaller risks is a doubtful control, although the number of countries in which suppliers and customers are located may mean that a hedge can be found for most risks. In addition, as mentioned in (a), the Treasury department's work does not appear to be **effectively monitored**.

> You would also have scored marks if you had discussed any of the following risks and controls.
>
> **Information technology risks**
>
> **Risks**
>
> ACB is vulnerable to the risks that the IT system will **fail to produce the information the board and managers need** to manage the business, either because the system is inadequate for their purposes or because it breaks down. It may also be vulnerable to problems with security and in particular **unauthorised access to data.**

Controls

The ERPS and EDI systems chosen should have the potential to **supply all the data required**. They should produce **custom-designed reports** and adopt an **integrated whole of business of approach.** The information technology department appears to have relevant controls in place, including **contingency arrangements** that are not apparent elsewhere in the organisation. However, there seems to be **no effective monitoring** of what the specialist department is doing by the **board or risk management group.** We are also not told about **recruitment and personnel controls.** It is particularly important that senior management ensures these controls are effective in the specialist departments, because of the risk management responsibilities that they have.

Accounting information risks

Risks

If the system produces unrealistic or inaccurate costing information, there is a danger that prices will be set at **inappropriate levels.** If prices are set **too high**, this means that ACB will be **more vulnerable to loss of sales to competitors**; if prices are too low, then the chances of **making losses** on products are increased. There is also the risk that the system will produce incorrect information for the financial accounts that will not therefore be **true and fair.**

Controls

ACB seems to place appropriate emphasis on financial performance information being accurate, with the **audit committee** and **internal audit** spending significant time on it. However, pricing is determined by estimates of costs occurring over a year ahead. There does not appear to be **monitoring of the accuracy of previous estimates of labour and overhead costs** (supplier costs are fixed by contracts), although **customer profitability analysis** will provide some indications. In addition although activity-based costing should provide a realistic method of allocating costs to products, it does not guarantee that **overheads** are being **controlled;** perhaps the emphasis on accuracy of data has meant there is too little focus on using the information for control purposes.

(c) **Risk treatment**

Risk response or treatment involves selecting appropriate measures to deal with risks that have been identified. What is an appropriate response will depend on the **risk appetite** of the company and the **likelihood and consequences** of each risk materialising. There are four basic types of risk response, corresponding to different levels of likelihood and consequences.

(i) **Risk acceptance**
This is appropriate for insignificant risks with **low likelihood and consequences**. The costs of dealing with the risk will not be worth the benefits of reducing or avoiding it.

(ii) **Risk transfer**
This is appropriate for risks that are **unlikely to materialise,** but have **serious consequences** if they do. The most important method of risk transfer is insurance.

(iii) **Risk reduction**
This is best for risks that will probably **materialise but will not have serious consequences.** Appropriate measures such as contingency planning will be used to limit the financial impact.

(iv) **Risk avoidance**
This would be chosen for **high likelihood-serious consequences risks**. Action ultimately may involve ceasing to undertake business that generates these sorts of risk.

Benefits of risk treatment

Clearly defined risk treatment policies and procedures have the following benefits.

Links to strategy

As we have discussed in (a), **appropriate risk treatment policies** are an integral part of risk management processes. The board needs to ensure that they are compatible with the company's strategy

Minimises shocks and costs

Treating risks appropriately should mean that the company is **prepared** for them when they do arise, and should avoid the costs that occur from failing to take action or taking the wrong action.

Individual accountability

Establishing individual accountability for managing specific risks should be easier if there are clear policies in place.

Effective monitoring

Clear procedures should enable **board monitoring** to be **more effective. Feedback and communication** to the board that **risks** have been **addressed** should be built into the risk treatment process. Clear policies will also provide **yardsticks** for internal and external audit to use for **independent verification work.**

Good corporate governance

Appropriate risk treatment policies help directors fulfil the **requirements of corporate governance guidelines** to establish appropriate control mechanisms for dealing with risks, monitor risks themselves by regular review and a wider annual review, and disclose their risk management policies in the accounts.

77 NOP

Text references. Chapters 1, 2, 9, 10

Top tips. This question is a reminder that one aim of P3 is to help you prepare for TOPCIMA. The scenario is a scaled down version of what you'll see in TOPCIMA, with plenty of information about the business that you have to analyse, and different proposals for change that you have to evaluate.

(a) requires some quite wide thinking about risks. You need to use knowledge from all three Strategic level exams; P6 knowledge will help you consider branding, marketing and procurement and P9 knowledge will help you discuss treasury. The main things to keep focusing on are the risks to shareholders – how do the risks limit or threaten sales? How might competitors benefit at NOP's expense? How could the risks result in increased costs, particularly unwarranted increases in costs (such as excessive directors' remuneration)? Note that our discussion under a number of headings includes increased costs of control resulting from the need to avoid more serious risks.

Ethics and reputation risk are significant elements in (a). NOP has maybe further to fall if it (or its suppliers) get caught out in unethical behaviour, and the fashion market may be particularly influenced by ethical consumption. However not having an ethical reputation at all can also create major risks (see Question 4 in this mock exam for an example).

Feedback on the exam suggested that some students struggled to come up with risks under some of the headings. Others by contrast generated plenty of ideas but ran into time problems as they spent too long on Question 1; certainly a risk on any question in this exam that involves identifying risks, where you can generate lots of ideas. In these circumstances you have to be **strict** on time; it's better to score 20 out of 30 on (a) and leave more time to obtain all the easier marks on the optional questions.

(b) (i) picks up the integral links between strategy and risk. Complexity means that central management coordination becomes a more significant control. In (b) (ii) we have tried to show the relative merits of the two proposals by discussing them both under the same headers. The key question is will the measures taken convince the stock market that the change in direction it regards as necessary has been made? Cost leadership and product differentiation, which you will have covered in P6, are important in this part.

Easy marks. The report format and the points in (b) (i) should have been straightforward marks.

Examiner's comments. (a) was done poorly by many students. In particular the discussion of branding and marketing strategy, and design and procurement were very weak and lacking in depth. Answers showed a lack of general business knowledge and a lack of awareness of recent business news. Many of the issues discussed in the question had been covered in the press in the last couple of years. Students would have benefited from thinking about the issues from the consumers' viewpoint. Discussion of sizing, culture, and ensuring comparable quality worldwide would all have gained marks. Discussion of social and environmental issues was better, although again many answers would have been improved if students had read the business press.

Answers to (b) were also weak. Many students failed to discuss risk ownership and instead discussed the control environment generally. Answers also needed to focus on the effect of the proposals on the share price fall and overall risk. Many students failed to mention the share price fall and instead produced general answers unrelated to the proposals.

Students should also remember that the examiner expects knowledge from managerial level papers to be used in P3. In particular use of knowledge from P5 *Integrated Management* would have improved many answers to (a).

(a) (i) **Branding and marketing strategy**

Risks of wrong branding

NOP's designers appear to have quite a **narrow branding strategy aimed at particular segments**. This requires good understanding of the different locations, ages, tastes, income and expectations of different customer bases. While NOP may be able to build this understanding up over time, it may be **less able to adapt to changes in customer profiles** and this may **threaten its market share**. In particular, the nature of the fashion industry means the **product life cycle** may be short; NOP's brands may become unfashionable, being seen as too safe by the youth market to which it is trying to appeal.

Risks of targeting wrong sector

NOP may have limited scope to expand at the upper end of the market, because of the presence of already **well-established quality labels**. NOP may need to offer products of significantly higher quality than these labels to expand its market, and this may be difficult given the other problems it faces.

Marketing risks

At present there does not seem to be a clear marketing strategy. Whatever the strategy, there is a **cultural risk** that the strategy will not be modified for the different worldwide markets and **marketing costs will generate insufficient sales**. The risk that marketing costs do not lead to increases in sales may be increased by the involvement of various **joint venture partners**. NOP may lack control over the messages that the joint venture partners give and hence the marketing messages may **not be consistent with the brand images and what is promised**. Also even if NOP introduces a new marketing strategy that works in the short-term, competitors may imitate it quickly and NOP soon lose competitive advantage.

Brand integrity

NOP may face the risk of having its products **copied illicitly** in certain areas of the world. Copying is rife in many of the areas in which NOP operates.

Reputation risks

NOP appears to be operating a 'me-too' strategy in design, following what the major fashion houses are doing. Whilst this may mean that they utilise designs that are likely to be popular, NOP will **not have a reputation for innovation**. This may limit potential sales growth, as a follower strategy may be difficult to market.

(ii) **Design and procurement strategy**

Competitor risks

Using the ideas of the top fashion houses may not be suitable for some of NOP's many brands, and sales from some of the brands may be **vulnerable to competitors** who are exploiting the market segment more imaginatively.

Cultural risks

The design strategy of only having London designers may limit the opportunities for development of brands. It ignores the creative potential in areas such as Thailand and Singapore that may be **better able to generate ideas** that appeal to NOP's non-European markets. **Costs of design** in these areas may also be **lower**.

Supply chain risks

To ensure quality is maintained, NOP may well be looking to **develop long-term relationships with suppliers**. These relationships may be jeopardised if there is **pressure on costs**. Not only may suppliers end contracts and switch legitimately to **supplying NOP's competitors**, NOP is at risk from disgruntled suppliers passing **confidential information about NOP's designs to competitors**.

Supplier quality risks

NOP faces the problem of monitoring quality in a situation where it has less control because the supplier is outsourced. Because much of the fashion trade is **seasonal**, even small delays due to production or quality problems could lead to the **brands arriving in the shops after competitors'**, and sales suffering significantly as a result. This risk will be greater if, as is likely, different suppliers specialise in **production of different brands**. This will magnify the impact of delays, as it may not be possible to substitute one supplier for another easily in the short-term.

(iii) **Remuneration of senior management and executive directors**

Lack of link between performance and bonuses

In theory the significant performance related element in directors' pay ought to encourage **goal congruence** – the directors striving to increase company performance to improve their own remuneration. However the **basis for determining the targets** that trigger performance related elements seem unclear. Large bonuses would seem to be appropriate in 20X6 with significant increases in sales and profits. In 20X7 conditions appear tougher, profit before tax would presumably be lower and generous bonuses should be unlikely; however have the targets set for 20X7 taken too much account of tougher trading conditions and hence been unduly lenient.

Encouraging undesirable behaviour

Although a significant performance element is desirable, the upper limits seem generous and this could encourage **manipulation of the accounts** to **achieve short-term profits**. The remuneration structure may encourage an excessive focus on achieving short-term profits, with half the remuneration being paid instantly in cash. Although there is a share element in remuneration, the lack of a time limit means that it is a short-term incentive for senior managers, and the three year holding period for directors is not a very long time. Also directors may be encouraged to **inflate profits and hence share price short-term** at a time when they can sell a significant quantity of shares obtained from previous bonuses.

Reputation risk

Because of the emphasis on ethics, there is a further risk to reputation if **large remuneration packages are paid**. Consumers may be less willing to buy if they feel that directors are benefiting at everyone else's expense.

(iv) **Corporate treasury function**

Speculation risks

It seems that the results of finance directors' treasury activities are measured as part of the overall assessment of profits from their division for remuneration purposes. This means that finance directors may be tempted to use derivatives to earn **profits through speculation**. This could potentially result in **large losses for NOP**; even if directors make profits through speculation, the risks they undertake may **exceed the risk appetite** of the group that the board has defined.

Knowledge risks

Even if finance directors do not speculate with derivatives, if they arrange hedging themselves they may incur losses through **lacking experience in treasury activities**. There appears to be no requirement for the finance directors to employ specialist treasury expertise.

Risks of failing to hedge

Although group policies are in place, there is no indication that they are being **enforced effectively** and so NOP may still be bearing currency risks. Finance directors may be unclear when they have to hedge or may simply fail to do so, and the group's treasurer may not have the information to enforce NOP's policies.

Risk of over-hedging

By contrast, if the treasurer's instructions are followed conscientiously, there is a risk of incurring **excessive hedging costs**. £100,000 equates to one futures contract. This figure does not seem material in the context of a 20X6 gross profit of £625 million.

Lack of goal congruence

Having the finance directors arrange **hedging independently** may mean **opportunities are lost** for **cost reduction through internal hedging arrangements**. If hedging can take place between different divisions, there may be no need to use expensive hedging arrangements such as option contracts.

(v) **Social and environmental policies**

Control risks

The board may have **problems enforcing the rigorous ethical code** and the **monitoring costs** of doing so may be high. Finance directors may be tempted to **avoid some requirements** to improve the profits of their division, and there will be costs such as **internal audit costs** in checking what they are doing. It may be even more difficult to enforce all aspects of the code on **suppliers**; checking up on what suppliers are doing again may be costly.

Business risks

Labour costs at the moment appear high, but NOP may have limited scope to reduce them due to the ethical code of conduct. NOP may be **vulnerable to competition** from other manufacturers who are not committed to a code, hence have a **lower cost base** and can **price more competitively**.

Waste disposal risks

NOP's commitment not to send waste to landfill sites and recycle everything again is beyond what it needs to do legally. Cost seems to have been a minor factor in this decision; whatever the environmental benefits, **significant costs of waste disposal** may threaten profit levels.

Reputation risks

Because NOP has signed up to the **ethical code**, the **risk to its reputation** if there are problems is **greater**. How serious the threat is depends on how much **consumer decisions** are influenced by **ethical issues**. However some lapses, for example use of forced labour or poor working conditions, may have a very serious adverse impact on sales.

(b) To: Board
From: Consultant
Date: 4 December 20X7
Subject: Risk ownership and profile

You asked me to prepare a report commenting on the board's role in risk management and the impact on risk profile of the suggestions made by the directors

(i) **Risk ownership**

Links between risks and strategy

NOP's risk appetite and risk management procedures should depend on the decisions directors take about the **strategic objectives** of the group. Part of the strategic decision-making process should be assessing what the accompanying risks of strategic decisions are, and whether the returns that the group can earn justify the risks it is taking. The board thus needs to develop **effective risk management mechanisms** to ensure risks are not greater than is necessary.

Stewardship

The directors also have a responsibility to shareholders to take appropriate care of the group's resources and to minimise the threats to them. The corporate governance reports stress the need for certain **decisions to be reserved for the board or individual directors**. These include directing when risk management is necessary to counter serious risks. The instruction of the treasurer that all open positions in excess of £100,000 be hedged is an example of this sort of decision.

Organisational environment

In a large group such as NOP it may be very difficult to define who is responsible for different aspects of **risk management**. Acknowledgement by the board of **risk ownership** is an essential factor in defining responsibilities clearly.

Intergroup coordination

The complexity of business arrangements, including the involvement of joint venture partners and outsource suppliers, increases the significance of the board's role as **coordinator**. The board needs to ensure that there is a **consistent outlook** towards risk management across the group, and, where relevant, with its suppliers. Board effort is needed, as otherwise risk outlook and management may differ significantly worldwide, **reflecting different attitudes to risk** in the countries in which NOP operates. The board may also be able to **identify opportunities for risk reduction between different parts of the group**, for example matching of exchange risks.

(ii) **Need for change**

Strategic direction

A poorer performance than the rest of the sector indicates that the market believes that NOP's **strategy needs to change**. The stock market may be focusing on both sales and costs. It may regard design and marketing as unimaginative; it may also regard labour costs of 18% of sales compared with an industry average of 12% as excessive.

Financing arrangements

If share price continues to fall, then it may be difficult to obtain sufficient equity funding to **finance significant new business developments**. The Group may have to use significant debt funding, and therefore **increase gearing** to a higher level than currently deemed desirable by the directors.

Impact on board

A major fall in share price may threaten the directors' position, with **shareholders forcing change** in the company rather than selling their shares.

Threat of takeover

If the share price falls far enough, if for example **market capitalisation** falls below the value of net business assets, then NOP will be **vulnerable to takeover**. Alternatively the group's shares may attract speculators, **increasing the volatility** of the share price.

Finance director's suggestion

Cost reduction

The stock market needs to be convinced that NOP will **achieve the desired cost reductions**. Investors may however doubt how much labour costs can be limited given NOP's commitment to a strong code of ethics.

Supply

Investors may also question whether the **cut in supplier costs** will have a **big enough impact**. Cutting supplier costs may also impact adversely on **product quality**; this may be a significant risk for NOP, given that it is positioned at the higher quality end of the market. Investors might also be sceptical whether NOP can achieve significant cuts in **transport costs**; the main influence on costs will still be the **long distances** between NOP's suppliers and customers. Cuts in transport costs may also mean changes in delivery planning, resulting in delays at key times of the year.

Increase in sales

The finance director's suggestion may have a positive impact on sales. NOP could differentiate itself from competition by being able to charge lower prices as a result of **cost leadership**, being a lower cost producer than competitors. However, this would seem to be inconsistent with NOP's desire to aim at the mid to high price sector of the market. Nevertheless the falls in share prices in fashion retail and retail overall may well indicate an economic slowdown and poor consumer confidence; in these circumstances a cut in prices may be more effective.

Impact on risk profile

The finance director's suggestion may have some appeal as it should lead to some reduction of costs. However the stock market may feel that the finance director's approach will **not enhance competitive advantage**, as it does not address the design and marketing issues that appear to be impacting on sales. If the market believes this, or if the fall in share price is primarily due to other causes such as a **lack of confidence in the board**, then the finance director's proposals will have little impact on the share price.

Marketing director's suggestion

Cost reduction

The marketing director's suggestion will not result in a fall in costs; if investors are looking for a **short-term boost in profits**, then they may not be satisfied if they believe that the increased costs will take some time to work through to increased sales.

Supply

A focus on certain ranges will put pressure on the suppliers who manufacture those ranges if demand **significantly increases**. The **importance of maintaining quality** to meet the expectations generated by the advertising campaign will be increased, and there is a risk that suppliers will not be able to deliver both quality and quantity of garments. Possibly NOP may need to improve its **supply chain management**.

Increase in sales

The advertising campaign could be seen as a clear indication to investors that NOP is developing a **stronger competitive strategy**. This will be important if, as seems likely, the market views NOP's current strategy as merely holding its position and thus being unsatisfactory. NOP is attempting to **differentiate itself on grounds of image**, and the high advertising costs could be a **barrier** to new or existing competitors responding effectively. Marks and Spencer, for example, have employed a similar strategy with some success.

However investors may doubt the long-term impact on sales for a number of reasons. Firstly concentrating on high-price products may be the wrong tactic if there is a **recession** with limited consumer spending. The **boost to the brand may not last very long**; it may be dependent on the **longevity of the celebrity's time in the media spotlight**. Product differentiation often requires more than just promotion; NOP may need to be **more innovative in design** as well. Investors may feel that as Glamour is only currently **15% of group revenue**, that the uplift to sales will make an insufficient difference. Investors may also be concerned about the **impact on brands that aren't being pushed**. One impact of the campaign may be to make these other brands look **tired**.

Impact on risk profile

Although NOP will continue to sell the same range of products, concentration of efforts on a few products will result in **less risk diversification**. Directors will have to weigh the relatively more serious consequences of a promoted product failing to deliver expected sales, against the problem that if the group aims to promote all its products equally, it will not have enough resources to do so effectively.

Conclusion

Although the marketing director's suggestion is speculative and will increase costs and risks, it seems a more positive way of addressing the business risks that seem to have led to the fall in share price. I recommend therefore that the marketing director's approach be adopted.

78 MFT

Text references. Chapters 1,2,6,7,9

Top tips. It is understandable if you found the wording in (a) (i) unclear; the question asks for a 2×2 matrix, but talks about high, medium or low risks. Our answer to (a) (i) reflects what the examiner seemed to want. The examples given in (a) (ii) do not necessarily have to relate to the scenario; application to the scenario comes in (a) (iii).

If your assessment of the risks differed from ours in (a) (iii), you still would have gained credit if you'd provided good reasons. Possibly the most debatable assessment is the variation in customer spend, as the performance of certain restaurants is highlighted in the scenario as causing concern. However as only 5 to 7 restaurants out of 74 are affected, this seems to indicate that the problem is not High Likelihood. Most of the problems are High Likelihood, Low Consequences problems, which can be dealt with by internal controls, hence the importance of the external auditor recommendations in (b).

Points to bring out in (b) are the differences the recommendations will make, whether other controls will be effective, the cost-effectiveness of the suggestions (particularly IT investment) and the need for central intervention.

(b) also gives 5 marks for the 'style' of the report. In another recent question, the 5 marks for the report were awarded for the style, structure, coherence and presentation of the report. Style would probably include these other factors as well in this question.

You need to head the report formally, address it to the board and include an introduction and conclusion. Obviously (hopefully) the structure of the report is based around the seven recommendations. You would have gained style marks for constructive comments, particularly being tactful and setting out your reasons if you didn't agree with the external auditors' recommendations.

(c) raises independence as well as competence issues.

Easy marks. As always, you should be able to gain maximum marks for report style.

Examiner's comments. The mark allocation for (a) was generous and most students scored well. Students needed to read the question and justify their answers, since some of the risks could have been placed in different places on the diagram.

Students generally scored well on (b); answers needed to discuss the costs and benefits of external auditors' recommendations to achieve a good mark.

(c) was done poorly. Students showed a worrying lack of knowledge of ethics and failed to identify the problem over objectivity. Many answers just recited words such as integrity and honesty rather than addressing the issues in the question.

(a) (i)

		Consequences	
		Low	**High**
Likelihood	Low	**Low risks** Risks which are unlikely to materialise and will not cause significant financial losses Misuse of credit cards	**Medium risks** Risks which are unlikely to materialise, but which may cause heavy one-off losses if they do Variation in customer spend
	High	**Medium risks** Risks which will not cause large one-off losses, but over time may cause significant losses because they frequently materialise Order taking process Misappropriation of inventory Time recording Short delivery of food and alcohol	**High risks** Risks which have a high change of materialising and will probably lead to heavy losses when they do Customer dissatisfaction

(ii) **Likelihood Low Consequences Low**

Accept risks. The costs of taking measures to avoid or reduce these risks will outweigh the benefits.

Likelihood Low Consequences High

Transfer, spread or share risks. Risks may be transferred to a customer by a **purchase agreement** or shared with a partner in a **joint venture.** The organisation may take out **insurance** against the consequences of risks materialising. Adopting a **portfolio approach** means taking action according to how risks are spread over the whole organisation.

Likelihood High Consequences Low

Reduce risks. Measures should be taken to control these risks, with the aims of:

- **Reducing the chances that the risks materialise** (for example obtaining reference for all new credit customers)
- **Reducing the financial consequences** (for example setting a maximum credit limit for customers)

Likelihood High Consequences High

Avoid risks. This can include abandoning business activities, for example ceasing to operate in **countries with severe political instability**. It can also mean **not undertaking certain activities at all,** for example using derivatives for speculative purposes.

(iii) 1 **Variation in customer spend**
Given that the group's strategy is based on maximising the value from each customer (there does not appear to be much recognition of customer segmentation), considerable variations in expenditure appear to represent a **failure of strategy.** If too many restaurants are failing to maximise spend, this may lead to the group being seen as under-performing, and its **share price falling.** However 5-7 restaurants out of 74 under-performing is not enough to warrant a High Likelihood Assessment.

2 **Order-taking process**

Problems with orders may occur if the recording by waiting staff is unclear; however problems will be mostly be corrected by customers and the **financial effect of problems** with individual orders will be **tiny**. Poor recording may also lead to disappearance of some cash proceeds. However as most bills are **paid by credit card,** the financial consequences should be limited.

3 **Misappropriation of inventory**

Poor kitchen security may give employees the chance to take some items of food, but the **value of foodstuffs** taken is likely to be **low;** not all food can be **easily concealed**. The risk of alcohol being stolen is limited by it being kept in a **locked storeroom,** although there may be a risk of **theft by employees who have the right of access to the storeroom**.

4 **Time recording**

It may be easy for many employees to claim for a little more time than they have actually worked. However **claims for unrealistic hours** are likely to be easy to spot. Restaurant managers will be **motivated to identify incorrect claims**, since employee costs are a very significant element in gross profit figures by which managers are judged.

5 **Customer dissatisfaction**

This is a high risk because customer dissatisfaction could have a **significant impact on demand**. Customers who have eaten in the restaurants and been dissatisfied may not return; potential customers may be deterred by word-of-mouth reports or reviews on the internet. If the problem persists, it could lead to **poor brand awareness** and adverse consequences in the long-term for MFT.

6 **Misuse of credit cards**

No restaurant spends more than 1% on local purchases, so the consequences of managers using corporate credit cards for this purpose are insignificant. Most other expenditure on the corporate credit cards will not be for large amounts. It is unlikely that restaurant managers will include personal items, since they would be **visible on monthly credit card statements**; the expenditure would also reduce gross profits, and **reflect adversely on the managers' performance.**

7 **Short delivery of food and alcohol**

This risk may well materialise frequently as **any member of staff can sign for deliveries,** and some staff may not be conscientious. However the amount delivered on each occasion will not be material for the whole group.

(b) **Report**

To:	Audit committee of MFT
From:	Internal Auditor
Date:	20 Aug 20X8
Subject:	Management letter from external auditors

Introduction

This report details my comments on the suggestions made in the letter by the external auditors. I believe that in general the comments have given a helpful external perspective on how the restaurants are operating and certainly warrant serious discussion.

1 **Variation in customer spend**

Variation in spend between MFT's restaurants has been identified as an area of **concern**. I need to take a **risk-based approach** and concentrate audit work on underperforming restaurants. The recommendation of **benchmarking** against best practice in the top performing restaurants is sensible, although local conditions may mean that variations remain. Depending on the level of work required, **additional internal audit resources** may be needed. **Staff secondments** from better-performing restaurants may also help to raise standards.

2 **Order-taking process**
The board needs to consider very carefully the need for significant IT investment to see if the benefits really justify the **purchasing and running costs**. It may be possible to trial a new system over a few restaurants to see if they do. A computerised ordering system will go some way to combating the problems identified, although other measures will be needed to supplement it. The system should ensure that kitchen staff understand the order and the pricing of the items entered is correct. However the wrong items may still be entered just as they could be written down wrongly; having staff repeat the order to customers is likely to be a more effective control.

3 **Misappropriation of inventory**
The computerised system recommended will help keep track of inventory levels. However a computerised system will not solve the problems of inventory being **incorrectly recorded** when delivered. Keeping alcohol in locked storerooms should be a **more effective physical control** to **prevent theft** and the **weekly inventory counts** should also deter theft.

4 **Time recording**
Again the costs of an automated time recording system may not be warranted by the benefits it brings. A central review of existing records should highlight **unusual patterns**, and managers have the incentive to ensure **staff hours** and hence **costs** are **correct**. The external auditors have not provided any evidence that staff have been claiming excessive staff hours, having reviewed records of hours worked; they have only said that there may be a problem.

5 **Customer dissatisfaction**
Customer dissatisfaction appears to be at a potentially serious level and is possibly the only issue of strategic relevance for MFT. Therefore the external auditors correctly suggest **action is needed**, certainly research by the market research consultancy to determine the cause of this dissatisfaction. However the board will need to decide whether local management will be responsible for taking steps to improve satisfaction or whether central intervention, supported by internal audit work, will be needed. This decision should be influenced by whether restaurants that have received poor customer ratings are **under-performing in other ways**, for example low customer spend. We need to examine whether **bad satisfaction ratings** are **correlated with poor performance**, and derive ultimately **from a poor control environment** and **poor restaurant management generally**.

6 **Misuse of credit cards**
This control is unlikely to be worthwhile. Managers are unlikely to be motivated to put through personal expenditure on their credit card, since it will **worsen their restaurants' results**. As no more than 1% of sales is on local produce, breaches of corporate guidance will not be financially significant. Any petty cash held will be **vulnerable to theft**, and balances held may be insufficient for one-off expenditure that is necessary in an emergency.

7 **Short delivery of food and alcohol**
Regular short deliveries of food and alcohol could lead to **significant financial losses** for individual MFT restaurants. I would endorse the external auditors' recommendation that **each delivery should be checked and evidenced**, as this control is effectively **cost-free**. Given other pressures on the restaurant manager's time, this task could be delegated to another reliable member of staff.

Conclusion

The external auditors have raised a number of very valid points. The key areas that the board needs to examine are how much the improvements can be **delegated to local managers**, and how much **central intervention** (including increased internal audit work) will be required. We need to be sure that the reliance on long serving restaurant managers has resulted in an **effective control environment**, and has minimised the possibility of **fraud or theft** by employees.

The external auditors have also highlighted the need for an **overall review of information technology systems**, to see if further investment will be **cost-effective**.

I hope this report has been helpful and I shall be willing to discuss my recommendations further if required.

(c) **Objectivity**

The main ethical issue is that the internal auditor lacks **objectivity**. As he designed the system, he may not see the problems identified by the external auditors as being serious or justified. Obtaining advice on the validity of the internal auditors' suggestions from someone with a **fresh perspective** may provide valuable insights.

Professional competence and due care

Objectivity is also linked to the internal auditor's professional abilities. The internal auditor has an incentive to play down criticisms by the external auditors, since they may cast doubt on his work designing the control and reporting system, and hence on his **professional competence**. Also if the system designed by the internal auditor was deficient, this may raise the issue of whether the internal auditor has the competence to make **a reliable assessment** of the external auditors' comments.

Mock exams

CIMA – Strategic level

Paper P3

Management Accounting – Risk and Control Strategy

Mock Exam 1

You are allowed three hours to answer this question paper
In the real exam, you are allowed 20 minutes reading time before the examination begins during which you should read the question paper, and if you wish, make annotations on the question paper. However, you will **not** be allowed, **under any circumstances**, to open the answer book and start writing or use your calculator during this reading time.
You are strongly advised to carefully read all the question requirements before attempting the question concerned (that is all parts and/or sub-questions).
Answer the ONE compulsory question in Section A.
Answer TWO questions only from Section B

DO NOT OPEN THIS PAPER UNTIL YOUR ARE READY TO START UNDER EXAMINATION CONDITIONS

SECTION A – 50 marks

Answer this question

Question 1

About 25 years ago, two people visiting a mountain range discovered a large underground cave. The find was considered to be 'exceptional' by the scientific community as the cave was the largest and best preserved example of a 'living cave', that is a cave where specific underground formations such as stalactites were still growing. Years of secret development, involving significant costs that frequently exceeded budget, meant that the cave was opened for public view last year. The development was funded mainly by the national government of the country the cave was located in and a bank loan. The cave is now maintained as a non-profit making Trust, (The CAVE Trust) controlled by a mixture of local people interested in maintaining the cave as well as experienced mountaineers and cave explorers.

Visitors to the cave now pay a fee of about €40 for access to the cave; the fee includes the services of an experienced tour guide. The fee of €40 was derived by the Trust as appearing to be good value for money for guests as well as providing some income to pay for the new tour guides etc. Tickets for cave access are sold near the cave entrance, where a museum and small shop are also located. Visitors pay for tickets using cash, cheques, debit or credit cards. Tickets are issued in numeric sequence, although only a limited number are available for issue each day due to space considerations in the cave. Other income is available from government grants.

Other items of expenditure within the cave include air conditioning and humidity systems to maintain the cave environment, wages of staff, light, heat and power and computer based security systems. Additional expenditure will be required in the next 18 months for extensions to the museum, a restaurant and research areas for school children as well as further development of access to the extensive cave system.

Partly due to lack of experience in the board of management, the actual management accounting system for the Trust is minimal. Information is provided on ticket sales, and expenditure totals at the end of each month.

The national government that provided part of the funding for development of the cave complex has recently indicated that funding will be withdrawn in six months. Unfortunately, the Trust does not have any contingency plan to overcome this loss of income.

Required

(a) (i) Explain how risks are identified and managed within a company, providing examples from the CAVE Trust where possible. **(14 marks)**

(ii) Evaluate the risk management strategy for income maintained by the Trust, suggesting how the Trustees should amend the strategy following the decision of the government to withdraw funding. **(7 marks)**

(b) Evaluate the management accounting system at the CAVE Trust and recommend improvements which will help to overcome any weaknesses you identify. **(13 marks)**

(c) Explain the audit process for accounting for ticket income in the Trust, recommending the audit tests to be carried out that will help to limit fraud. **(16 marks)**

(Total = 50 marks)

SECTION B – 50 marks

Answer TWO questions

Question 2

(a) Assume you are the Treasurer of AB, a large engineering company. You have forecast that the company will need to borrow £2 million by the end of September 20X3 for at least 6 months. The need for finance will arise because the company has extended its credit terms to selected customers over the summer period. The company's bank currently charges customers such as AB 7·5% per annum interest for unsecured fixed rate borrowing and LIBOR + 0.3% for unsecured floating rate borrowing. You believe interest rates will rise by at least 1·5 percentage points over the next 6 months. You are considering using one of three alternative methods to hedge the risk:

(i) Forward rate agreements
(ii) Interest rate futures
(iii) An interest rate guarantee (a short-term cap)

You can purchase an interest rate cap at 7% per annum for the duration of the loan to be guaranteed. You would have to pay a premium of 0·1% of the amount of the loan. As part of the arrangement, the company will agree to pay a 'floor' rate of 6% per annum.

Required

Discuss the features of each of the three alternative methods of hedging the interest rate risk and advise on how each might be useful to AB, taking all relevant and known information into account. **(12 marks)**

(b) You are contacted by the company's bank and informed that another of the bank's clients, a smaller company in the same industry, is looking for a swap partner for a similar amount of borrowing for the same duration. The borrowing rates applicable to AB and RO are as follows:

	Floating	*Fixed*
AB	LIBOR + 0.3%	7.5%
RO	LIBOR + 0.5%	8.5%

Required

(i) Demonstrate whether a swap would be beneficial to both companies in the situations described below. If a swap is beneficial, recommend how the two companies could co-operate in a swap arrangement to their mutual benefit. The situations are as follows.

(1) RO prefers floating rate finance, AB prefers fixed rate finance.
(2) RO prefers fixed rate finance, AB prefers floating rate finance.

Support any recommendations you make with appropriate calculations.

(ii) Discuss the advantages and disadvantages of arranging a swap through a bank rather than negotiating directly with a counter-party. **(13 marks)**

Note: A report format is NOT required in answering this question. **(Total = 25 marks)**

Question 3

Assume you are the newly-appointed treasurer of ZY, a medium-sized exporter and importer of goods, based in Singapore. The company imports mainly from Australia and New Zealand and exports to the USA. It has a subsidiary based in Melbourne, Australia which is partly financed by a loan from a local (Australian) bank. ZY usually hedges its foreign currency exposure by using the forward or money markets. Most customers are allowed, or take, 3 months' credit.

You have received the following memo from your managing director.

MEMORANDUM

From: The Managing Director
To: The Treasurer
Date: 21 May 20X2

I have been reading the financial section of the daily newspaper and note the following in respect of exchange rates and other economic data:

Exchange rates	*Sing $/US$*	*Aust $/US$*	
Spot rate	1.8126	2.0367	
1 month forward rate	1.8101	2.0350	
	Singapore	*USA*	*Australia*
Central bank base rate per annum	2.25%	4.25%	3.75%

A recent economic forecast for the South East Asia region, published in a local business journal, suggested that annual inflation over the next 12 months in Singapore is expected to be 1%, while in the USA it is expected to be 3.25%. I have a number of questions:

1. As interest rates are higher in the USA than here, surely the US$ should be trading forward at a premium to the Sing$, not at a discount?
2. The newspaper did not quote a 3-month forward rate. We have recently sold equipment to a customer in the US valued at US$ 2 million. What 3-month forward rate of exchange is implied by the information we do have, and therefore what Sing$ receipts can we expect in 3 months' time?
3. If we buy Aust$ on the spot market as and when we need them to pay for our imports rather than taking out forward contracts, it should surely save us a lot of money?
4. Would a potential policy be to buy Aust$ on the spot market now and place them on deposit until we need them?
5. Would it be in our interests to borrow Sing$ and pay off our Aust$ loan? This would save us money on interest payments.

Please let me have your comments.

Required

Write a report to the managing director discussing each of his questions. Include appropriate calculations, where relevant, to aid your discussion. **(25 marks)**

Question 4

You are a manager in the internal audit department of TB1, a large listed company employing 7,000 staff in your country including an internal audit department of 30. During the course of the audit of the computer-based financial control systems, you have discovered that €1.1 billion of revenue expenditure has been treated as capital spending. You have reported this finding to the head of internal audit and then to the chief accountant, but as far as you are aware, no action has been taken by the company. The external audit is due to commence in 7 days, and you have been instructed by the head of internal audit not to disclose this information to the external auditors.

Required

(a) Explain the composition of the audit committee in a listed company and outline its main tasks. **(10 marks)**

(b) Discuss reasons why whistleblowing has become more important in recent years. **(6 marks)**

(c) Evaluate the alternative actions available to you now, and how these may conflict with CIMA ethical guidance. **(9 marks)**

(Total = 25 marks)

Question 5

The FF Airline Company operates approximately 60 flights each day to a variety of destinations. The company was formed as a low cost 'budget' airline a few years ago following deregulation of the airline industry. While profitable, the company operates on extremely narrow margins; this means that any expenditure is carefully vetted by the Board and approval is only given for projects with a positive result in a cost benefit analysis.

Information Systems in the company are focused on providing a high level of customer service. Online booking, seat reservation and real time status information on all flights is available via the company's web site. Internal management accounting systems are restricted to provision of summary data each month end. Details on total income can only be obtained when sales information from FF's 10 regional offices is amalgamated at Head Office at the end of each month.

Each regional office is located in one of the airports served by FF. The office receives income from customer bookings and pays local wages, airport expenses such as landing fees and aircraft maintenance for planes in that location. Information is transferred weekly to head office on CD ROM due to the cost of installing a network. A number of regional offices have used their small delegated budgets to implement limited MIS systems, although these tend to be little more than basic spreadsheets.

Required

(a) Explain how an IS strategy should be developed. Use examples from FF Company to illustrate your answer. **(10 marks)**

(b) Explain the strengths and weaknesses in the IS strategy in the FF company, and provide recommendations on how to overcome the weaknesses. **(15 marks)**

(Total = 25 marks)

Answers

DO NOT TURN THIS PAGE UNTIL YOU HAVE COMPLETED THE MOCK EXAM

A plan of attack

We know you've been told to do it at least 100 times and we know if we asked you you'd know that you should do it. So why don't you do it in an exam? 'Do what in an exam?' you're probably thinking. Well, let's tell you for the 101st time. **Take a good look through the paper before diving in to answer questions.**

First things first

What you must do in the first five minutes of reading time in your exam is **look through the paper i**n detail, working out **which questions to do** and the **order** in which to attempt them. So turn back to the paper and let's sort out a plan of attack.

We then recommend you spend the remaining time analysing the requirements of Question 1 and highlighting the key issues in the question. The extra time spent on (a) will be helpful, whenever you intend to do the question, If you decide to do it first, you will be well into the question when the writing time starts. If you intend to do it second or third, probably because you find it daunting, the question will look easier when you come to back to it, because your initial analysis should generate further points whilst you're tackling the other questions.

The next step

You're probably either thinking that you don't know where to begin or that you could have a very decent go at all the questions.

Option 1 (if you don't know where to begin)

If you are a bit **worried** about the paper, it's likely that you believe that case study question 1 looks daunting. We therefore recommend that you do one or both of the optional questions before tackling the case study. Don't however fall into the trap of going over time on the optional questions because they seem easier. You will need to spend half the time available on the case study.

- If you think you can describe interest rate hedging instruments well, but are not sure of the mathematics, do think about attempting **Question 2.** Your answer to (a) can be purely descriptive, and the numbers make up less than half the marks in (b).
- **Question 3** on currency hedging gives a significant number of marks for calculations, some of which are not signposted that clearly in the question. If you're not sure what calculations to do, or do know but think you may struggle to do them, it's best to avoid this question.
- Part (a) of **Question 4** may appear to be one of the easiest sections of the paper. However you will also need to think about wider issues in (b) when discussing whistleblowing and make practical recommendations in (c). Remember in (c) that you have to discuss a number of possibilities and will get two to three marks for each.
- **Question 5** isn't about the technicalities of IT, but is more about the general management issues such as centralisation which you can bring in not just from this paper but other management and strategic papers. The details in the question will give you a lot of help in part (b). (b) represents the sort of question that might come up a lot in this exam – using the question details to identify weaknesses and linking in recommendations for improvements.
- When tackling case study **Question 1**, don't be put off by the number of marks given in total. Instead break the question down by focusing on the requirements of each part. If you read the question carefully you'll find that some of the question parts have more than one requirement. Take a few minutes to plan your answer, jotting down the different types of threats and risks involved as a start to (a). These should help you answer the rest of the question. You can gain credit for a number of points about risk management, provided you illustrate them by examples quoted from the case material.

Option 2 (if you're thinking 'I can do all of these')

It never pays to be over confident but if you're not quaking in your shoes about the exam then **turn straight to compulsory Question 1**. You've got to do it so you might as well get it over and done with. Make sure you answer every requirement and sub-requirement in the question and also make sure you include plenty of examples from the case study. Bear in mind that one thing you are being tested on is an ability to identify and discuss in detail how you would deal with the most important risks.

Once you've done the compulsory question, choose two of the questions in Section B.

- **Question 2** is more of an explanation than a numbers question, so you need to be clear on your terminology. The swap calculations should be fine if you've practised the questions in the body of the kit.
- Again if you've practised currency hedging calculations, you should cope well with **Question 3**, although make sure you can explain the relevant theories as well.
- You may think you know enough about audit committees to tackle a 25 mark question on the subject. However part (a) of **Question 4** is only worth 10 marks so take care! You have to discuss wider issues in (b) when considering whistleblowing, and discuss a number of alternatives in (c), coming up with some practical arguments.
- The dangers when answering **Question 5** are firstly to concentrate too much on technicalities at the expense of discussing strategy, weaknesses and control, the key concepts in this paper. The second danger is not to bring in the detail given in the case study. Although (a) is quite general, you won't pass that part if you don't mention FF.

No matter how many times we remind you...

Always, always **allocate your time** according to the marks for the question in total and for the parts of the questions. And always, always **follow the requirements exactly**.

You've got free time at the end of the exam.....?

If you have allocated your time properly then you **shouldn't have time on your hands** at the end of the exam. If you find yourself with five or ten minutes spare, however, go back to **any parts of questions that you didn't finish** because you ran out of time.

Forget about it!

And don't worry if you found the paper difficult. More then likely other students would too. If this were the real thing you would need to forget the exam the minute you leave the exam hall and think about the next one. Or, if it's the last one, celebrate!

Question 1

Text references. Chapters 1 and 2 cover the main risks and risk management methods. Chapters 7 and 8 are useful on the audit implications and Chapter 4 on the management accounting aspects.

Top tips. In (a) (i) it is important to identify the two key words of **identified** and **managed** in the question requirements, as this provides the basic format for the answer. The syllabus guidance notes provide examples of the kind of risks that a company may face, and this can be used as a framework for the answer. The management of risk implies looking at the various strategies in this area – the link to the scenario being that the Trust appears to have effectively ignored risk and that this is inappropriate.

(a) (ii) builds on (a) (i) by checking what remedial action is now required to overcome the weakness of lack of risk analysis in the Trust. The answer must focus on the loss of income; you need to specify what its income might be as you're asked to evaluate, and you should also provide additional relevant and realistic comment on whether other income sources can be found.

(b) is potentially very difficult to 'get into' simply due to the lack of information provided. However, given that scenarios may be relatively short, you will have to draw on your theoretical knowledge to provide outline answers in some situations. The basic sections of a management accounting system in terms of setting sales and expenditure budgets will be known, so these can be mentioned in the answer. Difficulties with the setting of budgets for these areas can then be determined from the scenario to provide useful, if relatively brief, examples to support the comments made.

In (c) you should remember that the main focus on audit work in the syllabus is identifying risk and then testing to ensure that the risks identified do not occur. The main sections of the answer therefore revolve around these two areas. The documentation of systems and internal control are mentioned in the syllabus content, hence require comment in the answer. However, lack of detail is justified partly from the note in the scenario that there are few controls, and partly because documenting and recording controls will be similar for most systems. Audit tests are linked to specific risks, and you should take care to ensure that the question requirement of showing how fraud can be limited is clearly spelt out in the answer.

Easy marks. Identifying threats and risks is generally the easiest part of a question like this, and forms the basis of the rest of your answer, so be very alert for risks when you're reading carefully through the scenario, particularly risks to income here and also problems of limited management systems.

(a) (i) **Identify the sources of risk**

A business review will be carried out by appropriately trained staff or external consultants to determine the business risks facing the company, or in this case the Trust. Specific risks that could affect the Trust could include:

Financial risk

An example would be **loss of key income or unidentified or unbudgeted expenditure** being incurred. The Trust is currently facing loss of key income as noted in the scenario, although unbudgeted expenditure in terms of collapsing roofs in the caves would also fall into this category.

Business risk

This includes **employee fraud or loss of reputation**. Employee fraud is possible in the Trust, although this is likely to be limited to unauthorised removal of cash takings or products from the shop. Loss of reputation could include visitors being lost or injured in the caves.

Technological risk

This results from **new or improved technology** that the company does not have access to or chooses not to use. While the Trust appears to lack some management information systems, there does not appear to be lack of any specific technology that would cause the risk of the company ceasing operations.

Corporate reputation

This relates to the **economic or political actions of a company**. In the case of the Trust there is the possible risk that the cave becomes contaminated in some way, thus losing its unique selling point of being the largest living cave open to the public.

Determine how the risks can be managed

There are four basic strategies for managing risks:

Avoidance

That is **removing the factors** that give rise to a risk. In the case of the Trust the risk of income sources could not be removed so this is not a viable option.

Control

The reason for the risk cannot be removed, but methods are identified to **reduce the risk to acceptable levels**. In the case of the Trust, this should have meant that **alternative sources of income** were identified prior to the situation becoming critical.

Transference

In this option, the risk is **transferred to a third party**, normally by the taking out of a suitable **insurance** policy. While the Trust could obtain insurance for business being affected by factors such as poor weather or strikes, it is less likely that insurance against sources of income not being available could be obtained.

Acceptance

The **risk is accepted** in the hope that it will not occur or that the consequences of the risk can be coped with if it does occur. This appears to have been the policy adopted by the Trust, given the problem that removal of the government funding is now causing.

Prepare an action plan for risk

For each identified risk, an **appropriate action plan** needs to be **determined**, based on the strategy adopted for that risk. Initial focus will be on those risks that have the **most adverse business impact** for the company, such as the **loss of income or loss of reputation** noted above. However, no action plan has been produced by the Trust, at least for the loss of income.

Appropriate actions for other risks identified would include:

(1) **Implementing appropriate internal controls** to limit employee fraud

(2) **Ensuring that the reputation of the Trust was maintained** by good management of the cave system

(3) **Obtaining public liability insurance against risks of the public** suffering injury while visiting the caves

The overall lack of risk management is worrying and needs to be addressed urgently by the Trustees.

(ii) **Risk management in the Trust**

The risk management strategy for income in the Trust does not appear to be fully developed. It would appear the Trustees have become **complacent** in their **management of income** and the withdrawal of funding from the government was therefore a surprise.

Actions to be taken by the Trustees

Determine the effect of the loss of income on the Trust

No information is provided regarding the **extent of income** provided by the **government**, but it would appear to be important given that the cave system was partly developed using that income. Amendments will have to be made to the management accounts to show the effect of losing this income. A decision may have to be taken regarding the **viability of the Trust** keeping the cave open. Expenditure appears to be **high and relatively fixed**, in terms of the air conditioning system for the cave, staffing, etc. If fixed costs cannot be covered in the medium term, then the cave will have to close.

Investigate other income sources

Other sources of income should be investigated as a matter of urgency.

(1) **Charging a fee** to schools for the use of the research area

(2) **Approaching universities** for grants to develop the cave system or to allow students of mineralogy to work in the caves

(3) **Approaching the public** for donations to maintain the cave

(4) **Obtaining additional bank finance**

(5) **Increasing entry fees**

An alternative may be to **reschedule the repayment of the bank loans** to decrease current expenditure.

For the future, the Trustees must also **undertake a full risk review** for the Trust, identifying other sources of risk and providing contingencies to overcome those risks.

(b) **Weaknesses in and improvements required to the management accounting system**

Lack of a management accountant

Possibly the main weakness in the management accounting system is the lack of a management accountant! While some system may have been established in the past to provide basic management information, the lack of appropriate reporting clearly identifies a **lack of expertise** in the Trust. Any revisions to the system will need to be extensive, implying the appointment of a management accountant.

Quality of information

The current system appears to provide some basic monitoring of expenditure only, which will not be sufficient for the future. A **more detailed analysis of costs and income will be needed**. Establishing a new system also implies purchase of additional computer hardware and software, so an appropriate budget will be needed.

Budgets

Given that the Trust will still try to obtain government funding in the future, then **expenditure budgets** will be necessary **to show exactly how the funds would be spent**. Until recently, budgeting would involve cave development and building of the various visitor amenities only. The new management accounting system will have to record the budget initially, and then report expenditure across appropriate budget headings as cave development progresses. The development is likely to involve a high degree of risk, as cost **overruns** were noted in the scenario, so the budget reports would need to show these overruns and provide a basis for further funding applications.

Variance analysis

Monitoring day-to-day running of the Trust should be relatively easy as most of the expenditure is fixed. Budgetary reports will need to **focus on variances** from budgets, although these should be identifiable as increases in staff numbers, additional expenditure on cave humidity control etc.

Determining costs

The current method of setting the ticket price as 'good value' is unlikely to be sufficient, given the reliance on ticket income that the Trust will have in the future. Setting the price will involve determining the following costs:

- **Fixed costs** of running the cave including air conditioning, wages etc.
- **Additional costs** of expanding the cave network

- **Any variable costs**, although these are likely to be limited to light and heat
- **Other discretionary costs** such as marketing may also be included

Total costs are therefore easy to determine and can be used as input into the management accounting system to assist in determining the ticket price in the future.

Setting the ticket price – recommendation

It appears that the total number of tickets that can be sold is already known. Assuming all tickets were sold, then the total costs divided by number of tickets would give the ticket price. However, there is **no information on the demand for the tickets**, meaning that this calculation will not be accurate. Some element of non-sale will have to be determined taking the past 12 months sales since the caves opened, and an estimate of falling demand as the ticket price may well be higher than the current 'good value' price. An initial assumption may be necessary, with subsequent close monitoring of sales following this to determine if the assumption was accurate.

Monitoring guest numbers

The Trust needs to **monitor guest numbers closely** to determine whether **income will be sufficient to meet actual and proposed expenditure**. This information does not appear to be available from the current system. Additional development and therefore costs will be incurred, establishing the link between the guest booking system and the revised management accounting system.

Any new management accounting system will have to **integrate** with the **current guest booking system** to obtain this information. Total income from ticket sales can then be compared to budget in the management accounting system and variance analysis used to determine any deviation from budget.

(c) **Audit process for the audit of ticket income in the CAVE Trust**

Audit planning

Audit planning is associated with **determining the business risks** for the Trust as a whole and any specific inherent risks and control risks for ticket sales.

Business risk – going concern

The overall business risk relevant to the CAVE Trust is **going concern**. The **withdrawal of funding** from the local government is likely to result in the **closure of the Trust** unless other income sources can be generated. This risk may mean that the Trustees would like to inflate sales income or attempt to minimise costs to try to show the results of the Trust in a favourable light, should negotiations with other providers of finance become necessary.

Inherent risk – cash sales

As some of the ticket sales are made for cash, there is an inherent risk that cash may be either **recorded incorrectly** or **misappropriated** (or both). Cash is a risky asset simply because it can be hidden and moved easily. Audit testing will need to focus on checking that all cash is recorded.

Control risk – lack of management experience

There appears to be **no audit experience** amongst the Trustees of the Trust. This implies that the **control system** will be **weak**, simply because setting up controls is **not a main focus of management**; they are more interested in the cave itself. It is possible that the auditor will not be able to rely on any internal controls, because they will either be missing or inadequate.

Summary of risk analysis

The main area of audit testing must therefore be **checking the completeness of income** – partly because of the potential going concern situation of the Trust and partly due to the nature of cash meaning it is easy to steal. Lack of management controls will affect audit work more from the point of view of limiting control testing and expanding the amount of substantive testing.

Documenting systems

Documenting systems means **recording the accounting system** so that individual transactions can be **followed from their start to end**. The auditor would prepare some form of system notes showing clearly the systems for recording ticket sales from cash and debit/credit cards, along with the controls expected over those systems.

Internal controls

As noted above, the internal control system is likely to be weak. A limited number of reconciliation controls such as agreement of total amount in till to the till roll each day by a person not actually selling tickets may be available. However, the auditor is **unlikely to rely on controls** for testing due to the inherent weaknesses noted above.

Audit testing

Audit testing will focus on ensuring that all transactions are **completely and accurately recorded** in the accounts of the Trust. Additional testing will be required over those areas where cash fraud could take place. Specific tests that will be carried out include:

Risk: Cash income incomplete

(i) For a number of days, **check the cash received in the till to the till roll**. This test will highlight cash fraud because any difference between the cash and the till could indicate cash being removed from the till.

(ii) For the same days, **agree the total amount of sales to the register of tickets actually sold**. This determines tickets sold and provides a check regarding the total income expected to be received.

(iii) **Agree the total cash sales to the bank paying in book**. This test may also identify fraud and money could be removed from the day's cash takings between being taken from the till and recorded on the paying in slip.

(iv) **Agreeing the total of the paying in slip to the bank statement**. This test could, in theory, identify fraud if the whole day's taking were stolen as the money would not appear on the bank statement.

Evaluation of results

If cash fraud is found then the auditor will need to carry out the following additional procedures:

(i) **Ask staff involved** with the sales system **why** the errors could have **occurred** – in other words check that the errors did not simply relate to unintentional mistakes rather than fraud.

(ii) **Attempt to determine the amount of cash fraud** by performing additional tests.

(iii) **Inform the Trustees** verbally of the situation.

(iv) **Make a report** to the relevant authorities for potential fraud.

(v) **Recommend** to the Trustees that **controls noted above are implemented** to try to minimise the likelihood of repeat fraud.

Question 2

Text references. Chapters 13 and 14.

Top tips. Answers to discussion questions like (a) should concentrate on the levels of interest the company will have to pay, the risk of suffering from adverse interest rate movements, the flexibility of the instrument and the cost of using it. You would have been given credit in (a) for using a graph to illustrate your answer.

(b) presented a major problem when it was set. The original wording only covered the situation in (i) (1) where that neither party would benefit, and it was clear that you would need to undertake some sort of swap calculation rather than just saying that neither party would benefit. If you are faced with this situation in an exam, and identify the problem before you get very far into the question, it may be best to do another question. If here however you had already done (a), you would be better off making an attempt at (b), explaining clearly what you had done, the assumptions you made and the problems that you had identified.

(b) mentions that the companies are of different size; in a swaps question this generally indicates that the gains should not be split evenly, but in favour of the larger company. We have split the gains 0.6:0.2, although 0.5:0.3 would have been fine as well. In many questions however you will be told how to split the swap (generally equally).

Easy marks. (a) is quite general; if you tackle it successfully, you can pass the question without scoring very well on the calculations.

Examiner's comments. Generally answers to (a) were good and related well to the question's scenario. Mistakes included failing to recognise that interest rate futures can be traded, commenting that forward rate agreements and futures are options, and not understanding that interest rate guarantees are options.

(a) (i) **FRAs**

A forward rate agreement (FRA) would **fix the interest rate on borrowing** at a certain time in the future. If the actual rate is higher than the rate agreed, the bank would pay AB the difference; if lower, AB would pay the bank the difference. FRAs are usually available only for borrowings above $1 million, and AB's borrowing is much larger than that.

Advantages of FRAs

FRAs are **flexible**; they can be arranged for any amounts and any duration. An FRA would protect AB from **adverse interest rate movements** above the rate negotiated. **No premium** is payable on a forward rate agreement.

Disadvantages of FRAs

However the rate the bank will set for the forward rate agreement will reflect expectations of future interest rate movements. As interest rates are expected to rise, the bank may set a higher rate than the 7.5% currently available. AB will **not be able to take advantage if interest rates fall unexpectedly**. It may also be **difficult to arrange a FRA for a period longer than one year**.

(ii) **Interest rate futures**

If AB purchases a future, it will be contracting to buy a **specific interest rate commitment** at an agreed price. The terms, amounts and periods of the contract will be **standardised**. The futures price is likely to **vary with changes in interest rates**; as interest rates increase, the price of the future will fall. This acts as a **short hedge** against adverse interest rate movements.

Advantages of futures

AB should be able to hedge the £2 million for a **relatively small outlay**. AB should also be able to obtain futures for the **exact amount** of the borrowing, as the **standard size** of a LIFFE futures contract is £500,000. Futures contracts are easy to liquidate on the open market.

Disadvantages of futures

Interest rate futures are for **fixed periods** with a **fixed settlement date**, so the hedge may need to be adjusted. AB may be liable to **basis risk**, the risk that the price of the futures contract may not move in the expected direction. Futures contracts require a **margin or deposit payment**.

(iii) **Interest rate guarantee**

The cap means that the **maximum interest rate** that AB will have to pay during a specific period is 7%. The floor means that the **lowest interest rate** that AB will pay is 6%.

Advantages of guarantee

The cap seems to offer better terms than the forward rate agreement, the rate of which is likely to be above 7.5%. AB will be able to **benefit from falling interest rates**.

Disadvantages of guarantee

The **premium** of 0.1% will be payable whatever the movement in interest rates, and whether or not the option is exercised. The cap also sets a **minimum rate** that AB will have to pay, and AB will not be able to take advantage of interest rates below 6%. However it seems unlikely, given current expectations, that rates will fall that low. The maturity of guarantees is **limited to one year**.

(b) (i) (1) **Recommendation**

As illustrated below, in this instance the parties will not benefit from a swap and should not therefore undertake one.

	AB	*RO*	*Total*
Company wants	Fixed	Floating	
Would pay	(7.5%)	(LIBOR + 0.5%)	(LIBOR + 8%)
Could pay with swap	(LIBOR + 0.3%)	(8.5%)	(LIBOR + 8.8%)
Potential loss			0.8%

(2) **Recommendation**

A gain of 0.8% in these circumstances could be made if a swap arrangement was undertaken. As AB is the **larger company**, able to obtain more favourable terms in both markets, the swap has been structured so that it receives 0.6% of the gain and RO receives 0.2%. Under the terms of the swap AB pays 7.5% and RO LIBOR + 0.5%. They then swap amounts, AB paying over LIBOR + 0.5% to RO and receiving 8.3% from RO.

	AB	*RO*	*Total*
Company wants	Floating	Fixed	
Pay to bank without swap	(LIBOR + 0.3%)	(8.5%)	(LIBOR + 8.8%)
Pay to bank if swap agreed	(7.5%)	(LIBOR + 0.5%)	(LIBOR + 8%)
Potential gain			0.8%
Split	0.6%	0.2%	
Expected outcome	(LIBOR – 0.3%)	(8.3%)	(LIBOR + 8%)
Swap			
Pay to bank if swap agreed	(7.5%)	(LIBOR + 0.5%)	(LIBOR + 8%)
Swap terms			
Swap floating	(LIBOR + 0.5%)	LIBOR + 0.5%	
Swap fixed(bal fig. working)	8.3%	(8.3%)	
Net paid	(LIBOR – 0.3%)	(8.3%)	(LIBOR + 8%)
Pay to bank without swap	(LIBOR + 0.3%)	(8.5%)	(LIBOR + 8.8%)
Gain	0.6%	0.2%	0.8%

Working

(7.5%) + (LIBOR + 0.5%) + X = (LIBOR – 0.3%)
(LIBOR + 8%) + X = (LIBOR – 0.3%)
X = 8.3%

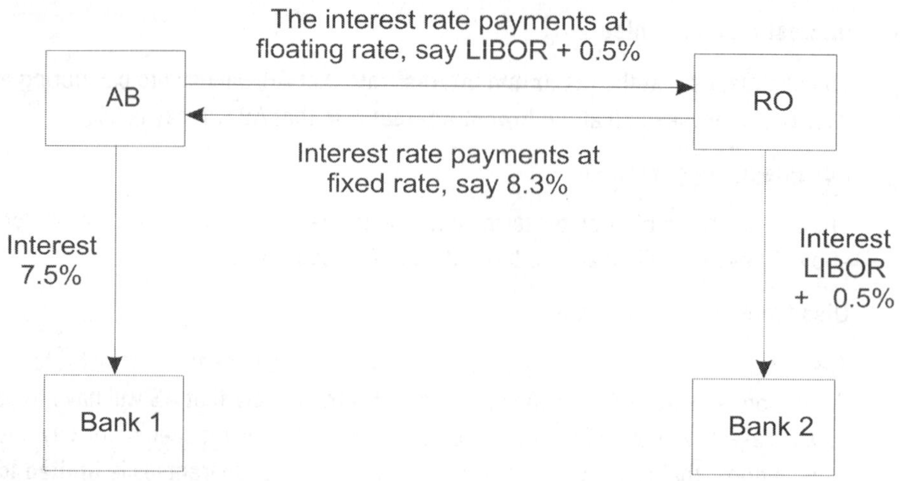

(ii) **Advantages of using bank**

(1) **Finding a counterparty**
A bank may be able to find a **counterparty more easily and quickly** than if the company searched for a partner itself. It may also be easy for a bank to reverse a swap if necessary.

(2) **Access to counterparty**
A bank may have **access to more counterparties** in more markets than if the company tried to find the counterparty itself

(3) **Reduced risk exposure**
The company is likely to be **less exposed to credit risk** if it deals through a bank. Banks are likely to have better information about the credit risks of counterparties.

Disadvantages of using bank

(1) **Cost**
Arrangement fees will have to be paid; these will not be necessary if a third party is contacted directly.

(2) **Timing**
Use of a bank leads potentially to **timing problems** if the company is settling before the counterparty, and the counterparty then defaults.

Question 3

Text references. Chapter 11.

Top tips. This question involves discussion of various issues raised by the managing director, who lacks full understanding of how foreign exchange markets work.

The information you are given indicates that you will need to discuss interest rate parity and/or purchasing power parity. Since these concepts are relevant throughout the answer, our answer explains them in detail in the introduction, and refers to them more briefly later on.

The level of detail you are given should have indicated that calculations should be used to support the points you made as relevant.

When dealing with continuously compounded interest rates for part of a year, it is more correct to use x to the power y calculations, but you would also have gained credit if you had adjusted the interest rates by dividing (see the alternative solutions).

You need to assume that there is no concern about the bid/offer spread on the forward exchange rates.

Easy marks. Explanations of purchasing power and interest rate parity should be fairly straightforward, also why it is risky not to hedge at all; this will often be a possibility that you have to discuss.

Examiner's comments. Answers to this question varied widely. Some candidates showed a serious lack of comprehension of the theories, and a few failed to mention interest rate and purchasing power parity. Others provided detailed discussions backed up by calculations. Candidates from non-UK centres tended to do very well on this question.

MEMORANDUM

From: The Treasurer
To: The Managing Director
Date: 22 May 20X2
Subject: Financial data

I am writing in response to the questions you raised about the financial data relating to South-East Asia published in a business newspaper. There are two important theories linking exchanges rates, interest rates and inflation which need to considered when determining strategies in this area.

Interest rate parity

Interest rate parity is based on the hypothesis that the difference between interest rates in the two countries should offset the difference between the spot rates and the forward foreign exchange rates over the same period. The formula is:

$$\text{Forward rate currency a/b} = \text{Spot a/b} \times \frac{1+\text{nominal A interest rate}}{1+\text{nominal B interest rate}}$$

Purchasing power parity

Purchasing power parity predicts that the exchange value of foreign currency depends on the relative purchasing power of each currency in its own country, and that spot exchange rates will vary over time according to relative price changes. The formula is:

$$\text{Forward rate currency a/b} = \text{Spot a/b} \times \frac{1+\text{A inflation rate}}{1+\text{B inflation rate}}$$

Note

1 **US $ trading forward**

The forward rate between the Singapore and US dollars is nearly as predicted by interest rate parity.

$$\text{One month forward rate} = 1.8126 \times \frac{1+0.0225/12}{1+0.0425/12}$$

$$= 1.8096$$

> **Top tips.** Because the exchange rates are quoted as Sing \$ to US \$, that means Singapore is Country A in the interest rate parity calculation, the US is Country B.

The reason why the US dollar is quoted forward at a discount or cheaper is that the market has acted to offset the desire that investors in Singapore \$ would have to switch to US\$, a currency associated with higher interest rates. The Singapore \$ has become more expensive in the forward markets to compensate for the lower interest rates in Singapore, a process known as **arbitrage**.

2 **Forward exchange rates**

Again interest rate parity can be used to estimate the forward rate.

Three month forward rate $= 1.8126 \times \frac{1+0.0225/4}{1+0.0425/4}$

$= 1.8036$

We can therefore expect US\$ 2,000,000 × 1.8036 = Sing \$ 3,607,200. This compares with a receipt of US\$ 2,000,000 × 1.8126 = Sing \$ 3,625,200 on the spot market.

> **Top tips.** As the currencies are quoted at Sing\$ X: US\$ 1, you have to **multiply** amounts quoted in US\$ to calculate what they are in Sing\$.

To guarantee that we receive the minimum of \$ 3,607,200 we should take out a forward contract for the expected receipt at a rate of \$1.8036, the contract to be performed in three months time.

3 **Buying Aust\$ on spot market**

We need to calculate the Aus \$: Sing \$ crossrates.

Aus \$: Sing \$ = US \$: Sing \$ × Aus \$: US \$

For current spot rates

Aus \$: Sing \$ $= \frac{1}{1.8126} \times 2.0367$

$= 1.1236$

For one month forward rates

Aus \$: Sing \$ $= \frac{1}{1.8101} \times 2.0350$

$= 1.1242$

Purchasing power parity indicates that the forward rates should in real terms be the same as the spot rates. In practice spot rates will differ from forward rates and the company could make **gains from favourable spot rate movements**. However the company may equally make **substantial losses** if rates move **adversely**, and because there is no specialist foreign currency manager, the risks of losses will be **too great. Transaction costs** may also be **higher.**

By contrast the company's use of forward contracts allows it to **limit its exposure to losses** by fixing in advance the rates it will use when it comes to pay for imports.

4 **Placing Aust\$ on deposit**

The arrangement you have described is a **money market hedge**, buying the currency, putting it on deposit and using the principal and interest to make the Aust \$ payment when it falls due.

Money market hedging may be slightly more beneficial than using the forward exchange markets, but the difference is likely to be small, as the premium or discount on the forward exchange rates will reflect interest rate differentials. Money market hedging is currently a strategy that the company uses.

5 **Borrowing Sing $ to pay off Aus $**

It is true that we would be paying lower interest rates on a loan in Sing $ than a loan in Aus $. However the difference in the forward rates compensates for this, so it would be more expensive to buy Aus$ now (each one would cost Sing $ 0.89) than it would be to set a forward rate to buy them in say a month's time (when each Aus $ would only cost Sing $ 0.8894)

In addition if the company hedges on the money market by buying Aus $ and placing them on deposit, the company would be **matching** the amount deposited with the Aus$ loan. Although the company would suffer higher interest rates than on a Sing $ loan, it would also **benefit from higher interest rates** on the deposit. **Matching** is a further way in which the company can limit its exposure to losses from exchange rate and interest rate movements.

If you have any further queries, please do not hesitate to get in touch.

Treasurer

Question 4

Text references. Chapter 5 covers corporate governance, Chapter 9 ethical codes.

Top tips. In (a) the role and composition of an audit committee are matters of fact. It is important to recognise the role of NEDs and the internal reporting function of internal audit as the latter ties in with section (c) of the question.

In (b) whistleblowing can be addressed as risks to the company, or as in this situation, why it is currently important. Knowledge of issues such as Enron and the note in the small scenario about computerised accounts provides links to points that can be made to support your discussion.

In (c) you need to show that some form of disclosure should be made while maintaining the ethical guidance of the Institute. An alternative approach to the answer would be to discuss the different disclosure options and then show how these affected integrity and confidentiality. However, explaining the ethical issues first does allow these to be applied to the reporting alternatives, reducing the amount of potential repetition in the answer. The requirement to evaluate may seem strange as there are no numbers, but what it means here is assessing how effective the different reporting options might be in resolving the problem.

Easy marks. If you have a reasonable knowledge of corporate governance, you should score high marks on (a), and should therefore pass the question comfortably.

(a) **Membership of audit committee**

According to the Combined Code, the **audit committee should have at least three members**, all independent Non Executive Directors. At least one member of the audit committee should have **recent and relevant financial experience**. The head of the internal audit department and the external auditor may also attend committee meetings, especially where internal and external audit reports are being discussed.

Tasks of audit committee

Monitoring financial statements and announcements of financial performance

The audit committee should review all announcements, concentrating in particular on the **significant financial reporting judgements**, also **key accounting policies** and the **overall appearance and presentation** of the accounts.

Reviewing internal controls and risk management

The committee should review the **system of financial controls** and may also be responsible for **reviewing internal control and risk management systems**. This includes continual monitoring of the **overall adequacy of the internal control systems** and **management's attitude towards control**.

Review of internal audit

As part of their review of the adequacy of internal controls, the audit committee should **assess the need for an internal audit function** in the context of the overall risk management framework. The committee should **approve the appointment of the head of internal audit** if it decides it is appropriate to have an internal audit function. If the organisation has internal auditors, the committee should supervise its work including the **standards** it follows, its **scope**, its **resources, work plan, liaison with external audit** and **results.** The committee should **monitor management's responsiveness** to internal audit's work.

Liaison with external audit

The audit committee should be responsible for **recommending the appointment, reappointment and removal of external auditors.** The audit committee should be particularly concerned with the **independence and objectivity** of external audit. The committee should especially consider whether it is appropriate to use external audit to **supply non-audit services.**

As regards the external audit itself, the committee should **discuss** its **scope with the external auditors** before it starts. The committee should also act as a **forum for liaison** between the external and internal auditors and audit committee, and be available for consultation with external auditors. The audit committee should **review the results of external audit's work** and **pursue any serious concerns** the external auditors have.

Dealing with staff concerns and investigations

The audit committee should review arrangements by which staff can raise concerns about **improprieties.** The committee should be able to ensure that appropriate **investigations** are made of concerns, whether raised by staff or through other sources.

(b) Whistleblowing has become more important in recent years for three main reasons:

(i) **Accessibility of information**
Firstly, an increasing amount of information is held on **computer files** that are in turn **accessible to many employees**. Certainly in the use of internal audit techniques where many transactions can be analysed by computer audit programs, the discovery of unusual or potentially incorrect transactions is more likely. Outside of the internal audit department, employees may **encounter information inadvertently**, simply because it is easily accessible. Whistleblowers are therefore more likely to find potentially unlawful or fraudulent transactions.

(ii) **Loyalty**
There is a **strong culture of loyalty** within many companies so that employees blowing the whistle may be seen as **traitors**. Although many countries have enacted laws to protect whistleblowers, they may still face retaliatory action by the company up to and including dismissal for making potentially false or malicious allegations.

(iii) **Whistleblowers**
Whistleblowers play an important role in uncovering mismanagement. Some recent financial scandals including Enron (2001) and WorldCom (2002) were bought into the public domain partly as a result of the actions of whistleblowers.

(c) **Importance of ethical code**

Actions that the audit manager can take must be **weighed against the CIMA ethical code**. While disclosing information about financial irregularities to a third party may appear to be attractive, the manager must bear in mind the overall ethical principles of integrity and confidentiality.

(i) **Integrity**
The principle of integrity implies that the manager will **act honestly** and that any action can be trusted. Any disclosure must therefore be made in good faith and not for financial gain and without malicious intent.

(ii) **Confidentiality**

The concept of confidentiality implies that **information obtained during the course of employment** in a company will be **kept confidential**, unless there is an appropriate reason to disclose this information. 'Normal reasons' will include client authorisation, breach of specific laws such as money laundering, and due process of law in a court.

The manager must therefore consider whether any disclose will be believed and whether breach of duty of confidentiality is appropriate in this situation.

Possible actions

Assuming that **disclosure is thought appropriate**, then the manager can consider the following reporting options:

(i) **To the board of directors or the chairman**

However, these people may be swayed by the **opinion of the chief accountant** and may not wish disclosure due to the adverse impact on TB1.

(ii) **To the external auditors**

Disclosure to a third party would appear to go against the **explicit instructions** of the head of internal audit. There is also no guarantee that the external auditors will be able to obtain appropriate audit evidence due to limited audit procedures or alteration of evidence prior to their visit.

(iii) **To the audit committee**

Given that TB1 is a listed company, then the principles of good corporate governance should be followed. Specifically, there should be procedures within the company to allow employees with genuine concerns about the operations of the company to make a **confidential approach** to the audit committee. As the committee is comprised of non-executive directors, then they should be able to take **appropriate investigative action** without conflict of interest regarding their stewardship of the running of the company.

Recommendation

It is therefore **recommended that the manager** make **disclosure to the audit committee**. This action will **not breach confidentiality** against the company as **no external disclosure** has been made, and given that disclosure is made in good faith, then it will also **maintain the manager's integrity**.

Question 5

Text references. Chapter 16.

Top tips. (a) relates to the overall model of determining the business strategy first and then ensuring that the information system strategy supports this. In this sense the question is relatively basic and few if any alternative answers would be expected.

(b)is the more difficult of the two sections. Information in the scenario must be used to provide the initial reason for the comments made in the answer. However your answer must give a good explanation of what you know and not just reproduce the facts in the scenario.

Note that the answer does not just cover the information technology aspects, but also considers wider management systems issues such as problems with the management accounting information and whether decentralisation is appropriate.

There may be alternative points that can be included in the answer, although initially these must be linked to the scenario.

Easy marks. (a) should be quite reasonable especially if you appreciate the links with Business Strategy.

(a) **Development of IS strategy**

IS strategy will normally be developed to meet the overall business strategy and requirements.

Steps in development

(i) **Determine the business strategy**
This is the **overall mission** of the **company**. In the case of FF this is the provision of flights between different locations.

(ii) **Determine the overall objectives of the company**
Objectives support the mission by showing exactly what the company expects to do. For example, FF has decided to be a low cost airline with a fairly good choice of routes.

(iii) **State the Critical Success Factors (CSFs)**
CSFs are those things that the company **must do well** in order to be a success. Rockhart identified that both internal and external CSFs would be expected in most companies. Internal CSFs for FF appear to be obtaining a given net profit and spending a minimum amount on IT. An external CSF will be related to customer satisfaction with the ease of use of the web site.

(iv) **Develop programme indicators**
Having identified the CSFs, individual **performance Indicators** can be developed to monitor the success or otherwise of achieving each CSF. For example, reports can be provided showing whether or not the target net profit has been achieved.

(v) **IS support overall strategy**
By following this process the information systems developed will automatically **support the overall business strategy**. Developing information systems first would not necessarily provide this support as there is no guarantee that the information provided would be relevant to the business objectives.

(b) **Strengths of IS strategy**

(i) **Customer focus**
Appropriate IS systems are available to allow customers to book and monitor details of flights operated by FF. This means that **bookings are not lost** due to poor IS. Provision of good customer facing systems will also hide the fact that the Company may lack appropriate in-house systems.

(ii) **IS Strategy**
The overall IS strategy may also be of benefit to the company in that it helps to ensure that there is **no excessive expenditure** on IS. However, the lack of expenditure causes other problems, as noted below.

Weaknesses in the IS strategy

(i) **Poor budgetary control**

In FF, new information systems are only implemented where a positive result is provided on the cost benefit analysis. While this helps to ensure that the benefit of each system outweighs the cost, it is not clear either **which costs and benefits are included** in the analysis or how intangible costs are measured. In other words, there is a danger that some of the **necessary information systems are not implemented** simply because they do not meet the investment criteria.

This problem could be remedied by **taking into account intangible benefits**. This may amend the investment decision and allow systems such as a company MIS with more frequent management information to be implemented.

(ii) **System incompatibility**

Lack of an appropriate IS system for the regional offices has led to some offices implementing their own systems. While these systems will be **correctly focused on user requirements**, they are unlikely to be the same and will **use different data formats and files**. Individual provision at each location will also lead to **duplication of effort** in system development, wasting resources within the company.

The problem could be **resolved** by **providing a design of a basic information system** for use in each of the 10 branches. It appears that the cost would not be significant, given that spreadsheets are currently being used. Details on user benefits will be required to show whether the system can be implemented using FF's current system development requirement.

(iii) **Decentralised IT system**

The overall IT system between branches and head office makes data transfer to head office **time-consuming and potentially dangerous**. Not only could the CD ROM be lost in the post, causing problems including loss of client sensitive data, but it is also not clear what backup systems are in place in FF in case of loss of data from one branch.

IS strategy could be amended to provide a **network**, allowing **daily secure transfer of data as a means of backup**. If the cost of a private network is considered too expensive, then use of a broadband connection with encrypted data transfer would be a cheaper option.

(iv) **Lack of overall strategy determination**

Allowing new systems to be developed without overall **control** is also a sign of **lack of overall IS strategy determination**. In theory, IS strategy should be set centrally to ensure that business objectives are achieved. Lack of central strategy determination has led to the problems noted above.

Even though the board takes a 'necessary evil' stance regarding the use of IS in-house, **review** of the board's policy may enable FF to provide additional useful IS systems.

[illegible]

CIMA – Strategic level

Paper P3

Management Accounting – Risk and Control Strategy

Mock Exam 2

You are allowed three hours to answer this question paper
In the real exam, you are allowed 20 minutes reading time before the examination begins during which you should read the question paper, and if you wish, make annotations on the question paper. However, you will **not** be allowed, **under any circumstances**, to open the answer book and start writing or use your calculator during this reading time.
You are strongly advised to carefully read all the question requirements before attempting the question concerned (that is all parts and/or sub-questions).
Answer the ONE compulsory question in Section A.
Answer TWO questions only from Section B

DO NOT OPEN THIS PAPER UNTIL YOUR ARE READY TO START UNDER EXAMINATION CONDITIONS

SECTION A – 50 marks

Answer this question

Question 1

The SPV Company is listed on the stock exchange of a central European country. The company manufactures a wide range of pharmaceutical products including modern drugs used in preventing and treating cancer, AIDS and similar diseases. SPV has three factories where drugs are produced and one research and development facility.

New R&D facility

The company needs to raise €400 million to open a new research and development facility in the south of the country it operates in. The company's credit rating is good, and the MSC bank is prepared to offer a loan at a rate of LIBOR + 0.5% as SPV prefers to take a floating rate loan. A fixed rate loan would be at 7.5%. However, a smaller company, HGS, is also looking to raise finance with a fixed rate loan. As HGS has a lower credit rating the MSC bank is only prepared to offer a rate of 9.5% or a floating rate of LIBOR + 1.0%. The bank proposes that the two companies arrange an interest rate swap for which the bank will charge 0.15% fees to each party. The two companies agree to split any benefit 2/3 to SPV and 1/3 to HGS.

The new facility is being designed to take advantage of recent theoretical advances in the use of potentially lethal varieties of bacteria to treat cancer and AIDS. Scientists have discovered that under certain conditions, these bacteria can be used to attack cancerous cells, effectively removing the cancer.

However, production of new drugs is potentially hazardous as lethal varieties of bacteria have to be used to manufacture the drug. These viruses and bacteria will be harmful if released into the general environment. This means that there are many precise requirements that must be followed in building the factory, such as provision of air conditioning, air filtration systems, emergency doors and 'negative pressure' systems to ensure that virus and bacteria are contained within the building, even if an accident occurs.

The project to build the new facility has been divided into a series of sub-projects. While each sub-project tends to follow on from the last in a linear fashion, overall control must still be maintained to ensure that delays do not occur between one sub-project finishing and the next beginning. Costs involved will relate to external contractors as well as use of SPV employees temporarily seconded to the construction project.

Expenditure on the construction of this factory will need to be monitored closely, with appropriate control action being taken if any stage of the project falls behind schedule. Detailed financial variance analysis reports will be available at the end of each phase of the project. This information will be summarised and distributed to project stakeholders.

Corporate governance

The board of directors comprises the chairman/CEO, three executive and two non-executive directors (NEDs). Separate audit and remuneration committees are maintained, although the chairman does have a seat on both of those committees. The NEDs are appointed for two and usually three 4-year terms of office before being required to resign. The internal auditor currently reports to the board (rather than the financial accountant) on a monthly basis, with internal audit reports normally being actioned by the board.

Required

(a) Discuss the corporate governance arrangements within SPV, briefly explaining any amendments you consider necessary to those structures. **(15 marks)**

(b) (i) Explain the principle and benefits of using interest rate swaps to reduce interest charges. **(6 marks)**

(ii) Calculate the interest rate benefit to SPV and HGS if the swap is arranged. **(6 marks)**

(c) (i) Describe the elements of a basic single loop control system showing how they can apply to the building of the new R&D facility in SPV. **(11 marks)**

(ii) Discuss the problems that could occur when attempting to use a control system to monitor the building of the new R&D facility. **(12 marks)**

(Total = 50 marks)

SECTION B – 50 marks

Answer TWO questions

Question 2

LP manufactures and supplies a wide range of different clothing to retail customers from 150 stores located in three different countries. The company has made a small net profit for the last three years. Clothes are made in three different countries, one in Europe, one in South America and the last in the Far East. Sales are made via cash, major credit cards and increasingly through the company's own credit card. Additional capital expenditure is planned in the next financial year to update some old production machinery.

In order to increase sales, a new Internet site is being developed which will sell LP's entire range of clothes using 3D revolving dummies to display the clothes on screen. The site will use some new compression software to download the large media files to purchasers' PCs so that the clothes can be viewed. This move is partly in response to environmental scanning which indicated a new competitor, PVO, will be opening an unknown number of stores in the next six months.

As a cost cutting move, the directors are considering delaying LP's new range of clothes by one year. Sales are currently in excess of expectations and the directors are unwilling to move away from potentially profitable lines.

Required

(a) Describe a process for managing risk that could apply to any company of a similar size to LP. **(7 marks)**

(b) Explain the business risks affecting LP and recommend how these risks can be managed. **(18 marks)**

(Total = 25 marks)

Question 3

Internal control systems are designed, amongst other things, to prevent error and misappropriation.

Required

(a) List the errors and misappropriations that may occur if purchases and capital expenditure are not properly controlled. **(5 marks)**

CMO is a high-quality, private motor manufacturing company. It has recently joined a consortium for the purchase of parts. CMO's purchases and capital expenditure systems are not integrated.

Purchases and capital expenditure

There are complex internal rules relating to what constitutes a purchase, and what constitutes capital expenditure and the budgets for both are tightly controlled. Problems associated with the internal rules result in a significant number of manual adjustments to the management accounts which take up an excessive amount of management time.

The system for authorising capital expenditure is not well controlled which results in some capital items being acquired without proper consideration, at the monthly meetings of the capital expenditure committee.

Purchase orders

Purchase orders are generated automatically by the computerised inventory system when inventory levels fall below a given level in the context of scheduled production. This system does not work well because the system uses outdated purchasing and production patterns and many manual adjustments are required. The orders are reviewed by the production controller and her junior managers and changes are made informally by junior clerical staff in the production controller's department.

Some of the purchases are input into the buying consortium system which shows the optimum supplier for any combination of cost, delivery time and specification. This system has only been in operation for a few months. The system takes up a substantial amount of disk space on the company's computers and is suspected of causing problems in other systems. It is difficult to use and so far, only two of the production controller's junior managers are able to use it. As a result, the parts ordered through the system are sometimes of the incorrect specification or are delivered late. The remaining purchases are ordered directly from manufacturers, as before, through a reasonably well-controlled buying department.

Required

(b) Explain, in a form suitable for inclusion in a report to management, the weaknesses, potential consequences and your recommendations relating to the purchases and capital expenditure systems of CMO. **(15 marks)**

Having received your report the directors have not only decided to act on its recommendations, but also to review the need for improving controls over the purchase of services.

Required

(c) Identify the main controls that should be exercised over the purchase of services. **(5 marks)**

(Total = 25 marks)

Question 4

You are in charge of information security in ROS Inc., a company which writes bespoke computer applications for a number of clients. The most recent application is production of a software control program for nanotechnology used in medical research. The software is highly confidential and has only been used on the internal private network in ROS; this network has no connections outside of the company.

As part of your monitoring, you have noticed private emails being sent by one employee Mr X, to a series of apparently related addressees in the BSTR company, a firm in competition with ROS. On further investigation, you found that the emails contained sections of the code of the new software control program. When challenged Mr X confirmed that the emails did contain sections of the code and asked you for a reference of good conduct prior to leaving the company. Mr X indicated that if this reference was not forthcoming, a timebomb virus hidden in the software control program would erase the entire program sometime in the next two weeks. You are informed that the virus can also be activated immediately by a series of keystrokes on the keyboard.

Required

(a) Recommend the actions that must be taken as a result of the breach of security up to and including removal of the virus. **(11 marks)**

(b) Discuss the main features of a personnel security policy that would be appropriate for ROS Inc, indicating the likely effectiveness of each section of the policy in preventing the introduction of a virus into the software control program. **(7 marks)**

(c) Describe the main elements of a software testing strategy designed to prevent a virus being included in software, and explain the problems in implementing this strategy successfully. **(7 marks)**

(Total = 25 marks)

Question 5

RP is a medium-sized importer and exporter of textile and other heavy machinery. It sells its products worldwide and has a policy of hedging all its overseas transactions in excess of a sterling equivalent of £100,000. Typically the company uses money market hedges or forward contracts. Below £100,000, the company bears the exchange risk itself.

The company's profits after interest for the past two years were as follows:

Year to	*30 September 20X8*	*30 September 20X9*
	£ million	£ million
Profit after interest	2.919	2.026

If the company had *not* hedged its currency risks, the profits would have been £2.141 million in 20X8 and 2.373 million in 20X9.

The Chief Executive is concerned about the effect hedging costs have had on the bottom line, especially as a hedging operation for a large contract is currently being arranged. He has asked for a report with a view to considering changing the company's policy on hedging.

The details of the proposed hedge are as follows.

The company is due to pay a Norwegian supplier 2.5 Norwegian million Kroners in three months' time for machinery for which RP has already found a buyer within the UK for £300,000. Today's exchange rate is NKr 8.9321 to the £1. On the advice of the Treasurer, the company is proposing to take out a contract to purchase NKr 2.5 million in three months' time at the forward rate of NKr 8.8820

Required

As Financial Manager with RP, write a report to the Chief Executive explaining:

(a) The purpose of hedging and the advantages and disadvantages of the company's current policy **(5 marks)**

(b) The financial implications of the hedging contract currently being considered. For the purposes of illustration and comparison, assume the NKr:

(i) Weakens against the £ sterling in three months' time to 8.9975, and

(ii) Strengthens against the £ to 8.6500 **(6 marks)**

(c) The factors the company should consider before changing its policy, in particular taking a decision not to hedge future foreign currency transactions **(8 marks)**

(d) Alternative methods of managing currency risks which might be available to the company **(6 marks)**

(Total = 25 marks)

Answers

DO NOT TURN THIS PAGE UNTIL YOU HAVE COMPLETED THE MOCK EXAM

A plan of attack

We've already established that you've been told to do it 101 times, so it is of course superfluous to tell you for the 102nd time to **Take a good look at the paper before diving in to answer questions**.

The next step

You may be thinking that this paper is a lot more straightforward than the first mock exam; however, having sailed through the first mock, you may think this paper is actually rather difficult.

Option 1 (Don't like this paper)

If you are challenged by this paper, it will be best to get the optional questions done before tackling the case study. Don't forget though that you will need half the time to answer the case study.

- Part (a) of **Question 2** is fairly general, but you do have to bear the company's details in mind. Although the scenario is quite short, there are lots of ideas in it that you can use to generate points for (b).
- Part (a) of **Question 3** is quite straightforward; all that's required is a general list. There is quite a lot of detail in (b); if you think about it, you'll be able to identify plenty of points. Remember the format for setting out answers: weakness, consequence, recommendation. You may not be able to think of too much to say about services in part (c), but bear in mind that it is only for 5 marks.
- If you're not sure how to approach **Question 4**, try thinking what the company has got to protect and what the timeframe is for the steps it must take (what does it need to do immediately). (b) brings in wider control systems issues and your knowledge of systems development can help you generate some ideas for (c).
- Although you may be put off **Question 5** by seeing it's a hedging question, the calculations are fairly straightforward (no derivatives) and they are only worth 6 marks; the rest of the marks are available for discussion.
- Every detail in the corporate governance paragraph is significant to your answer to part (a) of **Question 1**; keep asking yourself what's wrong with this. Even if you don't like the swap calculations in (b), you should still be able to pick up the discussion marks. (c)(i) requires a description of the main features of systems theory and mention for SPV's circumstances. If you keep making references to SPV, you will do better that many other candidates who won't have done. The key to (c)(ii) is thinking through the various stages of presenting and acting upon management information.

Option 2 (This paper's all right)

Are you **sure** it is? If you are then that's encouraging. You'll feel even happier when you've got the compulsory question out the way, so you should consider doing **Question 1 first**.

- Note the mark allocation for **Question 1** and make sure you allocate your time carefully between each part; don't focus too heavily on the parts you like best. Another trap to avoid is failing to mention the scenario details at all when answering (c)(i).
- Remember to bear in mind the circumstances of the company when answering part (a) of **Question 2**, although your answer can be fairly general. Analyse the scenario carefully in part (b) to ensure you've identified all relevant risks.
- You may think there's lots to say in all parts of **Question 3**, but bear in mind the marks and hence time allocation for each part. You will also lose marks in the most important part ((b)) if you don't present your answer in an appropriate format.
- Note that **Question 4** isn't just about IT specifics (although you do need a critical understanding in (c)); (b) is about wider control systems issues.
- If you've revised hedging, you should cope very well with **Question 5**.

Once more

You must **allocate your time** according to the marks for the question in total, and for the parts of the questions. And you must also **follow the requirements exactly**.

Finished with fifteen minutes to spare?

Looks like you slipped up on the time allocation. However if you have, make sure you don't waste the last few minutes; go back to **any parts of questions that you didn't finish** because you ran out of time.

Forget about it!

Forget about what? Excellent, you already have.

Question 1

Text references. Chapter 3 covers general systems issues. Chapter 5 gives detail on corporate governance and Chapter 14 shows you how to deal with interest rate swaps.

Top tips. (a) is designed to allow you to discuss the weaknesses in SPV's corporate governance. The points made state the relevant corporate government requirement, but then go on to explain why it's important, and to contrast what SPV does with best practice. Remember that the bulk of the marks will be for application to the scenario. The weaknesses are mainly directed around the composition of the board and its major sub-committees.

(b) is a basic swap calculation with the relevant information provided in the question. The spilt of the swap savings is not 50:50, providing a small complication. Although not required by the question, we have included a diagram of the swap in the answer to illustrate how it will work.

(c) (i) asks for an explanation of a single loop control system. The term single loop is included in the requirement to identify the type of control system required. Each element of the system is described and applied to SPV in turn. As with (a), most of the marks given for (c) (i) will be for application to the scenario. A common failing of answers to questions like this is to spend most of the answer on a general description of control systems and only talk about the organisation briefly at the end of the answer.

For (ii), the scenario includes some pointers to problems with the control system that you need to identify and include in the answer. The things to look out for are how each stage of the project will be organised, the management accounting information provided, and how progress will be measured. Knowledge brought forward from Paper P1 will be of help here. The examiner has recently emphasised the importance of being able to call on Managerial level knowledge in this exam. Since RCS is part of the management accounting pillar of the CIMA qualification, knowledge from P1 or P2 could be especially relevant.

Easy marks. If you have a good understanding of the corporate governance requirements, there is enough material in the scenario to enable you to score well on (a). (b) (i) would represent easy marks in any swaps question.

(a) **Suggestions for corporate governance**

Composition of the board

Corporate governance requirements normally indicate that the board of directors should comprise **equal numbers of executive and non-executive directors** to ensure no one group dominates, and that non-executive directors provide an effective presence on the board. By having only two non-executive directors, SPV may not be following requirements.

SPV needs to appoint at least one more non-executive director to the board.

Lack of financial experience

There is also a **lack of any relevant financial experience** amongst the non-executive directors. Again, corporate governance regulations normally suggest that at least one NED should have **financial experience** so they can monitor effectively the financial information that the board is reviewing.

Making the new appointee an accountant would also help to fulfil this requirement.

Role of chairman/CEO

Corporate governance regulations normally require that the roles of the **chairman** (the person running the board) and the **CEO** (the person running the company) are **split**. The reason for this is to ensure that no one person has too much influence over the running of the company. The only exception to this rule is that the roles can be combined for a short period of time where the company faces significant difficulties and giving more power to one person will assist in overcoming those difficulties.

As SPV does not appear to have any significant difficulties at present, then the roles of chairman and CEO should be split at the earliest opportunity.

Audit and remuneration committees

The chairman of the board is sometimes allowed to sit on the audit and remuneration committees to ensure that decisions made are in agreement with the overall objectives. Issues that are not clear with the current structures relate to the **composition of those committees.**

Corporate governance requirements indicate these committees will normally comprise **NEDs**, including the senior NED. This is to limit the extent of power of the executive directors. SPV needs to ensure that this requirement is being followed.

NEDs' terms of appointment

NEDs are **normally appointed for three year terms** at maximum. The re-appointment provisions apply to ensure that new NEDs are being appointed as directors on a regular basis. NEDs who have been on the board for a few years may become **too familiar with the operations** of the company and therefore not provide the necessary external independent check that they are supposed to do.

NEDs need to be appointed for **three year terms**, with re-appointment for a third term being exceptional rather than the norm.

Internal audit

The internal audit department should not usually report to the financial accountant as that person may have a **vested interest** in not taking any action on the reports, especially where reports are critical of the accountant. In that sense, reporting to the board is acceptable. However, the board as a whole may **not have the time to review internal audit reports** and again may be tempted to ignore them if they are critical of the board itself.

Corporate governance regulations indicate that the internal audit department **should report to the audit committee** with reports being forwarded to the board. This ensures that the report is heard by the NEDs, who can then ensure that internal audit recommendations are implemented where appropriate, by the board. In SPV, the internal auditor needs to report to the audit committee, for reasons already mentioned above.

(b) (i) **Principle of interest rate swaps**

Borrowing costs

An interest rate swap occurs where two companies (or a company and a bank) **swap interest rate commitments** with each other. The aim of the swap is to **reduce overall borrowing costs** for both parties. Swaps allow companies with **different credit ratings to borrow in the market that offers them the best deal** and then to swap this benefit to reduce overall borrowing costs. Each company essentially **simulates the borrowing costs of the other party**, while **maintaining their original obligations** to the provider of fixed or floating rate loans. The swap means that each party must accept **counterparty risk**, that is the risk of having to accept the other party's obligations on the loan should the other default.

SPV and HGS

In this situation, SPV can borrow at 7.5% in the fixed rate market compared to 9.5% being offered to HGS – that is a 2% difference. However, HGS can borrow in the fixed rate market at LIBOR + 1.0% compared to SPV who can borrow at LIBOR + 0.5%. HGS can borrow at 0.5% more than SPV. This provides an overall benefit of 1.5% (2% less 5%). Interest rate swaps therefore work on the principle of comparative advantage.

Flexibility

Swaps are **relatively flexible** as they can be arranged in any size and can be reversed if necessary.

Restructuring

Swaps also **allow some element of capital restructuring** by changing the nature of interest rate commitments. In this example, HGS will find it difficult to raise finance at favourable interest rates.

Transaction costs

The **transaction costs** for establishing the swap is relatively **low**. The only fee is the cost to the bank.

(ii) **Swap calculation**

	SPV	*HGS*	*Total*
Wants	Floating	Fixed	
Pays without swap	LIBOR + 0.5%	9.5%	LIBOR + 10%
Pays with swap	7.5%	LIBOR + 1.0%	LIBOR + 8.5%
Bank fee	0.15%	0.15%	0.3%
Potential gain			1.2%

Split of swap gain

Total gain = 1.2%
Split 2/3 to SPV and 1/3 to HGS
= 0.8% to SPV and 0.4% to HGS

Rate for SPV = LIBOR + 0.5% – 0.8% = LIBOR – 0.3%
Loan for HGS = 9.5% – 0.4% = 9.1%

	SPV	*HGS*
Pays to bank if swap agreed	(7.5%)	(LIBOR + 1.0%)
Details of swap		
Floating	(LIBOR + 1.0%)	LIBOR + 1.0%
Fixed (bal.fig. working)	8.95%	(8.95%)
Bank fee	(0.15%)	(0.15%)
Net outcome	(LIBOR – 0.3%)	(9.1%)

Working

(7.5%) + (LIBOR + 1%) + X + (0.15%) = (LIBOR – 0.3%)
(LIBOR + 8.65%) + X = (LIBOR – 0.3%)
X = 8.95%

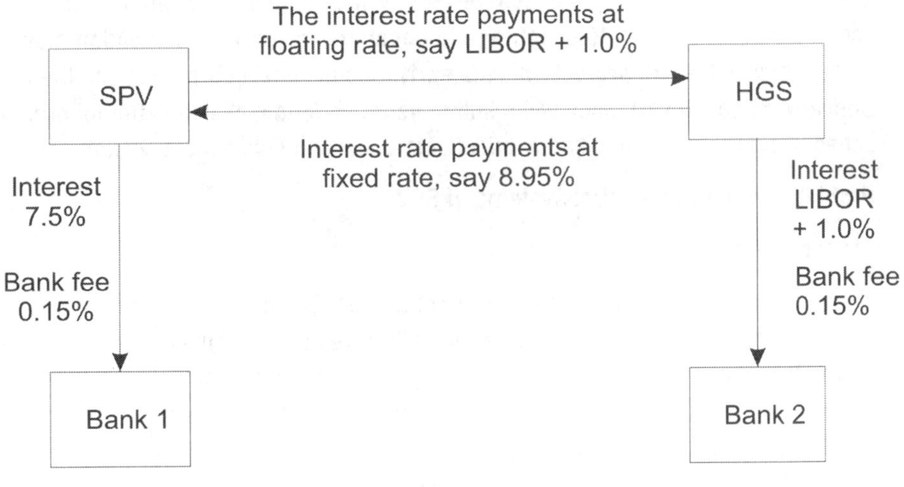

(c) (i) **Elements of a control system**

Plan

The first part of any control system is to **set a plan or budget** to show exactly what the system is attempting to achieve.

For SPV, there is a need to build the new factory with a specific budget. As there are several different steps to building the factory, then the plan can be divided into a series of **specific milestones** with **sub-plans** for each section being produced. The plan will involve **setting time and cost budgets** for each sub-project.

Process

The process is where the actual work is undertaken to manufacture the goods.

For SPV, this is the actual building of the new R&D facility. Actual **costs and time** in building each section of the facility will have to be **recorded**.

Sensor/Outputs

There must be some way of **measuring the outputs** from the system, with those outputs being quantifiable. The outputs will be collected by the **sensor**.

For SPV, the outputs from each sub-project are essentially the **time taken to complete each section of the project along with the costs to date**. Costs will be **accumulated by the management accounting control system** and reported as part of that system along with **variances against budget**. Time will also be measured against budget and reported using GANTT charts or similar project management tools.

Comparator

A comparator **measures the actual outputs** from a system **against the budget** for that system. Results are presented as positive or negative variances against budget.

SPV's management accounting control system will **present an analysis of budget against actual expenditure** while **GANTT charts** show budgeted against actual time taken.

Effector

An effector provides the **control action to change the actual system behaviour**. Control actions can include **changing the inputs to the system or the process itself**. Control action will be either to **return the actual time or costs taken to budget** (negative feedback) or in some situations where the variance is positive, take **control action** to increase the variance (positive feedback).

For SPV, control action will be needed when the **actual expenditure or time taken** on a sub-project moves away from the **budgeted cost or time**. Where time or costs are less than budget, control action will be taken to try to **encourage the positive variance**. The situation must also be monitored closely in case the **sub-project finishes early**, and the next sub-project can therefore **start early**. Similarly, **negative variances** will result in **negative feedback** in an attempt bring the project back on schedule and so avoid any 'knock on' effects of making subsequent sections of the project late.

(ii) **Problems with using control systems in SPV**

Preparing the plan

It may be **difficult to prepare the different budgets**. The new testing facility is expensive and currently has a round sum figure of €400 million as the cost. This figure is likely to include **many estimates** as the expenditure relates to the future. If the plan contains estimates then it may be difficult for individual managers to accept it or use the plan as a base against which to measure actual expenditure.

Measuring results

Building the new testing facility will involve **many difficult inputs** over a considerable period of time. Measuring the actual costs may be difficult because they involve a **variety of internal and external sources**. Cost allocation will be particularly difficult where **salary costs** of SPV staff have to be **allocated** between the project and their 'normal duties'. There may even be a tendency to allocate fewer costs to the project to avoid overruns.

Taking control action

To be effective, **control action should be taken** as soon as any **deviation from budget is identified**. However, in this project, **variance analysis reports** will only be **available at the end of each phase** of the project. This implies that cost or time overruns will not be identified until it is too late to take any effective control action.

Provision of non-accounting information

To fully understand the reason for variances, **non-financial information** is **normally provided** to explain why the variance has occurred. The supporting analysis helps to **determine the control action necessary** as a result of the variance. However, in the R&D project, it appears that **only financial information** will be **provided**. This means that **reasons for variances** will be **difficult to determine** and as a result inappropriate control actions may be taken.

Cause of variances

Variances are **normally split** between those that are under the **control of the manager** and those over which the **manager has no control**. Again, without supporting explanation for the variances, the reason for each variance will be difficult to determine, including whether managers are **responsible for each variance**. This may also lead to **lack of care** in managing the project as managers know they will not be 'blamed' for any adverse variances.

Project reports

Reporting to stakeholders

Regular reports on project progress are **essential** so that all stakeholders are **aware of the progress of a project** and can understand the reasons for any delays or alternatively time and cost savings. **Limiting reporting information** to financial comments only **decreases the effectiveness** of any project report. This may also **increase the work of the project managers** as they will now have to provide verbal explanations of variances to any stakeholder requesting this information.

Question 2

Text references. Chapters 1 and 2 cover the main risks and means of dealing with them. Chapters 11 and 13 cover the financial risks in more detail.

Top tips. In (a) the answer follows a standard method for effective risk management. While the question requirement leaves open the possibility of using other processes, the idea of identifying the risks, assessing the likelihood of occurrence, limiting the risk and control and review should be identifiable in the answer.

In (b), the scenario provides some useful hooks on which to base the main points in the answer. However, the list of risks could be applied to many other different companies. Identification and explanation of the risk and coming up with reasonable risk management suggestions is vital in this examination. As a lot of the scenario is about LP's business and commercial environment, it therefore follows that to score well in (b), you'll need to cover the main business risks in detail.

Easy marks. (a) is a straightforward discussion.

(a) **Risk appetite**

How organisations deal with risks will depend on the appetite managers have for taking risks. This may be determined by management inclinations, shareholder views or the history of the organisation. Managers should ensure that risk appetite is directly **related to the organisation's strategy** and balances growth, risk and return. It should feed into the organisation's policies and procedures.

Risk identification

Any organisation needs a procedure for **reviewing the risks it faces and to identify what those specific risks are**. The board of the company also needs to be aware that those risks will change over time, so it must be on the lookout for new risks. Risks may also **vary depending on the country** in which the company operates. For example it may be difficult to establish a new brand in a new country, or there may be different employment, environmental or other legislation that must be followed.

Risk assessment

Risk evaluation involves the use of various procedures to assess **the nature of the risk** and the **consequences** of the risk materialising. For a downside risk, the extent of any loss depends on:

(i) The **probability of the outcome of the loss making event**, and
(ii) The **size of the loss in the event that the risk crystallises** – that is occurs

Risk profiling

Risk profiling involves **mapping different risks** in terms of the **frequency** that they will crystallise, and the **severity** of the outcome if they do. Where the probability of the outcome is remote and the actual loss small, then no action may be taken regarding that risk. However, a high probability of the event and potentially large losses will mean that serious risk management measures are required.

Risk quantification

Managers will then assess the **scale of significant risks** in **quantitative terms**. They will try to assess the **expected loss**, the **probability that losses will occur** and the **largest predictable loss**. Possible methods include expected value and value at risk calculations, also simulations.

Risk management measures

Risk management measures are the **responsibility of managers and the board in an organisation**. The actual measure taken vary depending on the risk:

- **Abandonment/avoidance** of risks with high likelihood of occurring and serious consequences if they do occur – for example selling a loss-making subsidiary
- **Transfer**, for example by insurance, risks that have little chance of occurring, but will have serious consequences if they do materialise
- **Control** measures to reduce risks that are likely to materialise, but with limited consequences if they do
- **Acceptance** of risks with insignificant consequences, and little possibility of materialising

Risk control and review

Control systems should be **established to monitor risks** and to **identify new risks** or **existing risks** that are becoming **more significant.** The risk management and internal control systems and procedures may need to change to counter these sorts of risk.

(b) **Business risks**

These are risks that a **company's performance could be better or worse than expected.**

(i) **The new business venture to sell clothes on the Internet using 3D models to display the clothes.**

There is the risk that **demand will be far short** of that anticipated or that costs of developing the Internet site will significantly exceed budget. The dot.com company Boo.com collapsing after only a few weeks trading due to lack of ability of servers to cope with demand.

LP should have assessed the 3D project for feasibility. **Budgets** should have been established and **actual expenditure** regularly **compared with budgets**. If actual expenditure is unavoidably significantly in excess of budget, the board should consider whether the project should continue.

Thorough **testing procedures** should have been built into the plan, and these should ensure that the site is **capable of coping with anticipated demand.** Once the site is operational, LP should **monitor the level of sales** generated by obtaining customer feedback through the site, and **comparing sales generated** with the **costs** of keeping the site updated.

(ii) **Product obsolescence**

The decision to lengthen the time of sale for each product may appear to decrease development costs. However, the board of LP must also take into account **demand for the goods**. The fashion industry tends to issue new clothes and designs every few months, and certainly in temperate climates, fashions will change according to the season. There is a risk, if LP's clothes are perceived as unfashionable, that not changing products sold will **reduce sales** far in excess of the reduction in expenditure.

LP should **monitor the performance of products** in detail, and look for evidence of falling sales and other evidence that its products are **viewed as old-fashioned**, for example adverse customer or press comment. The board should also consider whether **work on developing new products** should continue, so that new lines can be launched quickly if demand falls.

(iii) **New competition**

The new company PVO appears to be aggressively attacking LP's market place. While the overall effect of the new competitor is difficult to determine, having a new range of clothes available is likely to attract customers with **little if any brand loyalty** to LP.

LP should make sure that **competitor activity is carefully monitored** and responses are made to known or predicted competitor activity, for an example an advertising campaign to counter new products being launched by the competitor. LP's board should also **review very regularly the performance of products** which are **most vulnerable to competitor activity** and decide whether to invest more in these or concentrate on other less vulnerable products.

The overall going concern of the company may again be affected.

Financial risks

Financial risks arise from the **possibility that the financial situation of the company will be different from what was expected**. Financial risks will include:

(i) **Credit risks**

These arise from the use of the **company's store card**. If there is an economic depression then there may be an **increased risk of card holders defaulting** on their payments.

LP should carry out **credit checks** before consumers are allowed a credit card. The **initial credit limits** should be **set low**, and increased over time if the customer's level of business and repayment record warrant it. The company's systems should **reject payments** that take customers in **excess of their credit limits**. LP should insist on a **minimum amount** being repayable on the card each month. There should be **specified procedures** for pursuing **overdue debts**.

(ii) **Foreign exchange risks**

These occur because LP purchases raw materials and some finished products from overseas. Depending on how these purchases are financed, there will be a risk of **exchange rate losses** if the main currency LP uses moves adversely compared to the supplying country's currency.

LP's board should consider changing purchasing arrangements, so that more purchases are made in countries where LP has significant sales, thus reducing exchange risks by **matching**. However this should be weighed against the possibility that purchase prices may increase from using different sources. Payments on large purchases not made immediately could be covered by **forward contracts**.

(iii) **Interest rate risk**

This results from an **increase in bank base rates**. An increase in rates may **increase LP's finance costs significantly**, especially where there are significant **loans or overdrafts** where the interest rate follows the base rate.

LP's board should review the company's pattern of lending. Ideally if interest rates are expected to rise, it should look to replace **overdraft and floating rate finance** with **fixed rate loans**. LP may also hedge borrowing that will be required in some months' time by means of **interest rate futures and options**.

Question 3

Text references. Chapter 6.

Top tips. Read through the examiner's comments about the real answers to this question (below). Notice the examiner emphasises that candidates should answer the question set. This is a point which it is pretty easy to get right in the exam and will therefore gain you marks and also save you wasting time and irritating the examiner. Always read the requirement carefully once or twice to make sure that you are not suffering from a case of wishful thinking. It sometimes helps if you read a requirement before reading through a scenario attached to a question as well – although you have to beware answering the question without reference to the scenario; the examiner hasn't just put it there for fun.

The main focus in (b) is on problems with the way the system has been designed; clearly if staff are forced to circumvent the system, there are major problems. Note that much of (b) is concerned with operational and managerial inefficiencies, and it does fall within internal audit's remit to consider these. Using the 'weaknesses, consequences, recommendations' format in (b) ensures you approach analysing the scenario systematically.

Remember in (c) that the controls must be appropriate for services. Think about the main objectives, that the company obtains the best terms and appropriate performance from the supplier, that only the services needed by the company are supplied and invoices are only authorised if evidence of the provision of services is provided.

Easy marks. (a) is a standard list of potential problems with purchasing (goods wrongly ordered, goods ordered on poor terms, problems with recognition of liabilities).

Examiner's comments. This was a question in a recognised format, that could have been answered very well but, surprisingly, was not. In part (a), many candidates properly identified the wide variety of errors and misappropriations that could occur if purchases and capital expenditure were not properly controlled, but a number of candidates did not read the question properly and instead suggested internal controls that should be in place in such systems. In part (b), almost all candidates included a 'covering note', which was not asked for and for which no marks were awarded. The question asked for weaknesses, potential consequences and recommendations in a form suitable for inclusion in a report to management. There was also a great deal of repetition in answers to this question. The overall impression was that answers were sloppy.

(a) **Errors and misappropriations – purchases system**

- **Goods** could be **bought** which are **not genuinely for the company**
- **Goods** could be **bought** at **inappropriately high prices**
- **Goods** which have **not been ordered** could be **accepted/paid for**
- **Genuine liabilities** might be **unrecognised**, resulting in loss of supply
- **Liabilities** which are **not genuine** might be **created** as part of a fraud

(b) **REPORT**

To: Management
From: Internal auditors
Date: 16 September 20X8
Subject: Purchases and capital expenditure systems

Complex purchasing system

Weakness

The purchasing system is **complex**. This can be seen in the distinction between capital and revenue purchases and also the use of two systems to purchase goods running in parallel.

Consequence

The complexity of the system **wastes management time** and at worst, could in itself result in **errors being made in classification or purchase** which could result in business interruption or dissatisfied suppliers.

Recommendation

The purchases system should be **revisited and simplified**. This could be done by the internal audit department. Alternatively, we would be happy to be engaged separately to provide advice on the simplification of your system.

Consortium system

Weakness

The new system of purchasing is **not used comprehensively** for all purchases.

Consequences

This is likely to lead to **confusion** and could lead to the company making **necessary purchases twice** or **not at all**.

Recommendation

Steps should be taken to **integrate the entire purchasing function** with the consortium system to avoid confusion.

Weakness

The **consortium system** can only be **operated by two of the production controller's junior managers**.

Consequences

This has two significant consequences:

(i) There are **insufficient people trained to operate the major purchasing system** and the company may find that they could be unable to operate their systems if those capable are absent.

(ii) The people who can use the system are employed in the production department, meaning that there is a **lack of segregation of duties** in the purchasing function, which could lead to error and/or purchasing fraud.

Recommendation

The purchasing department staff should be **trained to use the new Consortium system** and they should be the only people who use the system, so that they operate as an authorisation function to purchases.

Circumvention

Weakness

The **automatic re-ordering system** and the **capital expenditure system** both **operate inefficiently** and staff members are required to circumvent the system in order to be able to get on with their jobs.

Consequence

Staff may become **accustomed to habitually overriding the systems**, which will cause systems to be inefficient and fail to achieve company objectives.

Recommendation

The **system should be improved** and **staff reminded** that **circumvention** of the system is **not acceptable**. This is likely to have to be an initiative led by senior staff, who may have permitted/encouraged circumvention of systems in the past.

Information Technology Systems

Weakness

The **new purchasing system** appears to take up a **significant amount of disk space** and cause problems to other programmes.

Consequence

This may result in a **significant 'jam'** in the company's overall system, or even cause errors in related systems.

Recommendation

Technical advisers should be engaged to review the system and discover whether there is an **error with the new system**, or whether the **capacity of the company's infrastructure is sufficient**. It may be that the **company's IT policy** needs to be **reviewed**. Again, we could provide such a service for the company, if required.

(c) **Controls over services**

(i) **Segregation of duties**
The person who deals with the service suppliers **should not be the same person** that authorises the invoice.

(ii) **Terms of business**
The company should have terms of business and internal regulations in place which specify that suppliers of services are **only allowed to deal with authorised company staff.**

(iii) **Supplier monitoring**
Different means of monitoring the performance of suppliers should be used, for example **actual costs measured against budgeted costs** on a quarterly basis, or regular meetings with the supplier.

(iv) **Internal monitoring**
The accounts department should **monitor** whether **other departments' use of services is appropriate** by reviewing detailed bills, for example a breakdown of telephone charges.

(v) **Record-keeping**
Records should be **kept** of **specific services** at the time they were provided, for example records of visits by photocopying maintenance staff should record length of visit and work done. These records should be subsequently matched with invoices.

(vi) **Billing**
When authorising invoices for payment, the authoriser should **check recent payables ledger details** to ensure that the invoice has been presented when expected (for example utility providers would send invoices quarterly).

Question 4

Text references. Chapter 18.

Top tips. The main advice in (a) is don't jump to conclusions. Remember that although this situation is serious, there are basic techniques and procedures that must be carried out to assess the likelihood of the risk materialising. You have to provide **reasoned** recommendations in the answer rather than resort to inappropriate action with little or no justification.

In (b) it is important to know the main settings of a personnel security policy; however you will gain few marks unless you commented on how effective each section was. Again, be realistic and make practical comments where possible. Remember that programmers are clever people; don't focus the answer on inappropriate actions like simply watching the computer screen to check what they are writing.

(c) emphasises that testing is likely to be ineffective when certain types of viruses are involved. As in previous sections, don't jump to conclusions that the virus will be found – think through the situation carefully and document your answer with clear reasons why testing may not be effective.

Overall this question is quite specific, but it does bring in areas other than computerised systems (fraud, personnel controls), and possibly in the exam a computer fraud may be used as the basis for discussing wider issues.

(b) and (c) are also good examples of questions with complex requirements, and you need to ensure that your answers fulfil the whole requirement. Planning what you'll write, and asking yourself before you start writing whether what you're planning to say answers the question fully, will help you do this.

Easy marks. All parts require careful application to the scenario.

(a) **Actions to be taken now regarding the breach of security**

The immediate action is to minimise the threat to the company's computer systems.

(i) **Dismissal of Mr X**
Mr X must be asked to **leave the company immediately** pending further investigation of his claims. He should be escorted from the premises without being allowed to return to his desk or touch any ROS computer. This is to ensure that the virus is not activated.

(ii) **Personnel checks**
Checks must be made with the personnel department to ensure that **Mr X has signed the standard contract of employment** including the non-disclosure agreements concerning company software. This action will confirm that Mr X was in breach of contract, even if it is later determined that no action can be taken.

(iii) **Backup**
An **immediate backup** of the software control programme must be taken onto CD-ROM or similar storage media and **stored in a safe**. While backups will be taken each day anyway, this is a precautionary measure to ensure that the most recent copy of the software control program has been duplicated and stored securely.

(iv) **Program analysis**
The **software control program must be analysed** to try and determine whether Mr X's claims are correct regarding the virus. We should **load the program onto a 'dirty computer'**, that is standalone computer that has no links to any other computer. This will minimise any loss of programs or data caused by the virus. There is no reason to believe that the virus will only destroy the software control program.

(v) **Code identification**
The **software control program** must be **checked by other programming staff** to see if any of the code appears to relate to a virus. Many viruses have specific signatures which identify them. However, Mr X may well be a skilled programmer and so the virus may be well hidden within the software. If

necessary, other programming staff with skill in detecting and removing viruses can be hired to perform this check.

(vi) **Program changes**

It may be possible to **review recent changes** made to the software control program from the daily system backups. If so, amendments may be traceable to Mr X and then reviewed to determine whether they contain any virus.

(vii) **Removal of code**

If **suspicious code is detected**, then **attempt to remove it** on the dirty computer. Check that the software still operates after removal.

(viii) **Legal advice**

If **suspicious code is not detected, take legal advice** on the situation. If necessary, **agree to the terms of Mr X**, asking him to **remove the virus** on the dirty computer. As part of any severance agreement, tell Mr X that he must agree to amend the software at his own cost should any other trace of the virus be found.

(b) The personnel security policy in ROS must include the following features:

(i) **Recruitment**

Initial recruitment must include the taking of **references from previous employers**. While this will not stop implementing virus software, it will provide an indication of the trustworthiness of the employee. For confidential projects, telephone references may also be obtained to confirm written details.

(ii) **Job rotation**

Job rotation is important to ensure that **one person does not work too long on one section of code** and possibly implement viruses, and to **ensure that the code is checked** by other individuals. Checking may identify errors in program code as well as viruses.

(iii) **Supervision and observation**

Supervision may not be effective initially as it is a passive and relatively general activity and may not initially detect any wrongdoing. However, **monitoring of emails** did detect the illegal copying of the program code indicating that this system may be an **effective detection control**.

(iv) **Review of computer usage**

Reviewing computer usage may be effective where programmers suddenly start to work long or particularly unusual hours, especially with no colleagues around. It is generally easier to amend the code without the concern of someone overlooking the screen while the amendments take place. **Reasons for unusual working hours** must therefore be sought, although many programmers do work unusual hours. **Actual review of code** may be necessary to try and detect any incorrect programming.

(v) **Enforced vacations**

As in any job, **lack of vacations** can be **suspicious** simply because it appears the person does not trust anyone else to continue their work. Lack of vacation may indicate that the code has been amended illegally. However, there is **no guarantee that forcing staff to take vacations** will allow supervisors or other staff **to detect illegal amendments to software**, especially where those amendments are well hidden.

(vi) **Termination procedures**

These appear to be adequate in ROS, with Mr X being **denied access to the computer system as soon as the virus situation was discovered**. Allowing any programmer back to a computer after termination of contract may allow them to write new virus code or trigger previously written code.

(c) **Aim of testing strategy**

A testing strategy is designed to ensure that **software meets pre-determined objectives** without errors occurring in the input, processing or output of data.

(i) **Strategy approach**

The testing strategy is formulated detailing the **approach to be taken to testing**, the **tests conducted**, and the **techniques** to be used. The strategy will ensure that basic objectives are met; however, virus code may not be detected during normal processing so the strategy may fail to test for this.

(ii) **Test plan**

The plan **explains what will be tested and when the tests will take place**. If the plan is known in advance then the **virus code** could be **hidden or simply programmed** to remain inactive during testing. Even if the virus can be activated, the test plan may not include appropriate tests, as noted above.

(iii) **Test design**

Tests are designed to **check basic input, processing and output** are in accordance with any specification. As a virus will not be on any specification, test design is likely to be ineffective in identifying the virus.

(iv) **Performing tests**

Tests are actually carried out. The only possibility of detecting the virus will be if the **results are not exactly as expected**, although given that a timebomb virus will only be active on a given date, actual testing is unlikely to be of any use.

(v) **Documentation**

The documentation will simply **show the results of the test**. Although useful in providing a record of testing carried out, if no errors are found then no virus will be recorded.

(vi) **Re-testing**

Re-testing, including regression testing, will be performed where **one section of code has been amended**. If the amendment was unauthorised then reviewing the amendment itself will be more effective than actual testing for reasons noted above.

Question 5

Text references. Chapter 11.

Top tips. In (a) you need to describe clearly why hedging, despite its costs, is necessary in some circumstances; and in (c) why transactions cannot be looked at individually when deciding whether to hedge. The arguments in favour of reducing hedging in (c) are that matching is a better method, and that risks are minimised if the company is diversified or currency movements are predictable. (c) mentions both one-off transactions and longer-term risks.

When you plan your answer, make sure that the points you mention in (a) are not duplicated in (c).

With questions like (d), it's important to pick up scenario details to judge what methods are most appropriate for the organisation. The company isn't big enough to warrant maintaining a significant treasury function, so therefore you need to concentrate on simpler methods, and only mention more complex techniques briefly.

Easy marks. (a) is a discussion about basic points in this area (why you manage risk and the features of key risk management instruments).

To: Chief Executive
From: Financial Manager
Date: 31 October 20X2

Subject: The company's foreign exchange risk management policy

This report compares the company's existing foreign exchange risk management policy with alternative approaches.

(a) **Purposes of hedging foreign exchange risk**

Need for hedging

Our company sells world-wide, invoicing for most transactions in the currency of the foreign country rather than in pounds sterling. Some of our foreign suppliers also invoice in their local currencies. Sales transactions may suffer from **exchange losses**, if the foreign currency weakens between the date of the contract and the date of cash settlement. Likewise, exchange losses on **purchases** can be made when foreign currencies strengthen.

Forward contracts

The purpose of hedging is to **limit or eliminate these exchange losses** on transactions. The main hedging technique we use is the **forward foreign exchange contract**, in which the exchange rate is agreed in advance for future receipts or payments in foreign currencies. The hedge is applied to individual transactions over £100,000.

Advantages of forward contracts

The advantages of this policy are that the cash flows for all material foreign transactions are **predictable**, **exchange losses** are **eliminated** and cash **planning is made easier** because of this.

Disadvantages of forward contracts

(i) The **bank commission payable** and **exchange rates obtainable** on forward transactions **significantly erode our profits**, and

(ii) **Potential exchange gains** are **eliminated** along with the losses. In the year to 30 September 20X8, hedging eliminated £778,000 of foreign exchange losses, but in 20X9 potential exchange gains of £347,000 were forgone.

(b) **Financial implications of hedging the purchase of Norwegian machinery**

Purchase price

Whereas the UK sales price for this machinery is fixed at £300,000, the purchase price depends on how the Norwegian Kroner moves against the pound sterling over the next three months. At today's spot rate of 8.9321, NKr 2.5 million is £279,889, giving a trading profit of £20,111.

Top tips. As the exchange rate is quoted at NKr 8.9321:£1, you need to **divide** the NKr amount NKr 2.5 million by the exchange rate to arrive at the amount in £.

Kroner weakens

For the purpose of illustration, assume (a) that the NKr weakens in three months time to 8.9975. The supplier's invoice would be settled by a payment of £277,855, giving an exchange gain of £2,034 and a total profit on the transaction of £22,145.

Kroner strengthens

However, if we assume (b) that the NKr strengthens to 8.6500, the payment is £289,017, resulting in an exchange loss of £9,128 and a net profit of only £10,983.

Forward contract

If the transaction is hedged using a forward contract, the payment is known in advance to be 2,500,000 / 8.8820 = £281,468, giving a profit of £18,532 which is not affected by any future exchange rate movements. A small amount of the target profit is sacrificed in order to reduce risk.

(c) **Factors to consider before changing foreign exchange risk management policy**

Factors in favour of reducing hedging

(i) **Matching**
Because we import and export, there will be instances where receipts and payments in the same currency can be **matched**, reducing the requirement for hedging, because any losses on the imports will be offset by gains on the exports, or vice versa. Even if the transaction amounts and dates do not match exactly, the **amount**, **duration** and **cost of hedging** can be significantly **reduced** by planning along these lines.

(ii) **Portfolio effect**
Because we trade in many countries world-wide, the portfolio effect will automatically **reduce some of our currency risk**: gains from some currencies will be offset by losses from others.

(iii) **Longer-term movements**
Although many short-term currency movements are unpredictable, there are various factors which cause longer term movements and which can be predicted. For example, if there is **high inflation** in a country from which we are purchasing, the currency is likely to devalue, and there will be little sense in always hedging against purchase transactions for that country.

Arguments in favour of hedging

(i) **Embarrassment factor**
Although currency losses may be offset by gains in the longer run, the 'embarrassment factor' of a **significant loss** in any one year might cause customers to lose confidence in our management ability.

(ii) **Threat to existence of company**
In extreme cases, currency losses may **threaten the company's continued operations**. Sudden **dramatic realignments of currency** are not uncommon and, although predictable with hindsight, can take firms by surprise and cause huge losses.

(iii) **Large transactions**
For very large transactions, even small currency movements can create **significant losses**. It is wiser to hedge these transactions (assuming that matching cannot help) even if losses are not predicted.

Attitude to risk

The company's **attitude to risk** for foreign transactions therefore needs to be evaluated. The consequences of making currency losses, compared with the advantages of gains, need to be debated. For transactions that cannot be matched, the alternative to our existing policy is not necessarily to abandon hedging altogether, but to develop a policy which takes into account both predicted currency movements and the size of the transactions involved. It is likely that the threshold figure of £100,000 needs to be increased.

(d) **Alternative methods of managing currency risks**

Matching receipts and payments

As indicated above, one of the most powerful techniques for managing currency risk is to **match receipts and payments in the same currency**. The company should consider opening bank accounts in several major currencies (eg euros, US dollars and Japanese yen).

Matching transactions

Progressing this argument, we should also think more about trying to **match both sides of our import-export transactions** in the same currency. For example we may be able to pay a German supplier in US dollars and sell the product to the USA, invoicing in dollars. We should also consider **sourcing more products** from those countries for which our **sales are highest**.

Borrowing

When financing our working capital, we should **not be limited to loans in pounds sterling**. For example, if our main assets (receivables) are mainly designated in US dollars, we should consider borrowing in dollars to offset the currency risk.

Other methods

There are many alternatives to the forward contract for managing currency risks. I will be pleased to write a paper on the alternatives, which include **money market hedges**, **futures markets** and **option contracts**. These instruments can be used to reduce risk to whatever level the company deems appropriate.

CIMA – Strategic level

Paper P3

Management Accounting – Risk and Control Strategy

Mock Exam 3 (November 2008)

You are allowed three hours to answer this question paper
In the real exam, you are allowed 20 minutes reading time before the examination begins during which you should read the question paper, and if you wish, make annotations on the question paper. However, you will **not** be allowed, **under any circumstances**, to open the answer book and start writing or use your calculator during this reading time.
You are strongly advised to carefully read all the question requirements before attempting the question concerned (that is all parts and/or sub-questions).
Answer the ONE compulsory question in Section A.
Answer TWO questions only from Section B

DO NOT OPEN THIS PAPER UNTIL YOUR ARE READY TO START UNDER EXAMINATION CONDITIONS

SECTION A – 50 marks

Answer this question

Question 1

PLM: Background, organisational structure and financial controls

PLM is one of the world's largest manufacturers of energy saving products for use in construction. The group specialises in the manufacture of timber framed sections and of insulated panels, both being used in domestic and commercial construction. The insulated panels take the form of a "sandwich" of outer layers of wooden board with a polystyrene core, and so PLM is very dependent on access to timber supplies for the manufacture of both of its products.

PLM owns manufacturing plants and distribution centres in various locations around the world. The group is largely based in Europe, and has its headquarters and Research and Development Unit in Germany, as well as manufacturing sites in Germany, Scotland and Poland. The European manufacturing operations are supported by distribution centres located in each of Germany, France and Scotland. An additional manufacturing plant and two distribution centres are located in Canada, to serve both the Canadian and US markets. PLM sells to customers located in 15 different countries in Europe and North America.

The control structure in PLM is regionally rather than product based. Manufacturing and distribution centres are managed in combination as regional profit centres, whilst the Research and Development Unit is treated as a cost centre. For example, the Director of Operations for Western Europe is responsible for a single profit centre that covers the German and Scottish manufacturing plants together with the distribution centres in Germany, France and Scotland. Similarly, the Director of Operations for North America is responsible for a profit centre that includes all of the Canadian manufacturing and distribution centres. The Polish manufacturing plant is a separate profit centre managed by a UK based Director.

Profit centre results are calculated before inclusion of the impact of any foreign exchange or interest rate movements.

Product Development

The Board of Directors regards new product development as vital to the continued success of the business, and 5% of group profit is allocated to Research and Development. All new products have to obtain certification on their suitability for purpose and compliance with health and safety and building regulations. Certification is granted by an internationally approved body such as the UK based Building Research Establishment, but obtaining certification can take up to three years to complete.

Environmental Issues

PLM's timber based products appeal to customers because of the fact that timber is a renewable building material. There is, however, growing consumer concern about illegal logging and global depletion of major forestry resources.

In response to these concerns, PLM's strategic plan states that it aims, within two years, to have 75% of timber supplies sourced from sustainable woodland. The timber used for both the timber framed sections and the insulated panels is primarily softwood which, in forestry terms, is fast growing. Trees reach the necessary level of maturity in approximately 20 years. Reliable market forecasts suggest that demand for sustainably produced timber is growing faster than its supply, and that severe competition for this resource will emerge over the next five to eight years.

A number of international schemes have developed with the aim of providing customer assurance on the sustainability of a timber source. PLM uses suppliers which are registered under a number of different such schemes including the Forestry Stewardship Council, Sustainable Forestry Initiative, and the Canadian Standards Association. Consumers, however, appear to be poorly informed about the different assurance systems and are unable to clearly distinguish between genuine and "rogue" assurance schemes.

Market Conditions

The business has expanded very rapidly over the last 10 years as a result of a growing awareness amongst architects of the need to use environmentally friendly building systems, combined with the potential of both product types to halve construction times.

20 to 30 years ago there was a degree of mistrust within the industry about the use of timber frame construction techniques, and in Europe there were only a small number of contractors who were knowledgeable and experienced in their use. In contrast, the Canadian market for the product has been well established for over 50 years.

Insulated panels have also been in widespread use in North America for many years, but PLM was the first company to introduce this building system into Europe 10 years ago. Since then a number of competitors have entered the European market, some of which provide customers with on site installation services as well as acting purely as panel manufacturers. An important reason for the market appeal of the panels lies in the fact that they offer very high levels of insulation, and the European market has expanded hugely following the introduction of strict new regulations on the energy efficiency of new buildings. The MD is aware of the impact of the current credit crunch and has taken that into account when preparing the budget for next year by suggesting that there will be zero sales growth.

The customer base for both timber framed sections and the insulated panels is highly concentrated. For timber framed sections, 40% of global revenue is earned in Canada, whilst 80% of PLM's substantial European revenue from the sale of the insulated panels comes from ten main construction companies. Retention of key customers is pursued by PLM through its policy of guaranteeing delivery, anywhere in the world, of all orders in excess of €0·5 million, within six weeks of the order being received. As a result, there are times when PLM is manufacturing in Canada for delivery in Europe and vice versa.

Sales Mix and Profit Margins for the last two years

Year ended 30 June	**20X6**	**20X7**
Sales:	*€m*	*€m*
Global	350	420
North America	150	175
UK	45	65
France	10	10
Germany	60	70
Other countries	85	100
Global Ratio of timber frame to panel sales (by value)	60 : 40	52 : 48
Average profit margin on panels	9·5%	9·0%
Average profit margin on timber framed sections	12·5%	14·0%

Risk Management in PLM

Overall responsibility for risk management systems within PLM rests with a senior manager (ranked immediately below Board level) who holds the title of Group Risk Controller. He was appointed five years ago, after promotion following 20 years service as PLM's Head of Group Insurance. He works closely with the Head of Internal Audit, although their respective roles are not clearly defined and documented and they jointly report monthly to the Audit Committee and the Finance Director.

The Board of Directors' approach to risk management is to either avoid risk or transfer it. One consequence of this policy is that the insurance bill for the group is extremely high in comparison to its peers. The existing risk averse culture also means that all overseas customers are billed in Euros, and the Treasury unit is barred from using derivative financial instruments, even for hedging purposes, because they are "too risky."

The Group Risk Controller of PLM is due to retire next year, and in its most recent review of internal controls within PLM the Audit Committee recommended that the Board of Directors should work with the new appointee to undertake a major review of current risk management practice within PLM.

Required

Using the information provided in the above scenario you are required to:

(a) Discuss the extent to which each of the following aspects of the operational and business environment of PLM creates potential risks for the group's shareholders:

(i) Product development
(ii) Environmental issues
(iii) Market conditions
(iv) Sales mix and profit margins
(v) Financial controls **(20 marks)**

(b) Recommend, with reasons, a risk management control system that could be used by PLM as a mechanism for recording, prioritising and managing the group's risks. **(20 marks)**

ERM

(c) Explain why the role of the Group Risk Controller extends beyond issues of insurance and conformance and is also concerned with performance against strategic objectives. **(10 marks)**

(Total = 50 marks)

SECTION B – 50 marks

Answer TWO questions

Question 2

Required

(a) The shift towards fair value accounting has potentially increased the financial risks faced by companies that own high volumes of financial assets.

(i) Discuss the above statement. **(6 marks)**

(ii) Explain the tools that might be used to monitor such risks. **(4 marks)**

(b) KRL plc is a UK based transport company that specialises in large scale business to business contracts, delivering items from original manufacturers to assembly plants across the whole of Western Europe. Fuel is one of the company's main costs, and the Treasurer has decided to purchase oil futures to try and protect the company from the risk of rising fuel prices. The aim is to use any gains on the futures price to offset any increase in costs resulting from a fuel price rise. KRL forecasts that it will consume approximately 158,000 US gallons of fuel over the three month period to 1 March 20X9 at an average cost of £5·45 per gallon.

Crude oil futures are traded in the market in units of 1,000 US barrels (42,000 gallons) and today (1 December 20X8) the price for delivery in three months' time is US $116·00 per barrel. The current spot rate is US$ = £0·504.

Assume that on 1 March 20X9 the spot exchange rate is US$ = £0·51 and KRL is able to close out its contracts at a value of US$118·92 per barrel.

Required

(i) Calculate, ignoring transaction costs, the profit or loss arising from the decision to use futures contracts to hedge fuel costs. **(10 marks)**

(ii) Discuss the risks associated with hedging fuel prices via the purchase of crude oil futures. **(5 marks)**

(Total = 25 marks)

Question 3

FDS is a large diversified company whose information technology and information management activities are carried out by a shared service centre. FDS 25 is one of many business units operating as an investment centre within FDS. FDS 25 has developed a new business strategy which requires a major new investment in information technology to support its business strategy. FDS 25 needs to implement the new system as quickly as possible and within budget in order to meet its objectives.

Required

(a) Recommend the controls that could be implemented by a business unit like FDS 25 to mitigate against risk at each stage of information system design and implementation. **(15 marks)**

(b) From the perspective of FDS 25, identify the risk management advantages and disadvantages of each of

(i) utilising the shared service centre; and

(ii) outsourcing for the design and implementation of a new information system.

(10 marks)

(Total = 25 marks)

Question 4

HFD is a registered charity with 100 employees and 250 volunteers providing in-home care for elderly persons who are unable to fully take care of themselves. The company structure has no shareholders in a practical sense although a small number of issued shares are held by the sponsors who established the charity many years previously. HFD is governed by a seven-member Board of Directors. The Chief Executive Officer (CEO) chairs the Board which comprises the Chief Financial Officer (CFO) and five independent, unpaid non-executive directors who were appointed by the CEO based on past business relationships. You are one of the independent members of HFD's Board.

The CEO/Chair sets the Board agendas, distributes Board papers in advance of meetings and briefs Board members in relation to each agenda item. At each of its quarterly meetings the Board reviews the financial reports of the charity in some detail and the CFO answers questions. Other issues that regularly appear as agenda items include new government funding initiatives for the client group, and the results of proposals that have been submitted to funding agencies, of which about 25% are successful. There is rarely any discussion of operational matters relating to the charity as the CEO believes these are outside the directors' experience and the executive management team is more than capable of managing the delivery of the in-home care services.

The Board has no separate audit committee but relies on the annual management letter from the external auditors to provide assurance that financial controls are operating effectively. The external auditors were appointed by the CEO many years previously.

HFD's Board believes that the company's corporate governance could be improved by following the principles applicable to listed companies.

Required

(a) Recommend how HFD's board should be restructured to comply with the principles of good corporate governance. **(16 marks)**

(b) Explain the aspects of CIMA's ethical principles and the conceptual framework underlying those principles which you would consider relevant to continuing in your role as an independent member of HFD's board. **(9 marks)**

(Total = 25 marks)

Question 5

SRN is a small listed clothing retailer operating a chain of 18 stores in suburban shopping centres together with a city-based Head Office. Orders for stock are placed centrally by Head Office and are delivered to Head Office by suppliers. Details of goods received are entered by Head Office employees to the company's computer system. The goods are then despatched to the retail locations.

There are typically between two and three full-time employees in each store (one of whom is the store manager) plus part-time employees during the busiest periods. They are responsible for display and sales. All sales are processed using the electronic point of sale (EPOS) terminals which have the facility for cash, and debit and credit card sales. Cash sales are banked daily by store employees and each day Head Office reconciles bank deposits with the EPOS reports for each store.

Sales through the EPOS terminals automatically reduce stock levels and support Head Office purchasing and stock replenishment decisions. A physical stocktake is carried out by store employees six monthly. Usually the stocktakes reveal stock shortfalls for almost half the stores. Store employees attribute this to theft.

Prices are set initially by Head Office as a standard mark-up on the purchase cost. This price is automatically displayed on the EPOS terminals. However, employees have the authority to discount prices based on the length of time stock has been in their store and the need to ensure constant stock rotation. Sales revenue and price discounts are monitored weekly by Head Office to ensure that sales levels and margins are on target and that excessive discounting does not take place.

Sales, gross profits and net profits are reported quarterly for each store. A Head Office manager visits each store once per week, typically on the same day and at the same time, so that store employees can discuss any problems with the Head Office manager.

Required

(a) Identify the risks of fraud and theft faced by SRN in relation to its employees. **(6 marks)**

(b) Recommend (with reasons) the policies and internal controls that SRN could implement to prevent employee fraud and theft. In making your recommendations, you should consider both

(i) Working conditions and the role of the Human Resource function; and

(ii) Operational internal controls. **(19 marks)**

(Total = 25 marks)

Answers

DO NOT TURN THIS PAGE UNTIL YOU HAVE COMPLETED THE MOCK EXAM

A plan of attack

Yes we know you've heard it 102 times but just, just in case for the 103rd time **Take a good look at the paper before diving in to answer questions**.

The next step

You may be thinking that this paper is OK compared with the previous two mocks; alternatively you may like this paper a lot less than the other two.

Option 1 (Don't like it)

If you are think this paper is quite tough, it my be best to do one of the optional questions before the case study **Question 1**. However there is a lot of information in Question 1 that you will need to go through carefully. It's therefore best to spend the reading time going through the requirements and analysing the information, thinking carefully about how the data you're given will help you fulfil the requirements. Then whilst you're answering an optional question, further ideas may come to you on Question 1 which you can jot down for later use.

- Maybe **Question 2** is one that you instantly decided not to answer. However it's often the case that students do better on unexpected optional questions than on more mainstream ones. Points in Questions 2's favour include not having to take into account a scenario in (a). It is nevertheless true that you need to feel that you can attempt **both** parts if you are to choose this question.
- If you have a broad knowledge of the topics of systems development and outsourcing, that should certainly help you pass **Question 3.**
- The scenario in **Question 4** does provide some fairly obvious hints about problems with the governance of the organisation that correspond with key recommendations in the corporate governance reports. Don't be put off by the terminology in (b); the question is about the qualities you must display and the ethical threats you must consider.
- The scenario in **Question 5** is also quite helpful in terms of generating ideas and the requirements to (b) hint about the broad areas you need to cover. Certainly if you can think of a few risks for (a), that should help you think of enough controls in (b) to pass the question.
- When you answer **Question 1**, you're looking to generate 2 or 3 risks under each heading in (a); you should obtain 1-2 marks for each risk provided you show how it's relevant. Don't worry that you find some headings more difficult to generate risks for than others. Try to bring in your P6 knowledge as well. Don't spend time worrying if there are one or two bits of information in the question that you can't tie up to specific question requirements – just make sure that you make maximum use of the information you can link. (b) is about remembering a risk management model and demonstrating how it's useful. If you can remember what the risk management function does in (c) that should form the basis of generating some ideas.

Option 2 (It's a pleasant surprise)

Really? Then you can feel boosted. Best then to get the most important question over and done with, so you should be doing **Question 1 first**.

- A danger with **Question 1** is most of the scenario relates specifically to (a). It provides lots of material to help you answer (a), but that does mean you could risk going over time on this part. As more than half the marks are available for (b) and (c), you need to give yourself time to make a reasonable attempt at both parts.
- If you feel that you can see what the calculation requires in (b) (i), you should consider attempting **Question 2**. However don't forget you need to answer (a) as well, so need a knowledge of IAS 39.
- Knowledge of systems development and outsourcing should help you achieve a good mark for **Question 3,** although your answer to (a) needs to take account of who is carrying out the development.

- There are a number of shortcomings identified in the scenario to **Question 4** that link in obviously with the requirements of the corporate governance reports. Possible dangers with this question include not limiting your answer to what (a) requires and spending too much time on (a). There are one or two clear hints in the scenario that you can link in with CIMA ethical guidance in (b).
- Likewise in **Question 5** the scenario offers helpful hints about what can go wrong. Don't forget in (b) however to link suggestions with the risks you identify in (a) as much as possible, and to cover clearly all the areas specified in the requirements to (b).

Once, once more

You must **allocate your time** according to the marks for the question in total, and for the parts of the questions. And you must also **follow the requirements exactly**.

All finished and quarter of an hour to go?

Your time allocation must have been faulty. However make the most of the 15 minutes; go back to **any parts of questions that you didn't finish** because you ran out of time.

Forget about it!

Just wipe it from your mind.

Question 1

Text references. Chapters 1 and 2

Top tips. (a) is similar in format to Question 77 (a) in the kit from November 2007. It is a reminder that one aim of P3 is to prepare you for TOPCIMA; you need to consider the same sorts of risks as you're looking at in (a) when you analyse the TOPCIMA preseen. You may find that you can generate lots of risks under some of the headings but remember that the marks available will be no more than 5 per header. It's easy to run over time on (a) and put yourself under time pressure for the rest of this question and the rest of this exam.

Other risks you could have discussed in (a) (iii) include whether in general the market for energy efficient products was meeting maturity, and the need to cut construction times may be less relevant if the construction firms currently have spare capacity. Other issues that you could have mentioned in (a) (v) include the regional control structure, possible transfer pricing between divisions (when products are made in one centre for transport to another), and budgeting.

In (b) there are various features in the scenario that mean that COSO's enterprise risk management model is a good one to use, including the importance of strategic and compliance risks which are highlighted in the model, the need to consider risks at profit and cost centre level as well as for the group as a whole, and the unimaginative management of risk. The trap in (b) is to spend time giving a lengthy description of what is involved in each stage and not provide any justification for using the model. It would be OK to list each stage of the model and then show why you're recommending it. However it would be better to do as we've done and incorporate the model into your answer, showing how each stage would enhance risk management for PLM.

You would certainly get marks for justifying an alternative risk management model, as many stages should be similar to the COSO model. CIMA's risk management cycle is one possibility. You should have scored well on (b) if you had explained the need for most of the following stages:

- Establishment of risk management appetite
- Risk identification
- Risk assessment
- Risk profiling
- Risk quantification
- Risk management
- Review process and feedback

The points you make in (c) need to link with the company's strategy. You may have found this the hardest part of the question for generation of ideas if you were not familiar with the term group risk controller. If you knew what the main tasks of the risk management function were, that should have helped you answer this part.

Easy marks. If you'd learned the list of advantages COSO identified with their risk management model that are covered in Chapter 2 of the text, you should have scored a good mark in (b).

(a) (i) **Product development**

Costs exceed benefits

An obvious risk for shareholders is that the costs of research and development will exceed the benefits. The costs at **5% of profits** will have a significant impact on profit level and potentially on dividends. The benefits are uncertain, as there is **significant competition** in all areas of activities.

Costs without benefits

Before products enter the market, they have to be approved, and **consent by the certification body** cannot be taken for granted. There is a risk that costs will yield no benefits, or extra expenditure on products may be required to obtain approval, depressing points and hence dividends.

Failure to fulfil need for innovation

However if PLM fails to commit enough resources it is likely to **lose market share** to competitors who are introducing more effective products, or innovations that reduce their cost base and hence the price to consumers. In addition to the direct impact on sales, PLM **may be seen by the stock market** as a company that is **not adapting quickly enough** to changing conditions. This threat to reputation may **depress its share price** and **increase its cost of capital.**

Short-term returns

Relying on the activities of research and development to underwrite the company's future may particularly impact on shareholders who are looking for **high short-term returns.** While the long-term benefits of research and development may comfortably exceed costs, the development and approval process means that the **payback period** on specific research and development projects will be **lengthy**. It may be regarded as possibly excessive by shareholders who are looking for high short-term income and **increase its cost of capital**.

(ii) **Environmental issues**

Government action

If governments crack down on rogue certification schemes, PLM may benefit from **increased demand from ethical consumers** because its suppliers are all registered under genuine schemes, unlike its competitors.

Demand for sustainable timber

Concerns over the environment may also provide **opportunities** for PLM. Increased consumer **awareness of, and preference for, timber registered under genuine certification systems** will benefit PLM, who appear to use suppliers registered by reputable bodies. Legal crackdowns on rogue assurance schemes will also help PLM to **increase its income** and **profitability** for shareholders.

Shortage of supply

However by making a commitment to source from sustainable woodland, PLM may risk limiting its sales if it cannot **readily obtain all the supplies it needs**. Alternatively the competition in demand for the wood may mean that **raw material costs increase significantly**. PLM may not be able to pass on this cost increase to its customers, and thus its profits may fall.

Reputation risk

PLM's **reputation as an ethical manufacturer** may be **damaged** if it **fails to reach its 75% target** within the two years, or its suppliers are found to have breached sustainability standards. Consumers may switch to more ethical products, causing demand and income to fall.

(iii) **Market conditions**

Impact of credit crunch

The credit crunch is likely to result in **reduced demand** for PLM's products by construction companies that are **building fewer properties** and by individual consumers who **cannot afford to enhance their properties**. Customers may also become less concerned with energy efficiency and green issues as a result of the credit crunch, and this may allow PLM's competitors to **undercut it on price or quality**. There may be an **overall fall in sales** rather than the zero growth assumed by the MD.

Over-trading and working capital problems

PLM's **rapid expansion in revenue** in recent years may have meant that the company **lacks a sufficient working capital base**, potentially leading to **future liquidity problems** and threats to shareholder investment. PLM is making great efforts to retain customers and one aspect may be that it has to give **longer credit periods**. If it does face future problems with suppliers, it may have to accept **shorter credit periods** from them. A significant fall in demand due to the credit crunch may leave PLM with large levels of **unsold inventory**.

Competitor action

Competitors may decide to expand what they offer (for example more competitors providing on-site installation services). Alternatively the other services may become a **more significant factor in consumer purchasing decisions**, perhaps due to lack of time or willingness to install the panels themselves. This may adversely affect PLM's sales if it does not offer the same services,

Changes in foreign exchange markets

PLM's insistence on billing in Euros may cause its **income and profits to fall** if the Euro strengthens against the dollar and pound in PLM's major markets, making its products more expensive and reducing demand. The effect of market movements on PLM's **costs of supply** will be **uncertain**, depending on the currency in which supplies are billed, and the movements of the suppliers' local currencies against the Euro.

(iv) **Sales mix and profit margins**

Change in product mix

A comparison of recent figures shows that **panel sales** appear to be contributing a **greater share of sales revenues**. If this trend continues, profits will not increase at the same rate as sales, as the **profit margin on panels** at 9% is **lower than** the 14% on **timber framed sections**. In addition the **profit margin on panels fell** from 9.5% to 9%, whilst **the timber profit margin rose** from 12.5% to 14% between 20X6 and 20X7.

Geographical markets

The geographical split of sales indicates that PLM remains **very dependent on sales in North America**. This is a much more mature market than PLM's other geographical markets; the Canadian market for panels has been established for over 50 years. It thus may have **little scope for expansion in sales and profits.** However possibly the market can be seen as a cash cow which is less vulnerable to the credit crunch; PLM may be able to use its **brand image as a barrier to competition in this market**.

Customer mix

80% of PLM's European revenues from insulated panels come from sales to 10 main construction companies. This means that it is **significantly dependent on demand from these customers.** If the credit crunch causes even one or two to go out of business or reduce their demand, this will have a significant impact on profits available for distribution.

Fixed cost base

PLM appears to have a **large fixed cost base** due to the manufacturing and distribution centres it operates. A fall in sales, augmented by an increasing dependence on products with a lower profit margin, could therefore have a very significant effect on profit margins.

(v) **Financial controls**

Use of profit centres

The use of profit centres may lead to a **poor allocation of resources** as using profits as a measurement takes no account of the **capital employed**. Given that manufacturing and distribution centres are managed as profit centres together, it would be better to treat them as **investment centres** and measure their return in the light of the capital employed in each.

Accounting for foreign exchange and interest rate movements

Failure to take into account foreign exchange or interest rate movements at divisional level may also distort the results of regional centres. Foreign exchange movements may have quite a **significant impact on profits** as all overseas customers are billed in Euros. Interest costs should be the responsibility of regional centres if they have some discretion about the sources of finance they use.

Treatment of research and development as cost centre

Treating research and development as a cost centre and allocating a fixed proportion of profits may result in its expenditure being controlled too loosely. Research and development may feel **obliged to spend up to its expenditure allocation**, and is not judged by any method that measures return on its expenditure; there is **no system of transfer pricing** which could be used to establish a notional selling price for research and development's activities.

Costs of financial controls

The board's aversion to **risk** may mean **costs are higher** and **profits lower** than they need to be, because the financial controls are excessive. For example it will not be cost-effective to employ treasury function staff with specialist expertise if the restrictions they operate under, such as banning the use of derivatives, mean they cannot use that expertise.

(b) **COSO's enterprise risk management model**

The advantages of following a model like COSO's is that it should ensure that the **objectives and risk management mechanisms** that directors establish are **compatible with PLM's risk appetite**. The COSO model is a systematic method of **assessing and managing risks,** and provides criteria for **judging the effectiveness of risk management and control systems.**

International model

The COSO model is designed to be applied across different global cultures. As such, it is appropriate for PLM, which has a **significant presence on different continents**.

Focus on different risks

The COSO model highlights four categories of risk, all of which are significant to PLM

(i) **Strategic risks**

PLM faces a number of issues in relation to the **products** it offers, the action of **competitors** and the **availability of supplies.**

(ii) **Operational risks**

The tight guarantees PLM has provided about **delivery of supplies** means that delays in operations could have serious impacts on its ability to meet its commitments.

(iii) **Financial reporting risks**

PLM may face various problems relating to **over-valuation of working capital**, including the possibility of bad debts, and the valuation of unsold inventory.

(iv) **Compliance risks**

PLM is particularly concerned with the **compliance of suppliers with sustainability standards** and the **certification of its own new products** by internationally approved bodies.

Focus on risk at different organisational levels

The COSO model emphasises the importance of a coherent approach to risk management not only at entity level, but also at business unit, subsidiary or divisional level. This is particularly important for PLM. Its regional structure means that regional management are responsible for managing across all areas of operations rather than for particular products or activities. The model emphasises the risk management aspect of regional management's role. However it also stresses the need for effective management at the entity level. It shows how experience and practice should be shared across the organisation, and a common set of tools and techniques should be used.

Features of COSO's model

Each of the elements that the COSO model highlights are features that PLM's board and management particularly need to consider.

Internal environment

The internal environment includes the way **PLM is structured**, the **lead management give** and the **company's culture**. The COSO model shows **how risk management** is a key part of the **culture** of the organisation, embedded into all its processes and activities. The internal environment sets the basis for how risks are viewed and addressed. If senior management do **not clearly establish a risk philosophy**, the risk culture may be **haphazard**, and result in significantly differing attitudes to risk throughout PLM.

Objective setting

Perhaps the most important feature of the COSO model is that it emphasises how **risk attitudes and management** should be **integrated** with strategic objectives. The COSO model stresses that senior management need to consider the **risk appetite** of the business when taking strategic decisions. PLM's directors will need to assess whether their aversion to risk may be a drag on expanding the company. The model also emphasises the importance of **establishing strategic objectives** that **align with mission** and are **consistent with risk appetite. Business objectives** must be established before management can identify which events affect their achievement and what processes are required to deal with the potential consequences of those events.

Event identification

The COSO model demonstrates that PLM's board needs to **identify and record potential loss-inducing events** to reduce the likelihood that unexpected problems will occur. There seem to be problems which could occur quite suddenly, such as **disruption to supply arrangements**. A comparison of the results of systematic event identification with current insurance arrangements may identify risks that are being **insured unnecessarily**, and removal of these from insurance may reduce premiums. Event identification may also **identify opportunities** as well as potential losses, and enable the company to take advantage of developments in its environment.

Risk assessment and prioritisation

Following a structured programme of risk assessment should ensure not only that individual risks are assessed, but they are **profiled** and **prioritised** according to their importance (the likelihood and consequences of their materialising). This should enable PLM's directors to take a **portfolio view of risk** across the whole organisation and deal with multiple risks.

Risk response and management

Using the COSO model should help PLM adopt a more prioritised approach to responding to all risks. Its risk management policies appear to have been designed with **high severity risks in mind**, that are either transferred or abandoned. Using the COSO model should prompt PLM to identify and deal with **events** which have **low individual impact**, but which **frequently occur**. Their responses should be determined by the risk tolerances determined by the directors, and the costs and benefits of responses that follow from these. Details of the risks and the action taken to manage them should be recorded in a risk register.

Control activities

This follows on from the previous stages, in that **well–directed control activities** should **reduce risks** arising from low severity, high frequency events. Not only should control activities reduce losses, they can be presented as evidence to insurance companies that PLM is taking appropriate steps to deal with risks. This should help **reduce insurance premiums**.

Information and communication

Communication is also important to ensure **best risk management practice** is disseminated across the group; it should provide support for line managers and staff to enable them to exercise their responsibilities.

Monitoring

The COSO model stresses the need for management at all levels to **monitor changing risks continually**, to ensure that risk management structures and procedures remain appropriate. Fulfilling the requirements of the COSO model also enables PLM to **comply with best practice requirements** in corporate governance reports such as the UK Turnbull report, which stresses the need for risk management to be a major item on board agendas.

(c) **Differentiation between risk management and internal audit**

At present there is a lack of clarity between the roles of Group Risk Controller (GRC) and Head of internal Audit. The two roles need to be clearly differentiated for both to add maximum value. The GRC needs to play a **proactive role in risk management.** Since, as described in (b), risk management structures, policies and insurance need to be based on risk tolerance and strategic objectives, the GRC's main objective will be to ensure that risk management achieves this aim. The GRC should not be responsible for overseeing the testing of conformance with company policies or quality standards; that should be the **responsibility of the Chief Internal Auditor**.

Establishing enterprise risk management policies

The GRC has prime **responsibility for establishing risk management policies** and **responsibilities throughout the organisation** and will be involved in **setting implementation goals**. He needs to ensure that the policies and goals are **compatible** with the strategic objectives established by the board.

Allocating capital

The risk assessments that the GRC is **responsible for across the business** should enable the board to **allocate capital to business units based on risk**, aiming to **optimise PLM's risk portfolio**.

Establishing risk management environment

The GRC will have the main responsibility for **establishing key aspects of the internal environment** within which risk management is conducted. These include establishing a **common risk management language** that includes risk categories that relate to the key strategic risks the business faces.

Risk competence

The GRC should provide a **source of expertise** that line managers use to help them ensure their risk management activities are appropriate for the level of risk tolerance they should have.

Interface

The GRC should help ensure that enterprise risk management is **integrated** with other key strategic activities such as **business planning**.

Monitoring progress

The GRC will be responsible for **reporting to management** on progress in implementing risk management. The GRC will also assist line managers in **developing measures** that show how their risk responses have assisted in fulfilling business objectives.

Communication

The GRC should play an important role in **communicating PLM's risk profile** to key stakeholders such as institutional shareholders and stock analysts. Clarity on PLM's risk position should give these stakeholders more confidence, and thus reduce the company's **cost of capital**, which in turn will impact upon its investment strategies.

Question 2

Text references. Chapter 12

Top tips. (a) is about IAS 39 requirements; it would have been helpful if the question had made that clear. However it's also about the problems of what value to quote for something (here financial assets) surrounded by considerable uncertainty, so is a more general risk question as well. A significant problem is deciding what market values represent – an expected value over the longer-term or a figure that is more like a current worst case estimate.

The calculation in (b) (i) is rather unexpected, though hopefully you should be able to work out the futures part from your knowledge of futures. The second part, the loss caused by the price rise, appears to follow from the information given.

Note in (b) (ii) that high cost is not a risk as such, if you know in advance precisely what the costs will be. The possibility that costs will be higher than anticipated is a risk though.

Easy marks. You can use your knowledge of currency futures to answer (b) (ii) as most of the problems with currency futures also relate to commodity futures.

(a) (i) **Market values and financial risk**

Fair value accounting involves the **marking to market** of certain financial assets and thus requires **market values to be obtained or ascertained**. **Financial risk** is the **volatility in income, assets and company market value** as a result of this.

Investor confidence risks

The main problem many companies with high proportions of financial assets face is a investor uncertainty in the company's underlying valuation. Investors may not be sure if **low market valuations of financial assets are temporary or permanent**.

Valuation problems

Critics of fair value have highlighted various problems with the valuations as discussed below.

Assets wrongly valued

Considerable doubts have been raised over how reliable estimates of market value are for many financial assets. Some argue that there will always be considerable uncertainty affecting assets valued at market prices when **little or no market currently exists** for those assets. The problem is **enhanced for financial products** which are not **tradable** and therefore have **no market value**. The distinctions between different types of financial assets may be difficult to apply, and assets may be accounted for incorrectly as a result.

Assets under-valued

Some commentators have argued that market values are only realistic in **buoyant, liquid markets**; in slow markets use of market values underestimates long-term asset values.

Assets with temporary falls in value

The assets stated in the balance sheet are stated at their value on a particular day, the year-end. If there are **significant fluctuations in value around the year-end**, the assets may be understated compared even with their valuation when the accounts are published over the next few months. Although the accounts can draw attention to this fluctuation, investors may see the figures in the balance sheet as the ' headline' figures and base their judgements on those.

Disclosure risks

Some commentators have suggested that uncertainties over the fair value of assets can be **resolved by more disclosure**. Others though have asked whether more disclosure may confuse investors further, and that extra disclosures may **not be good information**.

Income risks

Under IAS 39 changes in the fair value of many financial assets have to be included in the income statement. Income may become **increasingly volatile** depending on the market data and models being used. This volatility is due to a focus on assets and liabilities rather than accounting for income. This may have an **adverse impact on the ability of companies to pay dividends** and on **companies' share price and cost of capital.**

(ii) **Monitoring of markets**

Companies should **continually measure activity** on markets where assets with significant value are actively traded. Where assets are not actively traded, they should monitor activity on similar assets or take into account past price movements and quotations.

Financial techniques and models

Companies can base their valuation of risks on risk measurement techniques such as **net present value analysis**, or on financial models such as the **Black-Scholes model**.

Quotes from experts

Quotes from experts such as brokers may provide valuable assistance in measuring risk. However when markets are not active, brokers may rely on **models** rather than **actual market data**, and their opinions may be of less value unless the assumptions behind the models are made clear.

Trading limits

Companies can ensure risks are effectively monitored by **setting trading limits** such as **maximum value at risk**.

(b) (i) **Futures market**

- Buy crude oil futures
- Number of contracts

  $\frac{158,000}{42,000}$ = 3.76, say 4 contracts.

- Over-hedge = (4 × 42,000) – 158,000

  = 10,000 gallons

- Outcome

	$
Cost of buying	
4 contracts × $116.00 × 1,000 gallons	464,000
Proceeds from selling	
4 contracts × $118.92 × 1,000 gallons	475,680
Gain on futures transaction	11,680
Gain on futures transaction in £ 11,680 × 0.51	£5,957

Actual purchases

Extra cost per gallon caused by rise in exchange rate = 5.45 ((0.51 – 0.504)/0.504) = £0.0649

Total extra cost = £0.0649 × 158,000 gallons = £10,254

	£
Extra cost of fuel	(10,254)
Profit on futures	5,957
Net loss	(4,297)

(ii) **Uncertainty about requirements**

KRL is **uncertain** about its **exact requirements** over the next few months, and so the amount **it hedges using futures** may not **correspond to its eventual requirements**.

Hedge problems

Even if KRL was certain about its future commitments, having to deal in a whole number of contracts means that there may be an amount that is **not hedged or is overhedged by futures**. The futures commit KRL to making a transaction in the future. This means that if prices move in KRL's favour, it will **still have to undertake the unnecessary transaction**. Purchasing crude oil options would give KRL the chance to decide whether or not to go ahead with the transaction.

Basis risk

Hedge inefficiencies are also caused by **basis risk**; the risk that the futures contract price will move by a different amount to the price of the underlying commodity. Crude oil is not fuel; fuel is subject to many other factors that can cause fluctuations in cost such as **changes in tax and duty and processing costs**. These factors will have differing impacts in the different countries where drivers will buy fuel while they are on the road.

Cash flow

Futures require a **margin payment corresponding to daily price changes in the futures market.** If the market is volatile, the margin payments may be for significant amounts.

Impact of exchange rate changes

The futures calculation in (b) (i) has taken into account the impact of the changes in the £/$ exchange rate. However **other exchange rate changes** will also affect the price of fuel, as drivers will be buying fuel across Western Europe.

Question 3

Text references. Chapters 17 and 18

Top tips. At first glance there does not appear to be much scenario to use, which may be a problem given that both question parts demand consideration of the scenario. However analysis of the limited information does yield various important points:

- We are looking at the situation from the viewpoint of FDS 25, a business unit which is using internal services
- The scenario emphasises FDS 25 is an investment centre and that meeting budget is a significant issue, so cost control will need to be considered in your answer

In (a) you need to go through the main stages of systems development. Remember that the shared service centre will be carrying out the detailed development work, but FDS 25 should be able to specify the controls it wants, obtaining advice from the service centre as required. FDS 25 needs to have control mechanisms in place for guiding and monitoring the development. In particular it will want to ensure that the system develops in line with its requirements.

The verb identify in (b) is a lower level verb, limiting what you say about each advantage and disadvantage. Clear headers and short paragraphs will help you score as many marks as possible in this section.

Easy marks. The advantages and disadvantages of outsourcing should represent easy marks as they have been examined before.

(a) **Control framework**

Steering committee

FDS 25 should set up a steering committee to oversee the **design and implementation** of the **new system**, ensuring that it meets **quality, timing and cost requirements**. The committee should be chaired by a senior manager, and should include a project manager, representatives from the shared service centre and user group representatives from FDS 25.

Role of management team

Given the importance of the investment to support FDS 25's business strategy, FDS 25's management team should be involved in approving the systems before development commences. Management should receive **regular reports** from the **steering committee** about the progress of the project, and **internal audit** about the checks they have carried out. Management should **sign off the project** before it is implemented.

Budgeting

Bringing the project within budget has been highlighted as very important. With the assistance of internal audit, the steering committee should review the **justification on cost grounds** for the **system chosen** and **how realistic** the **detailed budgets** are. The steering committee and senior management should **monitor the progress of costs against budgets** and **discuss overruns** with the service centre if they arise.

Systems design

Analysis

To be effective the design process needs to be based on a detailed analysis of requirements. A **feasibility study** should cover the **benefits and drawbacks** of the **current system, business and user needs**, particularly regarding future developments. The analysis process should examine the extent to which alternative solutions fulfil the **objectives** that the steering committee has defined, and the **costs and time to completion** of each option.

Specification

A key control in the design process is that it should result in a **detailed specification** for approval of the new system covering program and file design, data security and levels of authorisation. **Internal auditors should review the specification** for FDS 25 to ensure the system appears to be providing **complete information**, is **compatible with other systems** within FDS and has **sufficient security controls**. They should also obtain **evidence from users within FDS 25** that they will be happy with the system.

Systems implementation

Testing

The steering committee should specify to the shared service centre the **testing** that it requires to be carried out. As well as **comprehensive testing** by the service centre team, **internal audit** and **FDS 25's users** should test the system and confirm that they are happy with the results of the testing. This is important as FDS 25 is **keen to implement the system quickly to achieve its business objectives**, and so may be tempted to curtail testing.

Organisational controls

Before the new system is implemented, the steering committee needs to obtain evidence that it has been **adequately documented**. FDS 25's staff need to have received **appropriate training** before the system is implemented.

Initial running

The steering committee should ensure that **sufficient time** is planned for the changeover process and that controls over the actual implementation process are adequate, given the method of implementation chosen. Controls will have to ensure that **data is transferred correctly** and that **back-up arrangements** are in place should problems occur when the system goes live.

Post-implementation review

As it seems likely that the system will need to **develop further over time**, the internal auditors should carry out a post-implementation review for FDS 25 to establish whether the new system has **fulfilled users' needs** and whether the **system is performing in accordance with the specification**. The committee should also make a **final comparison of budgeted costs with actual costs**.

(b) (i) **Shared service centre**

Advantages

Provision of required services

Shared service centres exist to provide **only those services** that their 'customers', here investment centres such as FDS 25, **use**. FDS 25 should not be wasting money paying for unnecessary **risk management and controls** that it doesn't require.

Responsiveness to demands of FDS 25

FDS 25 should be able to **specify** to the service centre the **controls** it wishes to be implemented over **design and implementation**. The service centre should be able to provide expert help in deciding what controls are **appropriate to counter risks**, from staff's knowledge of other projects within the FDS group.

Disadvantage

Availability and cost of service

FDS 25's requirements may be subordinated to those of other parts of the group, and there may be little FDS 25's managers can do. In addition it may not be possible to specify **long-term pricing**. The cost of the services may be determined by group transfer pricing arrangements, and these may mean that the cost increases significantly over time.

(ii) **Outsourcing**

Advantages

Removal of cost uncertainties

An outsourcing arrangement will mean **costs of purchasing the service should be easy to predict**, and **budgets easy to control**. This is important for FDS 25 as it operates as an **investment centre**.

Service level agreement

A service level agreement should limit uncertainty by setting out the **facilities and level of service** that the service supplier will provide.

Available expertise

The specialist service supplier may well have developed and implemented similar systems for other companies, and thus will have **expertise and experience** in developing the system. This should mean that the system is developed efficiently, with little chance of error.

Disadvantages

Dependence on supplier

FDS 25 may become very dependent on the outsource supplier as the system is core to its future strategy. If the outsource supplier goes out of business, the loss of IT facilities may mean that FDS 25 may **not be able to achieve its objectives** and its **competitive advantage** may be damaged.

Locked into long-term contract

The service provider may not fulfil the terms of the service level agreement. Also because the system is core to FDS 25's future strategy, it may mean that FDS 25's needs change over time and in the future a **new supplier** may be best able to fulfil FDS 25's requirements. However FDS 25 may not be able to extract itself easily from its contract with the existing supplier.

Confidentiality

Loss of confidential information to a competitor may have severe consequences for FDS 25 given the high-level nature of the system. FDS 25's directors may be reluctant to transfer responsibility for the data outside FDS, however strong the guarantees provided by the outsource supplier.

Monitoring costs

The indirect costs of the arrangement may be higher than expected, including **other transaction costs such as insurance and the internal time resource** involved in monitoring the arrangement.

Question 4

Text references. Chapters 5 and 9

Top tips. (a) requires some care. The board wants to be more like a listed company board, so you can discuss many of the provisions in the Combined Code. However you need to remember that HFD is a fairly small charity, so you should be careful what you recommend. For example it would be fine to recommend the charity appoints 1 or 2 more executive directors but not 7 or 8.

If you struggled with (b), the fundamental principles and conceptual framework (based on ethical conflicts) are covered in Sections 7.3 and 7.4 of Chapter 9 of the Study Text. Using the OPPTIC mnemonic would have helped you remember the relevant ones. The great majority of the points in these two sections are relevant; the main omission from our answer is confidentiality. To score good marks you need to use material in the scenario to show why they are relevant. Given that the question is concerned with whether you should continue, you also need to bring in the safeguards that are designed to counter the threats identified in the conceptual framework. Knowledge of the Combined Code can be used to reinforce your answer in (b), as well as being very important in (a).

Easy marks. Hopefully you picked up the more obvious hints in (a): CEO/Chairman being the same person, questionable independence of NEDs, lack of scrutiny by NEDs of operational matters.

(a) **Split of role of chairman and chief executive**

Governance reports recommend that the roles of chief executive and chairman should be split between different individuals. It seems best for one of the existing NEDs to be appointed as chairman. Splitting the roles emphasises the two jobs are distinct, with the **chief executive running the charity** and the **chairman running the board**. The chairman can ensure the chief executive is **accountable** for his actions, by for example ensuring the board **has enough information** to exercise oversight of the chief executive. At present the chief executive is able to **manipulate the information** the board receives, to protect his position.

Appointment of secretary

The board's functioning would be better if someone acted as company secretary. The secretary could undertake a number of tasks currently undertaken by the CEO including **distributing board minutes** in advance of meetings and **briefing board members in relation to each agenda item**. This would free up the time of the CEO or chairman. The secretary should be accountable to the board collectively, and should if necessary have the **independence** to come into conflict with the CEO if the secretary believes it is in the interest of HFD.

More executive directors

The UK Higgs report commented that there is a greater risk of distortion or withholding of information, or lack of balance in the management contribution, when there is only one or a very small number of executives on the board. HFD should consider appointing one or two more executive directors, for example an

Operations Director; this would also help with **succession planning**, and lead to a greater emphasis on **risk management** and **operational control** at board level.

Establishment of board committees

HFD should establish a **system of board committees** along the lines recommended by governance reports. A committee structure enables different NEDs to concentrate on different areas of governance, perhaps in accordance with their different areas of expertise.

Audit committee

Appointing a **separate audit committee** will enable the main board to concentrate more on strategic and operational matters, leaving the audit committee to undertake the **detailed financial review** that is a major part of current board meetings. The audit committee should also be **responsible for appointment of auditors** and **liaison with them about further work**. At present the auditors' ability to exercise independent scrutiny could be questioned, since they have been appointed by the CEO. Governance reports recommend that all members of the committee should have sufficient financial expertise to contribute effectively, and that one member should have **relevant and recent financial experience**. New directors may therefore need to be recruited to fulfil this requirement or existing members **receive training**.

Nomination committee

A nomination committee of NEDs would **oversee the appointment of the new directors** that HFD's board appears to need. The committee would also review other important issues of board functioning that have not been considered recently, such as:

- The **balance between executives and NEDs**
- Whether there are **gaps between the skills, knowledge and experience** possessed by the current board and what the board ideally should have
- The need to **attract board members from a variety of backgrounds**
- Whether HFD will need to pay some NEDs to attract the right candidates

Remuneration committee

Since the duties of a remuneration committee of a charity should be less complex than for many listed companies, HFD might not establish a separate remuneration committee; however its key duties will need to be undertaken by another committee of NEDs. The **most important duty is to scrutinise the remuneration packages of the executive directors**. Whilst these may not be complex, stakeholders will wish to be sure that the charity's resources are not being used to provide over-generous remuneration packages.

Independent NEDs

Governance reports recommend that at least half the board are **independent NEDs**, without business or financial connections. It is possible that none of the current NEDs can be classed as independent, since they have all been appointed on the basis of previous business connections. Independent NEDs will be particularly important for HFD as it is a charity, and stakeholders will rely on NEDs to provide unbiased scrutiny of how the executive directors are conducting its affairs.

Expert NEDs

NEDs with **experience of the charity sector** need to be appointed. The reason given for not discussing operational matters, that these are outside the directors' experience, indicates that as a body the NEDs have **insufficient expertise** at present. The CEO's belief that the executive management team is more than capable of managing the delivery of the in-home care services misses the point. NEDs should **scrutinise**, and if necessary **challenge**, the way the CEO is running operations, drawing on their own experience.

Stakeholder representation

There appears to be a **lack of stakeholder representation** on the board; with fund providers, volunteer helpers and users of HFD's services not being represented. Having a user representative on the board would mean that the board received **direct feedback on the effectiveness of the charity's activities**. Stakeholder representatives could also **provide feedback** to the stakeholders they represent on the reasoning behind board decisions and HFD's current strategy.

Changes in board membership

It seems that new NEDs need to be appointed to provide the **expertise and independence** the board is currently lacking. Corporate governance reports recommend that the board should not be so large as to be unwieldy; therefore some of the new board members may have to replace existing board members.

(b) **Fundamental principles**

Objectivity

My **objectivity** may be seen to be threatened if I have a relative or close friend who is dependent on the care HFD provides. This need not stop me acting as a director; however I should register an **interest** with the rest of the board and **not participate in discussions** on matters that affect my relative or friend.

Professional competence and due care

I need to ensure that I have **sufficient knowledge** about charities generally and the sector in which HFD operates. At present the chief executive does not believe I or the other NEDs have the knowledge to **scrutinise the charity's operations effectively**. **Appropriate training** should help remedy the deficiencies in my experience.

Professional behaviour

As a practising accountant I should **comply with relevant laws** and avoid any action that discredits the profession. Thus again I should consider very carefully whether I can continue as a director if the other directors **take actions** which appear to be **contrary to charity laws**.

Integrity

As a practising accountant I should be straightforward and honest in my dealings. Thus I should consider resigning as a director if the other directors **take actions** which appear to be unethical, such as **approving funding applications** which are untrue or misleading.

Conceptual framework

CIMA's conceptual framework states that accountants may face threats to compliance with the fundamental principles and need to **identify, evaluate and respond appropriately to these threats**.

Self-interest

I need to consider whether my **business relationship** is significant enough to mean that my **personal interests would be seriously threatened** if a disagreement with the CEO severed the relationship. The existence of the business relationship could mean that I could not be seen as an independent non-executive director.

Self-review

Self-review may possibly be an issue if, for example, I am responsible as a board member for reviewing information in funding applications that I have helped to prepare. This participation should **limit my involvement in board discussions** to clarifying what I have done; I should not vote on the decision on whether to approve the application. Alternatively my work should be **reviewed** by a third party such as the **external auditors**.

Advocacy

The fact that I have agreed to be appointed as a non-executive director shows that I agree with HFD's **aims**. The danger here is that I may be such a strong supporter of HFD that I fail to scrutinise HFD's activities effectively. However this is potentially a danger with **whomever is appointed** as a NED; anyone acting on a voluntary basis for a charity like HFD is likely to be in sympathy with the charity's aims. This issue should therefore not prevent me from acting.

Familiarity

Corporate governance reports suggest that **NEDs** may no longer be considered independent if they have served for too long on the board and thus have built long-term relationships with HFD and the other directors. The Combined Code suggests independence will be **compromised after nine years**, and that **any term beyond six years** for a NED should be subject to a **rigorous review**. My length of service will therefore eventually affect my decision to continue as a director, but may not be relevant at present.

Intimidation

Intimidation may become an issue if I feel that the CEO is being unduly **aggressive** in his attempts to prevent the NEDs from discussing important operational matters. A possible solution to deal with this problem is to **resign** and **publicise the reasons for resignation**, maybe reporting to the appropriate regulatory body. However stakeholder interests may be better served by my continuing on the board and **standing up to the chief executive**.

Question 5

Text references. Chapters 3,6 and 9

Top tips. In (a) the verb identify is a lower level verb, suggesting one mark per point and that you need to identify six different risks. One way to generate ideas in (a) is to think where in the process fraud and theft can occur; there are opportunities at Head Office, between Head Office and the stores, and at the stores.

In (b) the best way to ensure you score marks for the operational controls you give is to link those controls as directly as possible with the risks identified in (a). The number of suggestions we make may be in excess of what you need to obtain full marks on this section. CIMA's post-exam guide was not available at the time of publication and is not always clear on how many marks are awarded per valid point. The fact that you are asked to recommend with reasons suggests that more than one mark is likely to be available per point.

Easy marks. Hopefully there are fairly obvious hints in the scenario that you should have been able to identify to use in your answer, for example:

- The apparent readiness of head office to accept (external) theft as an explanation for inventory losses
- Inventory being counted by the stores staff in charge of holding the inventory
- Store discretion to set discounts
- The predictability of current checks (store staff always know when the head office manager will visit and inventory will be counted)

You can assume in scenarios like this that if a control is not noted in the question, that it does not operate.

(a) Surprisingly it seems that theft (presumably by external parties) is accepted at present as a valid explanation for inventory losses. This allows staff a number of opportunities for theft.

Theft by head office staff

It appears possible for head office staff to receive and enter the goods, and then despatch them. Head office staff could **enter the amount received, steal some of that inventory and send a lower amount to the stores**. There is no evidence that anyone reconciles the inventory received by stores with the inventory received by head office.

Theft by delivery drivers

The failure to reconcile the inventory received by head office with the inventory received by stores also provides opportunities for **those responsible for delivering the inventory to stores** to steal some of it.

Theft by stores staff blamed on third parties

It appears that stores staff can **simply blame third parties** for the theft of inventory that they themselves have stolen.

Theft covered up by stores staff

The responsibility stores staff have for counting inventory means that they have the **opportunity to steal inventory but report it as still present** at the stores.

False discounts

Store staff could offer **discounts on inventory** to friends who could then sell this inventory at a higher price and share the proceeds. If store staff knew what was considered as 'excessive' discounting by head office, they could set these discounts so that they were within the limits tolerated by head office.

Pocketing discounts

Again providing they kept discounts within reasonable limits, stores staff may be able to **record sales as discounted on EPOS terminals** but **charge customers full price** and **retain the difference**. This would allow **theft of cash** rather than inventory.

(b) (i) **Working conditions and the role of the human resources function**

Zero toleration of theft

Head office management should try to deter theft by making it clear that **theft of inventory or cash is unacceptable** and staff who are discovered stealing anything will be **dismissed and prosecuted**.

Conditions and pay

Staff may be less inclined to steal inventory if **working conditions and pay** are **comparable with, or better than, competitors**. Instances have been publicised of staff theft of inventory being regarded as a fair perk in stores where pay and conditions were very poor. These thefts were **condoned by management**, demonstrating a **very bad control environment**.

Recruitment

All staff recruited should provide **references** and be asked when they apply if they have been **convicted of any indictable offences**. Human resources staff should confirm **references** are genuine by **contacting referees themselves** and should investigate any details about referees that appear to be unusual (for example a school head teacher's address not being the address of his or her school).

Training

Staff training should include **training about fraud and theft**, and the steps they should take to prevent it. In particular store managers should be made **aware of the risks of fraud** by the staff they manage.

Observation by human resources

By visiting stores and reviewing appraisal records, personnel staff should look out for **signs of discontent or low morale**, and should, if possible, be aware of **close personal relationships** between staff who work together.

Whistleblowing

The human resources function should **operate and publicise a channel of communication** so that staff who know that other staff have been **stealing inventory** can report thefts in confidence. Staff should be assured that they will not be victimised for reporting instances of theft.

Staffing levels

If stores are understaffed, staff may be **too busy to keep track of inventory** when it is delivered. Human resources need to assess whether staffing levels are adequate, in order for the **operational controls** described below to be effective.

Performance measures

The **performance measures used to judge the performance of store managers should include the % of inventory recorded** as stolen in their stores. The human resources function could benchmark practices at other store chains to see if manager and staff remuneration might be linked to the % of inventory stolen at their stores.

(ii) **Operational internal controls**

Segregation of duties at head office

To limit the opportunity for theft of inventory at head office, different staff should be responsible for **receiving inventory from suppliers** and **despatching it to stores**. Other staff should reconcile the **amounts shown as received by head office** with the **amounts shown as supplied on supplier documentation**.

Reconciliation of amounts received and despatched by head office

Inventory is not held at head office but **immediately despatched to stores once deliveries to Head Office are recorded**. It should therefore be possible to compare easily the inventory delivered and then despatched. This should prevent inventory being stolen at head office. A simpler solution may be to cut out the seemingly superfluous delivery to head office and have the **suppliers deliver directly to stores**.

Reconciliation of amounts despatched by head office with amounts received by stores

To **deter delivery staff** from **stealing inventory on route**, the **inventory despatched** to each store and the **inventory received** by each store should be **recorded**, and the **amounts compared** by separate head office staff.

Independent inventory counts

To remove the opportunity for **stores staff** to **record higher amounts in count records** to those held in inventory, each store's **regular counts** should be **conducted by staff from another store** or **head office**.

Surprise inventory counts

To deter staff from stealing inventory between counts and seeking to cover up theft at the counts, **surprise inventory counts** could be **carried out** by other staff more frequently than every six months. These counts should not follow a predictable pattern, both in terms of **how frequently they happen** and the **items counted**.

Improved security arrangements

To limit the opportunity for inventory theft by staff, **access to shop inventory store rooms** could be **limited to store managers. Closed circuit television recordings**, reviewed by head office, could be used to **spot theft by staff of inventory on display in stores. Security tagging** of inventory with tags being removed at the point of sale would make it harder for staff to steal goods. Although it may offend some staff, management should consider introducing **random checks on staff bags and lockers**.

Head office authorisation of discounts

To ensure that illegitimate discounts are not given by stores, head office could remove from stores the discretion to give discounts on slow-moving inventory. Head office could **prescribe a set scale of discounts**, or **approve in advance any discounts store managers recommended**. This would also help store to store benchmarking as all % would be the same, so **making it easier for Head Office to spot theft.**

Mathematical tables and exam formulae

PRESENT VALUE TABLE

Present value of £1 ie $(1+r)^{-n}$ where r = interest rate, n = number of periods until payment or receipt.

Periods (n)	Interest rates (r)									
	1%	2%	3%	4%	5%	6%	7%	8%	9%	10%
1	0.990	0.980	0.971	0.962	0.952	0.943	0.935	0.926	0.917	0.909
2	0.980	0.961	0.943	0.925	0.907	0.890	0.873	0.857	0.842	0.826
3	0.971	0.942	0.915	0.889	0.864	0.840	0.816	0.794	0.772	0.751
4	0.961	0.924	0.888	0.855	0.823	0.792	0.763	0.735	0.708	0.683
5	0.951	0.906	0.863	0.822	0.784	0.747	0.713	0.681	0.650	0.621
6	0.942	0.888	0.837	0.790	0.746	0.705	0.666	0.630	0.596	0.564
7	0.933	0.871	0.813	0.760	0.711	0.665	0.623	0.583	0.547	0.513
8	0.923	0.853	0.789	0.731	0.677	0.627	0.582	0.540	0.502	0.467
9	0.914	0.837	0.766	0.703	0.645	0.592	0.544	0.500	0.460	0.424
10	0.905	0.820	0.744	0.676	0.614	0.558	0.508	0.463	0.422	0.386
11	0.896	0.804	0.722	0.650	0.585	0.527	0.475	0.429	0.388	0.350
12	0.887	0.788	0.701	0.625	0.557	0.497	0.444	0.397	0.356	0.319
13	0.879	0.773	0.681	0.601	0.530	0.469	0.415	0.368	0.326	0.290
14	0.870	0.758	0.661	0.577	0.505	0.442	0.388	0.340	0.299	0.263
15	0.861	0.743	0.642	0.555	0.481	0.417	0.362	0.315	0.275	0.239
16	0.853	0.728	0.623	0.534	0.458	0.394	0.339	0.292	0.252	0.218
17	0.844	0.714	0.605	0.513	0.436	0.371	0.317	0.270	0.231	0.198
18	0.836	0.700	0.587	0.494	0.416	0.350	0.296	0.250	0.212	0.180
19	0.828	0.686	0.570	0.475	0.396	0.331	0.277	0.232	0.194	0.164
20	0.820	0.673	0.554	0.456	0.377	0.312	0.258	0.215	0.178	0.149

Periods (n)	Interest rates (r)									
	11%	12%	13%	14%	15%	16%	17%	18%	19%	20%
1	0.901	0.893	0.885	0.877	0.870	0.862	0.855	0.847	0.840	0.833
2	0.812	0.797	0.783	0.769	0.756	0.743	0.731	0.718	0.706	0.694
3	0.731	0.712	0.693	0.675	0.658	0.641	0.624	0.609	0.593	0.579
4	0.659	0.636	0.613	0.592	0.572	0.552	0.534	0.516	0.499	0.482
5	0.593	0.567	0.543	0.519	0.497	0.476	0.456	0.437	0.419	0.402
6	0.535	0.507	0.480	0.456	0.432	0.410	0.390	0.370	0.352	0.335
7	0.482	0.452	0.425	0.400	0.376	0.354	0.333	0.314	0.296	0.279
8	0.434	0.404	0.376	0.351	0.327	0.305	0.285	0.266	0.249	0.233
9	0.391	0.361	0.333	0.308	0.284	0.263	0.243	0.225	0.209	0.194
10	0.352	0.322	0.295	0.270	0.247	0.227	0.208	0.191	0.176	0.162
11	0.317	0.287	0.261	0.237	0.215	0.195	0.178	0.162	0.148	0.135
12	0.286	0.257	0.231	0.208	0.187	0.168	0.152	0.137	0.124	0.112
13	0.258	0.229	0.204	0.182	0.163	0.145	0.130	0.116	0.104	0.093
14	0.232	0.205	0.181	0.160	0.141	0.125	0.111	0.099	0.088	0.078
15	0.209	0.183	0.160	0.140	0.123	0.108	0.095	0.084	0.074	0.065
16	0.188	0.163	0.141	0.123	0.107	0.093	0.081	0.071	0.062	0.054
17	0.170	0.146	0.125	0.108	0.093	0.080	0.069	0.060	0.052	0.045
18	0.153	0.130	0.111	0.095	0.081	0.069	0.059	0.051	0.044	0.038
19	0.138	0.116	0.098	0.083	0.070	0.060	0.051	0.043	0.037	0.031
20	0.124	0.104	0.087	0.073	0.061	0.051	0.043	0.037	0.031	0.026

CUMULATIVE PRESENT VALUE TABLE

This table shows the present value of £1 per annum, receivable or payable at the end of each year for *n* years $\frac{1-(1+r)^{-n}}{r}$.

Periods (n)	Interest rates (r) 1%	2%	3%	4%	5%	6%	7%	8%	9%	10%
1	0.990	0.980	0.971	0.962	0.952	0.943	0.935	0.926	0.917	0.909
2	1.970	1.942	1.913	1.886	1.859	1.833	1.808	1.783	1.759	1.736
3	2.941	2.884	2.829	2.775	2.723	2.673	2.624	2.577	2.531	2.487
4	3.902	3.808	3.717	3.630	3.546	3.465	3.387	3.312	3.240	3.170
5	4.853	4.713	4.580	4.452	4.329	4.212	4.100	3.993	3.890	3.791
6	5.795	5.601	5.417	5.242	5.076	4.917	4.767	4.623	4.486	4.355
7	6.728	6.472	6.230	6.002	5.786	5.582	5.389	5.206	5.033	4.868
8	7.652	7.325	7.020	6.733	6.463	6.210	5.971	5.747	5.535	5.335
9	8.566	8.162	7.786	7.435	7.108	6.802	6.515	6.247	5.995	5.759
10	9.471	8.983	8.530	8.111	7.722	7.360	7.024	6.710	6.418	6.145
11	10.368	9.787	9.253	8.760	8.306	7.887	7.499	7.139	6.805	6.495
12	11.255	10.575	9.954	9.385	8.863	8.384	7.943	7.536	7.161	6.814
13	12.134	11.348	10.635	9.986	9.394	8.853	8.358	7.904	7.487	7.103
14	13.004	12.106	11.296	10.563	9.899	9.295	8.745	8.244	7.786	7.367
15	13.865	12.849	11.938	11.118	10.380	9.712	9.108	8.559	8.061	7.606
16	14.718	13.578	12.561	11.652	10.838	10.106	9.447	8.851	8.313	7.824
17	15.562	14.292	13.166	12.166	11.274	10.477	9.763	9.122	8.544	8.022
18	16.398	14.992	13.754	12.659	11.690	10.828	10.059	9.372	8.756	8.201
19	17.226	15.679	14.324	13.134	12.085	11.158	10.336	9.604	8.950	8.365
20	18.046	16.351	14.878	13.590	12.462	11.470	10.594	9.818	9.129	8.514

Periods (n)	Interest rates (r) 11%	12%	13%	14%	15%	16%	17%	18%	19%	20%
1	0.901	0.893	0.885	0.877	0.870	0.862	0.855	0.847	0.840	0.833
2	1.713	1.690	1.668	1.647	1.626	1.605	1.585	1.566	1.547	1.528
3	2.444	2.402	2.361	2.322	2.283	2.246	2.210	2.174	2.140	2.106
4	3.102	3.037	2.974	2.914	2.855	2.798	2.743	2.690	2.639	2.589
5	3.696	3.605	3.517	3.433	3.352	3.274	3.199	3.127	3.058	2.991
6	4.231	4.111	3.998	3.889	3.784	3.685	3.589	3.498	3.410	3.326
7	4.712	4.564	4.423	4.288	4.160	4.039	3.922	3.812	3.706	3.605
8	5.146	4.968	4.799	4.639	4.487	4.344	4.207	4.078	3.954	3.837
9	5.537	5.328	5.132	4.946	4.772	4.607	4.451	4.303	4.163	4.031
10	5.889	5.650	5.426	5.216	5.019	4.833	4.659	4.494	4.339	4.192
11	6.207	5.938	5.687	5.453	5.234	5.029	4.836	4.656	4.486	4.327
12	6.492	6.194	5.918	5.660	5.421	5.197	4.988	4.793	4.611	4.439
13	6.750	6.424	6.122	5.842	5.583	5.342	5.118	4.910	4.715	4.533
14	6.982	6.628	6.302	6.002	5.724	5.468	5.229	5.008	4.802	4.611
15	7.191	6.811	6.462	6.142	5.847	5.575	5.324	5.092	4.876	4.675
16	7.379	6.974	6.604	6.265	5.954	5.668	5.405	5.162	4.938	4.730
17	7.549	7.120	6.729	6.373	6.047	5.749	5.475	5.222	4.990	4.775
18	7.702	7.250	6.840	6.467	6.128	5.818	5.534	5.273	5.033	4.812
19	7.839	7.366	6.938	6.550	6.198	5.877	5.584	5.316	5.070	4.843
20	7.963	7.469	7.025	6.623	6.259	5.929	5.628	5.353	5.101	4.870

AREA UNDER THE NORMAL CURVE

This table gives the area under the normal curve between the mean and the point Z standard deviations above the mean. The corresponding area for deviations below the mean can be found by symmetry.

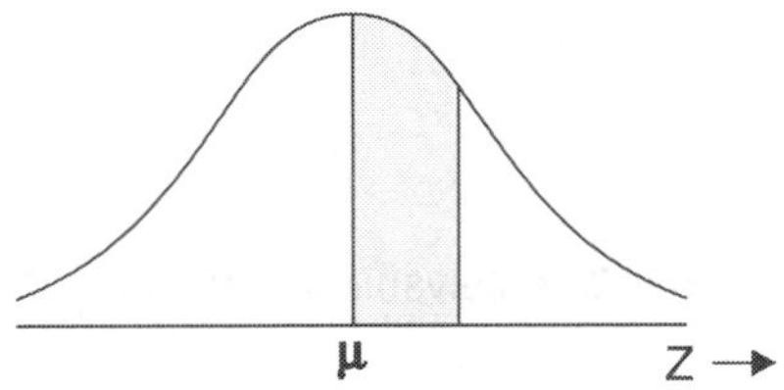

$Z = \frac{(x-\mu)}{\sigma}$	0.00	0.01	0.02	0.03	0.04	0.05	0.06	0.07	0.08	0.09
0.0	.0000	.0040	.0080	.0120	.0160	.0199	.0239	.0279	.0319	.0359
0.1	.0398	.0438	.0478	.0517	.0557	.0596	.0636	.0675	.0714	.0753
0.2	.0793	.0832	.0871	.0910	.0948	.0987	.1026	.1064	.1103	.1141
0.3	.1179	.1217	.1255	.1293	.1331	.1368	.1406	.1443	.1480	.1517
0.4	.1554	.1591	.1628	.1664	.1700	.1736	.1772	.1808	.1844	.1879
0.5	.1915	.1950	.1985	.2019	.2054	.2088	.2123	.2157	.2190	.2224
0.6	.2257	.2291	.2324	.2357	.2389	.2422	.2454	.2486	.2517	.2549
0.7	.2580	.2611	.2642	.2673	.2704	.2734	.2764	.2794	.2823	.2852
0.8	.2881	.2910	.2939	.2967	.2995	.3023	.3051	.3078	.3106	.3133
0.9	.3159	.3186	.3212	.3238	.3264	.3289	.3315	.3340	.3365	.3389
1.0	.3413	.3438	.3461	.3485	.3508	.3531	.3554	.3577	.3599	.3621
1.1	.3643	.3665	.3686	.3708	.3729	.3749	.3770	.3790	.3810	.3830
1.2	.3849	.3869	.3888	.3907	.3925	.3944	.3962	.3980	.3997	.4015
1.3	.4032	.4049	.4066	.4082	.4099	.4115	.4131	.4147	.4162	.4177
1.4	.4192	.4207	.4222	.4236	.4251	.4265	.4279	.4292	.4306	.4319
1.5	.4332	.4345	.4357	.4370	.4382	.4394	.4406	.4418	.4429	.4441
1.6	.4452	.4463	.4474	.4484	.4495	.4505	.4515	.4525	.4535	.4545
1.7	.4554	.4564	.4573	.4582	.4591	.4599	.4608	.4616	.4625	.4633
1.8	.4641	.4649	.4656	.4664	.4671	.4678	.4686	.4693	.4699	.4706
1.9	.4713	.4719	.4726	.4732	.4738	.4744	.4750	.4756	.4761	.4767
2.0	.4772	.4778	.4783	.4788	.4793	.4798	.4803	.4808	.4812	.4817
2.1	.4821	.4826	.4830	.4834	.4838	.4842	.4846	.4850	.4854	.4857
2.2	.4861	.4864	.4868	.4871	.4875	.4878	.4881	.4884	.4887	.4890
2.3	.4893	.4896	.4898	.4901	.4904	.4906	.4909	.4911	.4913	.4916
2.4	.4918	.4920	.4922	.4925	.4927	.4929	.4931	.4932	.4934	.4936
2.5	.4938	.4940	.4941	.4943	.4945	.4946	.4948	.4949	.4951	.4952
2.6	.4953	.4955	.4956	.4957	.4959	.4960	.4961	.4962	.4963	.4964
2.7	.4965	.4966	.4967	.4968	.4969	.4970	.4971	.4972	.4973	.4974
2.8	.4974	.4975	.4976	.4977	.4977	.4978	.4979	.4979	.4980	.4981
2.9	.4981	.4982	.4982	.4983	.4984	.4984	.4985	.4985	.4986	.4986
3.0	.49865	.4987	.4987	.4988	.4988	.4989	.4989	.4989	.4990	.4990
3.1	.49903	.4991	.4991	.4991	.4992	.4992	.4992	.4992	.4993	.4993
3.2	.49931	.4993	.4994	.4994	.4994	.4994	.4994	.4995	.4995	.4995
3.3	.49952	.4995	.4995	.4996	.4996	.4996	.4996	.4996	.4996	.4997
3.4	.49966	.4997	.4997	.4997	.4997	.4997	.4997	.4997	.4997	.4998
3.5	.49977									

This table can be used to calculate N(d_1), the cumulative normal distribution functions needed for the Black-Scholes model of option pricing. If $d_1>0$, add 0.5 to the relevant number above. If $d_1<0$, subtract the relevant number above from 0.5.

EXAM FORMULAE

Valuation models

(i) Present value of an annuity of £1 per annum, receivable or payable for n years, commencing in one year, discounted at r% per annum:

$$PV = \frac{1}{r}\left[1 - \frac{1}{[1+r]^n}\right]$$

(ii) Present value of £1 per annum, payable or receivable in perpetuity, commencing in one year, discounted at r% per annum:

$$PV = \frac{1}{r}$$

(iii) Present value of £1 per annum, receivable or payable, commencing in one year, growing in perpetuity at a constant rate of g% per annum, discounted at r% per annum:

$$PV = \frac{1}{r - g}$$

Review Form & Free Prize Draw – Paper P3 Management Accounting – Risk and Control Strategy (1/09)

All original review forms from the entire BPP range, completed with genuine comments, will be entered into one of two draws on 31 July 2009 and 31 January 2010. The names on the first four forms picked out on each occasion will be sent a cheque for £50.

Name: ______________________ **Address:** ______________________

____

____

How have you used this Kit?
(Tick one box only)

☐ Home study (book only)

☐ On a course: college ______________

☐ With 'correspondence' package

☐ Other ______________

Why did you decide to purchase this Kit?
(Tick one box only)

☐ Have used the complementary Study text

☐ Have used other BPP products in the past

☐ Recommendation by friend/colleague

☐ Recommendation by a lecturer at college

☐ Saw advertising

☐ Other ______________

During the past six months do you recall seeing/receiving any of the following?
(Tick as many boxes as are relevant)

☐ Our advertisement in *Financial Management*

☐ Our advertisement in *Pass*

☐ Our advertisement in *PQ*

☐ Our brochure with a letter through the post

☐ Our website www.bpp.com

Which (if any) aspects of our advertising do you find useful?
(Tick as many boxes as are relevant)

☐ Prices and publication dates of new editions

☐ Information on product content

☐ Facility to order books off-the-page

☐ None of the above

Which BPP products have you used?

Text	☐	*Success CD*	☐	*Learn Online*	☐
Kit	☑	*i-Learn*	☐	*Home Study Package*	☐
Passcard	☐	*i-Pass*	☐	*Home Study PLUS*	☐

Your ratings, comments and suggestions would be appreciated on the following areas.

	Very useful	*Useful*	*Not useful*
Passing CIMA exams	☐	☐	☐
Passing P9	☐	☐	☐
Planning your question practice	☐	☐	☐
Questions	☐	☐	☐
Top Tips etc in answers	☐	☐	☐
Content and structure of answers	☐	☐	☐
'Plan of attack' in mock exams	☐	☐	☐
Mock exam answers	☐	☐	☐

Overall opinion of this Kit *Excellent* ☐ *Good* ☐ *Adequate* ☐ *Poor* ☐

Do you intend to continue using BPP products? *Yes* ☐ *No* ☐

The BPP author of this edition can be e-mailed at: nickweller@bpp.com

Please return this form to: Nick Weller, CIMA Publishing Manager, BPP Learning Media Ltd, FREEPOST, London, W12 8BR

Review Form & Free Prize Draw (continued)

TELL US WHAT YOU THINK

Please note any further comments and suggestions/errors below.

Prize Draw Rules

ng date for 31 July 2009 draw is 30 June 2009. Closing date for 31 January 2010 draw is 31 December 2009.

ed to entries with UK and Eire addresses only. BPP employees, their families and business associates are

e necessary. Entry forms are available upon request from BPP Learning Media Ltd. No more than one per person. Draw restricted to persons aged 16 and over.

notified by post and receive their cheques not later than 6 weeks after the relevant draw date.

promoter in all matters is final and binding. No correspondence will be entered into.